P9-DHP-802

Macedonia

the Bradt Travel Guide

Thammy Evans

edition
3

www.bradtguides.com

Bradt Travel Guides Ltd, UK
The Globe Pequot Press Inc, USA

KOSOVO

Priština ↑

Belgrade ↑

Kumanc

Šarena Mosque & Bektaši Teke
page 223

Mt Tito
2748m
▲

Tetovo

SKOPJE

**Matka Dam &
Vrelo Cave**
page 148

Vardar

Matka

Treska

Vardar

**Jasen
Forestry
Range**

MACEDONIA

Gostivar

Kazluk

Mt Korab
2753m

Mavrovo
Anovi

Mt Solunska Glava
2538m

**Mavrovo
National
Park**

Kičevo

Debar

Treskavec Monastery
page 208

Crni drim

Ohrid Lake & Town
page 159

Kruševo

PRILEP

Globočka

Struga

ALBANIA

Tirana ←

OHRID

Resen

Galičira
National
Park

**Pelister
National
Park**

BITOLA

Lake
Ohrid

Lake
Prespa

Crna

POGRADECI

Golem Grad
Island

Thessaloniki,
Athens →

Kajm
2520

Korça

Brajčino eco–village
page 199

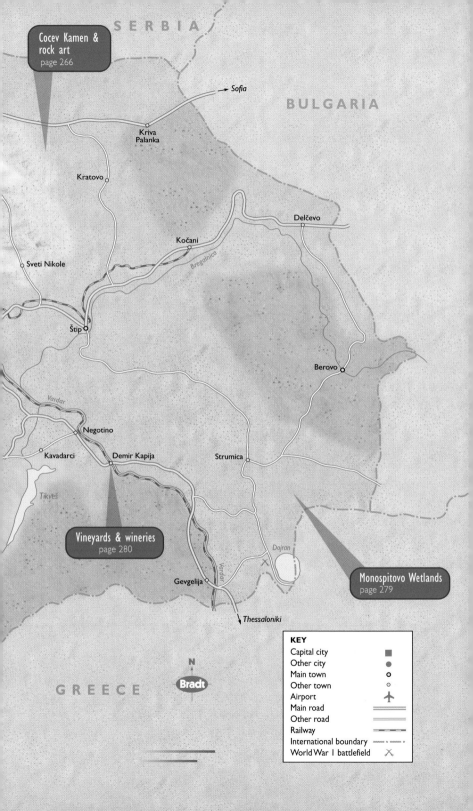

SERBIA

BULGARIA

Cocev Kamen &
rock art
page 266

→ Sofia

Kriva
Palanka

Kratovo

Delčevo

Kočani

Bregalnica

Sveti Nikole

Štip

Berovo

Vardar

Negotino

Kavadarci

Demir Kapija

Strumica

Tikveš

Dojran

Vineyards & wineries
page 280

Monospitovo Wetlands
page 279

Vardar

Gevgelija

↓ Thessaloniki

N

Bradt

GREECE

KEY

Capital city	■
Other city	●
Main town	◉
Other town	○
Airport	✈
Main road	═══
Other road	━━━
Railway	▦▦▦
International boundary	▬·▬·▬
World War I battlefield	✕

Macedonia
Don't
miss...

Wineries The rich Tikveš plain running from Veles along the River Vardar to Demir Kapija is renowned for its wines (BJ) page 269

People and culture The future mother-in-law hosts a dance in traditional dress with the closest relatives at the Galičnik Wedding Festival (SL) page 231

Ohrid Lake and town
Lake Ohrid is the jewel of the Macedonian crown — both the lake and Ohrid town are UNESCO World Heritage sites (BJ) page 159

Art and architecture
Pre-20th-century art mostly took the form of church frescoes, icons and woodcarvings, of which there are a great many in Macedonia (BJ) page 60

Hiking Macedonia is brimming with beautiful countryside that makes splendid hiking for a range of fitness and experience levels (BJ) page 295

above The southern side of the Vardar River is home to Skopje's main business district (V/D) page 115

left Kale Fortress, Skopje — continuing excavations of the site have revealed artefacts dating back to the Thracian era of 200BC (BJ) page 138

below Čifte Amam National Art Gallery is a former Turkish bathhouse that now houses various travelling exhibitions (BJ) page 134 *right* The Mustafa Pasha Mosque is the largest and most ornately decorated of all the mosques in **Skopje** (S/D) page 137

below The Bit Pazar is the biggest outdoor market in Skopje and has been held in the same location for over 600 years (BJ) page 132

bottom The 214m Kamen Most bridge was first built in the late 15th century and joins the old Turkish town to the new centre of Skopje (BJ) page 138 *above left* Paragliding is very popular in Macedonia, which is crammed with great accessible take-off sites, such as Mount Vodno (BJ) page 42

above right Swimming at Lake Ohrid, one of the oldest lakes in the world (TE) page 159

below Skiing at Popova Šapka, Tetovo — the resort offers 20km of groomed ski runs and over 35km² of terrain for off-piste skiers (TE) page 225

AUTHOR

Born in London, of Welsh and Malay Chinese parents, Thammy Evans has travelled and lived abroad for over 20 years, especially in China and southeast Europe. Professionally, her career lies in the field of political analysis. Her first overseas trip was to Malaysia at the age of eight, and she has been dabbling in numerous foreign languages ever since. Amongst her many other travels, her most memorable are the Trans-Mongolian Railway from Tianjin to Moscow in 1991, mountaineering in Bolivia in the summer of 1999, and doing the field research for her second Bradt travel guide *Great Wall of China* in 2005. Despite many forays to far-off lands, she feels most at home in the southern climes of wider Europe and has lived and worked in Macedonia for five years. She and her family now have a small stone house by the sea in Istria.

DEDICATION

To my mother

AUTHOR'S STORY

I ended up back in the Balkans (which is another story), with my husband in Macedonia. Not good at twiddling my thumbs, I had already sought advice from a travel writer friend (Cam Burns) about doing some freelance travel writing. 'Why don't you update a travel guidebook on Macedonia?' he suggested. 'What a brilliant idea!' I replied; and off I went to Stanford's, the biggest map and travel bookstore in the UK, to survey the many guidebooks on Macedonia and to choose the one closest to my style of writing to update. After about five minutes of research in the Europe section, I quickly came to the conclusion that there was a grand total of zero guidebooks on Macedonia, and that *ipso facto* I myself would be writing the very first one! Another five minutes of research lead me to the further deduction that the only publishing house crazy enough to tackle such a proposition would be Bradt Travel Guides.

I contacted Bradt, and to cut a very long story short, the then Chief Editor, Tricia Hayne, wrote back and said 'Yes!' Bradt was looking to expand its Balkan titles and I was very lucky to be in the right place at the right time.

Gathering accurate information on Macedonia, however, was not easy. In 2003 there was little published in English, and what was on the internet was sparse, outdated and contradictory. More was available in Macedonian, but was hyperbolic and did not meet the needs of an independent traveller. So, armed with tipoffs, mostly from the international community there at the time, I set off every weekend to conduct primary research. The result, several editions later and much fact checking by some very knowledgeable Macedonians, is the guide you have in your hands today. Enjoy!

PUBLISHER'S FOREWORD   *Hilary Bradt*

The first Bradt travel guide was written in 1974 by George and Hilary Bradt on a river barge floating down a tributary of the Amazon. In the 1980s and '90s the focus shifted away from hiking to broader-based guides covering new destinations – usually the first to be published about these places. In the 21st century Bradt continues to publish such ground-breaking guides, as well as others to established holiday destinations, incorporating in-depth information on culture and natural history with the nuts and bolts of where to stay and what to see.

Bradt authors support responsible travel, and provide advice not only on minimum impact but also on how to give something back through local charities. In this way a true synergy is achieved between the traveller and local communities.

* * *

Macedonia remains the Cinderella of the former Yugoslavia, attracting fewer visitors than its high-profile neighbours. Readers are fortunate to have Thammy Evans to guide them; she is one of our most highly praised, enthusiastic and conscientious authors. Users of this new edition have a treat in store.

Third edition November 2009
First published 2004

Bradt Travel Guides Ltd, 23 High Street, Chalfont St Peter, Bucks SL9 9QE, England.
www.bradtguides.com
Published in the US by The Globe Pequot Press Inc, 246 Goose Lane,
PO Box 480, Guilford, Connecticut 06475-0480

Text copyright © 2009 Thammy Evans
Maps copyright © 2009 Bradt Travel Guides Ltd
Illustrations © 2009 Individual photographers

British Library Cataloguing in Publication Data
A catalogue record for this book is available from the British Library
ISBN-13: 978 1 84162 297 2

Photographs Dickie Duckett/FLPA (DD/FLPA), Thammy Evans (TE), Gorgev/Dreamstime.com (G/D), Blagoja Jankoski (BJ), Philip Lampron (PL), Samir Ljuma (SL), Salahudin/Dreamstime.com (S/D), Jurgen & Christine Sohns/FLPA (J&C/FLPA), Vvvladimir/Dreamstime.com (V/D), Winfried Wisniewski/Minden Pictures/FLPA (WW/MP/FLPA)
Front cover St Holy Mother, Matka (BJ)
Back cover Zurla player (SL), Matka Lake (BJ)
Title page Ohrid Lake (SL), Girl in traditional dress (PL), Grapes for winemaking (BJ)

Maps Dave Priestley

Typeset from the author's disc by Wakewing
Printed and bound in India by Nutech Print Services

Foreword

A stay in Macedonia offers a feast for the senses. A quick glance at the history of the country gives clues as to the variety of cultures that are still represented today, through archaeological remains; historical and modern buildings – civil, military and religious; and in a diverse society.

The setting is a quite breathtaking landscape: mountains rising to 9,000ft; villages perched on the sides of valleys; freshwater lakes and reservoirs. It varies constantly through the seasons, and is always dramatic, whether you are up close, hiking, skiing or driving, or enjoying its majesty from a distance.

Macedonia does not stand still, so I am very glad Thammy has returned, two years on, to update and add to the guide in this third edition. Whether it's new leisure facilities and restaurants, a renovated church or mosque, the developing wine industry, a restored monument to British soldiers killed in action in World War I, or the evolving political situation, she has captured it here for the benefit of longer-term residents and visitors alike.

I am sure that many people will come to Macedonia clutching a copy of this guide and depending on it. I hope they will make their own personal discoveries too. For there is much waiting to be discovered and, wherever you go, you can be confident of a warm and generous welcome from the Macedonian people.

Andrew Key
British Ambassador

Acknowledgements

So many people have helped with this third edition, especially all the friendly people of Macedonia who have willingly or unwittingly helped me.

Specifically for this edition I would like to thank (any mistakes in the text are purely my own): Mimoza Gligorovska for her contribution on Mijaks and for chasing endless questions; Samir Ljuma for help in Tetovo and for many beautiful photos; Goran Miševski, Zoran Bogatinov, Bridget Trazoff-Blagoevski, Gerard McGurk, Sanne van den Heuvel, Ramadan Berat, Elizabeta Koneska, Darko Gavrovski, Perica Sardžoski and Nikolina; Beni Arjulai for help with the Albanian language section; Sally Broughton, Tome and a whole host of people on our adventures on Kožuf; Alison, Iskandar and Artemis Thorpe for giving me a home from home; Lee Hart Weber and Aubrey Harris for much improving the Strumica section; Kyungah Suk for introducing me to Monospitovo Blato; Reubin Thorpe, and Andriana Dragovik and Nikica Korubin of the Macedonian Centre for Archaeology Research for updates to the archaeology sections; Blagoja Jankovski for corrections to Chapter 12 on hikes; Sašo Dimeski and Beti of SAGW for help with maps; Katerina Hristovska for her insights and tour of the Museum of Coinage; Headmistress Seba Ibraim of Brakja Ramiz i Hamid School; Ajet Osmanovski and Azdrijan Memedov of Romaversitas; Pierre Oldini for help with the French; Romeo Drobarov, Simon Moody, John Durance, Andy Lennard and Jonny Lowe for traipsing around Dojran battlefield with me in the sleeting, freezing snow; Borce and Zoran Apostolov for yet another gorgeous suit; Risto Janakievski of Makadonska Kukja-Kale for dinner for my friends; Lazar Petrov at Popova Kula winery, my favourite hotel in Macedonia, for accompanying me through dinner and several courses of wine; Furkan, Oliver and Ivan Panovski (CEO) of Lotus Transport, the best taxi company in Macedonia, for driving me around obscure parts of the country and coming to the rescue when the train broke down; Slave Tomov and Ace Stojanov of Atlantis; Dimitar Gjorgievski of Go Macedonia; Džingis of Dea Tours; Maya and Ace of Simonium Travel for all sorts of help, skis and good food; Alison White of Regent Holidays for my flight to Skopje; my book distributor in Macedonia, Sašo Kuzmanovski; Omi for helping with Dani; and my mother for her tireless care of my affairs and family.

I am particularly thankful to all those readers who have found the time to write in with corrections: Barry Wilson, Dennis Verzijl, Nick Hunt, Jennifer Arnold and Rubin Zemon. I am also dearly grateful to all of the Bradt team for their help and understanding throughout the writing and sale of the book.

Finally I must once again thank my husband, Vic, who despite not being able to accompany me to even more obscure parts of Macedonia, still took care of me whilst I locked myself away in the evenings to write up my research, and whose only lucid conversation with me in those busy days was to read out the Macedonian train timetable to me in its entirety. Only love. We look forward to our first trip to Katlanovska Banja for a hot spring to share.

LIST OF MAPS

NOTE ABOUT MAPS

Several maps use grid lines to allow easy location of sites. Map grid references are listed in square brackets after listings in the text, with page number followed by grid number, eg: [156 C3].

FEEDBACK REQUEST

At Bradt Travel Guides we're aware that guidebooks start to go out of date on the day they're published – and that you, our readers, are out there in the field doing research of your own. You'll find out before us when a fine new family-run hotel opens or a favourite restaurant changes hands and goes downhill. So why not write to us and tell us about your experiences? We'll include you in the acknowledgements of the next edition of *Macedonia* if we use your feedback. So email e bradtmacedonia@yahoo.co.uk or write to us at Bradt Travel Guides, 23 High Street, Chalfont St Peter, Bucks SL9 9QE – we'll look forward to hearing from you! You'll also find regular updates from the author on our website. To check these out before you travel just click on 'author updates' at www.bradtguides.com.

Contents

Introduction

As I travelled around Macedonia to update the third edition, I found a Macedonia on the verge of becoming a western European standard tourist destination. At last, there are tourist information bureaux outside Skopje; many more of Macedonia's hiking trails are marked and signposted; there are boutique hotels outside Skopje (Popova Kula Winery at Demir Kapija, Kalin Hotel in Lazaropole, two small inns in Vevčani); and Katlanovska Banja (despite its continued dilapidating exterior) is a beautiful hot spring experience.

And I am still discovering new places and new experiences in Macedonia, just as Macedonia is also discovering what it has to offer and, what is most important to outsiders, is offering it in a way attractive to the first-time visitor. In this third edition, there is more on World War I battlefields; Macedonia's fantastic wines; castle bagging; people who have been inspired by Macedonia such as Edward Lear, founder of Save the Children Eglantyne Jebb, and the American hostage Miss Stone; and a much needed improved section on the Strumica area.

There is so much in this small land. It is not a place of extremes, but it is an area filled with intoxicating untold stories. Long lost in the battles of neighbouring states and their Great Power backers, Macedonia has often been seen as the ugly rump of another's desires, be they of Greece or Bulgaria or Serbia or Albania. Most people don't even know where Macedonia is and it was once described to me as the greatest 'non-destination' country. But if you care to scratch beneath the surface, you will find a Macedonia brimming with history, artefacts, rich local culture and beautiful scenery.

This guide, however, is just a starter kit, leaving plenty to be discovered, and plenty to be created. Geographically and historically there is much more to Macedonia if you veer off the tarred and hardened road, and you will only ever be rewarded for taking the bumpy side road. A Macedonian friend is invaluable to help find your way around and introduce you to your own adventure, especially once you wander off the edges of this book. You will pick up many of these friends along the way who will go out of their way to help as if it is really nothing at all, and many of whom will speak excellent English or German. Talk to the people and you will find them a fount of knowledge on the region, happy to give you their version of events – for what is written here is certainly not the last word on the subject.

Part One

GENERAL INFORMATION

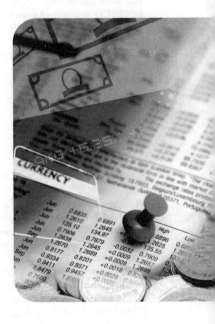

Country name (as recognised internationally) Former Yugoslav Republic of Macedonia (FYROM)

Constitutional name Republika Makedonija (**Република Македонија**)

Status Independent republic since 1991 through referendum

Languages Macedonian (Cyrillic alphabet), Albanian, Turkish dialects, Roma, Serb dialects

Population 2,022,547 (2002 census): ethnic Macedonian 64.2%, Albanian 25.2%, Turkish 3.9%, Roma 2.7%, Serb 1.8%, other 2.2%

Religion Orthodox Christian, Roman Catholic, Methodist, Sunni and dervish Muslim

Government Parliamentary democracy

Main political parties Governing coalition: VMRO-DPMNE (Internal Macedonian Revolutionary Organisation-Democratic Party of Macedonian National Unity), DUI (Democratic Union of Integration), NSDP (New Social Democratic Party); in opposition: SDSM (Social Democratic Party of Macedonia), LDP (Liberal Democratic Party) and DPA (Democratic Party of Albanians)

President Gjorge Ivanov (next presidential elections 2014)

Prime Minister Nikola Gruevski (next parliamentary elections 2012)

Municipalities 84, plus the City of Skopje = 85 (next municipal elections 2013)

Capital Skopje

Other major towns Bitola, Kumanovo, Ohrid, Prilep, Štip, Strumica, Tetovo

Border countries Albania, Serbia, Bulgaria, Greece

Area 25,713km²

National parks Three: Mavrovo, Galičica, Pelister

UNESCO protected area Ohrid lake and town

World Monument Fund site (2008 list) Sv Bogorodica Perivleptos Church, Ohrid

Total length of roads 10,591km (surfaced: 6,000km)

Total railway 922km

Airports 17 (international airports are Skopje and Ohrid)

Highest point Mount Korab 2,753m, bordering Albania

Lowest point River Vardar at Gevgelija border crossing 45m

Time GMT+1

Currency Denar (MKD)

Exchange rate £1 = 74.00MKD; US$1 = 43.60MKD; €1 = 62.80MKD (August 2009)

GDP Official: US$8bn (World Bank, 2007); Purchasing Power Parity (PPP): US$17.4bn

Average annual income US$3,470 (World Bank, 2007)

International telephone code +389

Electricity 220 volts AC. Sockets are round two-pin.

Flag A yellow oval at the centre emanating eight yellow segments against a red background

National anthem 'Today above Macedonia' (**Денес над Македонија**)

National holidays 1–2 January (New Year), 7 January (Orthodox Christmas), April (usually) (Easter), 1–2 May (Labour 'Day'), 2 August (Ilinden), 8 September (Referendum Day), 11 October (National Day)

History and Politics

And she, Deucalion's daughter,
of Zeus, the thunderer,
bore two sons:
Magnet and Macedon – a cavalryman, a warrior ...

Catalogue of Women, Hesiod (7BC)

HISTORY

The Republic of Macedonia achieved independence from Yugoslavia on 8 September 1991. The word 'Macedonia', however, has been associated with a much larger area than that represented by today's republic. 'Macedonia' has meant many things and had a multitude of changing boundaries across the millennia, but at its core is a geographical area upon which most historians and geographers are united. Geographical Macedonia, covering a large swathe of land from the source of the River Vardar (Axios in Greek) to its estuary at Solun (Thessaloniki in Greek), has a very rich and varied history, which is reflected in the present-day political climate and division of the geographical region.

Macedonia had its heyday during the build-up of its ancient empire, ending with the sudden death of Aleksandar III of Macedon (also known as Alexander the Great). Macedonia's claim today to this period of history is hotly disputed by the Greeks (see pages 23–4). As a recognised state, Macedonia rose for a short while again in the 11th century during the reign of Tsar Samoil (hotly disputed by the Bulgarians, see page 10). The region exerted an influence variously through its status as the Archbishopric of Bitola and Ohrid, but as an independent state, Macedonia did not emerge again until the ten-day Kruševo Republic of 1903.

Today's (internationally named 'Former Yugoslav') Republic of Macedonia gained independence from Yugoslavia in 1991. Geographical Macedonia is now made up of four political entities: Vardar Macedonia, which is the Republic of Macedonia; Pirin Macedonia, which is in Bulgaria; Aegean Macedonia, which is in Greece; and a tiny sliver north and south of Debar, which is in Albania.

CHRONOLOGY

Pre-9500BC	Palaeolithic (Old Stone Age) findings yet to be confirmed at Cocev Kamen
9500–6000BC	First traces of human existence in northern Macedonia date back to the Mesolithic (Middle Stone Age) period – discoveries confirmed only in 2009
6000–4000BC	Neolithic (New Stone Age) period, Gorlevo seal and Golemata Majka found near Skopje
4000–2200BC	Aneolithic (Bronze Age), including the use of Kokino observatory

GEOGRAPHICAL MACEDONIA

2200–600BC	Iron Age and rock paintings in Cocev Kamen
600–217BC	Paeonian kingdom
Mid-4th century BC	Paeonia vassaled to the Macedon royal dynasty
294–168BC	Antigonid dynasty
168BC–AD395	Roman period
395–1204	Byzantine period
6th century	Invasion of Goths, Huns and Avars
7th century	Beginning of Slavic immigration
976–1014	Reign of Tsar Samoil
1096–97	Crusaders cross Macedonia
1018–1767	Archbishopric of Ohrid
1371–94	King Marko's Kingdom of Macedonia
1394–1912	Ottoman rule
1877–78	Russo–Turkish war
March 1878	Treaty of San Stefano gives most of Macedonia to 'Big Bulgaria'
July 1878	Treaty of Berlin returns Macedonia to the Ottoman Empire
1893	Formation of the Internal Macedonian Revolutionary Organisation (VMRO) separatist movement
3 September 1901	Kidnapping of American missionary Miss Ellen Stone
3–10 August 1903	The Kruševo Republic
1912	First Balkan War sees Serbia, Greece and Bulgaria defeat Turkey; Macedonia is divided between Serbia and Greece
1913	Second Balkan War – Bulgaria tries to retake Macedonia
1914–18	Macedonia ruled by Bulgaria during World War I in return for supporting Axis
1918–41	Came under the rule of the Kingdom of Serbs, Croats and Slovenes

1920	Ruled for six months by the Yugoslav Communist Party
1941–44	Ruled again by Bulgaria
1944–91	Socialist Republic of Macedonia (within Federal Republic of Yugoslavia)
1991–present	Independent (former Yugoslav) Republic of Macedonia
2001	Six-month internal conflict between the National Liberation Army (ethnic Albanian) and state security forces
13 August 2001	Signature of the Ohrid Framework Agreement ends the conflict
15 December 2005	Macedonia receives EU candidacy status
April 2008	Greece denies Macedonia invitation to NATO due to name dispute

STONE AGE PREHISTORY Accurate history on this period of Macedonian history is sketchy. However, there is increasing speculation and some evidence that prehistoric Macedonia (6500–3500BC) may have had a matriarchal society worshipping female lineage and deity until their demise through the arrival of male-dominated Vinca-Turdas Neolithic tribes around 4500BC (established through pottery findings). The discovery of the *Golemata Majka* (Great Mother, not to be confused with the much later *Magna Mater* worship of the Romans from around the 2nd century BC) statue of 6500BC in Tumba Madžari in southeast Skopje in 1981 is cited as evidence of this.

The Aneolithic stilt water village, the Bay of Bones (see page 173), near Gradište, Ohrid, is another example of human settlement in Macedonia from prehistory.

PAEONIA According to Homer's rendition of mythical times in the *Iliad,* before Macedonia and the Macedonians came Paeonia and the Paeons. This land stretched from the source of the River Vardar to its estuary at Thessaloniki and across the River Struma to the Rhodope Mountains in the east. The legend goes that the Paeons themselves were direct descendants of the river god Axios. They were culturally quite close to their Illyrian, Thracian and Greek neighbours, and even took part in the siege of Troy around 1200BC. Later, other Greek historians such as Herodotus, Livius, Strabo and Thucydides described Paeonia and the Paeons in their writings.

It is now known that the Paeonian tribe existed from at least the late 6th century BC when the tribe started to issue its own coins, some of which are on display in the Museum of Coinage (see page 136) in Skopje. The first known capital of the Paeonians was Vilazora (today's Veles), and this was later moved to Stobi. By that time (mid 4th century BC) Philip II (Alexander the Great's father) brought Paeonia under his rule as a vassal state. It was completely subsumed into Macedonia by 217BC. Traces of their walled towns can still be found around Macedonia, where tumbled piles of limestone blocks tell of the cyclopean masonry techniques used to build their mighty fortresses. Vajtos, Matka, Mariovo and Demir Kapija were four such sites.

There is also mention during this time that in the southwest of the land lay an area called Pelagonia. Named after Pelagon, the son of Axios, this land was located around the River Crni Drim, which runs from Struga at Lake Ohrid through Debar into present-day Albania.

Further descriptions are made of other tribes bordering on, and fighting with, the ancient Macedonians who came to dominate the region. These tribes include the Lyncestis, who used to live in the area around Heraklea (now Bitola); the Brigians who spread out in pockets all over Macedonia, modern-day central

Albania and northwest Greece; the Enhelians centred around southeast Macedonia; the Dassaretians settled around Ohrid (then Lichnidos); the Illyrians who moved into present-day Albania and therefore bordered on western Macedonia; and finally the Dardanians who originated from a similar area to the Illyrians, and who some believe may have been related to the Illyrians. All these tribes are mentioned by Thucydides in his famous *History of the Peloponnesian War*, a war fought between Athens and Sparta in 431–404BC.

HOUSE OF MACEDON Legend says that the Macedonians came from Macedon, the grandson of Zeus (the Greek god of thunder) by his first daughter. Hesiod's epic, *Catalogue of Women*, goes on to say that Zeus's second daughter also bore two sons: Graecian and Latin. Thus the Greeks and the Romans, according to legend, were brothers, and cousins to the Macedonians. Some might say this is the origin of the animosity between the Greeks and the Macedonians. Indeed, at the time, the Greeks had gone to some lengths to keep their 'barbarian' cousins out of the Delphian Amphyctionic Council and from participating in the Olympic Games. Only in the early 5th century BC was the Macedonian royal family finally permitted into the Olympics, having been ordained 'sufficiently' Greek because of their common ancestry and worship of the same Greek gods. Common Macedonians were not allowed to compete until another century later.

How much the Macedons mixed with the Paeonians after they were made a vassal state by Philip II is not known. Philip II, who ruled 359–336BC, did found the city of Heraklea, near Bitola, and this probably brought with it a certain amount of associated Hellenic city culture.

Compared with other tribes in the Balkans, the Macedonians, allegedly by virtue of being mountain people, were renowned hunters and fighters, who also took a liking to drink and dance. These traits were equally matched by their desire for political power, which allowed the Macedonian dynasty to expand its empire gradually over the course of almost seven centuries. At the pinnacle of its existence during the reign of Aleksandar III of Macedon (known to Hellenites as Alexander the Great), the former Macedonian dynasty had gone forth in the name of spreading Hellenism and encompassed geographical Macedonia, most of the Hellenic city-states under the League of Corinth, the Aegean islands, Egypt, Asia Minor, eastern Iran and western India. In 331BC, Babylon (now in modern-day Iraq) was made the capital of Aleksandar's vast pan-Hellenic empire.

In the course of his ambitious campaigning, Aleksandar III of Macedon had squandered the previously good relations with the Greeks won by his father Philip II. Aleksandar's sudden death from fever left behind a weak and unprepared heir, and without the mighty backing of the Greek city-states the empire soon crumbled as a result of fighting between Aleksandar's generals. Eventually divided into four main territories, Macedon was already in the care of Regent Antipater. His son Cassander ruled after him, but on his death Macedon fell into civil strife.

ANTIGONID EMPIRE With the ancient royal house of Macedon long in tatters and the kingdom in civil war, another of Aleksandar III's generals, Antigonus I Monophthalmus, tried to retake Macedon. He had been ruler of Syria and Asia Minor after Aleksandar III, but was not able to recapture Macedon and died fighting for it at the Battle of Ipsus in 301BC. His son, Demetrius, did succeed in taking Macedon a few years later and thereby established the Antigonid Empire over Macedon and many of the Hellenic city-states for the next 125 years.

THE EMPIRE OF ALEKSANDAR III OF MACEDON

Route taken by Aleksandar III
of Macedon

0   1,000km
0   600 miles

294–277BC	Demetrius I Poliorcetes
277–239BC	Antigonus II Gonatas
239–229BC	Demetrius II
229–221BC	Antigonus III Doson
221–179BC	Philip V of Macedon
179–168BC	Perseus of Macedon

ROMAN RULE The Antigonid dynasty was no match for the emerging empire of Rome. Three devastating Macedonian–Roman wars ensued over a 50-year period: 215–205BC, 200–197BC and 171–168BC. On 22 June 168BC, Perseus, the last Macedonian king, was finally defeated at the Battle of Pydna. The land of ancient Macedon was incorporated into the Roman prefecture Macedonia, which also included Epirus, Thessaly, Vetus, and some of Thrace and Illyria.

ALEKSANDAR III OF MACEDON (THE GREAT)

Born in Pella (in modern-day Greece) in 356BC, Aleksandar III of Macedon was the son of King Philip II and his wife Olympias, a Molossian princess from neighbouring Epirus. Although both of the royal houses of Macedon and Molossia were probably begrudgingly accepted as Greek by ancestry by the time Aleksander was born, it remains much debated in today's Hellenic Republic and the Republic of Macedonia as to whether Aleksandar was half Macedonian and half Epirian/Molossian or truly Greek. In either case, his father Philip II, who learnt to highly appreciate the Greek military and diplomatic education he was given as a hostage in Thebes, passed his love of Greek culture and education onto the young Aleksandar.

Aleksandar became famous for continuing his father's dream of a united and expanded pan-Hellenic empire. Philip was assassinated in 336BC before he could realise his plans. But, at the age of 20, Aleksandar continued to strengthen his father's gains. A fearless fighter and far-sighted tactician, he spoke both Greek and his native Macedonian, and had been taught in his early years by Aristotle. In the name of spreading Hellenic culture and practices, Aleksandar's empire stretched all the way to the River Ganges in India. In his reign of 12 years his victories were numerous and are legendary:

336BC	Wiped out all remaining contenders to the Macedonian throne from within Macedon
335BC	Destroyed the town of Thebes in Greece
334BC	Defeated the Persians in Asia Minor
333BC	Defeated Darius, King of Persia, at Issus
332BC	Conquered Egypt and founded the town of Alexandria
331BC	Defeated Darius again at Babylon, which Aleksandar then made capital of his empire
327BC	Defeated King Pora, thereby acquiring the Punjab
325BC	Died on 10 June on his return to Babylon

His body was eventually interred by Ptolemy in Alexandria in Egypt. However, his tomb has since disappeared without trace. Some believe his body now lies at Idomena near Gevgelia in Macedonia, but it has yet to be discovered.

The 2004 Oliver Stone movie, *Alexander the Great*, and the 1998 Michael Wood BBC documentary, *In the Footsteps of Alexander*, are two succinct, popular sources on the man and his achievements. A website pooling a vast number of sources on Aleksandar is www.isidore-of-seville.com/alexander.

Pondering how to rule over the unruly Macedonians, the Amphipolis Council of the Roman Empire declared that Macedonia would be divided into four regions (*meriden*) but that each region would be free to elect its own magistrates and laws. It was forbidden, however, for the regions to co-operate at any level.

Unused to, and unhappy with these limited freedoms, Andriskos, also known as Phillip the False, led a rebellion of Macedonians against the Roman dictators in 149BC. The rebellion was resolutely put down and Macedonia's former freedoms were revoked. The Macedonians themselves were largely left alone, but a garrison of soldiers was permanently stationed there in order to fight off marauding neighbours.

As the Roman Empire grew bigger, so did the importance of various towns in Macedonia that lay on key trading routes. The most famous route was the Via Egnatia, which joined the Illyrian port of Durres (now in Albania) with Pelagonia on the Crni Drim, Heraklea near Bitola and on to Thessaloniki on the Aegean coast. Later the road extended even further to Constantinople. Another important route, the Diagonal Way, linked Heraklea with Stibera near Čepigovo (Prilep), Stobi, Bargala and on to Pautalija (now Kustendil in Bulgaria). There was also the Axios Road linking Skupi near Skopje with Argos south of Veles, Stobi and Dober near Valandovo. These important trade and military routes developed significant garrison and trading depots which soon developed into an intricate system of towns and villages throughout Macedonia, the stories of which remain largely untold. See the text box on page 32 for more on Roman archaeological sites and page 31 for a map of Roman roads and towns in Macedonia.

The expansion of the Roman Empire under Illyrian-born Diocletian (who killed St George, see page 235) reduced the size of the prefecture of Macedonia to make way for the new prefectures of Thessalia and Novus Epirus. Later, Macedonia was divided into Macedonia Prima, covering most of present-day Macedonia, and Macedonia Secunda, which covered Heraklea and Dober and the land to the south of these cities.

BYZANTINE MACEDONIA In AD395, the Roman Empire was divided into west and east, with the Greek-language-dominated eastern empire becoming commonly known as the Byzantine Empire. At this time, Macedonia became part of the Byzantine Empire and was ruled from Constantinople.

After Diocletian's death in AD305, Christianity slowly settled in Macedonia. Early in the 4th century, Skupi became the seat of the bishopric for the province of Dardania. In the year AD325, Stobi also acquired its own bishop at the Council of Nicea. Finally, Heraklea was also appointed bishop later in the century. The ruins of their early Christian basilicas can be found now in Heraklea, Stobi, Skupi and Ohrid.

After over 800 years of Roman and Byzantine rule, the orderly life of the Roman towns in Macedonia fell victim to the Huns, the Goths and the Avars. Attila the Hun and his men ransacked almost a hundred towns in the year AD447. Stobi and Heraklea survived these attacks fairly well, but a few decades later they fell to the Goths of Theodorik the Great. What the Huns and the Goths hadn't destroyed, the Avars (tribal brothers of the Mongolian hordes) finished off. And then, as if to add fate's final signature, the earthquake of AD518 undermined any attempt by the formerly great Roman towns to re-establish themselves.

SLAVIC MACEDONIA After the Huns, Goths and Avars had left the land in ruins, life in Macedonia fell to subsistence farming around small mountain towns and churches. Into this unguarded territory towards the end of the 6th century roamed the Slavic tribes from beyond the Carpathian Mountains (today's Poland,

By the end of the 10th century, one family's aspirations for their own state were such that the four sons of the Bryzsak Duke Nikola started to rebel against the feudal rule of Bulgarian authorities that were also ruling over Macedonia. Embroiled in its own fight with Byzantium, Bulgaria had little time for the four brothers, Aron, David, Moses and Samoil. But Bulgaria fell to Byzantium in AD971 and with it Macedonia came under Byzantium rule. Five years later in AD976, the Byzantium emperor John I Tzimisces died, and the four sons succeeded in taking Bulgaria and Macedonia back.

When the four brothers became two, after David was killed by Vlach travellers and Moses was killed in the Battle of Serres, Aron and Samoil quarrelled. Soon Samoil had Aron and his family killed, leaving Samoil as the sole ruler of an expanding empire. He brought most of Bulgaria under his rule and most of Macedonia minus Thessaloniki, as well as large parts of Greece, Albania, Dalmatia, Bosnia and Serbia as far as the Danube.

Samoil was crowned king by Pope Gregory V at Golem Grad on Lake Prespa. For many Macedonian historians this symbolises the official break with the Bulgarian, quasi-Russian, Orthodox Church, and marks the start of a Macedonian branch of the Church headed by the archdiocese of Ohrid. Others see Samoil and his achievements as the first of many attempts at Bulgarian domination. Weighing slightly more in favour of the argument that Samoil was seen by himself and others as Bulgarian is the evidence of the Bitola inscription (found in 1956, see page 195) and the fact that Samoil's arch enemy, Emperor Basilius II, was known by the nickname Bulgar Slayer, 'Boulgaroktonos'.

Tsar Samoil later moved his capital to Ohrid, where he built the great fortress being rebuilt today. But by 1014, the new Byzantine emperor Basilius II had had enough of this young upstart and sent troops to take back Samoil's empire. At the Battle of Belasica on 29 July 1014, Samoil's troops were resoundingly crushed by the Byzantines. Basilius (also written as Vasilius, Vasilie and Basil) then ordered that the 15,000 troops remaining should be blinded, leaving only one eye per hundred soldiers so that they could make their way back to Samoil (who had escaped during the battle) and he could see their defeat. The battle was at present-day Vodoča near Strumica. Vodoča means 'plucked eye'.

It is believed that when Samoil saw his blinded troops returning to him at Prilep on 6 October, he collapsed from a heart attack and died shortly afterwards. Macedonia then fell under Byzantine control and the people had to pay severe reparations to Constantinople for several decades to come.

Ukraine and Moldova). The Draguvite and Brysak tribes of the south Slavs settled in the northern Macedonian and western Bulgarian regions. Over the next three centuries they integrated with the local Greek-speaking tribes and eventually adopted Christianity, which had already taken a strong hold on the indigenous population. Some Macedonian historians claim that Macedonia's Slavs came from a unique Slav tribe and had their own language and aspirations for a nation state. There is little evidence, however, to back this.

Shortly after the fall of Tsar Samoil's empire (see box above), the Normans came riding into Macedonia under Robert Giscard (1016–85) to plunder and loot. The crusaders followed in 1096–97 on their way to pit the strength of Christ against that of Muhammad in the Middle East, levying war taxes as they went. Later on, Giscard's son, Boemund of Tarent (1050–1111), returned in 1107, replaying the plundering and looting of his father.

All the while, the locals tried repeatedly to rise up against their Byzantine rulers. In 1204, the Norman crusaders succeeded in sacking Constantinople and the Byzantine Empire fizzled into a few renegade dukes in Epirus and Nicea. The new states of Bulgaria and Serbia moved in to try to re-conquer parts of Macedonia.

FIVE HUNDRED YEARS OF OTTOMAN RULE The fall of Byzantium was eventually replaced by another empire, this time the Ottomans (for more on the Ottoman rulers, their rules and the ruled see box, page 48). Despite King Marko of Prilep's brave attempts to keep back the Turks (see box, page 186), his defeat at their hands in 1394 signalled the completion of Ottoman victory over Macedonia. Skopje had already been taken in 1392. Debar regained some independence under Gjergj Kastriot's Albania from 1444 to 1449, but then fell to Ottoman rule along with all Albania.

With the Ottomans came Islam and the building of mosques, covered markets, balconied houses, an increase in trade and eventually clock towers and railways. As when the Romans arrived all those centuries earlier, Macedonians did not take kindly to these new foreign rulers and many fled the country. Whilst the Ottomans encouraged the rule of the Orthodox elite over its millet (see box, *The millet system of governance and its aftermath,* page 56) and even went to some lengths to help preserve and protect some churches, such as Lešok and Joakim Osogovski, other churches of particular significance, such as Sveti Sofia and Sveti Pantelejmon in Ohrid, were converted into mosques.

In the wake of emigrating Macedonians, the Turks themselves moved into fertile Macedonia in droves to build new villages and towns. This influx built up ethnic tensions and despite the superficial improvement in trade and town life, Macedonians rose up repeatedly against their new masters. Macedonian bandits did all they could to oust the Turks and many were outlawed and hunted down by Ottoman *janissaries* (the military elite, see page 13) and their *arnauts* (special forces largely recruited from Albanian communities).

The Ottoman rulers adhered to the Sunni school of Islam, and therein to the Hanafi legal code. They also, however, tolerated and legitimised the Sufi side of Islam, which hailed from the more folklorish beliefs of Islam and emphasised the mystic communion of its disciples with Allah. Many Macedonians converted to

KING OF KUMANOVO

In 1689, Austrian emperor Leopold I of the Habsburg Empire sent General Piccolomini towards Macedonia to beat off the Ottoman army which had been encroaching upon Habsburg lands. Karpoš, chief of a band of outlaws based in the mining village of Kratovo, was quick to respond to the general's call for war and decided to rebel against the Ottoman overlords. The outlaws first rose up against the Ottoman stronghold of Kriva Palanka, and this started what came to be known as the Karpoš Uprising. More bandits joined Karpoš and the rebellion next took Kumanovo, then spread east towards Kustendil (now in Bulgaria) and west towards Skopje.

When Leopold heard that Karpoš had taken Kumanovo, the emperor promoted him and named him King of Kumanovo. But Leopold's further assistance to the new king, after Piccolomini had to beat a hasty retreat later that year, came too late. Six weeks after taking Kriva Palanka, Karpoš and 200 of his men were brutally killed and then impaled on the Stone Bridge in Skopje. Leopold's letter of encouragement to the Macedonian people a year later in 1690 fell on deaf ears.

THE FIVE VILAYETS OF THE OTTOMAN EMPIRE IN 1880

KEY TO BOUNDARIES

1880 Vilayet bdy	- - - - - -
1880 Historic bdy	-·-·-·-
1991 International bdy	-··-··-

Islam during the Ottoman period, either as Sunnis, or to a Sufi order. The Sufi orders, being less strict and more tolerant of individual expression, were more open to converts from other faiths. This was particularly true of the Bektaši order (see box, page 000) who were appointed the priests of the *janissaries*.

Towards the end of the heyday of Ottoman power, the British landscape artist and travel writer Edward Lear, better known today for his nonsense poetry and limericks, travelled through the Balkans in 1848 and 1849. He spent one week painting and writing in Monastir (Bitola) and Akhrida (Ohrid – at that time a part of Albania) in September 1848. His travelogue reveals a Macedonia demographically very different from today's, in which Lear had to appeal for a guard from the local bey to protect him whilst he drew. (Because the sultan had banned life-drawing – only patterns were allowed – the local peasantry considered his paintings to be the devil's work, and stoned him for it.)

The treaties of San Stefano and Berlin By the second half of the 19th century, the Ottomans' iron-like grip over their empire was beginning to loosen. The Habsburg Empire had won back Serbia and Bosnia, and Greece was also independent again. The newly freed states in turn wanted their share of Macedonia. This played itself out first of all in the sphere of the Church. In 1870, Russia ordained the independence of the Bulgarian Orthodox Church, with rights of influence over Macedonia. The Greek Orthodox Church took umbrage with this turn of events, and pushed Turkey into taking the issue up with Russia. Among many other issues this prompted war between the two nations.

The Treaty of San Stefano was the result of Turkey's defeat by Russia in the Russo–Turkish war ending in March 1878. The treaty allowed Romania, Montenegro and Serbia to extend their borders to include much of the land that they now have. Bulgaria, however, was made an autonomous new state, whose new borders extended as far as Niš and Vranje in present-day Serbia, Mount Korab and Ohrid in today's Macedonia, and to the far side of Prespa and Mount Gramos in Greece.

The great European powers of Austro-Hungary, France and Great Britain were dissatisfied with Russia's new extended spheres of influence through Bulgaria, and they convinced Russia to redraw the map. The new treaty, put together in Berlin in June and July 1878, essentially returned Macedonia to the Ottoman Empire for

THE DEVŠIRME TAX AND THE JANISSARIES

When the Ottomans expanded into the Balkans they started to run out of the manpower needed to run their expanding empire, keep order and conquer new lands. As a result the Ottomans implemented a tax system in the 1380s that was levied on non-Muslim families within the new territories. This tax, called devširme, required between 2.5% and 10% of boys aged 7–14 (not usually the first born) to be taken for education and training to run the Ottoman Empire. The boys were encouraged to convert to the Islam faith and could be enrolled in either a civilian or a military capacity.

For many non-Muslim families this tax was understandably extremely unpopular, and certainly did not help to ingratiate the new rulers with their new subjects, no matter what other 'freedoms', donations and perks may have been given in return. But as time went on, non-Muslim families found that the devširme was also a means of advancement within the Ottoman system, and soon selection criteria were attached to the devširme in order to keep down the number of applicants.

On the military side these boys went into the elite troops of the janissary (literally 'new troops' from the Turkish yeni čeri). Their training was harsh; once in the janissary it was forever; and they were forbidden to marry. But these elite troops soon realised their own importance and in 1449 they rebelled, demanding higher pay, pensions and other rights. It took another century before, in 1566, they won the right to marry. By the middle of the 17th century the demand to enter the janissary, particularly from Albanian, Bosnian and Bulgarian families, was so high that the devširme could be abolished.

Although these troops were formed, supposedly as a more loyal section of the army, in order to serve as the sultan's personal household troops and bodyguards, they proved in the end to be no more loyal than the rest of the Ottoman army, which was also made up of conscripted soldiers and tribal warriors. By the 18th century the janissary practically held the sultan hostage against his own imperial affairs and even his daily household. The Bekteši order of dervishes, the appointed priests of the janissary, supported them in their efforts.

The empire was already beginning to shrink due to the ineffectiveness of combat troops and many of the janissary weren't even serving soldiers. By 1826 the janissaries were so out of control that Sultan Mahmoud II finally abolished them, after several years of wresting back power from them and creating a totally new army. Their end, in a bloody revolt of the old 'new troops' against the new 'new army', was a sign of things to come over the next century: the demise of the Ottoman Empire.

its fate to be decided upon later. Bulgaria was duly annoyed and saw this as an affront to their long-standing kinship with Macedonia.

The seeds of Macedonian nationalism Some see the Berlin Treaty as the seed for a sovereign Macedonian state. While Macedonians may not have cared about not being part of 'Big Bulgaria', for the most part they were unhappy to return to Ottoman rule. Macedonian nationalism grew and there were repeated protests and armed clashes by Macedonians throughout the three Macedonian *vilayets* (administrative regions) of Skopje (now lacking Kosovo and Metohia which had gone to Serbia), Bitola and Thessaloniki. At the same time, Bulgarian forces worked to annex Macedonia to Bulgaria.

The various uprisings against the Ottoman rulers led eventually to the formation of a group of intellectuals under the name of the Internal Macedonian Revolutionary Organisation (VMRO). The founding members, Dame Gruev, Petar Pop Arsov, Anton Dimitrov, Ivan Haži Nikolov, Hristo Tatarčev and Hristo Batanžiev, founded the organisation on 23 October 1893 in Thessaloniki, with the goal of creating an independent Macedonia according to its historical and geographical boundaries. Other Macedonian heroes joined up, such as Pitu Guli and Goce Delčev.

It took another ten years of internal and external dispute for VMRO to engineer the uprising that would hopefully secure Macedonia's independence. It was during this effort that Jane Sandanski engineered the first international hostage crisis of our modern era by kidnapping an American missionary in Macedonia, Miss Ellen Stone, in return for US$63,000 (see box, page 270). Finally, at the Congress of Smilevo (20km northwest of Bitola) the Bitola Revolutionary District set the ball rolling for an uprising in their district. This was later expanded to a general uprising throughout all of Macedonia set for the auspicious date of Sv Elijas Day (literally *Ilij den/Ilinden* in Macedonian), 2 August 1903.

In the end it was the Kruševo Revolutionary District, led by Nikola Karev, that gained the upper hand over the ruling Ottomans, and on 3 August they announced the formation of the Republic of Kruševo. Unfortunately, it was only to last ten days before a detachment of the Ottoman army, outnumbering the 1,200 rebels sixteen to one, surrounded Kruševo and brought it to heel. Pitu Guli among many others died in the fighting. Goce Delčev had already been killed three months earlier.

The terror wrought on the local population thereafter was without precedent and much of it was recorded in the photography of the Manaki brothers (see box, page 190). But this repression only succeeded in indelibly marking in the minds of the Macedonian consciousness that freedom and independence from foreign rule was the only way out.

20TH-CENTURY MACEDONIA
The first and second Balkan wars By the 20th century, weakened at last by economic fraud, political in-fighting and a costly war with the Italians in 1911, the Ottoman Empire fell prey to the territorial ambitions of its remaining Balkan neighbours. Serbia, Montenegro, Bulgaria and Greece declared war on Turkey on 18 October 1912, and signed up the help of the Macedonian people by declaring that their anti-Ottoman league was for the liberation of the Macedonians. No such thing was to transpire, but instead the four nations divided Macedonia amongst themselves as soon as the defeated Ottoman armies finally retreated to Turkey.

Bulgaria, with rekindled memories of a Greater Bulgaria, took the lion's share of Macedonia, to the annoyance of the remaining nations of the anti-Ottoman league. Macedonian expatriate communities appealed to the Great Powers in London, and the Macedonian refugees in St Petersburg, Russia, even sent ahead a map made by Dimitrija Čupovski proposing the ethnic and geographical boundaries of an independent Macedonia in order to bolster their case. The neighbouring Balkan states, however, would have none of it. Serbia was vying for an outlet to the Aegean Sea, and Greece wanted control of Thessaloniki. Thus they decided the following year to challenge Bulgaria militarily for the land.

MACEDONIA AND THE RIGHTS OF THE CHILD

Abridged text from The Woman Who Saved the Children: A Biography of Eglantyne Jebb, by Clare Mulley

Eglantyne Jebb was born in 1876 to a family of social reformers in Shropshire, England. Her brother-in-law Charlie Buxton, a Liberal Member of Parliament, had founded the Balkan Committee in 1902 to campaign against the repressive policies of the Ottoman government in Macedonia. The committee's independent relief arm, the Macedonian Relief Fund (MRF), was set up a year later.

In February 1913, between the two Balkan Wars, Eglantyne travelled to Macedonia and Kosovo to deliver aid to the tens of thousands of mostly Muslim refugees displaced as the Balkan League (of Serbia, Bulgaria, Greece and Montenegro) advanced south to oust the Ottoman administration. This Orthodox Christian League resented Muslims for supporting Turkey, and resented Catholics for supporting Austria, a country with its own designs on Macedonia. Thousands of Muslims and Catholic Albanians were massacred by the victorious Serbian army and, in a systematic programme of what would now be called ethnic cleansing, villages and crops were also destroyed.

Eglantyne delivered funding and provided assistance to the MRF agents in Üsküb (Skopje), Prizren and Monastir (Bitola). Over half of the refugees in Monastir were on the verge of starvation. Some 5,000 were being fed by the MRF, through the distribution of 100,000 loaves of bread between January and April 1913, and the provision of a soup kitchen for 200 children daily for a month between February and March. Monastir was at that time a city of 50,000 inhabitants, and would have to absorb 30,000 refugees before the end of the conflict. But funds were never enough, despite the fact that, as the British Consul told her, just two pence a day could keep a man alive.

'Practically all the babies died,' Eglantyne wrote in her reports. Among the misery of starvation and disease, her most powerful recollection was that of 30 Turkish boys who had been abandoned at a boarding school when their teachers went to fight. When their food ran out the boys had simply gone to bed to die.

Narrowly escaping her own death from influenza on her return to England, Eglantyne did not venture back to the Balkans. She saw her role very much in policy development rather than in service delivery, and immediately urged the MRF to organise repatriation and resettlement of refugees in addition to relief work. From now on international security, sustainable development and citizenship became a fundamental part of her vision, without which relief, however essential, could only be a palliative measure.

Frustrated by the short-term effect of relief work, and spurred by the further agony wrought on German and Austrian orphans of the Great War, Eglantyne co-founded Save the Children in 1919 with her sister Dorothy. In 1923 she authored the five principles of the Declaration of the Rights of the Child, which was adopted by the League of Nations (the precursor to the UN) a year later.

History and Politics HISTORY

Unlike the first Balkan War of 1912, which had the strategic goal of ousting the Ottomans in order to divide the land up later, the second Balkan War of 1913 was all about gaining land and advancing the front line. Macedonian villages were razed and their inhabitants massacred in an effort to eliminate insurgents. It was during this time that the founder of Save the Children, Eglantyne Jebb, made her journey to Macedonia for the Macedonian Relief Fund to deliver relief from England to war-torn Macedonians (see box, page 15). And even after the Bulgarians lost the battle for the land they had gained under the Treaty of San Stefano, the suppression did not stop as the new masters of Macedonia (Greece and Serbia) continued to put down any hint of independence by the Macedonians.

The Great War In 1914 the Great War broke out following the assassination of the Austrian archduke Ferdinand in Sarajevo. The Central Powers of Germany and Austro-Hungary sided with Bulgaria against Serbia and Greece over the division of Macedonia. Macedonia, for the most part, chose the lesser of two evils by siding with only one of its former oppressors (Bulgaria) against Serbia (backed by France) and Greece. In reality Macedonians were drafted into all three armies to fight against each other. But Germany also enlisted the help of VMRO by financing the formation of a 'Macedonian' army, which fought alongside the Bulgarians on the condition of independence for Macedonia.

But the Central Powers lost the Great War, and the Paris Peace Conference set to negotiating the 'Macedonian Question', already an institution and a headache since the Berlin Treaty 40 years earlier. Of the three proposals put forward by Great Britain, France and Italy, it was the French proposal in favour of the Serbs that won out. The British proposal that Macedonia become a protectorate of the newly formed League of Nations, and the Italian proposal for autonomy were rejected as too risky. So without heed of what the Macedonians wanted, Macedonia was returned to the 1913 borders of the Treaty of Bucharest. Vardar Macedonia belonged once again to the enlarged Kingdom of Serbs, Croats and Slovenes (later Royal Yugoslavia) and a repressive colonisation of Macedonia by the Serbs began.

VMRO, however, would not be silenced and continued to fight for freedom from the Serbs. This led in 1934 to the assassination of the Yugoslav king Aleksandar Karagjorgjevic I by the Macedonian-born Vlada Georgiev. The fighting continued and when in early 1941 Yugoslavia refused to side with the Germans, Germany declared war on Yugoslavia, bringing Vardar Macedonia into the fray.

The communist struggle for Vardar Macedonia Inviting its allies to re-divide Macedonia yet again, the Germans, Italians and Bulgarians surrounded and then moved into Vardar Macedonia in April 1941. A secret British military organisation (see page 236), established to bring down the Axis forces through sabotage and subversion, was parachuted into Macedonia in order to help fight the fascist forces. Working initially with VMRO they later switched to the partisan forces of the Communist Party of Macedonia (CPM), set up in October 1941, when it became clear that the communist forces were the more coherent and successful.

Promising national liberty, the CPM managed to recruit many Macedonians to swell their ranks, despite the fact that it was formerly a sub-group of the Communist Party of Yugoslavia under Tito. Most Macedonians feared returning to a rule under anything relating to Royalist Yugoslavia and fought with the CPM, therefore, for the liberation of their nation rather than for any communist ideology. Under the auspices of the CPM, the Macedonians even set up their own government, the Anti-fascist Assembly of the National Liberation of Macedonia (ASNOM), on 2 August 1944, exactly 41 years after the Ilinden uprising of 1903. The government was headed by the pro-independence politician Metodija Andonov, more commonly known as Čento.

One month later, in September, the Bulgarians withdrew from Vardar Macedonia, suffering heavy losses to partisan forces. The Germans followed in their wake, beating a hasty retreat towards Greece, and ordering the deaths of hundreds of Macedonians after the failed attempt to bring a puppet government into Macedonia through the right-wing faction of VMRO. As it turned out, fewer than 300 Macedonians were actually killed under German Captain Egbert's orders, as many German soldiers let the Macedonians escape.

With the end of World War II, the CPM, with a decidedly pro-Yugoslav leadership, reneged on its promises of independence for Macedonia. The new borders around Vardar Macedonia enclosed the new People's Republic of Macedonia (later the Socialist Republic of Macedonia – SRM) firmly within communist Yugoslavia. Čento and his supporters were removed from office and replaced by the pro-Yugoslav Lazar Koliševski, who remained in power until the fall of Yugoslavia 55 years later.

As the capital of the SRM, Skopje, formerly a political backwater, was firmly orientated towards Serbia for leadership, and its pro-Serb partisan leaders were not well versed in government. Meanwhile, Bitola, traditionally the powerhouse of the region, languished in the shadows. Cut off from its usual orientation towards the southern regions of geographical Macedonia, Bitola's previous political and intellectual capacity was lost on the partisan government of the SRM. Any hint of dissension by Macedonia's pro-independence intellectuals was firmly put down.

Under Tito's communist Yugoslavia, although the SRM was nominally given the status of a federal republic, thereby giving it the right to decentralised government of its own people, this was not the case in reality. Limited autonomy was a move by Tito to divide up Serbian ambitions to take over Yugoslavia as a whole. Interdependence was brought to the federation, however, by dividing up its economic capabilities among the republics. The SRM became a popular tourist destination as part of the Yugoslavia package. Mining and tobacco production were encouraged, and Tito even started a tobacco museum in Prilep in 1973 to celebrate 100 years of the tobacco industry there (see box, page 208).

For the first time in the region's history, ethnic Macedonian arts and literature were encouraged, for which a distinct Macedonian language was recognised and strengthened. The man most known for this was Blaže Koneski (1921–93, confusingly also known under the names Blagoje Konjevic when studying in Belgrade, and Blagoy Konev when studying in Bulgaria), who became the head of the Macedonian Academy of Arts and Sciences (MANU). Some have criticised him for deliberately 'Serbifying' the Macedonian language in order to further differentiate it from Bulgarian influences. Others herald him as one of the greatest Macedonian poets and writers in living history.

Despite efforts to revitalise SRM's economy, Macedonia remained the poorhouse of Yugoslavia. This was not helped by the isolation of SRM by three of its neighbours: Albania became deeply introverted, Bulgaria shunned the pro-Serb authorities, and civil war raged in northern Greece until 1949. At the end of the civil war, the border with Greece was closed as Greek authorities tried to stamp out any further spread of communism or secessionist claims by Aegean Macedonians for an independent Aegean Macedonia.

Life in communist Macedonia followed a similar path to that of many other communist countries, although to much lesser extremes. The 1950s saw experimentation with collective production farms and state ownership of land and property. Many officials used these measures to line their own pockets, and although collective production had to be abandoned and a limited private business model was re-introduced in 1965, corruption in state-owned industries remained endemic.

Yugoslavia's break from Soviet tutelage allowed Macedonia to benefit from Yugoslavia's greater freedom of movement and other civil liberties. Nevertheless, one-party rule remained and any talk of an independent Macedonia or a reunification with the other parts of Macedonia was not entertained.

From Tito's death in 1980 and the decline of the Yugoslav economy throughout the 1980s, the Yugoslav republics and their many nationalities started to vie for greater degrees of autonomy and power in the federation or even out of it. As Serbia's president, Slobodan Milošević, became more belligerent at the end of the 1980s, the end of Yugoslavia became increasingly inevitable. Despite Lazar Koliševski's attempts to keep the federation together, the decision to move to a multi-party democracy in 1990 essentially spelt the end of one-party communist ideals in Macedonia.

In January 1991, Kiro Gligorov was appointed president of the SRM by the new multi-party parliament of Macedonia, and on 8 September 1991 the people of Macedonia voted in a referendum for the independence of the Republic of Macedonia and bloodlessly left the Federation of Yugoslavia. The Yugoslav army, needed elsewhere in dying Yugoslavia to fight Croatians and Bosnians, left Macedonia in April the next year.

Turnout for the referendum was 74% of which 95% voted for independence. The Albanian community claims that most of the remaining 26% of the non-voting citizenry were ethnic Albanians who did not want to live under the alternatives being offered, ie: as a minority within an independent Macedonia, or as a minority within Yugoslavia. It was later to turn out significant that this hefty percentage of Macedonia's citizens felt disenfranchised from the political developments of the country.

THE FORMER YUGOSLAV REPUBLIC OF MACEDONIA

Troubled first years With the additional difficulties of a disenfranchised Albanian community, the infant years of the Republic of Macedonia have been fraught with the usual transitional problems of high corruption and over-centralisation in what was essentially a nanny state. In Macedonia's case this was compounded by its formerly strong dependence on Belgrade. In the first multi-party elections of 1991, voters were faced with a bewildering plethora of parties and candidates, who were divided along political as well as ethnic lines.

The election produced neither a clear winner, nor a clear opposition, so a governing coalition of three parties was formed (the Social Democratic Party of Macedonia – SDSM, and the Liberal Democratic Party – LDP, both from the old communist leaders, along with the leading Albanian party, Party for Democratic Prosperity – PDP. The nationalist centre-right VMRO-DPMNE (Internal Macedonian Revolutionary Organisation-Democratic Party of Macedonian National Unity) took up parliamentary seats in opposition along with several other parties. As head of the leading party in the coalition, Branko Crvenkovski, at the young age of 27, became prime minister.

Two and a half years of political in-fighting ensued until October 1994 when new elections were held. But the bickering continued over the cast of the votes and it was not long before the main party in opposition, VMRO-DPMNE, and others withdrew from the election altogether. As a result, the existing governing parties, presenting themselves for one vote together, won three quarters of the vote. Forming a government in coalition with the Albanian majority vote, the new government took 112 of the 120 seats in parliament, leaving any form of opposition essentially untenable.

The Albanian community had long been unhappy with their representation in the new Macedonia, which many had not voted for in the first place. In November 1993, Macedonia's police force, strongly linked to the SDSM, arrested 12 people in Tetovo, allegedly for attempting to form an Albanian paramilitary organisation. The police claimed to have found hideouts, weapons caches and other incriminating evidence. Nine of the 12 were jailed for conspiracy and other related charges.

This did not deter the Albanian community, however, who continued to demand greater representation and started to set up their own university in Tetovo in 1995. Considering this a breach of the constitution, in which Macedonian was the only officially recognised language of the new republic, the authorities declared the university illegal and tried to close it down. In the ensuing public demonstrations, three Albanians were killed and ten policemen injured. Shortly thereafter an assassination attempt on President Kiro Gligorov was carried out. He lost one eye in the incident and his driver was killed outright. The unknown assassin has still not been apprehended, even after the government offered US$530,000 in 1999 for information leading to his arrest.

Despite the Liberal Party leaving the governing coalition in early 1996 in order to join the non-parliamentary opposition of VMRO-DPMNE and the attempt by the opposition to call for new parliamentary elections, the governing coalition continued to hold on to power. But international observers were at last allowed to monitor the local elections held that year which resulted in an even greater division between the ruling coalition in parliament and the opposition, who had won most of the main local elections. Tensions increased and in 1997 the mayors of Tetovo and Gostivar were jailed for raising the double-headed eagle flag of Albania over government buildings in their respective towns.

During the course of 1998, the National Liberation Army (NLA), a newly formed rebel group fighting for the liberation of Albanians, made its first public

WHAT'S IN A NAME?

The Former Yugoslav Republic of Macedonia – this is the international name for Macedonia as recognised by the UN and all major international organisations according to the 1995 interim agreement between Macedonia and Greece. Occasionally, but rarely, drop-down boxes on webpages when selecting a country file Macedonian under 'T'. For more on the name dispute see page 23.

Former Yugoslav Socialist Republic of Macedonia – the Socialist Republic of Macedonia (SRM) was one of the republics making up the Socialist Federal Republic of Yugoslavia (SFRY). Formed from the remains of the pre-war Kingdom of Yugoslavia in 1943, Yugoslavia was proclaimed the **Democratic Federal Yugoslavia**. In 1946, it became the **Federal People's Republic of Yugoslavia** and in 1963 the **Socialist Federal Republic of Yugoslavia** of which the SRM was a part. SFRY disintegrated in the Yugoslav wars of the 1990s and in reference to the period from 1991 until the recognition of all the former Federal Yugoslav republics as independent the area is collectively referred to as the Former Republic of Yugoslavia or FRY. The many abbreviatons are admittedly confusing.

A new documentary on the name dispute between Macedonia and Greece, titled *A Name is a Name*, and produced by Jason Miko, the biographer of the late President Trajkovski, is due out in 2010. It should prove controversial, to say the least.

announcement by claiming responsibility for the bombings of several police stations and judicial courts in the lead-up to the internationally observed parliamentary elections of autumn 1998. Their tactics did not succeed in bringing greater autonomy to the Albanian community, but the ineffectiveness of the ruling coalition to alleviate tensions between ethnic communities and to curb the economic difficulties of the transition to a post-communist system brought the electorate to vote in a new government. The winners, VMRO-DPMNE and the DPA (Democratic Party of Albanians), were both right-wing nationalist parties. Ljubčo Georgievski, aged 32 and leader of VMRO-DPMNE, became prime minister.

The new government was not given an easy start. A crisis was raging in neighbouring Kosovo. In spring 1999, some 360,000 Kosovar Albanians fled into northwestern Macedonia before the NATO bombing of Serbia later that year brought an end to Milošević's offensive in Kosovo. Although most refugees eventually returned to Kosovo or went on to other countries, the Macedonian authorities still feared a rise in the number of Albanians claiming citizenship in Macedonia and forcibly bussed tens of thousands of refugees into neighbouring Albania in April of that year. This fear was aggravated by several factors: firstly, the Albanian community claim that they made up to 40% of the population in Macedonia (as opposed to 19% in the 1994 census); secondly, the unclear status of ethnic Albanians who had failed to change their Yugoslav passport to a Macedonian one in the allotted timeframe of the early 1990s, but who were still claiming citizenship; thirdly, widespread electoral fraud in northwestern Macedonia in the local elections of 2000.

Throughout 2000, attacks on the police continued until, on 26 February 2001, the Macedonian authorities retaliated against suspected armed rebels in the village of Tanuševci, north of Skopje on the border with Kosovo, for an attack by the NLA on the police station there. Armed conflict between the authorities and the NLA raged for the next six months, both sides taking casualties and alleging war crimes for the deaths of civilians and the desecration of churches and mosques.

A peace deal and amnesty After President Trajkovski (elected after Gligorov stepped down in 1999) requested help from NATO on 20 June 2001, the international community managed to broker a ceasefire and a peace agreement. The Ohrid Framework Agreement was signed on 13 August 2001 by a new unity government, comprising VMRO-DPMNE, the SDSM, DPA and PDP. The agreement essentially gave the Albanian community much greater representation in state institutions as well as recognition of their language and culture (see box, opposite).

At the end of August, Operation Essential Harvest was launched by NATO troops upon invitation by the government to collect arms from rebel forces. Almost 3,500 weapons were collected in the month-long operation, which was half the number that the government had claimed were out there, but twice what the rebels had claimed they had. Another 7,571 were handed in to authorities in another weapons amnesty in 2003.

In addition to the Ohrid Framework Agreement, the government agreed an amnesty for all former rebel fighters except for those who had committed war crimes. The Albanians read this, as was clear in their negotiations with NATO, to mean an amnesty on all crimes except those cases taken up by the International Criminal Tribunal of Yugoslavia (ICTY) in The Hague. The Macedonian authorities interpreted the amnesty clause to mean that they could prosecute those cases not taken up by ICTY. Of the 100+ alleged cases, most were thrown out of court for lack of evidence.

Only five war crimes allegations were considered serious enough to be taken up by ICTY. These include the massacre at Ljuboten, north of Skopje, where at least six men of Albanian ethnicity were found shot in suspicious circumstances, and the mass grave found in Neprošteno containing four Macedonian bodies. After UN Security Council Resolution 1534(5) requested the ICTY to consider only the most senior and most responsible leaders in all Yugoslav wars for further

THE OHRID FRAMEWORK AGREEMENT

In the relative calm and cool of the breezes off Lake Ohrid the international community brought the government and rebel leaders together to thrash out their differences around a table and a piece of paper. The result brought greater rights for the Albanian community and hopes of guaranteed peace for all Macedonians. Although adoption of all the legal provisions envisaged in the agreement was completed with the Law on Flags and Symbols in July 2005, there is still a long way to go on full implementation of these laws in the spirit of the agreement.

CONSTITUTIONAL CHANGES The preamble of the new constitution of November 2002 deleted references to Macedonia as the 'national state of the Macedonian people' whereby Albanians and other minorities were singled out as only having rights as equal citizens, without being acknowledged as actual Macedonian people. The new constitution refers to all Macedonia's population as 'citizens of the Republic of Macedonia', equal before the law.

DEVOLUTION OF AUTHORITY In line with the wishes of the Albanian community for more say over their own affairs and also in line with European Union requirements for increased local self-government, limited powers of authority are being decentralised to the local administrative level throughout the country.

BADINTER MECHANISM Laws directly affecting culture, language, education and issues of local self-government are required to go through the Badinter mechanism in parliament. Named after Robert Badinter, born in 1928 and an experienced leading legal expert on minority rights, the mechanism requires a double majority to pass these laws: an outright majority, as well as a majority of those claiming to belong to the communities not of the majority population of the country.

EQUITABLE REPRESENTATION Equitable representation is now sought throughout all state institutions, and especially in the judiciary and the police. With a lack of sufficiently qualified minority citizens due to previous educational biases, it is proving difficult to increase minority participation in state institutions. It has been even more difficult with the need to downsize bloated institutions, effectively resulting in jobs for Albanians and job losses for ethnic Macedonians. Nevertheless, advances in ethnically mixed policing, for instance, are returning citizens' confidence to institutions of law enforcement.

THE RIGHT TO MINORITY EDUCATION AND LANGUAGE USE Non-majority ethnicities of at least 20% of the population have the right to use their language in state institutions alongside Macedonian (but not in foreign affairs). Although the Albanians are not singled out in the Ohrid Framework Agreement document, this provision has essentially brought the right for the use of Albanian in parliament amongst other institutions, in bilingual identity papers and other official documents, and has eventually legitimised the long-disputed Albanian university of Tetovo.

indictments, only one indictment was made from the 2001 conflict. This was against the former Minister of Interior, Ljube Boškovski, for his involvement in the massacre at Ljuboten. His command responsibility over the crime could not be established by the ICTY, however, and so he was acquitted in 2008. The remaining four allegations were returned to national jurisdiction in late 2007, but local courts have not taken the allegations any futher.

In comparison, over 40 indictments for war crimes committed in Bosnia during the early 1990s were prosecuted at the ICTY. These include that of the massacre at Srebrenica, where almost 8,000 Bosnian men and boys are alleged to be buried. Many hundreds of bodies have been found, but up to 20,000 remain missing from the war. Twenty-two people went missing in the Macedonian conflict, of which six are ethnic Albanians and one a Bulgarian national. Eight bodies have been found to date.

Accession years Parliamentary elections were held in September 2002. The electorate, disillusioned by the nationalist rhetoric of the VMRO–DPMNE coalition with the DPA and by the ineffectiveness of the unity government to move forward the Ohrid Framework Agreement, brought back the SDSM government of Branko Crvenkovski. Together with a new party, the Democratic Union for Integration (DUI), led by the former rebel leader Ali Ahmeti representing the majority of votes from the Albanian community, the new government made significant inroads in achieving the Ohrid agenda.

The country's situation has improved. Although economic growth has not caught up with pre-conflict figures, it reached 5% in 2007, which is three times that of some of the countries of 'old Europe'. Post-conflict agencies are moving out, or have scaled down considerably. NATO's forces turned their security mandate over to the first EU military deployment ever under Operation Concordia (350 soldiers), which was deployed on 31 March 2003. This was replaced on 15 December 2003 by an EU police mission, Proxima, comprising only 200 mostly unarmed EU police. Proxima was reduced to a small 30-man police advisory team one year later, which by mid-2006 was replaced by a twinning project with the German police of Brandenburg in line with EU accession practices.

In August 2004, the country succeeded in passing a controversial law to reduce the then 123 municipalities to a more manageable 84. Of the 84 municipalities, 15 are run by ethnic Albanian mayors and one by a Roma mayor. Since local elections in March 2005, the government has been moving slowly towards decentralising power. So far, limited decentralisation seems to be having the desired effect of some rejuvenation of the local economy. Some fear that decentralisation will increase the opportunities for institutional corruption, which is already high at the central level. Some also fear that greater autonomy is in fact polarising the ethnicities rather than uniting them.

Macedonia received EU candidacy status on 15 December 2005, but may not get a start date for negotiations until it has resolved its name dispute with Greece (see page 23), regardless of how well it achieves reforms in the 35 chapters of the EU *acquis* (areas of legal conformity). Macedonia's accession path to NATO was blocked by Greece for the same reason at the April 2008 Bucharest NATO Summit, as a result of which Macedonia now lags behind the other Adriatic Partnership countries (Albania and Croatia) in its bid to join NATO. The European Agency for Reconstruction, which has been in the country since June 2001, has poured significant funds into Macedonia to help bring its institutions towards European standards. This has been matched by bilateral financial aid from the European nations as well as by America.

The parliamentary elections of July 2006 brought in the opposition, VMRO-DPMNE, who were re-elected in a snap election in 2008 after Greece blocked Macedonia's entry to NATO. DUI, who won the majority of votes among the ethnic Albanian community, was sidelined in favour of DPA to join VMRO-DPMNE in the 2006 government, but were brought back into government in 2008, reducing fears that a politically disenfranchised Albanian community could agitate unresolved tensions.

The transition from one-party rule to a multi-party democracy has brought its usual share of troubles to Macedonia, compounded by inter-ethnic problems and a lack of support from neighbouring countries. Some of the problems which Macedonia is still tackling range from the lack of a fully participating civil society, the lack of independence of state institutions and with that the lack of public faith in those institutions, the problems of transition from state to private ownership and an antiquated education system. Finally, the lack of an independent civil service able to keep the country running effectively whilst parties argue out their differences deprives the country of the continuity needed to keep policy agendas on track.

NOT TO BE CONFUSED WITH GREECE Greece and Macedonia have had strained relations since time immemorial. Most Hellenic city-states viewed Macedonians as drunken barbarians from the north. (The word 'Greek', incidentally, was not used until the Romans used this name of a single Hellenic tribe and the closest geographically to Rome to refer to all of the Greek-speaking tribes on the Balkan peninsula.) Philip II brought Paeonia (the upper Vardar region), Pelagonia (the Prilep area) and Lyncestis (the Bitola area) into his expanding empire and united the constantly warring Greek city-states in the League of Corinth in 338BC to fight the Persians. Upon Philip's assassination, Aleksandar III of Macedon (see box, page 8) completed his father's dream in the name of a new pan-Hellenic era, and the Greeks have since claimed him as Alexander the Great. While most Greek historians would not dispute Aleksandar's lineage from the royal house of Macedon, they see Aleksandar's Macedon firmly as part of Greek heritage and not part of that of the geographical entity that now claims to be the Republic of Macedonia.

Maps from Roman, Byzantine, Ottoman and Yugoslavian times have included the geographical area of the Republic of Macedonia firmly under the label 'Macedonia'. Greek nationalist history, however, does not include the geographical area of the Republic of Macedonia in its view of Macedonia.

History aside, what is most in dispute is the use of the word 'Macedonia' in naming the country. When Yugoslavia named Vardar Macedonia the 'Socialist Republic of Macedonia' after World War II, the Hellenic Republic protested and asked Tito to rename the republic 'Vardar Macedonia' or 'Skopje Macedonia'. This was not accepted and Greece had enough to do fighting its own civil war and keeping out communism to worry too much about the name of its neighbour. But, internally, Greece continued its policy since the end of World War I of moving ethnic Greeks and Greek-speakers into Aegean Macedonia and moving Macedonians out whilst suppressing the use of their language and traditions. In this way Greece could at least control from its side any irredentist tendencies that Aegean Macedonia might have towards the SRM.

However, when the Republic of Macedonia claimed itself as the independent 'nation state of the Macedonian people' writ large in its new constitution of 1991, this was too much for the Greeks. Some Macedonian politicians started to call for reunification with Aegean Macedonia, and Athens feared an uprising in Aegean Macedonia and a desire by the two sides to rekindle long-lost dreams of the ancient royal dynasty of the Macedons. Newly independent Macedonia did not help matters by adopting the star of Vergina, formerly the flag of the ancient Macedonian kingdom, as their flag and stamping the star on their coins. Greece slammed a unilateral economic boycott on the fledgling state.

Fearing more troubles in the Balkans the international community worked hard for a solution. The interim title 'former Yugoslav Republic of Macedonia', or 'FYROM' for short, has been agreed for international official use while diplomats work harder for something less contentious. Especially since the final demise of the Federal Republic of Yugoslavia in 2003, the name 'FYROM' is as unsuitable today as giving the Hellenic Republic the name of 'former Ottoman Protectorate of Greece' or FOPOG for short.

In a spirit of compromise in 1995, the flag was changed to its present amended form and the coins were reissued without the star of Vergina. The boycott was lifted and relations between the two states have slowly started to improve. An interim accord was brokered that allowed Macedonia to use its constitutional name in bilateral relations with other countries, but Former Yugoslav Republic of Macedonia in international organisations until another name was agreed on by both countries. In addition, the interim accord agreed that Greece would not block Macedonia's entry to any international organisation on account of the name dispute. As of 2003 and for the first time since World War II, Greece has begun to issue visas to Macedonians who had previously lived or had family on the Greek side of the border. Tearful reunions on Aegean soil have abounded.

The dispute over the name gave way to Greece becoming one of the top three investors in the country. Encouraged by new members in the EU and NATO, Macedonia is working away to have countries recognise it under its constitutional name, or even simply as Macedonia. As more and more countries bilaterally recognise Macedonia under its constitutional name, Greece has once again become more vociferous on the issue and many in Greece still refer to the state as simply Skopje. In addition, Greece refuses to officially recognise Macedonians in Greece as an ethnic minority in their own right, but recognises them as Bulgarian.

Although the returning VMRO-DPMNE government in Macedonia has dropped its original irredentist claims towards Aegean Macedonia, Prime Minister Gruevski has blatantly riled Greece by naming the country's international airport Aleksander the Great (confusing the matter even further with Greece's Macedonia airport at Thessaloniki), and announcing that Macedonia will seek compensation for Macedonians who were forced out of Greece and thus lost land after World War II and the Greek civil war. Prime Minister Gruevski's mother, incidentally, hails from Aegean Macedonia.

International patience with this dispute is growing thin, especially since the EU revealed late in 2004 that Greece had been under-reporting its economic figures in order to get into the euro zone in 2000. Greece's blockade of Macedonia into NATO, and most likely into the EU, breaks the 1995 interim accord between both countries. As a result Macedonia is taking Greece to the International Court of Justice.

GOVERNING INSTITUTIONS

The governing system in Macedonia is a parliamentary democracy. Due to the infancy of Macedonia's democracy, political parties, and therefore government, are still very new to the political, economic and legal intricacies of successfully governing the country. As a result, and as a remnant from communist times, government institutions are not particularly transparent, and engender little public faith. Macedonia's fledgling civil society has a long way to go to achieve full participation in local and national governance, and a paucity of dialogue between government and civil society does not help.

In addition, political parties, electoral practices and the parliamentary system are in a fairly regular state of flux. Recent wide-reaching changes to the electoral system have been successful in ensuring fairer and more transparent elections, but there are still many problems especially regarding the voting rights of non-resident citizens, and the elimination of family and proxy voting.

HEAD OF STATE The current head of state, President Gjorge Ivanov, was elected in March 2009, succeeding Branko Crvenkovski, who was elected after the previous president, Boris Trajkovski, died tragically in a plane crash in February 2004. As Macedonia is a parliamentary democracy, the president holds little real power and the post is largely ceremonial. In Macedonia's volatile ethnic environment, however, the president can, and does, play an important role in inter-ethnic and inter-party relations.

LEGISLATURE Parliament is a unicameral assembly (*sobranje* in Macedonian), which consists of 120 seats. Parliamentary elections are held every four years based on multi-district proportional representation. Registered parties or coalitions put forward closed candidate lists in six electoral districts in one round of votes. The six districts are a new innovation as a result of the Ohrid Framework Agreement in an attempt to more fairly represent minority communities. In addition, the elimination of a second round of voting has helped to reduce political intimidation against election officials and the electorate. Professionalisation of the electoral boards (previously run by mixed party appointees) has also helped to eliminate intimidation and collusion in fraud. Since 2001 there has been no threshold for winning a seat in parliament.

In 2008, early parliamentary elections re-elected VMRO-DPMNE and its coalition. VMRO-DPMNE has been somewhat reformed since it ruled at the outbreak of the 2001 conflict. This has largely come about with the break-off of its more nationalist element in 2004 into the new VMRO-Narodna (VMRO People's Party under the continued effective leadership of former prime minister Ljupčo Georgievski). In addition, a breakaway party from SDSM, under the leadership of one of SDSM's original founders, Tito Petkovski, has also joined the coalition.

As of August 2008, the number of Assembly seats by party are as follows:

- 63 For a Better Macedonia coalition (consisting of the main party VMRO-DPMNE, the Liberal Democrats, the New Social Democratic Party, VMRO-Narodna and a number of small parties)
- 27 Sun Coalition for Europe (consisting of the Socialist Democratic Party of Macedonia (SDSM in Macedonian), Social Democratic Party, Liberal Democratic Party and other smaller parties)
- 18 Democratic Union of Integration
- 11 Democratic Party of Albanians
- 1 Party for European Integration

EXECUTIVE The head of government is currently Prime Minister Nikola Gruevski; the prime minister is elected by majority vote by the Assembly, as is his cabinet, the Council of Ministers. Of the 17 cabinet posts, four are held by Albanians: Culture, Education, Health and Environment. One of the four deputy prime minister posts is held by Imer Selmani, also an ethnic Albanian. Ethnic

25

Albanians also occupy a number of deputy minister posts, but these hold little real authority, as it is the state secretary of each ministry who actually has the most authority, after the minister.

JUDICIARY Constitutional and Supreme court judges are appointed by the Assembly. Lower (first-instance) and appellate (second-instance) court judges are appointed by the State Judicial Council, whose 15 members are elected by a mixture of judicial election, Assembly appointment, presidential appointment and ex-officio posts. Although the court system in Macedonia is designed to be independent of politics, there is in fact still much overlap and low self-regulation. This is not helped by the fact that there is no independent protection for judges who want to go against the political line. A national strategy for reform of the judiciary was adopted in 2004, but the full benefits of these reforms have yet to materialise. Unfortunately, Macedonian courts and law enforcement mechanisms tend to shy away from responsibility, not least because criminal pressures to do so are high. As a result the confidence of national citizens and international investors in the legal system in Macedonia is low. Progress in closing the chasm between legal reform and implemented reality is glacial.

ECONOMY

Macedonia's economy has been slow to improve. Already the poorhouse of Yugoslavia, Macedonia's economy deteriorated even further in the early 1990s through the sanctions imposed on Serbia, a unilateral economic boycott levied against Macedonia by Greece, inimical relations with Bulgaria and minuscule trade relations with even poorer Albania. Although all these areas of trade relations have improved, the conflict of 2001 did not help to alleviate the situation and like many post-communist countries, Macedonia is experiencing the brain drain so familiar when the country's young and educated, needed to revitalise the economy, leave for more lucrative jobs abroad.

In 2009 the estimated official unemployment figure for Macedonia was 35% of the working population, although surveys show that half of these do have part-time work of some nature, or work on the black market. Over 20% of the population lives in poverty (United Nations Development Programme, 2006). Macedonia's currency, the denar, has remained fairly stable as it has been pegged to the euro since 1998. Inflation in 2007 was 4%.

Macedonia exports a number of raw materials such as iron and zinc, but it has very few exports from skilled labour or light industry, never mind anything high tech. Textile manufacturing had been developed during the 20th century but, although Macedonia continues to export some clothing, it has proved difficult to compete against the likes of China and India. Macedonia imports almost twice as much in dollar value as it exports.

Macedonia's natural metallic resources have included copper, gold, iron ore, manganese, nickel, tungsten, lead, silver and zinc, but these resources are dwindling. For the building industry it also has abundant granite, gypsum, lignite, siliceous and quartz sands, as well as marble for which there is a large quarry and factory near Prilep.

Being located so far south in Europe but with ample rivers and water resources Macedonia also grows large quantities of corn, grapes, peppers, rice, tobacco, tomatoes and wheat. Unfortunately, without suitable cooling houses to store this produce out of season, Macedonia's agricultural industry remains tied to the seasons. It has to sell far too cheaply in the summer and has little to sell in the winter. In order to join the EU Macedonia will also have to start regulating produce size and quality, which will require expensive changes to agricultural practices and probably put small farms out of business.

Tobacco has been one of Macedonia's main exports, and during the summer harvests you can see it drying almost everywhere, but especially in Prilep where Macedonia's main tobacco factory is located. In recent years though, with the trend towards producing less harmful cigarettes, Macedonia's heavy-tar tobacco has become less popular.

Grapes on the other hand are on the rise as Macedonia's wines and liquors become more popular. The wine industry is poised to take off, and so now is a good time to get in if you want to try Macedonian wines whilst they are still inexpensive and unadulterated. For more information on Macedonia's wines including wine tours see page 284.

Much of Macedonia's farming is still done by hand, and although the industry is slowly becoming more mechanised, you can often see animals used for ploughing the fields and hauling crops. Land is terraced in many of the mountain areas and families and neighbours will resource labour during intensive planting and harvesting times. Macedonia is full of contrasts like that – one week you will see snow on the mountaintops, and the next week families are planting rice in the paddy fields.

2

The Outdoors

> The landscape here needed to be read, not just looked at ... When no longer a
> reality but a lost ideal, the precious beauty of the land increased: I saw why its poets
> spoke bitterly and in hyperbole.
>
> *Balkan Ghosts*, Robert D. Kaplan, 1993

TOPOGRAPHY

Geographical Macedonia is bounded by the Šar and Osogovska mountains to the
north, Lake Ohrid and the Pindus Mountains to the west, the Rhodope
Mountains to the east, and by Mount Olympus and the Aegean Sea to the south.
This area was divided into four parts after the Berlin Treaty of 1878, and although
Vardar Macedonia in particular may have changed hands several times since then,
the division of the four parts has largely stayed the same. The four parts are now
Vardar Macedonia in the northwest, Pirin Macedonia encompassing the Pirin
Mountains in the northeast (now part of Bulgaria), Aegean Macedonia to the
south as part of Greece, and a tiny sliver of land north and south of Debar and
part of Lake Ohrid, which now belong to Albania.

Vardar Macedonia, which is the land around the upper reaches of the River
Vardar, is divided from Pirin Macedonia in the east by the peak of Mount Ruen
and the Vlaina Mountains above the River Struma in Bulgaria. The mountain
ranges of Kožuf and Nidže divide the northern Vardar region from the southern
plains. This area is completely landlocked and is divided almost in half by the
River Vardar, which runs south to the Aegean Sea. Only the River Crni Drim,
which starts in Lake Ohrid and ends in the Adriatic, and the Strumica, which
drains into the Struma in Bulgaria, also lead to a sea port.

As is already evident, there are numerous small mountain ranges in Vardar
Macedonia, and in fact 80% of the country is considered mountainous. This is due
to the fact that three tectonic plates, African, Asian and European, meet in this
region. It is mostly the work of the African plate sliding beneath the Eurasian
plates under Greece that caused the geographic formation of Macedonia that we
see today, and it is also the reason why there are frequent earthquake tremors in
the region and many hot springs.

The friction between the plates has brought about a number of fault lines that
run across Macedonia approximately along the course of riverbeds. The one
under Kočani along the River Bregalnica contributed to the 1904 earthquake,
and the Skopje fault line along the Vardar contributed to the 1963 earthquake that
destroyed most of the city. The earliest well-recorded earthquake in the region
was in AD518 when Heraklea was destroyed, and it is likely that earthquakes will
continue for centuries to come. Scientists claim that these earthquakes are moving
eastward in intensity, and with the earthquake of 2009 in Italy, this doesn't bode
well for Macedonia.

Macedonia is absolutely littered with old castles. As a constant front over the millennia – between the Paeonians and the ancient Macedonians, then the Romans and the ancient Macedonians, then from maurading Gauls, Slavic tribes and crusaders, later between the crumbling Byzantine empire and the Ottomans, and finally the crumbling Ottoman Empire and the new nation-states of the 19th century – the southern border of Macedonia in particular has repeatedly seen strong fortification.

Sadly, Macedonia's position on the cusp of the European and African tectonic plates means that its regular earthquakes have all but destroyed all Macedonia's castles. The remains of a few are undergoing archaeological excavation and renovation, such as the Kale (castle) at Skopje, Ohrid, Strumica, Prilep, Tetovo, Štip and Gradište. The Carevi Kuli (towers) at Strumica form part of a very clear fortification line along the border, while Markovi Kuli in Prilep were once the pinnacle of an entire fortified town.

Many castles, such as at Otunje and Stenje near Tetovo, Kozle and Veles along the River Vardar, and at Kičevo, have little to show and can be quite hard to find. Others such as the once mighty cyclopean masonry of the Paeonian castles at Varoš near Oktisi, Prosek near Demir Kapija, and others at Matka and in Mariovo are but scars in the ground unless you know what you are looking for.

There are eight well-developed hot springs in Vardar Macedonia and dozens more that are undeveloped. The former have all been developed for medicinal purposes, although moves are afoot to open them up for recreational use. The medicinal qualities of the water depend on the mineral deposits beneath the spring, which the water has been forced through in order to reach the surface. Yugoslavia put a lot of research into understanding the medicinal properties of these hot springs and Macedonian doctors will frequently prescribe a sojourn at a particular hot spring for its healing qualities in relation to all sorts of maladies, from broken bones to pneumonia. Only Katlanovska Banja near Skopje offers western European spa-type standards, although there are plans also for Negorski Banja near Gevgelija.

The border of Vardar Macedonia shares three tectonic lakes, Ohrid, Prespa and Dojran, with it neighbours Albania and Greece. As their names imply, these lakes were formed millennia ago from movements in the tectonic plates. Lake Ohrid in particular is so old and the life forms in the lake so unique that it is comparable to Lake Baikal in Russia and Lake Titicaca in Peru/Bolivia, and it is under UNESCO protection. There are also ten manmade lakes, which were formed to create a hydro-electric production capability under Yugoslav Macedonia, and a number of glacial lakes high up in the mountains of the Baba, Jablanica and Šar ranges.

The longest river in Macedonia is the Vardar, which starts in the mountains above Gostivar and drains out at Thessaloniki in Greece. The Vardar collects 80% of the water run-out of Macedonia. The next longest rivers are the Bregalnica and Crna, both of which empty into the Vardar.

The highest peak in Macedonia at 2,753m, Mount Korab, is on the border with Albania. The highest peak wholly within Macedonia is Titov Vrv at 2,748m in the Šar Planina range, which is surpassed in the former Yugoslav states only by Mount Triglav in Slovenia. The lowest point in Macedonia is where the River Vardar exits into Greece at 45m above sea level.

Years of communist neglect and a poor economy have done little to improve transportation lines within the country. The only international railway line that presently runs through Macedonia, stopping in Skopje, is from Ljubljana to Thessaloniki. The lines to Priština and Kičevo have been sporadic since hostilities in the 1990s, and the line to Greece via Bitola does not run trains beyond Bitola. The original line to Ohrid was not updated with the wider-gauge rails beyond Kičevo and so stops there. The line from Kumanovo, planned to go to Bulgaria, stops 40km short of the border. A working passenger line runs from Veles to Kočani via Štip, but the side line from Prilep to Sopotnica is no longer working.

In line with preparation for EU entry, the European Agency for Reconstruction is pouring money into the main highways through Macedonia, so Motorway 1 (E75) along the Vardar, Motorway 2 from Kumanovo into Bulgaria and the E65 from Skopje through Tetovo, Gostivar and Kičevo to Ohrid and Bitola are in good condition, with dual carriageways on portions of those roads leading out of Skopje. With decentralisation other roads are being improved, but many are in a bad state of repair and some fairly well-used roads are still mostly cobbled (which have the advantage at least of being hard wearing), such as from Strumica to Radoviš, the roads around Lake Prespa, and the roads on either side of Kočani. A great many villages in Macedonia are still only accessible by dirt track or goat path, although these tend to be way up in the mountains where village life is dying out (partially because of lack of accessibility).

ANCIENT ROADS IN MACEDONIA

As Rome advanced its empire across the Balkan peninsula and beyond, a number of key trade and military routes were developed. Serving these routes were numerous small towns and settlements. Their whereabouts are well documented in Macedonian, but little information is available on them in English and their full significance is even less understood (see box, pages 32–3). Key ancient towns are detailed in individual chapters of this book, but roads are described below.

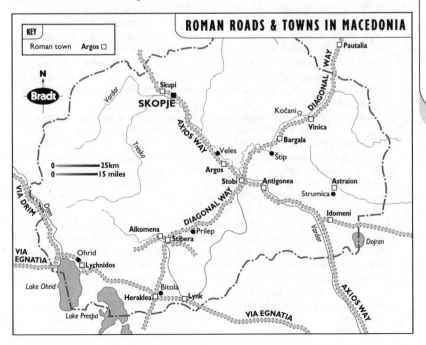

VIA EGNATIA The Via Egnatia connected Italy via the port of Durres in Albania to Elbasan and Ohrid, mostly along the River Shkumbin on the Albanian side. The Via Egnatia entered Macedonia near the village of Radožda on the western side of Lake Ohrid, then went around the north side of the lake to Ohrid and around the north side of the Galičica and Baba mountains to Heraklea near present-day Bitola. The road exited Vardar Macedonia via the ancient city of Lynk on the River Crna and then went on to Edessa, Pella and Thessaloniki, and eventually to Constantinople (today's Istanbul; Carigrad or Tsar's Town in Macedonian).

If any of the Roman surfaces still exist in Macedonia, they either remain buried or have been resurfaced. The most well-known section of the road in Macedonia is the cobbled section between Magarevo and Turnovo to the west of Bitola. This road was cobbled by French troops during World War I offensives. Some of it can still be seen but the remainder has since been tarmacked.

There are claims that sections of the Via Egnatia are visible between Oktiši and Gorna Belica at a stopping point called Vajtos, which some believe is the eighth stopping point on the road. But this location would be a complete dog-leg off the Radožda to Ohrid route and it is more likely that this section of ancient Roman road belonged to the road which followed the River Crni Drim from Enchelon (now Struga) via Debar to the mouth of the Crni Drim in present-day Albania.

AN UNTOLD STORY – ARCHAEOLOGY IN MACEDONIA

Andriana Dragovic and Nikica Korubin

Macedonia has a rich and varied archaeological resource. Of all the periods to be found in the country (from the mesolithic to the more recent archaeology of the cold war) it is the Roman sites that are the most monumental and most visible in the landscape. Remarkably little archaeological research has been undertaken however, and the management, curation and presentation of archaeological sites is universally poor. Nevertheless the situation is changing (though maybe not for the better) and a great deal of state funding is pouring into excavation campaigns. Conversely work in the realms of heritage management and resource quantification is being undertaken largely by the NGO sector with geo-physical surveys at sites such as Skupi, Bargala near Štip and Konjuh near Kumanovo.

Macedonia sits astride the land routes from western Europe into Asia and indeed the conquest of Macedonia was the key to the spread of Roman influence and later military occupation in the east. The ancient territories of Macedonia and Alexander the Great were of particular significance to the Romans because the emulation and surpassing of the feats of Alexander were a visible testament, both in the wider world and more importantly at home in Rome, to the greatness of Rome, the Senate (and later the Emperor) and Roman civilisation.

The Romans were extremely familiar with the Hellenic way of life, thought, architecture and urban living, and claimed much of it as their own. Hellenic colonies were interspersed in the western Mediterranean and much of southern Italy was influenced by Macedonian colonies, the most famous of which being the city of Pompeii. Much of the design of Roman houses aped Greek or Hellenic forms. As a result, the Hellenistic world created by Macedonian military might have appeared familiar to the Romans, as if Macedonia itself was a part of Rome's back yard. When Augustus conquered the modern-day areas of Serbia and Bulgaria, establishing the province of Moesia, the frontier of the Roman world in the Balkans became the River Danube. Macedonia in the

VIA AXIOS AND THE DIAGONAL WAY The Diagonal Way linked Heraklea with Stibera, which lies halfway between Bitola and Prilep, with Stobi, Bargala near Štip and Pautalija (now Kustendil) in present-day Bulgaria. It was an important road linking the Vardar Valley with the Struma Valley (now in Bulgaria) and crossed other important roads along the way. At Stibera it met the road from the mining town of Demir Hisar which followed the River Crna. At Stobi it crossed the Via Axios (the ancient Greek name for the Vardar River), which ran along the Vardar, and at Bargala it crossed the road from Strumica to the Ovče Polje plains around Sveti Nikola.

CLIMATE

Macedonia has a relatively dry Mediterranean climate with the full array of four seasons, although spring can be quite short, and each season is tempered by the altitude. In the Vardar Valley, Ovče Polje and the lower Pelagonia plains, temperatures are roasting hot in the summer and relatively mild in the winter. Skopjites tend to empty out of the capital during the hottest months of July and August, when temperatures can reach 40°C. These summer highs are infrequently punctuated by summer storms, but they do occur, especially in the mountains. Favourite summer retreats to the cool and welcoming mountains are Mavrovo National Park, Pelister National Park, Popova Šapka, Kriva Palanka, Berovo and

hinterland of this important frontier was thus one of the keys to military and civilian control of both the northern frontier of the Balkans and a gateway to the ancient Mediterranean world.

The significance of the archaeology in Macedonia is global, not least because the historical region of Macedonia was Alexander's manor and he still occupies a pre-eminent role in the psyche of northwest Europe and the US.

Funding for archaeological research is derived entirely from the Ministry of Culture. In a country with serious economic problems the realisation of the potential of the archaeological resource to entice the tourist dollar is growing, but as yet lacks the sophistication of approach found in many other European countries. Local archaeological organisations and NGO's are trying to build international co-operation with foreign institutions with some success. There are a number of examples of collaborative archaeological excavations with foreign (usually American) and Macedonian teams working in tandem.

Looting of archaeological sites is a big problem in Macedonia but identifying the scale is difficult for two reasons. Firstly, looted artefacts are whisked away to foreign markets in Europe, America and the Far East and secondly the precise provenance of any artefacts can seldom be established because so many of the sites of discovery are unknown to the archaeological community in Macedonia and thus cannot be policed. There is a robust legal framework to protect the archaeological sites of Macedonia, but the actual process of enumerating, identifying and characterising where the undiscovered archaeological sites are is yet to commence in any seriousness and the possibility of state provison for such a process has been called, from within the archaeological community of Macedonia itself, a 'science fiction'. There are, however, a plethora of iconic archaeological sites to visit with excavations underway at Plaošnik in Ohrid, Markovi Kuli, Visoka and Stibera in the Prilep region, Stobi near Veles, Heraklea in Bitola, Skupi outside Skopje.

For those who want to visit the archaeological site Vardarski Rid near Gevgelija there is a useful web page: www.vardarskirid.org.mk. Possibilities for volunteering on archaeological excavations may appear soon.

Kruševo. Bitola, a mere 380m above Skopje, is usually a good 10–12°C lower in temperature year round than the city itself.

Although the winters are mild in the low areas along the River Vardar, rarely getting below freezing, there are occasionally freak winters, such as in 2001–02, which saw Skopje come to a standstill when snow and ice blocked the roads for weeks. The mountains, however, regularly see 1–2m of snow. This makes for decent skiing, limited only by the standard of facilities or a skier's own abilities to go off-piste. Regions above 2,000m will see pockets of snow as early as August, and the peaks are certainly dusted with a light coat of snow by early November.

September and April may see longer spells of cloud and rain. In general though, the weather is warm and sunny from March through to November and perfect for outdoor sports. October–November is when the mountain trees turn colour before they shed their leaves and this is the time to take a drive or hike

WILD PLANTS   *Sanne van den Heuvel*

If you leave early for a hike in the Macedonian mountains, you will definitely meet a couple of older men and women collecting whatever the season offers. Macedonians still use a wide variety of herbs and teas for their medicinal properties and most people will be able to inform you about the characteristics of these plants, where to find them and how to use them. The pleasure of collecting nettle in early spring, wild strawberries in high summer and chestnuts in autumn creates an intimate relationship with nature, enriching the experience of walking in the mountains. Collecting herbs must be done in agreement with existing regional and national laws for protection and sustainable usage of plant species. Always pick only small parts from each plant to make sure that it is still able to grow.

An excellent book on collecting edible wild plants and mushrooms is Richard Mabey's *Food for Free* (Harper Collins 2003). The overview below (courtesy of the Berovo Hiking Trail map) provides a list of the most common herbs in Macedonia and their uses. The Berovo map is published by the Tourism Information Point (❧ 033 471 287; e *julijanab@yahoo.com; www.berovo.gov.mk*). They offer different programmes about rural and ecotourism and can also arrange activities such as hiking, walking, biking and camping.

Latin name	Common name in English and Macedonian	What and how it is collected	Uses
Thymus spp.	Thyme *Majčina dušica*	Young, green parts of the stem with leaves and flowers	Pneumonia, bronchitis and sore throat, nervousness, insomnia
Convalaria majalis	Lily of the valley *Momina solza*	Section above ground when buds begin to show	Heart problems
Rosa canina	Rose-hip *Šipka, diva roza*	Mature and hard fruits without stem, clean or sift out the centres which contain sharp hairs	In jams and tea, rich in vitamin C
Primula veris	Primrose *Jaglika aglička*	Flowers in dry, sunny weather the plant is rare and should only be collected in small batches	Coughing, running nose, cleaning of the blood
Chamomilla vulgare	Chamomile *Kamilica, vrtipop*	Flower and section about ground from spring until end of the summer	Inflammation of the mouth, dry lips, sore throat

through the ravines of Mavrovo, the Radika, Treška, Babuna and Maleševo. Skopje can get caught in fog during this time, but 20 minutes outside of the capital usually reveals bright sunny weather.

FLORA AND FAUNA

Due to Macedonia's location between the Mediterranean and Euro-Siberian regions, the variety of flora and fauna is extensive. During the 1970s and 1980s research and records were made of all the animals and plants in the Yugoslav Federation. Since then, however, Macedonia has had few resources to spend on maintaining these records and so even approximate figures on how many of each type of animal there are in Macedonia are few and far between. Macedonia has worked jointly with other countries, such as Greece, to try to establish

Latin name	Common name in English and Macedonian	What and how it is collected	Uses
Origanum vulgare	Wild marjoram Planinski čaj, rigjen	Section of plant above ground and the flower	For the throat, pains in the kidney and stomach
Urtica dioica	Nettle Kopriva	Leaves and herb are collected in July and August; roots are collected in the fall and in the spring	Cleaning of the blood, a homeostatic and for kidney disorders
Sambucus nigra	Elder Bozel	Collected when blossoms begin to open in May and June	Given for colds, flu, pneumonia and other respiratory illnesses
Achillea millefolium	Common yarrow Bela rada, ajdučka treva	Above ground section collected when it blossoms from May to September	Pains from diabetes and in the liver
Juniperus communis	Juniper Cmreka	Fruits are collected when they become dark blue from the end of August to September	Improving appetite, pains in gastro-intestinal track and respiratory illnesses
Plantago lanceolata	Narrowleaf plantain Tesnolisten tegavec	Leaves are collected from May to October when the plant blossoms	Cold, diarrhoea and ulcers
Viscum album	Mistletoe Bela imela	Leaves and the stem are collected from November to March; plant grows very slowly and large collections are tough on the plant	Regulation of blood pressure, makes blood vessels more elastic, increases metabolism and processes in the digestive track
Rubus idaeus	Raspberry Malina	Leaves are collected in summer from June-July to September	Nervousness, pre-menstrual tension, diarrhoea and dysentery
Mentha piperita	Peppermint Nane	Leaves are collected before blossoming in May	Used against gastro-intestinal pains and gases
Erythraea	Centaury/ red gentian Crven kantarion	The upper section is collected before blossoming	Increasing appetite and gastro-intestinal pains
Hypericum	St John's Wort Kantarion	Leaves and flowers	In tea and as an oil; an all round immune booster, antiseptic and anti-depressant

approximate numbers of wolves for instance, but more research needs to be done in order to confirm these figures.

A number of hotels and travel agencies, such as Hotel Bistra in Mavrovo, Go Macedonia and Adventure Guide Macedonia in Skopje, can arrange hunting and wildlife observation trips by jeep if you are interested. Lake Dojran and Golem Grad Island in Prespa Lake are havens of water wildlife, insects and birds, and if you take a guided tour in one of the national parks, such as from the village of Brajčino, your guide will be able to show you the tracks and beds of the local animals. Bats can often be seen in the evening around many of Macedonia's caves such as at Leskoec, Matka and Treskavec.

If you just want a quick overview of Macedonia's wildlife then the Natural History Museum in Skopje houses everything (stuffed) in one convenient location. Although the museum is in desperate need of attention and a good English brochure, it is quite interesting and also houses the skeletons of prehistoric animals that used to roam through Macedonia. For the most current information on Macedonia's wildlife contact Dr Ljupčo Mejolovski or Slavčo Hristovski at the Macedonian Ecology Society (*Institut za Biologija, Prirodno-Matematički Fakultet, Ul Gazi Baba bb, 1000 Skopje;* ☏ *02 3249 611;* e *mes@iunona.pmf.ukim.edu.mk, contact@mes.org.mk; www.mes.org.mk*).

MAMMALS There are eight protected species in Macedonia, among which is the **brown bear** (*Ursus arctos*). The last study in 1997 assessed their figures at somewhere between 160–200, of which there were around 70 in Mavrovo National Park, 30 in Pelister, and only three or four in Galičica. Since brown-bear hunting became illegal in 1996, it is believed that the bear population has slowly increased.

ENCOUNTERING BROWN BEARS

Taken from Bradt's Central and Eastern European Wildlife, *by Gerard Gorman*

Much has been written and said about what a person should and should not do when meeting a bear face to face. In most cases nothing at all needs to be done as bears usually do their utmost to avoid confrontation with humans. However, in the event of a physical confrontation humans stand almost no chance at all, as brown bears are incredibly powerful and fearless. Most confrontations between humans and bears involve animals which have been startled when feeding or mothers who sense their cubs are at risk.

- Give bears plenty of respect and space
- Never run from a bear, instead speak and move your arms to indicate you are human
- Alternatively, back away slowly and carefully
- If a bear stands up on its hind legs do not panic, it is merely assessing the situation
- Never walk directly towards a bear
- Never approach seemingly 'lost' cubs
- If a bear moves towards you stand your ground and stand as tall as you can
- Never look an approaching bear directly in the eye
- If a bear moves to attack hit the ground face-down and put your hands over the back of the neck
- When on the ground stay still, silent and 'play possum'
- Do not climb a tree to escape from a bear unless you are sure you can get above 4m high

Other protected species include the **jackal** (*Canis aureus*) for which there are no available numbers and the **Balkan lynx** (*Lynx lynx martinoi* – the national animal depicted on the back of the five denar coin). The Balkan lynx itself is poached for its gorgeous spotted golden-brown fur, even though poaching lynx can bring a sentence of up to eight years imprisonment. Its habitat, however, is also under continuous threat by illegal logging. In continuing decline, their numbers are believed to be fewer than 100 across Macedonia and Albania, with even fewer in Serbia and Kosovo. In an effort to reverse this phenomenon, the Balkan Lynx Recovery Programme (BLRP) has been set up across the Balkans to monitor and assist with protection. Thirty cameras have been set up in Galičica National Park alone, where the programme is monitored by Dime Melovski of the Macedonian Ecological Society (see contact details above).

Wolves on the other hand are not protected as they are considered a pest, preying on sheep and other farm livestock. Some 350 are killed every year, but their population remains stable at around 700. Since the government decreased the amount paid for a wolf skin (now about 700MKD), it has been assumed that the wolf population will increase.

The national parks and Jasen Forestry Reserve are home to many of the hunted species in Macedonia such as wolves, marten, wild boar, chamois, roebuck and other deer where their numbers are meant to be regulated through the use of a hunting licence system. Despite this, however, many of these animals are in decline. According to the Open Society Institute (*www.soros.org.mk*) most of the hunted animals' stocks have been reduced to less than 25% of their former numbers, and sightings are definitely not as common as they used to be. The deer populations in some gaming areas are less than 7% of their former numbers.

REPTILES AND INSECTS Macedonia does have some poisonous insects and reptiles, including some snakes and a few species of **spider**. Like most wild creatures, these will go in the opposite direction of a human being if given enough chance to do so. Many types of **lizard** will be seen scurrying from footpaths as you walk through the mountains, and **frogs** are abundant at Lake Prespa. **Mosquitoes** are common in marshy areas in the lowlands, but these areas are few and far between. Watch out also for **tortoises** crossing the roads – these are as much of a hazard here as hedgehogs are in Great Britain.

Among Macedonia's 17 different types of **snake** are the common (and poisonous) adder, field viper and sand viper (known as *poskog* or 'jumping snake' in Macedonian) as well as non-venomous water snakes and other more unusual species. The javelin sand boa, found in sandy areas around Lake Dojran, can reach up to 70cm in length and is one of the smallest of the boa and python family usually found in warmer parts of the world. The largest European snake, which can be found in the lowlands of Macedonia, is the large whip snake, *Coluber caspius*, which reaches up to 3m in length. Although non-venomous, it will bite in captivity or when frightened.

Two 'semi-venomous' snakes also live in Macedonia. The Montpelier snake, *Malpolon monspessulanus*, is found up to 2m in length in rocky limestone areas with dense vegetation. The cat snake *Telescopus failax* is up to 1m in length and prefers dry rocky lowlands, old walls and ruins. Both snakes are semi-poisonous because their venom produces only localised swelling and numbness and is difficult to eject from the small mouths of these snakes into a human arm or leg. Fingers might be tempting though.

FISH Macedonia's freshwater fish include carp, bream, catfish, barbell and perch. Dojran bleak, Strumica bleak and Macedonian dace are some that are peculiar to

Macedonia, as is the Dojran roach, *Ratilus ratilus dojrovensis*, and Ohrid trout, *Salma trutto letnica*. The latter are now endangered and fishing for them is illegal. Unfortunately, serving them in restaurants and eating them is not. The 10 August 2005 article from the Balkan Investigative Research Network (BIRN) highlights the problems of poaching and tourist demands (*www.iwpr.net/?p=bcr&s=f&o=257050&apc_state=henibcr200508*). Another type of Ohrid trout, *belvica*, is also served in restaurants and is a tasty alternative for a law-abiding tourist.

Eel, *jagula* in Macedonian, is common in Macedonia and a favourite dish of the locals. The eel from Lake Ohrid used to spawn in the Sargasso Sea until dams were built along the Crni Drim River. It is not yet clear how this is affecting their population, but they still seem abundant. Of the many small fish in Lake Ohrid, the *plašica* is the most famous, for its scales are used to make Ohrid pearls, using a painstakingly intricate technique the secret of which is fiercely guarded by the artisans of Ohrid.

BIRDS There are over 330 kinds of bird in Macedonia, and almost 100 migratory bird species that spend some of the year in Macedonia. Of Macedonia's native birds, 56 are protected. Amongst those protected are vultures and eagles. Vultures were undergoing study during 2003, when there was estimated to be between 35–40 pairs of Griffin vultures, 40–60 pairs of Egyptian vultures, and only one solitary male bearded vulture and one male black vulture. Both these last birds lost their mates well over a decade ago, and as they are monogamous creatures it is extremely unlikely that they will find new mates. There are plans afoot to introduce new pairs of bearded and black vultures into the country, but once again resources to fund such initiatives are limited.

Although eagles used to be abundant in Macedonia, only a dozen or so pairs can be found now around Mount Korab and the Šar mountain range. Storks, both white and black, are also on the decline, but you will still see them nesting in a number of villages and towns. Macedonian folklore claims they bring luck especially with regard to childbearing.

Pelicans and cormorants are quite common and fishermen use cormorants to catch fish on Lake Prespa. A wetland reserve at Ezerani is home to many of Macedonia's birds. Imported birds include peacocks, to be found at the monastery of Sveti Naum and at New Age Teahouse in Skopje; swans, introduced to Lake Ohrid in the early 1970s; black turkeys at the Monastery of Zrze; and ostriches farmed near Tetovo.

PLANTS AND BUTTERFLIES There are over 3,500 different plants in Macedonia. These include alpine flowers such as gentian and furry alpine bluebell as well as imported stocks of kiwi, pomegranates and rice, usually the preserve of more tropical climates. The great variety of flowers here also attracts an incredible number of different butterflies and moths. Look out particularly for the humming-bird hawk-moth, *Macroglossum stellatarum*, which is not commonly found in northern Europe.

Over 35% of the country is forest, most of which is deciduous. Less than 10% of Macedonia's forests are evergreen, but amongst that 10% is the Molika pine, which is unique to the greater Macedonia region, Bulgaria and Albania. In Macedonia the Molika pine is mostly found in Pelister National Park.

ENVIRONMENTAL EFFORTS

Despite views to the contrary, the communist period of Macedonia's history had gone a long way, both deliberately and inadvertently, towards helping preserve

Macedonia's rich wildlife and unspoilt natural environment. All three national parks, Pelister (1948), Galičica (1949) and Mavrovo (1958), were set up in this time, as well as Jasen Forestry Reserve (1958), and 48 natural monuments were designated for protection. Inadvertently, Macedonia's poor economy, low levels of tourism and lack of urbanisation have helped to preserve many areas of natural beauty.

Industrial pollution has been, and still is, a problem, as is the Macedonian disregard for litter, especially the non-biodegradable kind. The Macedonians may try to blame the government for a lack of litter bins and nobody to take the litter away (which is true) but Macedonians don't help themselves. As every responsible hiker knows, if you pack it in with you, then pack it out with you, and get rid of your rubbish through the waste disposal service rather than leave it as an eyesore and health hazard. There are efforts under way by NGOs to move the government towards better waste management, but it may be a few more years before the effects are seen.

Macedonia does have some environmental groups which go back to the communist era of social awareness, and even more are springing up now in the wake of international money earmarked for building civil society and civil participation. Although these groups do good work, and go some way towards educating local communities about environmental concerns in their area, to be effective a nationwide effort really needs to be led by the government.

RECYCLING Recycling does exist in Macedonia, although the service certainly doesn't come to the door, and won't even be in a nearby street. Newspaper and magazine recycling is the most ubiquitous, with large bell-like green drums in main streets in which you can slot papers and magazines. These are picked up by Skopje's paper recycling company, Komuna (*Ul Romanija bb, 1040 Skopje, behind the Skopje Fair;* \ *02 2551 081;* e *info@komuna.com.mk; www.komuna.com.mk;* ⊕ *08.00–14.00 daily*). They also collect office paper and will supply special cardboard cartons for offices for the purpose. Cardboard is also recycled there, and when you see it being collected by people on the streets, you'll be glad to know that it is not for the homeless to build a cardboard house under a bridge, but to be sold to Komuna for recycling.

Plastic bottle recycling is available for companies through a USAID-assisted project.

Whether you are living in or just visiting Macedonia, don't add to the rubbish which is already here, but follow these simple points:

• Reduce the amount you have to throw away, such as packaging
• Reuse disposable items, such as bags, paper and containers
• Recycle what you need to throw away
• If you pack it in, then pack it out
• Take your own bags (preferably cloth) with you to the shops
• Buy recycled and biodegradable products

LOCAL ENVIRONMENTAL ORGANISATIONS Macedonia's environment is at a critical point in its development and so now is the time to ensure that it gets saved for the likes of you and me to enjoy when we come to visit another day. If you would like to find out more about how you could get involved with environmental protection in Macedonia, contact one of the following groups:

Proaktiva (Contact Slavjanka Miladinova at) Dame Gruev 1–4/7, PO Box 695, 1000 Skopje; \/f 02 321 5881; e info@proaktiva.org.mk; www.proaktiva.org.mk. A young enthusiastic group that has worked hard to increase public awareness of the importance of Macedonia's environment.

Eco-sense 11 Oktomvri 125/12, 1000 Skopje; ☏ 02 3217 245/247; e info@ekosvest.com.mk; www.ekosvest.com.mk. Regularly seeks volunteers to help with clean-up days & other larger projects. **B Kozle** 100, PO Box 360, 1000 Skopje; ☏/f 02 3090 400; e contact@eko.net.mk; www.eko.net.mk. Dedicates itself to informing people about the environmental efforts ongoing in Macedonia.

Vila Zora 22 Trajko Panov, 1400 Veles; ☏ 043 233 023; e vilazora@mt.net.mk; www.vilazora.org.mk. Does major advocacy in remediating soil around the Veles area that has been contaminated by local industry. Also does a lot on preserving & presenting natural habitat & trails.

OUTDOOR PURSUITS

Macedonia is a haven for the outdoor sports enthusiast. Its mountains and waterways and lack of paved roads make it a pleasure to hike and bike in, and offer countless opportunities for paragliding, climbing, caving and kayaking. Many Macedonians themselves are keen outdoors people too, so although there is little in the way of ready-made outdoor package holidays or even just a bit of information in English, there are plenty of clubs which welcome outside interest and some are even opening up courses and guided tours. Information on how to get to the locations mentioned below is given in the individual chapters in Part Two of this guidebook.

HIKING AND MOUNTAINEERING These are by far the most popular outdoor sports in Macedonia. For more information on hiking clubs, huts and trails see *Chapter 12*.

ROCK CLIMBING This is a growing sport in Macedonia, and there are some excellent climbs to be had at Lake Matka near Skopje (traditional, multi-pitch), Kaneo at Ohrid (bolted), Pilav Tepe (Ploca) near Radoviš and Demir Kapija (bolted) right off the main road to Greece, amongst other places. For a guide to climbing routes at Matka see www.geocities.com/mkextreme2001/EngMatka.htm. For climbs at Pilav Tepe see below. Try also www.alpinizam.org for general information on other rock climbing areas. Active clubs include:

Everest Climbing Club Gevgelija; ☏ 034 213 743, 070 218 811. Club secretary Živko Murdžev.
Extreme Sport Climbing Club Boulder Hse Dzambaz, Ul 11 Oktomvri 42a, Skopje; ☏ 02 2432 503, (club secretary Martin Trajkovski) 070 242 028, (club president Vladimir Trpovski) 02 3111 460, 070 333 517; e shara@mt.net.mk or extremeclub@hotmail.com; www.fpsm-ska.org. The club has an indoor climbing wall in Skopje. They are also the authors of the first Macedonian climbing guide to Lake Matka (see above).
Issak Ruso Climbing Club Skopje; ☏ 02 3123 026, 070 617 821. Club secretary Dario.
Matka Climbing Club Franklin-Ruzevelt 68 1/2, Skopje; ☏ 02 2670 058, 070 34 28 28; e contact@matkaclimbing.org; www.matkaclimbing.org. Offer experienced guides for all of Macedonia & Bulgaria as well as rock climbing lessons at all levels of experience. The club can provide most of the necessary equipment such as ropes, helmets & other safety devices, but you

will have to provide your own footwear. Prices vary from €20 to €80 depending upon the duration & location of climbs & the amount of equipment hired.
Alpine Club Ploca Pilav Tepe, 17km west of Radoviš on the road to Štip & Skopje; e alpinistzm@yahoo.com for club president Zoran Majstorski; www.plocaclimbing.com. The rock climbing park at Pilav Tepe known as Ploca (Macedonian for slab or tile) is the most developed & most accessible climbing site in Macedonia. Golem Ploca features 12 bolted, multi-pitch routes. Mala Ploca has bolted & traditional routes. There are also 7 boulders below the big wall featuring bolted routes & bouldering problems. All the different sections are connected by maintained trails with signs & are a mere 10min walk from the Climbing Hut Ploca. The climbing hut complete with kitchen, bathroom (with hot water for showering) & 2 dorm-style bedrooms with a total of 12 beds is available for use by all. There are also opportunities for camping, hiking, &

mountain biking on marked trails around Lake Mantovo, the village Brest & the Monastery Sv Pantelejmon. The restaurant Pilav Tepe is located a stone's throw from the hut, offering traditional Macedonian cusine & a great view of the rock & its climbers.

Other indoor walls can be found at:

OU 'Toso Arsov' Borko Talev bb, Štip; ✆ 070 527 586
Ploca Climbing Hall Radoviš; www.plocaclimbing.com

Sport Hall 'Mladost' Negotino; ✆ 075 615 931
Sport Hall 'Nikola Karev' Negotino; ✆ 070 781 685

More information on climbing in Macedonia, but currently only in Macedonian, is at www.climbing.org.mk.

CAVING Macedonia is probably most well known outside the country for its speleology or caving. The karst formations of so much of Macedonia's ground structure make it ideal for caves. There are 346 registered caves (*peštera* in Macedonian) in the country, although the total of actual caves is probably somewhere between 400 and 500. Only four are protected: Pešna, Ubavica, Mlečnik and Gorna Slatinska. This number does not, however, reflect the amount of spectacular caves. Some of the caves have underground rivers, lakes, multiple caverns and of course stalagmites and stalactites. Many are home to rare underground life forms as well as prehistoric fossils. Most caves have not been made tourist-friendly yet and so most are really accessible only with the correct equipment, experience and preferably a guide. The only cave open daily to tourists (300MKD entrance fee) is Vrela at Lake Matka (see page 148 for more on the caves there), which is Macedonia's nomination for the New Seven Wonders of Nature.

By area the most well-known caves are at:

Gostivar The longest cave in Macedonia, at 1.2km, is Gonovica south of Gostivar, which has an underground river and the highest underground waterfall of 7m. Near here is also Ubavica Cave, almost a kilometre in length and boasting an underground waterfall.

Karadžica and Sopište The deepest cave in Macedonia is Solunska 4, just below Solunska Glava on Mount Karadžica. It is 450m in depth, with a single shaft of 250m in depth and contains the only ice cave formations yet known in Macedonia. Spela Bobguni near Patiška Reka is one of the more speleologically difficult and rewarding caves. There are about 50 other caves in the Sopište karst region.

Kavadarci Named the most beautiful cave in Macedonia is the 120m-long Gališka cave near Tikveš Lake. Its entrance at 10m high is easily accessible and its numerous water cascades and high humidity show off the colours of the various minerals inside. Bela Voda cave, 955m in length, with a lake at the end is near Demir Kapija.

Kičevo Slatinksi Izvor (meaning Slatino Springs) is near the village of Slatino south-southeast of Kičevo. It is over a kilometre in length and was been considered significant enough in caving terms (stalagmites, stalactites, river and lake features) to be submitted to UNESCO in 2004 for consideration as a World Heritage Site (see *http//whc.unesco.org/en/tentativelists/1917*).

Makedonski Brod Pešna Cave (page 210) near Makedonski Brod is the most accessible of caves, with a large entrance and the ruins of a medieval fortress. The

The Outdoors OUTDOOR PURSUITS

2

Slatino caves are also near here, as well as Golubarnik, Momiček and Laprnik caves near the village of Gorna Belica. In Golubarnik (meaning pigeon roost) have been found ancient human skulls and the largest (2m) cave pearl in Macedonia.

Other areas There are numerous other caves along Matka Dam, in Galičica National Park and around Lesnovo. Zemjovec cave near Krapa, Kumanovo, allegedly emits healing waters. The small cave of Alilica near Tresonče marks the start of the Biljana waterfall series along the River Tresončka. Some of the largest caves in the country include Dolna Duka and Krštelna.

For more information contact Ivan Žežovski of Speleology Club Peoni (↘ 02 2041 206 (answering machine) in Skopje, or English-speaking Divna Žežovska on 070 265 677).

SKIING There are three main ski resorts in Macedonia: Mavrovo, Popova Šapka and Kožuf. **Mavrovo** (www.zarelaz.com; see page 229) is the most popular by far, with a day pass costing 1200MKD. It is the most well equipped in terms of facilities, hotels, restaurants and bars, but it is also the lowest of the three ski resorts going up to only 1,860m (from a base lift of 1,255m). **Popova Šapka** (near Tetovo, see page 225) and Kožuf (near Gevgelia and on the border with Greece, see page 289) both offer more exciting terrain, but are also prone to high winds. Popova Šapka ski resort, set between 1,708m and 2,510m, is long in need of funds, and charges 800MKD for a day pass. **Kožuf** (www.skikozuf.com.mk), having only opened in 2007, is still in the process of being completed. It lies between 1,480m and 2,150m and charged 800MKD for a day ski pass in 2009. There is also some skiing on Pelister, Kruševo and Galičica.

BIKING Mountain biking is a growing sport in Macedonia, where there are literally thousands of off-road and dirt tracks. Energi mountain bike club (run from Bikestop shop (see below); e info@energi-cycling.com.mk; www.energi-cycling.com.mk) rents out bicycles and organises regional mountain–bike tours and smaller local tours. As a club they also promote developing biking trails in Macedonia as well as local sustainable tourism to historical and natural sites of interest. Bicycle rental is 1,000MKD per day. Go Macedonia (see page 70) hires out road bikes for 700MKD per day.

Bikestop, owned by Ljubče Kondev (Michael Sokov 6, Skopje; ↘ 02 3231 772; www.bikestop.com.mk (only in Macedonian); ☉ Mon–Sat 12.00–20.00) is all you'll need for parts, service or a whole bike. The Bicycling and Mountain Bike Association of Macedonia (↘ 02 3236 305) is at Rabotnički Sport Hall in the City Park Stadium. (This is also the number for the Chess Association of Macedonia.)

PARAGLIDING Paragliding is very popular in Macedonia, which is crammed with great accessible take-off sites, such as Mount Vodno outside Skopje, Popova Šapka above Tetovo, Galičica Mountain above Lake Ohrid, as well as sites in Kruševo, Strumica and Prilep. The interconnectivity of mountains, valleys, ridges and ravines here makes it possible to fly for several hours and up to 30km in one direction. It is also relatively cheap to learn to fly here compared with club rates in western Europe. Paragliding is overseen by the Aeronautical Society of Macedonia, whose webpage (www.vfm.org.mk/en_clubs.html) offers a host of information on more than just paragliding and list all the various clubs too. Here are some paragliding clubs offering courses and tandem flights:

Bukefal Struska 14b, 1000 Skopje; ↘ 02 3243 642, (club president Silvija Mitevska) 070 620 348, (club secretary Victor Boev) 070 279 088; e silvijafly@ yahoo.com, viktorboev@yahoo.com; www.sivacrosschool.com.mk

Delta Club Narodna Tehnikaul, Dimo Naredniko bb, 8000 Prilep; ☎ 075 410 393, 075 272 242; e spirkozam@yahoo.com; www.deltaparagliding.com.mk. Run by Zlako Spiroski, this club is the oldest in Macedonia & offers beginners courses as well as tandem flights. **Vertigo** Sv Mihail Cekov No.7-1/11, Skopje; ☎ 02 3239 502, (club president Sašo Smilevski) 070 650 080, (club secretary Karolina Smilevska) 70 650

226; e vertigo@mt.net.mk; www.vertigo.org.mk. Offers the full range of beginners, intermediate & advanced courses as well as tandem flights. All the instructors are nationally certified. A 5-day beginner's course costs €450 including loaning out equipment for you to learn to fly. The club meets every Thu evening around 21.00 at London Cafébar on the main square in Skopje. They also sell equipment.

SAILING There is only one lake really worth sailing on in Macedonia, and that is of course Lake Ohrid. AMAC SP-BOFOR Boat Club (*Kaj Maršal Tito bb, 6000 Ohrid;* ☎ *046 256 386;* e *stevco@amacsp-bofor.com.mk; www.amacsp-bofor.com.mk/ en/about.htm*) has been sailing on the lake since 1937 when it was established under the club's original name 'Strmec', a fast regional wind. They offer a variety of small to medium sail boats for hire at around 4,000MKD per day as well as reasonably priced sailing lessons. They also organise the annual Ilinden Sailing Regatta on Lake Ohrid on Macedonia's national day, Ilinden, on 2 August every year.

SCUBA DIVING If you fancy exploring the tectonic edges of Lake Ohrid then Amfora Dive Centre (*Lazo Trposki 35, 6000 Ohrid;* ☎ *046 254 900, 070 700 865; www.amfora.com.mk*) can take you; in the summer they also have a desk at Hotel Granit in Ohrid (☎ *046 207 100*). Lake Ohrid has a dramatic drop-off at its tectonic shelf, which is worth exploring, and there is also a Neolithic stilt village (Bay of Bones see page 173), which can be accessed with special permission. For a private club contact Ivan Mirkovski at Korali Dive Club (e *korali@mt.net.mk; www.korali.xmkd.com*). The club also arranges dives along the rest of the Balkan Adriatic and in Greece.

KAYAKING Once a big sport in Macedonia, kayaking appears to be on the decline, perhaps due to the expense of equipment and the upkeep of courses. Nevertheless, Macedonia offers numerous white-water rapids and a number of competition courses including those on the River Vardar in Skopje itself and at Lake Matka just outside Skopje. For more information contact the Association of Kayaking on Wild Waters Fans of Macedonia (*Rabotnički Sport Hall, 1000 Skopje;* ☎ *02 322 5234*). The Rabotnički Sports Hall also houses the Swimming Association of Macedonia (☎ *02 323 6223*).

FISHING Fishing in Macedonia is widely done, but only marginally successful. Despite boasting the first recorded instance of fly fishing (see *www.flyfishinghistory.com*), Macedonian rivers today tend to suffer from one of two conditions: overgrown or over-fished. Trees, shrubs and heavy overgrowth crowd riverbanks in many of the valleys, making casting nearly impossible and even if you do manage, odds are you'll lose your gear on a snag. Not that it's worth the hassle in any event, as over-fishing is so rampant in the open areas that 'keepers' are rare indeed. Lax enforcement of regulations and licensing mean that every kind of bait is used, limits aren't respected (or imposed), few buy a licence and it hardly matters – because they're rarely checked!

Still, for the avid fisherman, Macedonia does have trout, carp, bream and other freshwater species native to its streams, rivers and lakes. The Radika (see page 230), running from Mavrovo Lake to Debar and beyond, is a classic, albeit over-fished trout river. Running between craggy, forested mountains, it's got plenty of water and its deep holes hide some big fish – despite the proximity of the road along its entire length. The Crni Drim, running from Ohrid Lake to Debar, offers a number of choice spots, despite most of the river being inaccessible due to heavy overgrowth. The Treška, from Makedonski Brod north is accessible in several places, and therefore heavily fished. But fishing where it empties into the reservoir, or by boat on the reservoir itself, has brought considerable success. Finally, the Pčinja, starting just east of Kumanovo and emptying into the Vardar near Veles, has several accessible parts, including a glorious valley north from the village of Pčinja itself.

Lake fishing in Macedonia is subject to a prohibition on trout fishing in Lake Ohrid (see page 38). Still, the country has several bountiful lakes that offer decent sport fishing. Among the best are Debar, Dojran, Matka, Prespa and Mavrovo.

For more information contact the Sport Fishing Federation Združenija na Sportski Ribolovci na Makedonija (*Kočo Racin 75, Skopje;* \ *02 3164 539*). There you can get a licence for waters in the Vardar region of Skopje for 800MKD, or a nationwide licence for 1,690MKD. Licences last for one year and are available to foreigners who can show a passport. Various discounts exist for the young and the elderly, and licences for women are free.

Note that many waterways will have additional fees, ranging from 200–400MKD, that are levied in one of two ways: on site (*na lica mesto*) or by purchasing a sticker at the Federation to attach to your licence. On-site fees appear to be paid only if the warden finds you. At the time of writing, catch limits were 3kg of fish of all varieties, with the exception of trout, which carries a limit of two fish only, each of 30cm or longer.

EQUESTRIAN SPORTS There are two riding schools outside Skopje (see page 157) and numerous stables around the country. Local tour operators can arrange horserides outside Skopje and guided donkey rides to local sites are becoming increasingly available: see individual chapters for more.

GOLF The only (and brand-new) golf course in the country is the Petrovec Golf and Country Club, located 200m from the capital's airport. Set up around the old Norwegian army base at Banski Rid, it is due to open in 2010 with a nine-hole course, driving range and putting area. An 18-hole course, horseriding club and a five-star hotel with spa facilities are due to open in the coming years. Facilities are aiming to be the best and the most ecologically sustainable in the region and it is bound to do well. For more information contact Eco Sports International (\ *02 307 5316;* e *info@ecosportsintl.com; www.ecosportsintl.com*).

HUNTING AND WILDLIFE SAFARIS Game hunting is popular in Macedonia and the Jasen Forestry Reserve is still an exclusive wildlife range, once the preserve of the military and the president. The last president, Branko Crvenkovski, elected in 2004, dropped the annual diplomatic hunt, and took up tree-planting instead. At time of writing it is not known whether the new president Gjorgi Ivanov will resume the sport. Hunting and wildlife safaris can be arranged through local hotels, such as the Bistra in Mavrovo (see page 230) and the Molika on Pelister Mountain (see page 198). See page 35 for more on the types of wildlife to look out for on a wildlife safari.

ROAD RALLY RACING Mount Vodno is the location each year in mid-May (just as you might want to go out for your first hike of the year) for the Macedonian Hill Climb Championship. Hundreds of souped-up and stripped-down cars, including the odd Zastava or two, race up the winding road to the top. If you want a quiet hike or bike in the hills, this event makes for a thoroughly terrible day, otherwise it is quite exciting. For more info contact Velibor Kaevski (\ *075 894 577*).

3

People and Culture

In many parts of central and western Macedonia, a Slav, a Greek, a Vlach, a Turkish and an Albanian village would exist side by side in docile harmony. Quite simply, Macedonia was Europe's most enduring and complex multicultural region.

The Balkans 1804–1999, Misha Glenny

THE MACEDONIAN PEOPLE

The French rightly call a 'mixed salad' *une salade macedoine*. In fact anything mixed up is *macedoine*. Macedonia is arguably the most ethnically diverse country in the Balkans, if not in the whole of Europe; a quick look at Macedonia's history will show you why. (If you got this far without reading the first chapter then just take a look at the chronology on page 3 for a gallop through Macedonian history.) Macedonia has been anything but a homogeneous nation. Aside from various settlers in the Neolithic, Bronze and Iron ages, Macedonia has been invaded, starting with the Romans, by over a dozen tribes, races and empires. And those are the ones that didn't stay. Then there are those who made a home in Macedonia and added spice to the salad.

This has largely to do with the fact that Macedonia lies on the crossroads of important trading routes across Europe. The Via Egnatia linking the Romans via the sea port of Durres in Albania to Constantinople in Byzantium brought Romans, Albanians, Gauls, Crusaders, Byzantines, Turks, Bulgarians, Roma and Greek tribes. The crossroads linking northern Europe with Greece brought Vlachs, numerous Slav tribes, Goths, Huns, Avars, more Serbs and more Greeks.

The disputed question of Macedonian identity is one that numerous academics have written about, and there are many books on the subject too. If you want a lively discussion in Macedonia, then ask about this topic, and you'll find that your interlocutor will furnish you with a complicated family tree as long as your arm, and each person's background will be different.

If Macedonians and their overlapping neighbours cannot agree on who Macedonians are then I could not possibly hope to write an accurate account of such a topic. Nevertheless, from a lay perspective, which is often at least simple, I shall give an overview of some of the aspects which have contributed to Macedonian identity, and some of the arguments which are out there at the beginning of the 21st century, some 7,000 years after humankind is believed to have first settled in Macedonia.

Neolithic settlers into Macedonia from 5000 to 2500BC are believed to have spoken a Proto-Indo-European language, and by 2000BC Greek-speakers were settling in the area. According to Herodotus, the Dorian tribe moved up into southwest Macedonia sometime before the Trojan War, around 1200BC. There they became known as *Makedoni*. These may have moved on, but some remained to become and rule the Kingdom of Macedonia.

The royal house of Macedon, which ruled in the millennium before Christ, has legendary origins from the Greek god of thunder, Zeus. In reality, they are likely to have been a tribe who migrated up from beyond the Greek islands. In the 7th century BC the Makedoni started to mix with the non-Greek-speaking tribes of Paeonia and Pelagonia. Descriptions of these people from the classics of Thucydides, Herodotus and Tacitus show that the Paeons were mostly mountain people, strong and quick, who also influenced the language spoken by the Macedonians. As Professor Nicholas Hammond, the leading authority on ancient Macedonia, says, ancient Macedonian 'contained words of early Greek origin but was not intelligible to contemporary Greeks. The Macedonians in general did not consider themselves Greeks, nor were they considered Greeks by their neighbours.' The royal house on the other hand 'being of foreign extraction and divine descent' (Hammond) were confirmed as Greek in the 5th century BC when they were allowed to compete in the Olympics.

When the Romans invaded in the 2nd century BC, they most certainly left their seed in Macedonia. The invaders from the north, however, Goths, Huns and Avars, seem to have left nothing behind, not even a village or a crop, but razed everything in their way.

The next most influential invasion was by the Slavic tribes from beyond the Carpathian Mountains. There are many of these tribes, tall and hardy, but those thought to have settled in northern Macedonia were the Mijaks in the Debar and Galičnik region west of the Vardar and the Bryzaks to the east of the Vardar. They came as pagans and were gradually Christianised by the indigenous folk of Macedonia. They were allegedly also quite different Slavs from the Slavic tribes of Serbia and those of Bulgaria, although they all spoke a commonly rooted language.

The creation in AD862 by the monks Cyril and Methodius of a script for the Slavic language (Glagolitic, which was later superseded by Cyrillic) helped them to convert many Slavs to Christianity, and helped to formalise the language of numerous Slav tribes. Bulgarian and Macedonian tribes spoke a very similar language due to the influence of the Bulgarian Empire over Macedonia.

Slav origins remain the base of the Macedonians today, despite Ottoman rule over Macedonia from 1392 to 1912. Although many Slavs converted to Islam they continued to speak Macedonian (now known as the Torbeši – see below). It wasn't until the Serb annexation of northern Macedonia to the Kingdom of Serbs, Croats and Slovenes at the end of the second Balkan War of 1913 that the Serb people and language started to gain a serious foothold in northern Macedonia. This was continued during communist Yugoslavia with the Serbification of the Macedonian language under Blaže Koneski, and the prominent influx of pro-Serb Yugoslav partisans into positions of power in the government.

A growing number of Macedonians prefer to see themselves and their country as a heterogeneous mix of the rich tapestry that makes up this crossroads in the Balkans. As a result some prefer not to be called 'Slav' Macedonian as they are no longer purely Slav. Foreigners have always come their way, some bringing products and prosperity, others bringing domination and destruction. New Macedonia wants peace, prosperity and freedom from persecution in a civic-based society rather than to get hung up on ethnic terminology.

MACEDONIAN MINORITIES NEXT DOOR The Hellenisation of Aegean Macedonia, the Serbification of Vardar Macedonia and the Bulgarisation of Pirin Macedonia are topics of continued dispute. Macedonians are not officially recognised as an ethnicity in either Bulgaria or Greece. Both countries recognise Macedonians as Bulgarians. This goes back to the historical quest for influence over, and division of, Macedonia between these two countries and, later, Serbia.

In Bulgaria, some Macedonians are trying to be recognised as an ethnicity and to gain greater autonomy for their culture and self-government. The Bulgarian court judgement banning the formation in Bulgaria of a Macedonian association under the name OMO Ilinden states that 'there is no Macedonian minority in Bulgaria. There are no historical, religious, linguistic, or ethnical grounds for such an assertion.' This judgement banning the formation of OMO Ilinden has been deemed contrary to the right of association under the European Convention of Human Rights, and Bulgaria was ordered (again) in 2006 to repeal the judgement. The EU is applying plenty of pressure on Bulgaria to have the party recognised but, at the time of writing, OMO Ilinden is still waiting to be allowed to register.

In Greece, slavophone Macedonians who were exiled and lost property in the civil war just after the end of World War II are also trying to seek recognition from the Republic of Greece, including a return of their property. The plight of slavophone Macedonians in Greece is well described in Anastasia Karakasidou's 1997 book *Fields of Wheat, Hills of Blood* (see *Appendix 3*, page 335). And as late as May 2006, Greek president Papulias said, 'there is no Slavic minority in Greece', despite the fact that if you travel in Aegean Macedonia (northern Greece) you can still find people in their late 50s and older who speak Macedonian.

In 2004, the Union of Serbia and Montenegro agreed with Macedonia to recognise each other's ethnicities as a minority in their respective countries. This was generally not a bone of contention. However, there are pockets of Macedonian-speaking Muslims in southern Kosovo and adjoining areas of Albania who are known as Gorani. In Kosovo, the Gorani have claimed that they were persecuted by the Kosovo Liberation Army after the Yugoslav army retreated under NATO bombing in 1999, and that they have since been marginalised further by the redrawing of municipal boundaries in Kosovo.

Macedonians have been recognised as an ethnicity in Albania since World War II, but figures are disputed and range from 5,000 to 350,000. The disagreement over figures, recognition and rights to land is largely a mutual recognition issue as well as a fear of the break-up of sovereignty and territorial integrity. These issues are typical of the Balkans and while they are progressing towards stability, they are some way from being settled. The issue over Albanian rights in Macedonia is still very current. For more on the Macedonian diaspora see en.wikipedia.org/wiki/Macedonians_(ethnic_group).

MINORITIES IN MACEDONIA TODAY Ethnic minorities in Macedonia are numerous. Their numbers have varied over the years and in Yugoslavia they often claimed different nationalities in order to avoid persecution. So the number of Turks, Albanians or any other ethnic or religious group fell or rose according to who was most in or out of favour with the authorities in the year of the census. Sadly this phenomenon has continued in the years since the independence of Macedonia.

Albanians Albanians have bordered on the northwest of Macedonia for millennia. Whether they are descendants of Illyrian tribes is disputed, but they have a unique language which, although it has adopted many words over the centuries from Greek, Latin, Turkish and Italian, remains for the most part grammatically distinct and one of the oldest branches of the Indo-European linguistic tree.

Albanians started to make serious inroads into northwest Macedonia and Kosovo, however, only in the 17th century when Ottoman persecution of the native Slav population emptied these areas of their inhabitants. After the fall of the empire of Gjergj Skenderbey (see box, page 234), the Albanians were largely loyal to the Ottoman *beys* (chieftains, lords). Most converted to Islam and were

It is important to note that the rulers of the Ottoman Empire were not necessarily Turkish. They were a ruling elite made up first and foremost of Muslims, and secondly of those who spoke Ottoman Turkish. As a result, Albanians such as Skenderbey (see box, page 234), and the Christian boys taken by the dervish orders of Islam under the devširme tax (see page 13) would become a part of the Ottoman elite who ruled the empire on learning Ottoman Turkish and converting to Islam.

Turks on the other hand were considered by the elite to be the uneducated masses of peasant Anatolia. It is from these masses that Atatürk rose up against the Ottoman sultans and pashas to bring about modern Turkey. The masses spoke a different Turkish from that of the Ottomans of the Osmanli elite, which acted as a class barrier in everyday life.

Ottoman Turkish, however, was a language of convoluted court phrases, with words and grammar borrowed from Persian and Arabic for which the Arabic script was used. Arabic words stress the order of consonants as their distinguishing framework, and have little representation for short vowels. This does not suit other languages very well, such as the Turkish of the masses, Macedonian or Albanian. As a result, towns like Debar could be transliterated back out of Arabic script as any variety of spellings such as Diber, Dibrah or Debar, so long as d, b and r were in the same order. The Arabic script seen today above many mosque doorways and windows is therefore the script of Ottoman Turkish, and not related to the modern Latin-script-based Turkish.

rewarded with new lands bordering Albania. Many also learnt the Ottoman elite language and were schooled in Anatolia, later becoming *beys* in their own right.

However, when the Turkish nationalism of the Young Turks emerged at the beginning of the 20th century, Albanians in Macedonia, fearing repression from the encroaching Serbs, rallied for their own cause. In 1912 at the end of the first Balkan War, Albania became an independent state and with it went a small slice of Macedonia that lay south and north of Debar.

Much of Macedonia's 'Albanian question' is linked with the rise of nationalism in neighbouring Kosovo in the face of Serbian persecution, rather than with any significant desire to join Albania. Communist Macedonia did not help this perception and Albanians were almost as badly persecuted in Macedonia as they were in Kosovo. Fortunately, Serbian/Yugoslav persecution of ethnic Albanians in Macedonia does not go back the centuries that it does in Kosovo, and so there is hope yet that a civic-based state (incorporating EU preferred rules of subsidiarity or local self-government) might work out for the Albanians in Macedonia.

Unfortunately, however, new Macedonia has inherited the discriminatory leftovers of the Socialist Republic of Macedonia (SRM), which have been compounded by the sudden curb on movement instigated by the erection of borders between the formerly borderless communist republics. So whereas ethnic Albanians used to be able to go to university in Priština in Kosovo to receive teaching in Albanian, suddenly they had no access to teaching in their own language. The number of schools where children could receive instruction in Albanian was also heavily reduced. Less than 5% of the police force were Albanian in a country where Albanians claimed they made up more than a third of the population, yet over 80% of prison inmates were from the Albanian community. Moreover, the 1991 constitution stressed the nationality of the Macedonians, with Albanians as equals, rather than that the new Macedonia was a home for a mix of ethnicities as it had been for many centuries.

Furthermore, disenfranchised from the emerging political process in the new pluralist republic, ethnic Albanians refused to take part in the referendum on independence. They also refused the census of 1991 that would have established their numbers, fearing that the manipulation of the figures by the government would be used against them. Instead the Albanian community carried out their own census of their population in 1992, and it is starting from this time that other Muslim groups in Macedonia, such as the Turks and the Torbeši (see below), have alleged that the Albanian community has pressured them to count themselves among the Albanian community in order to swell the numbers for their census.

The Ohrid Framework Agreement of August 2001 (see box, page 21) has brought many more civic rights to the Albanian community. The Albanian community itself is now split as to whether they have won enough rights through the conflict or whether they should keep on fighting. Further battles have stuck so far to political turf and the census of 2002, which numbered the Albanian community at 25%, appears to have settled any disagreements about population numbers. Undoubtedly, the lure of EU membership in the years to come will prove to be a stabilising factor in relations among the communities.

Turks After the demise of the Ottoman Empire and the withdrawal of the Ottoman elite, many Turks fled back to Turkey in the wake of widespread retaliation by the Serbs who replaced the Ottoman leaders. This policy of encouraging what can only be described as 'cleansing' was continued under communist Yugoslavia in the 1950s and 1960s through handshake deals with Turkey whereby anywhere between 80,000 and 150,000 'Turks' left Yugoslavia via Macedonia and Bulgaria for Turkey. Many were not in fact Turks at all nor did they speak Turkish, but were Albanians or Macedonian Muslims (Torbeši – see below) who took advantage of the offer to escape further persecution in Yugoslavia. At the last census of 2002, less than 4% of Macedonians declared themselves to be of Turkish descent. This 4% are spread throughout the municipalities of Čair, Vrapčiste, Gostivar, Plašnica, Radoviš and Centar Župa.

The true ethnic Turks of Macedonia are the Yoruks (see box, page 50). Yoruk villages are found in the Radoviš area, Vrapčiste and Gostivar.

Torbeši Interestingly, some of these 'Turks', such as the majority of the population of Plašnica, are in fact ethnically Macedonian Muslims. They cast themselves as Turks in the census because they do not speak Albanian, are not Orthodox Macedonian, but by religion are closer to the Turkish community.

Another minority sometimes singled out are the Muslims of Macedonian descent as opposed to Albanian or Turkish. These Muslim Macedonians are sometimes called *Torbeši*, although this is often seen as a derogatory term, and applies to Muslim Macedonians in Macedonia as well as those in Albania. The Albanians sometimes refer to Muslim Macedonians as *Pomaks* even though Macedonians might argue that this is a term reserved for Muslim Bulgarians who come from the Rhodope mountain region. Albanians have historically seen the Bulgarians and Macedonians as one and the same.

Roma The Roma, along with their Sinti cousins, total almost 14 million throughout Europe. They migrated from northwestern India between the 11th and 14th centuries as travelling labourers, and although most have settled, many still live transient lives. Sadly, the 20th century brought considerable misfortune to the Roma, and the wars throughout the former Yugoslavia in the 1990s caused the most significant Roma population movements since the end of World War II. Poorly portrayed in the Western mass media, the Roma have arguably been the most severely affected in the long term by the harsh consequences of war. This is in large part because of their lack of representation in modern-day governing institutions and interest groups: neither politician, soldier, businessperson nor cleric has come forward to defend them locally.

The Roma's origins in northwestern India are very obvious from their facial features and elaborate traditional dress. They are mostly dark skinned, speak their own language originating from Sanskrit and have distinctive customs and traditions. The main ethnic division of Roma can be further subdivided into Arli, Kovaci/Burgudji, Djambazi, Baruci, Juzari, Pristevaci, Gilanli and Topanli. All subdivisions speak a dialect of the Roma language (for more on the Romani language see text box page 154). In addition to sub-ethnic divisions, in Macedonia Romani identity is largely split into those of Muslim faith (Xoraxane Roma) or Christian faith (Dasikane Roma). Faith as a means of identity has changed over time and is likely to do so again in the future.

YORUKS – AN ETHNIC TURKISH COMMUNITY IN MACEDONIA

Abridged with permission from Yoruks *by Elizabeta Koneska, Museum of Macedonia, 2004*

In the eastern part of Macedonia lives the Turkish Yoruk ethnic population, concentrated mostly in the mountainous areas of the Dojran-Valandovo and Radoviš-Štip region. In the historic sources the Yoruks are referred to as nomadic tribes of Turkmen origin who had emigrated from the steppes of central Asia to Anatolia, and from there settled in the eastern part of the Balkans from the 14th to the 16th century.

The migration of the Yoruks was probably the most successful colonising strategy of the Ottoman authorities in the Balkans compared with their attempts at colonising other central Asian tribes. The reasons for their settling in the Balkans were of a socio-economic and military-strategic character. Some researchers suggest that the favourable climate and rich grazing pastures of Macedonia were the crucial motive for the Yoruk migration. In favour of this, some researchers argue that they settled in the areas of rich pastures abandoned by Vlach farmers.

The Yoruk population was tribally well organised and as such fitted easily into the Ottoman army, which led to organising special units for different military, semi-military and other duties (dragging cannons, transporting materials, working in mines, maintaining and securing fortresses, etc). The Yoruks had a privileged status and in order to be motivated for their duties they were exempted from certain state taxes. They were thus treated as 'children of the conquerors'.

In order to get some benefits, substantial parts of the Islamised population joined the Yoruks. The census records from the early 16th century registered the phenomenon of some Islamised Christians joining the Yoruks in the Prilep region, Ovčepole and Tikveš, after the Yoruks crossed from the left to the right bank of the River Vardar. One of the mitigating circumstances for adopting Islam through the Yoruks was the fact that they were organised in *tarikats* – dervish orders that were religiously more tolerant. In this regard, bear in mind that the religious rituals of both populations included numerous pre-Christian and pre-Islamic pagan shaman elements, which brought them closer together.

The Yoruk community transformed from a nomadic to a stationary way of life in the 15th and 16th centuries. As a result, the state passed laws ordering those who hadn't changed their abode for more than ten years to be deprived of the right of Yoruk status, which meant they had to fulfil their duties of paying taxes to the state.

As an individual Turkish ethnic group in Macedonia the Yoruks are distinguished by their language, customs and folkloric particularities and, considering contemporary times, their rather closed social community. The Yoruks of the Radoviš-Štip region who live in

According to the last national census of 2002 (based on official citizenship), the number of Roma in Macedonia is 53,879 or 2.66% of the total population. Field research indicates, however, that actual numbers are much closer to 150,000. In Macedonia the biggest built-up settlement of Roma in the world, some 13,300 people have their home in Šuto Orizari, north of Skopje (see page 151). They mix very little with the remainder of the Macedonian community and inter-ethnic marriages are extremely rare. Part of the reason that they have not mixed with their host communities has traditionally been because of their transient lifestyles.

In Macedonia in recent decades, however, many Roma have settled permanently all over the country. Now, it is discrimination and a significant difference in lifestyle and outlook that keep the Roma from acceptance by, and even wanting to integrate fully into, their place of settlement. Traditionally, the Roma have been skilled labourers in carpentry, copper and blacksmithing, leather upholstery, basket weaving, the repair of all these things and more. They are also renowned as skilled

the foothills of the Plačkovica Mountain, however, differ with their own particularities, not only from the other Turkish populations, but also from Turks living in the lowland villages in the same region. That's why the villages of Alikoč, Kodjalija, Kaluzlija, Supurge and Prnalija from the Radoviš district are particularly interesting.

The contradiction between the traditional and the contemporary way of life is reflected in the contrast between the male and the female Yoruk population. The women wear their colourful and archaic traditional gowns, and their means of communication is limited, mostly due to the language barrier (the female population, almost without exception, speaks only Turkish). The men, meanwhile, have already adopted modern behaviour, dress and mobile phones.

The unfavourable conditions and living standards in the Yoruk villages in the past decades gave rise to emigration, mainly to Turkey and to some western European countries. The Yoruks from Macedonia were not involved in the great migrations of the Turkish population typical for the period after the fall of the Ottoman Empire. The first massive emigration of the Yoruks from these villages occurred in the 1950s, together with the emigration of a considerable part of the Turkish population from Macedonia. The second emigration wave took place at the beginning of the 1990s, following the dissolution of Yugoslavia, and was motivated by economic conditions as well as the actual political events. Since the end of the 1990s emigration has slowed.

The present language of the Yoruks is a conserved, archaic Turkish language, a specific Turkish dialect that has endured thanks to the considerable isolation of this population and the minimal external influences. The folkloric particularities of the Yoruks are most impressively reflected through the colourful traditional gowns worn by the female population of all ages. The Yoruk women make all the parts of the gowns, through weaving to sewing and embroidering. From the period of adolescence to marriage, girls are constantly preparing their dowry. For everyday use women and girls usually wear colourful dresses of ready-made fabric.

According to the old tradition, on Bajram or for weddings the Yoruks organise wrestling (*pehlivan*) contests, stone-throwing (*tašitmak*) contests and horse or donkey races. The wedding customs are certainly the most impressive. Marriages between blood relatives are avoided, but it often happens that two brothers marry two sisters (a kind of an 'exchange' of a sister and a brother for another brother and a sister, which saves money).

Elizabeta Koneska is Macedonia's leading ethnologist on the Yoruk community and works at the Museum of Macedonia. She can be contacted at ekoneska@freemail.org.mk.

musicians and dancers. Their tendency towards a life-on-the-move has not led them to put much emphasis on formal education, and so as the 20th century moved away from a product-based economy towards a service and technology-based economy, the Roma and their skills have been somewhat left behind. The move towards a throwaway society has not helped either, and so the Roma are largely left to manual labour and menial jobs; many have taken to begging.

In Skopje, especially in the municipality of Šuto Orizari, there is quite a significant class difference among the Roma. Some have gone abroad, earned good money visible by their small well-kept houses, and have qualified in recognised trade skills. Within Macedonia, from a mere handful in tertiary education in the early 1990s there are now some 200 Roma studying at university level. Most of them are pursuing careers in human and social sciences and are actively taking part in various academic training modules, organised by Romaversitas (*www.romaversitas.edu.mk*, only in Macedonian at the time of writing; see also *Stuff Your Rucksack* on page 111 to find out how you can help Romaversitas directly). It is hoped that these students will be the driving forces behind reorganising and modernising their communities.

At the other end of the spectrum, there are those who live in slums, such as on the outskirts of Bitola or Prilep, or the 1,700-plus remaining refugees from the conflict in Kosovo who mostly beg or wash windscreens at the traffic lights in Skopje. You will also see many of the Roma hawking clothes, hats and alarm clocks on the Stone Bridge, or plying the street with their boxes of cigarettes, tissues and chewing gum. Often you can also see a matriarchal figure order children to beg from potential clients as they come along the street. Although these children are forced to beg, they can still appear happy, laughing and playing as children do even if they have been on their feet all day. Occasionally, if they receive no alms they will get angry, not exactly a good sales technique, but understandable when they are likely to receive a clip around the ear from mum or dad for not returning with cash. Then they will return to playing a game of tag or jumping in the water fountain. It is questionable how much of the money they receive from begging ends up in their pockets or is taxed from a cartel that 'runs' the area.

The spiral of poverty that the Roma have found themselves in has lead to international efforts to try to stop discrimination against them and to bring them back up above the breadline. The OSCE's Office for Democratic Institutions and Human Rights, based in Warsaw, does significant work in this regard throughout Europe, and a number of non-governmental international Roma networks have started up as the Roma try to lift themselves out of poverty. Macedonia has signed up to the Roma Decade of Inclusion 2005–2015 (*www.romadecade.org*), in which the government has pledged to tackle improvements for Roma in basic services, health, education, housing and employment. Improvments are not easy: the Roma themselves are not keen to adopt the trappings of conventional Western lifestyles, whilst developing (and especially former socialist) economies struggle to harness the potential of entrepreneurship for self-employment and small businesses.

For more on the Roma in Skopje see page 151 and for their background throughout Europe see www.romani.org. A good website on the human rights and legal struggles of the Roma can be found at the European Roma Rights Centre (*www.errc.org*). In Macedonia there are several charities – for more information see *Giving something back* on page 110. Donating to a charity that has long-term goals for the community as a whole has proved to be far more effective in reducing long-term poverty than putting money directly into a bottomless pit. Unfortunately, like most of those living on the breadline of poverty or below, the Roma see little use for training in computers and sewing when this may not get them jobs in the current climate and their immediate needs are for food and housing. Trying, therefore, to get past the initial stumbling block of teaching a man to fish rather than giving him the fish is still proving difficult.

Aromanians/Vlachs The Aromanians (known as *Vlach* in Macedonian) arrived in Macedonia in Roman times from the 2nd century BC onwards. They are not related to the Romanians of Romania in language or ethnicity, although many

THE MIJAKS OF WESTERN MACEDONIA   *Mimoza Gligorovska*

The Mijaks have lived in western Macedonia for at least five centuries. The Mijak region, Mijachija or the Reka region, is named after the Radika River and its tributary the Mala River. Broadly speaking the area is bound by the Šar Planina to the north; the Korab, Dešat and Krčin mountains to the west; Bistra and Stogovo to the east; and the Debar Valley to the south. Within this area, the Mijaks are pocketed into four smaller regions. The Gorna (Upper) Reka region, from the village Brodec to the village Volkovija is mostly abandoned today but, in the past, was inhabited by Albanian-speaking Macedonians, called *Shkreti*. The Dolna (Lower) Reka, from the village Žirovnica to the village Skudrinje, and the Golema (Big) Reka, from the confluence of Mala Reka into the Radika to the confluence of the Radika into Lake Debar, are barely much more populated. Only the Mala (Small) Reka from the village of Galičnik to the village of Gari is seeing a small revival of seasonal tourism.

Over the course of time, the Mijaks have become a mix of Orthodox and Islamic religion. Their Islamisation started in the 16th century but was not widespread, rather individual, and lasted for a long period of time. Some authors note cases where half of the family was Orthodox and the other half Muslim. The conversion to Islam divided the Mijaks into Mijaks (Orthodox Macedonians) and Torbeši (Muslim Macedonians).

Their main occupation was and still is cattle breeding, and some records say they herded more than 2.5 million sheep and 150,000 horses before World War II. They are also known as the best woodcarvers and icon painters in Macedonia. Petar Filipovski-Garka, his brother Marko Filipovski and Makarie Frčkovski, all from the village of Gari, are the sculptors of the iconostasis in the Sv Spas Church in Skopje, the Sv Gavril Lesnovski Church near Kratovo and the Sv Jovan Bigorski Monastery, near Debar. Another famous artist, icon and fresco painter Dimitrie Krstev (1819–72), known as Dičo Zograf, came from the village of Tresonče. He painted over 1,500 artefacts all over the Balkans, and his work is still exhibited today as an example of his then very unique style of combining harsh post-Byzantine symbolism with Baroque ornamentation.

The Mijaks speak the Mijak dialect, part of the Western-Macedonian dialects. Some of the main differences are the use of the consonant group 'šč' instead of 'št' – *ščo* and not *što* (meaning what); the replacement of consonant 'a' with 'o' in many words – *zobi* instead of *zabi* (teeth), *kode* instead of *kade* (where), *roka* instead of *raka* (arm); and the transformation of 'lj' into the palatal 'l'.

Finally, the Mijaks have a most intriguing flag, one of the oldest in Macedonia. It is white with a red and yellow border and a yellow cross inside a red and yellow circle. The yellow segments of the circle represent the rays of the sun, and of course, is not unlike the symbolism of Macedonia's star of Vergina. The cross divides the letters ИС ХР (IS HR standing for Jesus Christ) and НИ КА (NI KA meaning victory). Four symbols standing in each corner of the flag are the ancient Macedonian lion, the Byzantine double-headed eagle, the Bogomil star and prostrate half-moon, and a Celtic dragon.

did emigrate there over time. They have always spoken a Latin-based language and refer to themselves as Armčnji. There are a number of names for them, however: the word *vlach* comes from the Greek and, along with other derivatives, has a mostly derogatory meaning centred around 'idiot' or 'bleat'. The Greeks in fact call them *Koutzovlachs* (*koutzos* meaning 'lame') – connected to a story that the Aromanians refused to participate in the Greek wars by claiming to be lame in one leg! They are called *Ulah* in Turkish, *Tschobani* in Albanian and *Cincari* by the Serbs. *Cincari* denotes 'stingy' and is often confused with the Aromanian and Romanian word for 'five'.

The Vlachs have always been in the business of trade. Many did well out of sheep farming, and it is not difficult to suppose that they may have followed the Roman legions who needed supplies. Certainly the main Vlach settlements in Macedonia are along the Via Egnatia, and their traditional villages, such as Malovište, show a once wealthy standard of living.

Although the Vlachs today are well integrated into Macedonian society, and now mostly live in the towns rather than in their old villages, many Vlachs can still be found to the fore of prosperous local businesses and hotels. They remain well educated, often speaking a number of languages and have a knack for figuring out good market niches.

Due to their relatively recent assimilation into Macedonian life it is difficult to assess the exact numbers of Vlachs, not least because many Vlach descendants may no longer consider themselves Vlach, but prefer in these times of possible ethnic segregation to call themselves simply 'Macedonian'. The 2002 census numbered Vlachs at less than 0.5% of the population.

Other minorities There are lots of other very small ethnic groups in Macedonia due to the nature of its geographical location. The next most significant group are the Serbs who were encouraged to settle in Macedonia when Vardar Macedonia became a part of the Kingdom of Serbs, Croats and Slovenes after World War I. Serbs made up 1.8% of the population in the 2002 census, but they do not form a particularly homogeneous group as they are scattered throughout the country and are completely assimilated into Macedonian life. Nevertheless, the Serbs have their own political party, as do most of the ethnicities in the country, reflecting a politics divided along ethnic lines rather than along any real differentiation in political platform. There are also significant groups of Croats and Montenegrins from Yugoslav days; Greeks from the 19th century when the Orthodox church was governed from Athens; Armenians who immigrated during the Middle Ages; and Ashkali Egyptians, who immigrated along with the Indian Roma. The Ashkali Egyptians, and many of the poor Turks who were left in Macedonia after the demise of the Ottoman Empire (for instance parts of Strumica), are often discriminated as Roma.

The Mijak (see textbox on page 53) are the next most well-known minority. They are not officially counted in the census and so their numbers are unknown.

LANGUAGE

There are two official languages in Macedonia, the Slavic-rooted Macedonian spoken by most of the population, and Albanian, which has equal status alongside Macedonian in municipal and government affairs where Albanian speakers make up 20% or more of the citizens in a particular municipality.

The **Macedonian** language is firmly based in the Slavic family of languages. Traditionally written in Cyrillic, it is occasionally found in Latin script especially in advertising. In past centuries it was closely related to Bulgarian and remains very similar in certain aspects of grammar and some vocabulary. Macedonians and Bulgarians can usually understand each other even if they can't speak the other's language. During both world wars Bulgaria's short rule over Macedonia saw an attempt to sway the Macedonian language back towards Bulgarian. When communist Yugoslavia won Macedonia, it set about reversing this and Serbifying the language. Today, the Macedonian alphabet is more similar to Serbian but has 31 letters instead of Serbian's 30 and four differing letters. Macedonian grammar, however, remains closely linked to Bulgarian. Serbia is also now increasingly using the Latin script rather than Cyrillic.

The Macedonian brother-saints Kiril and Metodi, followed by saints Clement and Naum, invented and spread Cyrillic throughout Slavic-speaking countries (see *Religion,* below) from the 9th century onwards. Old Church Slavonic is still the language and script used in sermon books today in Macedonia.

Albanian belongs to the Indo-European family of languages, but its roots, going back to the ancient language of the Illyrians, are some of the oldest and as a result its basic grammar and vocabulary resemble no other in the same family. Since its evolution in Albania, however, it has come under the influence particularly of Greek, Latin and Italian, therefore you will find a lot of words which are similar to these neighbouring languages. There are also some Slav and Turkish words.

There are two main dialects in the **Albanian** language: *Gheg*, spoken in the north of Albania, Kosovo and northwestern Macedonia, and *Tosk*, spoken in southern Albania. Up to the 19th century, Albanian could still be written in five different alphabets. This made communication and learning difficult, and in 1908 at the Conference of Monastir (Bitola) the decision was made to try to unify the language under one alphabet and literary standard. The Latin alphabet was chosen to provide 36 letters.

It was not until the 1960s and 1970s that a standard literary form of Albanian was finally formalised. This standard form, which is taught throughout the Albanian-speaking world, consists mostly of the Tosk dialect and grammar, with some Gheg additions. The Albanian given here is the standard literary form.

Most young Macedonians below the age of 45 will speak at least a smattering of English and some are fluent. Among older Macedonians and especially in the Albanian communities German is more likely to be the second language of choice. On the odd occasion when you will find explanatory literature at a historic site or church, it will probably be in French rather than English.

RELIGION

Today, most of Macedonia is either Orthodox Christian or Sunni Muslim. There are some Roman Catholics, Evangelists, Jehovah's Witnesses, Bektaši and a good smattering of agnostics and atheists. Despite Yugoslavia's efforts to keep the states secular and to discourage religious life, the downfall of communism has brought about a revival in religion that is now proving to be both a unifier within a community, and a separator of those communities within the state.

Many Macedonians have rallied around the Orthodox Church as a means of expressing their hard-won national identity, a trend that was inadvertently encouraged through the Ottoman millet system (see box, page 56). The rise of the Orthodox Church is most obvious by the increasing number of huge metal crosses lit up across the country, and the number of new churches being built despite the terrible state of the economy (a lot of this money comes from the Macedonian diaspora). Monasticism has also been injected with a new lease of life as of 1995, with the revival and refurbishment of a great many monasteries in Macedonia.

Muslim Albanians have expressed their distress at the use of the Orthodox Church as a symbol of the Macedonian nation, and whilst this has fuelled the conflict between the Albanian community and the Macedonian authorities, Muslim Albanians have also retaliated with the construction of many new mosques. This has not helped matters, especially as non-Albanian Muslim numbers have been used to justify the need for new mosques, yet services are often only held in Albanian.

Both sides in the conflict of 2001 desecrated churches and mosques, which is a war crime under the Geneva Convention, and sadly reflects a history of such practices in the region. Many churches were destroyed or built over by the Ottomans during their time in Macedonia. Of note was Sveta Sofia in Ohrid (see page 170) – photographs of it as a mosque can still be found. Even more mosques were destroyed by the Macedonians when the Ottomans finally left in 1912.

HISTORY OF THE ORTHODOX CHURCH IN MACEDONIA Jesus's disciple Paul was called upon by the vision of the 'man of Macedonia' to spread the word of God along the River Vardar. His journey in the middle of the 1st century is detailed in Acts 16:10–17:15, and many believe he made it as far as northern Macedonia. Timothy and Silas stayed on in Macedonia after Paul left, and they may have made greater inroads into the wilds of the upper Vardar. But by the 4th century, Macedonia had an established Christian Church under the Metropolitan of Skopje. Aside from written records elsewhere, early evidence of Christianity in northern Macedonia can be seen by the remains of numerous Christian basilica across the country.

When the Slav tribes came in the 7th century, they too were converted to Christianity. These newcomers brought with them the problem of how to teach

THE MILLET SYSTEM OF GOVERNANCE AND ITS AFTERMATH

The Ottoman millet system, whereby people were classed according to religion rather than race, allowed Christianity to live effectively alongside Islam. For the Ottomans an elite ruling class was important, and so the Church's influence over its subjects was just as much an integral part of their rule over the empire as the Islamic faith was over its respective followers. Within each millet system, the Ottomans were just as likely to inflict havoc on the lower echelons of the Christian millet as they were on the Muslim millet or the Jewish millet. The corollary of this millet system was that several religion-based 'nation-states' grew up alongside each other. In addition, political in-fighting within each millet system caused even further rivalry in the power vacuum left by the Ottomans following their demise, as played out in the desire of various factions of the Orthodox Church and their national leaders to 'rule' over Macedonia in the Balkan wars of 1912 and 1913.

Whereas the Jews were deported en masse during World War II to gas chambers such as those in Treblinka in Poland, many Muslims remained, and some believe even today that they should still be allowed free rein over their followers as in the millet days. The Orthodox Church, already disunited by national factions within the Church, more easily made the transition to the Westphalian nation-state system, which upholds sovereignty and non-interference in internal affairs as the key pillars of government and international relations. Unfortunately, the Westphalian nation-state system does not sit alongside the millet system so well, as a nation-state must have complete jurisdiction over a geographical area, whereas the millet system allows for several separate jurisdictions to apply to different people within the same geographical area.

the Scriptures through a foreign language such as Greek or Latin. To alleviate this problem the Byzantine emperor Michael III summoned the monks Cyril and Methodius (Kiril and Metodi in Macedonian), who were natives of Macedonia, to go forth and teach the Scriptures to the many Slav speakers in their native language. This they did in the year 862, travelling along the River Bregalnica and to do so they created the Glagolitic and Cyrillic scripts, variations of which we are familiar with today.

Thus Byzantium increased its influence over the region by using what is now known as 'Old Slavonic' to win over the local slavophone population. Shortly afterwards, as Byzantium began to fall and Bulgaria was first made a state, Bulgaria continued this practice of exerting influence through the Church by establishing the Bulgarian Patriarchate, with its sphere of influence away from the Greek Orthodox Church and the influence of Byzantium.

The Bulgarian prince Boris ordained Clement in AD893 as the first Macedonian Slav Bishop of the Bishopric of Velika (believed to be around the River Treška). Clement had been a disciple of Kiril and Metodi during their travels in Macedonia, and so had much influence in the land. His seat was at Ohrid, and he brought his fellow disciple from those travelling days, Father Naum, with him to Ohrid. There they set up the first Slavic monastery and school.

Later in AD976, Tsar Samoil (see box, page 10), who had rebelled against Bulgarian authority and founded his own empire, also founded his own church, the autocephalous Ohrid Archdiocese, in order to bolster his own empire. But with the fall of Samoil in 1014, the Byzantine emperor Basilius reduced the new archdiocese to a mere archbishopric.

Thus the Archbishopric of Ohrid remained for seven and a half centuries until in 1767 the Turkish sultan Mustapha III gave in to Greek pressure and allowed the Archbishopric of Ohrid to be dissolved, and even the eparchy of Ohrid was reshuffled to have its seat at Durres in present-day Albania, thereafter known as the Eparchy of Albania. Along with the reshuffle, Greece bargained the right to administer the Orthodox Christian faith in upper Macedonia. New churches built in Macedonia during this period of the late 18th century and 19th century show a lot of Greek influence and engravings, as do older churches which were renovated or refurbished during this time, and many of them were refurbished purely in order to illustrate the authority of the Greek Church.

During the Russo–Turkish wars of the late 19th and early 20th centuries, Russia granted Bulgaria its wish for orthodox influence over northern Macedonia. Bulgaria then lost out to the Serbs at the end of the second Balkan War of 1913 and northern Macedonia fell under the influence of the Serbian Orthodox Church, long since separate from the Greek Orthodox Church.

It was not until March 1945 that the Archdiocese of Ohrid put forward a resolution to create an autonomous Macedonian Orthodox Church. The Serbian Orthodox Church, of course, refused. Thirteen more years of discussions ensued until finally, in 1958, the Serbian Orthodox Church gave in and the following year the Macedonian Orthodox Church gained its autonomy, although still under the patriarch and canonical unity of the Serbian Orthodox Church.

The Macedonian Church was still not happy, however, and after more heated debate, the Holy Synod of the Macedonian Orthodox Church proclaimed itself autocephalous and completely independent of the Serbian Orthodox Church on 19 July 1967, exactly two centuries after the Archbishopric of Ohrid had been dissolved by the Ottomans. The legality of this move under the respective constitutions of both the Macedonian and Serbian Orthodox churches is still a bone of contention between the two churches, and the Serbian Orthodox Church still doesn't recognise the independence of the Macedonian Orthodox

Church. For more about the Macedonian Orthodox Church visit their website at www.mpc.org.mk, which has information in English as well as some beautiful photographs, the Church calendar, and information about the lives of saints celebrated in the Orthodox calendar.

Whether you are a believer or not, the churches, mosques and monasteries in Macedonia are amazing treasures which deserve to be kept for posterity. Although monastic life and the Church have received a new boost since the independence of Macedonia, many of the churches and monasteries do not receive much funding. It is obvious which ones receive fewer donations by the state of disrepair that the churches and inns are in. The more remote and less well-known monasteries are particularly badly off. Well-wishers usually leave 10 or 50MKD at the church altars, and you might want to consider giving more generously to some others. If you would like to make a larger donation by banker's draft or international money order, the residing father or sister will be able to furnish you with suitable details.

THE ISLAMIC RELIGIOUS COMMUNITY IN MACEDONIA Of the two main Islamic groups of believers, Sunni and Shi'a, most Muslims (about one-third of the population) in Macedonia are Sunnis. Not all of these are Albanian or Turkish, but many are ethnic Macedonian Muslims (Torbeši, see page 49), Roma or other ethnicities. There are also a small number of dervish believers of different *tarikat* (subdivisions or orders of the dervish Muslim faith) such as the Bektashi, Helveti, Nash-Bandi, Qadiri, Rufa'i or Sinani. Officially, there are no Shi'a followers in Macedonia, but some of the orders, especially Bektashi, contain some Shi'a doctrinal elements. The connection stops there, however, and there is no contemporary hierarchical connection with the Shi'a in Iran.

During Ottoman rule over Macedonia, there was no separation of 'Church' and state, and the millet system (see box, page 56) was used by the Ottoman sultans to rule over the different religious communities. At that time, the sultan was the highest Muslim religious authority. From 1918 to 1927, the Islamic community in Macedonia came under the authority of the Great Mufti of Belgrade, after which the Islamic believers of all Yugoslavia were unified under the Great Mufti of Sarajevo.

When Yugoslavia was formed in 1944, the Islamic Religious Community (IRC) in Macedonia registered in its own right with the Socialist Yugoslav Republic of Macedonia as the sole representative of the Muslim faith. The IRC is built on the doctrinal foundations of Sunni Islam, and has about 450 registered mosques and some 500 clerics.

There is only one Islamic school in Macedonia, the Isa Bej Medrese in Kondovo. Originally established in the 15th century, and revived in the 1930s as a rival private school to the Royal Yugoslav state-run Big Medrese of King Aleksander set up in Skopje, the Isa Bej Medrese was re-opened in 1979 in Kondovo after a period of closure during early communist times. By then many believers had gone abroad (and still do) to receive their religious education before taking up religious leadership positions at home. Due, of course, to the strong influence of the Ottoman period and continued links with Turkey, most receive their religious education in Turkey. The Turkish school of Islam teaches a modern secular version of the Muslim faith and these teachings continue to dominate in Macedonia. As in many other countries in the region, however, reactionary leanings in the Islamic community have led some to seek more traditional schooling in Egypt, while others have gone to Syria and Saudi Arabia, which offered scholarships for students from abroad. Some students returning from Saudi Arabia have brought back the experience and preaching of Wahabi and Salafi

Islam, both of which teach relatively radical views and practices. Wahabi and Salafi preaching in Macedonia is weak although Wahabi- and Salafi-linked NGOs continue to try to further their influence through their work in poor communities and in building new mosques. Most mosques, especially in major towns, such as the Motley Mosque in Tetovo, are of the Turkish school, and open and friendly to (appropriately clad) visitors, including women.

The only other Islamic organisation in Macedonia that has tried to register itself separately from the IRC is the Bektaši dervish community. Macedonia's law on religion, however, stipulates that only one representative of each major faith is allowed to register. Whilst this arbitrary provision has allowed for Orthodox, Catholic and various Protestant branches of Christianity to register, only one organisation is allowed to represent the Muslim faith. This serves the IRC (and the Macedonian Orthodox Church) well as this way it has better control of the influence of various sects of Islam (and the considerable funding that can go with them). It clashes, however, with the European Convention on Human Rights and will probably have to change in due course if Macedonia wants to get into the EU (although Greece still has an equally restrictive law on religion).

The head of the IRC in Macedonia today is the Reis-ul-Ulema (president). He governs the Riyaset, which is an executive body responsible for religious and spiritual activities and which is answerable to the Meshihat (the Assembly of the Islamic Community consisting of 51 members). Below the Riyaset and Meshihat, mosque communities are divided into 13 religious committees, each of which is headed by a mufti.

CULTURE

The arts are up and coming in Macedonia. While there are no big, famous museums, art galleries or world-renowned festivals, there are always plenty of smaller events going on, in Skopje year round and all over the country during the summer festival season. Sadly, venues and playlists are usually announced only a few days before the event, so you need to keep your eyes peeled for the information or log on to www.culture.in.mk regularly. Festivals and saints' days also have a big following in Macedonia. A list with approximate dates is covered in *Chapter 4*, page 100. Skopje at least, and some of the other larger towns in Macedonia, have a small but thriving classical arts scene in music, ballet, opera and drama, as well as modern drama in Macedonian and minority languages. (See *Chapter 5* for more on when and where to see Skopje attractions.)

Local handicraft in Macedonia is plentiful, but in the past has been hard to find and generally over priced. Prices are coming down, but still not low. Indigenous handicrafts include ceramics, stained glass and terracotta as well as traditional icons, silver filigree jewellery, iron and copper work, carpets, embroidery, local musical instruments, woodwork and museum reproductions. The Christmas handicraft fair at Čifte Amam in Skopje is becoming a popular event for making timely and original Christmas purchases and there are sometimes stands in the Ramstore. Macedonia Direct (*www.macedoniadirect.com*) offers mail order delivery around the world. A few permanent places to get handicrafts are:

Arka Hotel Bitpazarski 90/2I, Skopje; ☎ 02 3230 603 (see page 124)
Ikona Ramstore & off the centre of Maršal Tito, Skopje

Slave Marin's Goce Delčev bb, Ohrid (by the Green Market); ☎ 046 251 719
Jugo Hotel Maršal Tito, Gevgelia; ☎ 034 213 222

RELIGIOUS ART The arts in Macedonia, like its nationhood and politics, are fractured. Certainly during Ottoman times they appear to have had as little chance to flourish as possible. Pre-20th-century art mostly took the form of church frescoes, icons and woodcarvings of which there are a great many in Macedonia that are literally priceless and uninsurable.

Makarije Frčkovski and the Mijak brothers Filipovski from Gari were famous in the early 19th century for their iconostasis carvings. In total they carved four iconostasis during their lifetime. Three can still be admired at Sv Spas Church in Skopje, the Monastery of Sv Jovan Bigorski near Debar, and Sv Gavril Lesnovski near Kratovo. The fourth in Sv Nikola Church in Kruševo was destroyed when the church was razed during the Ilinden Uprising in 1903. In 1999, a tourist is alleged to have offered the head priest at Sv Jovan Bigorski a blank cheque for the church's iconostasis. Aside from the fact that dedications to God cannot be bought at any price, the piece is irreplaceable and so it remains there today and hopefully forever.

Icons up until the 10th century were made of terracotta, such as those found in Vinica (see page 254) and many are now on view at the National Museum of Macedonia in Skopje. Thereafter they were generally paintings inlaid with silver and sometimes gold from the gold mine outside Radoviš. Most of these are still in their original churches, but some of the more important icons and frescoes, rescued from centuries of neglect during the Ottoman Empire, have been put on display in Skopje's and Ohrid's galleries.

MODERN ART Modern art has taken hold of Macedonian artists in a big way, as if trying to catch up with centuries of artistic deprivation. The Museum of Contemporary Art, which was set up in 1964 after the disastrous earthquake in Skopje the year before, houses a permanent collection of modern art as well as frequent travelling exhibitions. Many pieces were donated to the museum as a result of the earthquake, including a piece by Van Gogh, which is usually held down in the basement, but can be viewed on request.

The Museum of the City of Skopje (the old railway station) and the national galleries of Čifte Amam and Daud Pasha Amam, both former Turkish baths, also hold travelling exhibitions. Those living in Skopje will not have failed to notice the amount of modern art, alongside the compulsory icon or two, that adorns the walls of modern Skopje apartments. Today the works of Macedonians such as Iskra Dimitrova, Omer Kaleši and Ibrahim Bedi are beginning to travel the world.

Since Yugoslav times, and especially since independence, Macedonia has encouraged artist colonies to grow and flourish. Ohrid is home to many Macedonian artists and you will frequently see budding artists trying their hand at representations of city life. The monasteries have also encouraged art, where the tranquillity of monastic life is often conducive to artistic development. Several art colonies take place in Macedonia during the month of August, including those at the Monastery of Sv Joakim Osogovski near Kriva Palanka, the Mijak village of Galičnik, the Monastery of Sv Petka in Velgošti near Ohrid, and the village of Kneževo near Kratovo.

FILM Photography and photojournalism have strong pioneering roots in Macedonia going back to the early 19th-century days of the Manaki brothers (see page 190). Today, exhibitions of the works of Alexander Kondev or Samir Ljuma can be found around Macedonia, and the works of Rumen Kamilov and Marko Georgievski can be seen in numerous magazines and articles about Macedonia.

The Manaki brothers also experimented in film back in the early 1900s, and Macedonia had a vibrant film-making industry during Yugoslav times.

Unfortunately, the break-up of Yugoslavia put a dampener on the film industry for a while, when access to equipment shared with other republics in the Yugoslav Federation was cut off with the rise of borders and national agendas. In a recent turn of events, however, Milčo Mančevski's 1995 release of *Before the Rain* has breathed life back into Macedonian film-making, which is continuing its revival with *Dust* (Mančevski, 2001), *The Great Water* (Ivo Trajkov, 2004, based on the book of the same title by Živko Cingo), *Soul Hunter* (Oliver Romevski, 2004), *Secret Book* (Vlado Cvetanovski, 2004), *How I Killed a Saint* (Teona Mitevska, 2004), *Bal-Can-Can* (Darko Mitrevski, 2005) and *Shadows* (Mančevski, 2007).

For an interesting and thought-provoking insight into life in Macedonia, *Before the Rain* is an excellent introduction. *Dust* gives a view of early 20th-century Macedonia under the Ottoman Empire, while *Bal-Can-Can* portrays through black comedy the continued melee of relations in today's Balkans. *The Peacemaker*, featuring George Clooney, is a Hollywood blockbuster that draws on the recent difficulties and porous nature of Macedonia's borders as an excuse for excessive violence beyond anything ever seen here in reality. Fortunately for English-speakers visiting Macedonia, foreign films are usually given Macedonian subtitles rather than dubbed, so going to the cinema needn't be hard work if you don't speak Macedonian, and it is one of the reasons why so many young Macedonians speak such good English.

MUSIC The soundtrack for these films has also injected life into Macedonian musical compositions by bands who combine traditional music with modern sounds such as Anastasia (*Before the Rain*) and Olivier Samouillan and Project Zlust (*How I Killed a Saint*). Other popular new artists on the scene are Kiril Dzajkovski (*Dust, The Great Water*); Trifun Kostovski (Macedonian soul); Tоše Proeski (modern pop and fusion – sadly, Proeski was killed in a car accident in Serbia in 2008); Kaliope (a long-time favourite of the Macedonians); Synthesis, who use traditional Macedonian instruments and vocal tones (see box below); Tung Tung, an Albanian ethno jazz group (recent albums *Red Grapes*, 2003, and *Gold Coin*, 2005); and Adrian Gadja (modern Albanian).

Many of these new beats can be enjoyed in the summer at Skopje's outdoor nightclubs, such as the Coloseum, Element and Cabrio, where UK and US disc jockeys also regularly perform, or at the various summer festivals. One of the easiest introductions to the Macedonian modern/traditional music mix is the album *Treta Majka* (Third Mother) by the famous Serbian Leb I Sol lead guitarist Vlatko Stefanovski, the Macedonian guitarist Miroslav Tadic and the Bulgarian kaval player Theodosii Spasov. Equally good is the album *The Path in the Sun* by the Dragan Dautovski Quartet.

Unless you look out for these new sounds, however, you will find an overwhelming amount of traditional Macedonian music in restaurants and family gatherings all over Macedonia. This is an acquired taste and a must for traditional ceremonies where Macedonia's national dance, the *oro* (*kola* in Serbian), is compulsory for all participants. The *oro*, a circle of dancers holding hands, proceeds in an anticlockwise circle getting gradually faster. There are a number of different versions of the steps to the dance, the most basic being a three steps forward, one step backward arrangement. The *oro* generally comes across as quite a serious affair; I have yet to see anybody actually smile during the dance, although allegedly they are having fun.

Even more serious is *chalgia* music from the 18th and 19th centuries. Chalgia mixes secular Byzantine music with classical Turkish music from earlier centuries. It comes across as generally sober music and its lyrics frequently tell of loss and yearning. Chalgia was played on traditional Macedonian musical instruments such

Like its people, Macedonia's musical instruments have a mixed origin. Many were brought to this land with the various invaders passing through over the centuries, while others are home grown. Playing traditional instruments is seeing a small revival in fusion music and in the revival of ethnic festivities. It is a rare wedding, holiday or religious event that doesn't bring out one of these traditional instruments – or perhaps an entire band of them. To give you an idea of what they are and how they sound, below is a snapshot of the most common ones.

KAVAL Traditionally a shepherd's instrument, the kaval resembles a flute. It is made of one piece of wood about 70cm long, usually ash, open at both ends and ornately decorated throughout. It produces a lovely warm sound, almost melancholic. You can hear the kaval frequently played in pairs, with the first leading a melody and the second one droning along with a slightly lower key.

GAJDA Macedonia's version of the bagpipe – its origins are in Macedonia's mountain villages. Gajdas have four main parts: the chanter (*gajdarka*), a wooden tube with seven finger-holes in front and a thumb-hole at the back; the drone (*brchalo*) producing the constant sound; the duvalo, a wooden pipe attached to the bag where the musician blows air in; and of course the bag itself (*mev*), made of tanned sheep or goat skin. The Gajda is usually accompanied by a kaval or two, a tambura, and perhaps a percussion instrument like the tapanče, daire or tarabuka.

ZURLA Typically played at weddings, social occasions and Turkish wrestling matches (*pelivan*), the zurla has a distinct piercing sound that is usually heard well above the drum (*tapan*) that accompanies it. It is a wooden (walnut or plum) two-part, wind instrument, the body of which is a conical pipe. A beak (*slavec*) is inserted into the upper, narrow part. Zurlas originated in the Middle East and were brought to Macedonia either by the Turks or the Roma – the latter of whom most often play it today. The larger (male) zurla is ususaly found in Skopje, Tetovo, Veles, Prilep, Bitola and Kratovo, while the smaller (female) zurla is played around Gostivar and Kumanovo.

as the *canoon*, *kemane*, *oud*, tambourine and *tarabuka* (see box, above). A six-CD anthology was brought out in 2006, and can be bought from Jugoton in Skopje. If you don't fancy the six-CD set, there is an interesting, more modern rendition of chalgia in the album *Kaldrma* (referring to an old type of road construction from the Ottoman period) by the pop/modern jazz Macedonian group String Forces and the traditional Macedonian Pece Atanasovski Ensemble (see page 101). Chalgia is played live every Wednesday at Vinoteka Temov (see page 131) in Skopje old town.

A CD of Macedonian church music by the monks of Jovan Bigorski is also available at Jugoton if you don't make it to the monastery for the 05.30 liturgy.

Many of the bands hired for traditional functions and festivities are Roma bands (see page 52), and one of the songs almost invariably played is 'Mjesečina', meaning 'moonlight' by Goran Bregovič, made famous in the Yugoslav film *Underground* (Emir Kusturica, 1995). The Roma have a strong history of music making, immortalised in the songs of Esma Redžepova-Teodosievska, the queen of Roma music.

LITERATURE Macedonian literary history is also split into two sections. The spread of the Cyrillic and Slavic languages is very much connected to the saints Kiril, Metodi, Clement and Naum (see page 57) and the development of the

SUPELKA A shepherd's instrument that looks and sounds like a recorder.

DUDUK A blocked-end flute that can be found in two lengths: 70cm like the kaval, and 25cm.

TAMBURA Brought to Macedonia in the 14th and 15th centuries via the Turks from the Middle East, the tambura is a long-necked string instrument with a pear-shaped body, made of walnut. It produces a metallic, tingling sound, and is played both solo and as part of an ensemble.

TAPAN This is a good-sized drum. What sets it apart is that the musicians of Macedonia play it with two specially designed drumsticks – known as a *kukuda* and a *pračka*. The kukuda is a narrow pipe made of wood, while the pračka is more like a thin switch. Each one strikes a different side of the drum and the difference in sound is remarkable; together they produce an impression that something big is about to happen. The tapan is the traditional accompaniment for most folk bands playing at special occasions. You'll find it at the Galičnik wedding, for instance.

DAIRE Essentially a tambourine.

TARABUKA An hourglass-shaped drum, medium size, made of wood and animal skin. Its origins are uncertain, but it has been variously connected with Greece, the Middle East and India. It is quite often used as accompaniment to the tambura.

KEMANE An instrument similar to the violin or viola.

To find out more about these instruments, or to order them, see www.macedoniadirect.com/instruments.

Archbishopric of Ohrid. Ohrid's Museum of Slavonic Literacy is dedicated to the historiography of its development.

Whilst much of the rest of Europe underwent a great literary phase during the Renaissance, Macedonia was firmly under Ottoman and Greek influence which did not encourage indigenous writings. The 19th-century Miladinov brothers (see page 180) went a long way to cast off this dark period in Macedonian song, poetry, literature and literacy. A whole slew of authors and poets have appeared since then, most recently Živko Cingo, Radovan Pavlovski and Petre M Andreevski. The works of Božin Pavlovski, now living in Australia, are also available in English (see *Appendix 3* for titles).

ARCHITECTURE Macedonian architecture goes back a long way, the earliest discoveries of which date back to the Bronze and Iron ages. The ancient Paeons built fortresses out of huge limestone blocks, using a technique called cyclopean masonry. No mortar was used, but the precise joints of the rocks and their huge size kept these constructions together for thousands of years. Very little of this architecture is visible today, although some remains can be found at Prosek above Demir Kapija, Mariovo and Vajtos (see page 183).

Thereafter, Macedonian architecture is centred largely around the development of the Church, until the arrival of the Ottomans at the end of the 14th century when Turkish inns, baths, mosques and clock towers influenced the skylines of towns like Skopje and Bitola. During the 18th century the development of what has become known as the 'old style of Ohrid, with extended eaves, spacious and splendid, with two entrances' (Pavlovski, *The Red Hypocrite*) became common among the rich and influential, such as the Ottoman lords, monastery inns and wealthy traders. One of the finest examples of this type of house is the Robev residence, now the National Museum of Ohrid, but they can be seen all over Macedonia in various states of disrepair, desperate for renovation.

Sadly, the renovation of traditional houses is costly, and therefore largely left undone. In addition, many of the beautiful 19th-century buildings of the grand European style, which used to adorn most of central Skopje, collapsed during the earthquake of 1963. In the aftermath, the money donated by hundreds of international donors to rebuild Skopje was used to bring in the latest competitive craze in concrete creations, both communist and international, which is still to be seen today. A fine example of this is the main post office in Skopje next to the Stone Bridge.

Practical Information

> ... for one does not come to Macedonia every day, and time and opportunity are
> not to be thrown away.
>
> *Journals of a Landscape Painter in Greece & Albania*, Edward Lear, 1848

WHEN TO VISIT

Located so far south in Europe, Macedonia is great to visit most of the year round.
It is particularly welcoming during spring and autumn outside the high tourist
seasons and when the weather is at its most pleasant. Here are the main highlights
of Macedonia month by month.

JANUARY Macedonia is at its coldest this month, and the snow is at its freshest.
Skiing in Macedonia is very cheap, costing as little as 1,000MKD per day, and
facilities are improving every year. This is also the month that Orthodox
Christians celebrate Christmas, and Muslims celebrate Eid-al-Adha. Aside from
New Year's Day itself, Vevčani has its big Twelfthtide Carnival on 13–14 January,
and on Epiphany (*Vodiči*, 19 January) is cross-throwing day.

FEBRUARY The snow is still great for skiing at this time of year. The Day of Sv
Trifun (the patron saint of wines and vineyards), 14 February, is increasingly
celebrated with Macedonia's excellent wines.

MARCH By this time of year Macedonia is sunny and warm during the day and
still cool in the evening. There is still some skiing to be had, but hiking and other
outdoor pursuits are starting to come into their own. Alpine flowers are starting
to emerge. The Strumica Carnival takes place at the beginning of the Easter
fasting period.

APRIL Spring is taking full effect by April and everything is green again. Hot
spells make a welcome change from winter, but there are extended periods of
showers. April 1 is celebrated in fancy dress. Easter usually takes place some time
in April.

MAY A truly magnificent month in Macedonia filled with fields of bright red
poppies and trays of fresh strawberries sold along the roadside. It can get into the
high 20°Cs during the day, but the evenings are often still cool enough for a light
jacket, especially in the mountains. Macedonia's musical instrument festival takes
place on 22–23 May and it is another great month for outdoor pursuits.

JUNE A month for cherries and wild flowers. Paragliding takes off from all the
mountain outcrops at Vodno, Ohrid, Prilep, Kruševo, Bitola and Štip, as the

warm currents really start to swirl up from the valley floors. Time for the first dip in the 298m depths of Ohrid's tectonic lake, or try exploring some of Macedonia's many caves.

JULY This is when Macedonia hits its hottest, and it is also when Macedonians themselves will be crowding the lakes and other tourist spots. Hotel spaces are therefore at a premium and it is advisable to book several weeks ahead. Get to Galičnik to see the National Wedding Festival if you can, try the Pivofest in Prilep for local beer, or if you are in Skopje make the most of the Skopje Summer Festival.

AUGUST Festival month in Ohrid, Bitola, Strumica and Kruševo. August 2 is a national holiday celebrating the Ilinden uprising of 1903 when the Macedonians rebelled against Ottoman rule. Lake Ohrid holds the Ilinden Sailing Regatta on the same day and the 30km Ohrid swimming marathon at the end of the month. Government goes on holiday during the second week of August, as do a lot of other Macedonians, so Skopje is practically empty, but Ohrid is alive with the Ohrid Summer Festival. For a slightly more relaxed atmosphere, Struga is up and coming with its own festival celebrating ethnic Albanian culture as well as the Struga Poetry Festival at the end of the month. A number of places have international artist colonies for painters, clay potters, woodworkers and others.

SEPTEMBER The month of grape harvesting and the very youngest wines when all and sundry are collecting car-loads of grapes, from the wizened old farmer with his donkey and cart to the young policeman in his Lada policewagon. From here on in is the time to visit the vineyards of Bovin, Čekorov, Elenov, Fonko, Ezemit, Popova Kula, Skovin and Tikveš to name a few, and discover the best of Macedonia's little-known wines. By this time of year the local tourists are thinning out, although weekends can still be busy. The weather is no longer the scorching sun of July and August, but definitely still T-shirt quality.

OCTOBER This is one of the finest months of the year for visiting Macedonia, especially for touring round the country. The weather is still warm during the day, and as autumn takes hold of the trees the woods burst alive with startling reds, yellows and oranges. This is a fantastic month for hiking, wine tasting and taking dramatic photographs of Macedonia's mountainous scenery. October also sees the Jazz Festival in Skopje – where in previous years Manu Chao, Omara Portuondo and Natalie Imbruglia have played – for as little as €20 per ticket.

NOVEMBER Still a very pleasant month to visit Macedonia. The sun is bright and brings warmth to the skin, but atop the mountains fresh snow glistens, beckoning hikers to their first winter walk and exciting skiers for the months to come.

DECEMBER Winter has definitely settled in by December. The trees are bare and snow is on all the mountains and sometimes a metre deep in the towns. Despite the shortening hours of daylight, the local Christmas market brightens most towns, and so this is a good time to buy local crafts and handiwork. Steaming cups of mulled wine at local stalls help keep the cold at bay.

HIGHLIGHTS/SUGGESTED ITINERARIES

SCENIC The lake and town of Ohrid (see *Chapter 7*) are seen as the jewel of Macedonia's scenic crown. And it is not without reason that Ohrid's medieval architecture and pristine natural setting are preserved by UNESCO as a place of historic, cultural and scenic significance. Outside the height of the summer season it remains a wonderful little getaway spot, and should not be missed on any trip to Macedonia. The back route from Skopje through Debar to Struga and on to Ohrid is worth the extra time.

All three of Macedonia's **national parks**, Pelister, Mavrovo and Galičica, offer many hiking trails and beautiful scenic drives. The one hike not to miss though is the 10km hike from Mount Vodno just outside Skopje down to Lake Matka (see page 298), which also offers rock climbing, caving, camping, kayaking and yet more scenic hikes to local monasteries and beyond. There are also many beautiful hikes to waterfalls, glacial lakes and other scenic spots (see *Chapter 12*).

ARCHITECTURE AND HISTORICAL CULTURE Other spots though, which are equally stunning and unique to Macedonia and which are much less well known, are the 16th-century villages of the Macedonian minorities. **Galičnik** village of the Mijaks hangs on the edge of a deep ravine and by car or public transport can be accessed only from the Mavrovo Lake, over the plateau of Galičnik National Park. Every July, as in days of old, the local men who have gone away to work return to Galičnik to marry their beloved. The ritual continues today and is a festive occasion open to all.

Malovište village, located in Pelister National Park, is an old Vlach village, formerly housing rich Vlach traders. It is now being renovated to preserve its heritage and is a beautiful example of the rich variety of Macedonian culture. There are hundreds of other fine old villages off the beaten track that have yet to be fully discovered and you'll find that taking a trip away from your main route will always reap a reward.

Macedonia's Turkish history is well worth looking into, and is best preserved in Skopje's old town, **Čaršija**. See *Chapter 5* for details of the old trading inns of Suli An, Kapan An and Kuršumli An, the bathhouses of Čifte Amam and Daud Pasha Amam, and the mosques of Mustafa Pasha and Sultan Murat.

SPIRITUAL INNS A trip to Macedonia would not be complete without at least visiting one monastery. They are renowned for their intricate woodwork and delicate architecture and for some of their remote but beautiful locations. The country boasted over a thousand churches and monasteries at the zenith of Orthodox ministry in the region during the 14th to 16th centuries. Ohrid was the centre of the Orthodox Church at the time and still has over 200 churches and monasteries overlooking its shores. Some of the most spectacular working monasteries to visit are Sv Joakim Osogovski (page 261) near Kriva Palanki; Sv Jovan Bigorski (page 238) near Debar; the World Monuments Fund-listed Treskavec Monastery (page 208) near Prilep; Sv Gavril Lesnovski near Kratovo (page 266); KALIšta Monastery (page 182) for its nearby cave churches looking over Lake Ohrid; Sv Borgorodica Prečista (page 241) near Kičevo; and Zrze Monastery (page 241) set high on a cliff.

All these spiritual inns are covered in greater detail in the relevant chapters of this guidebook. For those who want to make churches and monasteries the theme of their visit, here are some further suggestions: the Monastery of Sv Naum (page 174) on Lake Ohrid; the women's monastery of Jankovec (page 202) near Resen; the Monastery of Sv Leonthius (page 277) near Vodoča village; the women's Monastery of Eleusa (page 277) in Veljusa village; the Monastery of the Archangel Michael (page 207) in Varoš, Prilep; the women's Monastery of Sv Gjorgi (page 236) in Debar; the Church of Sv Spas (page 136) in Skopje; the Church of Sv Gjorgi (page 180) in Struga; the cave Church of Archangel Michael (page 102) in Radožda on Lake Ohrid; the Christian basilicas in Heraklea (page 110); Oktisi (page 103); Plaošnik (page 170) for its early Christian mosaics; and of course all the churches listed in the chapter on Ohrid (page 169).

AN ADDITIONAL SCORE OF MUST-SEES AND MUST-DOS Aside from the outdoors, architecture and monasteries, here is a more eclectic list of Macedonian highlights.

- Ascend to the towers of King Marko in Prilep for a 360° view of the Pelagonia plains and visit Prilep Tobacco Museum (page 208)
- Hike and climb (both traditional and bolted routes) around the canyon of Lake Matka, then eat in the cave restaurant Peštera (page 148)
- Visit dying Lake Dojran before it disappears and the Dojran battlefield of World War I (page 290)
- Marvel at the Motley Mosque in Tetovo, beautifully painted on the outside resembling a house of cards and inside like a tea tray (page 223)
- Visit Kruševo (page 211), the capital of the ten-day Republic of Kruševo in 1903 where one of the most successful Macedonian revolutions against the Ottoman Empire took place, to see some of the best-preserved architecture from the 18th and 19th centuries, and a re-enactment of events on 2 August
- Bathe in the recently renovated local hot springs at Katlanovska Banja (page 150), communist style at Banjište (page 237) and visit the progressing renovation of the Roman baths in Bansko (page 278)
- Eat traditional Macedonian *ordever*, a selection of prepared creamed vegetable and cheese hors d'oeuvres, with tasty pizza bread and the local beer, Skopsko
- With over 30 mountain huts (page 296) and over a hundred peaks of 2,000m and higher to choose from, both low-level hiking and more challenging mountaineering are available for a range of abilities
- Taste a variety of trout unique to Macedonia, such as *letnica* and *belvica*, or eat some of the most smooth-tasting carp from Lake Dojran
- Visit the old Turkish trading inns, mosques and Bit Pazar market in Skopje's old town (page 135)
- Cast yourself back to Roman times in the barely uncovered ruins of Heraklea and Stobi, and stop at the local vineyards on the way
- Ski at Popova Šapka, Mavrovo, Kožuf, Kruševo or Pelister, and relax afterwards with a massage and a choice of local grills
- Ride Lipizaner horses, famous for their dressage at the Spanish riding school in Vienna, at the El Kabon stables, and eat in their famous Cherry Orchard restaurant featured in the Macedonian film *Dust* (page 157)
- Eat at the Monastery of Sv Pantelejmon with stunning views overlooking the Vardar Valley (page 151)
- Learn to paraglide for a mere €400 with Club Vertigo, Bufekal or Extrema over the mountains of Vodno and Kruševo, or the lakes of Ohrid and Matka (page 42)
- Visit the dervish Baba Arabati Teke spiritual inn in Tetovo (page 224)
- Hike from Demir Kapija Iron Gate ravine along the stream bed to the mountain villages of Čelevec, Iberlija and Košarka (page 286)
- Stay at the Monastery of Sv Petka in the old trading village of Brajčino, centre of ecotourism in Pelister National Park (page 198)
- Go caving in over 300 underground caves, such as Pesna, Slatinksi Izvor, Bela Voda, Ubavica and Alilica (page 41), and visit Vrelo cave, Macedonia's nomination for the New Seven Wonders of Nature (page 148)
- Visit the town of Kratovo, situated around an old volcanic crater, for its rock art and volcanic droplets (page 265)

- Sit in the Palaeolithic throne of Cocev Kamen sacrificial and megalithic ancient observatory (page 266)

And much more: summer festivals, kayaking, local art galleries, fishing, carnivals, hunting, Christmas fairs, village saints' days, glacial lakes, folk festivals, mountain biking, spit-roast lamb …

TOUR OPERATORS

Operators outside Macedonia who can book your ticket and hotel and make up an itinerary for you are few, but on the increase.

UK

Andante Travel The Old Barn, Old Rd, Alderbury, Salisbury, Wilts SP5 3AR; ☎ 01722 713800; f 01722 711966; e tours@andantetravels.co.uk; www.andantetravel.co.uk; ⊕ Mon–Fri 09.00–17.00. Specialising in archaeology & the ancient world, Andante has espied the potential in Macedonia by offering a tour of the best of the country's Roman ruins, medieval churches & Ottoman architecture.
Explore! Nelson Hse, 55 Victoria Rd, Farnborough, Hants GU14 7PA; ☎ 0845 013 1539; e res@explore.co.uk; www.explore.co.uk; ⊕ Mon–Fri 08.00–19.30, Sat & bank holidays 09.00–16.30. Explore! runs several interesting tours through Bulgaria, Macedonia & Greece focusing on ancient Macedonia & Europe's last frontier.
Imaginative Traveller 1 Betts Av, Martlesham Heath, Suffolk IP5 3RH; ☎ 0845 077 8802; f 01473 667349; e online@imtrav.net; www.imaginative-traveller.com; ⊕ Mon–Thu 08.30–21.00, Fri 08.30–17.30, Sat 09.00–17.00, Sun 10.00–16.00. This tour operator has just started a European Frontiers tour including Macedonia. In addition to all the usual tour operator facilities, Imaginative Traveller offers a carbon offset supplement.
Regent Holidays Mezzanine Suite, Froomsgate Hse, Rupert St, Bristol BS1 2QJ; ☎ 0845 277 3317; f 0117 925 4866; e regent@regent-holidays.co.uk; www.regent-holidays.co.uk; ⊕ Mon–Fri 09.00–17.00, Sat 10.00–16.00. The first UK tour operator to branch into the region, Regent Holidays can book you accommodation in Macedonia, book you on one of their special group tours or provide you with an individual tour package tailored to your wishes.
Reality & Beyond Quenington Old Rectory, Cirencester, Gloucs GL7 5BN; ☎ 01285 750 888; f 01285 750 540; e lucy@realityandbeyond.co.uk; www.realityandbeyond.co.uk. Historian & art historian Lucy Abel Smith provides high-quality individually tailored tours for the discerning, providing exclusive insight into the architecture, culture & history of Macedonia.

USA

Kutrubes Travel Agency 328 Tremont St, Boston, MA 02116; ☎ 800 878 8566, 617 426 5668; f 617 426 3196; e adventures@kutrubestravel.com; www.kutrubestravel.com. Has recently started tours including Macedonia, & can provide individually tailored packages, as well as just accommodation bookings.
Sophisticated Traveler PO Box 23673, San Jose, CA 95153-3673; no phone; f 815 301 3482; e streservations@gmail.com; www.s-traveler.com. Provide a brief stop-off in Ohrid on their Athens to Dalmatia tour.

LOCAL TOUR OPERATORS Macedonia's tourist industry is still recovering from decades of neglect. Nevertheless, its relatively new main 'National Tourism Portal' (*www.exploringmacedonia.com*) offers thousands of ideas, links and contacts for visiting the country. A complementary site linking much more about Macedonia is **www.macedonia-timeless.com**, with the introductory CNN advert filmed by Macedonia's internationally acclaimed film director Milčo Mančevski (see page 61).

In addition to the tour operators listed below, the **Association of Tourist Guides** (*Dame Gruev, Block 3, Skopje;* ☎ *02 3118 498;* f *02 3230 803*) can also help with guides. To arrange outdoor sports activities get in touch with the clubs themselves as listed in *Chapter 2*, page 40.

Adventure Guide Macedonia Gjuro Gjakovič 16, 1000 Skopje; ☎ 02 3298 455; e contact@ adventureguidemacedonia.com; www.adventureguidemacedonia.com. Offers individual & group arrangements in all the outdoor sports available in Macedonia, including bike tours, caving, wine tours & jeep safaris.
Atlantis Bojmija 1/17m, Skopje; ☎ 02 2400 940; m 075 252 212; e skopje@atlantis.com.mk; www.atlantismk.com. This chain travel agency also has branches in Bitola, Delčevo, Strumica & Radoviš (see respective chapters in this guide), & provides Western Union & FedEx services.
Go Macedonia Ankarska 29A, Skopje; ☎/f 02 3071 265; e gomacedonia@t-home.mk; www.gomacedonia.com. Go Macedonia cater almost exclusively for foreign tourists, & their website isn't even available in Macedonian; English only. They offer special monthly tours, but can arrange a tour or make individual arrangements. Bike tours also available.
Turist Bitola Krali Marko 16, 7000 Bitola; ☎ 047 202 777; f 047 202 776; e through their contact page on the Macedonian site; www.turist.com.mk.

Has extensive experience working with foreign tour groups & agents. Can find you accommodation throughout Macedonia as well as arrange trips to sites.
Savana Orče Nikolov 20, Skopje; ☎ 02 3115 825; f 02 3114 206; e savana@savana.com.mk; www.savana.com.mk. Savana has a good website on Macedonia in English & will even book your accommodation in a monastery.
Simonium Travel Taftadžiska 2, Čaršija, Skopje; ☎ 02 6121 076; f 02 6121 076; m 070 319 301; e contact@simoniumtravel.com.mk; www.simoniumtravel.com.mk; ⊕ Mon–Fri 09.00–17.00, Sat 10.00–14.00. Specialises in discreet travel for the discerning.
Tuymada Dame Gruev 16–2/14, DC Paloma Bjanka, Skopje (in the same bldg as Kibo Restaurant); ☎ 02 312 0255, 02 3211 3755; f 02 3213 8382; e info@tuymada.com; www.tuymada.com; ⊕ Mon–Fri 09.00–19.00, Sat 10.00–16.00. Offers monastery tours but overnight stays are in nearby hotels. Has good rental car rates.

RED TAPE

Members of the European Union, Switzerland, New Zealand, Australia, Canada and the US do not need visas at present for stays of less than three months, and it is so easy to cross the border to get a new stamp in your passport that it is not worth applying for an extension if you want to stay longer. For an up-to-date check on which countries do require visas, visit the website of the Ministry of Foreign Affairs (*www.mfa.gov.mk/default1.aspx?ItemID=307*). Visa requirements can tend to change with a change of government, so keep this in mind.

POLICE REGISTRATION By law, you must register with the police within three days of arriving in Macedonia. If you are staying in a hotel, the hotel will do this for you automatically, but if you are staying in private accommodation or a monastery then you must do this yourself. Ask at your place of stay for a registration card (which Macedonians must also fill out) and ask for the nearest police station at which to hand it in.

Some of the monasteries will insist that you go through this process, but most private rooms do not even have the cards. While the police appear not to check most foreigners or private rooms, this might change and if you are caught the police have every right to deport you, even if you do plead the innocent tourist.

CUSTOMS You can bring in as much personal luggage as you like, although expensive items such as laptops, cameras, musical instruments, sporting equipment, radios and jewellery should be declared on entry if you want to leave with them without any hassles. Having said that, I have never been given a customs declaration form to fill out, but if you want to be on the safe side then ask for one.

You can pretty much leave with what you like too, providing you can prove that it was bought with legally exchanged money! Antiques and icons require a certificate of approval from the Ministry of the Interior before they can be exported.

Duty free allowances are 1litre of spirits; 200 cigarettes or 50 cigars or 250g of tobacco; perfume for personal use.

The maximum amount of currency you can bring into the country without having to declare it is €10,000.

E EMBASSIES

MACEDONIAN EMBASSIES ABROAD For a full and up-to-date list of Macedonian embassies abroad see www.mfa.gov.mk or www.embassiesabroad.com/embassies-of/ Macedonia.

Albania Rr Kavajes, nr 116, Tirana; ✆ +355 4 230 909, 274 765; f +355 4 232 514; e makambas@ albnet.net

Australia 74 Banks St, Yarralumla, Canberra ACT 2600; ✆ +612 6282 6220; f +612 6282 6229; e info@macedonianemb.org.au; www.macedonianemb.org.au

Austria Maderstrasse 1/10, A-1070 Wien; ✆ +43 1 524 8756; f +43 1 524 8753. Visa section: Konsularabteilung, Maderstrasse 1/4, A-1010 Wien; ✆ +43 1 524 8757; f +43 1 524 8754; e vienna@ mfa.gov.mk, botschaft@makedonien.co.at

Bulgaria Frederic Joliot-Curie 17, Block 2, Floor 1, Suite 1, 1113 Sofia; ✆ +359 2 870 1560/5098; f +359 2 971 28 32; e sofia@mfa.gov.mk

Canada 130 Albert Sv, Suite 1006, Ottawa, ON K1P 5G4; ✆ +1 613 234 3882; f +1 613 233 1852; e emb.macedonia.ottawa@sympatico.ca; www.3.sympatico.ca/emb.macedonia.ottawa/

France 5 rue de la Faisanderie, 75116 Paris; ✆ +33 1 4577 1050; f +33 1 4577 1484; e paris@ mfa.gov.mk

Germany Koenigsallee 2–4, 14193 Berlin; ✆ +49 30 890 695 21; f +49 30 89 54 11 94; e berlin@ mfa.gov.mk. Visa section: Hubertusalee 5, 14193 Berlin; ✆ +49 30 890 69 511; f +49 30 890 94 141

Greece Liaison Office, Papadiamanti 4, P Psychico, 154 52 Athens; ✆ +301 67 49 585; f +301 67 49 572; e athens@mfa.gov.mk. Consulate in Thessaloniki: Tsimiski 43, Thessaloniki; ✆ +30 2310 277 347; f +30 2310 278 598; e dkpsolun@ mfa.gov.mk

Netherlands Laan van Meerdevoort 50–C, 2517 Am Den Haag; ✆ + 31 70 427 44 64–5; f + 31 70 427 44 69; e hague@mfa.gov.mk

Serbia Gospodar Jevremova 34, 11 000 Belgrade; ✆ +381 11 328 49 24; f +381 11 328 50 76; e belgrade@mfa.gov.mk

Switzerland Kirchenfeldstrasse 30, 3005 Bern; ✆ +41 31 352 0028; f +41 31 352 0037; e makedamb@bluewin.ch

UK Suites 2.1 & 2.2, Buckingham Court, 75–83 Buckingham Gate, London SW1E 6PE; ✆ 020 7976 0535–8; f 020 7976 0539; e info@ macedonianembassy.org.uk; www.macedonianembassy.org.uk

US 2129 Wyoming Av, NW Washington, DC 20008; ✆ +1 202 667 0501; f +1 202 667 2131; e washington@mfa.gov.mk; www.macedonianembassy.org

FOREIGN EMBASSIES AND CONSULATES IN MACEDONIA
Embassies in Skopje

Albania Majka Teresa 22; ✆ 02 3246 726; f 02 3246 727; e ambshqip@mt.net.mk

Austria Mile Pop Jordanov 8; ✆ 02 3083 400; f 02 3083 350; e skopje-ob@bmia.gv.at

Bosnia & Herzegovina Mile Pop Jordanov 56b; ✆ 02 3086 216; f 02 3086 221; e emb.bih@ neotel.net.mk

Bulgaria Zlatko Šnajder 3; ✆ 02 3116 320; f 02 3116 139; e secretary@bgemb.org.mk

China, People's Republic of 474 Ulica br 20; ✆ 02 3213 163; f 02 3212 500; chinaembmk@mfa.gov.cn

Croatia Mitroplit Teodosij Gologanov 44; ✆ 02 3248 170; f 02 3248 004; e croemb.skopje@ mvpei.hr; www.mvpei.hr

France Salvador Aljende 73; ☏ 02 324 4300; f 02 324 4315; e franamba@mt.net.mk; www.ambafrance-mk.org

Germany Lerinska 59/1; ☏ 02 3093 900; f 02 3093 899; e dtboskop@unet.com.mk

Greece Borka Talevski 6; ☏ 02 3130 198; f 02 3115 718; e grfyrom@unet.com.mk

Hungary Mirka Ginova 27; ☏ 02 3063 423; f 02 3063 070

Italy 8-ma Udarna Brigada 22; ☏ 02 3236 500; f 02 3236 505; e segretaria@ambasciata.org.mk; www.ambaskopje.esteri.it

Netherlands Leninova 69–71; ☏ 02 3129 319; f 02 3129 309; e nethemb@mt.com.mk; www.nlembassy.org.mk

Norway 8-ma Udarna Brigada 2; ☏ 02 3129 165; f 02 3111 138; e embskp@mfa.no; www.norway.org.mk

Poland Djuro Djakovic 50; ☏ 02 3112 647; f 02 3119 744; e ambasada@skopje.polemb.net; www.skopje.polemb.net

Romania Rajko Zinzifov 42; ☏ 02 3228 055; f 02 3228 036; e romanamb@cadis.net.mk

Russian Federation Pirinska 44; ☏ 02 3117 160; f 02 3117 808; e embassy@russia.org.mk; www.russia.org.mk

Serbia Pitu Guli 8; ☏ 02 3129 298; f 02 3129 427; e srbamb@unet.com.mk

Slovenia Vodnjanska 42; ☏ 02 3176 663; f 02 3176 631; e vsk@gov.si

Spain 27 Mart, 7; ☏ 02 3231 002; f 02 3220 612; e ambspanija@mt.net.mk

Sweden 8-ma Udarna Brigada 2; ☏ 02 3297 880; f 02 3112 065; e ambassaden.skopje@ foreign.ministry.se

Switzerland Maksim Gorki 19; ☏ 02 3128 300; f 02 3116 201; e vertretung@sko.admin.ch, visa@sko.admin.ch; www.eda.admin.ch/skopje

Turkey Slavej Planina bb; ☏ 02 3113 270; f 02 3117 024; e turkish@on.net.mk

Ukraine Pitu Guli 3; ☏ 02 3178 120; f 02 3178 068; e mk@mfa.gov.ua; www.mfa.gov.ua/Macedonia

UK Salvador Aljende 73; ☏ 02 3299 299; f 02 3179 726; e britishembassyskopje@fco.gov.uk; www.britishembassy.org.mk. Passport renewal only available in Belgrade.

US Samoilova 21; ☏ 02 3116 180; f 02 3117 103; e EmbSkoWebM@t-home.mk; http://macedonia.usembassy.gov/

Consulates in Skopje

Australia Londonska 11b; ☏ 02 3061 114; f 02 3061 834; e austcon@mt.net.mk

Belgium Koco Racin 14/4–3 9; ☏ 02 2043 314; f 02 2043 314

Canada Partizanska 17a, 1st Floor; ☏ 02 3225 630; f 02 3220 596; e honcon@unet.com.mk

Denmark Aleksandar Makedonski 12; ☏ 02 2614 332; f 02 2612 291; e dancons@unet.com.mk

State of Israel Podgradje 50, Stara Skopska Čaršija; ☏ 02 3113 978; f 02 3113 976; e viktoroffice@ gmail.com

Japan Bd Ilinden 9; ☏ 02 3117 440; f 02 3118 731

Slovakia Skopska Crvena Opstina bb; ☏ 02 3137 095; f 02 3122 105; e markoni@mt.net.mk

Spain 8-ma Udama Brigada 31a; ☏/f 02 3220 205; e castadiva@mt.net.mk; ⊕ Mon–Fri 16.00–18.00

Consulates in Bitola

Bulgaria General Consulate of the Republic of Bulgaria, Bulevar 1 Mai 53; ☏ 047 202 893/894

Croatia Maršal Tito 91; ☏/f 047 227 440

France Maršal Tito 42; ☏ 047 223 192; f 047 223 594

Greece Office of Consular Economic & Commercial Affairs, Tomaki Dimitrovski 39; ☏ 047 237 350; f 047 220 310; e grofficebitola@mfa.gr

Romania 29 Noemvri 4/2; ☏/f 047 233 937

Slovenia 29 Noemvri 4/2; ☏ 070 207 959; f 047 254 138; e miskomojsov@yahoo.com

Turkey Anesti Panovski 10/1-8; ☏ 047 254 944; f 047 253 435

UK Maršal Tito 42; ☏/f 047 228 765

GETTING THERE AND AWAY

Sadly, Macedonia is poorly served by good and inexpensive transport in and out of the country. Most regional public transport users travel by the frequent and cheap buses to Macedonia as budget flights are only just starting, and the train is slow. Aside from the car option, and if you are thinking of walking in, make sure you enter at a designated border crossing (see *Security and safety*, page 87).

✈ BY AIR For daily flight times in and out of Macedonia see www.airports.com.mk. At the time of writing, airlines that fly into Skopje are: Austrian Airlines, Adria, Bosnian, Lufthansa, Malev, Croatian Airlines, JAT, Helvetic Airways and Czech Airlines. In the summer Adria also does flights to Ohrid from Ljubljana, and Croatian Airlines does a once-a-week flight between Dubrovnik and Skopje. MAT (*Macedonian Airlines; Vasil Glavinov 3, Skopje;* ✆ *02 3218 077/8; www.mat.com.mk;* ⊕ *Mon–Fri 08.00–20.00, Sat 09.00–15.00*) does limited flights within Europe. Otherwise a flight from the UK to Skopje will cost in the region of £200–500 plus tax.

The alternative to expensive flights into Skopje is to look at neighbouring airports for cheap deals and then take the bus or the train from there. There are often inexpensive flights to Thessaloniki in Greece, and then the train (twice a day) costs €15. Or, if you are travelling in a group, you might want to consider taking a taxi from Thessaloniki for €130. British Airways does a direct flight to Priština in Kosovo, and the bus from there costs €6. There are also direct bus services from Sofia, but not Tirana.

Try the following agents for cheap flights:

Dial-a-flight ✆ 0870 333 4488; www.dialaflight.co.uk
STA Travel www.statravel.com. Many offices around the world.

Trailfinders www.trailfinders.com. Many branches worldwide.
Travelbag ✆ 0870 890 1456; www.travelbag.co.uk

Skopje Airport Skopje's airport is tiny with only two gates, so arriving 45 minutes before departure is usually sufficient. When the overseas Macedonians return for holidays in the summer months you might want to arrive a whole hour in advance for flights to Austria, Germany and Switzerland. There is a small shop selling souvenirs and Macedonian newspapers in the check-in area, as well as a coffee bar, a post office counter and two cash machines. Skopje Airport is not yet set up for e-ticketing, so these are not available for purchasing inside Macedonia. In addition, you will often have to collect your onward boarding-card on a multi-leg trip at the transit desk of your transit airport as Skopje Airport might not be able to issue these. This can be somewhat harrowing if you have a very short stop-over and don't know the transit airport, but it usually works. There is a small duty free section inside the departure lounge (no newspapers, and only limited Tikveš and Bovin wines on sale).

Unfortunately, there is still no mass public transport to and from Skopje. Therefore, the only way to travel the 25km into Skopje town is to take a taxi. Taxis picked up outside the airport charge an extortionate €25 or 1,500MKD to go into Skopje. Some hotels pick up and drop off guests for free if you book in advance. Alternatively book a taxi on line with Lotus (*www.lotustransport.com.mk*) who will pick you up from the airport into Skopje for 900MKD (€15). This is the same price as a taxi flagged down on the street going to the airport. When taking a taxi to the airport and if you are unlucky enough to get a driver who does not speak much English, make sure you ask for the '*aerodrom vo Petrovec*' not to be confused with a part of Skopje city which is also called *Aerodrom* after the old airport!

🚆 BY RAIL If you love rail travel, and hanker after those old eastern European trains, then of the four international trains that enter Macedonia direct every day (two from Thessaloniki, and two via Belgrade) you'll be glad to know that one is a 20-hour overnight train from Ljubljana. There is a daily service also to Priština, leaving mid-afternoon and departing Priština early in the morning.

The 2¹/₂-hour journey spends 40 minutes at the border changing engines. The train is well used on the Kosovo side, but few use it on the 35-minute Macedonian passage. If you get stuck at Blace border on the way to Skopje, then it is only a 20-minute walk to the road crossing where you can pick up a taxi back to Skopje for 900MKD.

The domestic timetable is on line at www.mz.com.mk/uploads/vozen_red.pdf and the 2009 timetable is available in the box below. On-line train bookings are not possible at the time of writing.

TRAIN DEPARTURE TIMES FROM SKOPJE

5901 02.22 Lisiče 02.28, Dračevo 02.34, Orešani 02.41, Zelenikovo Novo 02.43, Zelenikovo 02.45, Veles 03.10, Košulčevi 03.21, Jazla 03.29, Tošo Arsov 03.37, Orce 03.43, Ovče Pole 03.57, Štip 04.17, Balvan 04.28, Bančo Prkje 04.36, Zletovnica 04.41, Sokolarci 04.47, Obleševo 04.52, Kočani 05.01

6900 02.50 Skopje North 02.58, Gjrč Petrov 03.06, Raduša 03.22, Jegunovce 03.34, Tetovo 03.47, Gostivar 04.11, Zajas 04.32, Kičevo 04.45

991 06.09 Lisiče 06.14, Dračevo 06.20, Jane Sandanski 06.29, Orešani 06.31, Zelenikovo Novo 06.34, Zelenikovo 06.38, Kadina Reka 06.44, Pčinja 06.49, Rajko Žinzifov 06.54, Veles 07.05, Zgropolci 07.19, Nogaevci 07.24, Gradsko 07.30, Stobi 07.34, Kukuričani 07.39, Crveni Bregovi 07.44, Kirvolak 07.48, Negotino Vardar 07.52, Dubravo 07.58, Demir Kapija 08.08, Klisura 08.16, Miravci 08.28, Miletkovo 08.32, Smokvica Nova 08.36, Smokvica 08.40, Prdejci 08.42, Gevgelija 08.48

990 06.10 Madžari 06.16, Ilinden 06.25, Miladinovci 06.35, Deljadrovci 06.39, Agino Celo 06.43, Romanovci 06.47, Prevoj 06.51, Kumanovo 06.57, Karpoš 07.02 Tabanovci 07.07

4901 06.46 Lisiče 06.51, Dračevo 06.57, Jane Sandanski 07.02, Orešani 07.04, Zelenikovo Novo 07.06, Zelenikovo 07.12, Kadina Reka 07.18, Rajko Žinzifov 07.28, Veles 07.39, Toploka 07.49, Čaška 08.00, Stari Grad 08.09, Martolci 08.15, Vasil Antevski 08.22, Teovo 08.28, Sogle 08.31, Bogomila 08.39, Oreše 08.49, Gostiražni 08.59, Slenče 09.06, Brailovo 09.13, Senokos 09.18, Prilep 09.29, Galičani 09.36, Bakarno Gumno 09.42, Trojkrsti 09.47, Novoselani 09.51, Loznani 09.55, Dame Gruev 10.02, Bitola 10.17

335 07.20 Zelenikovo 07.37, Veles 08.02, Gradsko 8.24, Negotino Vardar 08.43, Demir Kapija 8.58, Miravci 09.15, Gevgelija 10.00, Solun (Thessalonica) 12.31

390 07.41 Madžari 07.46, Ilinden 07.53, Miladinovci 07.58, Romanovci 08.11, Kumanovo 08.13, Tabanovci 08.44, Preševo 09.15, Vranje 10.08, Leskovac 11.41, Niš 12.35, Stalakj 13.34, Lapovo 14.34, Mala Krsna 15.19, Belgrade 16.33

6902 08.00 Železarnica 08.04, Skopje Sever 08.08, Gjrč Petrov 08.16, Saraj 08.21, Sulari 08.26, Raduša 08.35, Orašje 08.41, Jegunovce 08.49, Jegunovci F-ka 08.51, Rataje 08.58, Tetovo 09.05, Žerovjani 09.14, Vranovci 09.20, Gostivar 09.27, Lakavica 09.34, Padalište 09.45, Zajas 09.53, Štrogomište 09.56, Dlapkin Dol 10.00, Kičevo 10.07

8931 10.10 Lisiče 10.16, Dračevo 10.22, Jane Sandanski 10.27, Orešani 10.29, Zelenikovo Novo 10.32, Zelenikovo 10.36, Kale na Reka 10.42, Pčinja 10.46, Rajko Žinzifov 10.51, Veles 11.00

336 13.11 Kumanovo 13.42, Tabanovci 14.15, Preševo 15.02, Vranje 16.03, Leskovac 17.03, Niš 18.35, Stalak 19.34, Lapovo 20.34, Mala Krsna 21.19, Belgrade 22.33

8933 13.20 Lisiče 13.26, Dračevo 13.32, Jane Sandanski 13.37, Orešani 13.39, Zelenikovo Novo 13.43, Zelenikovo 13.46, Kadina Reka 13.52, Pčinja 13.56, Rajko Žinzifov 14.01, Veles 14.10

4903 14.30 Lisiče 14.36, Dračevo 14.42, Jane Sandanski 14.46, Orešani 14.48, Zelenikovo Novo 14.51, Zelenikovo 14.55, Kadina Reka 15.01, Pčinja 15.06, Rajko Žinzifov 15.11, Veles 15.22, Toploka 15.31, Čaška 15.41, Stari Grad 15.50, Martolci 15.56, Vasil Antevski 16.03, Teovo 16.07, Sogle 16.10, Bogomila 16.18, Oreše 16.26, Gostiražni 16.37, Slepče 16.44, Brailovo 16.51. Senokos 16.56, Prilep 17.07, Galičani 17.14, Bakarno Gumno 17.21, Trojkrsti 17.26, Novoselani 17.30, Loznani 17.34, Dame Gruev 17.40, Bitola 17.55

BY BUS Due to the lack of cheap flights and frequent comfortable trains, Macedonia is well served by international-standard coaches. See www.sas.com.mk for complete bus listings. Destinations from Skopje include:

Belgrade 12 a day (6hrs, 1,300MKD)
Frankfurt Depart at 08.00, 09.30, 11.45 (24hrs, 6,850MKD) & many other locations to Germany & Switzerland.

Istanbul 16.00 (14hrs, 2,200MKD)
Podgorica 18.00 Wed & Sat only (10hrs, 1,850MKD)
Priština 09.00, 11.30, 15.00 (3hrs, 340MKD)

5903 15.30 Lisiče 15.36, Dračevo 15.42, Jane Sandanski 15.46, Orešani 15.48, Zelenikovo Novo 15.51, Zelenikovo 15.55, Kadina Reka 16.01, Pčinja 16.06, Rajko Žinzifov 16.11, Veles 16.21, Košulčevi 16.31, Jazla 16.39, Tošo Arsov 17.47, Orce 16.53, Ovče Pole 17.07, Štip 17.27, Balvan 17.38, Bančo Prkje 17.46, Zletovnica 17.51, Sokolarci 17.57, Obleševo 18.02, Kočani 18.11

892 15.35 Zelezarnica 15.39, Skopje Sever 15.44, Gjrč Petrov 15.53, Volkovo 16.00, Gj.Jankovic 16.56, Uroševac 17.37, Polje 18.07, Priština 18.13

6904 16.30 Zelezarnica 16.34, Skopje Sever 16.38, Gjrč Petrov 16.46, Saraj 16.51, Supari 16.57, Raduša 17.06, Orašje 17.12, Jegunovce 17.20, Jegunovce F-ka 17.22, Rataje 17.28, Tetovo 17.35, Želovjani 17.44, Vranovci 17.50, Gostivar 17.57, Lakavica 18.04, Padalište 18.15, Zajas 18.23, Strogomište 18.26, Dlakin Dol 18.30, Kičevo 18.37

392 16.32 Madžari 16.38, Ilinden 16.50, Miladinovci 16.57, Deljadrovci 17.01, Agino Selo 17.05, Romanovci 17.09, Prevoj 17.13, Kumanovo 17.19, Karpoš 17.24, Tabanovci 17.48, Preševo 18.20, Vranje 19.13, Leskovac 20.46, Niš 21.24

8935 16.40 Lisiče 16.45, Dračevo 16.51, Jane Sandanski 16.55, Orešani 16.57, Zelenikovo Novo 17.00, Zelenikovo 17.04, Kadina Reka 17.10, Pčinja 17.15, Rajko Žinzifov 17.20, Veles 17.30

337 17.15 Zelenikovo 17.33, Veles 17.57, Zgroploci 18.10, Gradsko 18.19, Kukuričani 18.27, Negotino Vardar 18.38, Dubrovo 18.47, Demir Kapija 18.57, Miravci 19.14, Gevgelija 19.55, Solun (Thessalonica) 22.34

4905 18.15 Lisiče 18.25, Dračevo 18.31, Jane Sandanski 18.36, Orešani 18.38, Zelemikovo Novo 18.41, Zelenikovo 18.45, Kadina Reka 18.51, Pčinja 18.56, Rajko Žinzifov 19.01, Veles 19.12, Toploka 19.21, Čaška 19.31, Stari Grad 19.41, Martolci 19.47, Vasil Antevski 19.55, Teovo 19.59, Sogle 20.02, Bogomila 20.25, Gostiražni 20.43, Slepče 20.50, Brailovo 20.55, Senokos 21.00, Prilep 21.07, Galičani 21.13, Bakarno Gumno 21.19, Novoselani 21.24, Bitola 21.45

992 18.40 Madžari 18.46, Ilinden 18.55, Miladinovci 19.02, Deljadrovci 19.06, Agino Selo 19.10, Romanovci 19.14, Prevoj 19.18, Kumanovo 19.24, Karpoš 19.29, Tabanovci 19.34

3903 19.42 Lisiče 19.48, Dračevo 19.54, Jane Sandanski 29.02, Orešani 20.04, Zelenikovo Novo 20.07, Zelenikovo 20.11, Kadina Reka 20.17, Pčinja 20.22, Rajko Žinzifov 20.31, Veles 20.41, Zgropolci 20.55, Nogaevci 21.00, Gradsko 21.06, Stobi 21.10, Kukuričani 21.15. Crveni Bregovi 21.20, Krivolac 21.25, Negotino Vardar 22.29, Dubravo 21.35, Demir Kapija 21.45, Klisura 21.52, Miravci 22.04, Miletkovo 22.08, Smokvica Nova 22.12, Smokvica 22.16, Prdejci 22.18, Gevgelija 22.24

334 20.40 Kumanovo 21.11, Tabanovci 21.55, Preševo 22.35, Vranje 23.28, Leskovac 00.58, Niš 01.45, Staljak 02.44, Lapovo 03.44, Mala Krsna 04.29, Belgrade 05.44

2902 22.37 Madžari 22.46, Ilinden 22.55, Miladinovci 23.01, Deljadrovci 23.05, Agino Selo 23.09, Romanovci 23.13, Prevoj 23.17, Kumanovo 23.22 8937 22.40 Lisiče 22.46, Dračevo 22.52, Jane Sandanski 22.58, Orešani 23.00, Aelenikovo Novo 23.02, Zelenikovo 23.06, Kadina Reka 23.12, Rajko Žinzifov 23.22, Veles 23.31

From	Arrival time
990 Veles 05.05, Rajko Žinzifov 05.14, Pčinja 05.19, Kadina Reka 05.24, Zelenikovo 05.31, Novo Zelenikovo 05.34, Orešani 05.37, Jane Sandanski 05.39, Dračevo 05.44, Lisiče 05.50	05.55
991 Tabanovce 05.05, Karpoš 5.10, Kumanovo 05.16, Prevoj 05.21, Romanovci 5.25, Agino Selo 05.30, Deljadrovci 05.34, Miladinovci 05.39, Ilinden 05.46, Madžari 05.55	06.00
4900 Bitola 03.33, Novoselani 03.55, Bakarno Gumno 04.00, Prilep 04.14, Senokos 04.21, Brailovo 04.21, Slepče 04.32, Gostiražni 04.39, Oreše 04.48, Bogomila 04.56, Sogle 05.03, Teovo 05.06, Vasil Antevski 05.12, Martolci 05.19, Stari Grad 05.25, Čaška 05.35, Toploka 05.45, Veles 05.55, Rajko Žinzifov, 06.04, Kadina Reka 06.13, Zelenikovo 06.20, Novo Zelenikovo 06.23, Orešani 06.26, Jane Sandanski 06.28, Dračevo 06.34, Lisiče 06.39	06.44
335 Belgrade 22.00, Mladenovac 22.59, Palanka 23.20, Lapovo 23.51, Stalakj 00.55, Niš 02.10, Leskovac 02.52, Vranje 04.20, Preševo 05.35, Tabanovce 06.10, Kumanovo 06.20	06.50
6901 Kičevo 5.10, Dlapkin Dol 05.16, Strogomište 05.23, Zajas 5.29, Padalište 05.36, Lakavica 05.50, Gostivar 05.52, Vranovci 05.56, Žerovjani 06.03, Tetovo 06.13, Rataje 06.16, Jegunovce F-ka 06.29, Jegunovce 06.32, Oraše 06.38, Raduša 06.42, Sulari 06.49, Saraj 06.55, Gjorče Petrov 06.59, Skopje Sever 07.07, Železnarica 07.11	07.15
3900 Gevgelija 04.59, Prdejci 05.05, Smokvica 05.07, Smokvica Nova 05.11, Miletkovo 05.15, Miravci 5.30, Klisura 05.31, Demir apija 05.39, Dubrovo 05.49, Negotino Vardar 05.55, Krivolak 05.58, Crveni Bregovi 06.02, Kukuričani 06.07, Stobi 06.12, Gradsko 06.17, Nogaevci 06.22, Zgropolci 06.28, Veles 06.42, Rajko Žinzifov 06.55, Pinja 07.00, Kadina Reka 07.05, Zelenikovo 07.11, Zelenikovo Novo 07.14, Orešani 07.17, Jane Sandanski 07.20, Dračevo 07.29, Lisiče 07.34	07.39
5900 Kočani 05.21, Obleševo 05.32, Sokolarci 05.37, Zletovica 05.43, Vančo Prkje 05.48, Balvan 05.56, Štip 06.98, Ovče Pole 06.26, Orče 06.40, Tošo Arsov 06.46, Jazla 06.54, Košulčevi 07.02, Veles 07.14, Rajko Žinzifov 07.29, Kadina Reka 07.43, Zelenikovo 07.50, Zelenikovo Novo 07.53, Orešani 07.56, Jane Sandanski 07.58, Dračevo 08.04, Lisiče 08.09	08.14
2901 Tabanovci 07.23, Karpoš 07.28, Kumanovo 07.34, Prevoj 07.39, Romanovci 07.43, Agino Selo 07.47, Deljadrovci 07.51, Miladinovci 07.59, Ilinden 08.06, Madžari 08.15	08.20
891 Priština 05.53, Kosovo Polje 06.02, Uroševac 06.33, Gj.Jankovic 07.33, Volkovo 08.04, Gj.Petrov 08.21, Skopje Sever 08.29	08.36
8932 Veles 11.30, Rajko Žinzifov 11.40, Pčinja 11.45, Kadina Reka 11.50, Zelenikovo 11.57, Novo Zelenikovo 12.00, Orešani 12.03, Jane Sandanski 12.05, Dračevo 12.10, Lisiče 12.15	12.20
336 Solun (Thessalonica) 09.45 Gevgelija 10.37, Miravci 10.51, Demir Kapija 11.09, Negotino Vardar 11.24, Gradsko 11.43, Veles 12.05, Zelenikovo 12.28	12.45
393 Niš 08.55, Leskovac 09.36, Vranje 11.11, Preševo 12.32, Tabanovci 12.53, Karpoš 12.58, Kumanovo 13.03, Prevoj 13.08, Romanovci 13.12, Agino Selo 13.16, Deljadrovci 13.20, Miladinovci 13.28, Ilinden 13.35, Madžari 13.34	13.49
6903 Kičevo 12.15, Dlapkin Dol 12.21, Strogomišta 12.28, Zajas 12.34, Padalište 12.41, Lakavica 12.48, Gostivar 12.55, Vranovci 13.01, Žerovjane 13.08 Tetovo 13.19, Rataje 13.25, Jegunovce F-ka 13.35, Jegunovce 13.38, Oraše 13.43, Raduša 13.47, Sulari 13.54, Saraj 14.01, Gjorče Petrov 14.06, Skopje Sever 14.14, Železarnica 14.18	14.22

Sofia 06.30, 08.30, 15.00, 16.00, 22.00, 23.00, 24.00   **Tirana** 19.00 (7hrs, 1,370MKD)
(5hrs, 850MKD)   **Zagreb** 13.00, 17.00 (15hrs, 2,860MKD)
Thessaloniki 07.00 Mon, Wed & Fri only (5hrs, 1,050MKD)

International coaches also serve other locations in Macedonia, especially between Germany and the northwestern towns of Gostivar and Tetovo. For bus station details in Macedonia see individual chapters. Timetables and price information from some countries to Macedonian are available at

From	Arrival time
8934	Veles 14.26, Rajko Žinzifov 14.35, Pčinja 14.40, Kadina Reka 14.45, Zelenikovo 14.56, Zelenikovo Novo 14.59, Orešani 15.02, Jane Sandanski 15.04, Dračevo 15.09, Lisiče 15.15 **15.20**
4902	Bitola 12.42, Dame Grueve 12.58, Loznani 13.03, Novoselani 13.07, Trjokrsti 13.11, Bakarno Gumno 13.17, Galičani 13.23, Prilep 13.32, Senokos 13.41, Brailovo 13.47, Slepče 13.53, Gostiražni 14.01, Oreše 14.11, Bogomila 14.20, Sogle 14.27, Teovo 14.30, Vasil Antevski 14.36, Martolci 14.43, Stari Grad 14.49, Časka 14.59, Toploka 15.08, Veles 15.23, Rajko Žinzifov 15.34, Pčinja 15.39, Kadina Reka 15.45, Zelenikovo 15.56, Novo Zelenikovo 15.59, Orešani 16.02, Jane Sandanski 16.04, Dračevo 16.09, Lisiče 16.15 **16.20**
337	Belgrade 07.50, Mladinovac 09.12, Lapovo 09.40, Stalakj 10.40, Niš 12.20, Leskovac 13.01, Vranje 14.29, Preševo 15.45, Tabanovci 16.20, Kumanovo 16.30 **17.00**
992	Gevgelija 15.52, Prdejci 15.58, Smokvica 16.00, Smokvica Nova 16.04, Milekovo 16.08, Miravci 16.13, Klisura 16.24, Demir Kapija 16.32, Dubrovo 16.42, Negotino Vardar 16.48, Krivolak 16.51, Crveni Bregovi 16.55, Kukuričani 17.00, Stobi 17.05, Gradsko 17.10, Nogaevci 17.15, Zgroploci 17.21, Veles 17.35, Rajko Žinzifov 17.48, Pinja 17.53, Kadina Reka 17.58, Zelenikovo 18.05, Zelenikovo Novo 18.08, Porešani 18.11, Jane Sandanski 18.13, Dračevo 18.18, Lisiče 18.24 **18.29**
8936	Veles 18.16, Rajko Žinzifov 18.25, Pčinja 18.30, Kadina Reka 18.35, Zelenikovo 18.46, Zelenikovo Novo 18.49, Porešani 18.52, Jane Sandanski 18.54, Dračevo 18.59, Lisiče 19.05 **19.10**
334	Solun (Thessalonica) 17.09, Gevgelija 18.05, Miravci 18.19, Demir Kapija 18.37, Negotino Vardar 18.52, Kukuričani 19.02, Gradsko 19.11, Zgropolci 19.19, Veles 19.33 **20.14**
2903	Tabanovci 19.55, Karpoš 20.00, Kumanovo 20.06, Prevoj 20.11, Romanovci 20.15, Agino Selo 20.19, Deljadrovci 20.23, Miladinovci 20.28, Ilinden 20.34, Madžari 20.46 **20.51**
6905	Kičevo 18.54, Dlapkin Dol 19.00, Strogomište 19.07, Zajas 19.13, Padalište 19.20, Lakavica 19.27, Gostivar 19.36, Vranovci 19.49, Žerovjane 19.47, Tetovo 19.58, Rataje 20.04, Jegunovce F-ka 20.13, Jegunovce 20.16, Oraše 20.21, Raduša 20.25, Sulari 20.32, Saraj 20.38, Gjorče Petrov 20.43, Skopje Sever 21.51, Železarnica 20.55 **20.59**
5902	Kočani 18.27, Oblaševo18.36, Sokolarci 18.41, Zletovica 18.48, Vančo Prkje 18.53, Balvan 19.01, Štip 19.13, Ovče Pole 19.31, Orče 19.45, Tošo Arsov 19.51, Jazla 19.59, Košulčevi 20.07, Veles 20.21, Rajko Žinzifov 20.30, Pčinja 20.35 Kadina Reka 20.40, Zelenikovo 20.47, Jane Sandanski 20.53, Dračevo 20.58, Lisiče 21.03 **21.08**
4904	Bitola 18.43, Dame Gruev 18.58, Loznani 19.03, Novoselani 19.07, Trojkrsti 19.11, Bakarno Gumno 19.17, Galičani 19.23, Prilep 19.32, Senokos 19.31, Brailovo 19.47, Slepe 19.53, Gostiražni 20.01, Oreše 20.11, Bogomila 20.20, Sogle 20.27, Teovo 20.30, Vasil Antevski 20.34, Martolci 20.40, Stari Grad 20.46, Časka 20.56, Toploka 21.05, Veles 21.16, Rajko Žinzifov, Kadina Reka 21.36, Zelenikovo 21.43, Jane Sandanski 21.49, Dračevo 21.54, Lisiče 22.00 **22.05**
391	Belgrade 14.05, Mladenovac 15.03, Palanka 15.24, Lapovo 15.52, Stalakj 16.49, Niš 18.00, Leskovac 18.41, Vranje 20.16, Preševo 21.28, Tabanovci 22.10, Kumanovo 22.20 **22.50**

www.eurolines.com. At the time of writing Macedonia had yet to put its international coach services on the Eurolines website. There is a left luggage service at Skopje Bus Station.

BY CAR The easiest and most convenient way to get around Macedonia is still by car, (a 4x4 if you plan to go anywhere off the beaten track). But driving to Macedonia from the further reaches of Europe, especially places like Britain and Finland, is an extremely long journey – at least three days, unless you don't intend to sleep (not advisable).

If you do intend to drive from Britain, for instance, a recommended route would be to cross at Calais for a cheap, short ferry journey, drive through the roads of France, which are usually fairly empty although there are road tolls to pay (German roads are toll-free, but packed, and speed restrictions are becoming more widespread), cross the Alps at the Simplon Pass and head for Venice. From here take the overnight car ferry to Durres in Albania, or Igoumenitsa in Greece. Either journey from these ports to Skopje is arduous mountain driving (six hours from Durres via Ohrid, or ten hours via Bitola from Igoumenitsa), but the scenery is fantastic. The drive down through Italy, whilst making the ferry journey shorter, is packed with other drivers, often resulting in traffic jams in boring scenery. For times and prices of ferries between Italy and the Balkans see www.cemar.it/ferries/1_ferries.html.

MAPS AND TOURIST INFORMATION

Tourist information centres are beginning to appear in major towns in Macedonia now, although some are an outlet for local souvenirs rather than useful maps and information. In some cases you might be much better off going to a travel agency for information, especially in towns outside Skopje.

Maps of Macedonia are becoming available in a variety of formats from most bookstores and big supermarkets, such as Vero, Ramstore or Tinex. Town maps of Skopje, Ohrid, Struga, Kruševo, Berovo and Prilep made by Trimaks (*www.3maks.com*) are available throughout Macedonia. Locally made maps of Bitola and Strumica are available in those places only.

Since topographical mapping was de-classified, new 1:25,000 hiking maps of Macedonia (map information as at 2004) have been available for 160MKD each plus tax. Only 75% of the country was available in paper map format at the time of print, and the remainder should be finished by the end of 2011. Note that these maps do not use the WGS84 military grid referencing system (MGRS), but the old Yugoslav Croatian-based referencing using the Gaus-Krüger (Krigerova) ellipsoid. The grid co-ordinates used in this guidebook are based on the old Yugoslav Croatian-based grid referencing system currently used by the new Macedonian maps. Eventually the maps will be available with WGS84 MGRS. For those of you who require a conversion visit the webpage in the box below.

The old 1971 Yugoslav military maps of the country are available direct from the State Authority for Geodetic Works (SAGW) for those areas not yet completed for the new maps. The new maps should be available soon over the counter in shops and hotels but if not they are available directly from SAGW head office (*Trifun Hadži Janev 4;* ↘ *02 3170 114/120;* f *02 3171 668;* e *prodazba@katastar.gov.mk;*

GRID REFERENCES USED IN THIS EDITION

Please note that contrary to the first edition, which gave grid references in what is slowly becoming the world standard (WGS84 Military Grid Reference System or MGRS as used on NATO mapping), this edition has all its co-ordinates in the Croatian map datum (ellipsoid used) and Macedonian position format. This is so that they can be used directly with the new Macedonian 1:25,000 maps currently being released. For the few who have access to the NATO military mapping of the country, please see the following webpage http://homepage.mac.com/thammyevans/ BradtMacedonia for the WGS84 MGRS grids and how to convert between both systems. The page also gives instructions on how to set your GPS for use with Macedonian maps.

www.katastar.gov.mk/en/cartography). Known locally as the *katastar*, the head office is in Avtokomanda district (not in Karpoš, which is the local municipal office for Skopje only), and its entrance is actually on Jani Lukrovski where there is a statue of Atlas opposite a primary school. As stated on their website under 'pricelist', payment for the maps needs to be made through the post office. This can seem a bit daunting, but is in fact very easy. At SAGW, when you go to get the maps, their English-speaking staff will furnish you with a photocopy of a payment slip with all the details that you require. At the tiny post office five minutes by foot further down the street on Jani Lukrovski, the friendly staff will often help you fill out the real form, and all you have to do is provide your name and address and passport number. Pay in cash and take your receipt back to SAGW, who will then give you your maps.

Street names in Macedonia can make your stay a bit like playing hide and seek. Many streets don't have a name, but simply a number. In addition, some street names have changed at least twice since independence and the name given on the map may not correspond to the name actually signposted and used by the locals. Maršal Tito Street in Skopje, the main pedestrian street, is a case in point. On the Trimaks map of the city it is named Makedonija. On the street itself it retains its old name and that is still what people call it.

This guide follows Macedonian common usage as much as possible and street names are in their Macedonian spelling followed by the house number. If it is a numbered street then it is given as, for example, *Ulica 000*, followed by the house number (*broj*) *br0*. Many streets are named after dates in history, so house number 60 on the street of First of May is written here as '1st Maj 60'. As if all this is not confusing enough, some buildings, especially large factories or institutions, do not have numbers at all, in which case the street name is followed by *bb*, indicating *bez broj* meaning 'without number'.

Note that some streets have been renumbered several times due to new building work; as a result several buildings have the same number or have their old number still showing!

✚ HEALTH with Dr Felicity Nicholson

IMPORTANT PHONE NUMBERS
Ambulance ➘ 194
Fire service ➘ 193
Police ➘ 192
(A new combined number 112 should come into use soon.)

Make sure you get health insurance that is valid for Macedonia before arrival, unless you are prepared to pay for any mishaps yourself. Macedonian doctors and hospitals expect to be paid in cash on the spot by foreigners seeking treatment, and once furnished with your receipt, appropriately translated, you can reclaim your money back from your insurer. Most travel agents abroad will be able to sort you out with the appropriate health insurance, and some give a good deal, combining health and travel insurance with insurance against theft.

It is usually a good idea to get any treatment that you need before you go travelling. Compared with some countries, medical treatment is cheaper in Macedonia than in, say, the US, and standards can be as good as at home. Most doctors speak English. Nevertheless, it is always more comforting to get treatment at home.

Common illnesses can be treated in Macedonia by the pharmacists in any local pharmacy (*apteka*). Many have English-speaking staff, and they can also advise you of the nearest family practitioner if you are in need of a doctor. If you need hospitalisation, this is best left till you get home, unless it is an emergency, in which case either call 194, or it may be quicker to get a taxi to take you to the nearest hospital (*bolnica*). In Skopje, City Hospital (Gradska Bolnica), the red-brick building on 11th Oktomvri opposite the parliament, deals with all emergencies requiring anaesthesia. The emergency outpatients' entrance is around the back. There are several 24-hour pharmacies in big towns. In Skopje there is one on Dimitri Čupovski between McDonald's and the traffic lights.

VACCINATIONS Vaccinations are not legally required for entry into Macedonia, but doctors will advise the following to be on the safe side: tetanus, diphtheria and polio (this comes as an all-in-one injection – Revaxis – and lasts for ten years), hepatitis A and typhoid. It is wise to visit your doctor or a travel health clinic about four to six weeks before travel. If you are going to be in the country for a long time (four weeks or more) or are dealing with refugees or children or working in a medical setting then immunisation against hepatitis B and meningitis is worth having. For hepatitis B ideally three doses of vaccine should be taken before travel. These can be given at 0, 1 and 6 months; 0, 1 and 2 months; or if time is short at 0, 7 and 21–8 days. Only Engerix B is currently licensed for the last schedule.

Tick-borne encephalitis (TBE) This potentially fatal disease is spread by bites from infected ticks. Vaccination would be recommended if you are intending to walk through forests, or are likely to be a long-term resident in rural areas. Three doses of vaccine are ideal and can be given over a three-week period if time is short. At the time of writing only Encepur is licensed to be used in this way. TBE vaccine can be obtained only on a named-patient basis in the UK, which means that you have to pre-order the vaccine from either your GP or a travel clinic. It is not always possible to get vaccinations before you go so there are sensible precautions you can take.

Always wear long-sleeved clothing, trousers tucked into boots and a hat. Ticks can drop from overhanging branches onto your head and this is particularly a problem with children. Ticks should ideally be removed as soon as possible as leaving ticks on the body increases the chance of infection. They should be removed with special tick tweezers that can be bought in good travel shops. Failing that you can use your fingernails by grasping the tick as close to your body as possible and pulling steadily and firmly away at right angles to your skin. The tick will then come away complete as long as you do not jerk or twist. If possible douse the wound with alcohol (any spirit will do) or iodine. Irritants (eg: Olbas oil) or lit cigarettes are to be discouraged since they can cause the ticks to regurgitate and therefore increase the risk of disease. It is best to get a travelling companion to check you for ticks and if you are travelling with small children remember to check their heads, and particularly behind the ears.

Spreading redness around the bite and/or fever and/or aching joints after a tick bite imply that you have an infection that requires antibiotic treatment, so seek advice.

Tuberculosis Experts differ over whether a BCG vaccination against tuberculosis (TB) is useful in adults; discuss with your travel clinic. However, it may be recommended for children who have not yet been vaccinated especially if they are likely to be mixing closely with the local population. This is more important for longer-stay trips. Tuberculosis is spread through close respiratory contact and occasionally through infected milk or milk products.

Rabies Rabies is carried by all mammals. It is not common in Macedonia but it can be passed on to man through a bite, scratch or a lick of an open wound. You must always assume any animal is rabid and seek medical help as soon as possible. Meanwhile scrub the wound with soap and under a running tap or pouring water from a jug. Find a reasonably clear-looking source of water but at this stage the quality of the water is not important; then pour on a strong iodine or alcohol solution or gin, whisky or rum. This helps stop the rabies virus entering the body and will guard against wound infections, including tetanus.

Pre-exposure vaccinations for rabies are ideally advised for everyone, but are particularly important if you intend to have contact with animals and/or are likely to be more than 24 hours away from medical help. Ideally three doses should be taken over four weeks, though even taking one or two doses of vaccine is better than none at all. Contrary to popular belief these vaccinations are relatively painless.

If you are bitten, scratched or licked over an open wound by a sick animal, then post-exposure prophylaxis should be given as soon as possible, though it is never too late to seek help, as the incubation period for rabies can be very long. Those who have not been immunised will need a full course of injections. The vast majority of travel health advisors including WHO recommend rabies immunoglobulin (RIG), but this product is expensive (around US$800) and may be hard to come by – another reason why pre-exposure vaccination should be encouraged.

Tell the doctor if you have had pre-exposure vaccine, as this will change the treatment you receive. And remember that, if you do contract rabies, mortality is 100% and death from rabies is probably one of the worst ways to go.

TRAVEL CLINICS AND HEALTH INFORMATION A full list of current travel clinic websites worldwide is available on www.istm.org/. For other journey preparation information, consult www.nathnac.org/ds/map_world.aspx. Information about various medications may be found on www.netdoctor.co.uk/travel.

UK

Berkeley Travel Clinic 32 Berkeley St, London W1J 8EL (near Green Park tube station); ☎ 020 7629 6233; ☺ Mon–Fri 10.00–18.00, Sat 10.00–15.00.

Cambridge Travel Clinic 41 Hills Rd, Cambridge, CB2 1NT; ☎ 01223 367362; f 01223 368021; e enquiries@travelcliniccambridge.co.uk; www.travelcliniccambridge.co.uk; ☺ Mon, Tue & Sat 10.00–16.00, Wed/Thu 12.00–19.00, Fri 11.00–18.00.

Edinburgh Travel Health Clinic 14 East Preston St, Newington, Edinburgh EH8 9QA; ☎ 0131 667 1030; www.edinburghtravelhealthclinic.co.uk; ☺ Mon–Wed 09.00–19.00, Thu/Fri 9.00–18.00. Travel vaccinations & advice on all aspects of malaria prevention. All current UK prescribed anti-malaria tablets in stock.

Fleet Street Travel Clinic 29 Fleet St, London EC4Y 1AA; ☎ 020 7353 5678; www.fleetstreetclinic.com; ☺ Mon–Fri 08.45–17.30. Injections, travel products & latest advice.

Hospital for Tropical Diseases Travel Clinic Mortimer Market Centre, 2nd Floor, Capper St (off Tottenham Ct Rd), London WC1E 6AU; ☎ 020 7388 9600; www.thehtd.org; ☺ 9:00–16:00. Offers

consultations & advice, & is able to provide all necessary drugs & vaccines for travellers. Runs a healthline (tel: 020 7950 7799) for country-specific information & health hazards. Also stocks nets, water purification equipment & personal protection measures. Travellers who have returned from the tropics & are unwell, with fever or bloody diarrhoea, can attend the walk-in emergency clinic at the hospital without an appointment.

MASTA (Medical Advisory Service for Travellers Abroad) London School of Hygiene & Tropical Medicine, Keppel St, London WC1 7HT; ☎ 09068 224100 www.masta-travel-health.com; e enquiries@masta.org. This is a premium-line number, charged at 60p/min. For a fee, they will provide an individually tailored health brief, with up-to-date information on how to stay healthy, inoculations & what to take.

MASTA pre-travel clinics ☎ 01276 685040. Call or check http://www.masta-travel-health.com/travel-clinic.aspx for the nearest; there are currently 30 in Britain. They also sell malaria prophylaxis, memory cards, treatment kits, bednets, net treatment kits, etc.

NHS travel website www.fitfortravel.nhs.uk. Provides country-by-country advice on immunisation & malaria prevention, plus details of recent developments, & a list of relevant health organisations.

Nomad Travel Stores Flagship store: 3–4 Wellington Terr, Turnpike La, London N8 0PX; ☎ 020 8889 7014; f 020 8889 9528; e turnpike@ nomadtravel.co.uk; www.nomadtravel.co.uk; walk in or appointments ⏰ daily 09.15–17.00, Thu late night. 6 stores in total countrywide: 3 in London, Bristol, Southampton, Manchester. As well as dispensing health advice, Nomad stocks mosquito nets & other anti-bug devices, & an excellent range of adventure travel gear.

Irish Republic
Tropical Medical Bureau Grafton St Medical Centre, Grafton Bldgs, 34 Grafton St, Dublin 2;

USA
Centers for Disease Control 1600 Clifton Rd, Atlanta, GA 30333; ☎ (800) 232 4636, (800) 232 6348; e cdcinfo@cdc.gov; www.cdc.gov/travel. The central source of travel information in the USA. Each summer they publish the invaluable *Health Information for International Travel*.

Canada
IAMAT (International Association for Medical Assistance to Travellers) Suite 1, 1287 St Clair Av W, Toronto, ON M6E 1B8; ☎ 416 652 0137; www.iamat.org

Australia, New Zealand, Thailand
TMVC (Travel Doctors Group) ☎ 1300 65 88 44; www.tmvc.com.au. 22 clinics in Australia, New Zealand & Thailand, inc: *Auckland* Canterbury Arcade, 170 Queen St, Auckland; ☎ 9 373 3531; *Brisbane* 75a Astor Terr, Spring Hill, Brisbane, QLD 4000; ☎ (07) 3815 6900; e brisbane@ traveldoctor.com.au; *Melbourne* Dr Sonny Lau, 393

South Africa
SAA-Netcare Travel Clinics e travelinfo@ netcare.co.za www.travelclinic.co.za. 12 clinics throughout South Africa.

Switzerland
IAMAT 57 Chemin des Voirets, 1212 Grand-Lancy, Geneva; e info@iamat.org; www.iamat.org

InterHealth Travel Clinic 111 Westminster Bridge Rd, London SE1 7HR; ☎ 020 7902 9000; e info@interhealth.org.uk; www.interhealth.org.uk; ⏰ Mon–Fri 08.30–17.30. Competitively priced, one-stop travel health service by appointment only.

Trailfinders Immunisation Centre 194 Kensington High St, London W8 7RG; ☎ 020 7938 3999; www.trailfinders.com/travelessentials/ travelclinic.htm; ⏰ Mon, Tue, Wed & Fri 09.00–17.00, Thu 09.00–18.00, Sat 10.00–17.15. No appointment necessary.

Travelpharm The Travelpharm website (*www.travelpharm.com*) offers up-to-date guidance on travel-related health & has a range of medications available through its on-line mini-pharmacy.

☎ 1 671 9200; www.tmb.ie. Useful website specific to tropical destinations.

IAMAT (International Association for Medical Assistance to Travelers) 1623 Military Rd, 279 Niagara Falls, NY 14304-1745; ☎ 716 754 4883; e info@iamat.org; www.iamat.org. A non-profit organisation with free membership that provides lists of English-speaking doctors abroad.

TMVC Suite 314, 1030 W Georgia St, Vancouver, BC V6E 2Y3; ☎ 905 648 1112; e info@tmvc.com; www.tmvc.com. One-stop medical clinic for all your international travel medicine & vaccination needs.

Little Bourke St, 2nd Floor, Melbourne, VIC 3000; ☎ (03) 9935 8100; e melbourne@ traveldoctor.com.au; *Sydney* Dr Mandy Hu, Dymocks Bldg, 7th Floor, 428 George St, Sydney, NSW 2000; ☎ 2 9221 7133; f 2 9221 8401
IAMAT PO Box 5049, Christchurch 5, New Zealand; www.iamat.org

TMVC NHC Health Centre, cnr Beyers Naude & Waugh Northcliff; ☎ 0 11 214 9030; e traveldoctor@wtmconline.com; www.traveldoctor.co.za. Consult the website for details of clinics.

COMMON PROBLEMS Without stating the absolutely obvious, it is a good idea to be fit and healthy before going on holiday! Many of us though have usually just raced through a work or college deadline before leaving and the time to unwind and relax is just when the common cold or stomach flu takes hold. Food hygiene standards and tap drinking water in Macedonia are safe for the average traveller. If you are one of those fussy types, who have never allowed their stomach to harden to foreign bacteria, then drink the ubiquitous bottled water, and avoid drinking from mountain streams and water fountains. Water fountains in towns are usually from the same source as tap water and therefore safe.

Diarrhoea Unless you are a seasoned world traveller and have a stomach like cast iron, you may get a small bout of the trots on coming into contact with new foods, water and cooking. In Macedonia this is unlikely to turn into full-blown diarrhoea requiring antibiotics to clear it up. If it does, the pharmacy can sort you out, or, if you are prone to a bit of Delhi belly, bring some suitable medication with you from home.

There are many old wives' tales that are alleged to help you avoid this phenomenon. In Macedonia they believe that if you eat the onions of the new country within 24 hours of getting there, then your stomach will settle into the new environment. A good remedy I have found for the trots that just keep trotting is to restrict yourself to a diet of well-boiled salted carrots and salted white rice for a day or two. This will bung you up in no time at all. If that doesn't work try Imodium. Keep off dairy products, eggs and fresh fruit or juice for a few more days and things should return to normal. Always drink plenty of water if you have diarrhoea, and take in plenty of salt. The locals will recommend tea, others recommend flat Coca-Cola.

MOSQUITOES These not prevalent in most of Macedonia as the country is so mountainous, but in the low-lying areas around Skopje and south along the Vardar, you might find one or two. You'll find many more to the north and south of Macedonia in Serbia and Greece. Malaria in Macedonia was last seen in World War I, so it is no longer necessary to take anti-malarial tablets.

FIRST-AID KIT As with any travels away from your medicine cabinet at home, it is a good idea to have a small first-aid pack with you. You can buy these ready made from any good pharmacy at home, such as Boots in the UK, or Walgreens in the US, or you can just make up a small kit yourself from the following items:

- plasters/Band-Aids
- painkillers such as aspirin, paracetamol or Tylenol
- lipsalve
- sunscreen
- antiseptic cream (diluted tea-tree oil works well)
- mosquito bite cream (this should ideally contain DEET or a natural-based insect repellent containing citronella or eucalyptus)
- spare contact lenses if you are a contact lens wearer
- and I usually throw in a small sewing kit for when I've eaten too much of the local food and need to re-sew on a button, or my trousers have ripped on a hike in the forest.

WOMEN'S HEALTH If as a female traveller you find yourself, expectedly or unexpectedly, with health problems peculiar to the fairer sex, you will be glad to know that there are some good English-speaking gynaecologists in the capital. A

It is dehydration that makes you feel awful during a bout of diarrhoea and the most important part of treatment is drinking lots of clear fluids. Sachets of oral rehydration salts give the perfect biochemical mix to replace all that is pouring out of your bottom but other recipes taste nicer. Any dilute mixture of sugar and salt in water will do you good: try Coke or orange squash with a three-finger pinch of salt added to each glass (if you are salt-depleted you won't taste the salt). Otherwise make a solution of a four-finger scoop of sugar with a three-finger pinch of salt in a 500ml glass of clean water. Or add eight level teaspoons of sugar (18g) and one level teaspoon of salt (3g) to one litre (five cups) of safe water. A squeeze of lemon or orange juice improves the taste and adds potassium, which is also lost in diarrhoea. Drink two large glasses after every bowel action, and more if you are thirsty. These solutions are still absorbed well if you are vomiting, but you will need to take sips at a time. If you are not eating you need to drink three litres a day plus whatever is pouring into the toilet. If you feel like eating, take a bland, high carbohydrate diet. Heavy greasy foods will probably give you cramps.

If the diarrhoea is bad, or you are passing blood or slime, or you have a fever, you will probably need antibiotics in addition to fluid replacement. A dose of ciprofloxacin or norfloxacin repeated twice a day until better may also be appropriate (if you are planning to take an antibiotic with you). Note that both norfloxacin and ciprofloxacin are only available on prescription in the UK. If the diarrhoea is greasy and bulky and is accompanied by sulphurous (eggy) burps, one likely cause is giardia. This is best treated with tinidazole (four x 500mg in one dose, repeated seven days later if symptoms persist).

private practitioner is Dr Biljana Davčeva (*101 Orče Nikola;* ℡ *02 311 0113;* ◷ *Mon–Fri 09.00–17.00*).

Common remedies for cystitis, such as cranberry juice or Emergen-C, are hard to find. Uve-Mix herbal tea, available in most supermarkets, is the local solution. It tastes horrible, but mixed with dried basil (*basilikum*) and St John's wort (*kantarion*) is quite effective. Your first remedy should be 48 hours of heavy drinking (of water and Uve-Mix herbal tea), with absolute abstinence from caffeine and tannin (for another week). Avoid long journeys where you can't get to the toilet frequently. If you still have problems after a 48-hour concerted effort, then you will almost certainly need antibiotics. Amoxicillin, a form of penicillin good for waterworks and intestinal problems, is available over the counter cheaply.

Condoms are readily available in Macedonia, but tampons with applicators are not. OB tampons without applicators and regular sanitary towels are ubiquitous.

HEALTH AND SAFETY IN THE MOUNTAINS In the mountains, health and safety go hand in hand. Although Macedonia's mountains are not very big, they are sufficiently remote, and trails sufficiently obscure, so that without a good hiking map (preferably 1:25,000, 1cm = 0.25km) it is very easy to get lost. Make sure you are a proficient hiker before venturing for long hikes into the mountains here, otherwise a two-hour walk in the park could turn into an eight-hour mountaineering ordeal. Alternatively, and preferably, go with a guide, the tour operators above, or the clubs in *Chapter 12* will be able to find a guide for you.

Know the potential dangers of mountaineering and how to deal with them before you venture out on a hike, and preferably be first-aid proficient. If you've no idea what you are getting into and have come to Macedonia for the mountains, then there are safer playing grounds than these for an introduction to mountaineering, but the list of health and safety considerations below will give you an idea of what you are up against. If you get into trouble, call 192 for the police who will be able to get the mountain rescue service out.

Your medical pack for any extended hiking trip (more than two hours) should contain at least the following:

- large plasters/Band-Aids, and surgical gauze
- antiseptic cream and wipes
- painkillers
- crêpe bandages x 2
- surgical tape and zinc-oxide tape
- Compeed for blisters
- iodine-based water purification tablets (available from any good mountaineering shop, and hard to find in Macedonia)
- emergency blanket and inflatable splint if you are going on a long trip.

Dehydration In these untamed mountainous regions, the going can get tough, and like all mountains, water can sometimes be hard to find when you need it. Bring plenty of water with you, at least a litre per hour of uphill in the summer, and especially if you don't know where your next water source will be. It is very arid here and the lack of overhead cover can cause excess sweating. Dehydration will make you tired and prone to injury, and makes some people's vision blur. If you find yourself short of water, try to conserve what you have left, and take small sips every now and again. Don't over-exert yourself, and breathe through your nose rather than your mouth to stop excess moisture escaping. Keep covered to prevent excess moisture being lost in sweat.

Injury Injuries are usually caused when you are tired and/or hiking beyond your limit. It is, therefore, important to know what your limits are, and those of your travelling partners, and to recognise when it is time for a rest. Come properly equipped for the task at hand, with good hiking boots and an appropriate overcoat as a minimum. Many Macedonians wander around in flimsy, inappropriate shoes. This may suffice for a hike to a popular monument, but will get you in trouble further afield. If you do sustain an injury that would normally require stitching, then bind the wound with a large plaster or surgical tape and then secure it laterally with zinc-oxide tape.

Sunburn Do wear a hat, sunglasses and plenty of sunscreen (available in the pharmacies). The sun here is stronger than in northern Europe and it is easy to forget that point until it is too late. If you do get badly burnt, apply an after-sun cream or calamine lotion, cover up and don't go back out in the sun without a total sunblock. A cold wet teabag also works well for sunburn.

Sunstroke After the onset of dehydration and sunburn you are heading for heat exhaustion and then sun/heatstroke. While heatstroke can be fatal, if you recognise the early-stage symptoms soon enough you should never get that far. It is usually more difficult to tell in oneself than in others, so watch your hiking partner carefully. The easiest signs to look for are muscle cramps or numbness, dimmed or blurred vision, weakness, irritability, dizziness and confusion. If any of your hiking partners are talking utter drivel (more than normal anyway), are not able to have a logical conversation with you, and particularly if they say they don't need water or to get out of the sun, then sit them down in the shade immediately, loosen any tight clothing, sprinkle water on them and fan them to cool them down. They should take regular sips of water, but not drink a pint down flat. If your hiking partner shows the above signs, and feels sick, and particularly if their skin feels hot and dry, then the body has gone into shutdown mode. They may soon fall unconscious and medical attention is required quickly. Phone 194 for help.

Altitude sickness You are unlikely to suffer from altitude sickness in Macedonia, as it is difficult to gain enough height to do so. Nevertheless, altitude sickness does not discriminate, and should you decide to climb Mount Korab or Titov Vrv in one day from Skopje, no matter how young you are, nor how much mountaineering you have done sometime in the past, it may still hit you. The best way to avoid altitude sickness is to acclimatise. If you don't have that option open to you, and you start to feel dizzy, sick and overly short of breath, then the next best thing to do is to stop and rest. If this doesn't help then descend slowly to a lower level (500m is usually enough), and consider doing something else for the day. Sadly, there is no coca tea in Macedonia to help with altitude sickness.

Hypothermia Hypothermia occurs when the body loses heat quicker than it can make it. This is most likely to happen when the body is wet and cold, inactive, hungry and tired. Uncontrollable shivering, drowsiness and confusion are telltale first signs. If the person has stopped shivering, is physically stiff, and indifferent to their surroundings, then the body is already in shutdown mode. The person's body temperature must be raised immediately with plenty of warm, dry clothing, shelter and warm sweet drinks to increase the blood sugar level. Exercise will not help. At severe levels, skin contact with another warm body, preferably in a sleeping bag, might be required. At this point the medical services should be brought in. Do not heat the person with anything hotter than body temperature, nor immerse the person in hot water as this might simply cook outer extremities. Do not rub or massage the person, but warm the core of the body first.

Wild and deadly nasties Some poisonous snakes and spiders do exist in Macedonia, such as black and brown widow spiders, and some adders and vipers. They do not seek out humans, so you are extremely unlikely to come across any.

You are less likely to get bitten if you wear stout shoes and long trousers when in the bush. Most snakes are harmless and even venomous species will dispense venom in only about half of their bites. If bitten, then, you are unlikely to have received venom; keeping this fact in mind may help you to stay calm. Many so-called first-aid techniques do more harm than good: cutting into the wound is harmful; tourniquets are dangerous; suction and electrical inactivation devices do not work. The only treatment is anti-venom. In case of a bite that you fear may have been from a venomous snake:

- Try to keep calm – it is likely that no venom has been dispensed
- Prevent movement of the bitten limb by applying a splint
- Keep the bitten limb BELOW heart height to slow the spread of any venom
- If you have a crêpe bandage, wrap it around the whole limb (eg: all the way from the toes to the thigh), as tight as you would for a sprained ankle or a muscle pull

And remember:

- NEVER give aspirin; you may take paracetamol, which is safe
- NEVER cut or suck the wound
- DO NOT apply ice packs
- DO NOT apply potassium permanganate

If the offending snake can be captured without risk of someone else being bitten, take this to show the doctor – but beware since even a decapitated head is able to bite.

FURTHER READING

Wilson-Howarth, Dr Jane, and Ellis, Dr Matthew *Your Child Abroad: A Travel Health Guide* Bradt Travel Guides, 2005
Wilson-Howarth, Dr Jane *Bugs, Bites & Bowels* Cadogan, 2006

SECURITY AND SAFETY

The security situation in Macedonia has calmed down significantly since the end of the hostilities of 2001 (see page 20) and foreigners have never been a target. In fact, you are undoubtedly safer in Macedonia than you are in most major Western cities, from both theft and terrorism.

To be on the safe side, avoid areas known to be unsafe and large public demonstrations which may get heated. The website of your embassy in Macedonia will usually carry the most up-to-date information on the security situation, and the US embassy site also has comprehensive security and safety advice on their Consular Information Sheets at www.travel.state.gov. Many embassies advise their citizens to register at the embassy if they intend to stay in the country for any length of time, and to phone for the latest security advice on a particular area if you are going off the beaten track.

INTERNATIONAL TRAFFICKING OF WEAPONS, DRUGS AND PEOPLE While national crime levels are relatively low (see *Personal safety* below), international trafficking of humans more than makes up for the deficit. The porous, forested mountain borders of Macedonia are easy trafficking routes and have long been a route for heroin and opium from Afghanistan to Europe.

Poor border controls and high taxes make smuggling cigarettes and other goods in and out of Kosovo a profitable business for people in a country where unemployment even by conservative figures is around 25%. Illegal wood-cutting is also a problem (and to animal habitat) especially when Kosovo continues to have an abysmal supply of electricity. If you are hiking up in the border areas, the chances of you stumbling across illegal trade are very slim. Always bring ID with you, however, just in case, and looking very obviously like a hiker will ensure that any smugglers will keep out of your way.

Illegal trade in weapons has decreased since the end of hostilities and the lifting of sanctions against Serbia, but trafficking in women is on the increase. Macedonia is both a transit country and an end user of trafficked women. Very few Macedonian women end up being trafficked, but it is not without precedent. Most of the women come from countries even poorer than Macedonia and, tempted by the lure of easy money abroad waitressing or as a domestic help, they are often beaten, raped and forced into prostitution. Victims include minors who believe they are going for better schooling. In January 2003, MSNBC carried a very good article on this very issue in Macedonia, which can be found at www.msnbc.com/news/sexslaves_front.asp.

Gone Without Trace (Orion Books), a thriller by C J Carver based on extensive research and plenty of truth, centres around the trafficking of women through the northwest of Macedonia and Kosovo.

Because of the difficulty of policing this issue, foreign visitors who bring their children with them are advised to bring the appropriate documents proving the legal relationship of parent and child. A passport may suffice, especially if the child is on your passport, but if you have separate passports with different names then you may want to bring additional proof. Although traffickers don't usually take children so blatantly over an established border crossing, border police may suspect the worst. The same goes for young couples entering Macedonia. I've been asked my relationship to my husband more than a few times, and I'm not even that young! If you would like to help with the anti-trafficking effort here in Macedonia see the *Giving something back* section at the end of this chapter, page 110.

PERSONAL SAFETY In many respects crime is lower in Macedonia than in many countries in western Europe or in America. Nevertheless, you should take the usual precautions: this is not a country where you can leave your house unlocked when you are out, and you should keep your valuables close if you are going through a crowded place or travelling by public transport.

If you come to live in Macedonia as part of the international community then, as with a move into any new property, you may want to make sure the locks are changed in case former tenants have a key that falls into the wrong hands. Car theft is generally not a problem in Macedonia.

If you get stopped or detained by the police, for any reason whatsoever, remember to stay calm and polite. In any nation, smart-alec wisecracks, sarcasm, anger and lack of co-operation are seen as suspicious behaviour. You do have the right to ask why you have been stopped or detained, however, and, of course, the right to legal representation once you have been charged. You can be detained for up to 24 hours without being charged, by which time your embassy or consulate should have been informed of your detention. You also have the right to be spoken to in a language that you understand, so you might be better off waiting for an interpreter or a policeman who speaks your language rather than digging yourself into a bigger hole. The interpreter may take a while getting to you!

DRIVING AND ROAD SAFETY Speed restrictions are enforced here, and it is illegal not to wear a seat belt in the front seats of your car. You will find, however, that few Macedonians heed these rules or any form of lane discipline and driving etiquette. Some drivers here don't have licences and some cars wouldn't pass a road test without a bribe. If you are a Brit and have never driven on the right-hand side of the road, I would not advise Macedonia as a good place to start. If you are going to drive here, then don't be surprised to find vehicles without headlights at night, extremely little use of indicators, lorries backing down the road when they have missed their exit, parking on the pavement and two cars stopped in the middle of the road for a chat.

As a pedestrian, you'll also have to keep your wits about you when crossing the road, as drivers often don't heed traffic lights, and certainly pay no attention to zebra crossings.

If you are fined by the police, remember to make sure you are given a ticket/receipt for your fine so that you can be certain the money is going into the government coffers not the policeman's pocket.

SEXUAL HARASSMENT This is not usually a problem in Macedonia, and women here dress as skimpily as in the West. Macedonians think it is a bit strange, however, to travel on your own, especially as a woman; and keeping in mind the high level of trafficking in women which goes on in Macedonia, you'd better have your wits about you if you travel alone as a woman in strange places after dark. There are no obvious red-light districts in Macedonia, as prostitution is illegal, but there are bars and hotels that service this trade.

As with anywhere in the rest of the world, if you are a single female driver and an unmarked police car indicates that you should pull over, you should turn on your hazard lights and drive slowly to a public area such as a station before stopping. You could also phone the police on 192 to check if the police car is genuine.

PERSONAL HARASSMENT Don't expect to always be left alone as you wander around Macedonia looking at antique treasures and antiquated institutions. You will almost definitely come across two situations where you will wish that you could be left in peace. The first form of harassment will come from begging Roma (see page 52) who may follow you around for up to 15 minutes quietly begging for money, and may even get angry, though rarely if at all physically violent, if you don't give them money. Macedonians get this treatment too, and the best thing to do is not to give them any (giving money tends to encourage more begging); you can try what most Macedonians do, which is to say sternly '*begaj, odmah*', meaning 'scram, immediately'. If this does not succeed then dive into a café where the waiter will take care of the little beggar for you.

The second form is really just an uncomfortable invasion of personal space, usually from teenage boys who are bewildered and defensive about what on earth you think you are doing on their turf. Trying to engage them in friendly conversation with a winning smile (which often works, see page 109) may only raise their defences as a battle of hormones, pride and stubbornness ensues. This is how fights start, and no matter how much you might want to push them away or punch them in the face for getting too close to you, your belongings or your car, you are, after all, a guest in their home town or street, so back off confidently, and remember that locals at home probably aren't too friendly either; the difference is that you don't usually wander into that part of town at home.

DOGS There are a lot of stray dogs in Macedonia, and while they don't tend to be savage, or even a nuisance; some of them do carry disease and infections, so don't approach them, or take them in. Rabies is not common here, but leishmaniasis is more prevalent. Leishmaniasis is transferred by sandflies from host to new prey, and can be deadly if left untreated. Dogs with a mangy appearance and losing clumps of hair could have leishmaniasis.

If you do take in a stray dog, take it to the vet immediately for a check-up and all the necessary injections. There is no animal home here in Macedonia, and most dogs are not treated too well, so you probably have more to fear from a kept dog than a stray dog. The big shepherding dogs here, the *šarplaninec*, are well trained to guard their flock, so don't approach them or the flock, no matter how docile they may appear from several metres away. You may not return with your hand, and the dog won't be put down.

WHAT TO TAKE

CLOTHING Unless you know you are staying only in Skopje and Ohrid in the summer, then bring an overcoat or jacket, and it is cold enough for a fleece in the mountains no matter what time of year. Casual dress is the norm on the streets. Businessmen tend to wear short-sleeved shirts in the summer, and you may wish to pack such a shirt or polo shirt if you intend to go to one of the nicer restaurants in

Skopje. Nightclubs here don't have a dress code, but some churches and mosques do. Bring a pair of long trousers, shoulder covering, and for women, a headscarf, in case these are needed. In spring and autumn it may be very warm during the day, but in the evening it can also get quite cold, and some hotels may have not yet turned on or already turned off the central heating, so bring warm enough clothes.

PLUGS, ADAPTORS AND CONVERTERS Macedonia's electricity is 220 volts and uses two types of plug, both with the same two round pins commonly used in northern Europe. Plug casings come in the round-case variant as well as the six-sided flat-case variant.

There are a number of great travel adaptors available now which take a multiple choice of plugs and give multiple options in pins. If you are coming from North America and wish to bring American electrical appliances with you, then you can also purchase a power voltage converter which will convert the 220 volts of European electricity into 110 volts for your appliance.

Bring a universal sink plug, especially if you will be staying in lower-end accommodation.

TOILETRIES AND MEDICINES You can buy all the basics in Macedonia, although if you are coming here to live for a while you may wish to bring your favourite face cream or aftershave lotion. Contact lens solutions are expensive here, and contact lenses can take a while to order, so bring plenty with you. Always bring spare glasses if you wear them; it is a nightmare anywhere in the world if you break your only pair.

Bring clothes washing powder (unless you want to buy a large tub in the supermarket here) as launderettes are almost impossible to find, although there are dry-cleaners. The Western four- and five-star hotels have a laundry service. A basic first-aid pack as mentioned above under *Health* (see page 79) is also useful.

DOCUMENTS Obviously a passport, with visa if required, ticket and money (see below) are essential. If you are travelling with children, then some sort of proof that you are their legal guardian is advisable to stop a potentially harrowing ordeal at the border when police might think you are trafficking children. If you are bringing your own car, then make sure you have the right insurance. The international blue or green card insurance, which does not have Macedonia (MK) or any other countries you want to visit or travel through struck off, is valid here. A photo ID driving licence is required here, for both hiring and driving a car.

GIFTS It is always a good idea to bring family photos and postcards of your home town with you on holiday. They make good talking points and you can give the postcards out as a small gift. If you are invited into a Macedonian home, you may be given sweet syruped preserved fruits as a welcome. It is also a good idea to give something in return, and sweets from your home country are an ideal gift. Note that Macedonians can get all the German chocolates and many others besides, and anyway chocolate is not a good thing to bring in the summer as it will almost definitely melt. More permanent small souvenirs are ideal.

For an idea of gifts to bring back home from Macedonia see the *Culture* section of *Chapter 3* (page 59).

SPORTS GEAR Light sports shoes or open-toed hiking sandals like Tevas are fine for walking around or a short hike to a popular monument, but anything more arduous requires suitable hiking boots. You may also find a long pair of hiking trousers useful as the paths here are often overgrown and prickly, thorny or full of nettles. Dock leaves can be a remedy for nettle stings but unlike in the UK they rarely grow next to nettles. A hiking pole (or a stick picked up at the beginning of your hike) is a useful nettle and bramble whacker and helps to scare away snakes and dogs. Hiking without a stick is bound to elicit the comment from locals who meet you on your hike that you should have one.

Bring a good daypack and your favourite water container: wide-mouthed Nalgene bottles are far easier to fill from a local mountain stream than reused plastic water bottles. The Camelbak (*www.camelbak.com*) is very useful in this arid climate. You'll need to bring your own climbing boots if you intend to do any rock climbing, but the rest you can hire here from one of the clubs. Ski hire, including carving skis, is reasonable, but tele skis, ski de randonée or cross-country skis are seldom available to hire.

CAMPING There are no dedicated basecamp stores here, so you'll need to bring outdoor accessories with you. There is only one type of bottled stove fuel here, and it is not the butane/propane self-sealing screw-on Coleman type, so you'll either need to bring plenty of canisters (and most airlines won't let you bring them any more) or buy one of the local stoves which you can find in any outdoor market here. Alternatively, bring an all-purpose fuel stove and buy petrol.

It does get very hot in the summer, so bring enough changes of clothing so that you can swap out of your sweaty T-shirt when you get to the top of your hike. This helps to prevent you from getting a chill, which can easily happen when you reach the colder climes of the summit.

$ MONEY

The Macedonian denar has been pegged to the euro since 1998, and is therefore very stable. There is no smaller division of the denar. MKD is the international three-letter currency code, which is also used when Latin rather than Cyrillic script is used.

The denar comes in 10, 50, 100, 500, 1,000 and 5,000 notes, although you'll often find the 1,000 denar note hard to change. The 5,000MKD note usually stays firmly on the cashier's side of the bank counter. Macedonian shops never seem to have much change, so hoard your small notes, and change large notes whenever you can. Coins come in one, two and five denar.

There are no money changers on the street here, so money is either changed in banks or in the many legal money-changing booths in the main towns. Travellers' cheques are good for back-up funds, but if you have a debit card or credit card then you'll find lots of cash machines available in Skopje and Ohrid, and increasingly in other towns. Not all ATMs take international credit cards, so look out for the Visa/MasterCard and other labels indicating that they can do international transactions. You can change money at the airport both before you exit the arrivals lounge and in the departure hall.

Euros are the foreign currency of choice here. All the main hotels, restaurants and even a lot of the bed and breakfasts, especially in Skopje and Ohrid, will accept euros, although they may not always be able to give you all the right change in euros.

BUDGETING

On the most meagre of budgets, staying in local rooms, at monasteries, mountain huts and campsites, buying from the market or *kebapci* stalls, and using public transport, you could manage on around €10 a day, excluding your ticket to

Macedonia. Trains are cheaper than buses, but there are few trains. Most museums in Skopje and a lot of the churches in Ohrid charge a 100MKD entrance fee, but many things are also free. Hiking in Macedonia's beautiful mountains and national parks doesn't yet require an entrance fee, but wild camping is also forbidden.

Some €20 a day would just about bring you into the bed and breakfast bracket and it is hard to pay more than €10 for a meal, except in Skopje. At the other end of the scale you would be hard pressed to spend €300 a day here even if you were staying at the Aleksandar Palace Hotel in Skopje for your entire trip and hiring a 4x4 vehicle. Macedonia's local gifts (wood carving, Ohrid pearls, filigree, embroidered linen) are not all that cheap by comparison, and buying these items could deprive you of several hundred more euros.

GETTING AROUND

In the summer, some MAT international flights also connect Ohrid and Skopje. Check with a travel agent for times. Most people travel by bus or car, although

DISTANCES BETWEEN TOWNS AND BORDER CROSSINGS IN MACEDONIA

Blace	Tabanovce	Delčevo	Dojran	Bogorodica	Medzitilija	Kafasan	Berovo	Bitola	M.Brod	Gevgelia	Gostivar	Debar	Delčevo	Kavadarci	Kičevo	Ko…
70																
187	166															
188	183	142														
179	174	150	38													
208	204	259	198	189												
202	237	330	268	259	111											
178	155	44	98	106	248	318										
183	181	239	177	168	16	92	227									
156	177	243	181	170	91	99	226	78								
175	171	146	34	4	185	258	102	166	166							
86	117	246	248	229	138	119	240	124	75	225						
150	183	312	291	282	150	65	300	134	115	278	68					
178	155	11	131	239	248	319	35	228	232	137	230	297				
122	118	161	94	79	110	183	138	90	86	75	167	202	150			
131	162	263	209	191	91	73	255	78	25	187	46	89	252	111		
132	102	64	146	149	196	278	52	178	178	145	180	245	53	90	222	Ko…
121	70	162	205	212	262	286	151	241	227	208	166	234	151	172	211	9…
115	63	118	168	174	212	280	107	196	197	170	160	224	107	137	205	5…
178	173	230	174	165	65	166	218	52	55	161	140	154	219	81	62	17…
62	10	156	176	170	189	227	139	176	162	166	107	172	145	113	152	9…
111	107	143	82	68	121	195	127	100	98	64	156	214	132	10	201	8…
193	224	305	249	194	79	28	293	56	86	190	107	66	294	155	61	25…
142	140	199	143	128	61	134	187	41	37	125	108	153	188	49	62	14…
142	112	124	80	94	166	244	82	147	147	90	177	253	113	49	232	6…
218	213	267	214	232	44	63	255	30	108	228	142	102	256	120	96	21…
102	54	118	138	147	162	267	107	149	149	143	147	210	107	82	192	4…
22	49	179	171	162	182	187	163	176	137	160	67	134	168	105	112	1…
193	224	317	264	249	92	13	305	79	86	245	106	52	306	170	60	26…
171	141	95	51	55	188	268	54	175	173	51	216	281	85	82	261	9…
61	92	221	223	204	162	145	217	149	99	200	24	94	210	147	70	15…
70	65	120	124	110	133	203	111	120	116	106	110	184	109	52	155	6…
108	75	94	109	122	163	243	83	150	155	118	157	219	83	63	181	3…

train, bicycle or walking are also options. Macedonians do hitch around, but usually only locally, so you can get a ride.

BY TRAIN There are fairly limited options available for travel by train. There is a line from Skopje to Kičevo through the northwest of the country, which will take you to Tetovo and Gostivar, but not to Mavrovo and Debar. The line to Bitola via Veles and Prilep is a pretty ride, and certainly a recommended route to Prilep. The line to Gevegelia and Thessaloniki is also a pretty ride although there is not much to stop for on that route unless you want to get out at Demir Kapija for some hiking in the area. The lines to Kumanovo and Kočani also don't hold much attraction and you would be better off taking buses direct to places further afield like Kriva Palanka or Berovo. The maximum one could pay for a train ride anywhere in Macedonia at the time of writing was 420MKD for a Skopje–Bitola return ticket. The domestic timetable can be found at www.mz.com.mk/uploads/vozen_red.pdf and is in English on pages 74–7.

Car-hire agencies
Avis ↘ 02 3222 046; www.avis.com.mk
Budget ↘ 02 3290 222; wwww.budget.com.mk
Europcar ↘ 02 307 6425; www.europcar.com
Sixt ↘ 02 306 4666; www.e-sixt.com
Tuymada ↘ 02 3120 255; www.tuymada.com

	K.Palanka	Kratovo	Kruševo	Kumanovo	Negotino	Ohrid	Prilep	Radoviš	Resen	Sv.Nikola	Skopje	Struga	Strumica	Tetovo	Veles
Kratovo	44														
Kruševo	220	190													
Kumanovo	60	53	162												
Negotino	157	103	93	97											
Ohrid	273	266	138	214	167										
Prilep	195	160	32	130	61	106									
Radoviš	132	88	141	102	37	211	110								
Resen	256	231	103	206	132	35	71	181							
Sv.Nikola	103	57	144	44	73	213	112	58	183						
Skopje	99	93	159	39	95	174	131	125	198	80					
Struga	273	267	153	214	182	15	121	231	50	254	174				
Strumica	156	117	166	131	75	237	134	29	205	87	149	255			
Tetovo	141	135	164	82	136	132	132	167	184	122	44	132	196		
Veles	116	86	111	55	41	180	79	77	145	33	50	190	113	85	
Štip	90	52	151	66	51	215	119	37	180	25	86	230	66	128	40

BY BUS The bus service is the preferred mode of transport for Macedonians because it is frequent and cheap. That said, there is only one bus a day to Brajčino and Kruševo from Skopje, although towns are also served by buses from other towns. Buses are not air conditioned and do sometimes break down; few of them have on-board toilet facilities either, so you may have to wait for the toilet break along the road. There is no bus service from the airport. For more on bus times and prices, see individual towns in the following chapters.

BY CAR This is still the easiest way to get around Macedonia, especially by 4x4 if you want do a bit of exploring and are not so keen on hitchhiking. See the section on *Driving and road safety* above before considering driving, especially if you are not used to driving on the right-hand side of the road. There are many places to hire clean, reliable, modern cars in Skopje and other big cities, as well as at the airport. **Tuymada** (↘ *02 311 3755; www.tuymada.com*), in the Kibo Restaurant building in Skopje rents out a Ford Focus for as little as €55 per day for a long weekend or week. For road distances and listings of car-hire agencies see page 92. You'll pay about 60MKD per litre for unleaded petrol in Macedonia, and about 50MKD per litre for diesel.

BY TAXI Taxis are often a quick and cheap way to get around town, but also to places further afield. Taxis in Skopje have a minimum fare of 50MKD for the first 2km. Outside Skopje the minimum fare is usually 30MKD. All official taxis should be metered and carry a taxi sign on the roof of the car. A taxi ride from Ohrid to Brajčino, which is a one-hour journey, is €40. Make sure you agree the price before taking a longer journey as the driver may turn the meter off and pocket the money.

If you are going to a remote part of town, there's quite a high chance that the taxi driver taking you there will not know where it is, so you may wish to ask a few drivers until you get one who knows, or make him (there are extremely few female taxi drivers) phone into his radio centre so that they can give him directions. Otherwise they may drive around for a while and charge you the extra time.

A good, clean, and reliable taxi firm, based in Skopje, who can drive you anywhere in Macedonia or transport personal items (including pets) on your behalf are **Lotus Transport** (↘ *15157 for taxis in Skopje or* ↘ *02 3109 116 for other services;* f *02 3122 174;* e *contact@lotustransport.com; www.lotustransport.com*).

BY BICYCLE Biking tours are a great way to get around Macedonia, but you do need to be fit as it is a hilly little country. For an insightful personal account into bicycling around Macedonia see Professor Mark Boyd's webpages of his 2005 European tour for days 8–12 (*www.cs.unca.edu/~boyd/touring/tour05/tour.htm*).

To hire a bike, join or arrange a bike tour in Macedonia, see the biking section in *Chapter 2* (page 42).

ACCOMMODATION

Accommodation in Macedonia is generally cheap, but the standard you receive for the price you pay can be a bit of a lottery.

HOTELS Generally speaking, state-run hotels built before the 1990s are in pretty bad shape and not worth the money. In addition, and irritatingly, they tend to charge foreigners more than they charge Macedonians. On the few occasions that such hotels have been included in this guide, the price discrimination is indicated. Many state-run hotels are now being privatised and with that will hopefully come some improvements. Between late spring and early autumn (15 April to 15 October), state-run hotels may get a bit cold as the heating is turned off during this period.

Family-run or boutique hotels are excellent value for money but few and far between, although their numbers are increasing. Many petrol stations have small motels on the side and as most of them have been built fairly recently they are usually clean and tidy if basic, but reasonably priced. Hotel prices usually include breakfast, although only the top-notch hotels will manage to serve a buffet breakfast or provide room service.

In this guide, unless otherwise stated, all rooms have an en-suite bathroom, and all prices are per room. If you ask for a room for two people you will usually get a twin room with two single beds. To get a room with a double bed in, you must ask for '*soba co eden krevet za dvojica*', 'a room with one bed for two people', sometimes called a '*francuski krevet*' meaning 'French bed'. Even if you ask for this, don't be surprised if you end up with a twin room in which the hotel staff expect you to simply push the beds together. Or they may give you the *apartman* which is the Macedonian equivalent of the honeymoon suite and usually much more expensive. Rooms with three single beds are also quite common.

Top 12 The following is a list of recommended 'boutique-type' hotels, chosen in part for their strategic locations around the country so that you can visit all of Macedonia in comfortable value-for-money accommodation, but also in part for their peculiarities. Anticlockwise around the country starting in the capital, they are:

Hotel Jadran, Skopje Armenian-style grandeur in the centre of town. See page 125.

Bistra, Mavrovo A fireside over the lake by the ski-resort. See page 230.

Hotel Kalin, Lazaropole Beautifully refurbished, beautiful setting. See page 230.

Kutmičevica, Vevčani Small & quaint in the Republic of Vevčani. See page 183.

Villa Sveta Sofia, Ohrid The Ottoman period, lavish style. See page 163.

Hotel De Niro, Bitola Petite & central. See page 194.

Podgorski An, Strumica Out of the way but worth the stay. See page 279.

Hotel Monastir, Berovo Comfort in the wild east. See page 256.

Hotel Šagal, Kočani The first modern hot-spring spa hotel. See page 253.

Joakim Osogovski Monastery, Kriva Palanka Peaceful & cool in the mountains. See page 261.

Popova Kula Vineyard, Demir Kapija I rate this the best hotel offer in Macedonia, & the wine too. See page 287.

Villa Germanoff, Ohrid The piano suite has a balcony & a lake view. See page 163.

BED AND BREAKFAST In days gone by there was a whole bed and breakfast world in Macedonia. The collapse of the Yugoslav economy and the recent conflict in Macedonia have all but killed off this industry and as a result they are difficult to find outside Ohrid. Travel agents will say they'll try to find bed and breakfast

4

ACCOMMODATION PRICE CODES

Based on a double room per night.

Exclusive	$$$$$	€136+; £111+; US$181+; 8,500MKD
Upmarket	$$$$	€76–135; £61–110; US$101–180; 4,500–8,500MKD
Mid-range	$$$	€36–75; £26–60; US$41–100; 2,000–4,500MKD
Budget	$$	€16–35; £13–25; US$21–40; 1,000–2,000MKD
Shoestring	$	up to €15; <£12; <US$20; <1,000MKD

options for you, but will probably cajole you into a hotel as they don't make much money off the bed and breakfast industry. Once again, however, the nascent tourist industry in Macedonia is trying to encourage this sector. Sometimes the bed comes without breakfast, so make sure you ask what your options are. Bed and breakfast usually starts at about €10–15 per night.

SELF-CATERING ACCOMMODATION There is actually quite a lot of this in Macedonia as it is popular with Macedonians, but they are not well advertised in English. Some private accommodation (ie: self-catering) is listed at hotels.exploringmacedonia.com and local tour operators listed in each chapter in this book will also have some contacts.

MONASTERIES The monasteries are usually excellent value for money, even if you are not on a shoestring budget. As most of them were only revived 15 years ago, accommodation in their new inns is generally better than in most state-run hotels and half the price. Prices range from about 250MKD for a bed in the old quarters with bathroom on the corridor, to 700MKD for a bed in an en-suite room in the new quarters. Treskavec Monastery doesn't charge anything at all, although a donation is kindly received. The monasteries don't usually have a restaurant attached, but, as they are remote, they usually have cooking facilities available to guests.

The catch with staying in the monasteries is that they are not always very convenient to book into and as they are popular with Macedonians they are often booked up quite early. Very few of the staff/monks/nuns in them speak any English so you may need to get a Macedonian friend to help you, or a tour operator. If you can't get a tour operator to help you book in (eg: Go Macedonia, see page 70) or opt to do so yourself, try to phone during normal working hours. If you want to try turning up without a booking, then at least try to get there before 17.00 otherwise the inn staff may have gone home already, as they usually only stay around until all the pre-booked guests have arrived. Finally, soon after you arrive, you will need to get a registration card from the inn staff and go and register yourself at the local police station. Unlike in hotels, the inn staff will not do this for you. Some monasteries expect you to attend a church service if you are staying the night.

⛰ CAMPING Yugoslav-style camping is not always public transport friendly. People usually come in their car, hence they are called *autocamp*, and they are not, therefore, necessarily close to public transport. They are often large, full of old caravans, and not always scrupulously clean. Facilities and amenities, such as showering blocks and shops are also not good or nearby. They are cheap, however, and 500MKD will usually get you a tent space for four plus your car. Tourism tax is an additional 40MKD per person.

Strictly speaking wild camping is illegal, but many Macedonians do it, especially at a local festival or event. If you are going to camp wild, then please take away all your rubbish and leave the place in a good condition.

MOUNTAIN HUTS Most of the 30 mountain huts in Macedonia are listed in *Chapter 12*. They cost about 300MKD for a bed with bedding. It is best to phone ahead (Macedonian usually required) as most of the huts are not permanently staffed or go with one of the many hiking and mountaineering clubs. The huts rarely provide food, so you will need to bring all your provisions, but there is always plenty of water.

YOUTH HOSTEL There is only one true youth hostel in Macedonia, the Ferialen Dom (page 126) in Skopje. It is no cheaper than some of the bed and breakfasts, but if you are a YHA member then it is the cheapest accommodation in Skopje.

It is popular in the summer so book ahead. The official Hostelling International website lists a number of hostels although you can't book most of them on line (*www.hihostels.com/dba/country-MK.en.htm*).

A variety of former state-run hotels, family guesthouses and hotels have cottoned onto the hostel website networks, however, and advertise on other hostel websites as youth hostels (where you can get your International Youth Hostel Association discount) or as independent hostels, even though many of them are in fact mid-to-expensive hotels. A couple of the sites advertising the more budget end of the spectrum are www.hostelsweb.com and www.hostelworld.com/countries/macedoniahostels.html, the latter including a price comparison.

HOSPITALITY CLUB The Hospitality Club is a worldwide network, whose members are ordinary private citizens offering a place to stay in their home for free. You have to be a member of HC and agree to abide by the network's rules in order to use their services, which are run on an honesty basis. For more information and a list of hundreds of places to stay in Macedonia for free, visit secure.hospitalityclub.org/hc/hcworld.php?country=118.

✘ EATING AND DRINKING

Macedonian cuisine combines simple, healthy Mediterranean cooking with centuries of spicy Ottoman influence. It is a celebration of fresh, organic, small-scale produce, and even its wine is traditionally made with no sulphites. Summer markets teem with good local fruit and vegetables, whilst the winter holds crisp pickles (*turšija*) and jars of tasty red pepper spreads. Restaurants are getting better at offering some of the delicious *domašni* (home-style) dishes, but outside the main towns simple restaurants might only serve grilled chicken breast or pork chops and a few basic side dishes.

Macedonian **meze** (from the Turkish, and ultimately Persian *maze*; also known as *ordever*, literally 'hors d'oeuvre') is the best-kept secret of Macedonian cuisine. Usually served at the start of a banquet, *meze* is so tasty and varied that it can make a whole meal on its own. The Macedonian *meze* are a variety of cold 'creamed' vegetable spreads, initially cooked till soft and then hand blended with herbs and spices, onions and garlic, and doused with not too much oil. The most common are *ajvar* (see below), *pindžur* (roasted aubergine and peppers), *tarator* (yoghurt, cucumber, walnuts and garlic), *kajmak* (a type of clotted cream, often mixed with hot chillis and potatoes), egg and mushroom, and sweet grilled red peppers doused in garlic and oil (when they can be found in late summer). Eaten with pizza bread, *sarma* (stuffed vine leaves), local cured ham, Parmesan and a strong local drink like *mastika* or *rakija*, it is a real treat.

The most famous of these *meze* is **ajvar**. This is made every autumn when red peppers are at their most abundant. The best, of course, is homemade (*domašni*). To be invited into a Macedonian home to make *ajvar* is quite a privilege, and will give you an idea of the meticulous preparation that must go into preparing this Macedonian speciality. Some say that to be invited to make *ajvar* is like being offered the possibility of citizenship.

Without giving away the secret recipe, in essence the peppers must be softened to remove their skins and then simmered for hours, whilst stirred constantly, so that the peppers plus other added ingredients become a rough paste. The prepared *ajvar* is then sealed in jars for use throughout the coming year till the next pepper harvest. Macedonians will make *ajvar* by the vat-load, and family members will often come home from distant lands in order to partake in the occasion.

4

The main fare of any Macedonian meal is either meat or freshwater fish. **Lamb** is the most expensive and therefore not often served in cheaper restaurants. It comes roasted either in the oven or on a spit, and served in a big chunk on your plate, usually without rosemary, never mind mint. Otherwise the staple meat dish for most Macedonians is *skara*. This is plain grilled pork or chicken, usually salted and basted. *Skara* is so popular that you can buy it from street stalls by the kilo! Veal (*teleško meso*), beef, eel (*jagula*), stroganoff, thinly sliced garlic liver (*džigr*), schnitzel, pork chops (*kremenadle*) and skewered kebabs (*ražnič*) are also prolific. *Kebapči* are an extremely popular form of *skara*. They are a Balkan speciality of small sausage-shaped burger meat, well seasoned and very tasty with a beer and some good bread. Other popular traditional meat dishes are stuffed peppers, pork knee joint and *selsko meso* (village meat), which is a stew of different meats and sausages in an earthenware pot. *Makedonsko meso* is a variation of this with Macedonia's famous capsicum peppers.

Freshwater fish, either trout or carp (*krap* in Macedonian), is abundant in Macedonia. Ohrid is most famous for its *letnica* and *belvica* trout, and Dojran for its native carp. These particular fish varieties are peculiar to the lakes and cannot be found outside Macedonia, and for this reason (among others) Ohrid is protected under UNESCO. Ohrid trout, which has been caught in the past at over 20kg in weight, has been over-fished (see *www.guardian.co.uk/international/ story/0,3604,1007062,00.html*) and this is not helped on the Albanian side of the border by lakeside boys selling trout by the bucketful. You may, therefore, want to think twice before partaking too often of this famous and increasingly rare Ohrid dish. It is now illegal to fish for Ohrid trout (see page 38).

If you are ever invited into a family home you will likely be offered syruped and candied fruits and a glass of homemade **liker** or **rakija** (see box, page 198) made from grapes. Macedonia's particular speciality is **žolta** (meaning literally 'yellow') which is *rakija* yellowed by the addition of extra wheat at a secondary fermenting stage. It is usually very strong, but often sipped rather than thrown back in one as *rakija* is in many other Balkan countries. *Mastika* is another Macedonian speciality liquor, which is remarkably similar to ouzo. If you stay to eat, the meal will start with salad, followed by a hearty soup, the main course and then a dessert.

Fresh **salads** in Macedonia, especially outside Skopje, are not very inventive. Your four main choices are: a green salad (lettuce); a mixed salad (cucumber, tomato, grated cabbage and carrot); a Šopska salad (cucumber, tomato and grated white goat's cheese); and Greek salad (cucumber, tomato, cubes of feta cheese and maybe some olives). Vinaigrettes and salad dressings are almost unheard of, so don't expect a choice of thousand island dressing, blue cheese or ranch, or even salad cream. There is usually olive oil and vinegar served alongside and balsamic vinegar available in Skopje.

Other Macedonian specialities include: **tavče gravče**, butter beans stewed in an earthenware pot; **pastrmajlija**, a famous bread dough, pork and egg dish from Strumica which seems to be the Macedonian equivalent of pizza; **turlitava**, a vegetarian baked mix of local vegetables; and **'piti'** (usually translated as 'pies'). These are not pies in the English sense with a shortcrust top and bottom and fruit or stewed meat in the middle, but a *burek*-type affair consisting of layers of filo flakey pastry or pancake interlaced with egg and cheese, or sometimes meat and the odd spring onion.

There are also plenty of other Macedonian dishes that are usually cooked at home rather than served in restaurants, as they are more labour intensive. These include: **juvki**, a semolina-based pancake which is allowed to dry crisp before being broken and re-cooked with milk and water for breakfast or lunch; **sirden**, which seems to be the Macedonian equivalent of haggis; **pača** (brawn), made from the boiled meat of a pig's head or knuckles, fried with onions and herbs, and served cold in slices; *mantiji*, a seasoned meat pasty; and *mezelek*, offal stew.

Macedonian **desserts** – if you still have room by the time you have eaten your *meze*, hearty soup (*čorba*), *skara* by the kilo served with fried chips and several glasses of Macedonian wine – are few and mostly borrowed from other cultures, such as pancakes, *baklava*, *sutljaš* (rice pudding cake), fresh fruit and ice cream. *Ravanija* and *gurabii* are two types of syrupy cake, which you may get served in a Macedonian house, but rarely in a restaurant. Mouth-wateringly delicious, dark red forest honey (*šumski med*) can be bought at roadside stalls on the way to the Ohrid – some of the best are at the stalls south of Kičevo.

The art of **breakfast** is slowly coming to Macedonia. Kaj Maršal Tito on Ohrid Klimentski, Trend café on the Ploštad and Mečo's on Leninova in Skopje serve breakfast from 08.00 every day. Mečo's even has three cooked choices with drinks and bread for 99MKD before midday. Tivoli's in Tetovo also serves omelettes first thing in the morning. Breakfast for Macedonians traditionally consists of a strong coffee before work possibly with bread and cheese or jam, and at the weekends *juvki* or *tarama* (a cereal-based baked dish), then a break at around ten for a *gevrek* or *kifla* (sesame bread ring) and plain drinking yoghurt or *ajran* before settling down for a long lunch around 14.00. In Skopje, bakeries serving delicious pastries are becoming common, but outside Skopje it is wise to make sure you have breakfast included in your hotel bill, or buy something in, as you'll find few places on the streets that will serve you anything to eat. In Ohrid you can get sweet and savoury muffins, including *proja* (corn muffin with spinach) at Dva Biseri café from 08.00 in the morning. And beware the hot chocolate – it is often a filling warm chocolate mousse served in a cup!

Otherwise the preferred **drink** in Macedonia is coffee, either the strong Turkish variety which is a challenge to drink without sugar, served in espresso-size cups, or the usual cappucinos, machiattos and espressos. Turkish tea, served in small glasses, is popular in Albanian areas, and you'll sometimes see servers on bicycles or rollerblades carrying trays of them through the streets to customers. Fruit tea is usually considered a drink for the sick, but don't be deterred! Macedonia has lots of fruit teas (*ovošen čaj*) and mint tea (*čaj od nane*), and their mountain tea (*planinski čaj*) is a refreshing drink served in all the mountain huts and many restaurants. *Majčina dušica* (mother's little soul) tea is also a very popular mountain herbal tea. *Salep*, a drink made of ground wild orchid root and hot milk, is of Turkish origin and usually served with a sprinkling of ground cinnamon. You won't find it everywhere, but it's very tasty and warming on a cold winter's day. Another Turkish drink plentiful in vitamin B and carbohydrates is *boza*, a thick tart drink made from slightly fermented wheat (4% alcohol content). Its origins go back to Mesopotamia and it came to Macedonia with the Ottoman Empire. Available in ice-cream parlours and sweet shops, it is also good mixed with blueberry juice (*borovnica*). For more on Macedonian wines see page 284.

RESTAURANT PRICE CODES

Based on the average price of main course.

Expensive	$$$$$	€15+; £13+; US$20+; 1,000+MKD
Above average	$$$$	€8–15; £7–13; US$10–20; 500–1,000MKD
Mid-range	$$$	€4–8; £3–7; US$5–10; 250–500MKD
Cheap & cheerful	$$	€1.50–4; £1.20–3; US$2–5; 100–250MKD
Rock bottom	$	€1.50; <£1.20; <US$2; <100MKD

PUBLIC HOLIDAYS AND FESTIVALS

NATIONAL HOLIDAYS Macedonian national holidays are as follows:

1–2 January	New Year
7 January	Orthodox Christmas
April (usually)	Easter
1–2 May	Labour 'Day', when everybody goes picnicking
2 August	Ilinden (see pages 14, 191)
8 September	Referendum Day
11 October	National Day

A variety of other celebrations are observed in Macedonia, but are not national holidays. These include Eid-al-Fitr and Kurban Bayran (moveable dates according to the muslim calender) and others are:

13 August	Ohrid Framework Agreement
22 November	Albanian flag day

SAINTS' DAYS Every saint has his or her festival day and these are celebrated by the locals at the church dedicated to the named saint. Usually, the villagers gather at the church or monastery with pot luck food dishes, drink and music, and make merry. Some of the bigger monasteries such as Sv Joakim Osogovski attract thousands of visitors on these days, and donations to the church funds are usually generous.

As the Macedonian Orthodox Church runs on the amended Gregorian calendar first adopted by the Eastern Orthodox Church in 1923, some of the saints' and holy days that western Europeans might know are celebrated in Macedonia 13 days later. Some have a completely different celebration day. Below are a few of the Orthodox saints' days with their western Gregorian dates, followed in brackets by the page number reference to the church where you can see the celebrations in action. For the full Macedonian Orthodox calendar see www.mpc.org.mk. The Macedonian for Saint is Sveti/a (Sv).

28 January	Sv Gavril Lesnovski (page 266)
14 February	Sv Trifun, the saint of wine (page 281)
22 March	Sv Leonti (Leonthius) (page 277)
6 April	Sv Metodi
6 May	Sv Gjorgi (George, Gjurgjovden) (pages 180, 236)
24 May	Sv Kiril and Metodi of Solun (Thessaloniki)
14–15 June	Sv Erasmus of Ohrid (page 176)
2–3 July	Sv Naum of Ohrid (page 174)
2 August	Sv Ilija
7–8 August	Sv Petka (Peter, or Paraškjevija in Vlach) (pages 184, 198)
9 August	Sv Kliment Ohridski (page 170) and Sv Pantelejmon (pages 151, 246)
14 August	Sv Stefan (celebrated on 26 December in the UK) (page 175)
28 August	Sv Bogorodica (the Virgin Mary) (pages 171, 241, 255, 262)
29 August	The 15 martyrs of Tiberiopolis (Strumica) (page 276)
10 September	Sv Jovan Krstitel (John the Baptist) (page 238)
8 November	Sv Dimitri
21 November	Sv Archangel Michael (pages 102, 207)

| 4 December | Sv Bogorodica Prečista (page 241) |
| 19 December | Sv Nikola (known to many of us as Father Christmas) |

FESTIVALS There are a number of festivals throughout the year, but the majority take place in the summer especially around Ohrid and Skopje. The year kicks in with an Orthodox New Year festival, also known as the **Twelfthtide Carnival**, in the village of Vevčani (see page 183) on 13 and 14 January. It is a colourful two-day event attracting several thousand visitors who dress up in fancy dress and masks. Later in the month, on 19 January, is the celebration of **Epiphany**, when Bishop Naum throws a golden cross into Lake Ohrid in honour of John the Baptist and thereby blesses the lake. The practice is repeated all over Macedonia at local lakes and rivers, where men dive in after the cross purely for the honour of retrieving it.

Sv Trifun Day, the patron saint of wines, is on 14 February. This is becoming an increasingly popular festival to celebrate Macedonia's wines. During the first three days of Orthodox Lent (usually the same time as the Catholic/Protestant Easter) is the **Strumica Carnival** (page 276), followed a few weeks later by **Orthodox Easter**. On the Saturday evening of Easter weekend, people go up to their local churches shortly before midnight with a coloured boiled egg, and, when the bells of midnight have struck, a competition ensues to see whose egg survives when cracked against another. Fancy dress is the way to celebrate **1 April**, which, however, has nothing to do with fools.

After Easter is the summer-long season of festivals. On 22–23 May every year is the Pece Atanasovski **Musical Folk Instrument Festival** (page 101) in Dolneni, near Prilep. For more on what some of Macedonia's native musical instruments are see the box on page 62. In July, Skopje and Ohrid both hold summer evening blues concerts, plays, ballet and opera in historical venues and open-air theatres. In Skopje these finish in early August when the government goes on holiday, but they continue in Ohrid, which also holds a **Folklore Festival** early in July. Ohrid finishes its summer of festivities on the last weekend of August with the **International Swimming Marathon**, a 30km course from Sveti Naum to the town of Ohrid.

The **Prilep Pivofest Beer Festival** takes place in early July (page 204) where you can sup Macedonia's local brews with *čevapi*, peppers and other local as well as more international accompaniments to beer (sausage and mustard). The second weekend in July is the very popular **Galičnik Wedding Festival** (see page 231) which attracts many thousands of visitors and it is well worth the visit up to this pretty mountain village. For Macedonians, one of the most important events of the year is **Ilinden** on 2 August (see page 191), when the people of Macedonia stood up against the Ottoman Empire and brought in the ten-day Kruševo Republic. The **Ilinden Sailing Regatta** is held on the same day on Lake Ohrid.

There are numerous **artists' colonies** throughout the summer including the International Pottery Workshop in Resen in early August, the Traditional Costumes Exhibition on the first weekend after 2 August in Struga, and the Painters' Colony in Kneževo. The Monastery of Sveti Joakim Osogovski holds a Young Artists' Convention in the last week of August, which is also when its very popular saint's day falls. At the end of August the **Struga Poetry Evenings** (see page 180) take place over the bridge where Lake Ohrid empties into the River Drim in Struga.

Štip holds its popular **Mackfest of International Music** in October (page 252). In September Bitola holds the **International Film Camera Festival** in honour of the Manaki brothers. Skopje holds its **International Film Festival** in October along with the **Skopje Jazz Festival**, which usually puts on some

4

excellent artists. September and October are also very good months for wine tours (see page 284).

December finishes up the year with **Christmas markets** selling local crafts and mulled wine. **New Year's Eve** sees fireworks over the River Vardar in Skopje and equally colourful celebrations in many other towns across Macedonia.

🛒 SHOPPING

The things to look for and buy in Macedonia are the intricately hand-carved woodwork, filigree silver jewellery, manmade pearls, earthenware, traditional blankets, hand-embroidered linen, fur, leather goods and paintings. Most of these items are best bought in Ohrid, which has lots of little craft shops in its meandering old town. Skopje's old town also has some linen, fur and leather shops. Skopje's Roma part of town (see page 151) is the best place to order their hand-embroidered costumes, but traditional Macedonian costumes, like you might see at Galičnik or Ilinden, are harder to find. For more on local handicrafts see page 59.

For those living and working in Skopje, *Chapter 5* covers more of the items that you may be looking for while living away from home. English books can be found at Ikona, Matica and the English Learning Centre. Skopje is a good place to get hand-made suits (see page 133), and Štip has a number of clothes and shoe outlets (see page 248) who supply Marks & Spencer and other European shops.

If you get hooked on the Macedonian starter *ajvar*, a delicious dish consisting of stewed red pepper and herbs, you can buy this in jars in the supermarket. However, the best *ajvar* would be homemade so try to buy it locally in places like Brajčino, where you can also buy local *rakija, liker*, jams, wild mushrooms and excellent homemade *baklava* if you eat in a local home (see page 198). The best *mastika* (aniseed liqueur) is bought at monasteries such as Sv Jovan Bigorski.

For more on local wines see page 284.

🎭 ARTS AND ENTERTAINMENT

Skopje is the best place for most arts and entertainment in Macedonia. With a population of only 500,000 it is not, of course, on a par with London, Paris or New York, but it does have a few drama theatres, its own philharmonic orchestra and a number of art galleries. For more information on all of these see *Chapter 5*, pages 131–6. For more details on Macedonian arts and culture see *Chapter 3, Culture*, page 59.

Summer festivals are plenty (see above) and most towns do something. You won't find the latest blockbusters in the cinemas, but they also won't be dubbed, so you will be able to hear them in their original language.

Macedonia's national football team, nicknamed the Red Lions, plays in Skopje throughout the football season, and the most popular match is usually the match against England, whenever that occurs.

PHOTOGRAPHY

It is forbidden to take photographs in churches, restricted military areas, and of military installations. Most people do not mind if you take their photograph, but you should always ask first, and if they say no, do not insist. In the more remote villages, farmers may also not agree to you taking photographs of their animals. They believe that if you take a photograph even of only one animal it will affect the whole flock.

Negative film is easy to get, and development costs around 350MKD. Slide film is more difficult to get and can cost up to 500MKD just for the development. A good photolab which also has a supply of Fuji Sensia, Provia and Velvia slide film is Digital Studio Profoto Zdravko (✆ *02 3227 080*) on Dimitri Čupovski in Skopje. Stanimir Nedelkovski (✆ *070 217 975*) also develops very high-quality colour, and black and white slide film. Developing black and white slide film costs €4, and colour is €10. He will also let you use his lab to develop your own film. Both places produce high-quality digital photographic prints.

For more top tips on photography, see box on page 104.

ℓ MEDIA AND COMMUNICATIONS

NEWS OUTLETS For such a small country, Macedonia has a lot of television and radio stations. On the one hand this could be a healthy indication of freedom of speech and freedom of the media, but quantity doesn't make quality. Many of the television and radio stations have strong links to political parties so their coverage of daily issues can be biased. At the time of writing, the most reputable television station to give relatively balanced news coverage is A1 Television.

There are six main Macedonian-language television stations – A1 (as above), Kanal 5, MTV (not Music TV!), Sitel, Skynet and Telma – and many more local channels. Macedonian Radio and Channel 77 are the two main news-heavy radio stations broadcasting in the Macedonian language, but there are dozens of local radio stations. Some of the most popular radio stations which a lot of the restaurants tune into are Antenna 5 (95.5), City Radio (94.7) and Radio Uno (103.3). BBC World Service is available on 90.8 between 22.00 and 08.00 with on-the-hour news.

The daily newspapers produced in Cyrillic are *Dnevnik*, *Večer*, *Nova Makedonija*, *Makedonija Denes*, *Vest*, *Vreme* and *Utrinski Vesnik*, which is the most serious of them all. There are five weekly Macedonian-language news magazines: *Denes*, *Aktuel*, *Start*, *Focus* and *ZUM*. *Forum* is a bi-weekly politics and life magazine which caters to a politically more analytical sector of Macedonians, and which critiques without necessarily being critical. *Forum* also has an interesting quarterly magazine.

The two main Macedonian-language news agencies are MIA (*www.mia.com.mk*) and Makfax (*www.makfax.com.mk*), both of which have very good news in English which is updated several times a day. MIA requires paid registration for expanded news articles, while Makfax does not.

MIA, A1 and Sitel provide mobile phone news updates to T-Mobile phone users.

On the Albanian side the news agencies include Balkanweb, Kosova Press, Kosova Live, Kosovo Information Centre and Albanews. There are two main newspapers, *Fakti* and *Lajm*; one weekly, *Lobi*; and one major national television station, MTV3.

There are also Roma and Turkish media stations and papers produced in-country, as well as most of the major international newspapers and magazines available in Skopje after 19.00 every evening.

✉ **POST** The post in Macedonia is relatively reliable for low-value items, although not very fast. It usually takes between one and two weeks for letters to be delivered between Europe or America and Macedonia by standard post. Stamps can be bought only at the post office, although there is a philatelic bureau at the Ploštad end of the Trgovski Centar in Skopje if you are looking for commemorative stamps.

Most packages are opened on arrival in the country and items of value may be stolen. As a result, high-value items, and even books, should be sent by FedEx or DHL. FedEx services in Skopje can be found at Boulevard Partizanski Odredi 17 (❧ *02 3137 233*); DHL can be found at City Travel on the ground floor of Paloma Bjanka business centre (❧ *02 3212 2034*).

If you want post sent to you whilst travelling, have it addressed to you at Poste Restante, Pošta, Town Name. You will be able to pick it up at the town's main post office. Make sure that your surname is printed clearly in capitals and underlined, and bring some identification with you when you go to pick up your mail.

TELEPHONE Phone booths accepting coins, credit cards and pre-paid phone cards are also available all over the country. Pre-paid phone cards can be bought at newsagents and are easily visible by the big phone-card advertising boards in the shape of a telephone.

Mobile phone providers are T-Mobile, Vip and Cosmofon, where you can purchase a local sim card with an initial few hundred minutes for as little as

PHOTOGRAPHIC TIPS
Ariadne Van Zandbergen

EQUIPMENT Although with some thought and an eye for composition you can take reasonable photos with a 'point and shoot' camera, you need an SLR camera with one or more lenses if you are at all serious about photography. The most important component in a digital SLR is the sensor. There are two types of sensor: DX and FX. The FX is a full-size sensor identical to the old film size (36mm). The DX sensor is half size and produces less quality. Your choice of lenses will be determined whether you have a DX or FX sensor in your camera as the DX sensor introduces a 0.5x multiplication to the focal length. So a 300mm lens becomes in effect a 450mm lens. FX ('full frame') sensors are the future, so I will further refer to focal lengths appropriate to the FX sensor.

Always buy the best lens you can afford. Fixed fast lenses are ideal, but very costly. Zoom lenses make it easier to change composition without changing lenses the whole time. If you carry only one lens a 24–70mm or similar zoom should be ideal. For a second lens, a lightweight 80–200mm or 70–300mm or similar will be excellent for candid shots and varying your composition. Wildlife photography will be very frustrating if you don't have at least a 300mm lens. For a small loss of quality, teleconverters are a cheap and compact way to increase magnification: a 300 lens with a 1.4x converter becomes 420mm, and with a 2x it becomes 600mm. NB 1.4x and 2x teleconverters reduce the speed of your lens by 1.4 and 2 stops respectively.

The resolution of digital cameras is improving the whole time. For ordinary prints a 6-megapixel camera is fine. For better results and the possibility to enlarge images and for professional reproduction, higher resolution is available up to 21 megapixels.

It is important to have enough memory space when photographing on your holiday. The number of pictures you can fit on a card depends on the quality you choose. You should calculate how many pictures you can fit on a card and either take enough cards or take a storage drive onto which you can download the cards' content. You can obviously take a laptop which gives the advantage that you can see your pictures properly at the end of each day and edit those you want to keep and delete rejects. If you don't want the extra bulk and weight you can buy a storage device that can read memory cards. These drives come in different capacities.

Keep in mind that digital camera batteries, computers and other storage devices need charging. Make sure you have all the chargers, cables, converters with you. Most hotels/lodges have charging points, but it will be best to enquire about this in advance. When camping you might have to rely on charging from the car battery.

354MKD. Monthly contracts are also available. The main T-Mobile outlet is on the ground floor of Skopje's Trgovski Centar. Top-ups are sold in 200, 300, 590 and 1,000 impulses (and cost that many MKD respectively). Your phone is usually topped-up for you electronically at the point of sale.

If you are thinking of using your own mobile phone from home with a local sim card, make sure that your phone is unlocked and enabled for use abroad and with non-service provider sim cards. This is usually done for free now by your home service provider, but may need to be sent away (recorded delivery) for a few days before you leave home.

Using internet telephony, eg: Skype (*www.skype.com*), is a cheap way to 'phone' home from internet cafés. An increasing number of travel agents and hotels in Macedonia now list their Skype username on their website.

A useful telephone directory website is 988.mt.com.mk. It has an English interface, and for instructions on how to input Cyrillic on a Latin keyboard, see the 'help' option. The local telephone directory is the local dialing code followed by 188.

DUST AND HEAT Dust and heat are often a problem. Keep your equipment in a sealed bag, and avoid exposing equipment to the sun when possible. Digital cameras are prone to collecting dust particles on the sensor which results in spots on the image. The dirt mostly enters the camera when changing lenses, so you should be careful when doing this. To some extent photos can be 'cleaned' up afterwards in Photoshop, but this is time-consuming. You can have your camera sensor professionally cleaned, or you can do this yourself with special brushes and swabs made for this purpose, but note that touching the sensor might cause damage and should only be done with the greatest care.

LIGHT The most striking outdoor photographs are often taken during the hour or two of 'golden light' after dawn and before sunset. Shooting in low light may enforce the use of very low shutter speeds, in which case a tripod/beanbag will be required to avoid camera shake. The most advanced digital SLRs have very little loss of quality on higher ISO settings, which allows you to shoot at lower light conditions. It is still recommended not to increase the ISO unless necessary.

With careful handling, side lighting and back lighting can produce stunning effects, especially in soft light and at sunrise or sunset. Generally, however, it is best to shoot with the sun behind you. When photographing animals or people in the harsh midday sun, images taken in light but even shade are likely to look better than those taken in direct sunlight or patchy shade, since the latter conditions create too much contrast.

PROTOCOL In some countries, it is unacceptable to photograph local people without permission, and many people will refuse to pose or will ask for a donation. In such circumstances, don't try to sneak photographs as you might get yourself into trouble. Even the most willing subject, however, will often pose stiffly when a camera is pointed at them; relax them by making a joke, and take a few shots in quick succession to improve the odds of capturing a natural pose.

Ariadne Van Zandbergen is a professional travel and wildlife photographer specialising in Africa. She runs 'The Africa Image Library'. For photo requests, visit the website www.africaimagelibrary.co.za or contact her direct at ariadne@hixnet.co.za

INTERNET Most towns will have an internet café or two, although they are usually slow, and may not have the latest internet browsers and software. The Contact internet café on the top floor of the Trgovski Centar in Skopje is at least on ISDN and has the latest software. They do charge 120MKD per hour though, whereas most other internet cafés will charge half that amount.

In theory Macedonia is the first country in the world to offer nationwide free Wi-Fi access. In practice this claim is limited to providing free Wi-Fi to 95% of the country's citizens using schools as the access points. As a result, you are unlikely to get Wi-Fi access in remote parts of the country or even in most parts of Skopje that are not near a school.

Almost all new or refurbished hotels, such as Dal Met Fu in Skopje, and Millennium in Ohrid, also have free internet hook-ups in every room, or free Wi-Fi. For those moving into Skopje to live, ADSL at 10mbps can be installed into your flat and is available for Apple Macs (see *www.t-home.mk*).

As with writing to any person in anything other than their mother tongue, Macedonians are unlikely to answer an email that is not in Macedonian. So don't expect a reply too quickly, or at all, unless you have already established contact with them by phone or in person (see *Business* below).

BUSINESS

Business hours in Macedonia are sometimes quite difficult to pin down. Opening times vary from 06.30 (post offices), 07.00 (banks), 08.00 (supermarkets and green markets), 09.00 (some shops) to 10.00 (other shops). Some places shut for lunch, especially in the summer when the day is hot, and some travel agents outside Skopje for instance will close from 11.00 to 17.00 and then open again till 20.00. Closing times also vary from 15.00 (some museums and repair stores, even if their stated closing time is in fact 16.00), 16.00 (government and media offices) to anything between 17.00 and 22.00. Bars, restaurants and nightclubs are required by law to be closed from midnight on weekdays and from 01.00 at the weekends. If you are trying to get hold of government officials it is best to do so between 10.00–12.00 and 14.00–15.00. Most shops are closed on Sunday.

If you have not done business in the Balkans before, and especially if you come from a time-driven and impersonal business culture like the US, UK, Germany or Switzerland, you'll probably find doing business in Macedonia utterly frustrating. First of all, Macedonians do not see time as a product, ie: as money, so don't be surprised if you don't get your delivery on time, invitations are made late, people schedule important meetings with little notice, are then late for meetings, or cancel with little or no notice, and don't meet deadlines. In that sense, Macedonia is very Mediterranean.

Secondly, while they may openly condemn nepotism especially in the government, they rarely carry out any business transaction that does not involve a friend or relative. This is not difficult in a country of only two million people. On the contrary, Macedonians think it mighty odd not to use their friend's service, even if this means receiving an inadequate, delayed and substandard product. Moreover, of course, because the transaction has been done through a friend, you can't exactly complain when things don't work properly without sacrificing a friendship. Beware, therefore, of the business associate who becomes too friendly – he (sadly, there are still few women in the upper echelons of business here) is almost definitely going to call you for a favour later, and if you refuse he may cut the 'favours' in return.

Thirdly, few Macedonians see service as a product that can earn money. This is a leftover from the communist days, when state-owned shops were the only ones you could shop in and so, because there was no competition, it didn't matter how badly the customer was treated; they didn't have anywhere else to purchase products from anyway. You'll find bolshy service and a complete lack of customer appreciation particularly apparent in so-called 'civil' services such as the post office, the police and almost any public business.

Finally, as another leftover from a centralised communist economy and government and probably from several hundred years of Ottoman overlordship, many Macedonians have simply got too used to state handouts and to not having to think laterally or for themselves, never mind in terms of a market economy and what makes business tick. What may seem like a blatantly obvious moneymaker and business opportunity to you will be shot dead in the water after an initially positive greeting. Follow-up and follow-through are not strong points in Macedonian business culture. Most Macedonians would rather wait for a financial initiative from the international community than put their own sweat and savings into a new idea. And even then don't expect the internationally financed idea to roll on once the funding has dried up.

In defence of this lack of initiative, it is admittedly difficult to be proactive in an unstable and insecure economic environment. Theft and fraud are currently endemic in the system, making it difficult to guarantee the arrival of a part from overseas or the secure delivery of an order to an outside buyer. The good news is that the business environment is slowly changing for the better. A surprising number of people below the age of 45 speak English and may have worked abroad. Unlike their older (usually Russian-speaking) colleagues, the younger generation are more open to new ideas and experimenting with change.

Of course, there are some successful business people. Macedonia has a thriving black market, so somebody must know how to make money. The Aromanians (Vlach) people have always been good at trade and you'll find them behind many of the successful, small, family-run businesses. The wine industry is also growing and many of the Albanian community who have worked abroad and come back, bring good earnings with them which they turn into cafés, bars and new homes, although rarely much beyond that.

On the whole though, business is done through personal contact. Don't expect a Macedonian business to answer your email or call (especially if it was in English) or to follow up on a contact if you did not personally introduce them. This may be time consuming, but time isn't money here anyway. Fortunately, unlike in most of the rest of former Yugoslavia, you won't usually have to start the meeting or seal the deal with a shot of local *rakija*.

BUYING PROPERTY

Buying property in Macedonia as an individual citizen became possible in August 2008. Foreigners can purchase from any estate agent, although few will speak English. Property prices in the capital are high considering where Macedonia is on its path to EU accession (2014 maybe?), its lack of accessibility and what it currently offers the visitor. Outside Skopje and Ohrid lakeside, prices are much lower, but attractive properties are in much need of renovation. Macedonians claim they are some of the best builders in the world, and that does not mean cheap, but there is relatively little substantial corroboratory evidence. Buying property in Macedonia can be very long-winded (over a year from initial offer to completion), and if you do not speak Macedonian, then you will need to pay out for the translation of key documents, even if you do use a local lawyer who speaks English. Make sure that the title of the property is verified independently in case there is an ownership dispute on the property.

CULTURAL ETIQUETTE

DRESS For the most part modesty is not an issue in Macedonia. That said, you'll find many Muslim women here of all ages dressed from head to foot in a long overcoat and headscarf no matter what time of day or year, and as a woman you may find it uncomfortable to wander around strongly Muslim areas in a crop top and low-cut shorts. Nudism is unheard of on the lake beaches.

RELIGIOUS ETIQUETTE You should certainly be modestly dressed to enter a mosque and its grounds, and while most churches don't seem to mind what you wear, there are a few which require decent dress, such as Treskavec, Lesnovo and Marko's Monastery. Decent dress means covered shoulders, torso and legs. It is forbidden to take photographs inside churches.

Although many Macedonians are atheist as a leftover from communist days, increasing numbers have retaken to the Macedonian Orthodox Church with renewed vigour. Aside from tourist-frequented Ohrid, Macedonians might find it odd if you don't cross yourself three times before entering the church and light a candle immediately on entering it. Practising Macedonians believe that you will not enter through the gates of heaven if you do not bring oil or wax with which to burn the light of God.

DRUGS As everywhere in the world, there is a drugs scene in Macedonia, although it is small. Drugs are also illegal, even marijuana, so don't use/deal unless you want to risk ending up in a Macedonian jail. Dealing in drugs carries a hefty penalty, doubly so if you are caught taking them over a border crossing. Finally, make sure you keep an eye on your bags at all times while travelling into Macedonia so that no-one can stuff anything illegal in there without you knowing.

TIPPING Tipping is not a necessity here, where most Macedonians can hardly afford more than a coffee in a bar. However, it is greatly appreciated by waiting staff, and as a foreigner if you can afford it, it's certainly a small boost to the economy, morale and attitudes towards tourists. An extra 10 or 20 denar is suitable on smaller sums of money up to 500MKD, usually rounded up to the nearest 50 or 100, and on larger sums, up to 10% is appropriate.

GAYS/LESBIANS The gay and lesbian scene is very limited in Macedonia and it would be considered most strange if not offensive for same-sex couples to walk hand in hand down the street, never mind kiss in public. Booking into a hotel would not be considered so strange unless you insisted on a *francuski krevet* (double bed), as double rooms normally come with twin beds.

Since being gay was decriminalised in 1996, the gay community in Macedonia has been cautiously taking steps to promote greater acceptance. Egal (*Kole Nedelkovski 12a/2, 1000 Skopje;* ✆ *02 3220 851*) is currently the only organisation in Skopje promoting gay and lesbian rights. There are only two bars in Skopje that will accept openly gay clientele. Indy Pub, right behind the Universal Hall, is open to gays every day, and Boni Bar (right across the main entrance of the Greek Embassy) holds gay parties on Sunday evenings. After hours, Boni clientele usually continue to the Priority nightclub at Beverly Hills shopping mall. It is not a gay venue as such and is very turbo-folk.

INTERACTING WITH LOCAL PEOPLE

MACEDONIAN HOSPITALITY Macedonian hospitality is extensive and often overpowering. Especially outside Skopje and Ohrid, where people are not used to contact with foreigners, Macedonians whom you meet will go out of their way to show you a site or monument and then insist on giving you a cup of thick, black, sweet Turkish coffee and a gift from their garden, or some other memento. They will do this, even if you speak no Macedonian at all and they do not speak your language, which can make the conversation somewhat one-sided! They are not looking for a passport to your home country or even any other favour, and if you exchange addresses they will not usually follow up on it unless you do.

Macedonians would simply consider it too rude not to answer a request to the fullest extent and offer you a coffee in their home, and of course they are inquisitive to know who you are, where you come from and how you live in your own country. Trying to say no is extremely difficult without being rude, unless you have some handy pressing excuse, like 'I will turn into a pumpkin at midnight if I don't leave right now' or 'We left my mother in the car and she needs to go to the hospital for brain surgery.' In other words, no excuse will be satisfactory and especially the lame excuse that you do not have enough time, for the one thing that Macedonians do have a lot of is time, and they know that if there's five minutes' leeway in the schedule somewhere then you can fit in a half-hour coffee, and if there isn't five minutes in the schedule then you wouldn't be visiting their remote village anyway.

My advice is to make the most of this laidback way of life. It probably won't be around for much longer, as the fast pace and impersonal attitudes of modern-day life catch up with Macedonia. You may have to reschedule your cramped itinerary and knock something else off the list in order to fit in that coffee, but an invitation into the tenth house is still a privilege and will give you a momentary snapshot of how Macedonians live today.

A SMILE As you travel around Macedonia, especially off the beaten track, you may be greeted at first with a cold, hard stare. Some communities are not often visited by outsiders and so the locals will be suspicious and inquisitive if not bewildered by your intentions to sightsee around their home. Even other Macedonians from a far-away town get this treatment. A smile, a wave and a greeting like '*Zdravo*', or '*Tungjatjeta*' in Albanian regions, or even just 'Hello' will miraculously make your intentions to the locals clear, and their hostile glare will instantly dissolve into a winning smile and a greeting in reply. Initiate a conversation and the obligatory coffee is bound to follow along with a personal tour of their home and town.

CULTURAL QUIRKS Every society has its little idioms and beliefs – here are a few from Macedonia.

Promaja is the Macedonian word for 'draught', not as in beer, but as in the wind/breeze that blows in through an open door or window. Many (particularly older) Macedonians, like a lot of people in the Balkans, believe that *promaja* is the root of all illness, so don't be surprised if you are asked to close a window or door even on a blistering hot day.

Le le is an exclamation which Macedonians say all the time to add emphasis to a sentence. It's not directly translatable into anything in English, but other languages use similar expressions, like *ahh yoaaaa* in some Chinese dialects. *Ajde* is another frequent exclamation. It means 'let's go' or 'come on' or 'you're kidding'. You'll hear these two exclamations in the Macedonian language all over the place.

POLITICS AND HISTORY Macedonians are painfully aware of their history and politics, and are extremely interested in the slightest rumour of political intrigue. Macedonians will happily talk politics and history with you, but beware that you may not get them off the topic once started, no matter how many times you've heard the same tale of oppression and inequality. This phenomenon is particularly Balkan, but in Macedonia it is exaggerated by the fact that Macedonia's national neighbours mostly do not believe (largely for political reasons) that there is such a thing as an ethnic Macedonian, and as a result some question whether Macedonia should even be a sovereign state. As a foreigner, you'll never be right, and whatever you read in *Chapters 1* and *3* of this book is bound to offend someone, be they Macedonian, Serb, Albanian, Turk, Bulgarian, Greek, Orthodox or Muslim. So take what you hear with a small pinch of salt and debate politics with great caution, even if you were a top scorer in the debating society at college.

There is a Macedonian proverb that goes 'If my cow dies, may my neighbour's cow die too.' This, sadly, does sum up a lot of the attitude of the people here. But, as Mahatma Gandhi said, 'An eye for an eye makes the whole world blind.'

GIVING SOMETHING BACK

The interaction of the outside world with Macedonia can have a variety of effects. Hopefully, your visit to Macedonia will have a positive impact on the tourist industry and, indirectly, on the economy and the people. If you have room in your rucksack or suitcase on your way out or have a load of stuff to get rid of when you leave Macedonia, then try bringing some things to the organisations listed on the Macedonian page of **www.stuffyourrucksack.com** (see box, opposite). These organisations are in dire need of some basics, like books, shoes, pens and other small items you might have lying around your house.

If you would like to get more personally involved with charities and institutions in the country then here are a few to start you off. For environmental protection organisations see *Chapter 2, Local environmental organisations*, page 000.

ROMA To read more about the Roma see page 52. There are a number of organisations that are trying to serve their needs and bring the very poor back out of poverty and into education and jobs. **ARKA** in Kumanovo has been instrumental in this regard. Contact the president Feat Kamberovski (*11 Oktomvri 17/1-1, 1300 Kumanovo;* ☏ *031 421 362, 070 629 105;* e *arka@arka.org.mk, arka_ku@yahoo.com; www.arka.org.mk*).

For a Roma organisation based in the Roma settlement of Šuto Orizari contact Ahmed Naser of **CDRIM** (*Vinička 10, Šuto Orizari, 1000 Skopje;* ☏ *02 2654 839, 070 544 266;* e *nasersept@yahoo.com*).

ANTI-TRAFFICKING The trafficking of women through and into Macedonia is a particularly entrenched problem (see page 000), not helped on the Macedonian side by a weak policing and judicial system, and on the international side by the difficulty that the international community has in classing it as a crime separate from slavery, abduction, rape, torture, theft and prostitution. The whole issue is driven by huge financial profits and made easy for traffickers by the lack of public awareness.

TEMIS (Macedonian Women Jurist Association) (*Vasil Gorgov 34, 1000 Skopje;* ☏f *02 3082 932/3;* e *info@temis.com.mk*), who provide legal protection for trafficked women's rights and campaign to raise public awareness of the issue, and **Open Gate** (*Otvorena Porta-La Strada Macedonia, PO Box 110, 1000*

Skopje; ☏ *02 2700 107/367;* e *lastrada@on.net.mk; www.lastrada.org.mk),* who are also campaigning and setting up a safe house and helpline for trafficked women in Macedonia, are two organisations who are helping to eradicate the trafficking of women.

CIVIL SOCIETY The role that civil society plays in any country is an important contribution to self-governance and to providing checks and balances on government and people's hard-earned taxes. In Macedonia civil society is weak by European and American standards. International funding is trying to develop the role that parliamentarians should play as the elected representatives of the people, as well as the role that non–governmental organisations can play. Sadly, the NGO scene is still largely supply driven by the amount of donor funding available rather than demand driven by the confidence that citizens can make a difference. What are sorely missing are skills and competent local stakeholders (and a responsive government). If you have the skills, the funding or the time to help with civil society development in Macedonia it would be greatly appreciated. A couple of the more proactive and impactful civil society movements are:

Wake Up! Zgjohu! Bitpazarska bb, 1000 Skopje; ☏ 02 2636 240; e zgjohu@zgjohu.com.mk; www.zgjohu.com.mk. Aims to promote tolerance & a greater civic spirit among the people of Skopje. It works closely with households to inspire citizens to personally engage in securing their own safer community, & has established a forum inviting all Skopje-based civil society organisations to co-ordinate & enhance their co-operation. Wake Up! has majored on the message of rejecting violence & promoting rule of law, a message that has reverberated well among everyday citizens.

Youth Forum Eye Dimče Kovečeski 1/13, 6330 Struga; ☏/f 046 789 360; e contact@ youthforumeye.org.mk; www.youthforumeye.org.mk. Run by & works predominantly with youth aged 18–26 to empower them in areas of European-standard multi-ethnic civil society, democracy development, ecology preservation & awareness, & youth mobility. They also promote international youth exchange programmes.

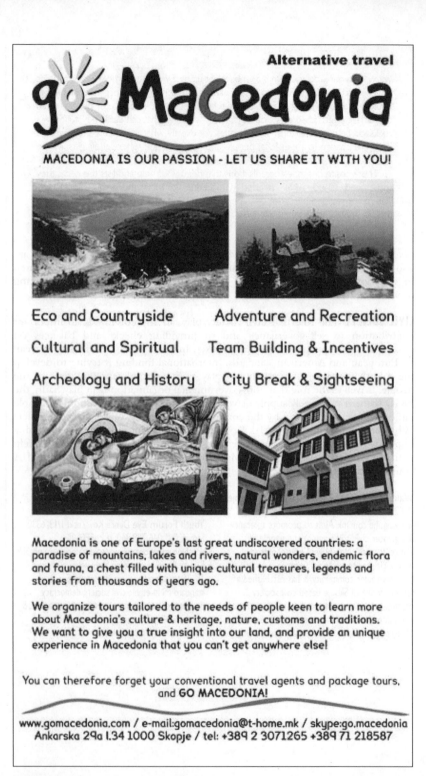

112

Part Two

THE GUIDE

114

5

Skopje

The Turkish residue was thick in Skopje. Men in white skullcaps played backgammon and drank rose-hip tea from small hour-glass-shaped receptacles … I crossed the flagstone bridge over the Vardar River, built on Roman foundations that had withstood major earthquakes in AD518, 1535 and 1963 … Ahead of me was 'new' Skopje …

Balkan Ghosts, Robert D Kaplan, 1993

The up-and-coming town of Skopje is divided by the River Vardar into the predominantly Muslim half to the north of the river, and the predominantly Orthodox Christian half to the south. Most government offices, main shopping centres, the main railway station and modern hotels are found on the southern side of town, although the old Turkish side of town, known as **Čaršija**, remains the main tourist attraction, with a large daily bazaar, a variety of interesting old buildings and cafés, and the remnants of the **Kale** fortress.

Foreigners from international organisations based in Skopje and Kosovo are still more abundant than pure tourists, and even though this international working community is decreasing, its spending power and Skopje's growing middle class are giving the city a slow and steady increase in amenities, shops and entertainment.

Skopje is a city of many cultures and is worth at least a couple of days itself. Don't miss out on **Vinoteka Temov** in Čaršija to try out Macedonia's wines and listen to live traditional music; and further just outside Skopje (see *Chapter 6*, page 150) the newly renovated **hot springs** at Katlanovska Banja.

HISTORY

Nestled in the valley of the Vardar River, Skopje has been a welcome respite from the surrounding mountains since Neolithic times. It first became a major settlement around 500BC when it formed part of the outer reaches of the Illyrian nation now known as Albania. As Rome moved its empire eastward, the settlement became known as Skupi, and later came under Byzantine rule upon the division of the Roman Empire. At the crossroads of two major trading routes, one between Constantinople and Rome, and the other between Thessaloniki and northern Europe, the area has constantly changed hands between nations vying for control of this geopolitically strategic area. Byzantines, Slavs, Greeks, Bulgarians, Austro-Hungarians, Serbs and Turks have all ruled the city. In 1392 began 520 years of Ottoman rule when the city became known as Üsküb and after further swaps among regional powers during and between both world wars, it was finally incorporated in 1944 into Federal Yugoslavia as the capital of the autonomous Republic of Macedonia. Skopje has been the capital of the independent Republic of Macedonia since 1991 when the fledgling state broke free from the Federation during the collapse of Yugoslavia.

CHRONOLOGY

6500BC	Neolithic tribes inhabited the Skopje region at Madžari and Govrlevo
700–500BC	Illyrians founded a settlement at present-day Zlokučani and a fort at Kale
148BC	Skupi made the seat of the Roman district government of Dardania as part of the larger province of Moesia superior
AD395	Under the division of the Roman Empire, Skupi became part of the Byzantine Empire ruled from Constantinople
AD518	Skupi almost completely destroyed by earthquake. Emperor Justinian rebuilt the town a few kilometres further south.
AD695	Skupi taken over by Slavs
10th century	Known as Skoplje under the Macedonian-Bulgarian Empire
1189	Became part of the Serbian Empire before reverting to Byzantine rule
1282	Conquered by the Serbian king Milutin II
1346	Milutin's grandson, Stefan Dušan, claimed Skopje as his capital and proclaimed himself Tsar
1392	Beginning of Ottoman rule over the Balkans for the next 520 years. Town known to the Turks as Üsküb.
15th century	Many Jews fled to Üsküb from Spain
1555	Earthquake destroyed much of the centre of Üsküb
1689	Occupied by the Austrian General Piccolomini. Plague infested the city and, on leaving, Piccolomini burnt it down.
1873	Üsküb to Saloniki railway line built
1910	Mother Teresa – Gondza Bojadziu – born in Skopje
1912–13	First and second Balkan wars
1914	Skopje ruled by Bulgaria
1918	Came under the rule of the Kingdom of Serbs, Croats and Slovenes
1920	Ruled for six months by the Yugoslav Communist Party
1941	Ruled again by Bulgaria
1944	Became the capital of the Federal Yugoslav Socialist Republic of Macedonia
1963	Earthquake razed much of Skopje
1991	Skopje became the capital of the independent Republic of Macedonia

THE ANCIENT SITES OF SKUPI AND KALE Kale, the Ottoman fortress that overlooks Skopje and the Vardar Valley, housed human settlements from as early as Neolithic times c3500BC. Geographic evidence shows that such prehistoric settlements would have been on the edge of a marsh, but the rise of the mountains surrounding Skopje turned the area into the fertile plains of the River Vardar. It became a natural route of passage between greater cities further east and west, and between the Aegean Sea in the south at Thessaloniki (earlier known as Saloniki and today still called Solun in Macedonian) and any travels further north.

In the 7th and 6th centuries BC many Greeks, tempted by trade and lands elsewhere, travelled and settled further north. The Illyrians settled in what is now known as Albania, and the outer reaches of their nation covered the source of the River Vardar all the way down to the foothills of the Vodno and the Skopska Crna Gore. They built the first fort at Kale, and others on Gradište above the present-day district of Dolno Nerezi, and later founded the town of Skupi in the area of the present-day Zlokučani village to the northwest of the town centre.

While other ancient cities of today's Macedonia, such as Hereaclea near Bitola and Stobi near Gradsko, came under the rule of the Macedonian Empire of Aleksandar III of Macedon, Skupi remained part of the Thracian earldom of Dardania until the 2nd century BC. Roman expansion east brought Skupi under Roman rule in 148BC when it became the seat of local government for the district of Dardania as part of the province of Moesia superior.

A PART OF THE BYZANTINE EMPIRE When the Roman Empire was divided into eastern and western halves in AD395, Skupi came under Byzantine rule from Constantinople (today's Istanbul) and became an important trading and garrison town for the region. The Byzantine emperor Justinian (AD527–65) was born in Tauresium (about 20km southeast of present-day Skopje) in AD483, and after Skupi was almost completely destroyed by an earthquake in AD518, Justinian built a new town at the fertile entry point of the River Lepenec into the Vardar. The town was known as Justiniana Prima.

By the end of the 6th century, Skupi had declined in prestige, although newer settlements were emerging on the northern slopes of Mount Vodno. These were destroyed, however, by invading Slav troops in AD695, who fortified Kale and the northern side of the Vardar.

The region soon came back under Byzantine rule. The town prospered and expanded, whilst many churches and monasteries were established in the tranquillity and remoteness of the surrounding hills.

MEDIEVAL SKOPLJE By the 10th century, Byzantine rule of Skupi was waning and the town was known as Skoplje under the Macedonian–Bulgarian Empire. In AD996 it fell within the breakaway state of Tsar Samoil (see box, page 10). Although Skoplje was not made capital of the new state, the town retained its strategic trading importance until Tsar Samoil's death in 1014, when Skoplje withered again into decline, aided by another earthquake levelling the town at the end of the 11th century.

The Byzantine Empire took advantage of the decline in Skoplje to regain influence in the area, but lost control of it once again in 1282 to Serbian king Milutin II. Milutin's grandson, Stefan Dušan, made Skopje his capital, from which he proclaimed himself Tsar in 1346.

FIVE HUNDRED YEARS OF OTTOMAN RULE Rolling back Byzantine rule across much of the Balkans, the Ottoman Turks finally conquered Skopje in 1392 beginning 520 years of Ottoman rule. The Turks named the town Üsküb. At first the Ottomans divided the greater Macedonian region into four *vilayets*, or districts – Üsküb, Kjustendil, Monastir and Saloniki – and as the northernmost of these, Üsküb was strategically important for further forays into northern Europe. Later Kjustendil was given back to Bulgaria, Janina to Greece and Shkodra went to Albania.

Under Ottoman rule the town moved further towards the entry point of the River Serava into the Vardar. It also became predominantly Muslim and the architecture of the town changed accordingly. During the 15th century, many travellers' inns were established in the town, such as Kapan An and Suli An, which still exist today. The city's famous Stone Bridge – Kameni Most – was also reconstructed during this period and the famous Daud Pasha baths (the largest in the Balkans and now a modern art gallery) was built at the end of the 15th century. At this time numerous Jews driven out of Spain settled in Üsküb, adding to the cultural mix of the town and enhancing the town's trading reputation.

At the beginning of Ottoman rule, several mosques quickly sprang up in the city, and church lands were often seized and given to ex-soldiers, while many churches themselves were converted over time into mosques. The most impressive mosques erected during this early period include the Sultan Murat or Hjunkar Mosque, Aladža Mosque and the Mustafa Pasha Mosque.

In 1555, another earthquake hit the town, destroying much of the centre. The outskirts survived and the town continued, nonetheless, to prosper with traders and travellers. Travel reports from the era number Üsküb's population anywhere between 30,000 and 60,000 inhabitants.

For a very short period in 1689, Üsküb was occupied by the Austrian General Piccolomini. He and his troops did not stay for long, however, as the town was quickly engulfed by the plague. On retreating from the town Piccolomini's troops set fire to Üsküb, perhaps in order to stamp out the plague, although some would say this was done in order to avenge the 1683 Ottoman invasion of Vienna.

For the next two centuries Üsküb's prestige waned and by the 19th century its population had dwindled to a mere 10,000. In 1873, however, the completion of the Üsküb–Saloniki (now Skopje–Thessaloniki) railway brought many more travellers and traders to the town, so that by the turn of the century Üsküb had regained its former numbers of around 30,000.

Towards the end of the Ottoman Empire, Üsküb, along with other towns in Macedonia – Kruševo and Monastir (now Bitola) – became main hubs of rebellious movements against Ottoman rule. Üsküb was a key player in the Ilinden Uprising of August 1903 when native Macedonians of the region declared the emergence of the Republic of Kruševo. While the Kruševo Republic lasted only ten days before being quelled by the Ottomans, it was a sign of the beginning of the end. After 500 years of rule in the area the Ottomans were finally ousted in 1912 during the devastating first Balkan War (see text box on page 15 for an eyewitness account).

THE BALKAN WARS AND THE WORLD WARS As the administrative centre of the region, Üsküb also administered the *vilayet* of Kosovo under Ottoman rule. This did not go down well with the increasingly Albanian population of Kosovo, who preferred to be ruled by Albanians rather than the ethnic Slav and Turkish mix of Üsküb. Albanians had started to intensify their harassment of Serbs in the area over the past decade, culminating on 12 August 1912 when 15,000 Albanians marched on Üsküb in a bid to take over the city. The Turks, already weak from other battles against the Balkan League of Greece, Serbia, Montenegro and Bulgaria during the first Balkan War, started to flee.

When Serb reinforcements arrived some weeks later, the 23 October Battle of Kumanovo (50km northeast of Skopje) proved decisive in driving out the Ottomans from all of Macedonia. Skopje remained under Serbian rule during the second Balkan War of 1913 when the Balkan League countries started to fight amongst themselves. Then World War I gave Bulgaria the opportunity to retake Skopje in 1914. By 1918, however, it belonged to the Kingdom of Serbs, Croats and Slovenes, and remained so until 1939, apart from a brief period of six months in 1920 when Skopje was controlled by the Yugoslav Communist Party. The inter-war period of Royalist Yugoslavia saw significant immigration of ethnic Serbs into the region. An ethnic Serb ruling elite dominated over Turkish, Albanian and Macedonian cultures, continuing the repression wrought by previous Turkish rulers.

During World War II, Skopje came under German fascist occupation and was later taken over by Bulgarian fascist forces. March 1941 saw huge anti-Nazi demonstrations throughout the streets of the town, as Yugoslavia was dragged into the war. But Nazi war crimes were not to be stopped and on 11 March 1943, Skopje's entire Jewish population of 3,286 was deported to the gas chambers of Treblinka concentration camp in Poland. Another year and a half later, on 13

November 1944, Skopje was liberated by the partisans, who wrested control after a bitter two-day battle.

THE FEDERAL YUGOSLAV SOCIALIST REPUBLIC OF MACEDONIA From 1944 until 1991 Skopje was the capital of the Federal Yugoslav Socialist Republic of Macedonia. The city expanded and the population grew during this period from just over 150,000 in 1945 to almost 600,000 in the early 1990s. Continuing to be prone to natural disasters the city was flooded by the Vardar in 1962 and then suffered considerable damage from a severe earthquake on 26 July 1963. Over 1,000 people were killed as a result of the earthquake, almost 3,000 injured, and over 100,000 were made homeless.

Nearly all of the city's beautiful 18th- and 19th-century buildings were destroyed in the earthquake, including the National Theatre and many government buildings, as well as most of the Kale fortress. International financial aid poured into Skopje in order to help rebuild the city. Sadly, the result was the many 'modern' concrete monstrosities of 1960s communism that can still be seen today and hundreds of now abandoned caravans and prefabricated mobile homes left to rot. Even Mother Teresa's house was razed to make way for a modern shopping centre (the Trgovski Centar). Fortunately, though, as with previous earthquakes, much of the old Turkish side of town survived.

INDEPENDENCE Skopje made the transition easily from the capital of the Federal Yugoslav Socialist Republic of Macedonia to the capital of today's Republic of Macedonia. The city livened up considerably when Skopje housed the headquarters of the NATO intervention into Kosovo in 1998 and 1999. Due to its proximity to Kosovo, the city will continue to see NATO troops and other international staff for as long as Kosovo remains a protectorate. The city saw some rioting during 2001 when internal conflict between the Albanian community and the Macedonian majority erupted over the lack of Albanian representation in government and other social institutions.

Today, Skopje is seeing a makeover in buildings, streets and shops. The new VMRO-DPMNE government, re-elected in snap elections in April 2008, has pledged to restore the Kale fortress and to rebuild the beautiful 19th-century Army House and the Old Theatre. The abandoned works of the facilities at Vodno cross are also undergoing a revival.

GETTING THERE AND AWAY

See pages 72–8 for getting in and out of Skopje, where links to both the full domestic train and bus timetables can be found. Skopje is well served by bus.

GETTING AROUND

TAXIS Taxis are plentiful and cheap at only 50MKD for a minimum fare for the first 2km. Taxis come in a variety of four-door sizes and makes, from old Skodas, former Yugoslavian Zastavas, Mercedes and BMWs to brand-new Skoda Octavias, VW Golfs and Passats. All are marked with lighted taxi signs on the roof, and you can flag them down almost anywhere on the street. Taxi ranks can be found at the main intersections of town, the central one being outside Barista at the pedestrian end of 11 Oktomvri near the Trgovski Centar [125 F2]. Taxis can also be ordered from any of the following telephone numbers: 15152 (Naše Taxi – all yellow cabs, *www.nasetaxi.com.mk*), 15157 (Lotus – all white cabs, *www.lotustransport.com*), 15177, 15190, 15192, 15193, 15194, 15195. The

↑ Kosovo,
Aqueduct

Šuto,
Orizari
(see page 152)

BD MAKEDONISKA KOSOVSKA BRIGAI

Tetovo,
Zlokučani,
Bardovci

Den i Nokj

Javor Mrzenci/
Meana B

HIGHWAY 2

Vardar

Aleksandar
Palace

BD NIKOLA KAREV

SAMOILOVA

Mladost Karpoš
swimming pool

Balkanika

City Park

Boris
Trajkovski
Stadium

Colosseum
Cabrio

Element

French cemetery

Tetovo

BD ILINDEN

Havana

Zoo

ABC Tennis
Club

Football
stadium

Kale
Ice Rink

LAZAR LIČENOSKI

Vardar

USA

Lira

Kvarner
Skopski Merak
Club Spa

Natural
History
Museum

Uranija

Marakana

City Park

Kale
Swimming Pool

Ezerce

Anja

Kale

8TH SEPTEMVRI

NIKOLA TESLA

Kanet

Tomče Sofka

Squash
courts

Dramski
Teatar

RUZEVELT

ORČE NIKOLOV

Ministry
of Defence

Tiglio's

Mala Stanica
restaurant (1km)

BD PARTIZANSKI

FRANKLIN

Angelkovski
Tailor

Idadia

Library

Juke Box

Universal
Concert Hall

Ambassador

OHRIDSKI

Jadran

Vero
Supermarket

McDonald's

Toscana

LENINOVA

Cox

BD METROPOLIT

Rose Diplomatique
Church
(RC)

VASIL GLAVINOV

SV KLIMENT

Dutch
embassy

Stonebridge

Makedoni
Square
Dal Me
Fu

TITO

Vuk

Kapištec

TEODOSIJ GOLOGANOV

IVO RIBAR LOLA

Dva Elena

Vodenica/Mulino

MILE POP
JO RDANOV

VASIL GJORGOV

Beverly Hills
Shopping Centre

Best Western Turist
Bristol

MARSAL

Dom na
Armija

Parliament

steps

KARAORMAN

ZAGREBSKA

KOZARA

DAME
GRUEV

MITO HADŽI VASILEV

City Museum
of Skopje

Tinex
Supermarket

ELISIE POPOVSKI- MARKO

Bombay

Seven

VODNJANSKA

see pages 124–5

ŽELEZNIČA

Flower
market

PITU GULI

ACO KARAMANOV

Victoria

Pansion Brateks

BELGRADSKA

Ministry
of Interior

BIHACKA

VODNO

Tasino
Češmiče

PARTENIJ ZOGRAFSKI

Villa Vodno

SALVADORE ALIJENDE

CRNIČE

Leonardo

N

Bradt

CRNIČE

0 ————————— 1,000m
0 ————————— 1,000yds

Panorama

UK embassy, French embassy,
UNMIK Liason office,
Vodno

BUTEL 1

BUTEL 2

DŽON KENEDI

ČAIR

CVETAN DIMOV

(PLASTIC ALLEY)

Gazi Baba
Woods

AVTO
KOMANDA

Yayha
Pasha

Arabati
Teke

see page 135

Museum of
Contemporary
Art

Aladža

Bit
Pazar

Kuršumli An

SAMOILOVA

Natl Mus of
Macedonia

Mustafa
Pasha

Gazi Isa-Bey

Saat Kula

Hjunkar

Church of Sv Gjorgji
& British cemetery

Faculty of
Forestry

SAGW
(Katastar)

Museum
of Skopje Bazaar

BD KRSTE

GAZI BABA

BD ALEKSANDAR MAKEDONSKI

Airport
Kamnik Hunting
Lodge & restaurant (1km)

Kale

Sv Spas

Čifte Amam
Gallery

Kapan An

University
of Kiril &
Metodi

Daud Pasha
Amam Gallery

Sv Dimitri

MISIRKOV

BD GOCE DELČEV

The Swan Pub

National
Theatre

NAUMOV

British
Council

Skopje Courts
Youth culture
centre

Macedonia
Television &
Radio (MTVR)

P

Continental

Skopje
Fair

STIV

Vardar

Frosina Cinema

Trgovski
Shopping Centre

Holiday Inn

National Bank
of Macedonia
Museum of
Coinage

BD KOČO RACIN

BELASICA

Vardar

Olympic
swimming
pool

Green market

Ferialen
Dom

KRUŠEVSKA REPUBLIKA

BD KUZMAN JOSIF PITU

Railway
station

Trimaks
Map store

Harmonija
(Vegetarian)

Skopjanka Mall

Macedonian
Mountaineering
& Sports
Federation

Borče Tailor

BD JANE SANDANSKI

McDonalds

Biser Shopping Mall

ANTON PANOV

II OKTOMVRI

KISELA
VODA

BD III MAKEDONSKA BRIGADA

FRANJO KLUZ

KOSTA NOVAKOVIĆ

AERODROM

Military Museum
of Macedonia

1st MAJ

Sopište,
Marko's Monastery,
Kitka Mountain

Bazen Biser
Swimming Pool

dispatchers at 15157 and 15177 speak English. Many taxi drivers also speak good English or German, and those who do will be quick to give you their business card for repeat business.

BUSES These can get very crowded during rush hour, but they are frequent and cover a wide area. The Trimaks Skopje map has a good inset of the city bus routes. See the map on page 146 for routes to outlying villages. City bus timetables and maps for both the inner city and to outlying villages are available at www.jsp.com.mk. The Inter Town Bus Station [121 F6] is located at the train station where the information desk staff speak good English (✆ 02 2466 011/313) and they also have a good website in English with all the bus timetables (*www.sas.com.mk*) including prices. Main times for direct buses are listed in the box below. Out-of-the-way places will require a change of buses at the local main

BUS DEPARTURES FROM SKOPJE

Berovo via Delčevo	07.30, 08.15, 12.30
Berovo via Vinica	09.30, 13.20, 14.15, 15.15, 16.30, 18.00
Bitola	06.00, 09.00, 11.00, 12.30, 13.30, 15.00, 16.30, 17.00, 19.00, 21.00
Bogdanci	08.30, 11.00, 14.00, 16.00, 17.00, 18.00
Debar	06.30, 09.30, 10.00, 13.00, 14.00, 14.15, 15.15, 16.30
Delčevo	07.30, 08.15, 11.30, 12.30, 17.15
Dojran	08.30, 14.00, 16.00 (Nov Dojran only)
Gevgelija	08.30, 11.00, 14.00, 15.30, 16.00, 16.30, 17.30, 18.00
Gostivar	07.00, 07.30, 08.15, 09.30, 10.30, 12.00, 12.30, 13.30, 14.30, 15.30, 15.45, 16.30, 17.15, 18.00, 19.30, 21.30
Katlanovo Spa (Bus 53)	05.05, 06.05, 07.00, 07.30, 08.25, 09.15, 09.55, 11.00, 11.35, 12.25, 13.40, 14.15, 15.20, 15.55, 16.35, 17.40, 18.25, 19.15, 20.20
Kavadarci (Negotino)	10.30, 12.00, 15.00, 19.30
Kavadarci (Rosoman)	09.00, 15.45, 17.00, 20.15
Kočani	07.30, 08.15, 08.50, 09.30, 12.30, 13.30, 14.30, 15.30, 15.45, 16.30, 18.00, 18.30, 19.30
Kriva Palanka	06.00, 07.30, 09.00, 10.30, 11.30, 12.30, 13.00, 14.00, 15.00, 15.30, 16.00, 17.00, 18.00
Kruševo	07.45, 16.15, 16.45
Kumanovo	every half-hour from 06.00 until 20.00
Ohrid (Kičevo)	06.00, 08.00, 10.00, 14.00, 14.45, 15.00, 15.30, 16.00, 16.30, 18.30
Prilep	13.00, 14.00, 14.30, 18.00
Probištip	07.30, 12.15, 13.00, 15.30, 16.00, 16.40, 18.00
Resen	06.00, 11.00, 12.30, 13.30, 15.30, 16.30
Štip	06.00, 07.30, 08.15, 08.50, 09.30, 10.00, 11.30, 12.05, 12.30, 13.00, 14.30, 15.00, 15.15, 16.00, 16.30, 17.00, 18.00, 19.00, 19.30
Stobi	08.30, 11.00, 14.00, 16.00, 17.30
Struga	05.30, 11.00, 12.30, 12.50, 13.15, 14.00, 14.30, 15.30, 16.10, 16.45, 17.30
Strumica (Radoviš)	06.00, 08.05, 10.00, 12.05, 13.00, 14.00, 14.30, 15.00, 15.30, 16.00, 17.00, 18.00, 19.00
Tetovo	every half-hour from 05.15 until 20.00
Veles	every half-hour from 06.00 until 21.00
Vinica	08.45, 09.30, 12.30, 13.20, 14.00, 14.15, 14.30, 15.15, 15.45, 16.30, 18.00, 19.30
Vinica (Kumanovo)	12.30
Zletovo	07.30, 12.15, 16.40

town; for instance, buses to Oteševo or Brajčino require a change at Resen. Prices are quite low (although more expensive than the train). A single to Dojran is 410MKD and a return is 590MKD. A single to Stobi is 210MKD.

For buses from Skopje to international destinations see page 122. There are no direct buses to Greece.

TRAINS The railway station on Bd Kuzman Josef Pitu [121 F6] (\ *02 3116 733, 02 0121 079*) is 15 minutes' walk southeast of the Stone Bridge. It is probably one of the sorriest main stations you will come across in the Balkans and is not located in a very inviting part of town, although it is as safe as anywhere else in Skopje. The information desk staff do not speak much English, but fairly good German. There are two trains a day going to Thessaloniki, one early in the morning and the other late afternoon, and there is an afternoon train to Priština (Kosovo) returning early in the morning. For train times see the table in *Chapter 4*, pages 74–7.

TOURIST INFORMATION

The Skopje Tourist Information Office is at Vasil Agilarski bb [125 G2] (*next to Restoran Nacional;* \ *02 3223 644;* ⏀ *08.30–16.30*). Tour operators specialising in Skopje are listed on page 70 in *Chapter 4*. Good maps of Skopje abound, and the Trimaks map includes all the bus routes.

⬆ WHERE TO STAY

Skopje offers a whole range of hotels and private rooms, as well as a youth hostel, and summer camping sites. If you would like to book on line and no website address or email is offered below then try under 'accommodation' on www.exploringmacedonia.com, where most of these hotels offer on-line booking.

HOTELS
Top end
⌂ **Best Western Hotel Turist** [125 F3] (85 rooms) Gjuro Sturgar 11; \ 02 328 9111; f 02 328 9100; e turist@bestwestern.at; www.bestwestern-ce.com/turist. The hotel's coffee shop entrance is on Maršal Tito near the centre of the city. Maršal Tito St is a busy pedestrian zone, which can be quite noisy. Western 4-star standards. $$$$$

⌂ **Continental** [121 G4] (230 rooms) Bd Aleksandar Makedonski bb; \ 02 3116 599; f 02 3222 221; www.contimak.com. A 4-star tower-block hotel. It has good conference facilities & a decent restaurant. $$$$$

⌂ **Holiday Inn** [125 G2] (178 rooms) Mosa Pijade 2; \ 02 3292 929; f 02 3115 503; e hiskopje@ holiday-inn.com.mk; www.holiday-inn.com/skopje. Another 4-star hotel conveniently located near the centre of town. It is next to the Trgovski shopping centre so is very close to amenities such as restaurants, supermarkets, underground parking, pubs & the Millennium Cinema. The hotel has an excellent fitness centre, which is not open to the public.

Reserve a room well in advance as the hotel is often booked with international conferences. During Aug prices can drop by up to 50% when Skopje empties for the summer. $$$$$

⌂ **Stonebridge Hotel** [125 F1] (41 rooms) Kej Dimitar Vlahov 1; \ 02 3244 900; f 02 3244 901; www.stonebridge-hotel.com. Opened in 2006, this top-quality hotel has an unrivalled view over the city & River Vardar from the top-floor dining room. Small pool, fitness room & very nice Turkish steam room. $$$$$

⌂ **Hotel Aleksandar Palace** [120 A2] (135 rooms) Bd Oktomvriska Revolucija; \ 02 3092 392/ 3092 200; f 02 3092 152; e info@ aleksandarpalace.com.mk; www.aleksandarpalace.com.mk. Located by the river, on the western outskirts of town. Its restaurant is good value, has reasonable food & is open to non-residents. Its fitness centre is also open to non-residents at 380MKD per session (800MKD including use of sauna & lukewarm jacuzzi) & is the best available, although its layout is not the best for privacy. There is no swimming pool, but there is an Olympic-size pool next door to the Aleksandar Palace. $$$$

🏠 **Hotel Arka** [135 D3] (26 rooms) Bitpazarska 90/2; ✆ 02 3230 603; f 02 3238 781; e info@hotel-arka.com.mk; www.hotel-arka.com.mk. Modern, well

Mid-range

🏠 **Hotel Ambassador** [124 C2] (35 rooms) Pirinska 38; ✆ 02 3121 383. In the courtyard next to the Russian Embassy. This is the hotel with the statue

maintained with good facilities for the price. Small pool on the 7th floor (also the dining area), Wi-Fi in rooms. Setting in the old town is a little bit tatty. Can be hard to find, but is signposted from Bd Krste Misirkov, or turn behind the small fountain on Bitpazarska. $$$$

of liberty on top & a couple of other Roman figures. Close to bars & restaurants. $$$$

SKOPJE TOWN CENTRE

🏠 **Hotel Bristol** [125 F4] (33 rooms) Maršal Tito bb; ☎ 02 3114 883; f 02 3236 556. A 3-star hotel at the end of Maršal Tito with an older feel to it, this was the original meeting place for the Skopje International Rotary Club starting in 1924 (now held in the Hotel Aleksandar Palace). $$$$

🏠 **Hotel Dal Met Fu** [125 F2] (6 rooms) Above the restaurant of the same name in the town square; ☎ 02 3239 584; www.dalmetfu.com.mk. Well furnished, including internet connection in each room. $$$$

🏠 **Hotel Jadran** [125 E2] (21 rooms) 27th Mart bb; ☎ 02 3118 427; f 02 3118 334. Formerly the stately home of an Armenian family, this small 3-star hotel is resplendent with 19th-century Turkish-style furnishings & is centrally located in the pedestrian heart of the city. $$$$

🏠 **Kamnik Hunting Lodge** [121 H4] (15 rooms) Kamnik bb; ☎ 02 252 3522; f 02 258 0540; e info@kamnik.com.mk; www.kamnik.com.mk. A great restaurant (if you like game) & modern rooms. Shooting range downstairs, tennis courts outside, fitness gym, & it is also the meeting location of the Wine Knights! For more on the restaurant & directions see under *Where to eat* opposite. $$$$

⌂ **Rose Diplomatique** [124 B5] (8 rooms) Roza Luxemburg; ✆ 02 3135 469; f 02 3129 058; e info@rosediplomatique.com.mk; www.rosediplomatique.com.mk. A very nice small hotel with an attractive interior & a good restaurant (for residents only). Free Wi-Fi, buffet b/fast. The hotel is often full so book well in advance. $$$$

⌂ **Victoria** [120 B6] (11 rooms) Slave Delovski 18; ✆ 02 3107 600; f 02 3107 610; e hotelvictoriaskopje@yahoo.com; www.hotelvictoria.com.mk. Nicely furnished new hotel in the quiet foothills of Vodno. Free Wi-Fi & transfer to & from the airport. $$$$

Not so expensive

⌂ **Hotel Seven** [124 D5] (9 rooms) Vodjanska 28; ✆ 02 3176 905, 070 671 587. Basic rooms, directly opposite the entrance to the main hospital. Secure parking available. B/fast can be brought up from Žužu bakery downstairs. $$$

⌂ **Kanet** [124 B1] (13 rooms) Jordan Hadžikonstantinov Džinot 20; ✆/f 3238 353; e contact@hotelkanet.com.mk; www.hotelkanet.com.mk. This clean basic hotel is located on the edge of the city park near the river, bars & restaurants. $$$

⌂ **Hotel Kapištec** [120 A5] (11 rooms) Mile Pop Jordanov 3; ✆ 02 3081 424/425; e kapystec@t-home.mk; www.hotel-kapistec.com.mk. Clean & quiet. $$$

⌂ **Hotel Square** [125 E2] (8 rooms) Nikola Vapcarov 2, 6th Floor (take the lift to the 5th & walk the final floor); ✆ 02 3225 090; f 02 3225 077; e hotelsquare@mt.net.mk;

⌂ **Villa Vodno** [120 B7] (12 rooms) Partenij Zografski 79a; ✆/f 02 317 7711; e villavodno@t-home.mk; www.villavodno.com.mk. An immaculate house with spacious apts in the foothills of Vodno. Fireplace downstairs, fitness machines available, free Wi-Fi, airport pick-up & drop-off for €15. $$$$

⌂ **Leonardo** [120 D7] (9 rooms) Partenij Zografski 19; ✆ 02 3177 517; e info@hotel-leonardo.com.mk; www.hotel-leonardo.com.mk. Small new hotel in the quiet foothills of Vodno. Small garden, free Wi-Fi, buffet b/fast. $$$

⌂ **Tomče Sofka** [124 C1] (17 rooms) City Park, near the stadium; ✆ 02 3117 250, 02 3127 293; e contact@tomcesofka.com.mk; www.tomcesofka.com.mk. Recently refurbished, this hotel is on a bustling strip of cafés & restaurants near the river. $$$

www.hotelsquare.com.mk. Nicely furnished small rooms with a good view over the square. $$$

⌂ **Hotel Tasino Češmiče** [120 C6] (59 rooms) Belgradska 28; ✆ 02 3177 333; f 02 3176 736; e tascinocesmice@t-home.mk; www.tasino.com.mk. A 3-star hotel at the foot of Vodno Mountain, looking more like a train station than a hotel. Quiet setting. $$$

⌂ **Ferialen Dom** [121 E6] (26 rooms) Prolet 25; ✆ 02 3114 849; f 02 3235 029; e hotelfsm@hotmail.com; www.myha.org.mk. The only youth hostel in Skopje offering discounts to Hostelling International members. Not far from the train station or the centre of town. Clean, tidy en-suite rooms. A lively restaurant downstairs. $$$

⌂ **Hotel RM** [135 B3] (8 rooms) Jorgandžiska 12/14; ✆ 02 3117 133, 02 3131 288. Right in the old town next to the *bezisten* old covered market. Small, old & tidy. $$

PRIVATE ROOMS AND PANSIONS If you would prefer to stay in a private room in order to get a more Balkan feel to your visit then these can be arranged through the Skopje Tourist Information Office (page 123). Make sure you ask for something near the centre of the city otherwise you may have a long walk into the centre. Private rooms start at 1,200MKD or €10 per person per night, excluding breakfast, and usually offer shared bathrooms.

Bed and breakfast-type lodges or *pansions* include:

⌂ **Pansion Brateks** [120 B6] (3 rooms) Aco Karamanov 3a; ✆ 02 3176 606, 070 243 232. Popular & therefore often full. A 20min walk from the centre & set at the foot of Mt Vodno among the houses of the rich & the diplomats, giving it an airy upmarket feel. German is spoken & only a little English. $$

⌂ **Boda** [124 D4] (3 rooms) Ivo Ribar Lola 32; ✆ 02 3221 023. Conveniently located near the centre of town. All rooms share a communal bathroom. $$

⌂ **Mlin Balkan** [124 D3] (4 rooms) Leninova 79; ✆ 02 3110 635. A 10min walk from the centre. All rooms share 2 communal bathrooms. $$

🏠 **Vuk Skopje** [120 A5] Mile Pop Jordanov 1;
📞 02 3081 426/427. A 20min walk from the centre.
Clean & basic. $$

CAMPING

🏕 **Autocamp Bellevue** At the Hotel Belleview,
site is 5km east of Skopje on the way to the airport;
Ul 32, br24; 📞 02 2572 277; f 02 2572 276;
e info@bellevue.com.mk; www.bellevue.com.mk. $
🏕 **Autocamp Boom** Stenkovec, 6km from the
capital; 📞 02 2053 848. $

🏕 **Saraj Campsite** On River Treška just before
Lake Matka; 📞 02 2047 307. Often very full in
summer. $
🏕 **Katlanovo Campsite** 30km southeast of
Skopje, near the hotsprings; 📞 02 2721 051 (see
Chapter 6, page 150). $

✕ WHERE TO EAT

Traditional food abounds in the city and, slowly, there is some variety moving in too,
including Japanese, Chinese and Indian, as well as Italian, Greek and Turkish. For an
overview of Macedonian cuisine see *Eating and drinking* in *Chapter 4*, page 97.

Eating out is still quite cheap, with a lunch dish often as little as 150–200MKD,
and evening meals going up to 1,000MKD or more if you eat on the expensive
side. Almost any menu in Skopje will appear in English as well as Macedonian.
All restaurants must now offer non-smoking seating (although its proximity to the
smoking seating sometimes makes the division irrelevant), and in the summer
there is an abundance of outdoor seating. Debar Malo has many restaurants
tucked away in its largely residential streets, while a few other good restaurants are
strewn around the rest of the city.

Most restaurants (unless otherwise stated) open at 12.00 and stay open until
midnight. Some restaurants open at 08.00 for breakfast, especially of the cooked
variety, such as at **Mecho's**, **Trend** and **Kaj Maršalot** (all detailed below). Unless
otherwise listed, all restaurants are open seven days a week.

THE BEST OF MACEDONIA'S TRADITIONAL MIX
Macedonia on show

✕ **Balkanika** [120 A2] Oktomvriska Revolucija 24
(as if heading for the Aleksandar Palace but in the
park); 📞 02 3073 712. Nice outdoor seating. Best
pastrmalija in town. $$$
✕ **Dab Pivnica** [125 E2] Gorki Maksim 1. Just off the
main square, & would be easy to miss if you were not
to look for the 2 huge dark brown wooden doors.
Don't miss a mixed platter of their cold creamed
starters (*meze*), Parma ham & chunks of Parmesan
cheese, with a side basket of their delicious sesame-
seed pizza-bread strips. This is often enough for a meal
on its own, but they have lots of other excellent dishes
including aubergine & mozzarella pizza, mixed grills &
an excellent rack of lamb ribs. $$$
✕ **Kamnik** [121 H4] Kamnik bb; 📞 02 252 3522;
www.kamnik.com.mk. Hidden in Avtokomanda
district, turn immediately before the Lukoil petrol
station on the way from the airport into town. Lots
of stuffed animal trophies deck the walls. Serves wild
boar sausages, Macedonian venison, rabbit bechemel
stew, & more. Try their cold cut sausages, salamis &

hams for a range of game choices. Also has a wide
choice of Macedonian & foreign wines. $$$
✕ **Makedonska Kukja** [120 A4] Bd Mitropolit
Teodosij Golaginov bb, opposite the Alumina factory;
📞 02 3296 415, 070 208 519;
www.makedonskakuka.com. Traditional Macedonian
décor & food; live music in the evenings. $$$
✕ **Pivnica** [135 E4] Inside the old Turkish inn of
Kapan in the old town; 📞 02 321 2111. An
atmospheric setting; offers a few vegetarian dishes.
$$$
✕ **Stara Gradska Kukja (Old City House)**
[125 G1] Pajko Maalo 14, opposite the east side of
the Macedonian National Theatre; 📞 02 3131 376.
This beautifully renovated old-style Macedonian
house from 1836 is atmospheric, complete with
intricate wooden ceiling & traditional food. $$$
✕ **Lira** [120 B3] Nikola Tesla 11; 📞 02 3061 726;
www.lyra.com.mk. Excellent traditional live music
every evening. Fireplace & patio. Good lamb in a
cream sauce. $$$

✘ **Kaj Maršalot** [124 D3] Bd Kliment Ohridski; ☎ 02 322 3829; ⊕ Mon–Sat 08.00–01.00, Sun 12.00–23.59. Decked out in true Yugonostalgia with busts of Tito & waiters in red pioneer scarves. Traditional music & food add to the atmosphere. Great full cooked b/fasts. $$

✘ **Makedonska Kukja** [135 B2] Slavej Planina 2, near the Kale & the Turkish Embassy; ☎ 02 3216 016.

Local atmosphere, local prices ($$)

✘ **Čamo** [124 B2] Mihail Sokov 6a, down a small garden path to the left of Bikestop on Michel Sokov; ☎ 02 316 1130. Čamo is another unassuming place which is so popular that you may need a reservation during peak lunchtimes. Try their *sarma*, braised tongue & *pavlaka* (sour cream cheese).

✘ **Dane** [124 D4] Božin Stijkov bb, opposite the Dutch Embassy; ☎ 02 3229 457. Dane serves very good *pleckavica* (hamburger patties) & *meso vo salamura* (pork preserved in salt vats).

✘ **Dva Elena (Two Deers)** [120 A5] Zagrebska 31; ☎ 02 3082 382. An excellent steakhouse.

✘ **Javor Mrzenci** [120 A2] Signposted as Meana B on Bd Oktomvriski Revolucija, near the Aleksandar Palace; ☎ 02 3097 070. Small & local. Very good lamb chops.

✘ **Kaj Jole** [125 E2] Maksim Gorki bb; ☎ 02 322 0529. This is the hangout of the Macedonian Writers' Association. Its basic décor & unassuming signage (Jole is written in Cyrillic above the entrance at the street, then take the 2nd door on the left down the corridor) belie its good, traditional food.

✘ **Kibo** [125 E3] Vasil Glavinov bb, Paloma Bjanka business centre, 2nd Floor; ☎ 02 3133 535. Good salad bar, hearty soups, fried squid, apple strudel & fresh sweet beetroot juice (*džus od cvekot*).

✘ **Krigla** [124 C1] Ohridski Kliment 8, cnr of Ilinden; ☎ 02 3117 869. National restaurant. Nice atmosphere.

✘ **Lutz** [125 G4] Železnička bb (noticeable by the smoke & steam pouring out of the coke-stove chimney by the front door); ☎ 02 3110 306. It serves particularly impressive *ražnič* (skewered meats & vegetables) on a small sword, which takes about

This building was the home of Josif Mihaijlovski, the 1st mayor of Skopje from 1929–41, who was appointed by the king of Royalist Yugoslavia. The interior has been beautifully restored to give a sense of royal times & displays a number of the achievements of Skopje's 1st mayor. The menu is not extensive but the food is excellent. Try their minced-meat stuffed aubergines with their toasted unleavened bread, *pishipishi*. $$

40mins to cook, so make sure you order a starter to stave off the hunger whilst wafts of your sizzling *ražnič* tantalise your taste buds. Also to be recommended is their thinly sliced *džigr* (liver). Fried to perfection in local herbs & seasonings, it is like liver you will never have eaten in an English-speaking country! No frills, but the real McCoy.

✘ **Mechos** [124 C2] Leninova 38 (next to the Chinese restaurant); ☎ 02 3166 659. Good pizzas & cooked b/fasts. The rest of the menu is average.

✘ **Mala Stanica** [120 A4] Moskovska 26 (not to be confused with the bar & art centre on Železnička); ☎ 02 3061 024. Run by the chefs of Macedonia's 1st president, the food here is exceptionally good, especially for the price. Richard Gere ate here when filming for *Hunting Party*, & his photo is on the wall as you enter. Try *tikvica meze* (courgette spread) to start, & *sutljaš* (rice pudding cake) for dessert.

✘ **Momir** [124 B5] Ivo Lola Ribar bb; ☎ 02 3211 011. Specialises in local fish & traditional dishes.

✘ **Nacional** [125 G2] Vasil Agilarski, opposite the park by the Trgovski Centar; ☎ 02 3214 200. Has excellent pizza bread served as a big domed spaceship accompanied by live elevator music. Lovely outdoor patio.

✘ **Orach** [124 C4] At the end of Ivo Ribar Lola opposite the Bulgarian Embassy; ☎ 02 3223 933. A cosy winter restaurant with a fireplace & serves great beef stroganoff. Sadly its patio seating is very noisy.

✘ **Žabar (Frog)** [124 D1] Kej 13 Noemvri bb; ☎ 02 3132 411. The only restaurant actually overlooking the Vardar River. Good spare ribs (*rebra*). No frog!

Slightly further out of town in the City Park on the street dividing the stadium from the park proper are a number of upmarket traditional restaurants, all of which serve good food:

✘ **Anja** [124 C1] ☎ 02 3161 377; www.anja.com.mk. Less traditional, more pizza-pasta. Popular place in the park. $$$

✘ **Ezerce** [124 A1] ☎ 02 3122 389. Surrounded by a small moat hosting ducks & swans. $$$

✘ **Tomče Sofka** [124 C1] ☎ 02 3117 250. Good traditional food & a small hotel upstairs. $$$

✘ **Uranija** [120 C3] ☎ 02 3118 030. Connected with the tennis courts. Traditional food. $$$

TURKISH ($) Turkish cuisine can be found mostly in Čaršija, the old Turkish side of town. *Kebapci* at any of these restaurants is very good especially if accompanied with grilled red peppers and a beer, but my personal favourite is at **Turist** [135 B4] at the north entrance to Kapan An, where the bread is always grilled with smotherings of *kepabci* dripping and plenty of *vegeta* seasoning. *Burek* and *baklava* are also popular. On the south side of the river, the *kebapci* at **Destan** [125 F2], next to Barista on 11th Oktomvri, is very good, and is claimed to use a special family recipe handed down over several generations. Their bread is not as good though and they only offer *kebapci*.

ITALIAN

✘ **Mulino** [124 B5] Ivo Lola Ribar bb; ✆ 02 3232 877. Vodenica in Macedonian, this restaurant sports a decorative waterwheel & fishpond. Very popular with government & ambassadors. If you want to eat during the popular eating hours after 20.00 you may need to phone in advance to reserve a table. $$$$

✘ **Vittoria** [125 F4] Mito Hadži Vasilev Jasmin 35a; ✆ 02 3227 266. Upmarket setting. Variety of salads, pizzas & fresh sea fish. $$$$

✘ **Miracoli** [135 D4] Mavrovka shopping centre; ✆ 02 3231 549. Good food at a good price, fast & usually busy. Staff speak good German. $$$

✘ **Tiglio's** [124 A3] Slavka Nedič 15, opposite the western end of Debarca St; ✆ 02 3124 073; ☻ 10.00–24.00. Difficult to find even with a taxi, but good food & an atmospheric quiet patio. Antipasto calabrese, roast pepper salad, pastas, gorgonzola beefsteak. $$$

✘ **Toscana** [120 A5] Ivo Lola Ribar 72a; ✆ 02 307 9994. By far the best Italian cuisine in town as recommended by Italians. Small & personable. The head Italian-trained chef & owner, Vlado, will recommend his freshest pasta of the day & latest culinary delights, & they also do a mean tagliata à la rosmarin. $$$

✘ **Da Gino's** [120 F2] Trgovski Centar, 2nd Floor; ✆ 02 3121 109. This place offers the best pizzas, made in true Italian style. Impressive fresh seafood platter, squid ink pasta & very good beef carpaccio. $$

✘ **Dal Met Fu** [125 F2] On the main square; ✆ 02 3112 482. Lots of outside seating from which to observe the square & even in the winter the glass-fronted restaurant offers lots of sunlit areas as well as upper seating in a more cosy atmosphere. Has an excellent salad bar of some of the best Italian antipasti. The owner has 2 other restaurants, **Dal Fufol** [125 E5] & a fast-food version **Fufufu** [125 E5], both on Vodnjanska St. $$

OTHER FOREIGN FARE AND BREAKING THE MOULD

✘ **Den i Nokj (Jour et Nuit, Day & Night)** [120 A1] Aco Šopov bb; ✆ 02 3096 096. Serves refreshingly small portions of good French food in a swanky upmarket atmosphere. Rather pricey. Traditional & slightly cheaper Macedonian food downstairs. $$$$

✘ **Nobu** [124 C2] Leninova 29; ✆ 02 3121 123. Sushi lovers can only hope that this place will stay open & expand its menu. Sake & salmon abound, but *tobiko*, *uni* & other rarer delicacies might take some years to tempt the Macedonian palate. Also serves some good stir-fries. $$$$

✘ **Shanghai** [124 C3] Leninova 36; ✆ 02 3228 100. Serves excellent Shanghainese food. Most of the rest of the food is imported from China, & the tofu is exquisitely fresh & made on the premises. Take-away service available. Try their salt & pepper fried prawns, fish or pork for something truly Chinese. $$$$$

✘ **Amigos** [125 F3] Maršal Tito/Makedonija 11; ✆ 02 3228 699. Less authentic Mexican, but a wide variety of cocktails for a very good price in a popular location. Also has a stall upstairs in Ramstore. $$$

✘ **Amika** [125 G2] Above the Irish Pub; ✆ 02 3113 488. Serves good quiche Lorraine, tagliatelle pesto Genovese & French onion soup. $$$

✘ **Bombay** [120 B6] Elisie Popovski 50; ✆ 02 306 7373. Serves good Indian food in a traditional setting, although their paneer is not authentic (probably a feta substitute). They also have a take-away menu. Buffet on Thu lunchtime. $$$

✘ **Stars Ocean** [124 C2] Pirinska 35; ✆ 02 3228 337. Authentic Chinese food, very reasonably priced & fairly popular. $$$

✘ **Garcia Mexican** [124 C5] Vasil Gjorgov (behind Beverly Hills shopping centre); ✆ 02 3128 280. The most authentic Mexican in town. Good value. $$

✘ **St Patrick's** [125 G2] Trgovski Centar, ground floor (facing the river); ✆ 02 3220 431. Aside from Guinness, this first of the Irish pubs to come to Skopje, has a surprisingly large menu of non-Balkan dishes, including stir-fries & curries. $$

✘ **Divino** [125 E3] Dame Gruev 7; ✆ 02 3296 588. Buffet style & reasonable quality for a decent price. Serves mostly traditional foods, sandwiches, soup, desserts & drinks. Nice seating area. Conveniently located. **$$**

✗ Trend [125 E2] Ploštad Makedonija, Nikola Vapčarov 2; ✆ 02 3132 425; ⊕ 08.00–04.00. As its name suggests, this is one of the places to be seen. Modern menu, 3 b/fast choices & lots of cocktails. **$$**

CROATIAN COAST

✗ Dalma [124 B4] 227 Ulica (cnr with Petar Poparsov); ✆ 02 324 6616; www.dalma.com.mk; ⊕ Mon–Sat 10.00–24.00, Sun 13.00–24.00. Very good Dalmatian dishes in a small exclusive atmosphere. Superb fresh octopus (best eaten with truffle oil), lamb chops & salt baked fish. **$$$$**

✗ McDonald's [125 E3] Dimitri Čupovski 13; ✆ 02 3130 131. Also on Jane Sandanski at Aerodrom & on Bd Metropolit Teodisij Gologanov next to the Vero hypermarket. If you're desperate there's always the familiar double cheeseburger with large fries & Coke. Ivo Ribar Lola has a kids' play area, & a drive-in. **$$**

✗ Kvarner [120 B3] Andon Dukov 27; ✆ 02 3090 752. Excellent Istrian seafood flown in fresh. Try their fish carpaccio, sea bass & Malvazia white wine. **$$$$**

✗ Frutti di Mare [124 B2] Rade Končar 5; ✆ 02 3132 145; ⊕ closed Sun. Specialises in Dalmatian & Mediterranean seafood dishes. **$$$**

VEGETARIAN Only **Harmonija** is dedicated to vegetarian food in Skopje. Some places, such as **Dal Met Fu**, **Kibo** [125 E3], **Divino** [125 E3] and **Dabnica An** [125 E2], also have good salad bars and dishes. **Pivnica An** [135 B4] in Čaršija offer a few vegetarian plates, and most *meze* choices will be vegetarian. A lot of Italian places will have non-meat pizzas and pastas.

✗ Harmonija [121 G6] Skopjanka Mall 37; ✆ 02 2460 985; ⊕ closed Sun. Offers a feast of macrobiotic meals. The owner & cook, Tanja, earned her degree in macrobiotic cuisine in the US & is able to give you a dietary consultation on appointment. **$$$**

CAFÉ BARS, WINE BARS, COFFEE SHOPS AND TEA HOUSES Skopje's popular strip is from Intro café bar and Buddha cabaret nightclub at the old railway station and current Museum of Skopje [125 F4] all the way along Maršal Tito Makedonija pedestrian area to the café bars on the ground floor of the Trgovski Centar facing the river, ending with Process nightclub and St Patrick's Irish Pub [125 G2]. The cafés along the pedestrian area often sport large comfortable armchairs outside under big shady umbrellas to help you while away a summer afternoon. Other popular places outside the pedestrian area include:

♀ Lezet [124 C3] Cnr of Nicola Trimpare & Leninova. Also runs a bohemian theme with intimate seating cubicles facing a small fountain in the middle of the bar. Slightly more well-heeled than New Age or Orient House (see below).

♀ Mr Jack's [124 D3] Partizanska Odredi 3; ✆ 02 3231 999. A true Irish bar, as even the Irish in Skopje would claim, but hard to find back off the main road at the bottom of a high-rise complex. Pleasant, relaxing & welcoming.

⬛ New Age [124 D4] Kosta Šahov 9. A welcome alternative to Skopje's usual smoke-laden cafés, offering a rich menu of black, green & fruit teas, milkshakes, *kefirs*, alternative coffees & cocktails in a garden atmosphere with low seats, floor seating & cushions. This is where you'll find that mix of East meets West, reminiscent of the great Viennese coffee houses, if a little more bohemian. The tea house has lots of board games to while away the hours, as well

as a pet black cockerel & a female peacock in the garden.

⬛ Orient House [124 D4] Ivo Lola Ribar. Very bohemian, very relaxed. Good *salep* (wild orchid root drink) sprinkled with chocolate.

♀ Piazza Liberta [125 E3] Dimitri Čupovski 24; ⊕ 08.00–24.00. Also known as Kikiriki, meaning peanut, due to the free peanuts served with your drinks, the shells of which are simply thrown on the floor. Old reading-room atmosphere with shelves filled with books & big upstairs windows that look out onto the street. Named after the square that used to be here before the 1963 earthquake.

⬛ Tito Broz [124 A3] Partizanska. Nothing Yugonostalgic about this place, which styles itself on a Starbucks-type atmosphere & menu with long flavoured coffees, hot chocolate (not the pudding type), cookies & cakes. Wi-Fi available for the addicted.

♀ **Vinoteka Temov** [135 B4] Gradište 1a, Stara Čaršija; ☎ 02 3212 779; ⊕ 11.00–01.00. At last a quaint wine bar in the old town, serving a wide variety of Macedonia's own finest wines as well as an extensive range of wines from abroad. Live music is played most evenings, including traditional *chalgia* on Wed. This place is so popular that you will need a reservation at least a day in advance for a table after 19.00.

ENTERTAINMENT

Despite its size, but being the capital, Skopje has a choice of theatre, dance, concerts and cinema, as well as pubs and nightclubs. The Skopje Tourist Information booklet, available free every month from many travel agencies and hotels, lists a full calendar of events in the city, as well as many useful addresses and telephone numbers.

THEATRES AND CONCERT HALLS

🎭 **Dom na Armija** (Army Hall) [125 F3] Maršal Tito bb; ☎ 02 3118 450. Holds classical concerts once a week on Thu at 20.00 except in Jul, Aug & Sep.
🎭 **Dramski Theatre** [120 A4] Šekspirova 15; ☎ 02 3063 453
🎭 **Macedonian National Theatre** [125 G1] Quay Dimitar Vlahov; ☎ 02 3114 060. Stages opera & ballet.
🎭 **Centar Teatar** [125 E4] Kliment Ohridski; ☎ 02 3164 667. Hosts modern drama & plays produced by the Macedonian National Theatre.

🎭 **Detski Teatr** [125 F2] Dimitri Čupovski 4; ☎ 02 3222 619
🎭 **Theatre of National Minorities** [135 D1] Nikola Martinoski 41, Čaršija; ☎ 02 3296 583. Holds plays in Albanian & Turkish.
🎭 **Universal Hall** [124 B3] Partizanski Odredi; ☎ 02 3224 158. Holds concerts 2 or 3 times a week, both classical & modern jazz/rock. Skopje's jazz festival is held here for a week every Oct.

CINEMAS Skopje has several small cinemas. Try:

◾ **Dom na Armija** [125 F3] Maršal Tito bb; ☎ 02 311 8450. Shows films on a projector screen in a large auditorium. All films are shown in their original language & tend to come out a few months after their release in their country of origin.
◾ **Frosina Cinema** [125 G1] Youth Culture Centre, Quay Dimitar Vlahov; ☎ 02 311 5805. Often shows art or foreign movies, usually a different one every evening at 20.00.
◾ **Millennium** [125 F2] Trgovski Centar, 1st Floor; ☎ 02 312 0389. The biggest & best at 150MKD.
◾ **Ramstore** [125 F4] ☎ 02 317 8030. Has 2 small new screens also at 150MKD.

NIGHTLIFE

Bars Many of the café bars mentioned above are popular all through the evening and into the small hours. Other tried and tested bars that draw a faithful crowd are:

♀ **Bastion** [124 C2] Pirinska 43; ☎ 02 3223 636; ⊕ Mon–Thu 08.00–24.00, Fri & Sat 08.00–01.00, Sun 10.00–24.00. Opposite Nobu sushi bar. Popular place & sometimes the hangout of the film director Milčo Mančevski.
♀ **Cox** [124 A5] Ivo Lola Ribar; ⊕ Sun–Thu 10.00–24.00, Fri & Sat 10.00–01.00. Salsa evenings on Tue & Thu. Free lessons for novices are given at 20.00. Free Wi-Fi available here.
♀ **Café Art** [124 D2] Partizanski; ⊕ 20.00–01.00. Has laidback music & old hits accompanying interesting artistic installations by the owner Malinski.
♀ **Havana Club** [120 C3] ⊕ 20.00–03.00. In the city park. Very popular in the summer with large outdoor area.

♀ **Jukebox** [124 B2] Orče Nikolov 99; ⊕ 20.00–03.00. Small & cosy with live jazz on Thu night, & dedicated DJs most nights. Named after the original 1940s jukebox still to be found there.
♀ **Mala Stanica** [125 E4] Zeleznička bb; ⊕ 20.00–01.00. An unimposing green front hides the relaxed atmosphere in this café bar serving the art centre that is also housed here.
♀ **Mama's** [124 D3] Kliment Ohridski 60; ☎ 02 3239 120; ⊕ Sun–Thu 10.00–24.00, Fri & Sat 10.00–01.00. Wonderful blues & jazz bar with comfortable seating & live piano or jazz trios providing an atmosphere in which you can still (just about) talk to accompanying friends.

♀ **Marakana** [124 A1] City Park; ⏰ 21.00–03.00, restaurant downstairs ⏰ 08.00–24.00. Live jazz upstairs every evening after 22.00.
♀ **Van Gogh** [124 B2] Next to Bikestop on Michel Sokov; ⏰ Sun–Thu 09.00–24.00, Fri & Sat 09.00–01.00. Another bar frequented by Mančevski when he is in town. Offers salsa on Wed & mixed/gay nights on Sun. Quiet setting spilling out onto the cobblestone road.

Clubs By far the most popular clubs in the summer are the outdoor nightclubs in the city park. **Colosseum** [120 B2] (*www.colosseum.com.mk*), **Cabrio** [120 B2] and **Element** [120 C2] (*www.element.com.mk*) all run a mixed programme over the summer inviting DJs from abroad such as Heaven and Pete Tong, as well as modern Balkan artists and sounds. Element retreats to its winter quarters under the TC Plaza when the weather gets too cold for the outdoor club. Coloseum's winter quarters are behind the post office at the railway station.

Hollywood [125 F2], on the top floor of the Trgovski Centar above the Millennium Cinema, offers dancing most nights. Next door to St Patrick's pub is **Process** nightclub [125 F2] (✆ *02 3215 476, 075 414 004;* e *contact@process.com.mk; www.process.com.mk;* ⏰ *Tue–Sun 23.00–04.00).* **Club MNT** and **Jazz FM**, both beneath the Macedonian National Theatre [125 G1], are also lively scenes after 22.00. **Buddha** [125 F4], underneath the Museum of Skopje, is not quite as laidback as its name might imply. For more information on Skopje's lively club scene see www.skopjeclubbing.com.mk.

SHOPPING

FOOD The **Vero supermarket** [120 A5] chain and the **Ramstore** [125 F4] on Mito Hadzi Vasilev have the widest range of food available in Skopje, including ginger, basil, fresh limes, mint and horseradish sauce and fresh seafood (from Greece). Another supermarket chain is **Tinex** [120 B6], which along with Vero and the Ramstore, also takes all major credit cards. Local fresh produce is best bought from the big fresh markets either at the Bit Pazar (see below) or the **Green market** [125 G3] on the western corner of Kočo Racin and 11th Oktomvri, or **Bunjakovač market** [124 B3] on Partizanski just after Leninova.

The **Bit Pazar** [135 D1] is the biggest outdoor market in Skopje. Not only does it have fresh vegetables, fruit, meat products, fish, spices, pulses and tea, it also has a large ironmongery section and, in fact, you can buy almost anything there. Now held every day, it used to be held on Tuesdays and Fridays only, following a 600-year-old tradition, first held by the monks of the Monastery of Sv Gjorgi Gorga. The monastery no longer exists but the market is still in the same spot and has expanded over the former grounds of the monastery.

There are a few **health food** stores in Skopje under the Biona chain. The closest to the centre of town is behind the hospital on 11th Oktomvri [125 G2].

Makedonska Vinoteka, specialising in all Macedonia's **wines**, is listed on page 284.

SOUVENIRS AND LOCAL CRAFTWARE Conveniently many souvenirs are now sold in a number of shops around the town, although these are still sometimes a little obscure. In addition to Hotel Arka [135 D3], **Ikona Souvenirs** [125 F3] at Lui Paster 19 has a wide variety of mementos including handicrafts, T-shirts, replica icons and golden masks, local wines and spirits and many other things besides. There is also a small souvenir shop on the ground floor of the Trgovski Centar [125 F2], and another on the corner of Maksim Gorki and Dame Gruev [125 E3].

The old town is the best place to get genuine locally made handicrafts such as leather slippers, hand-embroidered cloths, musical instruments and ethnic-style clothing. Šutka (see page 151) is the place to order lavish Roma costumes.

CLOTHES Skopje is awash with shoe shops and there are also plenty of clothes shops. Most of these products are mass produced in China and imported. The Trgovski Centar [125 F2], City Mall [125 F2], Sorabija [125 G2], Ramstore [125 F4] and the pedestrian area linking these main shopping malls offer the likes of Benetton, Wolfords, Hugo Boss and Mango. Local tailors in the old town are still cheap especially for repairs and copying, although the choice of materials from which to make clothes is not the best. For a top-class men's **tailor** used by the diplomatic community try Borče on 11 Oktomvri in Kisela Voda [121 E6] (\ 02 3133 065, 075 230 061, 070 278 585; e *apostolovzoran@yahoo.com*). He offers prompt service and a wide choice of materials. You can expect to pay €100–140 for a two- or three-piece suit. Women's suits are also available. Angelkovski [124 A4], used by the first president of Macedonia, pays good attention to detail and is slightly more expensive, although his choice of materials is not as wide as at Borče's.

BOOKS The best bookstore chain in Macedonia is Ikona Books. There are three stores in Skopje, on the ground floor of the Ramstore [125 F4], at Dimitri Cupovski 22 opposite McDonalds [125 E3], and at Partizanski Odredi 9 diagonally opposite the Orthodox cathedral Kliment i Ohridski [125 D2]. All are marked on the Skopje map on page 124. They carry an extensive range of English books, as well as Bradt and other travel guides. Ikona also has stores in Tetovo Ramstore, Ohrid, Bitola and Strumica.

OTHER PRACTICALITIES

POST The main post office, Post Office No 1 [125 E1], is the large building immediately to the east of the Stone Bridge on the south side of the river. It is open from 07.00 to 17.30 Monday to Saturday and from 07.00 to 14.30 on Sunday. The telephone centre located in the main post office is open 24 hours. Calls at the post office or at telephone kiosks on the street need to be made either with tokens or using a pre-paid phone card. Both can be purchased from post offices and newspaper stands. Mobile phone cards are 354MKD including several hundred minutes.

INTERNET There are numerous internet cafés around town and they are very cheap. Contact Café on the top floor of the Trgovski shopping centre [125 F2] charges 120MKD for one hour. For half that price you can use the internet centre opposite La Caffe on Maršal Tito [125 E2], or at Ivo Lola Ribar 22 [125 E3]. Black-and-white print services are available at both; colour is available at Contact Café. Some of the smaller internet cafés may not have the latest web browsers so if you are trying to access a fairly advanced site then you are better off going to the Contact Café. Wi-Fi is available at Barista [125 F2] and Dal Met Fu [125 F2] on the city square and at Tito Broz Café [124 A3] on Partizanski.

WHAT TO SEE AND DO

SUGGESTED ONE-DAY TOURS If you are in Skopje for just one day and do not have your own transport, the following itinerary will give you a good overview of the city: Kale – Sveti Spas – Mustafa Pasha Mosque – *kebapci* lunch outside Kapan An – Čifte Amam Gallery – Suli An – Kuršumli Han – Bit Pazar – dinner at Dab Pivnica or Pivnica An. You could also spend half a day taking the local bus to Katlanovska Banja hot springs (see *Chapter 6*, page 150).

If you have a car, or can afford a taxi or guided tour, then a trip up to Vodno, on to the Monastery of Sv Pantelejmon and back via Lake Matka in the morning is well worth the extra effort for a taste of the beautiful mountainous scenery of Macedonia (see *Chapter 6* for information on these places). The afternoon should take in at least Kale and Čaršija.

MUSEUMS AND GALLERIES

City Museum of Skopje [125 F4] (*Mito Hadzivasilev Jasmin;* ❏ *02 3114 742;* ⊕ *Mon–Sat 09.30–17.00, Sun 09.30–13.00; entry 100MKD*) The museum is housed in the old railway station on the southern end of Maršal Tito. The original Skopje–Thessaloniki railway started from this station in 1873, but the present building was built in 1940–41. The earthquake of 26 July 1963 destroyed a large portion of the building and station, leaving the station clock fixed at 05.17 when the earthquake hit. The clock hands have remained at this time ever since and the building became the city museum soon after. The new railway station is now 20 minutes' walk away further east. The museum exhibits a permanent history of the city through the centuries (although the 20th-century section has been closed for years) as well as temporary exhibitions of local artists, architects and designers. A small brochure in English can be obtained at the front desk.

Daud Pasha Amam Gallery [135 B5] (*Kruševska 1a;* ❏ *02 3133 102, 02 3124 219; entry 100MKD*) This is the obvious copper cupola building to your right as you enter the old town from the Stone Bridge. It is well worth a visit just for the building itself. Built in the 15th century as a bathhouse while Skopje was under Turkish rule, it was then one of the most magnificent of its kind, boasting 13 different-sized copper cupolas and varying degrees of hot steam rooms and cold baths separated for men and women. Nowadays only the beautiful roof and ceiling architecture remain. The gallery houses mostly contemporary art, although there are a few older pieces, one dating back to the 13th century. The art is an added bonus to the building if you like modern art, although a good working Turkish steam bath in Skopje is sorely missed.

Čifte Amam National Art Gallery [135 C3] (*Bitpazarska bb;* ❏ *02 3109 566, 02 3126 856; entry 50MKD*) This is another former Turkish bathhouse, the second largest in Skopje, built at the beginning of the 16th century under the orders of Isa Bey, the son of Isak Bey. It now houses various travelling exhibitions and lies immediately south of Suli An. Another old bathhouse in Čaršija is Šengul Amam (also known as Gurciler Amam) next to Kuršumli Han. Like Čifte Amam, it was badly damaged in the 1963 earthquake, but this bathhouse has not been repaired.

Museum of Contemporary Art [135 A1] (*Muzej na Sovrjeme Uumetnost, Samoilova bb, PO Box 482;* ❏ *02 3117 734; www.msuskopje.org.mk* ⊕ *Tue–Sun 09.00–16.00; entry 50MKD*) The museum lies to the west of Kale on top of the hill. As its name suggests, it houses contemporary art. A large, airy building, it holds 4,360 prominent international as well as national exhibits. Many of the exhibits are donations given to Macedonia after the 1963 earthquake when the 1963 New York convention of the International Association of the Plastic Arts called upon the artists of the world to support the city's reconstruction through associated artwork. The custom-built museum opened in 1970 with a remarkable collection of international donations created especially for this museum. Such pieces include a canvas named *Head of a Woman* (1963) by Pablo Picasso, which is usually stored in the basement, but can be viewed upon request.

National Museum of Macedonia [135 B2] (*Čurčiska bb;* ❏ *02 311 6044;* ⊕ *Tue–Fri 08.00–16.00, Sat 09.00–15.00, Sun 09.00–13.00; entry 100KD*) The museum

French cemetery, US embassy
Museum of Contemporary Art
SAMOILOVA
Turkish embassy
Makendonska Kukja
PROHOR
SLAVEJ PLANINA
PČINSKI
SVEKARSKA
ULICA 123
ULICA 121
ULICA 382
ULICA 122
Hidaverdi
ULICA 133
National Minorities Theatre
Aladža Mosque
Bit Pazar
NIKOLA MARTINOSKI
Kuršumli An
National Museum of Macedonia
OPINČARSKA
SARAČKA
ULICA 183
Mustafa Pasha Mosque
Kale entrance
Old post office
Arasta Mosque
Bezisten Covered Market
Museum of Skopje Bazaar
Kjuršiski An
MUTAVDŽISKA
TAFTADŽISKA
Kose Kadi
RM
LEB LEBDŽISKA
Cifte Amam
National Art Gallery
Fountain
BIT PAZARSKA
ULICA 116
ULICA 111
BD KRSTE MISIRKOV
Sv Spas
LAZAR
TANEV
Simonium Travel & souvenir shop
Murat Pasha Mosque
Arka
SAMOILOVA
Kale
Vinoteka Temov
JORGANDŽISCA
TAFTADŽISKA
Kapan An
Pivnica An
Turist (Kebapci restaurant)
Ilinden shopping centre
T'Ga Za Jug
KAZANDŽISKA
Miracoli
Skenderbej Monument
BD GOCE DELČEV
Sv Dimitri
Daud Pasha Amam National Gallery
CRVENA SKOPSKA
II MART
Vardar
Stonebridge Stone bridge
0 ——— 100m
0 ——— 100yds
Macedonian National Theatre
The Swan (English Pub)
STIV NAUMOV
Kiril i Metodi Library
British Council

lies between Mustafa Pasha Mosque and Kuršumli An in Čaršija. It is not marked up as the 'Museum of Macedonia' from the outside and the entrance is merely a break in the red railings on the southernmost side of the complex. If you haven't got much time to visit ancient sites in Macedonia, then the museum is a good way to get an overview of all the civilisations that have passed along the River Vardar. Many of the best iconostases in the country are also housed here, and there are some excellent exhibits of the world wars, including weaponry and ammunition. Many of the exhibits are being revised and the number of texts in English is increasing.

Some of the archaeological exhibitions are held in Kuršumli An, access to which can only be gained through the main museum. Originally a tavern and then for a long time a political prison (see below for a history of the inn), Kuršumli An is open Monday to Friday.

Museum of Skopje Bazaar [135 C3] (↘ *02 311 4742; entry free*) Suli An, another old trading inn, houses the Museum of the Skopje Bazaar which holds an interesting exhibition on trading life in Skopje during the Ottoman Empire. The museum and exhibits are in need of repair and all the text is in Macedonian but it is free to enter. The museum itself is upstairs, and downstairs is the university's Department of Applied Arts. You can walk around the courtyard to see the students working in the downstairs rooms and the department's entrance hall has several modern art paintings. Exhibitions and public lectures are advertised in Macedonian on the front door. Suli An lies in the centre of the old bazaar area and the front entrance to the inn often looks closed, but it is usually in fact open.

Military Museum of Macedonia [121 H7] (*Military Academy in Aerodrom;* ↘ *02 328 3624;* ⊕ *Mon–Fri 09.00–15.00; entry free*) The museum covers Macedonian military history in the broadest sense of the term, starting with the campaigns of Aleksandar the Great up until World War II.

Macedonian Museum of Natural History [120 B3] (*Ilinden 86;* ↘ *02 3117 669;* ⊕ *Tue–Sun 09.00–16.00; entry 30MKD*) There is not much to see in the museum and all the text is in Macedonian, but there are some impressive remains of prehistoric animals found in Negotino and other areas of Macedonia, and lots of stuffed eagles and vultures as well as other animals of the region. Make sure you have small change as the ticket attendant does not. Next door to the Natural History Museum is the **Skopje Zoo**. A visit here is not recommended unless you want to see how bad a zoo can be. Most of the safari animals are dead already, except for one chimpanzee and three baboons. There is also one very lonely white bear, lots of penned-in ruminants and birds, and several stray wild dogs. Entry (at 50MKD) will make you want to become an animal rights campaigner.

Museum of Coinage [121 F5] (*National Bank of the Republic of Macedonia, Bd Kuzman Josifovski Pitu 1;* ↘ *02 3108 108;* ⊕ *Mon–Fri 09.00–15.00; entry free*) A truly amazing collection which will take you through the history of coinage right from Paeonian times. This is by far the best presentational museum in Macedonia, with literature available in English. Bring ID in order to get through the main bank entrance.

CHURCHES, MONASTERIES AND CEMETERIES
Monastery of Sveti Spas (Holy Salvation) [135 B3] (↘ *02 3163 812, 02 3109 401*) This is the only remaining monastery in the centre of Skopje and houses one of the most beautiful churches. Its main entrance is at Makarije Frckovski 8 although it is easier to visit it from its top entrance on Samoilova opposite Kale. Some of the foundations of the monastery go back to the 14th century, before Ottoman times. Under Ottoman rule it became illegal for a church to be taller than a mosque, so the church was mostly rebuilt below ground in order to accommodate the height of the original church bell tower.

The present three-naved church dates from rebuilding in the 18th and 19th centuries. Three of the most famous woodcarvers of the time, Makarije Frckovski of Galičnik and the brothers Marko and Petar Filipovski from the Mijak village of Gari, worked for five years from 1819 to 1824 to create the 10m wide and 6m high iconostasis (the intricate woodwork divider between the nave and the main part of the church). The iconostasis is cut from the wood of walnut trees, and is made up of two rows of partly gold-inlaid icons depicting scenes from the Old and the New Testaments. Many of the scenes have been carved to reflect Macedonian traditions and folklore, such as the figure of Salome, who is dressed in traditional Macedonian garb. Among their more famous works, Frckovski and the Filipovski brothers carved even more stunning iconostases for the Monastery of Sv Jovan Bigorski in Mavrovo National Park and the Monastery of Sv Gavril in Lesnovo.

Sv Spas is also famous for housing the beheaded remains of the revolutionary Goce Delčev. Leader of the Independence for Macedonia Revolutionary Organisation (IMRO – to which the present-day government VMRO-DPMNE traces its roots), Delčev was beheaded in 1903, but his head, no doubt posted on the Stone Bridge as proof of his execution, was subsequently lost. His remains were exhumed and moved to the Sv Spas only in 1964.

Church of Sv Dimitri [135 A5] Also north of the river, the church is just west of the Stone Bridge. The original church was built in the 14th century and in typical Macedonian fashion the bell tower is separate from the main building. The present structure dates from the 19th century.

Cathedral of Sv Kliment of Ohrid [124 D2] (*Cnr Partizanski & Ohridski*) A modern 20th-century building shaped interestingly in the form of a dome with a smaller dome at each corner, making it easily mistaken as a modern mosque at a quick glance.

Church of Sv Gjorgi and British Cemetery [121 H3] (*First left off 16 Makedonska Brigada*) The cemetery houses over 100 graves of British servicemen who died during World Wars I and II. A service is held by the British Embassy there each November.

French Cemetery [120 D2] (*Samoilova bb, after the Museum of Contemporary Arts*) The cemetery houses the graves of almost 1,500 French servicemen who died in World War I. A tiny museum at the entrance displays documents and photos of the period.

MOSQUES The Čair and Čaršija districts of the old town have over 30 mosques. In the mid 17th century Evlija Čelebi, a famous Turkish travel writer of the time, noted 120 mosques in Skopje. Most were burnt down in the fire of 1689 started by the Austrian General Piccolomini in order to rid the town of a rampaging plague. A few of the mosques from that time remain.

Mustafa Pasha Mosque [135 B2] (*Samoilova, opposite the main entrance to Kale*) The largest and most ornately decorated of all the mosques in Skopje was built in 1492 at the order of Mustafa Pasha while he was Vizier of Skopje under Sultan Selim I. The entrance to the mosque is through a four-column porch, which is crowned with three cupolas and a 124-step white minaret rises from its western end. Inside, the pulpit and prayer recess is made from intricately worked marble and the walls are decorated with ornate paintings. The five windows in each wall are staggered, rising up the walls of the mosque to create a pyramid effect. Despite having stood the test of time well, the mosque did have to undergo major restoration after the earthquake of 1963 and still has a cracked dome. In the grounds of the mosque are Mustafa Pasha's mausoleum and his daughter Umi's sarcophagus.

Hjunkar Mosque [121 F4] Also known as the Sultan Murat Mosque, it pre-dates the Mustafa Pasha Mosque by some 50 years. It was built next to the Monastery of Sv Georgi Gorga near the present-day university of Sv Cyril and Methodius. At the time, the monastery was one of the most important monastic centres in the Balkans, but when Isak Bey, then commander of the Turkish army, built the **Aladža Mosque** [135 D1], the Pasha Bey Mausoleum (still visible in the grounds of the Aladža Mosque) and a *medresa* (school for teaching the Koran) on the actual grounds of the monastery, he effectively destroyed life at the monastery. The *medresa* no longer exists, nor the monastery, but both mosques remain on either side of Boulevard Krste Misirkov. The mausoleums of Sultan Beyhan and of Ali Pasha of Dagestan lie in the grounds of the Hjunkar Mosque.

Yayha Pasha Mosque [121 F3] Further north on Boulevard Krste Misirkov, it was built in 1504 for Yayha Pasha, the son-in-law of Sultan Bayazit II. Notable for its modern four-sided roof, it is the imposing mosque visible as you come off the highway from the airport into the centre of town. Originally, the prayer area was roofed with one large and five small domes, but these were destroyed in the last earthquake of 1963.

Murat Pasha Mosque [135 C3] Opposite Čifte Amam, this modern square-roofed mosque was built in 1802. The original 15th-century structure was burnt down when General Piccolomini set Skopje alight in 1689.

Kose Kadi Mosque [135 C3] At the western end of *Bezisten* (the covered market) above a passageway of shops, this 17th-century mosque was last renovated in 1993.

Hidaverdi Mosque [135 C1] Between Kuršumli An and the Theatre for Minorities, it looks more like a half-renovated shop front than a 16th-century mosque, despite having been restored in 1995. It lacks the usual distinguishing minaret.

Gazi Isa-Bey Mosque [121 F3] On Čairska, it once held one of the first libraries in Skopje. In the mosque grounds is a 560-year-old plane tree (*Platinus orientalis*).

HISTORICAL SITES
Kale Fortress [135 A3] The present-day site has probably seen some sort of occupied fortification since the Illyrians first came through from Greece to settle in Albania. Continuing excavations of the site have revealed artefacts dating back to the Thracian era of 200BC when the Dardanians fought from Kale to defend the surrounding area from the invading Romans.

The 1963 earthquake razed most of the fortress. Much of it is only now being restored. Some of the current visible structure dates from the 10th-century enlargement of the fort under Tsar Samoil. The ramp was partly built of stones from the ancient town of Skupi, which was destroyed in 518.

After crossing the Stone Bridge into the old town, the main gateway of Kale can be approached just after the flyover entering Čaršija, or a more scenic route can be taken a little further on by following the cobbled street up to Vinoteka Temov then taking the steps up to the forecourt of the Monastery of Sv Spas. The main entrance is opposite the old post office.

Now a well-kept tourist attraction (apart from the piles of rubbish thrown down from the top of the fortified outer wall), Kale served as a barracks to the Turkish army during Ottoman rule, and then to the JNA (Jugoslav National Army) until 1963. The restaurant, open in the summer to tourists, is the old army canteen. A drink there is welcome when the heat and exposure to the sun, making quite a difference in temperature between the river level and the top of the fortress, can parch the thirst very quickly most of the year round.

Kamen Most [120 D4] The 214m Stone Bridge, which joins the old Turkish town to what has now become the centre of town south of the river, was first built in the late 15th century under the orders of Sultan Mehmet II the Conqueror. By then the population of the city was increasing so rapidly, due to the draw of merchants to this important trading town, that people were already living beyond the original town walls. The only bridge across the river was many miles away further west, so a new bridge here, close to the main hub of the town, helped with the problem of overcrowding on the north side of the river as well as easing the arduous trading route into the town from the south.

The original stonework of 13 arches of travertine stone still stands, although the top of the bridge has been changed a number of times since it was built. Originally at a width of 6.33m, it was widened to 9.8m in 1909, and then returned to its original width in 1992. During the conflict of 2001 the bridge was badly damaged, and the fact that it has taken so long to be repaired (still missing its small lookout post in 2009) is a symbol of the difficult reconciliation between what has become the largely Muslim community in the old town and the remainder of the Macedonian community to the south of the bridge. Damage to the original lookout post during the first attempt to repair the bridge in 2002 has been a poor excuse, and even the Turkish Embassy demanded an explanation.

The bridge was originally built with stone pillar railings, used by the Ottoman rulers of Skopje to spike the heads of traitors and criminals. The bridge became a public execution place and, amongst many others, the Ottomans sentenced Karpoš, the 'King of Kumanovo', to death by impalement on the bridge in 1689.

Saat Kula [121 F3] The dark red-brick clock tower near Hjunkar Mosque (Sultan Murat Mosque) is the last remaining portion of the old city walls. Erected in the mid 16th century, the top half of the clock tower was originally made of wood and housed a clock brought over from Hungary. In 1904 the wooden structure was replaced with stone and a new clock was procured. That clock was then destroyed in the earthquake of 1963 and has not been replaced since.

Bezisten [135 C3] The covered marketplace of the old bazaar area is a courtyard-type building with more stores built inside the courtyard itself. It is located behind Čifte Amam to the northwest. Originally built in the 15th century for trading cloth and material, the store soon spilt outside the original structure, forming narrow little cobbled lanes between the one- and two-storey shops, which leaned onto each other. The old bazaar quickly became 18 different trading houses – goldsmiths, cobblers, ironmongers, corn exchange, etc – and the remnants of these can still be seen today. The Bezisten of today is a 19th-century structure, housing some non-governmental organisations, and is no longer reminiscent of its former glory.

Turkish trading inns Čaršija has a number of Turkish trading inns, which are well worth a visit, including Kuršumli An belonging to the Ragusan merchants, Suli An and Kapan An. These inns usually have one or two entrances but no windows on the outside. The entrances lead into a large courtyard, which is surrounded on all four sides on the first floor by wooden-balconied guest rooms looking out onto the courtyard. Underneath these, on the ground floor, were the stabling and storage quarters. There was often a well in the centre of the courtyard where guests would usually gather to while away the evening.

As you go past the old bazaar area of Čaršija from the Stone Bridge the first inn you will come to is **Kapan An** [135 B4]. Its walls now house several restaurants and bars both inside the inn and outside.

5

Further down the street towards Bitpazar is **Suli An** [135 C3], which is now the Museum of the Old Skopje Bazaar (see above).

Kuršumli An [135 C2], meaning Bullet or Lead Inn, to the northwest of Bitpazar is probably one of the most impressive inns of its period. At the time it was designed to stable up to 100 horses, and house their traders and owners. Some of the rooms even had their own fireplace, which was deemed quite a luxury in those times. In 1878 the building became the town prison. It now holds archaeological exhibitions as part of the Museum of Macedonia next door.

MONUMENTS AND STATUES Unlike many former communist cities, Skopje does not display the usual array of statues to communist heroes, although there are still plenty of communist/late 1960s–1970s-style buildings to be seen, such as the main government building [124 D1], main post office [125 E1] and the Macedonian National Theatre [125 F1]. There is a larger-than-life-size statue of Mother Teresa on Maršal Tito [125 F3], which was put up shortly after her house near the main square was demolished to make way for the Trgovski shopping centre. Her house has been reconstructed next to the statue and is now a museum. The site of her former house is marked with a small plaque at the western entrance to the Trgovski Centar.

After considerable controversy, a statue of Skenderbey [135 C4] (see box, page 234, for more about him) was erected on 28 November 2006 (Albanian Flag Day) in front of Ilinden shopping centre. An Albanian national hero, and a Catholic who stood up in the mid 15th century against the Ottoman colonisation of the area, the erection of his statue was controversial for three reasons. For many ethnic Macedonians, admitting the statue of an Albanian hero into Skopje touches upon a sore point regarding ethnic Albanian encroachment on ethnic Macedonian land, rights and nationhood. For the Turkish community (who once built the old town) Skenderbey is seen as the enemy. For the Islamic community, Skenderbey's reconversion back to Catholicism is seen as treachery. On the purely aesthetic side, the statue does a lot to enhance this modern concrete edge of the old town.

The centre-right government re-elected in 2008 has proposed to erect a statue of Alexander the Great in the main square. This is bound to cause problems with Macedonia's southern neighbour, Greece, just as the renaming of the airport to Alexander the Great has also increased friction between them recently (see page 23 for history of the issue).

ACTIVITIES

Aside from sightseeing, Skopje offers a host of sports facilities and outdoor pursuits. The southern bank of the River Vardar to the west of the Stone Bridge is paved all the way to the Aleksandar Palace Hotel and another 3km beyond. With views onto the surrounding mountains, the 6km stretch makes a wonderful walking, rollerblading, cycling or running route, and is a great place to see the locals taking a stroll too. It is lit at night most of the way.

The city **sports stadium** [120 C3] is on the river side of the city park. The Macedonian national football team can often be seen practising and playing there. Tickets for matches can be purchased at the stadium box office or from the Football Association of Macedonia (*8th Udarna Brigada 31a;* ℑ *02 3235 448, 02 3229 042*). The **Boris Trajkovski Stadium** [120 A2] (*Bd 8th Septemvri;* ℑ *02 3214 477*), named after the late president, who died in a plane crash in 2004, opened in 2008. It is an impressive building with four restaurants and a large sports bar, and is home to the Macedonian handball team.

Another big sports complex, including an outdoor swimming pool and an ice-skating rink in the winter, is **Kale Sports Hall** [120 D3] below the castle (⊕ *Mon–Thu 09.00–22.00, Fri, Sat & Sun 09.00–24.00*). There is an all-female gym, **Vitalis**, at Orče Nikolov 101 (✆ *070 268 559;* ⊕ *Mon–Sat 11.00–21.00*), near Juke Box bar. The **Olympiski Bazen–Prolet pool** [125 H2] at Kočo Racin bb (✆ *02 3162 958;* ⊕ *Tue–Fri 20.00–24.00, Sat/Sun 10.00–16.00, 20.00–24.00*). The pool complex also offers a fitness centre open every day 09.00–23.00, although it is not as pleasant to work out in as the fitness centre at the Aleksandar Palace Hotel (open to the public, see above). Next door to the Aleksandar Palace Hotel is the Olympic-size **Mladost Karpoš III indoor and outdoor pool** [120 A2] (✆ *02 3060 463*). A very nice bijou pool (good for practising turns) is downstairs in the **TCC Plaza Spa** [125 E3] at Vasil Glavinov 12 (✆ *02 3111 807*), including hot stone loungers and a gym (membership only). By far the nicest outdoor pool is the privatised army pool, **Bazen Biser** [121 H7], just off Kosta Novakovič in the Aerodrom part of town. It's open 10.00–18.00 and 21.30–01.00 every day and serves drinks and snacks. It's packed after midday so go early or in the evening. 100MKD entry fee.

For **horseriding** see page 157 in *Chapter 6*.

Tennis clubs are plentiful in Skopje, and private lessons cost 700–1000MKD per hour. Courts are an additional 300–450MKD per hour, with lighting adding another 100MKD. Try one of the following:

As [121 H6] Aerodrom; ✆ 02 240 3114. A big fitness complex with 10 tennis courts.
Forca [120 A4] Londonska; ✆ 02 306 0333. Two outdoor courts. Pleasant atmosphere.
Jug [120 C3] City Park; ✆ 02 3118 530
ABC [120 C3] Ilindenska; ✆ 02 3063 622. Also has a popular café & drinks bar.

Hipodrom [121 H3] ✆ 02 2521 444. Outdoor courts, summer only, near Avtokomanda.
Kamnik [121 H4] Kamnik bb (see page 127 for directions); ✆ 02 252 3522. Excellent restaurant.
Evroset [120 A1] Skupi; ✆ 02 309 5385. Nice viewing area & café looking down on the courts.
Squash Club [120 D3] Lazar Ličenoski 31; ✆ 02 322 7077. Nice café with a view on the courts.

There are two **bowling alleys** in Skopje. One is at the bottom of the Trgovski Centar [125 F2] and the other is at the Bellevue Hotel (see map on page 145) near the airport. Unlike in the US, bowling here is with slightly smaller balls that have no finger holes.

Finally, the **Aviation Association** [125 E3] on Dimitri Čupovski (✆ *02 3227 672; www.vfm.org.mk/en_clubs.html*) offers private flying, parachuting and paragliding courses.

For other sporting events and opportunities try contacting the Sport Association of Skopje at Jordan H Džinot 12a (✆ *02 3117 687, 02 3228 624*).

After a day of sports or hiking, a good opportunity to relax and pamper yourself, especially if you can't get as far as Katlanovska hot springs (page 150), is to go to **Aseana Royal Spa** (*Sv Apostol Guslarot 12;* ✆ *02 3246 442;* ⊕ *Tue–Fri 10.00–22.00, Sat–Sun 12.00–20.00*). Treatments include Balinese body massage, facials, body toning and pedicures. Prices range from 400MKD for a foot massage to 4,200MD for an exotic flower bath.

6

Outside Skopje

> After a ten-mile drive from Skopje we arrived at the little monastery which is
> called Matka, or the Mother, because it is so kind to barren women ... on a broad
> ledge under dripping cliffs, here hung with purple flowers, among wind-swept trees
> that leaned laterally over the abyss ...
>
> *Black Lamb and Grey Falcon*, Rebecca West, 1941

Most of Macedonia is accessible from Skopje in one day, depending on how long
you want to spend at a place, and whether you're prepared to return after dark.
Aside, then, from places covered elsewhere in this book, here are a few suggested
day trips closer to Skopje.

MOUNT VODNO

Mount Vodno at 1,066m is the prominent summit to the south of Skopje topped
by a 75m yellow steel cross. It takes almost three hours to walk up from the town
centre, and is a popular walk with Macedonians on a sunny weekend. It is possible
to drive up to the summit during the day in the winter or between 20.00 at night
and 09.00 in the morning in the summer, but on a popular walking day the road
is firmly closed at Hotel Vodno, and parking can overflow from the hotel car park
for hundreds of metres down the road.

The panorama of Skopje from the summit is spectacular and all the main
sites can be viewed easily. The mountain hut **Dare Djambaz** (☎ *02 3234 365,
02 3143 236*) at the summit offers 50 beds, basic food, a collegial atmosphere
and welcome shelter if the weather has turned foul on the way up the
mountain. It's well worth the visit just for the numerous photos of
Macedonians who have climbed mountains around the world to proudly fly
their flag, and also for the hot sweet mountain tea (*planinski čaj*) at a mere
15MKD per cup.

The steel cross at the top is quite the monstrosity and provoked a lot of
controversy among Albanians when it was first started in 2002. Some ethnic
Albanians, most of whom live on the opposite side of the valley, see the cross as
a reminder of their domination by the ethnic Macedonian majority. It costs
100MKD to take the lift up the cross, and a restaurant is due at the top of the
cross soon, as well as another at the bottom. Lit up at night, the cross is a
convenient orientation marker denoting the south of the city if ever you are lost
at night in the streets of Skopje.

The easiest and most popular route to the summit is from the entrance to
Vodno National Park on Ulica Salvadore Aljende. The westernmost road opposite
the turn-off to the Hotel Panorama takes you over a couple of small bridges, up
past a modern apartment block to your left, and then past some lovely old
farmhouses. This quickly leads up into the woods above the town, and the main

Kosovo

Bražda

Radišani

Kučkovo

Sv Ilija Monastery
& Cardak restaurant

Raduša

Trofta

Orman

Vardar

Cherry Orchard restaurant
& El Kabon Stables

Suto Orizari
Roma Town

Volkovo

Volkovo

Skopje Sever
(North)

Novo Selo

Ilinden
Riding Club

Aqueduct

Rašče

Bardovci

Skupi

Autocamp
Boom

Zlokučani

Kondovo

Gjorče Petrov

Saraj

SKOPJE

Svilare

Treska

Vardar

Tetovo

Pantelejmon
Monastery
& Klet restaurant

Mountain hut
Dare Dzambaz

Skopje
Central

Vodno
1066m

Saraj Recreation Centre

Govrlevo

Sopište

Sv Ana

Pestera

Dolni Sonje

Sv Bogorodica

Dam

Sv Nikola

Sv Andreja

Mountain hut
Matka

Treska

Matka Lake

Dobri Dol

Markova Sušica

Markov
Manastir

Gorni Količani

Crvena Voda

Crni Vrv
2352m

Aldinci

Ljuboten
Raštak
Bulačani
Creševo
Aračinovo
Autocamp Bellevue
Madzari
Skopje East
Ilinden
Miladinovci
Romanovce
Kumanovo
Vardar
Skopje South
Markova
DRAČEVO
International airport
Jane Sandanski
Petrovec
Katlanovska Banja
Katlanovo
Dolni Količani
Zelenikovo
Vardar
Mountain hut Kitka
Kitka 1569m
Paligrad
Kadina Reka
Sv Bogorodica
Pčinja
Pčinja
N
Bradt
0 _____ 10km
0 _____ 6 miles

path is easy to follow. There are numerous diversions off the main path, and almost all diversions heading upwards will pop out at the summit eventually.

The main path is marked with red and white painted stripes on trees, and joins the road again just before the turn-off to Sv Pantelejmon Monastery. From the Hotel Vodno many people simply walk along the tarmacked road and there are numerous tracks from the road where people veer off to gather chestnuts. The

0 ━━━━━━━━━ 10km
0 ━━━━━━━━━━━━━━ 10 miles

65 **RAŠTAK**

Kumanovo,
Belgrade

65a **STRAČINCI**

65b **SMILKOVCI**

55a **BRNJARCI**

66 **BUČINCI**

55 **ARAČINOVO**

STAJKOVCI

MRŠEVCI 66b **DELJADROVCI**

63a **AJVATOVCI**

63 **MARINO** **BUNARDŽIK**

10 **SKOPSKO POLJE**

GORNO KONJARE

Pčinja

55 **IZDRIŽOVO**

68 **SUŠICA**

31 **DOLNO LISIČE**

51a **DRAČEVO**

52 **RŽANIČINO**

69 **DIVLJE**

62 **OGNJANCI**

51 **STUDENIČANI**

Vardar

53 **KATLANOVSKA BANJA**

67 **ZELENIKOVO**

67 **NOVO CELO**

Gevelija,
Greece 67 **STRAHOJADICA**

dedicated hiking path through the woods, however, actually starts to the left of the restaurant and mountain hut Skopje 63 above the barrier in the tarmac road. It is marked with yellow and green painted stripes on the trees. The path joins the road again about 1,200m from the road's end at the mountain hut and cross.

A walk up to the summit in late autumn is spectacular for its vistas of vivid red and yellow foliage laced with clouds and evergreens. Sweet chestnuts can be harvested in abundance on an early morning walk up the mountain, but be prepared to compete with the many locals with the same idea. Wild mushrooms are also plentiful at this time.

Numerous routes lead from the top of Mount Vodno, including a lovely day hike to Lake Matka (see *Chapter 12*, page 298). Another popular hike close to Skopje is to Mount Kitka (see *Chapter 12*, page 314).

LAKE MATKA AND CAVES

Lake Matka is the beloved quick getaway retreat of most Skopjites. There is hiking, boating, restaurants, churches, monasteries, caves and a small hotel. The lake itself was manmade by damming the River Treška and before the river was dammed, Sv Andreja church and the old mountain hut, which is now a café and restaurant with rooms, used to stand 20m above the river. The steep-sided ravine is quite spectacular and the cliffs are popular with the sport-climbing crowd, who can often be viewed at their sport from the café terrace.

GETTING THERE It is a mere half-hour drive from the city and the number 60 bus from anywhere on Boulevard Partizanski goes there hourly for 60MKD. A taxi from the centre of Skopje costs 400MKD. It is a ten-minute walk along the River Treška from the parking area and bus stop to the foot of the dam, and then another ten minutes up past the dam where the path opens up to the grounds of the Matka Hotel and Restaurant and the Church of Sveta Andreja.

WHERE TO STAY AND EAT The old **Planinski Dom Matka** has now been turned into a proper restaurant, as well as the lakeside café, and offers five en-suite rooms with Wi-Fi and all mod cons (♪ *02 3052 655, 02 3022 922, 070 217 900;* e *contact@canyonmatka.com; www.canyonmatka.com;* $$$/$$). Take a look inside the restaurant to see some excellent photos of the nearby churches and caves.

Before the dam itself is the **Restoran Peštera** (♪ *02 2052 512;* $$$), also known as the Bear Cave, which has a nice outdoor patio and a small indoor restaurant set into the rock walls, making it rather cool inside. The food is traditional Macedonian including a good house stew and allegedly you can eat bear steak here too.

WHAT TO DO Small **boats** from outside Dom Matka café will take you down the lake for €10 a boat, where there is a small restaurant part way down the lake accessible by boat only. There is also a lot of **hiking** in the surrounding hills, which are home to over 50 species of protected butterflies and moths. Various paths lead to over a dozen churches and monasteries, some long abandoned, some in full working order.

Next door to Dom Matka is **Sv Andreja Church**, which was built in the 14th century by another Andreja (not the saint) who was the brother of King Marko (see page 186).

Near Restoran Peštera the bridge over the river takes you to a path leading up to the **Church of Sv Nikola**, which has an excellent view onto the hotel and café. Above the Restoran Peštera is the **Monastery of Sveta Bogorodica**. It is a working monastery with inns, which are not open to the public, and a small church. Above the entrance to the church is an inscription reading:

> By the will of the father, the son and the holy ghost and the divine temple of the Mother of God came Lady Milica. She found this church unroofed, built a roof for it, painted its frescoes and built a wall around it. Mention, Lord, that this took place in 1497.

The church itself may be older than this if she found it already without a roof.

To the left of the entrance to the monastery is a path marked red which leads up to the churches of Sv Spas (80 minutes) and Sv Trojica (85 minutes) and the ruined Monastery of Sv Nedela (95 minutes). The walk to these churches is beautiful, although the trail is steep and badly marked so patience is required to get there. **Sv Spas** was built in the 14th century on the foundations of an earlier church, and renovated in 1968. To the right of the church as you approach it (ie: to the northeast) are the large and overgrown limestone blocks of an ancient fortress. The site continued to be populated into Ottoman times when it was known as Markov Grad (Marko's Town). It was also a hideout for Macedonian revolutionaries, until it was discovered by the Ottomans and ransacked.

An alternative rendition to the end of this fortress comes in the form of a love story. Allegedly, an Ottoman *bey* fell in love with the beautiful Bojana from Marko's Town, and when she refused his overtures, the *bey* decided to take her against her will. The citizens of the fortress helped her and killed almost a hundred Turk soldiers before Bojana realised her fate was sealed and threw herself to her death from the steep cliffs of the canyon into the River Treška. Sadly for the rest of the citizens, the soldiers took revenge by razing the fortress to the ground. The only building still left standing (just about) is the **Church of Sv Nedela** (Sv Sunday) with its ruined archway and old fresco of the saint. Take care going up to this church as it stands on precariously steep ground.

There are two paths from here back down to the lake at Sv Andreja. The longer path marked yellow goes via Matkin Dol. It is very steep and should be walked with care. The name Matkin Dol means Torture Valley, which might give you an idea of how difficult it is. There are a few small caves along this path where monks retreated in order to find union with God.

There are several impressive **caves** around Matka. The main ones are Ubava, Vrelo, Podvrelo and Krstalna. Vrelo is Macedonia's nomination for the New Seven Wonders of Nature (*www.new7wonders.com/nature/en/nominees/europe/c/VreloCave*) and as a result has been made open to the public for a 300MKD entrance fee (per person, including 30 minute boat trip). Ask at Dom Matka for access, which is by boat only. Podvrelo is almost completely underwater: with a depth of well over 500m, it may be the deepest known underwater cave in the world, and so is for the accomplished cave diver only. Ubava (meaning beautiful) has the most stalagmites and stalactites, waterfalls, and colours, and archaeological findings in the cave indicate that it may have been used as a shelter during Palaeolithic (Old Stone Age) times almost 10,000 years ago. For more about the caves see Dom Matka's website.

To the left of the main restaurant are several boards showing the walks, animals and sites to be found in the area, as well as a climbing guide board showing the climbing routes on the large rock face on the opposite side of the lake. For those wishing to do some serious climbing or extended hiking and mountaineering in Matka or anywhere else in Macedonia or Bulgaria, **Matka Climbing Club** (contact details on page 40) can offer experienced guides as well as rock-climbing lessons.

The path along the river continues after the monastery, past a huge memorial of a carabiner hung on a piton stuck into the rock. The memorial was put up to commemorate the lives of climbers lost in a climbing accident at that spot in the early 1990s. The rest of the path along the lake is mostly good, but in some places it is crumbling and requires a bit of careful footwork. Again, it's not a walk for those with severe vertigo.

Eventually, the hike comes to the end of the lake and continues up the River Treška. Parts of the river cliffs are quarried for rock, so you may not be able to walk more than the first 3km as the cliffs become unsafe. The middle reaches of the Treška between Makedonski Brod and Lake Matka are meant to be good fishing, and these can be reached more quickly by driving around via Sopište.

KATLANOVSKA BANJA

The newly renovated hot springs at Katlanovska Banja (*banja* is Macedonian for 'thermal baths'), 30km outside Skopje near the airport, are well worth a visit as the only Western-standard spa in the country (↘ *02 2581 002;* f *02 2581 032;* e *katlanovskaspa@katlanovskaspa.com; www.katlanovskaspa.com*). The main sanitorium is still in need of much renovation, but the main baths rival those in western Europe or northern America. Since the area was essentially trashed after housing refugees and internally displaced people from the conflicts in Kosovo and in Macedonia, the area has been cleaned up, but still has a way to go to become the popular place it once was for a picnic, a walk in the countryside, or a fishing trip. Nevertheless, many locals come to collect the medicinal waters of the natural springs coming from the rock faces on the approach to the baths.

The baths themselves are open 07.00–21.00 and the restaurant until 23.00. Finally a spa in Macedonia open to both sexes at the same time, the main pool costs €4 per hour, and a private pool for two costs €15 per hour. Some excellent spa packages are available, including the full range of massage, body mudpacks and facials, as well as monthly special offers. See their website for specific details. A small shop is open for small snacks and supplies and there are a couple of old picnic gazebos in the grounds.

Bus number 53 goes to the baths from Skopje (see timetable, page 122). Return buses to Skopje run at 04.45, 05.20, 06.00, 07.10, 08.00, 08.45, 09.45, 10.25, 11.20, 12.55, 13.50, 14.45, 15.25, 16.25, 17.05, 17.40, 19.00, 19.35, 20.30, 21.15, with a reduced service on Sundays. An up-to-date timetable is also available on the spa website.

To get there by car there are two approaches, one from the north side when coming from Kumanovo and one from the south. To get to the south side, go east out of Skopje, past the airport as if going to Greece, and then take the Katlanovska Banja exit on the right. Keep following the signs and when you run out of signs, follow the river. If you get disoriented or lose the river on your right, just open the window and follow the sulphur smell. It is faint, but it will lead you to the Banja area.

THE OLD STONE AQUEDUCT

The 55-arch aqueduct is worth going out of your way for, as at least there is something there to see and to photograph. Some sources say the aqueduct goes back to Roman times; others, however, say it was built during Ottoman rule by Isa Bey in the 16th century. It was certainly used then, when the Ottomans required more water for the many Turkish baths in town, such as Čifte, Gurciler and Daut Pasha Amam, and maybe they built the present structure on the ruins of a Roman original. It is now in disrepair and completely unprotected, although attempts have been made in the past to keep it from falling down completely.

To get there, cross the river at the Aleksandar Palace Hotel and join the E65 highway going north to Kosovo. Just over 1km after turning onto the E65, turn right immediately after the railway flyover onto a dirt track. Pass back under the railway flyover for a few hundred metres until you reach the gates of the army barracks and then turn left, or park here if you do not have a 4x4. From the barracks gates it is a 500m walk to the aqueduct, which will have been visible from the E65 highway. You may not be allowed to take photographs of the aqueduct with the barracks in the background, so position yourself with the barracks behind you to take your shots.

SARAJ CAMPSITE AND WATER PARK

A few kilometres before Lake Matka is the Saraj Recreation Centre (✆ 02 2347 307). Right at the foot of the Matka cliffs, it looks as if it should be heavenly, and USAID has poured a lot of money into getting it back into some semblance of order. It is very popular with the local Albanian community, who spend large portions of their weekends at their caravans on the site. You can also set up a tent on the site; call to book a space.

There are plenty of swimmers diving off the edge of the huge outdoor pool at the deep end, but about half the large expanse of water is not even adult knee deep, so your young ones can splash about in it in relative safety. There are a few snack bars and ice-cream stalls about, but a distinct lack of public toilets. There are much cleaner pools in Skopje, and if you can get to Mavrovo or Ohrid lakes, the water there is much more inviting. The poor River Treška, which skirts around the edge of the recreation park, is sinking under trash, despite the new law against fouling the environment and a €50 fine if caught – proof that 'Keep Macedonia Tidy' has yet to become a firm part of the Macedonian psyche.

PANTELEJMON MONASTERY

In the village of Gorni Nezeri, halfway up Mount Vodno, is the Monastery of Pantelejmon. The present church dedicated to Sv Pantelejmon is built on the foundations of an older church dating back to 1164. The church is surrounded by inns (see below) and a restaurant, Klet (✆ 02 3081 255; $$$), offering traditional Macedonian fare. The restaurant has excellent views of the Vardar Valley, with a long outdoor patio area that promises a good sunset on a summer evening.

GETTING THERE It takes about 20 minutes by taxi to the monastery from the centre of Skopje, which should cost in the region of 300MKD. There are two routes to Pantelejmon Monastery from Skopje: the easiest route is to take the road just below Hotel Vodno around the mountain; the shorter route is to take Kozle Street all the way to the end past the long blue factory on the right, and at the end of the factory complex take a left turn marked Gorni Nezeri all the way up to the monastery.

WHERE TO STAY
Hotel Pantelejmon (12 rooms) ✆ 02 3081 255.
Expensive simplicity. $$$$

ŠUTO ORIZARI ROMA SETTLEMENT AND MARKET

Šuto Orizari, or Šutka for short, is the home of the sizeable Roma minority (see page 52) who live in Skopje. It is a part of Skopje that is little visited by tourists, and most Macedonians would think you were a bit crazy to want to go there. Nonetheless, the daily **market** is super-cheap (and filled with a lot of junk) and it's where you can get some of the hand-sewn and embroidered Roma clothing and shoes.

More interesting than a wander through the market (where even the Roma will tell you to keep a tight hold on your wallet) is a walk around some of the side streets off the northern end of Vietnamska. This area of their settlement will give you a feel of how the Roma live and love a carefree and artistic life. The closely packed one- or two-storey houses are usually immaculately whitewashed with a decorative fence of moulded concrete or ironwork, topped with whitewashed lions and Pekinese dogs pawing a ball. Wooden caravan wheels,

6

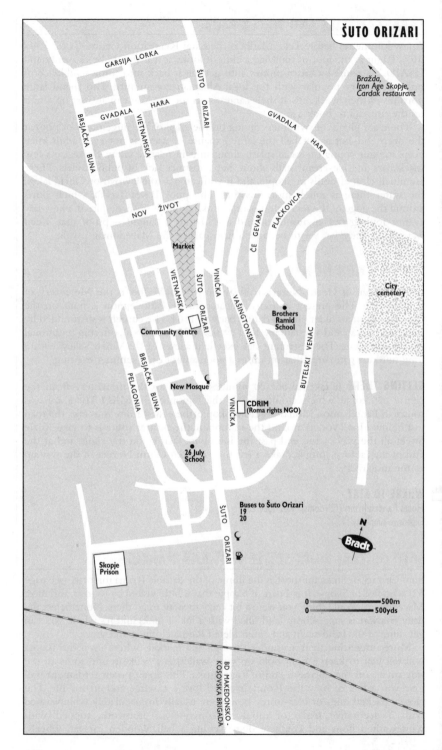

ŠUTO ORIZARI

GARSIJA LORKA

GVADALA HARA

ŠUTO ORIZARI

BRSJAČKA BUNA

VIETNAMSKA

Bražda,
Iron Age Skopje,
Cardak restaurant

GVADALA HARA

NOV ŽIVOT

Market

VIETNAMSKA

ŠUTO ORIZARI

Community centre

ČE GEVARA

PLAČKOVICA

VINIČKA

VAŠINGTONSKI

Brothers
Ramid
School

City
cemetery

BRSJAČKA BUNA

PELAGONIA

New Mosque

VINIČKA

BUTELSKI VENAC

CDRIM
(Roma rights NGO)

26 July
School

ŠUTO ORIZARI

Buses to Šuto Orizari
19
20

N

Bradt

Skopje
Prison

0   500m
0   500yds

BD MAKEDONSKO -
KOSOVSKA BRIGADA

harking back to the nomadic days of the Roma, adorn the walls and fences. Many of these lovely homes are not built from money earned here in Macedonia, but are the result of years away working in Germany and Austria.

The atmosphere and surroundings are not unlike a Chinese or Indian neighbourhood in Malaysia or some other southeast Asian country. Children laugh and play in the streets and this is a world away from the Roma who beg on the streets with their babies. But behind the laughter of children, the concerns of adults are not difficult to find.

In a community where education is not always highly valued, it is difficult enough to get the really poor of the Roma community to attend school. It is even more difficult when the main school in Šutka, Brakja Ramiz i Hamid, is filled three times over capacity and has few facilities and insufficient teaching staff. The school gymnasium has no heating in winter and most of the windows are broken. Water runs down the walls of the changing rooms and many of the corridors in the school.

On the bright side, the Roma are outstandingly talented in music and dance. The school has a few musical instruments of its own, but most of the children bring their parents' instruments into school, the very instruments that their parents earn their living from by playing in bands for hire at parties and festivals. In recent years, despite the poor teaching conditions and the other overwhelming concerns of poverty, Brakja Ramiz i Hamid has repeatedly won the first prize in the annual Skopje school choir and school orchestra competitions.

To find out more about the Roma see page 52, or to help Brakja Ramiz i Hamid directly see *Giving something back* on page 110.

GETTING THERE To get to Šutka take the number 19 or 20 bus heading north from Dame Gruev outside the main post office, or take the ten-minute taxi ride for less than 150MKD. Ask to be dropped off at the Šutka Pazar, which is on the main street through Šutka.

ARCHAEOLOGICAL SITES AROUND SKOPJE

NEOLITHIC SKOPJE – GOVRLEVO AND MADŽARI The history of greater Skopje spans more than 7,000 years. The oldest habitation in the area dates to the Neolithic or New Stone Age (5000–3000BC). Archaeological evidence from the sites of Tumba in Madžari and Cerje in Govrlevo (both to the east of Skopje south of the E65 highway) suggests a society of some sophistication with dwellings built of mud brick and/or wood. A small reconstruction of these early villages has been done at Madžari although it is nothing to write home about.

The people of these sites venerated the earth, as the sustainer and ultimate repository of all human life, represented by the 'Venus' figurine or Golemata Majka (Great Mother) found at Madžari in 1981. Copies of the figurine feature in all the craft and souvenir shops around the country. Part of a figurine of an inhaling male torso was found at Govrlevo as well as a manuscript seal. Both items show advanced use of pottery and the Govrlevo seal suggests a literate and administratively well-organised civilisation some 7,000 years ago. The male figurine has been named Adam of Macedonia. Recently, a reconstruction of the Neolithic village in Madzari has been made. For more information you can visit the following web-page: www.tumbamadzari.org.mk.

IRON AGE SKOPJE – BRAŽDA Some 10km north of Skopje, at the foot of the Skopska Crna Gora Mountain, lies the village of Bražda. The picturesque surroundings of this village host the Iron Age or proto-historic and early antique (800–300BC) antecedent to Skopje, which is situated on the top of a small hill covering some 4.5ha and is reputed to be the capital of the Agriani tribe. Details of the settlement morphology are rather poor and little is visible, but one monumental building, probably the tomb of a noble or a king, is extant. The Agriani, an ethnic community that lived in the northeastern part of modern-day Macedonia around Skopje, are frequently mentioned in inscriptions from the 4th century BC. Renowned for their fighting prowess they were one of the elite units in the Macedonian army of Aleksandar the Great. Čardak Restaurant near here is listed on page 157. To get there, take bus 61 (towards Pobožje), 71 (towards Banjani) or 81 (towards Blace), all of which go through Bražda.

ROMAN SKOPJE – SKUPI Skupi became the administrative, cultural, economic and religious centre of the entire region following the Roman victory over Perseus in the third Macedonian war of 168BC and the foundation of the Roman province of Dardania. In the year AD313, following the Edict of Milan, it became the seat of the episcopate. Skupi was razed by the earthquake in AD518, during the reign of Emperor Justinian, (himself born some 30km away from Skopje in Tauresium, today's village of Taor in Zelenikovo municipality) but did witness low level squatter re-occupation.

The extent of the Roman colony of Skupi is largely unknown, even after significant archaeological excavation, the most recent being in 2008 when a church was discovered. The buildings visible within the excavations are: a hall reputed to be the civil basilica, the centre of civil administration of the town, with its mosaic floors; a small Roman bath; a north–south-aligned street (or *cardo*), possibly the Cardo Maximus; a theatre, remnants of part of the city wall and the ground plan of a church or basilica.

Recent work undertaken at Scupi includes a geo-physical survey and fieldwalking by the Macedonian Centre for Archaeological Research (MACAR)

DID YOU KNOW? ROMANI LANGUAGE AND FAMOUS ROMA PEOPLE

The Romani language belongs to the North Indo-Aryan (Indic) languages and is close to Hindi, Punjabi and the Dardic languages. There are numerous Romani dialects, having been influenced by the Roma's place of settlement. For example Romani words of Iranian origin include *baxt* (luck, fortune), *ambrol* (pear), *khangeri* (church), *angustri* (ring), *ruv* (wolf), *vurdon* (wagon). Romani words of Greek origin include *drom* (path, road), *isviri* (hammer), *karfin* (nail), *klidi* (key), *kokalo* (bone), *papin* (goose), *petalos* (horseshoe), *tsox* (skirt), *(v)amoni* (anvil), and *zumi* (soup).

In return Romani has also contributed significant numbers of slang words to the languages of the countries where they have settled. The following slang English words (standard meaning in brackets) have come from Romani:

Bamboozle (cheat)	Dad (father)
Bosh (nonsense)	Lolly (money)
Bungaloo (one-storey house)	Nark (informant)
Busk (play music)	Pal (friend)
Char (clean)	Posh (classy)
Chav (youth)	Rogue (rascal)
Corker (tell a lie)	Rum (strange)
Cushti (good)	

A good website on the Romani language is www.rroma.org.

and the Centre for Cultural Heritage and Archaeological Resource Management (CHARM) in cooperation with UK institutions. More recent excavations by the Museum of Skopje have uncovered part of the city wall and have identified that the limit of the urban area (though still unknown) was greater than suspected. A basilica was also discovered along with a complete and rather beautiful statue of Venus Pudica associated with a possible bath building. The statue is 1.7m high, white marble and has a dolphin tatooed on the left leg. It is the only complete sculpture to be found on Macedonian soil yet and dates to the 3rd century.

By far the most remarkable discovery relating to Skupi, by dint of their preservation, are the standing Roman gravestones or *stele* some 150m further up the road towards Bardovci. What makes these gravestones unique is that they were found still standing in place, *in situ*, preserved by being buried under a later mound. This level of preservation of Roman monuments is paralelled no-where else in the Roman world.

The archaeological site is located next to the road to the village of Bardovci and has an obvious access. A newly constructed path leads the visitor around the excavations and along which a number of notice boards explain a little of what you are looking at. The site is 1.5km from the Aleksandar Palace Hotel. To get there take the bridge north over the river and turn left at the traffic lights 200m after the river. Take the second right turn 1km down the road to go towards Bardovci, and the ruins are on the right after another 100m.

MARKO'S MONASTERY (MARKOV MONASTIR)

Tucked in the foothills of Jakupica Mountains, south of Vodno Mountain, is the village of Marko Sušica, at the southwestern end of which is King Marko's Monastery. The monastery church dedicated to Sv Dimitri was started by Marko's

6

Here are a few phrases in the local Macedonian Romani language:

Lacho dive	Good day/Hello
Sar san?/So keres?	How are you?/What are you doing?
Ov sasto (m)/ov sasci (f)	Thank you
Naj pala soste!	You're welcome!
Katar aves?	Where are you from?
Sar si to anav?/Mo anav si ...	What's your name?/My name is ...
Va/Na	Yes/No
Tjiri familija si vi tusa?	Is your family with you?
Kaj djas?	Where are you going?
Na haljovava tut	I don't understand you
Haljoveja man?	Do you understand me?
Av mansa (sing)/aven mansa (plu)	Come with me
Ava kari	Come here
Roma	People
Achov devlesar	God be with you/Farewell

Famous Roma people or famous people of Roma origin are mostly musicians, dancers and actors. These include Elvis Presley, Django Reinhardt, Yul Brynner, Michael Caine, Charlie Chaplin and Bob Hoskins. Others include the footballer Eric Cantona. The new Roma Ambassador to the EU is the world famous Spanish flamenco dancer Joaquin Cortes.

father, King Volkašin, in the mid 14th century, and then finished by Marko after his father's death in 1371. This may have been as close as Marko's kingdom got to Skopje, and from here the border probably went through his brother's monastery of Sv Andreja at Matka and on to the Šar Mountains.

The monastery has frescoes of the king himself, as well as an interesting fresco of the three wise men visiting baby Jesus, and one of Sv Clement, the first archbishop of Ohrid. Although Ohrid was never a part of Marko's kingdom, the archbishopric was always behind the fledgling kingdom, and the absence of Serbian saints and church figureheads in Marko's monastery is seen as a good indicator that Marko adhered to the Church of Ohrid rather than the new Church of Serbia.

GETTING THERE To get there, take Ulica 11th Oktomvri southeast out of town and keep on this road as it becomes Ulica Sava Kovačevič and leads on to the village of Sopište. Take care to keep going straight on Sava Kovačevič and do not follow the main road around to the left when it turns into 1st Maj Street. After Sopište bear left towards Dobri Dol and Markova Sušica (signposted). At the crossroads just before the village, go straight on over the bridge and into the village until you reach the monastery on the other side. You will require shoulder and leg coverings to enter the church itself.

The small stream running below the monastery is a popular picnic site.

SV BOGORODICA MONASTERY NEAR KOŽLE

On the drive to Veles from Skopje, the road south follows the River Pčinja from Katlanovska Banja until it joins the Vardar. The road winds around the sides of a steep gorge making interesting driving and offering fantastic scenery. Fortunately, at this section there are (or at least should be) no oncoming cars as the road north takes a completely separate route further east. On this southerly road, a couple of kilometres before the River Pčinja joins the Vardar, there is a spacious stopping place on the right-hand side of the road with a couple of holy roadside shrines and a water fountain. This place also marks the stop for the Monastery of Sv Bogorodica which can be seen across the river from the roadside.

The 500m hike starts through a metal entrance to the left of the fountain, goes across a small wooden bridge crossing the river, and ends up in the courtyard of the monastery. It is no longer a working monastery, but is kept by two wardens who live there. They might join you at this juncture to explain the place.

The site was originally just a shrine in the rocks and, like many rock shrines in Macedonia, it eventually became a cave church. This one was built using old train rails from 1918 to help support the roof, but by the 1930s it was completely abandoned. It took another 40 years for the church to be rebuilt in 1976, thereby saving some of the original roof frescoes, and replacing the old iconostasis.

If you spy the monastery on the way down south, but don't manage to stop, remember you won't be able to see it on the way back north as the north road does not pass that way.

✖ WHERE TO EAT

Outside Skopje are several great traditional restaurants. Although they can be difficult to find and certainly quicker and more convenient to get to by car/taxi than by public transport, they are all set in beautiful scenery, where a hike in the local hills and woods is rewarding and helps to work up an appetite.

✗ **Čardak** Sv Ilija monastery, 5km north of Skopje; ✆ 02 266 665, 071 511 868. A good place to eat if you have been out walking in the Skopska Crnagore. To get there take the road through Butel & turn left before Radišani village & head towards Mirkovci. The restaurant & monastery are signposted. To get there by bus, the 61 (towards Pobožje), 71 (towards Banjani) & 81 (towards Blace) all go past the turn-off to Čardak. Ask the driver to let you off at Restoran Čardak Sveti Ilija. **$$**

✗ **Cherry Orchard** Volkovo; ✆ 02 2055 195; www.gastronomskivodic.com.mk/cherryorchard.html; ⏰ Tue–Sun 09.00–21.00. Set in the grounds of the El Kabon riding stables, which have a well-manicured terrace & lawns overlooking the exercise paddocks & a delightful children's play area. The restaurant building itself was used in the Macedonian movie *Dust* by Milčo Mančevski, & was reconstructed at the stables (whose horses were used in the movie) at the end of filming. The well-groomed interior offers fireside seating in the winter, but is sadly not well frequented, not least because it is complicated to get there by car. The number 22 bus from anywhere on Partizanski ends its journey 700m from the restaurant where it is signposted for the remainder of the dirt track to the stables.

To get there by car take Partizanski all the way to the end & at the crossroads, rather than turn left as if going onto the highway to Tetovo, continue straight ahead. At the next crossroads in 400m turn right opposite the church & go over the railway flyover. Follow this road through the village of Novo Selo for 3km until you cross the railway line again at Volkovo. Turn right immediately after the railway line. After almost 2km turn right at the crossroads & in 600m you'll cross back over the railway line. The road forks in another 400m & you will want to take the left fork to get to Cherry Orchard. From here there are signs for the restaurant, which is only another 700m away. **$$**

✗ **Trofta** Raduša village; ✆ 02 203 4444, 070 581 329. This trout farm, set in the disused quarry on the southern side of the village, is a good model of regeneration of an abandoned industrial site. The windy road to Raduša takes about an hour from Skopje & offers spectacular views on a good day of the pyramid-shaped Mount Ljuboten. The village is a mere kilometre from the border with Kosovo & saw the fierce Battle of Raduša on 13 August 2001, the same day as the signing of the Ohrid Framework Agreement. The train goes to Raduša several times a day. See timetable page 74. **$$**

✗ **Klet** (see page 151)

✗ **Dom Matka** (see page 148)

HORSERIDING

Horseriding is becoming increasingly popular around Skopje, especially among the expats. Riding fees are around €10 for 40 minutes, or €100 per month. Try:

El Kabon Stables Cherry Orchard in Volkovo district; ✆ 02 2055 195. To get to El Kabon see the details for Cherry Orchard restaurant above.
Ilinden Riding Club Hipodrom village, east of Skopje; ✆ 070 338 002. Claims to be the oldest horseriding club in Macedonia. It has some 20 horses, including Hanoverian, Holsteiner, Belgian & English breeds.

Other riding stables are in Stenkovec, and at Petrovec 20km outside Skopje near the airport.

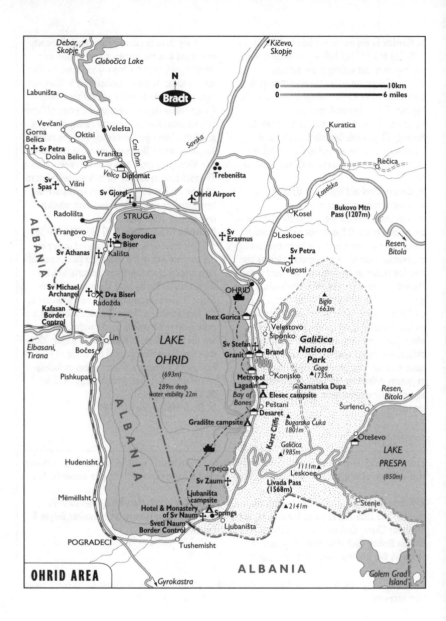

Debar,
Skopje
Globočica Lake
Kičevo,
Skopje

N
Bradt

0 ————————— 10km
0 ————————— 6 miles

Labuništa
Vevčani
Gorna
Belica
Oktisi
Velešta
Kuratica
† Sv Petra
Dolna Belica
Vraništa
Rečica
Velica Diplomat
Trebeništa
Sv
Spaš †
Višni
Ohrid Airport
Sv Gjorgi
Radolišta
STRUGA
Kosel
Bukovo Mtn
Pass (1207m)
Frangovo
† Sv
Erasmus
Leskoec
Resen,
Bitola
Sv Bogorodica
Biser
Sv Athanas †
Kališta
Sv Petra
Velgosti
Sv Michael
Archangel
† ♀× Dva Biseri
Radožda
Kafasan
Border
Control
OHRID
Bigla
1663m
Inex Gorica
Elbasani,
Tirana
Lin
Bočes
Velestovo
Šiponko
Galičica
National
Park
Sv Stefan
Granit
Brand
Pishkupat
**LAKE
OHRID**
(693m)
289m deep
water visibility 22m
Konjsko
Goga
1735m
Metropol
Lagadin
Samatska Dupa
Elesec campsite
Bay of
Bones
Peštani
Desaret
Šurlenci
Gradište campsite
Bugarska Čuka
1801m
Galičica
1985m
Oteševo
LAKE
PRESPA
(850m)
Hudenisht
Trpejca
1111m
Leskoec
Livada Pass
(1568m)
Sv Zaum †
Mëmëllsht
Ljubaništa
campsite
Hotel & Monastery
of Sv Naum
Springs
Sveti Naum
Border Control
Ljubaništa
Stenje
2141m
POGRADECI
Tushemisht
ALBANIA
Gyrokastra
Golem Grad
Island

OHRID AREA

158

7

Lake Ohrid and Galičica National Park

> The waters, limpid as the crystal of the rock, from which property the lake perhaps acquired its Greek name (for lychnis signified transparent), discover a bottom of clear sand, at even a depth of from nine to fourteen English fathoms.
>
> *Travels in Epirus, Albania, Macedonia and Thessaly*, FCHL Pouqueville, 1820

Lake Ohrid is the jewel of the Macedonian crown. Both the lake and Ohrid town are under the protection of UNESCO as a site of rare environmental, scientific and cultural significance. And not without due reason: the lake itself is one of the oldest in the world, belonging in the ranks of Lake Baikal in Russia and Lake Titicaca in Peru/Bolivia. The town has historic roots going back to Neolithic times and claims the longest continuous settlement of humans in the world dating back 7,000 years. Many of these historical remains are still being excavated and some can be seen in the museum or in the form of churches, castles and other architecture. Allegedly, there are **365 churches**, monasteries and holy sites around the lake, one for every day of the year. Aside from these attractions, Macedonians love Ohrid because it is their seaside: the waters are beckoning in the long hot days of July and August. Then there is **Ohrid Festival**, attracting world-renowned artists to perform in the **Roman amphitheatre**, medieval **fortress** and many other lakeside venues. The two main towns situated on the lake are Ohrid and little visited, but quaint, Struga.

And once you have partaken of the festivals and seen the sites of the town – Tsar Samoil's Fortress, Sv Sophia's Church and the Robevi House to name a few – there are plenty of things outside the town too: the **lake springs** at Sv Naum; cave churches at Kališta and Radožda; caving, hiking and paragliding in **Galičica National Park**, including to a panoramic point to see both Ohrid and Prespa lakes; diving in and sailing on the lake; the **Twelfthtide carnival** in the Republic of Vevčani; and day trips by jeep, donkey or foot to nearby mountain villages.

OHRID

HISTORY The shores of one of the oldest lakes in the world have been inhabited since prehistoric times. The earliest signs of humankind in the area have been found in Dolno Trnovo, to the north of the main town, and at the Bay of Bones at Gradište, dating from Neolithic times (around 5000BC). Although there is nothing of the graves left to see at Dolno Trnovo, the Bay of Bones stilt village has been reconstructed, and some of the related artefacts are on display in the Ohrid Museum.

Later, tribes known as the Brigians, Ohrygians and Enhelians settled in the area. These tribes neighboured the Illyrians of Grecian origin, who at that time had moved through Ohrid into areas further west (now Albania). They were displaced by the Desaretes, and it is as the capital of Desaretia that Lychnidos (present-day Ohrid) is first mentioned.

Lychnidos, meaning 'town of light' (in ancient Greek *lychni* = light, *dos* = town), was so named by Phoenician Cadmus, a Theban who settled in the town after he was banished from Greece. Later, in the 4th century BC, the town was inhabited by the Macedonians of Philip II, and then the Romans in the late 2nd century BC. The town was developed further during Roman times by traders travelling along the Via Egnatia (see page 32), which passed through Radožda and Lychnidos. A Roman fort also existed further around the lake at Gradište (the first half-metre of the outer wall of which has now been rebuilt for visitors to view). With these travellers came preachers of Christianity.

By the 5th century AD, the first early basilicas were being built in Lychnidos. Twelve are believed to have been built in total, although only six have been found so far. The largest and most significant of these is at the site of today's Monastery of Sv Kliment at Plaošnik. The large size of the basilica indicates the importance of this church and of the bishops who resided here, whose work grew with the arrival of pagan Slav tribes in the 6th century. Other basilicas found around Lake Ohrid are at Sv Sophia, Sv Erasmus and another in the hills above Biljana Springs.

By 879, the town was no longer called Lychnidos but was referred to by the Slavs as Ohrid, possibly from the Slav words *vo hrid*, meaning 'on a hill' as the ancient town of Lychnidos was at the top of Ohrid Hill.

A few years later, the missionaries Kliment and Naum came to Ohrid and set up the first monasteries that taught in Slavic (see box, above). This strengthened the already strong religious tradition in the town, and a century later, when Tsar Samoil (see box, page 10) moved the capital of his empire to Ohrid, he also made Ohrid the head of its own autocephalous archdiocese.

Tsar Samoil's fortress city at Ohrid is still visible today, although parts of it were destroyed when Samoil was defeated by the Byzantine emperor Basilius II in 1014. Ohrid then became a part of the Byzantine Empire again and the archdiocese of

Ohrid was reduced to an archbishopric. But it remained an influential archbishopric nonetheless, whose reach extended from the Adriatic in the west as far as Thessaloniki to the south and all along the River Danube in the north to the Black Sea, and the Archbishop of Ohrid was always a powerful political appointee.

The Archbishopric of Ohrid, although nominally under the patriarch of Constantinople, went from strength to strength as well as growing in geographical influence even under the Ottoman Empire (see box, page 56). By the end of the 16th century the jurisdiction of the Archbishopric of Ohrid went as far as the Orthodox communities in Dalmati and Venice in mainland Italy, as well as to Malta and Sicily.

Ohrid's privileged position within the Ottoman Empire through its seat as the archbishopric was rarely challenged, although in 1466 this was jeopardised when the citizens of Ohrid sided with the Albanian Lord Skenderbey (see box, page 234) against their Ottoman rulers. Several high-ranking Church officials and the archbishop were jailed as a result and died in prison.

When the Archbishopric of Ohrid was abolished in 1767 at the behest of the Greek patriarchate, Greek influence on Ohrid's religious life became pronounced, much to the dislike of the locals. It took just over a century for the locals to then convince the Ottomans to shut down Greek teaching in Ohrid in 1869. Thereafter, Ohrid's history follows a very similar pattern to the rest of northern Macedonia. VMRO's branch in Ohrid rose up on Ilinden in 1903 like the rest of the land, and was brutally put down again afterwards. Under Yugoslavia, Ohrid saw development in tourism, and Tito even had a summer residence on the lake, now reserved for Macedonia's president.

Tourism is picking up again now in Ohrid so many of the socialist-style hotels are being completely renovated and many smaller family-run hotels and new apartments are springing up along the lake. Sadly, however, none of the town's development is currently regulated, despite being a UNESCO heritage town, and so a few jet skis, raucous bars in the old town and rowdy disco boats on the lake can spoil for many an otherwise idyllic, culturally rich experience. Outside the peak season of July and August, it is quieter and cheaper.

GETTING THERE AND AWAY The railway line to Ohrid closed down in 1966 when the decision was taken not to upgrade the 60cm gauge line to the current 76cm gauge. Although trains and lines are to be upgraded in Macedonia, the Kicevo to Ohrid line is unlikely to receive funding. An excellent webpage on the old 17hr steam journey is at www.penmorfa.com/JZ/ohrid.html. Otherwise you may travel as follows:

By air Macedonia's only other international airport, aside from Skopje, is at Ohrid (↘ 046 262 503, 046 252 820; e ohdap@airports.com.mk). There are only a few flights a day in and out of the airport, which is 14km north of the town, and closer to Struga than it is to Ohrid itself. Macedonian Airways (MAT) (↘ 046 263 375, 046 254 151; f 046 254 241; e matohrid@freemail.org.mk; www.mat.com.mk) fly once a week to Zurich, Vienna and Dubrovnik in the summer. There are no flights from Skopje to Ohrid. Full flight details for Ohrid Airport can be viewed at www.airports.com.mk.

By car If you are driving to Ohrid from Skopje (around 2½hrs), you should consider taking the back road through Mavrovo National Park via Debar (3hrs 15mins). The dramatic tour through the mountains winds past four dams (Mavrovo, Debar, Golema and Mala Globočica) and close to the border with Albania. It is especially worthwhile in the autumn when the trees turn colour.

Belgrade, Serbia	15.30 & 17.30 daily
Sofia, Bulgaria	19.00 daily
Frankfurt/Dortmund, Germany	05.30 on Wed & Sat
Kičevo–Skopje	04.30 (summer only), 05.30, 07.30, 10.45, 12.45, 15.00
Bitola–Skopje	10.00, Bitola 07.00, 13.15
Kočani	06.00
Struga	05.30–22.30 every 15 mins
Elsani	13 buses every day 05.30–1930
Peštani/Desaret	16 buses every day 05.50–21.30
Trpejca/Sv Naum	05.00, 06.00, 12.15, 15.30, 18.30

By bus There are frequent buses to Ohrid from all over Macedonia with more frequent services in the summer. Buses leave at least every two hours from Skopje and cost around 600MKD. The inter-town bus station (ℐ *046 260 339*) is at Pitu Guli 4, from which frequent buses go towards Sveti Naum and Struga. A taxi ride to the bus station from the centre of town costs 100MKD. Up-to-date bus times can be found in Macedonian at www.ohrid.gov.mk/index.asp?novostiID=112. For the main bus times see the box above.

GETTING AROUND

By taxi The old town is small enough to walk around (but hilly) and driving is restricted. There are no town buses, so the best way to travel longer distances is by taxi, which has a minimum fare of 30MKD. If you can't flag one down on the street, try calling one of the following numbers (prefixed 046 from a mobile phone): 1580, 1583, 1591, 1592, 1585, 1588, 1595, 1599.

By boat A good way to get around the lake is by boat. During June to September a daily boat service runs from the main boat quay in Ohrid to Sv Naum and returns in the late afternoon. Most hotels post the boat times. The approximate times can also be found in the box below.

There are lots of boat taxis that will take one or a whole boat load of passengers for a ride for a minimum of €10. This is a great way to get from the centre of town to the Church of Sv Jovan at Kaneo on a hot day if you do not fancy the 1km hike over the hill. You'll see many a boat-taxi driver along the harbour and wandering the streets, often wearing a sea captain's hat, and they will probably ask you if you want a ride long before you have got around to asking them. €20 will take you for an extended tour around the harbour, €30 will take you to Struga, Kališta or Radožda where the view of the cave church from the water is quite striking (at least one hour's boat journey), and €45 will take you on the two-hour journey to Sveti Naum.

	Out	Return
Ohrid quay	10.00	17.15
Hotel Park	10.10	17.05
Hotel Granit	10.20	16.55
Hotel Metropol	10.25	16.50
Hotel Desaret	10.35	16.40
Sv Naum	10.45	16.30

For larger boats contact Vladimir Stojkovski (✆ *046 277 221, 046 277 222;* e *vstojosk@macedonia.eu.org*), based in the Hotel Ohrid, who will be able to sort out hiring a boat for the day or half day. A 30-passenger boat, for instance, including lunch on board with drinks, works out at about €45 per person.

TOWN MAPS Free town maps are available in some of the big hotels. A 1:6,000 map of Ohrid can be bought in most supermarkets and bookstalls, both in Skopje and in Ohrid itself. The Trimaks map also includes a 1:65,000 map of the lake on the back of the city map, as well as some useful information on sites, telephone numbers and street names.

TOUR OPERATORS For help with bookings, tours and further information once in Ohrid, contact:

Dea Tours Kej Maršal Tito 40; ✆ 046 265 251; f 046 230 648; e dagoli@doctor.com; www.deatours.com.mk; ⏱ daily 09.00–20.00. Friendly multi-lingual staff with a wealth of knowledge about the region. They can arrange various tours including ethno-tourism, donkey rides, adventure tours, mountaineering & other possibilities. Dea Tours can also help with finding accommodation in all price ranges.
General Tourist 2000 Partizanska 6; ✆ 046 260 423; f 046 262 516; e gen2000@mt.net.mk; www.generalturist2000-ohrid.com.mk; ⏱ daily 09.00–20.00. Aside from tours in the region they also offer all the usual travel agency services.

WHERE TO STAY
Old town
🏠 **Villa Germanoff** (3 rooms) Tsar Samoil 57; ✆ 046 266 831, 262 048; e tunte@ mezzoforte.com.mk. The Piano Room with a view onto the lake is one of the nicest rooms in Ohrid. Say in advance if you want b/fast included. Electric kettle & drinks in each room. $$$
🏠 **Villa Sveta Sofia** (5 rooms) Kosta Abraš 64; ✆ 046 254 370; f 046 254 363; e info@ vilasofija.com; www.vilasofija.com. Of traditional Macedonian architecture in the old town with its own restaurant & private bar. Exquisite service accompanies every room. $$$
🏠 **Villa Forum** (4 rooms) Kuzman Kapidan 1, Gorna Porta; ✆ 046 251 340, 070 819 713; e villaforumohrid@yahoo.com; www.villaforumohrid.com.mk. Brand-new rooms at the top of the old town overlooking the amphitheatre & lake. 1 twin, 2 dbls & 1 suite, all with an extra fold-out armchair-bed. $$$
🏠 **Hotel Aleksandrija** (15 rooms) Kosta Abraš bb; ✆ 046 258 860; e info@hotelaleksandrija.com; www.hotelaleksandrija.com. Overlooking the lake at the entrance to the old town, this brand-new hotel offers 2 deluxe apts with jacuzzi, & the remainder are all dbl-bed rooms. $$$
🏠 **Hotel Cingo** (25 rooms) Abas Emin 3 (behind the old town); ✆ 046 250 001/002; e hotelcingo@ mt.net.mk; www.hotelcingo.com.mk. Modern hotel.

Rooms have cable TV, AC, bathroom & internet hook-up. $$$
🏠 **Villa Kaneo** (4 rooms & 2 apts) ✆ 070 353 999, 046 265 583; e maslova@ohrid.com.mk; www.ohridaccommodation.com.mk. Nice tasteful rooms in 2 houses, one in Kaneo overlooking the lake & another in the centre of town, Villa Dudan. Private bathroom but not en suite. $$
🏠 **Villa Rustika** (5 apts) Hristo Uzunov 1; ✆ 046 265 511, 070 212 114; www.villarustica.com.mk. Fantastic 270° view of the lake from the top suite & a beautiful garden, below a massive kiwi tree, for b/fast in the morning or a nightcap. $$
🏠 **Lucija's** (7 rooms) Kosta Abraš 29; ✆ 046 265 608, 070 352 804; f 046 266 396. Excellent value for money for its location. The patio is right on the water so you can go for a quick swim before b/fast, & the house is right opposite the Jazz Inn, so you don't have far to stumble in the evening either! $$
🏠 **Dimče Kanevče** (3 rooms) Kočo Racin 39, Kaneo; ✆ 046 262 928, 070 800 760; e dkanevce@hotmail.com. Very nice rooms, simple & clean, right on the lake with a private jetty to swim from. Shared bathroom. $
🏠 **Stefan Kanevče** (9 rooms in various houses) Kaneo; ✆ 046 260 350, 070 212 352; e stefan_kanevce@yahoo.co.uk (see box, page 167). $

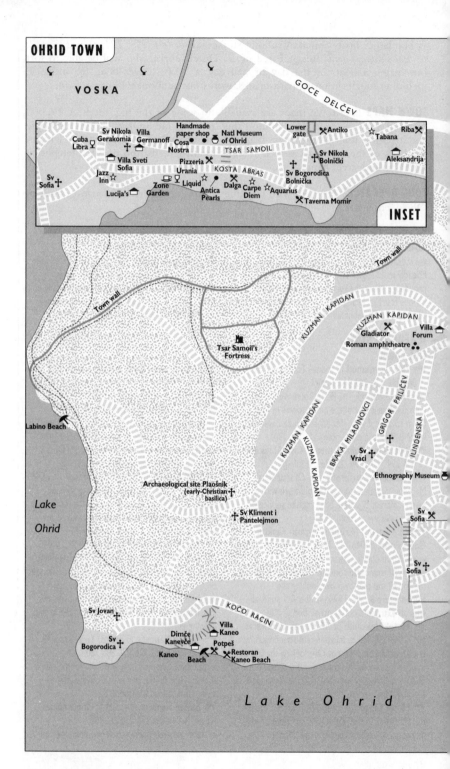

OHRID TOWN

VOSKA

GOCE DELČEV

INSET

Cuba Libra

Sv Sofia

Sv Nikola Gerakomia

Villa Sveti Sofia

Jazz Inn

Lucija's

Villa Germanoff

Zone Garden

Liquid

Handmade paper shop
Cosa Nostra

Pizzeria

Urania

Antica Pearls

Natl Museum of Ohrid

TSAR SAMOIL

KOSTA ABRAS

Dalga

Carpe Diem

Lower gate

Antiko

Tabana

Riba

Sv Nikola Bolnički

Sv Bogorodica Bolnička

Aquarius

Taverna Momir

Aleksandrija

Town wall

Town wall

Town wall

Kuzman Kapidan

Kuzman Kapidan

Kuzman Kapidan

Kuzman Kapidan

Kuzman Kapidan

Gladiator

Villa Forum

Roman amphitheatre

Tsar Samoil's Fortress

Braka Miladinovci

Grigor Prličev

Ilindenska

Sv Vraci

Ethnography Museum

Sv Sofia

Archaeological site Plaošnik
(early-Christian basilica)

Sv Kliment i Pantelejmon

Sv Sofia

Labino Beach

Lake Ohrid

KOČO RACIN

Sv Jovan

Sv Bogorodica

Dimče Kanevče

Kaneo

Beach

Villa Kaneo

Potpeš

Restoran Kaneo Beach

Lake Ohrid

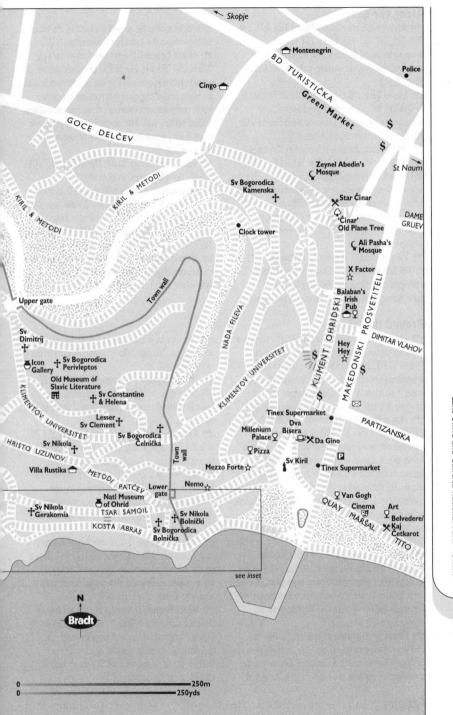

Skopje

Montenegrin

Police

BD TURISTIČKA
Green Market

Cingo

GOCE DELČEV

$

$

St Naum

KIRIL & METODI

KIRIL & METODI

Zeynel Abedin's
Mosque

Sv Bogorodica
Kamenska

Star Činar

Clock tower

'Činar'
Old Plane Tree

DAME
GRUEV

Ali Pasha's
Mosque

X Factor

Upper gate

Town wall

NADA FILEVA

Balaban's
Irish
Pub

KLIMENT OHRIDSKI

PROSVETITELI

DIMITAR VLAHOV

Sv
Dimitrij

Icon
Gallery

Sv Bogorodica
Perivleptos

Old Museum of
Slavic Literature

Sv Constantine
& Helena

Hey
Hey

$

$

$

KLIMENTOV UNIVERSITET

KLIMENTOV UNIVERSITET

MAKEDONSKI

Lesser
Sv Clement

Sv Nikola

HRISTO UZUNOV

Sv Bogorodica
Čelnička

Villa Rustika

METODI PATČEV

Tinex Supermarket

Millenium
Palace

Dva
Bisera

Da Gino

Pizza

Sv Kiril

PARTIZANSKA

Tinex Supermarket

P

Town
wall

Mezzo Forte

Lower
gate

Nemo

Natl Museum
of Ohrid

TSAR SAMOIL

Sv Nikola
Gerakomia

KOSTA ABRAS

Sv Nikola
Bolnički

Sv Bogorodica
Bolnička

Van Gogh
Cinema

QUAY MARŠAL

Art

Belvedere/
Kaj
Cetkarot

TITO

see inset

N

Bradt

0 _____ 250m
0 _____ 250yds

Along the quay

⌂ **Riviera** (36 rooms) Kej Maršal Tito 6; ☏ 046 268 735, 046 251 912; f 046 254 155; www.rivierahotel.com.mk. The hotel also has a restaurant with patio seating, a piano bar & mini-shop. $$$

⌂ **Hotel Tino** (18 rooms) Kej Maršal Tito 55; ☏ 046 261 665; e hoteltino@mt.net.mk; www.hoteltino.com.mk. Standard clean rooms with AC & bathroom. Prices inc b/fast. $$$

⌂ **Millenium Palace** (25 rooms) Kej Maršal Tito 110; ☏ 046 267 010, 046 265 414; f 046 263 361; e info@milleniumpalace.com.mk; www.milleniumpalace.com.mk. Standard smart hotel with internet connection. The hotel also has its own sauna, fitness centre & restaurant. A great buffet b/fast is 250MKD for non-residents. $$$

⌂ **Villa Biljana** (5 rooms) Kej Maršal Tito 111; ☏ 046 266 444, 070 833 130; e reservations@ vilabiljana.com.mk; www.vilabiljana.com.mk. Sandwiched between the Millenium & the Lebed,

these rooms offer the view & location of the other hotels without the extra hotel trimmings. $$$

⌂ **Hotel Lebed** (10 apts) Kej Maršal Tito 112; ☏ 046 250 004, 046 263 607; e tani@mt.net.mk; www.hotellebed.com.mk. The last accommodation at the quiet end of the quay, this recently renovated hotel, complete with internet connection, also offers private parking with 24hr surveillance. All prices inc b/fast & vary according to whether rooms have a lake view. $$$

⌂ **Villa Dea** (10 rooms) Kej Maršal Tito 40; ☏ 046 265 251; e info@deatours.com.mk; www.deatours.com.mk. Excellent value & location for the price. Rooms have balcony & view over the lake. B/fast available at Hotel Royal next door. $$

⌂ **Apartmani Agiroski** (8 apts) Kej Maršal Tito 26; ☏ 046 262 844, 070 743 576; www.agiroski.com. Set down the little alley on the way to the Catholic church, these apts are clean, modern & some have a view of the lake from the balcony. $$

Around the lake

⌂ **Hotel Inex Gorica** (125 rooms) In the same complex as the president's summer residence; ☏ 046 277 522; e bookings@inexgorica.com; www.inexgorica.com. Completely refurbished, the hotel is pleasant & high quality. Access to 3 small beaches & a café pavilion on the water. $$$$

⌂ **Hotel Granit** (233 rooms) Sv Stefan; ☏ 046 277 886/887; f 046 277 888; e hotelgranit@ europe.com; www.hotelgranit.com.mk. Despite its name, this is a pleasant, large hotel with direct access to the lake & a jetty for boats. Lakeside rooms are subjected to the café music & evening conferences or events spilling onto the lawn. Paddle boats on the beach are 150MKD per hour. Suites are better value for money for 2 people sharing. $$$

⌂ **Hotel Desaret** (252 rooms, 9 villas) near Peštani; ☏ 046 285 950/951; f 046 285 915. Despite its large size, a nice facility with a wide beach & more privacy in the little villa-type accommodation. For those hankering after well-kept communist décor, this is the place. $$$

⌂ **Hotel Sveti Naum** (30 rooms) ☏ 046 283 080. Your chance to stay in the holy grounds where Sv Naum himself taught & preached. Situated at the south end of the lake, the monastery is tranquil at

night but can be just as busy as Ohrid during the day with visitors. The peacocks crow loudly early in the morning. $$$

⌂ **Hotel Lagadin** (10 rooms) ☏ 046 285 227, 070 261 448; e info@hotellagadin.com.mk; www.hotellagadin.com.mk. Basic rooms above the restaurant. $$$

⌂ **Apartments Lagadin** (4 apts) ☏ 046 254 200, 070 307 460. Built in 2005, these apts are spacious & tastefully furnished, including all the usual hotel extras as well as a lounge & small kitchenette. View & sounds of the lake from the balcony. Lagadin Beach, a shop & restaurants are a few minutes away. Prices exc b/fast vary according to the season. $$$

⌂ **Studio Lagadin** (2-bedroom house & 1 apt) ☏ 046 285 041, 070 818 758; f 02 3177 746. Set up on the hill behind the main bustle of little Lagadin, these studios surround a pleasant garden & seating area with a view of the lake. $$

⌂ **Hotel Brand** (26 rooms) On the hill side of the road above Hotel Granit; ☏ 046 277 220–2; e hotel@tkprilep.com.mk. A friendly hotel that benefits from the beach access & some of the facilities of the Granit without the luxury cost & loud music in the summer. $$

Camping ($) All the sites listed here are 500MKD per tent space (maximum four people per tent space) plus 40MKD tourism tax per person.

⚑ Gradište (400 tent spaces, 25 caravans, 8 bungalows) 17km from Ohrid on the way to Sv Naum; ☎ 046 285 945/845. Huge, but with it comes a long stretch of beach & several ball courts. Conveniently located next to the Bay of Bones & Peštani village.

⚑ Ljubaništa (65 tent spaces) Close to the Sv Naum end of the lake; ☎ 046 283 240
⚑ Elesec (70 tent spaces) 10km on the eastern road of Lake Ohrid; ☎ 046 285 926

If you run out of options above, private rooms are available around the lake for as little as 350MKD without breakfast.

✗ WHERE TO EAT
Ohrid has a host of little pizzerias and fish restaurants along Tsar Samoil and Kosta Abraš, and fast-food joints and cafés galore along Kliment Ohridski. They can quickly become much of a muchness, and once you've eaten through the good few, fish again can become a bit boring. Despite the fact that Ohrid trout is endangered and illegal to fish, restaurants here still pride themselves on serving it. Ohrid is begging for some cuisine alternatives and a really good breakfast café in the centre. Here are some of the best available.

✗ Gladiator Brakja Miladinovci 14 (directly overlooking the amphitheatre); ☎ 046 266 942; ⊕ daily 11.00–24.00. Despite the bullish title, this charming restaurant has terrace views from up high of the lake & serves traditional Macedonian food in a traditional setting with the best of Macedonia's trad/mod ethno music. **$$$**
✗ Restoran Sv Sofia Tsar Samoil 88; ☎ 046 267 403; www.restoransvetasofija.com.mk; ⊕ daily 08.00–24.00. On the uphill side of Sv Sofia Church, has

a wonderful outdoor patio overlooking the church, & good food. Try their excellent fried squid. **$$$**
✗ Antiko Tsar Samoil 30; ☎ 046 265 523; ⊕ daily 12.00–24.00. An upmarket place to eat, with a wooden interior. Traditional Macedonian dishes take 3hrs to prepare so order ahead. **$$$**
✗ Dalga Kosta Abraš 3; ☎ 046 255 999; e dalga@restorani.com.mk; www.dalga.restaurants.com.mk; ⊕ Sun–Thu 10.00–24.00, Fri & Sat 10.00–01.00. Ohrid's original

500 YEARS OF THE KANEVČE FAMILY AT KANEO

The Kanevče family came to Kaneo from Kičevo over 500 years ago in the late 1400s. They settled in the sheltered nook of the rocks of Kaneo still protected within the town walls, and quickly became wealthy lake fishermen after they bought the fishing rights for the northern half of the lake from Peštani to Kalište from the Ottomans. The family soon outgrew the small settlement at Kaneo and expanded into Ohrid itself where some of the early 19th-century houses still belong to the family, such as the one below Sveta Sofia Church and their older houses on Kaneo beach. Ohrid's abundant fishing and its position on a major trading route kept the Kanevče family busy up until the beginning of the 20th century.

Then with the Balkan Wars, the division of Macedonia, the closed-door policies of early communism, and the negative effects of a bloated and over-centralised socialism, the luck of the Kanevče family went downhill. Stefan Kanevče, who remembers those days of good fishing with his grandfather, is still a keen fisherman and will happily take you out fishing on the lake if you want. He's also a mine of knowledge on many things in Ohrid and Macedonia. But the fishing trade isn't what it used to be, and he and his family have little money now to renovate the beautiful but crumbling houses at Kaneo. His, however, are the few rooms in Macedonia where you can actually stay in an original 19th-century house, complete with intricate wooden ceiling, closets and wardrobes. No heating and no television, only the sound of the waves of the lake to lull you to sleep at night.

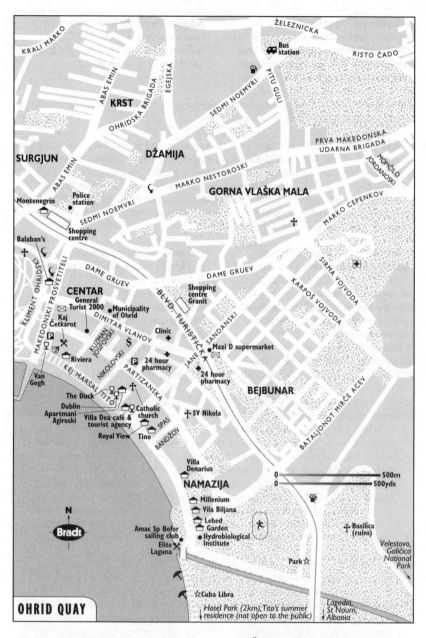

OHRID QUAY

Map labels:
ŽELEZNICKA · Bus station · RISTO ČADO · KRALI MARKO · ABAS EMIN · OHRIDSKA BRIGADA · EGEJSKA · SEDMI NOEMVRI · PITU GULI · KRST · DŽAMIJA · PRVA MAKEDONSKA UDARNA BRIGADA · MOMČILO JORDANOSKI · SURGJUN · ABAS EMIN · MARKO NESTOROSKI · GORNA VLAŠKA MALA · MARKO CEPENKOV · Montenegrin · Police station · SEDMI NOEMVRI · SIRMA VOJVODA · Balaban's · DAME GRUEV · DAME GRUEV · KARPOŠ VOJVODA · KLIMENT OHRIDSKI · MAKEDONSKI PROSVETITELI · CENTAR · General Turist 2000 · Municipality of Ohrid · Shopping centre Granit · BLVD. TURISTIČKA · JANE SANDANSKI · Kaj Četkarot · DIMITAR VLAHOV · Clinic · Maxi D supermarket · KUZMAN JOSIFOVSKI · Riviera · NIKOLOVSKI · 24 hour pharmacy · 24 hour pharmacy · BEJBUNAR · Van Gogh · KEJ MARŠAL TITO · PARTIZANSKA · BATALJONOT MIRČE ACEV · The Duck · Dublin · Apartmani Agiroski · Villa Dea café & tourist agency · Catholic church · SV Nikola · Royal View · Tino · SPAS · BANDŽOV · Villa Denarius · NAMAZIJA · Millenium · Vila Biljana · Lebed · Garden · Hydrobiological Institute · Basilica (ruins) · Amac Sp Bofor sailing club · Elite Laguna · Park · Velestovo, Galičica National Park · Bradt · N · Cuba Libra · Hotel Park (2km), Tito's summer residence (not open to the public) · Lagodin, St Naum, Albania

Shopping centre

0   500m
0   500yds

---

lakeside fish restaurant sporting photos of all the rich & famous who have ever eaten there. **$$$**

✕ **Taverna Momir** Kosta Abraš 1; ☎ 046 262 117; e momir@restorani.com.mk; www.momir.restaurants.com.mk; ⏰ Sun–Thu 08.00–24.00, Fri & Sat 08.00–01.00. Nice lakeside seating with more Macedonian food. **$$$**

✕ **Kaj Četkarot** Kaj Maršal Tito 3; ☎ 046 231 520; ⏰ 08.30–24.00. Named after the wagons (četkar) on the lawn outside the restaurant. Serves traditional food in a national-style setting, including cooked b/fasts. **$$$**

✕ **Restoran Kaneo Beach** Kaneo; ⏰ daily 09.00–01.00 in summer only. Right on the water, serving basic dishes, but you can't beat the location, even if it is only for a drink. **$$**

✗ Potpeš Kaneo; ⊕ daily 09.00–01.00 in summer only. Rivalling its neighbour, there is not much to choose between the two. Also open only in the summer, when both can become very crowded, so arrive early. **$$**

✗ Elite Laguna Kaj Maršal Tito; ⊕ daily 12.00–24.00. Pleasant little place overlooking the yacht club boats on Biljana Springs estuary, although the food is nothing special. Limited menu of traditional fare & pizzas. **$$**

✗ Star Činar 7 Noemvri 1; ✆ 046 260 890; ⊕ daily 12.00–24.00. Local food at local prices overlooking the old plane tree. Serves extremely strong green *rakija* (*zelena rakija*). **$$**

✗ Da Gino's Pizzeria in Skopje has a branch in Ohrid right on the main square; ⊕ Sun–Thu 08.00–24.00, Fri & Sat 08.00–01.00. Excellent pizzas with fresh mushrooms rather than tinned. **$$**

BARS AND CAFÉS These stretch all the way from Restoran Kaneo Beach (see *Where to eat* above) to Cuba Libra (see *Nightclubs* below) at Biljana Springs, although it is mostly hotel fronts along the quay.

♀ Balaban's Irish Pub Bd Makedonija Prosvotiteli. Just like you would expect an Irish pub abroad to be, but no draught Guinness.

♀ The Duck Pub Kaj Maršal Tito; ✆ 075 304 505. Plays classic blues & jazz, with a live band every night in the summer. Great for people-watching along the quay.

☕ Dva Bisera Café Kliment Ohridski bb, next door to the restaurant of the same name, near Sv Kliment's statue; ⊕ 08.00–24.00. Serves a variety of sweet & savoury pastries, fresh fruit juice, & the usual coffees. **$**

♀ Urania Kosta Abraš 60. Overlooking the lake, this place is slightly more laidback than some of the other bars along this street.

☕ Zone Garden Kosta Abraš 66. The only café to have a stretch of sand in the old town. Popular with the bronzed & beautiful.

NIGHTCLUBS These are abundant in Ohrid. Here are a few favourites.

☆ Aquarius Kosta Abraš 30; ⊕ 10.00–01.00. Very popular place right on the lake.

☆ Carpe Diem Kosta Abraš 32; ⊕ 10.00–01.00. Listen to Aquarius's music in the summer but at a slightly lower volume with a slightly less trendy crowd.

☆ Cuba Libra Biljana Springs Beach; ⊕ 11.00–04.00. The hottest place in town, & right on the water if you need a dip. Live bands most nights.

☆ Hey Hey Bd Makedonija Prosvetiteli; ⊕ 22.00–03.00. Popular dance tunes & turbo-Slav nightclub.

☆ Jazz Inn Kosta Abraš 80; ⊕ 22.30–01.00. Good, live music on Thu, Fri & Sat. Very popular.

☆ Liquid Kosta Abraš 17; ✆ 046 258 552; ⊕ 10.00–01.00; www.liquid.com.mk. Ultra trendy on the lakefront featuring live bands at the w/ends. Serves cocoa. Has Wi-Fi.

☆ Mezzo Forte Tsar Samoil 4; ⊕ 11.00–01.00. A happening little place.

☆ Nemo Tsar Samoil 20; ⊕ 11.00–01.00. Arguably one of the most popular places in the old town.

☆ Park Turistička bb, just past the petrol station; ⊕ 22.00–03.00. For a proper discotheque.

☆ Tabana Tsar Samoil 11; ⊕ 10.00–01.00. Has a fantastic rooftop pub overlooking the lake.

☆ X Factor Bd Makedonija Prosvetiteli; ⊕ 22.00–03.00. Rock & techno nightclub.

WHAT TO SEE AND DO Unlike the rest of Macedonia, Ohrid is cottoning onto how to make money from its tourist attractions, and almost all the cultural and historical sites require an entry fee of 100MKD per person. In those few churches that do not charge an entry fee it is customary to leave some money at the altar or icons anyway, and the money is definitely needed if Macedonia is to preserve these historical sites.

Churches and monasteries Of the 365 holy sites around the lake, here are six of the most important within the town to start you off. Details of many more of the lesser churches can be found in various booklets available in most of the church shops and bookshops in Ohrid.

Sv Kliment at Plaošnik Dedicated to saints Kliment (Clement) and Pantelejmon, this was completed in 2002. It stands beside the original site of Kliment's very own monastery school, started in AD893. Kliment had built the original church on the ruins of the early 5th-century basilica at Plaošnik, and had even built his own tomb into the church, in which he was buried upon his death in AD916. Almost 150 graves were recently found and suggest that the church was also a hospital during Kliment's time.

The church was renovated and enlarged three times in the 12th, 13th and 14th centuries, but during the time of Ottoman rule the church was transformed into the Imater Mosque. Sv Kliment's relics were then hastily moved to the 10th-century church of Sveta Bogorodica Perivleptos. The mosque did not survive the end of the Ottoman Empire and after its destruction only the legend remained that Sv Kliment's monastery and his tomb used to stand at Plaošnik.

Excavations started in 1943, and it was not long before the foundations of the church, the basilica and the tomb were found. Frescoes from the renovation and enlargement periods have also been found, but none from the original 9th-century church. The foundations of the 5th-century basilica have been preserved and are on display in front of the new church. Excavations continue, and there is discussion in the town about restarting a theological university at the site.

Sv Sofia The church was built in the early 11th century as a cathedral church for Archbishop Leo of the Archbishopric of Ohrid. It was also built on the remains of a former basilica and later became a mosque and then a warehouse during the Ottoman Empire. In 1912 it was re-converted to a church.

As a mosque the inside of the cathedral had been completely whitewashed and so it took extensive work during the second half of the 20th century to retrieve the 11th-century frescoes which lay underneath. Most of these are now on display again, as well as some of those from later renovations of the church in the 12th and 14th centuries. Sv Sofia is one of only two churches in the world to display such a high number of well-preserved 11th-century frescoes. The other is Sv Sophia in Kiev.

Sv Bogorodica Perivleptos (Sv Kliment's Church of the Holy Mother of God Most Glorious) This late 13th-century church took on the Sv Kliment prefix only when Sv Kliment's relics were transferred there during the Ottoman Empire. At the same time the church became the cathedral of the archbishop when the original cathedral at Sv Sophia was converted into a mosque. By the end of the 15th century the cathedral had started to become a collection point for historical records and artefacts saved from other churches around Ohrid. In 1516 the cathedral's collection and its library became the archbishopric museum, which is now the National Museum of Ohrid housed in the Robev residence (see below). In the 1950s, centuries of smoke and soot from candles and incense were carefully cleaned from the frescoes to reveal some interesting examples of late medieval painting. Look out for the fresco of the Last Supper, which is being eaten outside rather than inside, and note the use of perspective in this new style of painting which emerged in the late 12th century as opposed to the older style of more traditional churches.

Sv Jovan Kaneo This is the most frequently visited church in Ohrid because of its beautiful location on the cliffs directly above the lake. It was built at the end of the 13th century by an unknown benefactor, but shows signs of both Byzantine and Armenian influence. Inside, a group fresco of the 3rd-century Sv Erasmus, believed to be one of the first missionaries to the area, together with the 9th-century Sv Clement and the early 14th-century Archbishop Constantine Kavacila of Ohrid betray the eclectic nature of the church, which although built later than Sv Clement's Church of Sv Bogorodica Perivleptos, was painted in the older style of 11th- and 12th-century frescoes.

This church features visibly in Mančevski's *Before the Rain*, a must-see film about Macedonia (see page 61). Behind the church, a small path leads up to Sv Kliment's Church at Plaošnik. Tucked away in the rock below the entrance to the church grounds is also the very small cave church of Sv Bogorodica.

Sv Bogorodica Bolnička and Sv Nikola Bolnički These are to be found on either side of a small lane leading from the Lower Gate of the town wall to the lake. Both were built in the 14th century and were originally hospital churches (*bolnica* in Macedonian), separated into the women's hospital of the Virgin Mary, and the men's hospital of Sv Nikola. The men's hospital is some 70 years older than the women's hospital and is an interesting construction of an older church inside a newer church. Both back onto the town wall, parts of which can still be found in the church grounds. Sv Nikola is usually closed, but well worth a look into – ask Slavica next door at the women's hospital to open the heavy walnut doors for you.

Museums and galleries
National Museum of Ohrid (✆ *046 267 173;* ⊕ *daily 10.00–14.00, 18.00–21.00*) The museum was first established in 1516 in Sv Kliment's Church of Bogorodica Perivleptos as a museum to the Archbishopric of Ohrid. This must make it one of the oldest museums in the world. Now the collection is divided into the archaeological display housed in the Robev residence and the ethnographic display housed in the Urania residence. The Robev house on Tsar Samoil is the renovated wooden three-storey house, which is a museum piece in itself, and one of the finest examples of 19th-century Macedonian architecture in the land; well worth a visit. The Golden Room displaying the only golden mask allegedly still in Macedonia (see page 175) is due to open in 2009.

Icon Gallery (✆ *046 251 395;* ⊕ *daily 09.00–13.00, 17.00–20.00*) On the edge of the back wall of the old town, the gallery shows a range of some of the most valuable icons from the 11th to 19th centuries saved from churches all over Macedonia.

Local artisans Ohrid is home to many painters, sculptors, woodcarvers and other artisans hidden away in narrow streets. **Cosa Nostra** (*Kosta Abraš 48;* ✆ *070 623 939;* e *marinovamarija@hotmail.com;* ⊕ *daily 11.00–15.00, 18.00–23.00*) sells a wide variety of handmade local products, souvenirs and jewellery from many artisans all over Macedonia. The Sv Kliment Ohridski handmade paper makers at Tsar Samoil 60 (✆ *046 253 610, 075 465 131;* e *panevski@ohridpaper.com.mk*) is a fascinating little shop with one of only two replicas of the **Gothenburg press**. Paper is handmade, hand-printed in the press and sold in the shop. Vangel Dereban **silver filigree** workshop is at Sveti Kliment Ohridski 40. In the lower town, Vasil Malezan **packsaddle workshop** is at Goce Delčev 40, and Milan Belevski **cobbler** is at Goce Delčev 26 for handmade shoes and repairs.

Paintings and artwork can be found in many galleries in the old town; also:

Atelier Gallery Tsar Samoil 52. For the work of Živko Pejoski.
Gallery Ohridska Porta 29th November 3. For the work of Vangel Naumovski.

Gallery Upevče 7th November 10
Gallery Bukefal Sv Kliment Ohridski 54

Ohrid pearls made from the scales of local fish are sold in many shops along Kliment Ohridski and at:

Gallery Marija Dame Gruev 28

Antica Pearls Kosta Abraš 51 & Klimentov Univerzitet 87

Woodcarving workshops and wooden icons are available at:

Barok Tsar Samoil 24
Porta Tsar Samoil 32

Tron Tsar Samoil bb (nr Villa Germanoff)

Other sites of interest in Ohrid

Tsar Samoil's Fortress (⊕ *Tue–Sun 09.00–18.00*) The fortress dates only from the end of the 10th century, but records from Livy and other ancient historians tell that a fortress has stood on the top of Ohrid Hill since at least the 3rd century BC and other findings go back even further. In 2002, a golden mask and glove similar to those found in Trebenište (see box on page 175) from the Paeonian period were found behind the fortress walls.

Today much of the 3km fortified wall which enclosed the fortress can still be seen, although the inside of the fortress itself is mostly destroyed and still awaiting restoration. Up until the Ottomans arrived in Ohrid in 1395, the town was completely enclosed within these great city walls, and only two gates, the Upper Gate and the Lower Gate, existed by which to enter the town. The people of Ohrid must have put up an almighty fight against the Turks from within the walls. Once taken, though, the town expanded beyond the walls as the Turks and Ottomans moved into the Ohrid area. As in other towns like Skopje, the Ottomans kept the Christian population within the town walls. The town walls must then have felt more like a prison barrier than a defensive structure.

Mesokastro The Turks meanwhile built up what came to be known as the Lower Town of the Mesokastro area, which continues today to have a more Turkish feel to it. There you will find two working mosques, the Zeynel Abedin Mosque and Ali Pasha's Mosque, astride the **900-year-old plane tree** (*Platanus orientalis*) known locally as *Činar* in the middle of Kruševska Republika Square. Allegedly, this tree's hollow trunk used to house a barber's shop at some time in its history and later a very small café. As the old Turkish town winds around the back of the town wall you will see a number of old Turkish shops which are no longer in use, but their dust-covered artefacts and tools are still on display. These may not be around for much longer as a few new buildings are beginning to encroach.

Roman amphitheatre The Roman amphitheatre near the Upper Gate is just over 2,000 years old, but had been buried for centuries until, in the early 20th century, trial excavations confirmed its location. The next few decades of turmoil put the full excavation on hold, until in the 1960s the excavations finally got going again. By the 1990s the amphitheatre was fully uncovered and is now once again being used in the summer as in days of old for outdoor concerts and performances. If you manage to attend a concert there, take a close look at your seat to see if you can decipher the name of the season ticket holder who owned that seat some 2,000 years ago.

Walking along the lake Heading south out of Ohrid along Kej Maršal Tito is particularly pleasant in the evening when the sun is setting on the lake. Sometimes there are buskers and street performers on the quayside. At the end of the quay

(1.3km from the centre's main street, Makedonija Prosvetiteli) is the yacht club Amak CP-Bofor and the **Biljana Springs** estuary. The springs are renowned for their refreshing drinking water, which is bottled and sold throughout Macedonia. For more information on the yacht club's membership, docking fees and yacht hire see page 43.

On the far side of the small bridge over the Biljana Springs estuary is the Army Water Training Centre, which has a beautiful little beach with a view onto Ohrid town, Tsar Samoil's fortress and the Church of Sv Jovan Kaneo. Cuba Libra café

DIVING IN LAKE OHRID

A tectonic lake almost 300m in depth with endemic plant and animal life, Ohrid offers a number of underwater attractions to the scuba diver. Arguably one of the most interesting sites is the **Bronze Age** (3,500 years ago) **stilt-village** Michovgrad, also known as the Bay of Bones, near Gradište. Discovered in 1997 and named after the diver who discovered it (see below), the village had been built on stilts over the marshy edges of the lake when the waters were not as high as they are today. The stumps of former stilts can still be seen sticking out of the sand under the water, as well as many pieces of broken amphora and other pottery. The best finds are on display in the small museum at the Bay of Bones (page 173). The site is a nationally protected area, and experienced divers may go there with permission.

As a geological area, the lake is interesting because of its depth and steep drop-offs. The steepest drop-off closest to the shoreline is beneath the karst cliffs over Gradište and Sv Zaum Church. Here, a 20m sheer wall shelters endemic plants, freshwater mussels and sponges. *Plašica, belvica* and gudgeon are plentiful to see when diving, and occasionally it is possible to see some mrenka and crayfish. Ohrid trout on the other hand are rarely seen as they live deep in the lake. Night diving offers the best chance to see eels as well as chub and larger fish coming up to feed.

Just south of Struga is a sunken World War II German coastguard boat and two **World War I tugboats**. The latter were deliberately sunk during the war to stop them getting into enemy hands. An Ottoman Empire rifle has been found in the lake (see the town museum, page 171), and on the Albanian side of the water is believed to be a small **World War II aeroplane**. A project is also ongoing to try to find part of the Via Egnatia, which is believed to lie somewhere underwater between Struga and Ohrid around Sv Erasmus Church.

All of these sites (except the aeroplane) can be seen through Amfora Dive Centre, based at the Hotel Granit (✆ 046 207 100, 070 700 865; www.amfora.com.mk). Their chief instructor and divemaster, English-speaking Micho (the discoverer of Michovgrad), has done over 5,000 dives in Lake Ohrid, and is also the Macedonian army's special forces diving instructor. As with diving anywhere, take care not to disturb the lake bed: not only is the sandy bottom very easily disturbed, causing a deterioration in visibility, but the lake's endemic species are also vulnerable. Visibility is at its best in the lake (up to 22m) during May and September. You will need to purchase a yearly dive licence (valid for 365 days) before diving. Thereafter the dive fee to Michovgrad is €30; all other sites €20 – including all equipment. Tank refill is €10. Amfora Dive Centre is Scuba Schools International certified and will also accept PADI, BSAC and other licensed divers. Diving courses are available on request.

As with diving anywhere, check you are satisfied with the equipment provided before diving. A diving buddy of mine who is a British army diving instructor noticed on our dive that the tanks were out of date, hence this added word of caution.

bar and nightclub is also here. The next 1.7km along the lake goes through partially wooded grounds away from the main road to the Hotel Park. Cyclists and rollerbladers frequent the path and there are several little entry points to the lake. At Hotel Park, the path skirts around **Tito's summer residence**, which sits atop the promontory that marks the south end of Ohrid Bay. It is now the summer residence of the President of Macedonia and so is not open to visitors.

On the other side of Tito's summer residence is the four-star Hotel Inex Gorica and a number of holiday camps. A path along the rocky shore continues from inside the Inex Gorica complex for another 2km in front of other holiday camps and hotels until it meets up with the main road.

Heading north out of Ohrid old town past the Church of Sv Jovan Kaneo is a pleasant walk for about 500m to the back of the town. There is plenty of exploring to be done among the old wall and fortress, with splendid lake views.

FESTIVALS AND EVENTS IN OHRID Summer is the big festival season for Ohrid. In early July is the **Balkan Folklore Festival.** From mid-July to mid-August is the **Ohrid Summer Festival** now over four decades old. Classical concerts and plays are held in historical and outdoor locations around the town, such as in the amphitheatre, basilicas, churches and Tsar Samoil's fortress. Simultaneously through August there is also the **Ohrid Troubadour Festival** of popular and folk music. On Ilinden, 2 August, is the Ilinden Sailing Regatta. Usually the last weekend in August is reserved for the **Ohrid International Swimming Marathon** when, since 1962, swimmers have been invited to test their strength against the 30km course from Sv Naum to Ohrid. In September Ohrid holds the musical and folklore festival entitled '**Songs of the Old City**'.

OUTSIDE OHRID

SV NAUM MONASTERY The Monastery of Sv Naum is right at the other end of the lake near the border with Albania. It is a beautiful and popular site, with well-kept grounds that are home to a flock of peacocks, including an albino, and a source of the waters for Lake Ohrid. New inns built in the last decade make up the Hotel of Sv Naum (see contact details on page 166).

The actual early 10th-century Church of the Holy Archangels built by Sv Naum is in fact buried beneath the present 16th-century church, which stands in the middle of the monastery courtyards. The church had been destroyed during Ottoman rule and its remains were rediscovered only in 1955 when excavations beneath the present church floor were carried out. The original church was a typical trefoil or clover-leaf design and contained the tomb and relics of Sv Naum himself. These have been preserved and re-interred beneath the new floor of the present church, which is now marked with black and white marble to show the floor plan of the original 10th-century church.

The present church was enlarged in the 17th and 18th centuries, and in 1799 the tiny chapel over Sv Naum's underground tomb was built. When you enter the chapel, which is to the right as you enter the narthex, and listen very carefully above the tomb, you are meant to be able to hear Sv Naum's heart still beating. Touching the stone above the tomb is also meant to make a wish come true.

BOAT TRIPS FROM NAUM A boat trip down to the springs, which feed Lake Ohrid, is available from Sv Naum. Trips and boat numbers are limited by the Galičica National Park authorities as the springs are rare natural phenomenon and therefore it is important not to disturb the ecological balance in the waters. This doesn't stop unlicensed boatmen from trying to take surplus visitors in the busy summer months, so make sure you take a legal ride. The 45 springs, which bubble up from the bottom of the crystal clear stream bed, mostly bring water from the neighbouring lake of Prespa on the other side of Galičica National Park. Prespa lies another 157m above Lake Ohrid and so the water is effectively siphoned off through the bed of Galičica Mountains into the spring on the other lower side of the mountain.

A good boatman to go with is Nikola Pavleski. For 120MKD on your half-hour trip into the springs and back, he will give a constant stream of information in English and Macedonian, as well as stops just to listen to the tranquillity and the orchestra of birds, allow for photographs and of course see the bubbling springs themselves. He tops it off with a round of *rakija* for everyone.

SV STEFAN MONASTERY AND CAVE CHURCH Just 5km outside Ohrid is the Monastery and Cave Church of Sv Stefan, hidden away above the lake a 500m hike from the lake road. The little old lady, Raina, a wizened *baba*, almost bent in half from years of sweeping and caring for the grounds, is the only person now living in the monastery. She will tell you that the original cave church here was built in the 9th century at the time of Sv Clement. Villagers from the surrounding settlements of Šiponko, Gorica and Konjsko up the hill have since built the present walls and in the 15th century the church was painted with frescoes.

The best reason to go to the church is indeed Raina. She'll serve you coffee if you have time to stop and chat, and will try to sell you postcards from the last foreigners who stopped by. She doesn't like having her photo taken though.

To get there take the path uphill from opposite the Hotel Beton, 4.5km from the petrol station on the eastern edge of Ohrid. The path is marked with a hand-painted sign saying Sv Stefan in Cyrillic.

At the gateway into the monastery the path continues up above the monastery to the villages of Šiponko in the north and Konjsko in the south, and further

THE GOLDEN MASKS OF MACEDONIA

North of Ohrid Airport, outside the village of Trebenište, are the burial tombs of what have become some of the most important and richest archaeological discoveries ever to be made in Macedonia. The unearthing of ten chambers in 1918 revealed the lavish burial ceremonies of the ancient Paeons and Macedonians of the 1st millennium BC. Five golden masks were found in the graves as well as jewellery, pottery, ceremonial clothing and shoes. The burial chambers belonged to rich princes of the region who were cremated at death, so only the burial riches remain. Three of the masks are now in Belgrade and the other two in Sofia. Each mask is worth in the region of €18 million. Part of a sixth mask has been found at the Petilep tomb in Beranci, near Bitola, and more tombs, long since ransacked, exist all over Macedonia.

Sensationally in 2002, Pasko Kuzman made his name as Macedonia's leading archaeologist when he discovered a sixth complete golden mask during excavations at Tsar Samoil's fortress in Ohrid. No documentation of the find has been logged, and the mask has been kept since then in a cigar box in Kuzman's apartment. Now, however, that he has been re-instated as the country's top archaeologist since the re-election of the new centre-right government, Kuzman is due to put the mask on display in 2009 in the soon-to-be opened Golden Room at the Museum of Skopje. This will be the first time that any of the masks have been publicly seen in Macedonia. Little but age-old scars in the ground exist at the Trebenište tomb now, and the fortress is still under excavation.

hiking into Galičica National Park. Beware the Šarplaninec sheepdogs in the old and dying settlement of Šiponko, and the villagers don't like strangers wandering around on their own.

There are two more cave churches on the eastern side of the lake, one at Sv Erasmus and Sv Ekaterina between Ohrid and Struga, and one on Gradište II beach at Gradište campsite near Pestani halfway to Sv Naum. There are good views of Lake Ohrid from these churches.

STRUGA

On the northern shore of Lake Ohrid is the town of Struga. Also boasting human settlements going back to Neolithic times (3,000BC), the old name of Struga is Enchalon, the ancient Greek word for eel, which is still a popular food in the area (see page 38). The new name Struga comes from the old Slavic *straga* meaning 'cross', but some say it also comes from the word *struže* meaning 'blowing wind'. With just over 16,000 inhabitants in the town and 35,000 people in the municipality, Struga is less than half as populous as nearby Ohrid. Dwarfed in size and popularity by its neighbour, Struga is nevertheless an up-and-coming town and a delightful getaway from busy Ohrid in the height of the summer season. Its many cafés along the River Drim leading out of Lake Ohrid make a good day or night out and there are some pleasant places to stay and to visit in the vicinity.

GETTING THERE AND AROUND There are regular buses to Struga from all over the country. Many buses from north of Struga are on their way to Ohrid, and stop at the petrol station turn-off, where a *kombe* minibus is waiting to transport passengers for an extra 40MKD each the 15 minutes into town. It is less than half an hour's drive from Ohrid to Struga, which costs 300MKD by taxi. Ohrid Airport (see page 161) is only 15 minutes away by taxi. The minimum taxi fare in Struga is 30MKD. There are no town buses. The inter-town bus station (✆ 046 782 770) at the northern outskirts of the town is 1.5km from the centre. There are three international bus services leaving from Struga: the daily 17.30 bus to Belgrade, Serbia, via Skopje; the daily 12.00 bus to Istanbul, Turkey; and the Friday 18.30 bus to Sofia, Bulgaria. National and local bus times from Struga are listed below.

There are more buses to other destinations, such as Prilep, Štip, Strumica and Veles, during the summer months. For more information enquire at the bus station or check www.struga.org/eng/index_eng.html.

BUS DEPARTURES FROM STRUGA	
Kičevo–Skopje	06.00, 08.30, 10.30, 12.00, 14.00, 16.00, 17.30
Mavrovo–Skopje	05.00, 05.45
Bitola–Skopje	07.00, Bitola 10.00
Debar	05.45, 08.00, 10.00, 11.30, 13.00, 14.30, 17.30
Ohrid	from 05.00–22.00 every 15mins
Vevčani	from 05.00–20.00 every hr
Labuništa	from 05.00–20.00 every 30mins
Del. Korosišta	from 06.00–20.00 every 30mins
Oktisi	from 05.00–20.00 every 30mins
Nerezi	05.00, 15.30
Radožda	06.15, 09.00, 13.00, 15.00, 19.00

WHERE TO STAY Struga has a number of lakefront hotels ranging from 10 to 250 rooms. The nicer or more personal ones are:

🏠 **Drim** (205 rooms) Kej Boris Kidrič; ☎ 046 782 611, 046 784 327; e hdrim@mt.net.mk; www.hoteldrim.com.mk. Close to the centre of town, the quay & a long stretch of beach. Drim also owns the Hotel Belgrad at the edge of the old town & on the pedestrian area. But it is in dire need of renovation & is noisy even if it is cheaper than Drim. $$$

🏠 **Blue Sky** (23 rooms) Kej Boris Kidrič; ☎ 046 784 590, 070 757 999; www.bluesky-hotel.piczo.com. You can't get more central than this. Brand-new

rooms overlook the River Drim, but can be noisy on a w/end. All mod cons & free Wi-Fi. $$$

🏠 **Plaža** (20 rooms) Vlado Maleski bb; ☎ 046 786 126, 046 781 089. A Macedonian-style hotel built in the 1980s & yet to be refurbished. Close to the centre of town & overlooking the beach. $$

🏠 **Diplomat** (43 rooms) Velešta village, 4km north of Struga; ☎ 046 793 022/720; e info@ diplomatstruga.com; www.diplomatstruga.com. Clean new rooms in a pleasant setting, but can be popular with weddings & banquets. $$

WHERE TO EAT AND DRINK Along the River Drim and the pedestrian zone are lots of little pizza and snack places, cafés and bars.

✕ **Aquarius** 1.5km out of town on Vlado Maleski; ☎ 046 780 273; ⏰ daily 11.00–01.00. For an upmarket atmosphere overlooking the lake. $$$

✕ **Angela** Kaj Boris Kidrič west bank; ⏰ daily 11.00–23.00. A small restaurant with modern blues music & rough-hewn wooden tables & chairs. Serves local dishes including *furnagiska* (a *pastrmalija* or pizza bread base with pork or chicken, egg & cheese), *souflaka* (bowl of spicy pork or chicken), fresh grilled mushrooms, pizzas, & turkish coffee. $$

✕ **Sv Nikola Skara** Kaj Boris Kidrič west bank; ⏰ daily 11.00–23.00. A tiny grill joint on the river blessed with good food & friendly staff. $$

✕ **T'ga za Jug** Džumkarovski; ☎ 046 788 741; ⏰ Tue–Sun 11.00–01.00. For traditional food & setting in the centre of town. $$

✕ **Aleksandar Makedonski** Razme Maleski; ⏰ Tue–Sun 11.00–01.00. More traditional food & setting. $$

✕ **Taj Mahal** Kaj Boris Kidrič east bank; ⏰ daily 11.00–01.00. Not a curry in sight, but traditional Albanian food. $$

♀ **Harp** Kaj Boris Kidric east bank; ⏰ daily 11.00–01.00. 5 years ago there was only one Irish pub in Skopje, now they are in almost every town. This one offers the best margaritas in town, as well as a Guinness.

♀ **Alibi** Kaj Boris Kidrič east bank; ⏰ daily 11.00–01.00. A good bar for viewing the opposite busier side of the bank.

♀ **Soho** 15th Corpus 37; ☎ 071 396 575; ⏰ daily 11.00–02.00. Popular night bar & café during the day.

♀ **Tullimore Dew** 15th Corpus 39; ⏰ daily 10.30–02.00. More popular than the Harp, but the view is not as good.

♀ **Cinema** 15th Corpus 41; ⏰ daily 11.00–02.00. Busy café bar prior to going over to Glamour nightclub.

☕ **Admiral** 15th Corpus 43; ⏰ daily 11.00–02.00. Cool place to drink a coffee with a view onto the lake.

☆ **Glamour** 15th Corpus 40; ⏰ 22.30–03.00. The most popular nightclub in town.

Other restaurants and pizzerias such as **Konak** and **Tirona** are springing up near Aquarius.

WHAT TO SEE AND DO Struga offers a long pebble beach right in the centre of town, a lovely riverside walk from the lake through town along the Drim River, and a small compact pedestrian and old town area. Aside from wandering around the narrow streets, here are a few noteworthy sites.

Natural History Museum (*Boro Kalajdžioski bb;* ☎ *070 786 644, 070 782 487;* ⏰ *daily 09.00–17.00*) The legacy of Dr Nikola Nezlobinski (deceased), it has over 10,000 examples of flora and fauna from around Ohrid and Prespa. Mostly from his own collection and displayed in his original house, the collection is the best

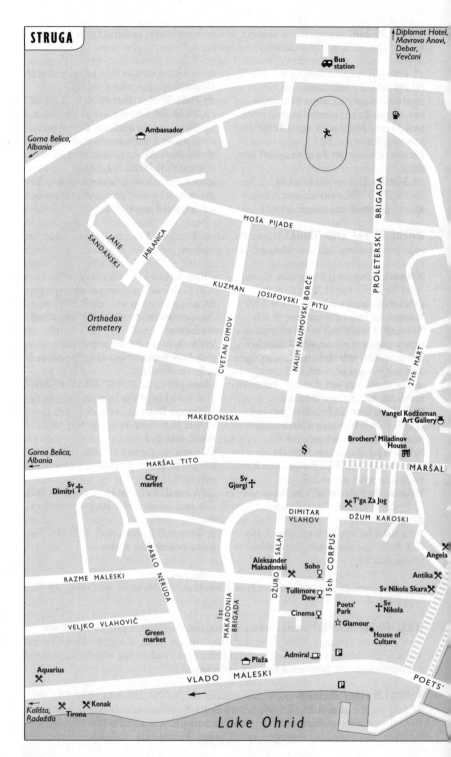

STRUGA

↑ Diplomat Hotel,
Mavrovo Anovi,
Debar,
Vevčani

Bus station

Gorna Belica,
Albania

Ambassador

MOŠA PIJADE

JANE SANDANSKI

JABLANICA

PROLETERSKI BRIGADA

KUZMAN JOSIFOVSKI PITU

NAUM NAUMOVSKI BORČE

Orthodox cemetery

CVETAN DIMOV

27th MART

MAKEDONSKA

Vangel Kodžoman
Art Gallery

Brothers' Miladinov
House

Gorna Belica,
Albania

MARŠAL TITO

MARŠAL

Sv Dimitri †

City market

Sv Gjorgi †

T'ga Za Jug

DIMITAR VLAHOV

DŽUM KAROSKI

PABLO NERUDA

DŽURO SALAJ

15th CORPUS

Aleksander Makadonski

Soho

Angela

RAZME MALESKI

Antika

Tullimore Dew

Sv Nikola Skara

1st MAKADONIA BRIGADA

Cinema

Poets' Park

† Sv Nikola

VELJKO VLAHOVIČ

Green market

☆ Glamour

House of Culture

Plaža

Admiral

P

Aquarius

VLADO MALESKI

P

POETS'

Kališta,
Radožda

Tirona

Konak

Lake Ohrid

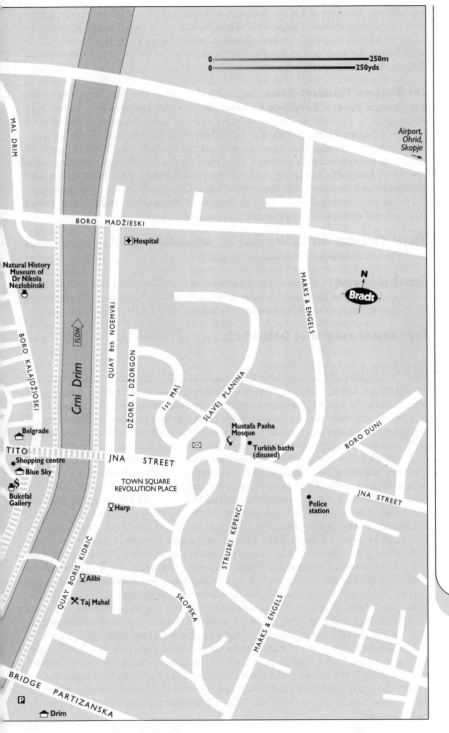

0 ——————————— 250m
0 ——————————— 250yds

Airport,
Ohrid,
Skopje →

N

Bradt

MAL DRIM

BORO MADŽIESKI

✚ Hospital

Natural History
Museum of
Dr Nikola
Nezlobinski

MARKS & ENGELS

QUAY 8th NOEMVRI

BORO KALAJDŽIOSKI

Crni Drim

FLOW

DŽORD I DŽORGON

1st MAJ

SLAVEJ PLANINA

Mustafa Pasha
Mosque

BORO DUNI

Belgrade

⊠

Turkish baths
(disused)

TITO

Shopping centre

Blue Sky

$

Bukefal
Gallery

JNA   STREET

TOWN SQUARE
REVOLUTION PLACE

Harp

Police
station

JNA STREET

STRUSKI KEPENCI

QUAY BORIS KIDRIČ

Alibi

✕ Taj Mahal

SKOPSKA

MARKS & ENGELS

BRIDGE   PARTIZANSKA

🅿

Drim

179

available on the region. Dr Nezlobinski, a Russian doctor who immigrated here in 1924 during Royalist Yugoslavia when Serbia encouraged many Russians to move to Macedonia, first put his collection on display in 1928. It is best to phone ahead to make sure or arrange for the museum to be open as it is often closed despite its alleged opening hours.

The Brothers' Miladinov House This old town house (see box, page 181) hosts the **Struga Poetry Evenings Collection** from the international festival held every year at the end of August. Always opened with Konstantin Miladinov's famous 'Longing for the South', the poetry evenings were started in 1962, exactly 100 years after the death of two of the brothers. Recitals take place throughout the town on the bridges over the Crni Drim. At the beginning of August is the festival of *Kengo jeho* (meaning 'Songs' Echo') **celebrating Albanian songs and dances** from Macedonia and the region. **Lake Day** is celebrated on 21 June with kayak races, music and food stalls. A festival of **Byzantine music**, the Struga Autumn of Music, takes place in the second half of autumn.

Vangel Kodžoman Art Gallery Near the Miladinov house, this gallery houses Kodžoman's paintings of old Struga.

Church of Sv Gjorgi On the western outskirts of the old town, it was built in 1835 on the grounds of an older 16th-century church, which contains a number of icons dating back to the 13th century, including one of Sv Gjorgi from 1267.

Town mosque and disused Turkish baths Next to the post office on JNA Street.

GALIČICA NATIONAL PARK

Founded in 1958, Galičica National Park extends from Ohrid Lake shore immediately west of Velestovo, through Velestevo village, around the peak of Bigla at 1,663m and then down to the shores of Lake Prespa just east of the village of Šurlenci. It includes all the land south of this line to the border of Albania. The park also includes the island of Golem Grad (see page 202) in Lake Prespa.

The park offers endless hikes in pristine countryside, although few of them are well marked so be confident of your orienteering skills before you go into the park, or take a guide. The top of the range plateaus out to a beautiful wide valley with a dirt vehicle track running through it. Some old ski lifts go up to some of the peaks. The highest peak completely in the park, Bugarska Čuka meaning 'Bulgarian peak', lies midway through the park, and from this peak there's a **panoramic view of both Lake Ohrid and Lake Prespa**. A new rangers' hut (grid 8914 4265) has been built along the plateau road, some 2.5km from which is the small **cave of Samatska Dupa**. A mere 235m long, but high enough to walk through for the most part, it is one of the few caves in Macedonia that has electric lighting. The entrance to the cave is locked off. To visit the cave with the lights turned on, arrange a tour with one of the tour agencies on page 163.

Almost 3km south of Trpejca village is the turn-off to the southern mountain pass of Livada at 1,568m. The winding asphalt road gives spectacular views of Lake Ohrid on one side and Lake Prespa on the other. From the pass, a two-hour hike south on a badly marked path leads to the peak of the range on the border with Albania. Both Prespa and Ohrid Lake can also be seen from this point.

On the Prespa side the road continues past the dishevelled holiday resort of Oteševo and on to Carev Dvor and Resen. The road is partly cobbled and partly badly paved.

RADOŽDA Radožda is the last village before Albania on the western side of Lake Ohrid. It's a sleepy fishing village right on the shores, which is renowned for the very best fish from the lake and for its **cave church** high on the cliffs overlooking the village. The cave church is dedicated to the Archangel Michael. Amongst the frescoes on the cave rocks is one of the archangel at the Miracle of Chonae. Some of the frescoes in this church date back to the 13th century. It's quite a steep hike up the steps to the church, and the door to the cave itself is usually kept locked. Ask for the key in the Dva Biseri Restaurant at the bottom of the steps.

Less well known is that sections of the Roman **Via Egnatia**, which followed the much older Candavian Way, can still be seen in the village. As they are mostly built of blocks some 3m wide and perfectly jointed, it is easy for the visitor to appreciate

MILADINOV'S 'LONGING FOR THE SOUTH'

The Miladinov brothers, Dimitrija (1810–62), Naum (1817–95) and Konstantin (1830–62), were pioneers in re-establishing the supremacy of the Macedonian language in Macedonia during a time when Greek had been brought into Macedonian schools and sermons (see page 44). Dimitrija was a prominent Macedonian-language teacher and struggled daily for the Ottoman authorities to recognise the Macedonian language. His brother Naum was a distinguished musician, and his youngest brother Konstantin became one of Macedonia's most famous poets with his poem 'Longing for the South' (T'ga za Jug, in Macedonian), written while studying in Russia. T'ga za Jug is now the name of a popular Macedonian wine and of numerous restaurants throughout Macedonia. Dimitrija and Konstantin both died in prison in 1862 for their efforts to bring the Macedonian language officially back to Macedonia. Their efforts were not wasted, however, and seven years later, in 1869, the Greek schools in the Ohrid region were finally shut down.

Longing for the South
If I had an eagle's wings
I would rise and fly with them
To our own shores, to our own climes,
To see Stamboul, to see Kukuš,
And to watch the sunrise: is it
Dismal there, as it is here?

If the sun still rises dimly,
If it meets me there as here,
I'll prepare for further travels,
I shall flee to other shores
Where the sunrise greets me brightly
And the sky is strewn with stars.

It is dark here, dark surrounds me,
Dark fog covers all the earth;
Here are frosts and snows and ashes,
Blizzards and harsh winds abound.
Fog everywhere, the earth is ice,
And in the breast are cold, dark thoughts.

No, I cannot stay here, no,
I cannot look upon these frosts.
Give me wings and I will don them;
I will fly to our own shores,
Go once more to our own places,
Go to Ohrid and to Struga.

There the sunrise warms the soul,
The sunset glows on wooded heights;
There are gifts in great profusion
Richly spread by nature's power.
Watch the clear lake stretching white
Or bluely darkened by the wind,
Look upon the plains or mountains:
Beauty's everywhere divine.

To pipe there to my heart's content!
Ah! let the sun set, let me die.

Konstantin Miladinov (1830–62)
Translated by Graham W Reid

what a feat of civil engineering the Via Egnatia was. This section of the road, however, is made of smaller blocks. It lies around 2km or a half-hour walk from the centre of the village. After the Dva Bisera Restaurant, at the first village shop, turn right up the hill to a small church where the tarmac runs out. A pleasant hike along a stone-walled road through the woods goes past a section of stone road and a small church dedicated to Sv Bogorodica. Until here the path follows a contour around the mountain and then rises for another ten minutes to the flagstones of the Via Egnatia. The exact lie of the road beyond this section has still not been uncovered, but part of it is now believed to be underwater below Sv Erasmus between Struga and Ohrid. To get to see the road ask for the *kaldrma* (meaning 'flagstone').

Where to stay and eat There are a number of small restaurants along the Radožda shore road. Looking onto the village square below the cave church is the small and cosy restaurant of **Dva Biseri** (*Two Pearls, village square;* \ *046 787 118;* ⊕ *Sun–Thu 08.00–24.00, Fri & Sat 08.00–01.00; $$*). The two old ladies who cook here hold the secrets of their fresh-cooked lake trout close to their heart. It really is the most divine trout you'll ever taste, as good as if you had caught it yourself and whisked it straight onto the barbecue. Further down the shore road are a village shop, the village hall, and a small café and upstairs restaurant called **Albatross**. The next restaurant is **Letnica** (Little Diver), which has a spacious glasshouse upper deck for a good view of the lake. (*Both* ⊕ *Sun–Thu 11.00–24.00, Fri & Sat 11.00–01.00. $$*)

After Letnica is another restaurant called **Aleksandrija** (\ *046 782 752;* m *070 212 613;* ⊕ *Sun–Thu 11.00–24.00, Fri & Sat 11.00–01.00; $$*) and then a small basic ten-bed hostel called **Lebed** (*Swan* \ *046 787 077;* $). Accommodation costs €15/person/night including breakfast, which you can take outside right on the shorefront. There is also a small swimming deck inviting you for a dip into the crystal-clear waters. The hostel (and all the other restaurants in town) is run by the Slavkovski family. The parents, Maria and Branko, are often to be seen sitting in traditional dress on the benches outside the hostel. They are very amenable to having their photograph taken if you ask nicely and especially if you can offer to send them a copy. They speak only Macedonian. The last restaurant on the shore road is the **Ezerski Raj** (Heavenly Lake). It has a beautiful wooden deck overlooking the lake as well as views onto the Albanian peninsula of Lin village. It is the last restaurant before the entrance to the **campsite** and the footpath to Albania.

KALIŠTA On the way to Radožda, 5km from Struga, is the small settlement and monastery complex of Kališta, located right on the shores of the lake and next to the Hotel Biser. The monastery is the summer residence of Archbishop Naum, the highest church official in the Holy Synod of the Macedonian Orthodox Church. Within the monastery complex is the cave church of **Sv Bogorodica**, whose frescoes date back as far as the 15th century. Access to the church is often closed, so ask at the Hotel Biser (see below) if they can open it for you.

A 500m walk south of the monastery along the shore is the tiny **cave church of Sv Atanas** set high in the cliffs. The steps up to the church are not for those who suffer with severe vertigo, and one would be hard pushed to deliver a service inside the church to a congregation of more than half a dozen people.

Where to stay

Hotel Biser (230 beds) On the lake front; \ 046 785 700; f 046 780 404; e info@ hotelbiser.com.mk; www.hotelbiser.com.mk. Built as a traditional Macedonian house, but much bigger. Open all year & recently refurbished, it is a tranquil place with a wide beachfront, a restaurant set into the rock wall, & a small pizzeria near the beach. $$$

Getting to Radožda and Kališta Both villages can be reached by car from the turn-off at Frangovo on the E850, or by taking the coastal road from Struga through Kališta. By far the most picturesque way to get there though is by boat taxi from Ohrid, as it is quite impressive to see the cliffs and church loom up over the village. A boat taxi will cost you €30 round trip whether there is one passenger or six, but the boat will wait for you and your party to finish your half day around Radožda to take you back to Ohrid. Buses to the villages leave from Struga bus station at 06.15, 09.00, 13.00, 15.00 and 19.00.

OKTISI, VAJTOS AND THE REPUBLIC OF VEVČANI
Less than half an hour north of Struga are the villages of Oktisi and Vevčani. The pretty old village of Oktisi lies along a tributary of the Crni Drim and has a number of old watermills hidden along its banks. On the outskirts of the village is a 5th-century Christian basilica with some excellent examples of late Roman mosaics. Above the village in the hills is also an overgrown site called **Vajtos Kale** where a castle is alleged to have stood from Paeonian times. Some say that Vajtos is the eighth stopping place on the Via Egnatia, and the last stop before Ohrid, but it is much more likely that this was a stop on the Crni Drim road to northern Albania. The rock outcrop shows little signs of having been a castle, but the vantage point is pretty and it is easy to imagine that the wide road up to Vajtos might have been the Via Egnatia. For a circular route description to Vajtos and Vevčani with a sketch map see page 305.

Turning right before the mosque in Oktisi, go over the bridge to get to the next village of **Vevčani**. Allegedly the villagers of Vevčani held their own referendum during the break-up of Yugoslavia for their very own republic. Although they didn't manage to gain independence, they nevertheless created their own coat of arms, passports and even printed specimen currency, replicas of which can be bought in the local shops (but not to be used as legal tender). The village is beautiful, with babbling brooks, old-style houses and proud people. Here there are a number of old *babas* and *tatkos* in traditional dress who will be happy to have their photograph taken. The spring at the back of the village erupts from the rock and the area has been maintained with a small bridge, walkways and benches for all to enjoy. Buses go to Vevčani from Struga every hour from 05.00 until 20.00.

Where to stay and eat
Premier (10 rooms) On the way up to the church; ☎ 046 790 620, 071 380 295; e hotelpremiermk@yahoo.com; www.hotelpremier.com.mk. Brand-new modern rooms, bar, & b/fast room. Wi-Fi, all mod cons. $$$

Kutmičevica (2 rooms) Near Sv Nikola Church; ☎ 046 798 399/626, 070 249 197.

Predominantly a traditional restaurant with indoor & outside seating, & 2 small rooms with fireplaces. $$

Domakjinska Kukja (4 rooms) Behind Sv Nikola Church; ☎ 046 790 505, 070 815 950. The 1st traditional inn to revive in the village, its restaurant has a fireside atmosphere, beer-barrel tables upstairs & good food. $$

GORNA BELICA
Another good day trip away from the lake is up to the village of Gorna Belica, 16km northwest of Struga. The village is now mostly the weekend residence of Strugites, but it has a fine Vlach church, a high view onto Lake Ohrid, proximity to the Via Egnatia and good hiking up to a glacial lake and a cave church. The village first became a settlement in 1769, when the Aromanians (Vlachs) of Moskopole, southern Albania, were driven out of that town by the destruction wrought by the local Ottoman *bey*, and moved up here with all their animals, belongings and families. They chose this spot along the River Belica, where villagers believe that the old crumbling **Church of Sv Clement** is no less

THE TWELFTHTIDE CARNIVAL

Vevčani has held a Twelfthtide carnival on 13 and 14 January every year since the middle of the 6th century. The 12 days after Christmas, which in the Orthodox calendar is on 7 January, are meant to be a time when evil spirits are at their most active with regards to wreaking havoc on the coming year. On New Year's Eve (13 January in the Orthodox calendar), the villagers start a two-day event designed to banish evil spirits from entering into the new year. People dress up in costumes and masks representing all things evil and unlucky in the hope that if evil is faced with its own reality this will scare it away. The costumes and disguises are a testament to what Macedonians find evil or unlucky. Typical costumes include policemen, soldiers, pregnant brides, an old groom, a funeral procession as well as ghoulish monsters of all varieties. Local politicians and international organisations are ridiculed, and the Ottoman times are also caricatured. A procession of floats starts at midday on the 14th when all sorts of ingenious horror stories are depicted and include tables of human heads, bird flu inspectors (including live chickens) and giant condoms. The procession ends in the village square in the late afternoon with a lot of parading around a fire in which all the costumes are ritually burned.

Concentrating on the banishment of evil as a serious business rather than on the celebration of the end of fasting, this festival has some sinister overtones mixed with alcohol. A fight or two usually breaks out between inhabitants of the upper village and the lower village and it is allegedly the time to punish dogs! Nevertheless, the carnival has started to become a popular national event, attracting over 2,000 visitors every year. When you arrive in the village on the carnival days, you will be stopped by masked men in camouflage uniforms who will ask to see your passport before letting you into the village. The correct passport to show is, of course, the Republic of Vevčani passport, which can be purchased from the masked 'police' for 150MKD. Grill and drink stands provide revellers with sustenance through the small hours, and if you have not managed to book yourself (well in advance) a room in the village, then try the Hotel Diplomat outside Struga (see page 177).

than his actual 9th-century summer monastery from before he moved to Ohrid permanently as bishop.

The Aromanians built their own church, **Sv Petka**, or Paraschevia, in Vlach, up above Sv Clement's Church, and it is a fine example of an early 19th-century Vlach church. By that time, 1829, the Greek influence on the old Ohrid archbishopric was all pervasive and so all the original inscriptions on the church are in Greek. The church is cared for by the Dunoskis and if they are around they will be happy to tell you more about it. Look out for the **wooden hawk** above the central lantern in front of the iconostasis. This original pulley system still flaps the wings of the hawk as the lantern is pulled up and down, making a loud clapping noise.

The village celebrates two festivals in honour of both patron saints, Sv Petka on 8 August and Sv Clement on 9 August. This double whammy fills the village up with visitors on those two days and it is well worth a visit if you can make it. Other patron saint festivals exist for neighbouring churches and holy sites, one of the most interesting being the dedication to the **Church of the Perumba**.

The tiny cave church was built in 1998 in honour of a local legend about a girl who, several centuries ago, was being chased by the local Ottoman thugs. The girl ran up against the steep cliff rocks where the church is now and fell to the ground exhausted, knowing that there was nowhere for her to escape. She prayed to God for deliverance and just as the thugs were catching up with her, they saw her *top left*   Ohrid Museum must be one of the oldest museums in the world — it was first established in 1516 as a museum to the Archbishopric of Ohrid (L/D) page 171

above   The crystal-clear calm waters of Lake Ohrid, a tectonic lake 289m deep that boasts indigenous species and Neolithic stilt settlements (SL) page 159

left   Statue of Sv Kliment — he was a missionary who came to Ohrid and was involved in setting up the first monasteries that taught in Slavic (TE) page 160

below   Fishing village Radožda, on the western side of Lake Ohrid, has the best trout restaurant on the lake and some cave churches too (G/D) page 181

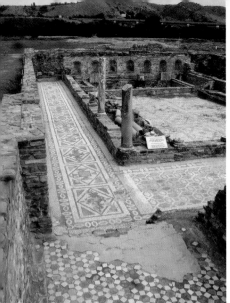

left   The Roman site of Stobi was first discovered in 1861, and even today only a fraction of the city has been uncovered (BJ) page 286

below   The megalithic observatory at Kokino dominates the surrounding area at a height of 1,013m above sea level (BJ) page 260

bottom Tsar Samoil's Fortress in Ohrid dates only from the end of the 10th century, but there is evidence that a fortress has stood on the top of Ohrid Hill since at least the 3rd century BC (BJ) page 172 *above left* Over 30,000 eggs were used to manufacture the paint and glaze of the Šarena Džamija (coloured or painted mosque) in Tetovo (S/D) page 223

above right Sv Kliment at Plaošnik was completed in 2002 and stands beside the original site of Kliment's very own monastery school, started in AD893 (G/D) page 170

below The remote Monastery of Treskavec has a beautiful setting under the summit of the impressive Zlatovrv (BJ) page 208 top   The Twelfthtide carnival is held in Vevčani on 13 and 14 January every year and is designed to banish evil spirits from entering into the new year (BJ) page 184

above left   House in Resava village — this is a typical house of the Tikveš area (BJ) page 269

above   Macedonian cuisine is a celebration of fresh, organic, smallscale produce (SL) page 97

left   *Baba* at the Church of Sv Nedela, near Lake Matka (BJ) page 149 *above*   Pelivan wrestling: in each round two men, smothered in sunflower oil and wearing only leather breeches, compete to tussle the other to the ground (SL) page 231

right   The *tapan* is played with two specially designed drumsticks — known as a *kukuda* and a *pračka* (BJ) page 63

below   Herding horses on Šar Planina mountain (BJ) page 226

right   Stone doll natural rock formations
        near the village of Kuklica — legend
        says the figures are the result of a
        petrified wedding (BJ) page 267

below   The Šar Mountains offer a host of
        hiking trails and are home to 49
        glacial lakes (BJ) page 226

bottom At 2,753m, Mount Golem Korab is
        the highest peak touching
        Macedonia and shares the border
        with Albania (BJ) page 297

Lake Debar, spread out magnificently below the town of Debar, is a 22km artificial lake built in 1964 as a means of producing hydro-electricity
(BJ) page 237

fragile body fly up into the air as a pure white dove (*perumba*). The dove flew away and locals have honoured the place as a holy site ever since.

The locals walk up to the site once a year on the first weekend in June. Due to the proximity of the site to the Albanian border, the hike takes place only with the accompaniment of local Macedonian soldiers. For more information on how to join the hike, ask in Gorna Belica or contact **Ohrid Climbing Group** (*Abraš 22, Galičica;* \ *046 262 458*). Any other hikes west of Gorna Belica and up to the glacial lake in the north are also best accompanied by a professional guide or other Macedonian who knows the area. The tracks are not well marked and encounters at the border could become difficult.

Getting there To get to Gorna Belica take the main road west out of Struga for about 2km and take the turning to the right signposted Zagračani. After 1.5km you will come to a T-junction immediately after a very small bridge. Turn right and then almost immediately left along an unmarked road. This road leads first of all up to the village of Visni. After the village follow the asphalt road around to the right and continue on another 5km to the village of Gorna Belica.

REČICA More as an aside on the way between Ohrid and Resen, if you want to see some natural, 100% ecologically sound **washing machines**, go to the tiny hamlet of Rečica. Essentially a local stream is siphoned off via a small wooden canal and allowed to drop a few metres into a huge wooden, lined bowl set in the ground. The rush of water swirls around in the bowl into which the blankets, rugs and some modern-day washing liquid are added. After the time taken to have a small picnic with *rakija* and a good chat, the rugs and blankets are hung up to dry on wooden poles in a nearby field and collected in a few days when the items are dry. This was once a centre for traditional blanket and rug making, and local people still come here to have their old rugs and blankets washed. Sadly, traditionally made rugs and blankets are not for sale here, although local honey is. Called *valavica* or *valajca* for short, they are also sometimes referred to as *virovčanka* (whirlpools).

Getting there To get to Rečica, take the road towards Resen. After 15km take the turning left towards Kuratica, and after 1km take the turning right through the working quarry. Less than 3km along this dirt track will take you to the *valavica* area just before the village. The village itself has a small church and several old watermills further upstream.

AROUND THE LAKE INTO ALBANIA A good half-day trip in the area if you have a car and car insurance to cover you in Albania (most hire cars from Macedonia aren't covered for Albania) is to drive around the lake. It is not uncommon for many countries to become 'blurred' at the edges: a little neglected by central administration and adopting some of the characteristics of the country next door.

The border crossing itself is relatively painless, and a short wait and €10 will get you the requisite visa. Once on the other side the full effect of former communist Albania's paranoia about foreign influence and invasion comes into plain view. The countryside is strewn with concrete dome lookouts and troop defences, which appear like giant molehills from a mole gone mad all over the hills. These defensive positions complete with rifle lookouts do not cease until you are back in Macedonia on the other side of the lake. Most have now fallen into disrepair, and some have even fallen into the lake.

Along the lake in summer, boys will hold up strings of fresh trout caught from the lake, and a number of nice-looking lakeside restaurants on the way around

After the death of Serbian Tsar Dušan in 1355, a mere ten years after he had been crowned king in Skopje, the Serb kingdom started to fall apart at the seams. Tsar Uroš took over, helped by the Mrnjavčevič brothers, Volkačin and Uglečа. They headed feudal kingdoms within the empire and in 1365 Volkačin proclaimed himself co-tsar and ruler of the western side of the empire with its seat of power at Prilep.

Volkačin had four sons by his wife Elena, and several daughters. Marko, the eldest, was born in 1335. Thirty-six years later in 1371, when Volkačin and his brother were killed fighting against the Ottomans in Thrace, Greece, the crown of the empire passed to Marko, as neither Tsar Uroš nor Volkašin's brother Ugleša had any heirs. Even though he was of Serb origin, King Marko is often viewed by the Macedonians as the stepping stone for Macedonian nationhood between Tsar Samoil (967–1014) and the ten-day Kruševo Republic of 1903.

Prilep was centrally placed within Marko's kingdom, which reached from the Šar Mountains in the northwest down the western bank of the River Vardar to Kastoria (in present-day Greece) in the south. Rarely did his kingdom include Skopje or Ohrid, and eventually Prilep fell to the Ottomans in 1394. A year later King Marko was killed in Romania while forced to fight for the Ottomans against the Vlachs.

will serve freshly caught fish and local vegetables. There are allegations that fish sold on this side of the border are sometimes caught using dynamite, but I have certainly seen no evidence of this on my way around.

At the southern end of the lake is Pogradec, which has a few shops and buffet bars along its main street and a lot of money changers who will buy your euros and dollars from you. Not a soul seems to speak anything other than Albanian, and, unless you've practised a lot, they probably won't understand your accent. On your way out of Pogradec on your way back to Macedonia make sure you head towards the lakeside road shortly after the centre of town before you go veering off on the main road into the wilds of central Albania. There are a couple of nice restaurants set in a park just before you get to the Sv Naum border.

It doesn't matter which way round you go, although the anticlockwise direction appears more of an eye-opener to me than the other way around.

Alternatively, for the fit and keen, a bike ride around the lake is almost 100km, including some pretty hard-core hills. One day for the super-fit; two or three days for a more leisurely ride. Bikes can be hired at Dea Tours in Ohrid.

8

Pelagonia, Prespa and Pelister

This is the story of Kruševo:

> Just after midnight on the morning of August 2, 1903 (this was the day that the general uprising was proclaimed), a rattle of rifles and a prolonged hurrahing broke the quiet of the peaceful mountain town. Some three hundred insurgents under 'Peto-the-Vlach' and four other leaders had taken the town by surprise.
>
> *The Balkan Trail*, Frederick Moore, 1906

This southeastern corner of Macedonia, known as Pelagonia in ancient times, is rich in history both natural and manmade. The **Via Egnatia**, a monumentally long Roman road linking the Adriatic crossing at Durres with Constantinople (now Istanbul in Turkey), traverses Pelagonia, which has traditionally been rich in trading towns. **Pelister National Park**, on the Baba mountain range, is the oldest national park in Macedonia. It conserves some rare glacial lakes, the Pelister Eyes, and is a haven of hiking and hidden Vlach villages. From up in its hills you can see both major and minor **Prespa lakes** (the latter lies in Greece and Albania) as well as the mountain range of Galičica National Park on the other side of the lake. In the north of the region around Makedonski Brod are several **caves**, including Pešna Cave, where the ruins of a medieval fort sit near the entrance.

There are a number of initiatives to revitalise the Pelagonia region with tourism and so you will sporadically find pockets of convenience and good signage. Hopefully this will further improve with time, making the area more accessible to the unaccompanied traveller and those who speak little Macedonian. If you visit nowhere else in this region, spend at least a couple of days in Prilep to see the ruined **Towers of King Marko** and the remote **Monastery of Treskavec**. The scenery at these two sites is magnificent and is the setting of the films *Before the Rain* and *Dust* by Macedonia's most famous film director, Milčo Mančevski.

BITOLA

The main town of the region is Bitola. Once a major trading town, it is currently the second-largest city in Macedonia with over 80,000 people, and is the seat of Macedonia's second university. It has managed to maintain its pretty 18th- and 19th-century architecture in the centre of town, and these buildings tell of the former glory of Bitola when every major European country had a consulate here due to the amount of trading and business conducted in the town. The River Dragor divides the old Turkish town from the 18th-century town and conjures up a beautiful tree-lined canal effect, drawing in the cool air of the Baba Mountains. Despite being further south

PELAGONIA & SURROUNDING AREAS

0 — 25km
0 — 15 miles

Bradt

N

Gostivar, Skopje

Zajas

KIČEVO

Ohrid

Makedonski Brod

Plasnica

Pusta Reka

Kruševo

Krivogaštani

Sopotnica

Suvodol

Pešna Cave

Tereska

Zrze

Ropotovo

Sekirci

Blato

Solunska 4

Solunska Glava
2538m

Nežilovo

Bogomil

Teovo

Izvor

Babuna

VELES

Skopje

E27

E75

Vardar

Štip

Gevgelija,
Thessaloniki

Rosoman
Kral Džo

Dam

Tikveš Lake

Raec

Raec

Restoran CE

Pletvar Pass
(994m)

Prisad Pass
(1093m)

Treskavec

Zlatovrv
1422m

Prilep Lake

PRILEP

Prilepsko

see page 205

188

189

than Skopje, Bitola is usually cooler year round, sometimes up to 12–15°C cooler – lovely in the summer when Skopje can get up to the high 30°Cs, but bring an extra sweater in the winter.

HISTORY OF THE REGION It is believed that a tribe known by the name of Linkestris were the first to inhabit the area south of Bitola around 4500BC. Just over 4,000 years later the first major town to be established in the rich Pelagonia Valley was the ancient Macedonian town of Heraklea Lyncestis. It was founded by Philip II of Macedon (the father of Aleksandar III of Macedon) in the middle of the 4th century and named in honour of Hercules, with whom the Macedonian royal dynasty of the Argeads identified. The additional name 'Lyncestis' in turn honours the ancient tribe of Linkestris. Although Philip lived there for some time, his son was eventually born in Pella over the present-day border in Greece.

With the fall of the ancient kingdom of Macedonia, Heraklea came under Roman rule in the 2nd century BC and continued to grow as an important trading town. By this time the Via Egnatia passed through Heraklea where it crossed with the Diagonal Way, another major north–south road joining Heraklea with Stobi, Štip and then Kustendil (now in Bulgaria).

Julius Caesar used Heraklea as a supply depot during his campaigns and many of his veterans settled there. Later, during the time of early Christianity in the 4th century, Heraklea developed as the seat of the regional bishopric. By the 5th century, Roman rule was in decline and Heraklea was ransacked several times by marauding Avars, Goths and Huns from the north. When a large earthquake struck in AD518, the inhabitants of Heraklea abandoned the city.

Later, in the 7th century the Dragovites, a Slavic tribe pushed down from the north by the Avars, settled in the valley and gave the river its present name of Dragor. Eventually a new town was established immediately north of Heraklea, mentioned under the name Obitel in one of the charters of Tsar Samoil, showing that even then the town was closely associated with churches and monasteries (*obitel* means family chamber of a monastery). The town continued to prosper from trading and eventually became the third largest city in the Balkans after Constantinople and Thessaloniki. The surrounding area also thrived as a centre of Christian worship, so that by the time the Ottomans came at the end of the 14th century they named the town Monastir due to the number of monasteries in the surrounding hills, which served the monks of the 500 churches in the region.

Soon, Monastir became so important that the French set up a consulate there. Eleven other countries followed suit. The influx of 18th- and 19th-century architecture can still be seen in Bitola today, despite artillery fire and bombing during the world wars. Mixed with the influence of Ottoman architecture in the form of mosques, covered markets and bathhouses, Bitola has a very cosmopolitan feel to it even today, and its inhabitants still pride themselves on their international heritage.

At the beginning of the 19th century, Monastir was at the zenith of its trading history and the railway even came to town, linking southern Macedonia with Skopje, Belgrade and beyond. French was widely spoken in the town, which included a number of foreign and international schools as well as a military academy that was attended by Turkey's pro-reform leader, Kemal Atatürk. The town boasted 2,000 households, and every second household owned a piano, on which many a song about Bitola was composed. Allegedly there are over 200 songs about Bitola.

The Manaki brothers (see box, page 190), famous for their pioneering work with the camera, opened their studio of art photography in Bitola in 1905. In honour of their work in photography and later cinematography, Bitola started the first international Manaki Film Camera Festival in the world in 1979, which continues every September.

At the end of the 19th century, revolution against the Ottomans was taking hold all over Macedonia, and Bitola was no exception. The Internal Macedonian Revolutionary Organisation (IMRO) was very active in Bitola and there are those who say that some of the guerilla warfare tactics developed in Bitola during those years were even exported to other nations rising up against dictatorial foreign rule. The Ilinden Festival every 2 August (a national holiday) celebrates the Ilinden Uprising of 1903 against the Ottomans. The Republic of Kruševo which was proclaimed the next day in nearby Kruševo lasted only ten days before it and all other regions of dissent were sharply put down.

The Balkan Wars of 1912–13 put an end to Ottoman rule in Bitola and all of Macedonia, but many more years of foreign rule still followed. Reprisals against the Turkish community were high and over 40 of the 60 Turkish mosques in the town were destroyed. Nazi occupation in the early 1940s annihilated Bitola's thriving Jewish scene when 3,011 Jews were deported on 11 March 1943 to Treblinka in Poland. Today, Macedonia's entire Jewish community is only around 1,000.

While Bitola has languished in Balkan obscurity during the 20th century, modern lines of communication and transport have bypassed the once important trading centre. To add insult to injury, the provincial town of Skopje was made capital of the Federal Yugoslav Socialist Republic of Macedonia. Since then, Bitola, far from the heart of Yugoslavia, has only ever been given secondary consideration. It has little chance now of regaining its importance in trade, but it may still become a prime cultural destination.

GETTING THERE AND AROUND There are only four trains a day to Bitola from Skopje and four back out (see table page 74). The train is slow and decrepit, but the journey at least between Prilep and Skopje is scenic. Average train journey from Skopje to Bitola is 3½ hours for 370MKD return. There were no trains to/from Greece at the time of writing.

BITOLA

Prilep, Skopje, French cemetery

Prilep, Skopje

NAUM NAUMOVSKI

MAKSIM GORKI

PRILEPSKA

Please note: The River Dragor runs between the carriageways of Boulevard 1st Maj.

BOULEVARD 1st MAJ

ŽELEZNIČKA

INDUSTRISKA

IVAN MILUTINOVIČ

EDWARD KARDELJ

Ajdar Kadi Mosque

KAVALA

PROHOR PČINSKI

ŽIKICA JOVANOVIĆ SPANAC

PIONERSKA

GAVRILO PRINCIP

Dragor

Yeni Mosque

City market

OLD TOWN

DALMATINSKA

ALEK SANDAR TURUNDŽEV

Antiko

BD 1st MAJ

see inset

4th NOEMVRI

SVETI NAUM

MAKEDONSKA

Sv Bogorodica

NIKOLA TESLA

SLAVE DŽURO DŽAKOVIČ

BORIS KIDRIČ

Sv Petra

KIČEVO

TESLA

II MART

Bezisten covered market

Izložbena Gallery

DOBRIVO E RADO

Grme

UK, French & Turkish consulates

Catholic church

RUŽVELTOV

NIKOLA KARAMANDI

ELPIDA KARAMANDI

Croatian consulate

MARKS & ENGELS

Korzo

SOLUNSKA

Isak Mosque

Kus Kus

MARŠAL TITO

Goce Delčev Square

29th NOEMVRI

Vero

Supermarket

METODI

Bure

Epinal

TITO

Icon & Woodcarving Gallery

IVO LOLA

Basic courts

Town Hall

Fire station

State Archive

BOULEVARD 1se MAJ

Dragor

Clock tower

Sv Dimitri

De Niro

OKTOMVRI

Ilit

LIMBARKO

LENINOVA

MARŠAL

Chinese

Ikona Books

PITU GULI

OHRIDSKI

Josip Broz School

University

Rector's House

Trnovo, Ohrid, German cemetery

OHRIDSKA

GEORGIEVSKI

STERO

OSMANO

SLAVKO

JOSIF

House of Culture

KIRIL

BELGRADSKA

LENINOVA

KLIMENT OHRIDSKI

KLIMENT

Vlach church

SOLUNSKA

KRUŠEVO

HRISTO UZINOV

PITU GULI

TSAR SAMOIL

TSAR SAMOIL

KUZMAN JOSIFOVSKI

192

BITOLA
Old Town

ALAKSANDAR
TURUNDZEV

R. ZINZIFOV

✗ Antiko

VELES

VELES

BOULEVARD 1ST MAJ

DUNAV

KR. DALMATINSKA

ALI MAKO
Turist Travel Agency

• Aries

Na
Muabet

KRALI MARKO

Drągor

TRST

ORDAN NIKOLOV

TRST

S. KOPANKI

M. TANCEVSKI

N
Brädt

DEBARCA

PELAGONIJA

ORDAN DZINOT

M. PIJADE

PANDA CESNOVA

Brioni ✗

✗

BRAKA MINGOVI

SKOPSKA

ZIKICA JOVANOVIC SPANAC

IVAN MILUTANOVIČ

PELAGONIJA

MAKEDONSKA

ŽELEZNIČKA

INDUSTRISKA

4th NOEMVRI

NIKOLA TESLA

PARTIZANSKA

RIBAR

PARTIZANSKA

Bitola Institute, Museum
and Art Gallery ⚑

Dom na Armija
(Military club)

P

Sports
hall

Bitola   Park

Sports
fields ✗

INDUSTRISKA

Railway
station

🅱

IVO LOLA RIBAR

Swimming
pool

Greece

BUKOVSKA

🏛 Zoo

Heraklea Linkestis ∴
(Roman ruins)

N
Brädt

500m
500yds

0
0

Skopje	05.00, 05.45, 06.30, 07.30, 09.00, 11.00, 11.50, 14.30, 16.30, 17.15
Ohrid	06.30, 09.00, 09.30, 13.15, 15.00, 16.00, 18.30, 19.30
Kičevo, Gostivar and Tetovo	05.00, 10.00, 14.00, 16.00
Strumica	07.00, 14.15
Gevgelija	15.00
Prilep, Negotino and Radoviš	14.00

Buses do exist but like most town buses in Macedonia their destination is not always well marked although they are frequent. Enquire at the bus station (047 231 420) on Ulica Nikola Tesla opposite the train station (047 237 110).

The main areas of Bitola are easily walkable, but taxis are cheap and abundant. Minimum fare is 30MKD.

TOUR OPERATORS

Turist Krali Marko 16; 047 202 777; f 047 202 776; e predrag@turist.com.mk; www.turist.com.mk. Located in the old town, has extensive experience working with foreign tour groups & agents. Can find you accommodation throughout Macedonia as well as arrange trips to sites. Friendly, English-speaking staff, & have maps of Bitola for sale for 100MKD.

Aries Dalmatinska 6; 047 224 155; e info@aries.com.mk; www.aries.com.mk. Also located in the old town, their website has a very good range of self-catering accommodation & beautiful small villas in Pelister National Park.

WHERE TO STAY Bed and breakfast stays can be arranged through Turist and Aries (see above) or try the hotels below. There are several more very nice hotels and villas less than 10km away in the villages of Trnovo and Magarevo in Pelister National Park (see page 196).

Epinal (175 rooms) On the cross of the pedestrian zone Maršal Tito & Leninova; 047 224 777; e reservation@hotelepinal.com; www.hotelepinal.com. Popular with tour groups of Greek visitors, it offers full comfort, including a gym, pool, sauna, jacuzzi & casino. $$$$

De Niro (18 rooms, 2 apts) Kiril i Metodij 5; 047 229 656; f 047 207 233; e hotel-deniro@mt.net.mk; www.hotel-deniro.com. In the centre of town. Nice bar & restaurant downstairs. Beautiful rooms if a bit small. $$$

WHERE TO EAT AND DRINK The main pedestrian area, **Maršal Tito**, known as Širok Sokak, hosts a number of café bars and restaurants. These change owners and names as frequently as the wind, so the best bet is to take a stroll with the Bitolans and pick whichever looks the best. Don't forget to look up at the 18th-century architecture as you walk by. There is a good Vero supermarket at the north end of Maršal Tito if you want to buy provisions for a day out or simply a snack and drinks. Try also:

✗ **Antiko** Bulevar 1st Maj 243, on the left bank of the river next to the old town; ⏰ Sun–Thu 12.00–24.00, Fri & Sat 12.00–01.00. Traditional restaurant with live music & good food. $$
✗ **Kus-Kus** Kiril i Metodij 2a; 047 222 603; ⏰ Sun–Thu 12.00–24.00, Fri & Sat 12.00–01.00.

Opposite Hotel De Niro, this is the 1st French restaurant to come to town. Boasts a wide range of salads, & does pizza. $$
✗ **De Niro** Kiril i Metodij 5; ⏰ from 08.00 for b/fast. Serves traditional Macedonian food throughout the day, & has a nice patio at the back. $$

✗ Chinese Solunska 234; ⊕ Sun–Thu 12.00–24.00, Fri & Sat 12.00–01.00. Good for a change of diet. **$$**

✗ Bure Maršal Tito 82–88; ✆ 047 236 519; ⊕ Sun–Thu 11.00–24.00, Fri & Sat 11.00–01.00. Quaint décor & serves very good pizzas. **$**

WHAT TO SEE AND DO Bitola is a pretty town to walk around. The long pedestrian street called **Maršal Tito** is lined with 18th- and 19th-century buildings and leads down past the **Bitola Institute, Museum and Art Gallery** (*Kliment Ohridski bb;* ✆ *047 233 187*) and the Dom na Armija concert house and officers' club. The museum holds the 'Bitola inscription' stone that marks the building of a fortress in Bitola in 1015. Interestingly, the inscription reads that the fortress was built by Ioan the Autocrator who was Bulgarian by birth and related to Samoil whose army was defeated by the Byzantine Tsar Vaslius II in 1014. This statement rather puts a hole in the Macedonian theory that Tsar Samoil was Macedonian rather than Bulgarian. Some say, on the other hand, that the stone is a fake. At the

---

IN SEARCH OF A WORLD WAR I PILOT

Abridged from text by Eric Allart, history teacher, former professional archaeologist
Translation by M. Marc

On 5 April 1918, Brigadier (Corporal) Pilot Léopold Michel Montoya was reported missing in action when his plane – a Nieuport 24 – was shot down by the German ace Gerhard Fieseler behind the Bulgarian lines, south of Caniste. (Fieseler, who later became an aerobatics champion, aircraft designer and manufacturer, was awarded the Golden Military Merit Cross and the Iron Cross, first and second class, for 19 aerial victories he won in Macedonia during World War I.) On 21 April 1920, the French court of Bordeaux officially declared Brigadier Montoya killed in action, and his family were informed by the German Red Cross. Although Montoya's wife died in childbirth, her daughter, Audette, survived her and was brought up by her grandparents. In between the two world wars, the family attempted in vain to have Léopold's burial place located.

In 2005, whilst off duty, Captain Fief, of the French gendarmerie, came across Montoya's identity disc at an antique dealer's shop in Skopje. On inquiring around the battlefield site where the disc had come from, a shepherd from Kruševica confirmed that his father had been requisitioned to bury 'both pilots' killed on the ground by Bulgarians in 1918. Another shepherd on the plateau south of Caniste was able to point out a bush commonly known as the location of the pilot's burial place. The topography of the site hardly allows an emergency landing and the plane is likely to have been seriously damaged before Montoya was killed on the ground by Bulgarian troops.

Back in France, Captain Fief found the pilot's grand-nephew, Christophe Montoya, who confirmed that Léopold's daughter was still alive. With the help of a war veterans' society, the Montoya family recontacted the French Ministry of Defence and the French Embassy in Skopje to ask for the location and repatriation of Léopold's body. The family hope to uncover, positively identify and repatriate Brigadier Montoya's body in the summer of 2009, but seeking funding and battling through government red tape is hindering progress. Ongoing archaeological and regressive mapping work with the aid of photos of the area taken in 1918 by an anonymous pilot of the 504th Squadron based in Bac, northeast of Bitola, which was Montoya's squadron, will help to solve much of the contradictory data surrounding the circumstances of the death of Brigadier Léopold Michel Montoya, killed in action, 'mort pour la France'.

end of the pedestrian street is the pretty city park. Beyond the park the road leads to Greece and a turn-off clearly marked shortly after the park leads to Heraklea, half an hour's walk from the centre of town.

Heraklea Linkestis (see *History of the region* above, page 190) is barely uncovered, so visits in future years may be more fruitful, but for now there are a number of important relics to be seen there including the amphitheatre, baths, basilicas and some impressive mosaics. There is a small museum and sometimes a snack and drink shop on the site, but most of the more important finds are in the town museum or in the National Museum in Skopje. Entry to the ruins costs 150MKD and permission to photograph the site costs another 500MKD.

The tree-lined **Boulevard 1st Maj** runs the length of the **River Dragor** and skirts the south side of the **old Turkish town**. Along the boulevard going west out of town are a number of the old consular residences. The present consulates of the United Kingdom, France and Turkey are on the corner of Maršal Tito and Kiril i Metodi.

In the centre of town at the north end of Maršal Tito is the **clock tower**, the **Izložbena Art Gallery** housed in a former mosque, and the covered **Bezisten**, which still houses one of Bitola's markets and whose gates are still locked at night.

Dating back to the Turkish period of Bitola's history are the **Isak Mosque**, built in 1508–09; the **Yeni Mosque**, built in 1559; and the **Ajdar–Kadi Mosque**, built in 1562 by Kodja Sinan, a prominent Ottoman architect. There are a number of churches in Bitola, the most significant being that of **Sv Dimitri**, renowned for being one of the biggest churches in the Balkans. It was built in 1830 during Ottoman times when churches were not allowed to be ornate or ostentatious on the outside. As a result the builders lavished the inside of the church, which has been well preserved to this day. The opulence of the church is captured in the opening scenes of *The Peacemaker* (1997) staring George Clooney, which were filmed in Sv Dimitri.

There are a number of festivals that take place in Bitola every year. Interfest is an international festival of classical music, held in August. Heraklea Evenings are a series of outdoor theatre and musical events held over the summer in places like the amphitheatre in Heraklea as well as other outdoor venues. Over the summer there is also the International Graphics Convention, the international children's festival, the Small Monmartre, and others.

PELISTER NATIONAL PARK AND ECOTOURISM

Opened in 1948, Pelister National Park is the smallest (12,500ha) but oldest national park in Macedonia. It is famous for its ancient molika pine trees (*Pinus peuce*), as well as rare lynx, bearded eagle, gentian plants and many other different types of flora and fauna. Mount Pelister, at 2,601m, is the summit of the Baba Mountains, which are in fact a part of the Rhodope range of mountains of Bulgaria.

WHERE TO STAY
Hotels
Šumski Feneri (4 dbls, 4 sgls & 4 apts of 5 beds each) Near Trnovo; \ 047 293 030; f 047 293 131; e sfeneri@t-home.mk; www.hotelimakedonija.com.mk/hotel_sumskifeneri.ht ml. Set around a cosy foyer & landings laden with well-kept plants & flowers. The hotel also has conference facilities for 40 & restaurant seating for 140. The Vlach family Musulanov have run the hotel for many years now, & their daughter, Ljubica, speaks good English & will give guided tours of Bitola & Malovište on request. To get to the hotel, head west out of Bitola along the river & turn left at the

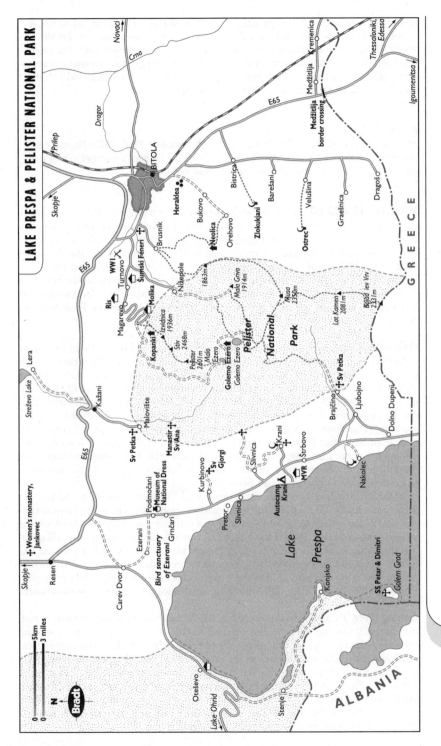

LAKE PRESPA & PELISTER NATIONAL PARK

Novaci

Crna

Dragor

Prilep

Skopje

E65

BITOLA

Dragoš

E65

Barešani

Velušina

Graešnica

Bistrica

GREECE

Kremenica

Thessaloniki, Edessa

Medžitlija

Medžitlija border crossing

Igoumenitsa

Brusnik

Bukovo

Orehovo

Zlokukjani

Ostrec

Heraklea

Neolica

Nižepole

1863m

Mala Griva 1914m

Musa 2350m

Lot Kamen 2081m

Bojad´iev Vrv 2331m

WWI

Šumski Feneri

Turnovo

Molika

Magarevo

Ris

Izvidnica 1936m

Kopanki

Stiv 2468m

Pelister 2601m

Malo Ezero

Golemo Ezero

Golemo Ezero

Pelister

National

Park

Sv Petka

Ljubojno

Dolno Dupeni

Braičino

Strežovo Lake

Lera

Kažani

Malovište

Sv Petka

Manastir Sv Ana

Kurbinovo

Sv Gjorgi

Silnica

Krani

Šrbovo

MVR

Nakolec

Skopje

Resen

Women's monastery, Jankovec

Carev Dvor

Ezerani

Podmočani

Museum of National Dress

Grnčari

Bird sanctuary of Ezerani

Pretor

Silnica

Autocamp Krani

Lake

Prespa

Konjsko

SS Petar & Dimitri

Golem Grad

Oteševo

Stenje

Lake Ohrid

ALBANIA

N

Bradt

0 5km
0 3 miles

197

battered sign for Pelister Park, & then right onto a cobbled road for 1km. The hotel is on the left. $$$
🏠 **Ris** (10 rooms) Magarevo, 12km outside Bitola; ☎ 047 293 901. A new, small hotel in the hills of Pelister with a nice little restaurant & very pleasant lawns. The hotel is 2km further up the road than Šumski Feneri. $$$

🏠 **Molika** (56 rooms) Pelister National Park, at the top of the mountain road; ☎ 047 229 406; e hmolika@mt.net.mk; www.hotelmolika.com.mk. This hotel, commanding amazing views, is almost ski-in ski-out. All rooms are en suite with TV & central heating. $$

Mountain huts

🏠 **Golemo Ezero** (45 beds) ☎ 047 221 605 (afternoons only). This hut lies 600m below Pelister peak at 2,000m. To arrange an overnight stay contact Sterjov Zlatko. $

🏠 **Kopanki** (110 beds) 1,600m Mountain Baba; ☎ 047 222 384. B/fast not included, so bring your own food. $

WHAT TO SEE AND DO Skiing is the favourite winter pastime in Pelister. To get to the ski lifts from Bitola, drive west out and turn off for the park after about 3km towards Trnovo. Keep driving through Trnovo and Magarevo until you get to the end of the road. Unfortunately, there is no public transport to the ski lifts, other than a taxi. Make sure you fix the price of the journey before you set off.

Hiking is the popular summer sport. The walk from Hotel Šumski Feneri in Trnovo village to Magarevo further up the mountain takes you along part of the Via Egnatia. Parts of the road still have the cobbles laid down by French troops fighting in the area during World War I.

Malovište A Vlach settlement that is well worth a visit and is a real museum piece is Malovište. It was once a rich trading village, and it is not difficult to see that some of the houses were once very stylish in their time. Most are now in various states of decay. The **Church of Sv Petka** is usually open and, unusually for most churches in Macedonia, its exonarthex is on the left of the entrance rather than on the right (it is also on the north side and a good place to cool off in the hot summer). The church sometimes allows stranded travellers to stay overnight in a couple of makeshift beds in the upper gallery. Behind the church is a graveyard containing some gravestones as old as the church itself. Forty minutes' hike from the village is the **Monastery of Sv Ana,** which houses guests for the moderate price of 150MKD per night per person.

Malovište has had some funding from the EU to spruce itself up and put out some advertising. There is a small information room just where the tarmac runs out (ask in the village to be let in) where you can buy a well laid-out book on the village (also available from Hotel Šumski Feneri). Unfortunately, the village is literally dying, as very few if any young people live there now, and despite the EU funding, not much seems to have been done regarding follow-up. No further money seems to be coming into the town and there isn't even a village shop or somewhere to buy a coffee, although there are drinking fountains near the church.

Getting there To get to Malovište from Bitola take the highway towards Resen for almost 20km and take the exit marked Kazani. At the crossroads turn left and then take the next left at the village shop. Follow this one-lane road some 5km until you get to the village. Back at the crossroads, if you take the road straight on north, you will drive along the River Šemnica to **Streževo Lake**, and turning left at the village of Lera and then left again at Sviništa, you can take a dirt track up to another formerly rich Vlach village, **Gopeš**. Gopeš has not had as much funding as Malovište, but is also a good potential museum town showing a glimpse of life back in the wealthier Vlach days.

ECOTOURISM DEVELOPMENT IN PELISTER NATIONAL PARK Less than 5km from the border with Greece, the village of Brajčino is courting an ecotourism initiative offered through the Swiss non-governmental organisation ProNatura. Brajčino was chosen for its pristine, picturesque setting on the edge of Pelister National Park. Its idyllic location is away from the hustle and bustle of city life and is protected by the Baba massif and with a view onto Lake Prespa. It has good access to the glacial lakes atop the range and from there to Pelister summit and the mountain huts. It is easily accessible by car or by bus from Resen (several buses every day).

EATING AT HOME

Brajčino offers the chance to eat with the locals. Some friends and I ordered a day ahead for the special set menu to be served at 19.00 upon our arrival in the village. There is no à la carte menu, but vegetarian food or other dietary requests can be included, if the order is placed in advance.

We arrived in good time and walked up the narrow winding roads of the village to Jadranka's little farm at house number 144 (the village is so small that there are no street names). The family were waiting for us and ushered us into their tiny Sunday room, the one reserved for guests and special occasions.

Sitting at the neatly laid table we were offered a shot of *rakija* or *liker* as an aperitif to welcome us to their home. I chose the *liker* made of a *rakija* base re-distilled with blueberries and sugar. Fortunately, the Macedonians take their time over their liqueurs, and this one was well worth savouring; accompanied by salad fresh from their garden, I could have drunk two or three glasses, but saved myself for the homemade wine which was to come with the main course.

We moved on to a country veal soup, so delicious that I asked the origin of the calf. 'Yes, it is our calf,' Jadranka replied. Feeling slightly guilty that I was eating from their larder, I continued the conversation enquiring if the calf had had a name. 'Rusa,' came the reply. 'Ah yes, well Rusa is indeed most delicious,' I added in my best Macedonian. Everyone burst out laughing at this point, probably at my attempt to speak Macedonian.

The next course included more of Rusa's melt-in-the-mouth offerings, accompanied by sweet roasted peppers and sautéed potatoes. Their homemade wine was fruity and mild, quaffable by the jugful, although we restrained ourselves to fit in some of their homemade peach juice, while we chatted away with the family about each other's lives. Formerly the area had lived well from sheep farming, but now Macedonia's depressed economy could not support the high price of sheep. With so little work in the locality, Jadranka and Jonce were glad to receive the extra income that ecotourism might bring their way. Jonce could be hired as a mountain guide by the day or half day (1,500/800MKD) and, in addition to set meals, Jadranka sells dried boletus mushroom (350MKD/500g), *liker* (400MKD/litre), *rakija* (150MKD/litre) and other homemade products such as jam, juice and wine.

We finished the meal with some homemade marble cake, cherries from their garden and a cup of coffee or mountain tea. Fully satiated, we then meandered back down the hill to our beds for an exquisite night's sleep.

The next evening we ate at Milka's house. We were greeted with the Macedonian tradition of candied fruits (locally grown and produced, of course) and shots of mint or cherry *liker*. More delicious homemade courses followed, ending with a *baklava* made of walnuts and poppy seed that was so tasty I'll be ordering a whole tray in advance next time to take home.

Formerly a rich trading village, it still has a small population of mixed ages despite the emigration of many of the villagers in the middle of the 20th century to Canada and Scandanavia due to lack of employment or in order to escape communist persecution. The departure of most of the business know-how from the village has left it in hard times, even more so since the break-up of Yugoslavia which has taken its toll on the village's formerly prosperous apple trade. Previously, apples from the area would be sold as far away as Zagreb and Ljubljana, whereas new borders and taxes have all but eliminated the apple export. Now the villagers, through the help of ProNatura and the local non-governmental organisations of DEM (Ecological Movement of Macedonia) and BSPM (Bird Society Protection of Macedonia), are trying to revive the local economy by offering visitors access to their pristine lifestyle in return for keeping it so. Ten percent of the income of the guides, accommodation and the village shop is reinvested into preserving the local area.

Where to stay and eat Accommodation is either bed and breakfast-style in a local house at 900MKD per person (or bed only for 420MKD) or dormitory style in the old Monastery of Sv Petka (24 beds) for 350MKD. The monastery is no longer a working monastery, but was renovated by the villagers in 2003 under the ecotourism project in order to accommodate visitors. It is set in a meadow above the village and offers utter tranquillity, a view onto Pelister and a fantastic night sky. The accommodation price at the monastery includes bedding and use of the bathrooms, but you will have to pay 30MKD extra for a towel if you need one, and another 60MKD for use of the kitchen. There is so far no heating, so once the weather turns cold you may prefer to seek accommodation elsewhere. Breakfast is not provided.

There is a small village shop and café just off the main square that also offers information on the village guides and tours, but no restaurants. A village lunch or evening meal can be arranged in one of the local houses, giving you that extra special local experience, eating almost entirely locally grown and produced food (see box, page 198). You can order three types of menu: a basic menu for 350MKD (three courses), a standard menu for 450MKD (four courses) and a special menu for 550MKD (for special occasions). Children aged between five and 12 years pay half price, younger than five years free. Wine with your meal is not included in this cost.

To find out more about Brajčino, book accommodation, a meal or a guide in Brajčino ✆ 070 497 751, 047 482 444; e info@brajcino.com; www.brajcino.com.mk.

What to see and do The village has done a lot of work to tidy up local hiking trails and to keep them well marked and signposted. Hiking guides can be arranged for 800–1,200MKD for a half day or 1,500–3,600MKD for a full day (depending on the number of people) to take you on less well-trodden trails and to give you an insight into local flora, fauna and history. It's a five- to six-hour hike to the mountain hut of Golemo Ezero at one of the 'Eyes of Pelister', and then another three-hour hike from there to the summit of Pelister.

The village itself is pretty to walk around and an ideal setting for walks with children. There are many animals to be seen in the village farmyards and a number of buildings are marked with information plates on the usage, architecture and previous owners of the building. Much of this information is from the book *Brajčino Stories* by the writer Meto Jovanovski from *Brajčino*, a former chairperson of the Macedonian Pen Club. He is now retired and returns to the village every summer. The **bey's house** (*Begot Kukja*), the house of the last Ottoman commander for the area from the end of the 19th century, can be viewed inside if you ask for the key in the neighbouring houses or at the village shop.

There are six churches near the village dating from medieval times through to the beginning of the 20th century. The medieval churches are those dedicated to Sv Petka, Sv Bogorodica and Sv Atanas. It's not known exactly when these churches were built or even in which order, but all contain frescoes of the same era and, like so many churches in Macedonia, are in various stages of disrepair.

The **Church of Sv Petka** lies in the grounds of the old monastery 15 minutes' walk outside the village. Sv Petka's holy day is 8 August, when as many as 600 of the local villagers gather in the monastery with food and drink to celebrate.

The small **Church of Sv Bogorodica** leans against a cliff above the village. The cliff can be seen from the village and, although the church itself is obscured by trees, the rock face is marked out with a cross at the top of the cliff. Set into the cliff are a number of 'cells' where local monks used to stay overnight in days of old.

The medieval church 15 minutes' walk to the south of the village is dedicated to **Sv Atanas**. It is mostly in ruins but has some graves possibly dating back to medieval times.

The church closest to the village and still used by its inhabitants is the **Church of Sv Nikola.** Built in 1871, it is in a pretty location with a good view onto Lake Prespa. The main nave of the church is usually locked, although you may be able to access the glass-fronted exonarthex. Ask in the village for the key. The bell tower is a recent addition, made of a simple metal frame but in the traditional Macedonian style of being separate from the church itself.

The churches of **Sv Ilija** (1915) and **Sv Archangel** (1919) are located outside the village and are very simple. They are also rarely used, making them musty and damp.

Further down the valley is the larger village of **Ljubojno**. It is made up of houses similar in style to Brajčino, although a few 19th-century town houses have also made it into the village square. The square is begging for a few good outdoor cafés and a piazza lifestyle … maybe in a few more years. Clearly seen above the village are the two churches of **Sv Petka** and **Sv Pavle**, which vigilantly watch over Ljubojno.

LAKE PRESPA

Lake Prespa offers a peaceful, cooler and cheaper alternative to Lake Ohrid, and is well worth a visit in July and August when even Ohrid can get blisteringly hot and the festivities can be too much. Combined with Pelister Mountain, which is exactly 800m higher than the Galičica Mountains running the length of Lake Ohrid, the area offers a lot for those who love the outdoors.

The lake is situated 850m above sea level, making the surroundings quite cool from the mountain air. But due to the relatively shallow depth of Prespa, only just over 50m, the lake itself can get quite warm, up to 25°C in the summer. A shallow sandy shoreline allows children to play and swim safely where their feet can still touch the bottom.

Sharing its borders with Greece and Albania, the lake is in fact closely connected on the Greek side to a smaller lake of the same name situated between Greece and Albania. The two lakes are separated only by a narrow strip of land in Greece, and in centuries gone by the two lakes used to be one. During that time, the name Prespa, meaning blizzard, came about because of the illusion created of an almighty blizzard when the lakes would freeze over; covered in snow, the lakes would appear like a white-out to anyone looking in their direction. Other legends abound as to how the lake actually came into existence (see box, page 203).

🏠 **WHERE TO STAY** There is a lack of good places to stay on the lake itself, in part because it is not as good a lake to swim in as Ohrid. Most Macedonians tend to stay in Pelister National Park (see page 196), in little villages like Brajčino (page 198). Ezerani bird sanctuary also offers basic accommodation (page 203) and try the following:

🏠 **Hotel MVR** (56 rooms) Krani; ☎ 047 483 247. This is arguably the safest hotel in Macedonia as it belongs to the Ministry of the Interior & is reserved primarily for use by the police. It is rarely anywhere near full, however, & it has a good location on the lake. With a small exclusive beach for hotel customers, it's good value for money. Rooms are basic in that very 'socialist' style, all en suite but no TV or AC (it rarely gets that hot there anyway). The hotel has a restaurant that seats over 100 guests & is sometimes booked up for weddings, but usually you will have the terrace to yourself. The hotel also has about 20 hook-ups for caravans & camping, with block showers & toilets. To get to the hotel turn towards the lake (signposted *Ezero*) from the main lake road where it is also signposted Krani in the opposite direction. This road will also take you to **Autocamp Krani** (which is not as nice as the hotel but is cheaper) but turn off left before you reach the gated entrance of the autocamp. $

WHAT TO SEE AND DO Aside from swimming in the lake and enjoying the cooler temperatures of Pelister Mountain, the must-do thing at Lake Prespa is to visit the **island of Golem Grad**, sometimes known as Snake Island for all the water snakes that live around the shores of the island. The island is now uninhabited and is part of the nature reserve of Galičica National Park. It contains endemic flora and fauna protected by the island's lack of contact with the rest of the world, so if you do get the chance to go, be sure not to disturb the ecosystem.

The island has been inhabited over the centuries going back to Neolithic times. It is believed that Tsar Samoil was crowned tsar on the island in AD976, and the remains of two 14th-century churches, dedicated to Sv Petka and to Sv Dimitri, are built on the foundations of 6th-century early Christian basilicas. Other ruins of an old village can also be found there.

If you can't find a local to take you out to the island, then boat trips can be arranged by Go Macedonia in Skopje (see *Tour operators* on page 70). On the trip you will see a variety of birdlife much of which gathers on the island. When you go back to your boat, look out also for all the water snakes, which may have gathered around the boat. As soon as you step into the water or move the boat, they will disappear and are perfectly harmless.

If you are approaching the lake from Ohrid via the E65 then it is worth a look into the **women's monastery of Jankovec**, a few kilometres before the town of Resen. This was the first women's monastery to be brought back to life after several decades of neglect during communist times. Sister Kirana, who heads the best group of fresco painters alive today in Macedonia, brought the nuns to the rundown 16th-century monastery in 1998. They have done a lot of work to it since then and their skills as fresco artists are in high demand throughout Macedonia. They also weave, and sometimes you can purchase their handicrafts at the monastery.

There are a number of access points to the shores of Lake Prespa where there are small beaches and resorts. The largest of these is at **Oteševo** on the northwestern side of the lake. Oteševo also houses the national centre for respiratory illnesses, due to the superb quality of the air at Lake Prespa.

There are smaller beaches at Konjsko, Asamati, Pretor, Krani, Nakolec and Dolni Dupeni right on the border with Greece (the border crossing here was still closed at the time of writing). Oteševo and Pretor also offer hotels and beach-style bungalows, but these are in some need of renovation.

Konjsko is on the western side of the lake near the border with Albania. It has a lovely little public beach, which is quite secluded, and the village itself is the site of an ancient settlement which is largely intact and now protected as part of Macedonia's cultural heritage. A small cave church dedicated to Sv Elias can also be found near the village. The asphalt road does not go all the way, so be prepared for a hike or take a 4x4.

Krani has a lovely small private beach available to those staying at the Hotel MVR (see *Where to stay* above), whereas the beach at **Dolno Dupeni** is larger and public, and has a small food and drinks hut.

The beach at **Nakolec** has the added attraction of being next to this small mixed-ethnicity village, one of the few in the area along with Krani, Grnčari and Arvati. The **Church of Sv Atanas** on the shore of Nakolec used to stand practically in the water, but now lies some way off due to the water loss from the lake. The receding shoreline has allowed for some excavation, however, which has revealed the foundations of buildings further into the lake. As measures are now being taken to refill the lake these excavations will undoubtedly be covered over once again but hopefully not before the research on them has been finished. Nakolec also used to have a number of wooden houses on stilts, but these are no longer standing. The old Bektaši *teke* in the village is being rebuilt.

At the northern end of the lake the village of Podmočani has a small **museum of national dress** and artefacts in a small house on the main road. Still the private collection of a local farmer, Jone Eftimoski, it is now open to public viewing for a small entry fee. There are over 140 costumes from all over Macedonia along with jewellery, weapons and coins. Just as you get to the start of the cobbled part of the road there is a small green sign marked 'museum' pointing to the house on the right of the main road. It may not look open, but there is usually someone around in the front garden who will let you in and give you a guided tour.

Further along the lakeside road is the **bird sanctuary of Ezerani**. As with any birdwatching it is best to go early during the day or in the evening, otherwise you may find only a herd of cows among the rushes, eating discarded apples. The bird sanctuary is home to over 115 different species of bird including wild geese, pelicans and local moorhens. It is a part of the University of Skopje and internationally protected by EURONATUR. University members can stay at the sanctuary for a discounted price, but non-members pay €15 per night for bed and breakfast. The rooms and facilities are in great need of attention.

A TALE OF TEARS

Legend has it that a town once stood in place of the great Lake Prespa. While walking through the local woods one day, the son of the king of the town chanced upon a wood nymph whose beauty surpassed that of any girl he had hitherto laid eyes upon. On asking her name, she replied in an enchanting voice 'Nereida'. The king's son fell immediately in love with the nymph and came to the woods many times to woo her and take her hand in marriage, offering her all the riches of his father's land and a place by his side as the queen of the kingdom. But the nymph turned down his generous offer, saying that she could not marry a mortal without sinister consequences befalling the groom and his homeland. Unable to imagine a deed so awful and unable to suppress his love for the nymph, he chose one night to have her kidnapped and kept her in confinement until she accepted his offer of marriage. Upon their pronouncement as husband and wife, however, the heavens opened and a downpour of rain ensued. The rain did not stop until the whole town was underwater and every citizen had drowned. The result is the present-day Lake Prespa. The moral of the story is that when a woman says 'no' she really does mean it.

The next turn-off on the left leads to the village of **Kurbinovo**. This is a typical working local village along a pot-holed tarmac road crowded with meandering sheep, goats and cows. At the second house on the left, a two-storey white building with a railed front lawn, ask for the key to the **Church of Sv Gjorgi** (*ključa Sveti Gjorgi*), and continue on up the road. At the crest of the hill in the village turn right through a narrow row of houses and continue another couple of kilometres until you turn into a large tarmacked parking area, obviously out of keeping with the surroundings. Above the car park is the 12th-century Church of St George. There are a number of medieval frescoes inside dating from when the church was first built in 1191. Some in Macedonia believe that the style of these frescoes was the seed of the **Renaissance** arts in Italy, where their painters were forced to flee with the invasion of the Ottoman Empire, who banned all still-life art. Unfortunately, of the many frescoes depicting the life of St George, few can be seen now.

PRILEP

If you are venturing beyond Skopje and Ohrid and are wondering where to go next, and/or want a compact representation of Macedonian life through the ages, then go to Prilep. The town is situated under the Towers of Marko, a medieval **fortress**, and has two worthwhile monasteries in the vicinity. The town also has a well-preserved, if small, old Turkish town and a pedestrian area where it is simply nice to drink coffee and relax. The area is so symbolic of Macedonian culture that it has been used twice by Macedonian film director Milčo Mančevski, as the setting for a couple of his films. The name of the city itself derives from the ancient tribe of the Pelazgi. Macedonia's fledgling **beer festival** takes over in July.

GETTING THERE AND AROUND

By train Prilep train station (☏ *048 412 660*) is 500m to the west of the centre of town. Four trains travel to/from Skopje every day (see times on pages 74–7). If you don't manage any other train journey in Macedonia, this is the one to do, as it takes you through some great mountain scenery. The section from Veles to Prilep is in parts not even accessible by road and midway between the towns of **Sogle** and **Bogomila** offers a fantastic view of the Solunska Glava Mountain

BUS DEPARTURES FROM PRILEP	
Belgrade	07.30, 09.40, 18.00
Sofia	05.40, 20.30
Skopje	14 buses a day from 05.30–17.15; 320MKD sgl, 500MKD return.
Bitola	14 buses a day from 05.30–23.00; 100MKD.
Ohrid	08.15, 09.40, 12.30, 16.30, 17.00, 18.40; 300MKD sgl, 500MKD return.
Strumica	06.45, 07.40, 15.15
Veles	05.30, 06.30, 06.40, 15.00, 15.15
Kičevo	05.30, 07.00, 09.00, 14.15, 16.00
Kočani	08.30, 15.40
Resen	10.00, 14.35, 18.35

And once a day to Brajčino 13.20; Gevgelija 15.40; Radoviš 14.40; Kavadarci 14.00; Probištip 16.00; Oteševo 16.00; & Struga 18.00.

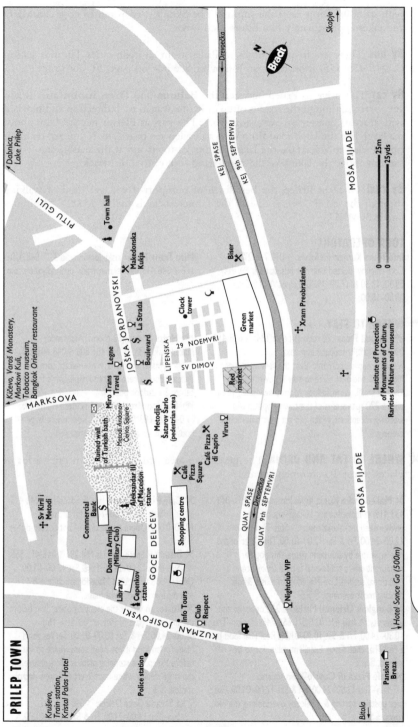

Kruševo,
Train station,
Kristal Palas Hotel

Police station

KUZMAN JOSIFOVSKI

Library

Cepenkov
statue

Dom na Armija
(Military Club)

Commercial
Bank

Info Tours

Club
Respect

Shopping centre

GOCE DELČEV

Aleksandar III
of Macedon
statue

Ruined wall
of Turkish bath

Metodi Andonov
Čento Square

Café
Pizza
Square

Metodija
Šatarov Šarlo
(pedestrian area)

Café Pizza
di Caprio

Virus

MARKSOVA

Miro Trans
Travel

Legne

La Strada

Boulevard

7th LIPENSKA

SV DIMOV

29 NOEMVRI

Red
market

JOŠKA JORDANOVSKI

Clock
tower

Makedonska
Kulja

Town hall

PITU GULI

Kičevo, Varoš Monastery,
Markovi Kuli,
Tobacco museum,
Bangkok Oriental restaurant

Dabnica,
Lake Prilep

✝ Sv Kiril i
Metodi

Green
market

Biser

✝ Xram Preobraženie

✝

KEJ 9th SEPTEMVRI

KEJ SPASE

Drevečka

N

Brač

Skopje

MOŠA PIJADE

Institute of Protection
of Monuments of Culture,
Rarities of Nature and museum

QUAY SPASE

QUAY 9th SEPTEMVRI

Drevečka

Nightclub VIP

MOŠA PIJADE

Pansion
Breza

Hotel Sonce Ga (500m)

Bitola

0   25m
0   25yds

with its 800m drop from the summit. The Skopje–Prilep return costs 300MKD and takes approximately two hours each way.

By bus There are frequent buses to Prilep from all main cities. The bus station (✆ *048 425 555*) is on Kuzman Josifovski. See box on page 205 for times.

By car The drive to Prilep between the **Babuna** and **Dren mountains** is also very pretty, although the road is often only one way in each direction and blocked with tractors, lorries or expansion work. The pass at Pletvar lies at 994m above sea level. For the back road from Veles to Prilep see page 248. If you are taking it from Prilep to Veles, take the lake road out of town and at the marble statue of a cannon above the lake take the right-hand fork onto a dirt track.

By taxi Once in Prilep, the best form of transport if you get tired of walking through the small town is one of the numerous taxis (*call* ✆ *15188*). Minimum fare is 30MKD.

TOUR OPERATORS
Info Tours Kuzman Josifovski; ✆ 070 741 275. Conveniently located near the bus station; ☉ daily 08.30–13.30 & 17.00–19.30, except Wed & Sat: 08.30–15.00.

Miro Trans Travel Joska Jordanovski 3; ✆ 048 410 166; f 048 415 392; e mirotrans_prom@yahoo.com

🏠 WHERE TO STAY
🏠 **Kristal Palas** (22 rooms) Lenin 184; ✆ 048 418 000; e info@kristalpalas.com.mk; www.kristalpalas.com.mk. Near the railway station. Modern & the best place to stay in town. Has a lovely if small, warm, indoor rooftop swimming pool with a 270° panorama of the town. Popular with wedding receptions, which can get a bit noisy in the evening. $$$

🏠 **Hotel Sonce** (52 rooms) Aleksandar Makedonski 4/3a; ✆ 048 401 800; f 048 401 801; e info@makam.com.mk; www.makam.com.mk. Pleasant rooms recently renovated. Large fitness centre & outdoor pool. $$

🏠 **Pansion Breza** (9 rooms) Moša Pijade 24a; ✆ 048 423 683, 071 214 071. Rooms in a large house with a nice small b/fast area. $$

✕ WHERE TO EAT AND DRINK
The pedestrian area and the old town offer a lot of places to eat. Recommended are:

✕ **Makedonska Kukja** Joska Jordanovski 4; ✆ 048 433 419; e makedonska_kuka@yahoo.com; www.makedonskakuka.com; ☉ Sun–Thu 12.00–24.00, Fri & Sat 12.00–01.00. The sister of the one in Skopje by the same name, this popular restaurant offers traditional food & ambience in a traditional setting. Live Macedonian music & folk dancing most evenings. $$$

✕ **Bangkok Oriental** Marksova 212 opposite the university; ✆ 048 425 027, 071 656 746; ☉ Sun–Thu 10.30–24.00, Fri & Sat 10.30–01.00. Real Thai food by a real Thai chef, Chen. Excellent value not to be missed. $$

✕ **Café Pizza di Caprio** Town square; ☉ Sun–Thu 12.00–24.00, Fri & Sat 12.00–01.00. Has nice upstairs seating & a balcony overlooking the old town. $$

✕ **Café Pizza Square** Jane Sandanski; ✆ 048 415 301; ☉ Sun–Thu 12.00–24.00, Fri & Sat 12.00–01.00. Offers a selection of hot & cold dishes. $$

✕ **Biser** Kej Spase, Kej 1st Maj 29; ✆ 048 415 366; ☉ Sun–Thu 12.00–24.00, Fri & Sat 12.00–01.00. Offers good traditional Macedonian cuisine & accompanying traditional music. $$

✕ **Restoran Ce** At the stopping place 5km before the mountain pass of Pletvar; ☉ Sun–Thu 08.00–24.00, Fri & Sat 08.00–01.00. Serves good Macedonian food if you need somewhere to eat before Prilep. The stopping place is recognisable by the large shining white marble cross & new petrol station. $$

♀ **La Strada** Goce Delčev; ✆ 048 414 212; ☉ Sun–Thu 11.00–24.00, Fri & Sat 10.00–01.00. A happening bar with a raised balcony off the street. It is also the sister company of **VIP Nightclub** on Kej 9th December, opposite the bus station, which plays live music Thu–Sun, & has its own pizzeria & bar food.

WHAT TO SEE The **old Turkish centre** of Prilep is small and can be walked around in about ten minutes, so it is best enjoyed over a drink break or lunch period. It borders on the pedestrian area Metodi Šatarov Šarlo, and towering over the old town is the **clock tower**. Next to the clock tower are the **ruins of an old mosque**, and the one remaining wall of another can be found in **Metodi Andonov Park**.

There are two churches near Prilep's centre. Behind the library is the **Church of Sv Kiril i Metodi**, which dates from 1926. It is a fairly modern church, with no frescoes. The **Church of Xram Preobraženie**, built in 1871, is located opposite the **Green Market** on Quay 9th December. The church is dark, no frills, and mostly locked although you can look through the glass doors. The courtyard, however, provides a welcome place to sit down and there are taps there for water.

The **Fortress Towers of Marko** (*Markovi Kuli*) stand prominently on the hill above Prilep. The fortress is named after King Marko (see box, page 186), the last Macedonian king, who died fighting the Turks. There is no information available at the site itself, but archaeological findings show that parts of the fortress date back to the Iron Age, the 3rd and 4th centuries BC and later periods during the Ottoman Empire. Most of what remains to be seen today is from medieval times. It is sadly mostly in ruins, but still well worth the hike, and the views from the top over the ruins and beyond are magnificent.

To get there from the centre of town take Ulica Markovska uphill and turn off to the right after about 1km where the road levels off, just after a small pharmacy and a car mechanic shop, opposite some conference halls. Keep going uphill until you get to the back of the houses that will lead you to the gravel road to the towers. The road passes the famous stone called Slon, meaning the elephant, which marks the beginning of the Markovi Kuli site and continues in a blaze of white crushed marble (Prilep is also a marble-mining town) around the back of the hill. This is the easy route up, suitable for a high-clearance vehicle, although whether you will find parking space at the top on a busy weekend is another thing.

Alternatively, you could take on a frontal assault of the towers and go straight up the middle of the rocks. A path eventually forms itself if you bear right of the entrance. It must have been suicidal as a foot soldier, even with armour and weapons, to attack the towers from this direction: hard work all the way up and raining arrows. Bring plenty of water with you, at least half a litre per person on a hot day, as there is none at the top and thirst would spoil an otherwise lovely gambol among the rocks.

The frontal assault and parts of the towers are steep, require some scrambling and have no handrails, so this is not advisable for those who are prone to vertigo. A watchtower has been recreated at the eastern end of the rocks using concrete, and it looks decidedly out of place. The highest part of the rock formation is marked by a metal-girder cross, similar to the one in Skopje but smaller.

From the top it is also possible to hike 8km north to Zlatovrv, where the monastery of Treskavec lies (see below and *Chapter 12*).

On the southeastern edge of the Marko Towers' rock feature, in a part of Prilep called Varoš, is the **Monastery of Sv Michael the Archangel**. It is perched between the rocks looking out to the Pelagonia plains, and now houses five nuns. As you enter the monastery take note of the 15th-century iron doorway. Little remains of the original church, built in the early 12th century, but two partial remains of frescoes and some of the original walls can be seen in the church vaults.

The church now standing in the monastery courtyard is made up of two parts built during medieval times and of three classical period marble columns, which were found by the monks who built the monastery. The second oldest Cyrillic inscription to be found in Macedonia is carved at eye level into the far right pillar as you stand in the exonarthex (the oldest inscription is the epitaph dedicated to Tsar Samoil's mother and father). The remaining housing for the nuns was erected in the 19th century. Underneath the main inn is a deep well that is entered via a small doorway.

Allegedly there were once 77 churches in the Prilep area, but only six were left standing after the Ottoman Empire moved in. The **Church of Sv Atanas**, which no longer has a roof, can be seen on the road approaching Sv Michael's Monastery.

To get to Varoš take Gorče Petrov out of town past the turning to Markovi Kuli. At this point the road turns into Orle Čopela, and very quickly you'll come to a bust of Orle Čopela on the right at the top of the rise in the road. Take the right turn just before this monument onto Borke Dopačot (in typical Macedonian fashion this is not marked as such at the turning!). Follow this asphalt road all the way to the monastery.

OUTSIDE PRILEP

PRILEP TOBACCO MUSEUM (\ *048 401 090, 075 461 945;* e *agtis@mt.net.mk*) Housed in the grounds of the Tutun Tobacco Institute, the Prilep Tobacco Museum was opened in 1973 to celebrate 100 years of the tobacco factory that now houses both the institute and museum. Especially for the occasion, Tito ordered the purchase of over 750 items for display in the museum ranging from German tobacco pots, Chinese cigarette cases, Russian snuffboxes and Ottoman pipes, to intriguing cigar cutters and ornate *nargilehs* (water pipes) for both scented tobacco and opium. The room housing the exhibits seems an anti-climax on first entry, but a closer look at the carved faces and scenes on the artefacts reveals an exquisite craftsmanship that is fascinating and compelling, even if you don't agree with smoking (and smoking had been banned in 1634 by a decree from the Ottoman sultan). Artefacts made from a variety of woods, bone, ivory, silver, gold inlay, pearl lacquer, silver filigree, silver nitrate inlay, semi-precious stone and glazed enamels are all on display. Sadly, very little information is available in Macedonian and none in English at the time of writing. However, many of the stories behind the pieces can be told by the museum curator Aleksandar Tretkoski if he is available. The museum is open by appointment only during the week.

TRESKAVEC MONASTERY The remote Monastery of Treskavec is 8km outside Prilep under the summit of the impressive Zlatovrv. It is a magnificent old complex of significant historical and cultural value that is in urgent need of renovation. The site is of such worth that it made the World Monument Fund's 2006 top 100 most endangered sites. In addition to the value of the site itself, its remote setting is beautiful and earned itself a central role in Mančevski's film *Before the Rain*.

The monastery is built on the ancient town of Kolobaise, which existed from the 3rd century BC until the 7th century AD. The name of the town is written in a long inscription cut into a stone used as the base of the cross on top of the central dome of the church. There are also other inscriptions around the church that date back to the 1st century BC, when a temple to Apollo and Artemis was first built on this site.

Further remnants of the town under Roman rule can be found in the present 14th-century church of Sv Bogorodica, which was built on the foundations of the original 6th-century basilica. There is a baptism font on the left of the narthex as you enter, and the walls of the narthex have a number of stone carvings and sculptures. As there are few lights in the church, it is a good idea to bring a torch with you or a lighter for the candles so that you can see the artefacts. The narthex goes around to the right, covering two sides of the church, at the end of which is a separate confessional room. This room is interesting for its fresco depicting the donors who paid to have the church built: the two old men dedicated their life to God and are shown, as is typical of frescoes of the original church donors, holding the church between them.

There is a secondary narthex before entering the nave, and from this narthex are some steps on the right that lead into a small chamber. Inside the cupola there is one of the few frescoes of Christ as a young boy (there is another in the Monastery of Sv Eleusa, also in the right-hand chamber). The church has a number of 16th-century frescoes with the typical greenish sheen on the face of the figures that was the hallmark of Macedonian rather than Greek artists. Also in the nave is a casket of the skulls of seven monks from the monastery who were executed, along with almost 200 other monks who lived there at the time, by the Ottomans.

To the right of the entrance into the monastery is the old dining hall. It contains the old stone tables and Roman jars and vats, but it is in a terrible state of repair, and the last fresco at the end of the hall is in dire need of help if it is to remain intact on the wall. The chips in it show that it is an older fresco that was deliberately chipped in order to apply plaster for a new one, which has long since gone.

Despite its former glory in the early Ottoman period, only one monk currently runs the monastery. Father Kališt, who speaks very good English, welcomes visitors to the monastery and especially to the Sunday service held at 11.00. It is forbidden to enter the monastery scantily clad, so make sure you bring coverings for shoulders and legs before you get all the way there only to find you are improperly dressed and refused entry.

Outside the monastery are ancient graves cut into the rock. Water wells are encased in the stone wall to the left of the monastery main gate which leads to the ancient graves. There are also caves and monks' cells up on Zlatovrv. The stone outcrops and the views are intriguing and there are thought to be 77 animal and human forms that one can find in the rocks, such as lions, people talking to each other, a sphinx, a frog and eagles.

Father Kališt has a meagre income from this remote monastery with which to do much needed renovation work, and he charges nothing to stay in the inns, so maybe give generously at the altar when you visit the church. State-run excavation work is ongoing around the monastery, after which Father Kališt hopes to start with renovation. The Macedonian Ministry of Defence had pledged years ago to fix the 4x4 road to the back of the monastery but by 2009 nothing had been done. For route descriptions and a map of the three routes to the monastery see *Chapter 12*, page 300.

Like many modern monks these days, Father Kališt (✆ *048 800 160;* e *treskavec@ gmail.com*) has internet access at the monastery and excellent mobile phone coverage.

MARIOVO To the southeast of Prilep towards the border with Greece is the region of Mariovo. This rugged, beautiful area straddles the River Crna, which is flooded to the north (forming the manmade Tikveš Lake), and to the south comes from Pelister National Park through Bitola and the ancient Paeonian city of Lynk, whose exact location is still not known. The river must have been an important one to the ancient Paeons, for outside the small village of Monastir is one of the finest examples of what little remains of their ancient cities. Built out of finely cut limestone blocks using what has become known as cyclopean masonry (ie: a masonry technique which uses no mortar, but precision cuts and the size of the blocks to keep a construction together), these fortified cities date back to Aneolithic times.

Evidence of other such cities have been found in Demir Kapija, Vajtos near Ohrid, Debar, Tetovo, Prilep and Skopje amongst other places, usually in high locations that are easy to defend. The site at Mariovo is unusual for being in the river valley, and archaeologists are still researching the site to see if they can find clues as to why it was located there.

To get to the site, take the road south out of Prilep towards Bitola and turn off southeast towards the town of Vitolište (signposted). After 5km the road passes the village of **Stavica**, a picturesque village used by Mančevski in *Before the Rain*. Another 25km later the road crosses the River Crna at the new bridge that replaced the old Ottoman bridge of Hasin Bey. The river crossing is popular with picnickers and fishermen, and parts of the old bridge can still be seen. After another kilometre the old road to Monastir village is signposted from the opposite direction. Turn south to follow the dirt track (4x4 only or walk) upstream for 4km towards the village of Monastir. The site of large old limestone blocks can be seen from this track. At the village the site is known as *stari grad* (old town) *arxeološko naogjalište* (archaeological site), and although the two very old men who live here know about the site they are past the age to be able to take you there. It is admittedly just a site of old limestone blocks, but if you want to see for yourself the closest thing you'll get to cyclopean masonry built by the Paeons, then let your imagination build the rest of the city for you. The new road to Monastir, 4km from the bridge, does not allow a vantage point onto this site.

STIBERA RUINS West of the highway between Prilep and Bitola, between the villages of Trojkrsti and Čepigovo, are the barely uncovered ruins of the Roman town of Stibera. Once a prominent urban centre in ancient Macedonia, the last Macedonian king, Perseus, had his military headquarters there, from where he conducted his campaigns against the Romans in 169BC. The Greek historian and geographer Strabo writing in the 1st century BC refers to Stibera by its ancient name of Stymbara as being one of three cities located along the River Erigon (today's Crna), in the ancient Paeonian region of Derriopos and Pelagonia. The archaeological remains in Stibera range in date from the 3rd century BC to the 3rd century AD. Among the remarkable finds are more than 30 marble statues and busts, many exquisitely carved, and about 20 pediments and inscriptions. Barely cordoned off, overlooking the confluence of the Blato and Crna rivers, are the Temple of Tyche (the Greek goddess of fortune) and the town school.

AROUND MAKEDONSKI BROD Another interesting monastery, halfway between Prilep and Kičevo, is the **Monastery of Zrze**, near the village of the same name. Quite spectacular to see from the approach, it is set into the cliffside as if it hangs there only by the will of God. The monks' cells are built precariously into the cliff walls under the monastery. The monastery inns and church are built at the site of an earlier Christian basilica, whose foundations can still be seen, along with a number of marble pillars and other artefacts.

The church dedicated to **Sts Petar and Pavle** contains frescoes from the 14th century and an additional nave, known as the Shepherd's Church, to the left of the main nave. The main church is famous for its icons, which show the Virgin Mary in profile rather than face on and on the right of Jesus rather than the left. Legend says that when the icons first came to the church they were placed, as is usual, with Mary on the left of Jesus. Every morning, however, the church's monks would come for morning prayers to find the icons reversed. Bewildered by this phenomenon the father prayed to Mary for enlightenment on the issue. She apparently told him that she had to be placed on the right of Jesus because otherwise her profile depiction would turn her back rather than her face to her son, which she would never do. The depiction of Mary in profile is unusual in Macedonia, but common in Russia. There are also the graves of two Russian nuns in the grounds of the monastery (recognisable by the Russian Orthodox-style gravestones), and so it is believed that these icons originally came from Russia with the nuns.

To get there, turn off the road to Kičevo from Prilep at the village of Ropotovo. The turn-off is signposted for Peštalevo. Go through these next two villages until you reach the first left turn in the village of Kostinci at what appears to be the mayor's house. There is a hand water pump at this corner. Here the road turns into a dirt track and leads only to the village of Zrze and straight on to the monastery which you'll be able to see long before you come to the village. The last turn before the monastery is very rutted, so park at the corner unless you have a 4x4.

Just before Makedonski Brod is the turn-off to Modrište. This area of Macedonia, like Matka and Lesnovo, is riddled with caves and underground tunnels. At the end of the road at Belica are Golubarnik, Momiček and Laprnik caves. Near Slatina are several more caves accessible only with equipment. However, very visible on the way to Lokvica is the entrance to Pesna Cave, where the medieval ruins of former residents still exist. The cave goes back a long way through the mouth of a small tunnel at the back of the main cavernous entrance.

In Makedonski Brod itself there is the **Church of Sv Nikola,** which used to be a Bektaši *teke* (monastery of the Muslim order of the Bektaši), and some pleasant walks along the river.

Where to stay and eat In nearby Plasnica, an ethnic Turkish village, the local restaurant is renowned for its excellent fish dishes straight from the River Treška. Near the village of Devič is **Mak Viking** (✆ *045 275 606, 071 371 169;* e *makviking@t-home.mk; www.makviking.com*). A small ostrich ranch, the restaurant serves ostrich steak and omelettes (among other dishes), and offers seven rooms at €25 for a double.

KRUŠEVO

Macedonians rave about Kruševo. Aside from being the place of Macedonian uprising against the Ottoman Empire in 1903, it is a very quaint Vlach town and thoroughly pleasant. At 1,250m, the town is the highest in the entire Balkans, and is a ski town in its own right, with ski lifts connecting the town to the slopes on Musica, Golomanica, Kozjak and Ručalo.

On 2 August 1903, the holy day of Sv Ilija, the Internal Macedonian Revolutionary Organisation (VMRO) rose up all over Macedonia to fight for independence from the Ottoman Empire. This day is known as Ilinden, literally *Ilija den* or Ilija's day. After fierce fighting, Kruševo succeeded in wresting power from the Ottomans and on 3 August the new government of Dinu Vangeli announced the independence of the Republic of Kruševo to a population of 14,000 (today there are only 10,000 in Kruševo). Nikola Karaev was made president.

However, it lasted only ten days before the Ottomans brought the new government to its knees and the Republic of Kruševo was no more. In 2003, the celebrations commemorating the centenary of independence (even though Macedonia has been shackled for most of the intervening years) were of the utmost national and cultural significance. For the Macedonians, 2 August is like 4 July for

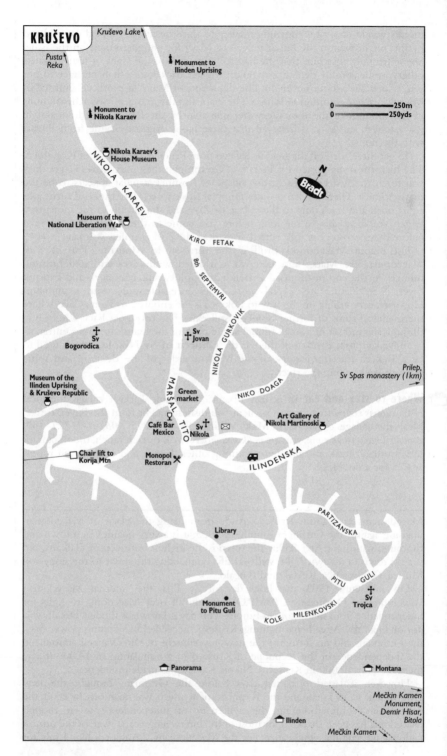

KRUŠEVO

Kruševo Lake

Pusta Reka

Monument to Ilinden Uprising

Monument to Nikola Karaev

Nikola Karaev's House Museum

NIKOLA KARAEV

Museum of the National Liberation War

KIRO FETAK

8th SEPTEMVRI

NIKOLA GURKOVIK

Sv Jovan

Sv Bogorodica

NIKO DOAGA

Prilep, Sv Spas monastery (1km)

Museum of the Ilinden Uprising & Kruševo Republic

MARŠAL TITO

Green market

Café Bar Mexico

Sv Nikola

Art Gallery of Nikola Martinoski

ILINDENSKA

Chair lift to Korija Mtn

Monopol Restoran

PARTIZANSKA

Library

PITU GULI

Sv Trojca

Monument to Pitu Guli

KOLE MILENKOVSKI

Panorama

Montana

Ilinden

Mečkin Kamen Monument, Demir Hisar, Bitola

Mečkin Kamen

0   250m
0   250yds

N

Bradt

the Americans or 14 July for the French, although much more solemn. A re-enactment of the uprising now takes place every 2 August, and is a massive attraction.

GETTING THERE AND AWAY The main bus station (✆ *048 477 102*) is on the far side of town on the road out to Demir Kapija. There are several buses a day to Skopje for 330MKD.

WHERE TO STAY AND EAT Two good places to stay in Kruševo are the hotels Montana and Ilinden at the ski side of the town (west). Sadly, there are no good places to eat in the town, choices being your hotel, the main dilapidated *restoran* in the centre, or a few *skara na kilo* places.

🏠 **Hotel Montana** (200 beds) ✆ 048 477 121, 048 447 522; e montilin@mt.net.mk; www.montana.com.mk. Has recently been refurbished. The Montana towers over the town & is well signposted: head left when the main road through town forks just after the centre. Rooms in

the refurbished part of the hotel include b/fast & jacuzzi bath. $$
🏠 **Hotel Ilinden** (50 rooms) ✆ 048 477 072. Much more downmarket & can be found on the right fork after the centre, next to the ski lift. $

WHAT TO SEE AND DO Even if you do not make it here for the main event of the re-enactment of the Ilinden Uprising, Kruševo has plenty to visit on all the other days of the year. Aside from taking in the architectural beauty of the old houses, the main attraction for Macedonians is the **Ilinden Uprising Monument** containing the tomb of Nikola Karaev. It's easy to find; just head for the large white concrete monument on the northern hill of the town. The **house of Nikola Karaev** is now preserved as a museum, and is well worth a look inside for the rich decoration of the era. Like most of the intellectuals who made up VMRO, Nikola was obviously not from a poor background. Two more museums in the town are the **Museum of the Ilinden Uprising** (✆ *048 477 177, 048 476 756*) and the **Museum of the National Liberation War** (✆ *048 477 126/197*). There is also an art gallery of the paintings of the local painter Nikola Martinoski.

An hour's hike uphill from the Hotel Montana is **Mečkin Kamen**, the site of one of the battles. There is a large statue there of a fighter throwing an extremely large boulder. This is where Macedonians gather on 2 August every year to pay homage to the early revolutionaries.

On the holy front, the **Monastery of Sv Spas** in Trstenik, on the outskirts of Kruševo, is relatively young by Macedonian standards having been built in 1836. The monastery stands out on the hill as you approach Kruševo from Prilep, but the turn-off for the monastery (signposted) is low down in the valley before you start climbing up into Kruševo on the main road. The monastery is a popular place for Macedonians to stay. Churches in the town itself include the **Church of Sv Jovan**, built in 1904, which houses a collection of old icons from Kruševo; the **Church of Sv Nikola** in the centre of town, which was built in 1905 during the restoration of the town after the Ilinden Uprising; and finally the youngest, **Church of Sv Bogorodica**, built in 1967.

DEMIR HISAR

Halfway between Bitola and Kruševo is the small town of Demir Hisar. There is not much, if anything, worthwhile stopping for in the town itself, but nearby are some historical villages and monasteries. Four kilometres to the west, outside the village of **Slepče**, is the monastery dedicated to Sv Jovan Preteča. The monastery was established in the 14th century although a newer church, dedicated to **Sv**

Nikola, was built in 1672. Further south into the Plakenska Mountains is the village of **Smilevo** where, at the Congress of Smilevo, the decision was taken to carry out the Ilinden Uprising that brought about the ten-day Republic of Kruševo. Nearby is also the Vlach museum village of **Gopeš**, practically in ruins and barely lived in now. There you will find what was the biggest church in Macedonia 200 years ago. To the north, halfway between Demir Hisar and Kruševo, is the **Monastery of Zurče** near the village Zurče. Its church, dedicated to Sv Atanas Aleksandriski, was built in 1617, although it took another century for the iconostasis to be put in.

The Northwest and Mavrovo National Park

... every inch of the [Šarena] mosque inside was painted with fripperies in this amusing and self-consciously amused style. There was a frieze of tiny little views, of palaces on the Bosporus with ships neatly placed around the sound, of walled gardens with playing fountains ... it was like being inside a building made of a lot of enormous tea-trays ...

Black Lamb Grey Falcon, Rebecca West, 1941

The northwest of Macedonia along the Vardar and Radika rivers is edged by the **Šar mountain range** bordering Kosovo, and by the **Korab** and **Dešat mountains** bordering Albania. The main towns of Tetovo, Gostivar and Debar are predominantly Albanian, with significant pockets of Turks in Vrapčista, Centar Župa, Plašnica and Vraneštica. If you don't speak any Albanian, you'll be more warmly welcomed among most of the Albanian community if you speak German as it is more widely spoken here than English as a second language. **Skiing** is available at Popova Šapka near Tetovo, and at Mavrovo. **Mavrovo National Park** is the home of some stunning mountain scenery, waterfalls and wildlife, and where the **wedding festival** of Galičnik takes place every July. The back road to Ohrid from Gostivar goes past Mavrovo Lake and down the Radika River into the manmade dammed valley of Debar Lake. From there it follows the Crni Drim River past the dammed Globočica Valley on to Struga. In the autumn it is probably one of the prettiest routes in Macedonia, when the densely wooded mountainside becomes a riot of red, orange and yellow. This is the area of Macedonia that could earn itself the name of 'Little Switzerland'.

TETOVO

With a population of 70,000, Tetovo is the gateway to the Šar Mountains and to the popular Popova Šapka ski resort. Towering above the town, covered in snow until July and as early as September, is Macedonia's second highest mountain, Titov Vrv (Tito's Summit, 2,748m). This is in fact the highest mountain that lies completely in Macedonia (and was also the highest in the whole of Yugoslavia, earning it its name). The higher peak of Mount Korab (2,764m) lies further to the south above Lake Mavrovo on the border with Albania.

Nestled close to Kosovo and Albania, Tetovo is the de facto capital of Macedonia's significantly sized Albanian minority. It is also the headquarters of the main Albanian-centred political parties, the Democratic Union of Integration and the Democratic Party of Albanians. Just outside Tetovo is the South East European University, Macedonia's third university after Skopje and Bitola.

HISTORY Tetovo is a relatively new town by Macedonian standards, although there have been archaeological discoveries near the town which date back to the

THE NORTHWEST AND MAVROVO NATIONAL PARK

Bronze Age (2200–1200BC). Macedonia's oldest artefact, a Mycenae sword from this period, was found outside Tetovo. It is now on show in the Museum of Macedonia in Skopje. Copper and gold in the local streams first attracted Greek settlers but during Roman and early Slav times there were few inhabitants here. The first signs of a significant settlement appeared as a small rural village served by the Church of Sv Bogorodica during the 13th and 14th centuries. At that time the village was called Htetovo. Legend says that the village got its name after a local hero, Hteto, succeeded in banishing snakes from the village. Thereafter it became known as Hteto's Place, or, in Macedonian, Htetovo.

Tetovo remained under Ottoman control from the end of the 14th century until the Ottomans were ousted from Macedonia in 1912. During that period the town was named Kalkandelen, which means 'shield penetrator', in honour of the local smithies' weapon making. Their superior craftsmanship extended to the advent of small firearms and cannons, which were traded all over the Balkans. The small hill above the town, near the present-day village of Lavce, has been fortified since Paeonian times and the Ottomans also built a substantial fortress there, the remains of which are some of the better preserved in Macedonia.

A number of mosques were built in the town, the most beautiful of which is the Šarena Mosque, built in the 16th century, which fortunately escaped the fire of the mid 17th century that destroyed most of the town. In the 16th century, the Bektaši order also settled in Tetovo, where they remain at the Bektaši *teke*.

During Turkish times Tetovo came under the *vilayet* of Kosovo and was strongly orientated towards its Albanian brothers and the Albanian struggle for independence from Ottoman rule. But the Serb victory in the Balkan Wars of 1912 and 1913 left the entire *vilayet* of Kosovo, including Tetovo, Gostivar and Debar, under the control of Royalist Yugoslavia. The resulting crackdown on Islam forced many Muslims from Tetovo to emigrate to the US and Canada, while thousands of Serbs were encouraged to move into the town to develop the mining and hydro-electric industries.

The town prospered: orthodox churches were built, skiing and pony trekking started in the Šar Mountains, and White Russian settlers arrived. The 1930s were good for the new Slav settlers of Tetovo; and then came World War II and Tetovo became a part of fascist Albania. In resistance, some of the new Serb settlers set up the Macedonian Communist Party, founded on 19 March 1943 in Tetovo, but by then the Albanian Communist Party was also fighting for the town.

Eventually, the town fell to Tito under the Socialist Republic of Macedonia (SRM), and Albanians in Tetovo were subject to much the same repression as the Albanians of Kosovo in Yugoslavia. More Muslims emigrated and those who remained demonstrated periodically but violently against the communist regime, notably in the Yucel Incident of 1957 and the Kalkandelen Incident of 1968. When the troubles in neighbouring Kosovo began in 1981, Tetovo had to be put under the control of paramilitary police due to the rioting and show of sympathy with the Kosovar Albanians. The same happened again in 1989.

When it became obvious in 1990 that Yugoslavia was about to fall, over 2,000 ethnic Albanians marched through Tetovo demanding secession from the Socialist Republic of Macedonia and unity with Albania. Self-determination of an ethnic minority within a state was not a right under the SRM constitution, and, protesting their lack of representation under the constitution of a new Republic of Macedonia (RM), the Albanians of Macedonia boycotted the referendum on independence from Yugoslavia and were thus excluded from almost any representation in the new government. Tetovo became the headquarters of the new Albanian political parties, which were regarded as unconstitutional by the new RM. Tensions worsened, and were fuelled by increasing lawlessness in

In the early 1990s, the Albanian community, self-selectedly disenfranchised from the democratic process in Macedonia, tried to start the first university in the country to offer courses in Albanian. The government disapproved, repeating that Macedonian was the only official language allowed under the then constitution (the writing of which the Albanians had not participated in), and with that the struggle for the right to learn in one's own mother tongue ensued. Eventually, after intense mediation from the OSCE's High Commissioner for National Minorities, Max van der Stoel, both sides agreed on a compromise in the form of the **South East European University** (SEEU, also known as the van der Stoel University) offering courses in Albanian, Macedonian and English.

In many ways SEEU was set up to be independent of the government by being a fee-paying establishment built with international money. In the academic year of 2004/05, SEEU enrolled 3,886 students, of whom 78% spoke Albanian as their first language. SEEU has the potential to be a role model for education among mixed ethnicities around the world, and could make for a valuable exchange year for students of Balkan history and language. For more information see www.seeu.org.mk.

With the rights enshrined in the Ohrid Framework Agreement, the Albanian community finally won their struggle for state funding for Albanian language tertiary education with the legal recognition of **Tetovo University** in 2003. The following year, 1,550 students enrolled. Annually, on average, there are 6,000 students in the Goce Delčev University in Štip, 15,000 students enrolled in the University of Bitola, and 37,000 in the University of Kiril i Metodi in Skopje.

neighbouring Kosovo. Prior to the NATO bombing of Serb forces in Kosovo, Tetovo became the rear supply base for the Kosovo Liberation Army, and then later home to thousands of Kosovo refugees.

In 1997, Ajladin Demiri, the mayor of Tetovo, was jailed for raising the double-headed eagle flag of Albania from Tetovo town hall, and by 2000 the outbreak of hostilities in Tanuševci, north of Skopje on the border with Kosovo, had spilled into the towns of Tetovo and Gostivar. Even after hostilities had ceased and a peace deal had been brokered by the international community, there was still inter-ethnic tension in the area. The old Tetovo–Gostivar–Debar highway (now the back road through Bogovinje and Vrapčiste), linking these predominantly Albanian towns, was the scene of many armed blockades in 2001/02.

Today, although some tensions remain, they are either inter-gang disputes, which are not aimed at the innocent tourist, or are purely of a political nature. Since the recent formation of two universities in the town (see box above), Tetovo has become a young and vibrant place that is welcoming and interesting.

GETTING THERE, AWAY AND AROUND Tetovo is a 40-minute drive from Skopje on the E65 highway (Motorway 2). There is also a **railway** service to the town three times a day from Skopje and from Kičevo (see train timetable on page 74). It costs 80MKD to Skopje and 82MKD to Kičevo. The train station (\ *044 336 660*) is on Ulica B Kidrič, almost 1km to the southeast of the town centre.

Buses, however, are the easiest form of public transport to reach the town. The inter-town and international bus station (\ *044 336 331*) is next to the train station, although most buses also stop and pick up in the centre of the town. Buses to Skopje start at 05.45 and run approximately every 45 minutes until 20.00. The one-hour journey costs 150MKD including the price for the toll booths. For times of main inter-town buses see box on page 222.

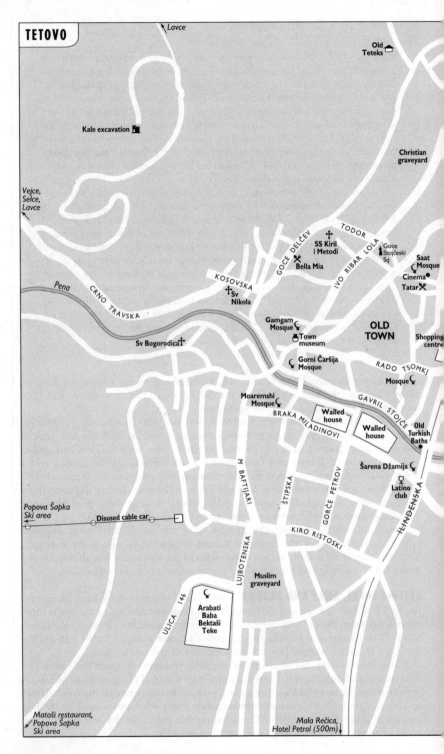

TETOVO

Lavce

Old Teteks

Kale excavation

Christian graveyard

Vejce, Selce, Lavce

Pena

CRNO TRAVSKA

TODOR

GOCE DELČEV

SS Kiril i Metodi

Bella Mia

Goce Stojčeski Sq

Saat Mosque

Cinema

Tatar

KOSOVSKA

Sv Nikola

IVO RIBAR LOLA

Gamgam Mosque

Town museum

OLD TOWN

Shopping centre

Sv Bogorodica

Gorni Čaršija Mosque

RADO TSOMKI

Mosque

Moaremshi Mosque

GAVRIL STOJČE

BRAKA MILADINOVI

Walled house

Walled house

Old Turkish Baths

M. BAFTIJARI

ŠTIPSKA

GORČE PETROV

Šarena Džamija

Latino club

HINĐENSKA

Popova Šapka Ski area

Disused cable car

KIRO RISTOSKI

LUJBOTENSKA

Muslim graveyard

ULICA 146

Arabati Baba Bektaši Teke

Matoši restaurant, Popova Šapka Ski area

Mala Rečica, Hotel Petrol (500m)

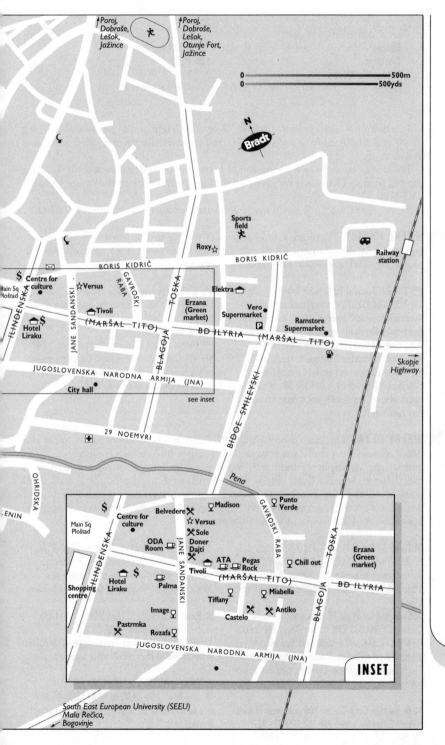

↑Poroj,
Dobroše,
Lešok,
Jažince

↑Poroj,
Dobroše,
Lešok,
Otunje Fort,
Jažince

0 ——————— 500m
0 ——————— 500yds

N
Bradt

Sports
field

Roxy☆

Railway
station

BORIS KIDRIČ   BORIS KIDRIČ

✉
Main Sq
Ploštad

$ Centre for
culture

☆Versus

🏠Tivoli

$
Hotel
Liraku

GAVROSKI
RABA

TOSKA

Elektra🏠

Erzana
(Green
market)

Vero
Supermarket

Ramstore
Supermarket

P

JANE SANDANSKI

(MARŠAL TITO)   BD ILYRIA   (MARŠAL TITO)

BLAGOJA

BRĐOE SMILEVSKI

Skopje
Highway

JUGOSLOVENSKA NARODNA ARMIJA (JNA)

City hall

see inset

29 NOEMVRI

✚

OHRIDSKA

Pena

-ENIN

$

Main Sq
Ploštad

Centre for
culture

Belvedere✕

Madison

Punto
Verde

☆Versus

✕Sole

ODA
Room

Doner
Dajti

🏠 ATA
Tivoli Pegas
Rock

GAVROSKI
RABA

Chill out

TOSKA

Erzana
(Green
market)

JANE SANDANSKI

(MARŠAL TITO)

BD ILYRIA

BLAGOJA

Shopping
centre

HINĐENSKA

$
Hotel
Liraku

Palma

Tiffany

Miabella

Image

Castelo

✕ Antiko

Pastrmka✕

Rozafa

JUGOSLOVENSKA NARODNA ARMIJA (JNA)

INSET

South East European University (SEEU)
Mala Rečica,
Bogovinje

221

Skopje	every 45 minutes 06.00–20.15
Gostivar	every half-hour 06.00–20.00
Struga via Kičevo	06.15, 13.20, 15.20, 18.20
Debar	07.15, 10.45

International destinations include Belgrade (eight-hour journey departing 09.00 and 20.00); daily to Sofia at 21.00; and regular daily journeys to destinations in Germany.

Local area buses to villages on the old road north to Vratnica and south along the old road to Debreše leave every 15 minutes from Potok in the centre of town 05.50–20.00.

Tetovo itself is a fairly small town. Taxis run for a minimum fare of 40MKD.

WHERE TO STAY There are few good places to stay in the town of Tetovo itself, and you may prefer to opt for Skopje only an hour away, or go right up into the mountains and stay at the Popova Šapka ski resort (see page 225).

Tivoli (18 rooms) Bd Ilyria 19; 044 352 370, 071 389 213; f 044 352 371; e tivoli@tivoli.com.mk; www.tivoli.com.mk. Opened in 2006; at last an up-to-date hotel in Tetovo run by one of the best restaurants in the town. All mod cons including Wi-Fi. Friendly, helpful staff, buffet b/fast & oranges at reception. $$$

Hotel Liraku (also known by its old name, Makedonija) (39 rooms) 044 338 586. In the centre of town, this hotel is well located but noisy & very rundown. $$

Elektra (5 rooms) Ulica 120, Broj 2; 044 339 190; f 044 339 455. Close to the centre of town & in a quiet area behind the OSCE offices. Basic, but clean & tidy rooms. $$

Motel Petrol (8 rooms) Ilindenska bb; 042 336 422. Clean new rooms above the petrol station on the busy Ilindenska, 1km from the centre. All rooms are en suite with TV & AC. $

WHERE TO EAT The main thoroughfare, Bd Ilyria, offers plenty of places to eat and drink, as does the parallel street to the south, Ulica JNA, which is slightly less busy and so the atmosphere along it is more relaxing. Tetovo's main green market, called Erzana, on Bd Ilyria side is packed with fresh local produce as well as all sorts of other knick-knacks and cheap clothing items. There are also some nice restaurants on the way up to Popova Šapka and some at the Šapka ski resort itself. Restaurants in Tetovo include the following:

Tivoli Bd Ilyria 19; 044 352 370, 071 389 312; ⏱ Sun–Thu 08.00–24.00, Fri & Sat 08.00–01.00. Serves a range of good salads, risottos & excellent b/fast omelettes. Pleasant atmosphere & fine service. $$

Sole Jane Sandanski 98 (opposite the House of Culture); 044 333 238; ⏱ Sun–Thu 12.00–24.00, Fri & Sat 12.00–01.00. Popular with businessmen, artists & local politicians. Delicious pasta & sea food. The focaccia with garlic is especially tasty but do not leave without trying the homemade crème caramel. $$

Bella Mia Goce Delcev 108 (just west of Kiril i Metodi Church); 044 331 332, 070 224 922; ⏱ Sun–Thu 12.00–24.00, Fri & Sat 12.00–01.00. Serves traditional Macedonian fare in a pretty, traditional setting in the old town with a nice čardak (patio) in the summer. Good Bela Mia tava & pindžur. $$

Pastrmka Pastrmka Ulica JNA 3; 044 335 633; ⏱ Sun–Thu 12.00–24.00, Fri & Sat 12.00–01.00. As the name (trout) suggests, specialises in fish as well as Macedonia's other traditional fare. $$

Tatar 114th Ulica 2; 044 333 430; ⏱ Sun–Thu 12.00–24.00, Fri & Sat 12.00–01.00. A nice family restaurant, with good tatar cold starters & rolled lamb. $$

CAFÉS, BARS AND ENTERTAINMENT Contrary to what people might think, Tetovo offers a great variety of places for entertainment, especially from Thursdays to Sundays.

Ata Caffe Bd Ilyria. New & popular near Tivoli restaurant & hotel.

Image Jane Sandanski. Attracts a slightly older ethnic Macedonian crowd.

Palma Bd Ilyria. A small cafeteria decorated in rococo style.

Pegas Rock Café Also near Tivoli.

Madison Lounge Boris Kidrič; 044 335 126. One of the entertainment icons of the town. Recently renovated, offers excellent music & a nice atmosphere, mainly frequented by people in their 30s.

Punto Verde Boris Kidrič. Another great bar with a huge terrace, normally packed on summer afternoons.

☆ **Roxy** An outdoor summer discotheque.

Rozafa Similar ambience to Tiffany.

Tiffany Bd Ilyria. A fun place popular with the trendy ethnic Albanian youth.

☆ **Versus** Jane Sandanski, next door to Sole Restaurant. Frequented by a young ethnic Macedonian clientele. Offers live music during summer w/ends.

WHAT TO SEE AND DO The **Arabati Baba Bektaši** *Teke* is one of the prettiest sites in the town, with well-kept gardens, old-style inns and meditation platforms. A *teke* is the Sufi equivalent of a monastery belonging to the Bektaši order of dervishes (Muslim mystics). Sufism is derived from the Sunni branch of Islam. This *teke* in Tetovo was built at the end of the 18th century and remained the seat of the Bektaši until 1912 when the Ottomans were driven out of Macedonia.

With the departure of the Ottoman rulers from the area in 1912 the dervishes were no longer welcome and most fled to neighbouring Albania or elsewhere. Although the *teke* saw a small revival between 1941 and 1945, the lands were taken as state property during Yugoslav times and made into a hotel and museum. In recent years, however, the Bektaši order has regained access to the *teke* and the site is being slowly refurbished. Although in considerable disrepair it is still the largest and most well-preserved *teke* in the western Balkans.

The prayer room and library are open to visitors if accompanied by the *baba* (priest), who will welcome any library donations of Islamic books to replace the many burnt in 1948 when partisan forces set the library alight.

Next to the *baba's* courtyard is the *meydan*, which used to be the main place of worship for the Bektaši. Now it has been converted into a Sunni mosque (much to the annoyance of the dervishes who would like to see their *teke* completely returned to the Sufi order).

The **Šarena Džamija** (meaning coloured or painted mosque and often called the Motley Mosque by English-speakers) is known locally as Pasha Djamija (Prince's Mosque). Its colourful exterior makes the building look like it is clad in a deck of playing cards. Over 30,000 eggs were used to manufacture the paint and glaze. The site used to include an inn as well as a bathhouse on the other side of the river (currently being renovated). The grounds of the mosque contain an octagonal *turbe* (grave) of Hurshida and Mensure, the two women who paid to have the mosque built in 1459.

Other mosques in Tetovo include the **Saat Mosque** which as its name implies used to have a clock in its minaret, the **Gorni Čaršija Mosque** so called for its proximity to the upper bazaar area, and the **Gamgam Mosque**. Churches in town include the **Church of Sv Bogorodica** near the river, the **Church of Sv Nikola** above the river and on the way to Lavce and the fortress remains, and the **Church of Kiril i Metodi**.

In the village of **Lešok**, 8km to the northeast of Tetovo, is a monastery of the same name housing the two 14th-century **churches**: **Sv Bogorodica** (the Holy Virgin Mary, built in 1326) and **Sv Atanas** (mid 14th century). The Church of the Holy Virgin contains frescoes from three different dates: the time of construction, the 17th century, and lastly 1879. The original iconostasis and several marble columns from the original church are now on show in the city museum. The monastery was one of several in the area favoured by the 19th-century Pasha Abdulrahman, who donated money to their upkeep. Later, he attempted an uprising against the sultan and failed (it wasn't just the locals who were unhappy with the Ottoman elite) and was packed off to fight in the Crimea, where he died. Unfortunately, during the conflict of 2001, the Church of Sv Atanas was severely damaged by a bomb. It is now being reconstructed with

ALI SERSEM BABA AND THE ARABATI BABA *TEKE*

Ali Baba (not Ali Baba of the *Arabian Nights*) was the brother-in-law of the Sultan Suleijman the Magnificent, and had been a high-ranking *baba* in the important Dimotika *Teke* (now in Greece) when his sister (who was one of the sultan's wives) fell into disfavour with her husband. This did not bode well for Ali Baba, who was sent to Tetovo at the outer fringes of the Ottoman Empire to live the simple life of a Bektaši monk.

Another version of the story goes that Ali Baba was an official of the Ottoman Empire who gave up his position in order to live the simple life of a Bektaši monk. The sultan, angered by the departure of one of his favourite officials, yelled after Ali as he departed Constantinople, 'If you will be a fool, then go.' Sersem, the old Turkish for 'fool', became Ali Baba's nickname thereafter.

Whichever is the true story (the Turks favour the first one), Sersem travelled the vast empire of Turkey until he came upon the River Pena in the tranquil mountains of Tetovo. There he settled until his death in 1538, quietly practising the 'way' of the Bektaši order. After his death, his only pupil to survive him, Arabati Baba, founded a monastery in Tetovo to commemorate Sersem's life.

The present-day buildings were built at the end of the 18th century by Rexhep Pasha, also a dervish, whose tomb lies next to that of Sersem's in the mausoleum of the *teke*. Not all the buildings are still standing today: in the courtyard can be seen the foundations of what might formerly have been the *teke* stables; a fountain, meditation platform and a watchtower are also original. Some say that the blue painted tower next to the *baba*'s private courtyard was originally built to house the sick daughter of Abdulrahram Pasha. The reception inn is still in disrepair, although the library is being refurbished. One of the buildings has been turned into a Sunni mosque, but the inns around the Bektaši graveyard have been preserved for the *baba*.

Many Sufi/dervish orders include a ceremony or dance ritual called *zikr*. This involves swaying movements in time to music and/or the repetition of Islamic texts by the lead dervish or *zakir*. The ceremony requires a lot of control and concentration in order to empty the mind of all but God himself, and can appear to result in an almost trance-like state. The *zikr* is performed on a meditation platform like the one at the Bektaši Arabati Baba *Teke*. (For the Rufa'i dervish order, renowned for their feats of walking on hot coals and swallowing swords, the *zikr* often appears quite frantic and it is from this order of *zikr* that the phrase 'whirling dervish' comes.)

At the Arabati Baba *Teke* another ceremony takes place once a year in recognition of the martyrdom of the Shia Imam Hussein family, who were stabbed to death in Kerbela, Iraq, for their religious beliefs. As in other Shi'a communities, worshippers beat themselves in order to relive the martyrdom of the Imam and his family.

international financing and work on new frescoes started in 2004. In the yard of the Monastery of Lešok is the tomb of the educator Kiril Pejchinovik, who was born in 1770. In his honour, the monastery hosts an International Meeting of Literary Translators every year.

Just above the small village of Lavce, above Tetovo, are the ruins of an **Ottoman fortress** or *kale*. The kale and its accompanying mosque were destroyed in the 1912–13 Balkan Wars. Although no longer the glorious fortress it once was, it remains one of the better-preserved remnants after Tsar Samoil's fortress in Ohrid and the kale in Skopje. It is also undergoing considerable excavation work in recent years, and it is likely to be rebuilt to its former glory.

In its heyday it was quite the construction with a series of tunnels from all the main Ottoman houses in the town leading to the fortress. The thinking behind the tunnel system was to allow the defenders of the fortress to escape behind enemy lines if the fortress was besieged, allowing the besiegers themselves to be encircled. The last tunnel collapsed in the 1960s and since excavation has started, two of the tunnels, to Selce and Lavce, have been found.

While the kale can't be seen from Tetovo, floodlights at night can be seen, and the views of Tetovo and the River Vardar from the kale are magnificent. The site remains strategically important and was used in the last conflict of 2001, as was the Pena Valley behind, for shoring up troops and supplies. In World War II the Pena Valley was bombed repeatedly by the Germans.

The paths up the River Pena lead to a number of mountain villages and past the **Iron Cave**, a large underground system popular with cavers and potholers. There are also attractive villages along the Tetovo road to Prizren in Kosovo. Orašje, close to the Kosovo border, has the remains of another once strategic **castle** guarding the Pena Valley. In villages such as Brezno and Varvara, you can still see good examples of traditional village architecture – wattle-and-daub houses with stone roofs. Some villages, such as Jedoarce, Setole and Otunje, are former weekend house retreats that were damaged during the conflict and are now slowly being rebuilt. While you are unlikely to come across many people, there are wonderful views over the Polog (Vardar) Valley as well as several mountain walks through mature beech and sweet chestnut forests onto the top of the Šar range.

POPOVA ŠAPKA SKI RESORT AND MOUNTAIN RANGE

Popova Šapka lies to the west of Tetovo 1,000m above the town. In days gone by it was the most successful ski resort in Macedonia, but it suffered during the conflict years for being in the heart of the predominantly Albanian region of the country and local economic renewal has been sporadic at best. The continued closure of the cable car from Tetovo town centre to Popova Šapka illustrates the problems at the local government level, while the arrival of cat-ski opportunities for off-piste skiers does at least show room for entrepreneurship. Overall, facilities are improving and it remains cheap.

GETTING THERE The road to Popova Šapka is well paved if long and zigzaggy and the snow at the top and the views of Kopilica mountain on the way up are well worth the drive, although parking is at a premium. During the winter there is a minibus that goes up at 08.00 and comes down at 15.00. It's hard to pin down as it picks up from various differing places depending on clients, so ask through your hotel. Alternatively a taxi ride from Tetovo to Popova Šapka is 500MKD. For the journey back down, ask a restaurant or café on the slopes to send up a taxi for you. A map of Popova Šapka is on the Titov Vrv map on page 313.

⌂ WHERE TO STAY

⌂ **Bora** (24 rooms) Signposted from the trail board by the cone-shaped ski rental shack; ↘ 044 361 106; f 044 361 107. Right at the top of Popova Šapka settlement, it has the great advantage of being ski-in & ski-out. Recently renovated, friendly, & frequented by the fit Nordic & Swiss off-piste skiers taking the cat-ski which is based there. Sunny restaurant overlooks the slopes. $$$

⌂ **Slavija** (35 rooms) On the way up to Bora; ↘ 044 361 030. In need of upkeep, but boasts a swimming pool. $$

⌂ **Popova Šapka** (80 rooms) At the end of the tarmac road & parking; ↘ 044 361 020. This state-run monstrosity has the advantage of always having rooms available. Ski-rental available in the lobby. $$

⌂ **Kaj Dule** (4 rooms, inc one 8-bed room) Just below Bora; ↘ 070 934 309. Basic, cheap & friendly. Shared bathrooms. $

⌂ **Šara Ski Planinski Dom** (mountain hut, 5 rooms inc one 8-bed room) Blagoja Toska 41/14; ↘ 070 329 898; e saraski_te@yahoo.com. Bijou & basic, but based right on the slopes at the popular little café next to the new church. $

⌂ **Smreka Planinski Dom** (mountain hut, 100 beds) the pink building beyond Hotel Slavija; ↘ 02 322 5958 for the hut warden Duško Boskovski in Skopje. $

✗ WHERE TO EAT AND DRINK

✗ **Bačilo** ↘ 044 361 001. Once you're in the village, take the first right & follow the road about a 3rd of the way up; ☺ daily 11.00–23.00. A very popular local restaurant with good views over the ski slope. Book a table in advance if you want to be guaranteed a place on a busy w/end. $$

✗ **Casa Leone** ↘ 044 361 002. Two-thirds of the way up the same road as Bačilo; ☺ daily 12.00–23.00. A delightful pizzeria with a sunny dining room & narrow balcony offering even better views of the slopes. Also does a very tasty džigr al Venezia (liver in red wine). $$

✗ **Matoši** Halfway up the 18km road to Popova Šapka; ☺ daily 12.00–23.00. This rustic restaurant offers a wide terrace, good views, & good food. $$

✗ **Mednes** Popular café next to the Teteks Hotel at the bottom of the ski-runs; ☺ daily 09.00–23.00. Accessible from the slopes, it is the perfect place to while away a hot chocolate or mulled wine whilst viewing the skiers below. $

WHAT TO DO Even if you don't ski or snow-shoe the views of the Vardar Valley from the drive up to Popova Šapka are outstanding. For **skiing** the resort offers 20km of groomed ski runs and over 35km² of terrain for off-piste skiers. A day ski pass costs 800MKD. Carving skis and snowboards are available for **renting** for as little as 400MKD including boots and poles (bring ID to leave with the ski rental hut) at either the orange 'cone'-shaped hut just before Hotel Popova Šapka, or from the shop in Hotel Popova Šapka's lobby. For the **off-piste** skier Eskimo Freeride (↘ 071 361 639; e info@eskimo-freeride.com; www.eskimo-freeride.com) offer a day package on their Snowcat (including accommodation and food) for €159–179. **Ski lessons** are available for 700MKD per hour from Zemri Beluli at Ski School Profi (↘ 070 981 395; e atomic_180@hotmail.com). **Snow-shoeing** and winter mountaineering guides are available through Ljuboten Planinarski Klub (see page 296).

In the summer the Šar Mountains offer a host of **hiking** trails, which have all recently been re-marked, maintained and signed. An excellent **trail map** is available in English from Ljuboten Planinarski Klub (see page 296), as well as **mountain guides** ranging from €15 per hour to €125 for the weekend. Sadly, 1:25,000 hiking maps need to be ordered in advance from the Katastar in Skopje (see page 78). The area has 49 glacial **lakes**, such as Golemo Ezero, Belo Ezero, Bogovinsko Ezero and Crno Ezero; several waterfalls at Lešnica and Kriva Šija (see *Chapter 12*, page 312) and there are also **rock-climbing** sections at Crnen Kamen, Kobilica and below Mount Plat. For most, though, the attraction is to reach the top of Titov Vrv at 2,747m (see *Chapter 12*, page 312). For those seeking a greater challenge there is the 80km ridge hike all the way from Ljuboten peak to Mount Korab near Debar.

GOSTIVAR

Today, Gostivar municipality has over 81,000 inhabitants. The town itself, while offering few renowned tourist sites, is pleasant, multi-cultural and a frequent location for seminars and conferences and a convenient stopping point on the way south. With the source of the River Vardar a mere 5km from Gostivar, the river is clean and rapid as it courses through the town. For these reasons and more, Gostivar is slowly becoming more popular.

HISTORY Habitation of the Gostivar area and the Polog Valley go back to the 7th century BC. In 170BC, the town of Draudak was built near Gostivar. The Roman historian Livy mentions that the last Macedon king, Perseus (ruled 179–168BC), attacked Draudak with 10,000 men. Later, Turkic settlers started coming to the region with the Hun settlement in the area dating to AD378. Avar, Bulgar, Kuman, Oğuz, Pećenek and Vardar Turks settled here throughout

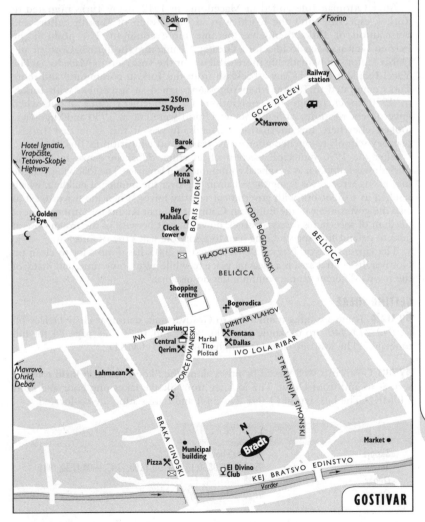

the next millennium. Later, Slav tribes came to the region and the town's current name Gostivar comes from the Slavic word *gosti* meaning 'guests' and the Turkish word *dvar* meaning 'castle' or 'fort'. In the first half of the 14th century, Gostivar is mentioned in the 1313 Bath Declaration of Serbian king Milutin, as well as by Tsar Dushan at the opening ceremony of the Hagia Maria Monastery in Kalkandelen (Tetovo).

The first Ottoman attack on Gostivar was in 1336, but it wasn't until the invasion of Yildirim Bayezid in the 1390s that the Ottomans took effective rule of Gostivar and the Polog Valley. Many Turkish families moved here from Turkey during the favourable emigration policies promoted by Sultan Murat II and Sultan Mehmet the Conqueror, and so the town grew. Over the years, Gostivar flourished as a cultural centre and by the late 19th century the town boasted seven inns, five mosques, three schools, two libraries, two dervish *teke*, a bathhouse and a clock tower. Of all of these, only the clock tower built in 1566 and the Beg Mahala Mosque built in 1688 remain today.

After Ottoman rule ended in Macedonia in 1912, many Turks migrated to Turkey, especially after the world wars as suppression of Turkish culture and persecution of Turks themselves became more common. The push of the Prizren Union's Megalo Idea for a Greater Albania into the Tetovo, Gostivar and Debar regions only made life more difficult for the Turks left in Macedonia. The Yucel Incident of 1947 saw a backlash from the Turkish community and more Turks emigrated to Turkey when Yugoslavia signed an agreement with Turkey in 1950 to encourage the emigration. The agreement came about when government relations with the Soviet Union were cut in 1950 and Yugoslavia looked elsewhere for international friends. It was at this time that Turkish primary schools re-opened after many years of no education in Turkish.

After the 1996 municipal election of an ethnic Albanian mayor in Gostivar, Turkish was forbidden as an official communication language. The following year the mayor was arrested for flying the Albanian flag over the municipal building, which resulted in a shoot-out with government security forces. When the mayor tried to take the government to the European Court of Human Rights for infringement of freedom of speech, his case was struck down, in part because of the mayor's use of guns to defend 'free' speech being seen to justify the state's use of force.

The current mayor, Nežvat Bejta, elected in 2005, has done a lot to clean up Gostivar. Its central area is a pleasant place to while away some time, and many of the town's different ethnic communities do just that.

GETTING THERE

By train There are three trains a day to Gostivar train station at Goce Delčev bb (☏ *042 213 440*) from Skopje at 03.00, 06.20 and 16.30 (see page 74 for full timetable). The journey takes 90 minutes and costs 110MKD.

By bus Gostivar is well served by buses along the Skopje–Struga/Ohrid route as well as to and from Debar. The journey from Skopje takes one hour and costs 140MKD. The bus station (☏ *042 217 344*) and train station are co-located.

BUS DEPARTURES FROM GOSTIVAR	
Skopje	every half-hour
Tetovo	05.15, 06.35, 08.30, 10.00, 11.30, 13.00, 13.45, 16.00, 17.30, 19.15
Debar	15.15
Ohrid	07.20 (seasonal only)

WHERE TO STAY AND EAT Gostivar is served by three hotels; all rooms are en suite:

Balkan (16 rooms) Ilindenska 165; ☎ 042 214 401. Decent rooms not far from the centre. $$

Central (27 rooms) Borče Jovanoski 56; ☎ 042 216 226. Basic rooms & no b/fast available so try the cafés & bakeries on the main square. $

Ignatia (34 rooms) On the east side of Highway 65, just after the last toll booth, 2km from the centre of town. New & clean, good value for money, some rooms have jacuzzi baths. $

The town centre has several pizzerias, *kebapci* diners and cafés. There are many more restaurants on the main street from the highway.

For a good trout farm restaurant outside Gostivar, try **Kaj Sime** (*Vrutok;* ☎ *070 888 690, 070 472 311; $$*).

WHAT TO SEE AND DO Gostivar is largely a people-watching town. The centre, with its cafés and bars surrounding tended greens and park benches, is where local people while away the day, meet friends and drink coffee. You are much more likely to see people here in remnants of local dress than in other big towns around Macedonia, especially men in Turkish waistcoats and a variety of local hats. The *plis*, a stiff white woollen domed hat, is worn by Albanian men. The white crocheted hat is worn by Muslim men who have done the hajj pilgrimage to Mecca, while a plain or an embroidered squarish hat is worn by a lot of Roma men of the Bektashi faith.

The Ottoman **clock tower** built in 1566 is on the street behind the municipality building. Next to it is the **Bey Mahala Mosque**, built in 1688 by Ebu Bekir, the son of Kara Mustafa Pasha, and rebuilt by Ismail Aga.

A walk along the quay is pleasant and it is good to see the Vardar so clean as it enters the town. By the time the Vardar reaches Skopje it is an even murky brown colour, indicating that Macedonia still has a long way to go in waste water treatment and environmental preservation.

The nearby village of **Vrapčište** is a Yoruk Turkish village (see box, page 50). The town hall has an ethnological museum and occasionally **pelivan wrestling** matches take place in the summer. For information on the next matches or more about Vrapčište contact the Millennium Association (☎ *042 332 326;* e *mngo@post.com*).

MAVROVO NATIONAL PARK

Ten kilometres south of Gostivar is the turn-off to Mavrovo National Park and lake. The park itself extends over the Bistra plateau across the Radika Valley and all the way up to the Dešat mountain range that forms the border with Albania. In the little town of Mavrovo there are a number of places to stay and the town makes a good base for hiking, skiing, watersports or simply as a quiet getaway.

GETTING THERE The little settlement of Mavrovi Anovi, on the road from Gostivar to Debar, is served several times a day by bus from Gostivar, Debar and Skopje year round. A taxi from here will take you over the dam for the 7km ride to Mavrovo itself for 250MKD, and during the ski season buses go all the way to Mavrovo.

WHERE TO STAY AND EAT

Radika (62 rooms) On the far side of the river; ☎ 042 223 300; f 042 223 399; e reservations@radika.com.mk;

www.radika.com.mk. The newest & most dazzling offer available near Mavrovo. Indoor & outdoor pool, spa, fireside bar. $$$$

Bistra (42 rooms) At the end of town; ☎ 042 489 027/219; f 042 489 002; e bistra@bistra.com; www.bistra.com. This is a true ski resort hotel, with spacious lounges & reception areas, welcoming open-hearth fire, good restaurant & bar, fitness centre, pool & conferencing facilities. All the rooms are en suite with AC & TV. They also have overflow accommodation down by the lake for the same price, but it is not nearly as luxurious even though you get to use all the facilities of the main hotel. $$$

Hotel Ski Škola (run by the Hotel Bistra, see above) Offers access to the Bistra facilities & is located right next to the ski lift. $$$

Srna (24 rooms) At the entrance to the village; ☎ 042 388 083. Good value for money. All rooms have newly refurbished bathrooms, TV & central heating. $$

Neda (25 rooms) Galičnik, 15km from Mavrovo; ☎ 046 831 307, 070 596 114; ⊕ 1 Jul–1 Oct. Rooms are basic with no TV or AC, & aside from 4 rooms that are en suite, bathroom facilities are on the corridor. $

Camping Camping is also available in Mavrovo town campsite, and many people camp almost anywhere in the surrounding hills.

Mavrovo does not yet offer a wide range of places to eat, and for the price you are best off eating at the Bistra for atmosphere and quality, or at the Hotel Srna for something a little cheaper. For those determined to try something really local, the village of Trnica on the River Mavrovo just before it joins the Radika offers sour cheese and ground corn as a speciality, allegedly the best in the region. The modest restaurant is nothing to write home about, nor is the food.

ACTIVITIES IN THE PARK Mavrovo is a small but popular local ski resort, offering black, blue and green runs accessible by chair lift. Oddly, the green runs are all at the top and the two black runs are the only way to ski/board down to the bottom. Unless there has been an exceptionally snowy winter, the blacks are quickly iced up and sporting bare patches that you might prefer to leave for your best rock skis. For those who would rather not risk the narrow and icy descent, the midway station picks up skiers. Many day trippers go up just to plod around at the top, admire the view and snack at the little restaurants. A day ticket to ski in the park is 1,200MKD, a week ticket is 5,000MKD and a season ticket is 20,500MKD. Hunting trips can be arranged through the Hotel Bistra, which also sells fishing permits. Fishing on the lake is from 1 February to 30 October, and on the River Radika it is from 15 January to 30 October.

There are many hiking trails throughout the park although they are not always well marked, and for mountaineering enthusiasts Mount Korab beckons alluringly above the lake. Due to the lack of good hiking maps of the area (not due to be published until late 2010) it would be best to take a guide with you on such hikes or take part in the annual outing organised by Korab Mountaineering Club (see *Chapter 12*, page 296).

WHAT TO SEE Mavrovo National Park is not only a preservation area for the rare wildlife that lives in this most mountainous area of Macedonia, but is also renowned for its culturally unique and isolated **Mijak villages** (see text box on page 53). The village of **Gari** is home to the famous iconostasis woodcarvers, the Filipovski brothers, who carved the iconostasis of Sv Bigorski, Sv Spas and Sv Gavril Lesnovski churches. **Tresonče** village is the gateway to **Biljani Slap Waterfalls** and **Alilica Cave** (see *Chapter 12*, page 310). **Lazaropole**, formerly a hunting village, with a small ski lift, is now promoting its clean air and its village tourism, where the beautifully refurbished **Kalin Hotel** is well worth staying in (*16 rooms;* ☎ *046 846 222;* e *info@kalinhotel.com.mk; www.kalinhotel.com.mk;* $$).

To get to these three villages, take the bus to Debar and ask to be dropped off at Mavrovo Nacionalen Park. Less than 2km along this road on the left-hand side

Nestled on a cliffside in Mavrovo National Park is the Mijak village of Galičnik. Tradition going back hundreds of years saw the travelling traders of Galičnik returning once a year in July in order to marry their sweethearts. Up to 40 weddings would take place on St Peter's Day (Petrovden), entailing a massive guest list and followed by a huge party. Village residents of Galičnik have dwindled since those giddy days and so from 1999 onwards couples from elsewhere in Macedonia have been allowed to apply to be the privileged bride and groom for the mid-July *Galičnika svadba* (wedding). Thousands of visitors flock every year to see the rituals, costumes, folk dances, traditional music, and of course the Orthodox wedding ceremony itself.

Preparations for the wedding start, like most weddings, some days in advance. People from surrounding villages gather for a sheep milking competition. One of the few of its kind in the Balkans, it is spectacular to see the milkmen and maids at their work. The milk is then used in a variety of local culinary specialities, including various cheeses, *kajmak* (sour clotted cream) and *sutlijaš* (sweet milk pudding).

With the gathering in the past of such a posse of men, the stag night equivalent was and continues to be a day of pelivan wrestling. In each round two men, smothered in sunflower oil and wearing only leather breeches, compete to tussle the other to the ground. The winner is he who beats all others in his weight class by keeping his opponent's back pinned to the floor for a count of three. Traditionally viewed by men only, it is increasingly drawing a female crowd.

On Saturday morning, the day before the wedding ceremony itself, the future son-in-law adorns the wedding hall with flowers and garlands. He then fires three shots to warn off any usurpers and to signal to the guests to make their way to the village. As guests arrive the future mother-in-law welcomes them with bread and water and hosts a dance in traditional dress with the closest relatives. Today, professional dancers are brought in for a colourful show of costumes and synchronisation. With the pressure mounting, the groom is then shaved in public at the village spring as a sign of the impending end of his bachelor days.

On the wedding day itself on Sunday, the day starts with the stormy arrival of the wedding party on galloping horseback to visit the bride. Reduced often to a slow trot through throngs of onlookers, the party brings a young boy with them, whom the godfather-to-be (*kum*) places with the bride's party, as a good luck charm to bring the couple a son. A bridle is then placed symbolically on the bride's head as a gesture of her devotion, faithfulness and obedience to her husband. Whilst the requirement for a son and unconditional love is no longer paramount, the tradition lingers on. The *kum* then delivers a finely adorned banner to the bride's house while she serves the guests local wine and *rakija*.

Afterwards at the village spring, mirroring the groom's ritual the day before, the bride fills jugs with water for her last time as an unwed maid. Another dance ensues at the village square, where the men dance the *teškoto*, a virile representation of the hardships of migrant workers.

Finally, clad in her finest, a Galičnik folk dress of silk and gold braid weighing almost 40kg, the bride is escorted to the central church of Sv Petar i Pavle where, in the eyes of the honoured few who can fit in the church, the wedding ceremony itself takes place in the late afternoon. Traditionally, the groom stayed until Mitrovden (8 November), but these days the groom leaves with the guests after the wedding and Galičnik returns to its sleepy self by Monday afternoon.

The Northwest and Mavrovo National Park   MAVROVO NATIONAL PARK

9

watch out for the 600-year-old **Deer Leap Bridge**. Legend has it that the bridge was built by the local *bey* (Ottoman lord) during the 14th century to commemorate the gallant death of a deer which he and his army had been hunting. Badly wounded, nevertheless the deer continued to elude the *bey* and his army, until it reached the Garska River. The deer leapt over the river but died on the other side. To commemorate the deer's bravery, the *bey* ordered a bridge to be built in the likeness of the deer's last leap. A shaded footpath on the far side of the river makes for a pleasant hike along the Mala River.

The most famous Mijak village in Mavrovo National Park, however, is undoubtedly **Galičnik** (see text box on page 231) for its nationally acclaimed annual wedding festival. The village is accessible by road only from Mavrovo town (15km) over the Bistra plateau, or by foot from Janče. The hike from Janče takes almost two hours and gives spectacular views of Mount Korab and the Radika Valley (see *Chapter 12*, page 308).

On the west side of the Radika River, opposite the Monastery of Sv Jovan Bigorski (see page 238), is a 40-minute hike from the village of Rostuše to **Duf Waterfall** (*Chapter 12*, page 308).

DEBAR

The road past Mavrovo Lake through the Mavrovo National Park snakes its way along the River Radika to the town of Debar (Diber in Albanian and also seen in older writings on the town as Dibri or Dibra). It is a fairly small town serving a municipality of 20,000 inhabitants. Although it lies in Macedonia and is only 137km from Skopje and 67km from Ohrid, its traditional cultural and economic orientation has been towards towns further afield in Albania. As a result of today's more open borders with Albania, life in Debar is reviving again, but the town is still in need of significant repair and rejuvenation. There is not much of note in the town itself, but it has a rich strategic history and lies in magnificent countryside. This is an area well worth exploring for the intrepid and is sure to be developed in time.

HISTORY The earliest recording of Debar is under the name 'Deborus' on a map drawn by the Greek astronomer and cartographer Ptolomy in the 2nd century. After Tsar Samoil was defeated in 1044 (see box, page 10) by the Byzantine emperor Basilius II, Debar was administered under the Bishopric of Bitola. In the latter half of the 14th century Debar was ruled by the Albanian Kastrioti clan, but fell under the rule of the Ottoman Empire in 1423 when the local Albanian ruler Gjon Kastrioti died shortly after his four children were taken hostage. His son, Georgj Kastrioti Skenderbey, survived to take back his father's land and unite all of Albania in 1444. A larger-than-life-size statue of Skenderbey adorns Debar's centre, showing the fondness which the locals have for his cause (see box, page 234).

Only a few years later in 1449, Debar was overrun once again by the Turks, and became known as Dibri or Debra in Turkish. The city constantly rebelled against Turkish rule, however, not least because of the wealth of the many Turkish *bey* and *aga* who lived there off local taxes and the fat of the land. But Turkish rule also brought trade to Debar and the city centre grew and became known for its crafts industry. Much of the architecture from that period still survives and if you can get a look into some of the older houses you will find the distinctive Turkish woodcarved *dolapi* (wardrobes), *minderliki* (built-in benches), intricate ceilings and doors as well as *cardaci* (enclosed porches on the second floor).

During the Balkan Wars of 1912–13 Debar was taken back by the Albanians, but was then handed over to the Kingdom of Serbs, Croats and Slovenes as a reward for helping the Allies during World War I. Thereafter many Serbs and

DEBAR

N

Bradt

0 ————————— 500m
0 ————————— 500yds

↗Krivci

⌂
Banjište
Hot springs↗

Pijanačka
Church ✝️▲840m

● Muslim
cemetery

▲824m

✕ Senad

STU SEPTEMVRI

Afrona
✕

Skenderbeg
Monument ●

Evropa
✕

BRATSTVO EDINSTVO

Pizza King
✕

▲789m

● Christian
cemetery

VELJKO VLAHOVIKJ

● Muslim
cemetery

Sv Gjorgi
Pobedonost ✝️

Dolno Kosovrasti,
Skopje, Mavrovo,
Restoran Besa,
Sv Jovan-Bigorski↗

↙Struga,
Ohrid,
Restoran Sami ✕

Lake Debar

Montenegrins were encouraged to settle in Debar, a common tactic to ensure that newly acquired land became more integrated with the motherland.

During World War II, Debar was again fiercely fought over by various partisan and fascist groups and their Great Power backers (see box, page 236) but in the end the Socialist Federal Republic of Yugoslavia won out, and Debar became part of the Socialist Republic of Macedonia in Federal Yugoslavia. Socialist Yugoslavia helped to develop the economy of the region with hydro-electric dams (Debar and Globočica lakes), local mines, quarries and tourism.

Sadly, the transition to an independent Macedonia has not helped Debar's economy in the same way the transition to communism did initially. Many minority communities left the town after the independence of Macedonia, and this trend was exacerbated by the conflict of 2001. Such high emigration has further dampened the town's chances of economic revival.

GETTING THERE AND AROUND There are two direct buses a day to Debar from Skopje at 10.00 and 14.14. The journey takes two hours and costs 280MKD. Debar is small enough to walk around. Taxis cost a minimum fare of 30MKD.

WHERE TO STAY AND EAT The old Debar Hotel has not been open for some years. These are the hotels in the area:

Banjište Hot Springs (75 rooms) Banjište, 5km north of Debar; ☎ 046 831 092, 046 842 095. Rooms at present are basic, with some converted to en suite with a TV, but as yet no AC.

The hotel side of the spa is being privatised but it will take some time for the hotel to see the benefits of this. For further details on the spa itself see page 237. $$

GJERGJ KASTRIOTI (SKENDERBEY)

Gjergj Kastrioti is known as the greatest hero of the Albanians for freeing and uniting all Albanians against the Turks in 1444.

Gjergj was born in Kruja, Arberia (today's Albania), to the Lord of Middle Arberia, Gjon Kastrioti, and Voisava, a princess from the Tribalda family of the Polog (Upper Vardar) Valley. Gjon had four sons, all of whom were kept hostage by the Turks in return for loyalty from the Albanian lord. When Gjon died, the Turks poisoned the four sons, but Gjergj managed to survive. He went on to convert to Islam and attend military school. He so excelled in swordsmanship and other military skills that he earned himself the title of Iskander Bey, meaning Lord Alexander. He then successfully led several Ottoman campaigns in Europe and Asia Minor, and was appointed general and then governor general of several provinces in Middle Albania.

But Gjergj missed his homeland, and in 1443, after being defeated by the Hungarians at Nišin Serbia, he deserted the Ottoman army and went back to recapture his home town of Kruja. On raising the Albanian flag, red with a double-headed black eagle, the flag that remains today, Gjergj claimed, 'I have not brought you freedom, I have found it here among you.' Less than a year later, having reconverted to Christianity, he united the Albanian princes against the Turks at the Assembly of Alesio (Lezha in Albanian) with an army of a mere 20,000. He won 25 out of his 28 battles against the Turks and was supported by the Italian princes and popes across the Adriatic for staving off the Turkish assault from western Europe for 25 years.

In 1468 Gjergj died of fever, but his army kept the Turks out of Albania for another 12 years. He is the national hero of Albania and all Albanians and his valour has been the inspiration of many national and foreign poets and writers.

Sv Gjorgj Pobedonoset, or St George the Victorious in English, is indeed the same patron saint of England who slayed the dragon from his gallant white horse in order to save the princess. St George is a legend in many countries and it is astounding that his benevolence should reach as far as the Russian, Greek and Macedonian Orthodox churches as well as the Church of England and many other churches around the world.

George was born in AD280 in Cappadociea, now in modern-day Turkey. He joined the Roman cavalry at the age of 17 and rose to become a great swordsman and favourite of the then Roman emperor, Diocletian. George had converted to Christianity, whilst Diocletian was a firm believer in the pagan traditions. Eventually this rift in their beliefs brought George to his death. After doing his best to save Christians who had been sentenced to death by Diocletian, George was cast in prison to be tortured until he renounced his belief in Christ. Despite extreme forms of torture he did not renounce his faith and finally he was beheaded on 23 April 303 in Nicomedia near Lydda, Palestine.

He became the patron saint of the little church in Debar because that church contains the only replica of St George's original icon that stands in the Zograf Monastery at Mount Athos in Greece. When the original icon appeared miraculously in the Zograf Monastery shortly after it was built, the local monks claimed that it had been sent from Lydda by St George himself. The local bishop did not believe in the veracity of this story and so touched the icon to check for telltale signs of fresh paint. As soon as he touched the nose of the icon his finger stuck fast and eventually it had to be chopped off when all other efforts at removal failed. It is claimed that the finger remains stuck to the original icon and a bloody digit represents this on the replica icon at St George's Church in Debar.

The church frescoes reveal the life and times of St George, including his many miracles. Depictions of the terrible Emperor Diocletian show him wearing a Turkish turban, indicating the locals' views of the Turks at the time.

Many of the nuns speak English and will be able to tell you much more of the history of the church and the frescoes if you have time.

🏠 **Restoran Besa** (50 rooms) Dolni Kosovrasti; ☎ 046 842 031, 071 656 852. A basic but pleasant hotel with a nice balcony restaurant serving locally farmed trout & traditional Macedonian food. Near the Kosovrasti hot springs (see below). $$
🏠 **Monastir Sveti Jovan Bigorski** (35 beds) 17km north of Dolni Kosovrasti; ☎ 042 478 675. Recently & exquisitely renovated inn. By far the most beautiful place to stay in Macedonia so long as you are inside the monastery gates by 21.00 & up

for prayers at 06.00. See page 238 for more on the monastery. Bring your own food for use in the communal kitchen at the bottom of the inn. $
✕ **Restoran Sami** ☎ 046 833 721, 070 241 205; ⊕ daily 11.00–23.00. A place to eat offering a wonderful scenic view of Debar Lake. The turn-off to the restaurant is exactly 3km southwest of town immediately after the dam. The food is average Macedonian, but the atmosphere is pleasant. $

WHAT TO SEE Debar is sorely missing a small museum that could tell the rich history of this strategically important town and its various rulers. There are two orthodox churches, whose priests can tell you a lot about the town, if you want to take the time. As you come to the centre of town from the Skopje road you will be faced by the statue of **Skenderbey** (see box on page 234), also written as Skenderbeu, Skenderbeg, and not to be confused with the Skenderbeg fascist troops of World War II. This is the town's main street and continues on to Banjište skirting the edge of the old town of Upper Debar.

Just before you exit Debar on the Skopje road is the **Nunnery of Sv Gjorgi Pobedonoset** (see box, page 235). The nunnery was completed in 2001 and is dedicated to the church of the same name. The grounds of the nunnery are small, but very well kept and hang on the edge of the cliffs of Lake Debar. If the main vehicle gate is closed, enter through the house door a little further down the nunnery outer wall. The effect of entering the door on a sunny evening

BRITISH OPERATIVES IN DEBAR

By 1943 the Axis advance into the Balkans threatened Macedonia. Albania was already held by the fascist Italian powers and the Allies were concerned that without help from special forces, the Macedonian region would also fall into fascist hands. As a result the British Special Operations Executive (SOE), a secret military branch set up by the British government in the 1940s to help defeat the enemy through sabotage and subversion, parachuted operatives into the Debar region. Their mission was to liaise between anti-Axis elements of the local resistance and the Allied forces in order to advise and see how best to help the resistance.

Major Richard Riddell, Captain Anthony Simcox, Flight Lieutenant Andy Hands and Lieutenant Reginald Hibbert were four such British SOE officers. They had been given only a few weeks' notice of their impending insertion into Debar and barely received enough language training or in-depth political background briefings, not least because their mission was to aid the resistance and not report on political developments.

The political situation there was complicated. Albania had divided into two main political factions, the pro-fascists of the puppet government under King Zog (who was living in London at the time) and the republicans, and the anti-fascist resistance of the National Liberation Movement (LNC) headed by Enver Hoxha. To complicate this otherwise clear division there were various tribal chieftains in the hills around the Debar region who were prepared to go with either party depending on who would give them the most autonomy. And then there was the Communist Party of Albania (CPA), an offshoot of the Communist Party of Yugoslavia (CPY), which had joint control with the LNC over the Albanian National Liberation Army (ANLA) otherwise known as the Partisans. In addition, having lost the Debar, Gostivar and Tetovo regions to Royalist Yugoslavia after the Great War, many Albanians were wary of the ANLA and their political masters the CPA and LNC for their close links to the CPY. It was difficult to know in the end who would help whom.

By early 1944 Debar was firmly in the hands of the Germans and it was impossible to drop supplies into Albanian territory to help any potential pockets of resistance. Nevertheless in July 1944, Mehmet Shehu, commander of the 1st Brigade of the ANLA, now holed up north of Peshkopia in the foothills of Mount Korab, decided to march 1st Brigade into Macedonia in order to try to regain Debar from the east. The British SOE officers went with him. In four days the brigade marched over Mount Korab, down to the Gostivar–Dibra road, then up to the Bistra plateau above Mavrovo and back down to the Dibra–Kičevo road, possibly close by Tresonče, Lazaropole and Gari. Finally, marching up again towards Struga and Ohrid, the British officers heard of a supply-drop base for the Macedonia partisans only four hours' march away from their position. They convinced HQ Balkan air force to drop 'Albanian' supplies into Macedonia from where they could reinforce the ANLA with ammunition, arms and equipment. With additional help from the Royal Air Force, Debar was finally brought back into the hands of the Allies on 30 August 1944.

For a lengthier account of this operation read Sir Reginald Hibbert's piece in *The New Macedonian Question*, edited by James Pettifer (see *Appendix 3*, page 335).

accompanied by the ding-a-ling-ling of the doorbell is like being transported to another world or a secret garden. The church itself is one of the best preserved in Macedonia, with all its 19th-century frescoes intact, giving it a much richer feeling than many of the churches in Macedonia which are obviously in great need of repair. Although this church dates back to only 1835, it is built on the foundations of a 16th-century church, which was destroyed by the Arnaut invasion. The 16th-century church had in turn been built on the grounds of the 11th-century castle of St George. The nuns sell a variety of handicrafts and are renowned throughout the churches of Greece and Macedonia for their excellence in making the ornate orthodox bishops' hats.

Lake Debar, spread out magnificently below the town of Debar, is a 22km artificial lake built in 1964 as a means of producing hydro-electricity. It's a popular lake for fishing and swimming although it is little visited from outside the local area. At the southern end of the lake is the Globočica power station, which also serves Globočica Lake further upstream towards Struga. At the northern end of the lake, where the Radika River enters, is Kosovrasti spa. This is also a favourite fishing spot for the locals, as the lake fish come up to the mouth of the Radika to feed. At the time of writing it's the largest artificial lake in Macedonia (of which there are ten) and at its deepest point the lake is just less than 100m deep. The reservoir at Lake Treška, which is still being filled, should surpass the Debar Lake by 8km when it has been fully flooded.

OUTSIDE DEBAR

DOLNI KOSOVRASTI HOT SPRINGS These hot springs like all the others in Macedonia are indoors. There are separate baths for men and for women (no mixed bathing) and each bath is about 3m by 4m. One hour in the bath will cost you a mere 10MKD. The baths are open every day 08.00–21.30. Sunday evenings tend to be pretty busy. Banjište hot springs (see below) is a better experience.

To get there turn off the Debar–Gostivar road at the northern end of Lake Debar, and cross the bridge back over the Radika River. Follow the dirt track on the left and over the small hill for 200m back towards the lake. Over the hill are the hot springs, now inside a concrete one-storey building. Next to it is a ramshackle old Turkish house that used to cater for the hot springs, but has long since fallen into disrepair. There is a small outdoor pool available occasionally.

GORNI KOSOVRASTI VILLAGE If you follow the tarmacked road straight up the side of the mountain for 20 minutes (two hours by foot), you'll come to the ethnic Albanian village of Gorni Kosovrasti. There's not much here except excellent views of the valley floor, the terraced fields on the way up and some fascinating wooden houses and barns. You'll get a real taste of mountain village life here, with cattle and goats wandering around in and out of houses and stables, and the local herdsmen riding mules and donkeys. There is a small mosque in the village.

BANJIŠTE HOT SPRINGS Banjište, 5km outside Debar, close to the Albanian border (so close that your mobile phone is more likely to pick up an Albanian signal than a Macedonian one), lies in the foothills of the Gole Krčin Mountain (2,341m). As you approach the village you can see the run-off from the hot springs tumbling down the ditch on the side of the road, and where it burbles over the hill the water minerals have formed deposits of calcium, lime and sulphur. The smell of sulphur is strong.

The springs themselves, of which there are three (Nova Kaptaža, Goren and Dolen), are quite well kept compared with a lot of other hot spring facilities in

Macedonia, although the paint is still falling off the walls and the experience is a far cry from anything you will find in Switzerland or Colorado. But the baths themselves (separated for men and women) are nicely sunlit, and the small lawn area outside the entrance to the baths is a pleasant place to sip a coffee and take in the magnificent view of the surrounding mountains.

The baths are open 07.00–21.00 every day, and cost a mere 30MKD to enter. Until 15.00 every day the baths are reserved for medicinal bathing and relaxing, but after 15.00 the spring turns into the local bathhouse, and the local community turns up en masse to scrub down with soap and shampoo and washcloths. This makes for a very convivial atmosphere, and the front lawn is filled with ethnic Albanian women in their scarves and long dresses chatting away with friends and neighbours.

THE MONASTERY OF SV JOVAN BIGORSKI (ST JOHN THE BAPTIST) This is a fully working monastery. It was first established in 1020 when the miraculous icon of St John the Baptist (also known as St John the Forerunner) first appeared at the spot where the church now stands. The present-day structures of the church and the surrounding monastery were built, however, in the 18th and 19th centuries. The church closely resembles those of Mount Athos in Greece, characterised by two octagonal domes, the smaller of the two near the main entrance, and the larger residing over the area of worship.

In its day this church's influence stretched over a large part of the region and into present-day Albania as far as Elbasan. Today the church is renowned for containing the final one of only four iconostases carved by the famous Makarije Frčkovski from Galičnik and the Filipovski brothers from Gari (two are in the monastery at Lesnovo – see page 266 – and the Church of the Holy Saviour in Skopje; the third in a church in Kruševo was burnt down after the Ilinden Uprising of 1903). The iconostasis has over 500 humans and over 200 animals carved into it depicting scenes from the Old and New Testaments, and also includes a representation of the woodcarvers themselves. Many of the people depicted in the iconostasis are wearing the traditional 19th-century Macedonian costumes despite the fact that the scenes herald an era many centuries earlier. The bishop's and prior's chairs are also carved by the Filipovski brothers and Frčkovski.

The chest of relics in the church contains a fragment of bone allegedly from the right humerus of St John, as well as bone fragments of the bodies of other saints. They are apparently preserved by their holy nature. The remainder of St John's forearm lies in the Cetinje Monastery in Montenegro.

Church services take place at 06.00, 16.00 and 19.00 every day. The brotherhood of Jovan Bigorski pride themselves on their revival of old Eastern Orthodox ecclesiastical liturgy, which is sung according to the Byzantine tradition as opposed to the Serbian tradition brought in after the fall of the Ottoman Empire. It involves no instruments and is very melodic. The liturgy is sung by the priests at 07.00 (after an hour of prayer) and at 19.00 to start the church service, and is well worth attending. Alternatively, a double CD set of the liturgy can be bought for 700MKD at the monastery shop after the services (also available in Jugoton in the Trgovski Centar in Skopje). Monastery *mastika* (Macedonian ouzo), icons and other religious items can also be bought there.

KIČEVO

Kičevo was known in ancient times as Uskana. It is mentioned by the Roman historian Livy when he records that the last Macedon king, Perseus, took Uskana with an army of 10,000 men during the third Macedonian War against the Romans. Kičevo became the current name of the town with the arrival of Slav settlers in the 7th century BC, although in the 11th century it was noted under the name of Kicavis in one of the documents of the Byzantine emperor Basilius II. In the 13th and 14th centuries during the reign of King Marko it was also known as Katin Grad, because this was where his sister Katina lived.

Kičevo became a part of Albania during World War II and is considered the first town in the Republic of Macedonia to be liberated by Macedonian forces when they defeated fascists here (it was retaken again later). Today the town continues to have a strong ethnic Albanian community and is the home town of Ali Ahmeti, the former National Liberation Army leader and current head of the Democratic Union of Integration. The municipality of Kičevo has just over 30,000 inhabitants.

GETTING THERE Kičevo is served by train (*station* ☎ *045 225 168*) and bus (*station* ☎ *045 223 900;* e *simeks-prevoz@hotmail.com*). The stations are co-located on the west side of Highway E65 less than 1km from the centre of town, which is on the east side of the highway. The last 60cm narrow gauge steam train to Ohrid sits outside the station. There are three trains a day to Kičevo from Skopje and three return. The section between Gostivar and Kičevo is the most scenic, running through close-knit mountains, numerous small tunnels, and alongside a clean pretty mountain river. A single fare Skopje to Kičevo is 182MKD. For trains times see table on pages 74.

Only the buses below stop at the bus station. There are more buses however, which pick up along the main highway between the station and the town. To get to Struga, take the bus to Ohrid and the driver will drop you off at the MakPetrol station at the junction near Struga. A minibus (*kombe*) will take you from there to anywhere in Struga from 40MKD.

WHERE TO STAY
🏠 **Hotel Kičevo** (22 rooms) Narodnička; ☎ 045 223 362. A basic hotel, clean & friendly, near the train station. $$$

🏠 **Kukja na Umetnosta** (20 rooms) Knežino; ☎ 045 262 061, 070 793 739. Completed in 2005 to take the strain off Knežino Monastery after the annual art colony there (Jul every year) became too secular. Beautiful surroundings. $$

🏠 **Panorama** (11 rooms) ☎ 045 222 434. Basic accommodation between Kičevo & the village of Krušino. $$

🏠 **Union** (33 rooms) Osloboduvanje 1; ☎ 045 220 711/712. In the centre of town; location makes up for standard. $$

WHERE TO EAT AND DRINK
Dining out and the café culture in Kičevo are distinctly male phenomena, but not unfriendly. You'll receive a better welcome if you speak Albanian, German or English rather than Macedonian. There are lots of little *ćevapi* stores in the backstreets around the town square or you can try one of the following:

✗ **Elita** Ploštad. The only restaurant on the town square, it offers traditional Albanian food. $
✗ **Pizzeria Roma** Osloboduvanje; ☎ 045 221 232. A new restaurant with a pleasant atmosphere. $

🍰 **Romansa** Osloboduvanje. A relaxed café offering sweet pastries & ice creams as well as the usual drinks.
🍷 **Piano Café** Osloboduvanje; ☎ 045 221 664. Not a piano in sight in this black leather lounge bar.

BUS DEPARTURES FROM KIČEVO	
Skopje	05.50, 09.00
Ohrid, Bitola, Prilep	07.00, 12.00, 14.00

KIČEVO

Clock tower

Kočanska

840m

Kale

Bigor/
Dolenci

Town museum

Kočanska

ALEKSANDAR MAKADONSKI

Elita

Sv Petar i Pavle
Church

$ Union

Masteon

Makedonski Brod,
Prilep

KUZMAN JOSIFOVSKI PITU

Romansa Piano Cafe

Basic
courts

OSLOBODUVANJE

Gravity

MIRKO MILESKI

Pizzeria
Roma

Police

Elite

$

Balkan

NARODNICKA

Kičevo

Railway
station

Struga,
Ohrid

STEFANOSKI

500m
500yds

Krušino

Kukja Na Umetnosta (2km),
Knežino (2.5km)

Motel
Biser

N

Bradt

Panorama

240

WHAT TO SEE The town appears uneventful, although it has seen new paving, benches and refurbished buildings around the tiny town square *ploštad*. The clock tower and **Kale** fortress are all that remain of note from the Ottoman period. The Kale is a short hike up the hill behind the **town museum** on the town square (⊕ *Tue–Sun 11.00–16.00*).

A few kilometres southeast of Kičevo is the Monastery of **Sv Bogorodica Prečista**, the Holy Immaculate Mother of God. Set high in the mountains, its tall majestic walls can be seen imposing over the landscape for some distance. Although the monastery originally dates back to the 14th century it is most renowned for Blagovestie Day on 17 April 1924, when Bishop Dositej entered the brotherhood. In 1963, Dositej became the first archbishop of the revived Ohrid Archbishopric, otherwise and now known as the Macedonian Orthodox Church. A few years later in 1967, Archbishop Dositej proclaimed the autocephaly (independence) of the Macedonian Orthodox Church from the Serbian Orthodox Church. This was without the consent of any of the other orthodox churches and has been a point of dispute ever since.

The monastery has also allegedly been the hideout of many an exile, including some of the Knights Templar, Richard Lionheart on his return from the Third Crusade in 1192, and the last Tsar of Russia Nicholas Romanov when he hid here during the Russian Revolution.

A legend of a flying icon accompanies the monastery: an icon of Mary has been taken three times to Knežino Monastery, northwest of Kičevo, and each time the icon has returned the same night via a ray of light. The icon is still on display in the church today. The church's saint's day is on the birthday of the Virgin Mary on 21 September.

To reach this monastery, head south out of Kičevo towards Ohrid and take the turn-off for Bitola. A few kilometres after the turn-off is a sign for the left-hand turn to Prečista.

10

The Northeast and Middle Vardar

Some archaeological findings suggest that the site was used in the first half of the second millennium BC as a 'holy mountain' where probably more than one cult were celebrated among which the cult of the Great Mother Goddess …

Information brochure on Kokino ancient observatory, 2006

The northeast of Macedonia is little visited, although it contains some great scenery, its fair share of churches and monasteries, hot springs and some very interesting rock formations. In the vicinity of the extinct volcanic crater of **Kratovo** there is **rock art**, large volcanic droplets, Stone Doll rock formations at **Kuklica**, cave dwellings near Konjuh, and a **megalithic sacrificial observatory** at Cocev Kamen. Closer to Kumanovo is another alleged **Aneolithic observatory** near Kokino.

The region's mountains rarely reach above 2,000m except in the Osogovski mountain range, which reaches 2,252m at the border with Bulgaria. But the valleys boast rolling hills and rich paddy fields, and are the wheat basket of Macedonia.

The main river dividing the region is the Bregalnica. Roughly running its course was the ancient road of the Diagonal Way joining Heraklea (near Bitola) and the valley of the River Vardar at Stobi to the valley of the River Struma near Pautalija (now Kustendil in Bulgaria). Another ancient road through the region was the Serres road, joining Ovče Pole in the north to Serres (now in Greece) via Štip, Radoviš and Strumica. Both roads crossed at Štip, making it an important trading town in times of old. Although there are fewer uncovered Roman ruins in the north of Macedonia than in the south, a **Roman amphitheatre** was unearthed near Klečovce in August 2003, adding to the list of important Roman ruins already found in the region at Vinica and Bargala.

The two most visited sites in this part of the country are the **Monastery of Sv Joakim Osogovski** outside Kriva Palanka, and the region of **Berovo** for its lake setting and forest hiking in the cool mountains. Rarely visited, but equally important for containing the last of four rare iconostases is the **Monastery of Gavril Lesnovski**.

VELES

Once an important Roman settlement going by the name of Vilazora, today this unassuming place, and despite its former grand title as Tito Veles, is barely more than an industrial transit town. Nevertheless, its old town is quaint, has a few cultural sites worth a wander past, and local trails have recently been upgraded. Pollution from the lead works outside the town is a concern, but the local environmental NGO Vila Zora (see page 38) has been running projects to remediate local soil pollution. Good news on the health side is that the industry is scaling down. This is bad news for the economy of the town, however.

THE NORTHEAST AND MIDDLE VARDAR

S E R B I A

Pǎnja

† Prohor
Pčinski

K o ž j a k   M t s   German

Žegljane

Taticev Kamen (Kokino)

G e r m a n

Arbansko

Tabanovce

Stepance

† Staro Nagoričane

Dragomance

Lipkovo Lake

Stracin Pass
(692m)

Rankovce

Kostoperska
Karpa

Zebrnjak

† Matejče

KUMANOVO

Kumanovska Banja
(hot springs)

Klečovce

Kriva

Kuklica

O s

Konjuh Cocev
Kamen

Kratovo

Gorni
Kratovo

Blace

Aračinovo

Pǎnja

SKOPJE

Vardar

Probištip

Hot springs Katlanovska Banja

Sveti Nikole

Mladost

Bregalnica

ŠTIP

VELES

▲ Solunska Glava
2538m

Argos

Bogomila

Izvor

Gradsko

Stobi

Vardar

Rosoman

Crna

NEGOTINO

Vardar

K o

Prilep↓

Kavadarci

Senokos↓Prilep ↓Prilep, Svinska Glava

Kustendil
(Bansko),
Sofia

0 |————————————| 25km
0 |————————————| 15 miles

BULGARIA

M t s

Kriva Palanka Varovište
Deve Bair

Toranica
✝
**Sv Joakim
Osogovski**

Kriva

*Mount Ruen
2252m*

N
Bradt

Drenak

*Carev Vrv
2084m*

o g o v s k i M t s

Sasa

✝ **Sv Gavril Lesnovski**

⊢ Lesnovo

⊢ Zletovo

Gratče

Istibanja

*Kalmansko
Ezero*

Kalimanci

Delčevo

Delčevo

Bansko

Hot springs ○
Banje

KOČANI

Orizari

Šagal

Sliv

*Cavka
1536m*

**Golak
Recreation
Centre**

Vinica
Leski

Zrnovci

Vidovište ○ Morodvis

Bregalnica

Bargala

Kozjak

Kozjak

*Pisec
1754m*

P l a č k o v i c a   M t s

Pehčevo

Idilija

○ Kežovica Spa

Kodžalija ○
Alikoc

Radoviš

Berovo

Bregalnica

*Berovo
Ezero*

**Klepalo
Pass**
(1290m)

*Goten
1420m*

*Petleč
1352m*

n e č k a *S m r d e š   M t s*

*Mantovsko
Ezero*

Strumica

*Turija
Ezero*

*Orgažden
1745m*

BULGARIA

STRUMICA Dabilja

Kukliš

Novo
Selo

Petrič

*Demir Kapija,
Gevgelija,
Greece*

Valandovo

Strumica

245

GETTING THERE Veles has an hourly train service to and from Skopje (see train timetable on page 74). The train station (✆ *043 231 033*) is 1km northwest of the centre. **Buses** ply frequently between Skopje, Veles and other parts of the country, starting at 06.00 from Skopje for 120MKD.

The last bus to Veles from Skopje is at 21.00. Veles bus station (✆ *043 234 550*) is on the left bank of the Vardar a few hundred metres from the centre of town underneath the bridge over the Vardar for the main road out of town.

WHERE TO STAY AND EAT

⌂ **Romantique** (26 rooms) Lake Mladost, 9km from Veles; ✆ 043 212 999; f 043 212 997; e info@hotelromantik.com.mk; www.hotelromantik.com.mk. Recently renovated with all mod cons, free Wi-Fi, a good restaurant, fireside bar, pool & private beach on the lake. $$$

⌂ **Brod Panini** (15 rooms) Lake Mladost; ✆ 043 211 444; e brodpanini@t-home.mk. Views from this boat hotel guarantee a lake view. $$

✗ **Parnak** Tito Gradska bb. Conveniently close to the town market, its patio spills onto the River Vardar. Best *skara* in town by far. Serves traditional Macedonian food. $$

✗ **Baže Piti** Alekso Demnievski 7 (opposite the post office); ✆ 043 234 056. Serves good pizzas, *piti* (Macedonian layered pies), *pastrmajlija* & *skara* (grilled meat). $$

✗ **Panini** Blagoj Gorčev bb; ✆ 043 233 615. Serves pizzas & *pastrmajlija*. $$

✗ **Amor** Maršal Tito 33; ✆ 043 233 287. Serves pizza, pasta & *skara*. $$

✗ **Snoopy** Blagoj Gorcev bb. A varied menu, including the house speciality of frogs' legs. Live music outdoors in the summer. Wide wine selection. $$

The main street Blagoj Gorcev is alive with café bars in the evening as people stroll up and down.

WHAT TO SEE

Right bank The town is claimed to be the site of the Paeonic fortress of Vilazora, but nothing of it remains to be seen. A few of the presumably extensive Roman ruins have been excavated. The Ottoman **clock tower** indicates where the centre of the town used to be, further south of the current centre. The **Veles Museum** is at Maršal Tito 20 (✆ *043 223 315*). The 14th-century **Church of Sv Pantelejmon** in the old town rises imposingly over Veles. Just to its south towards the river is the little 14th-century **Church of Sv Nikola**. More recently refurbished is the **Monastery of Sv Dimitri** to the south-southeast of the town past the River Topolka, which empties into the Vardar. This is also where the Ottoman Kale once stood, and now there are the remains of four old watermills scattered along the Topolka. Another 3km walk past Sv Dimitri on the old road is where the River Babuna empties into the Vardar. The trails along the Babuna up into **Pešti Canyon** have recently been upgraded with benches and multi-lingual panel boards indicating local fauna and flora. The 4km hike along the river and canyon is dotted with caves, some of which have churches and shrines.

Left bank The old town on the left bank of the Vardar boasts a unique **black and white mosque**, as well as the birthplace of the famous Macedonian revolutionary and poet Kočo Racin. The bus station and the market are here as well as the town theatre and the **Church of Sv Spas**.

OUTSIDE VELES Nine kilometres north of the town is **Mladost reservoir**. This is the poor man's Ohrid, but a popular place with visitors from the region. There are a number of busy little hotels and restaurants there in the summer (see *Where to stay and eat*, above).

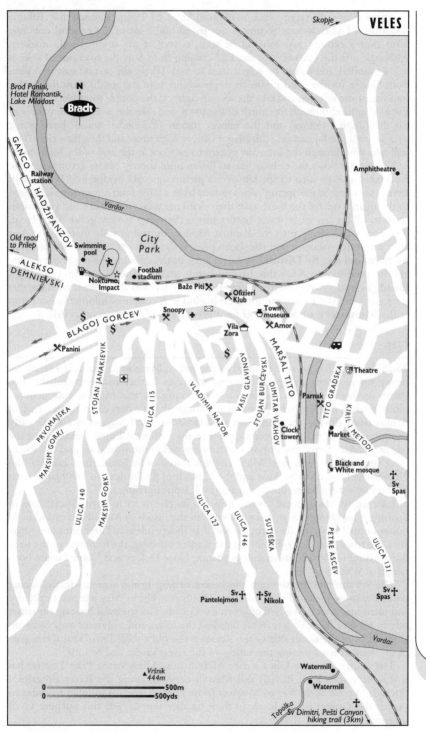

Skopje

Brod Panini,
Hotel Romantik,
Lake Mladost

N

Bradt

Amphitheatre

Vardar

Railway
station

Old road
to Prilep

City
Park

Swimming
pool

ALEKSO
DEMNIEVSKI

Football
stadium

Baže Piti

Nokturno,
Impact

Ofizieri
Klub

BLAGOJ GORČEV

Snoopy

Town
museum

Amor

Vila
Zora

Panini

Theatre

Parnak

Clock
tower

Market

Black and
White mosque

Sv
Spas

Sv
Pantelejmon

Sv
Nikola

Sv
Spas

Vardar

Vršnik
444m

0   500m
0   500yds

Watermill

Watermill

Sv Dimitri, Pešti Canyon
hiking trail (3km)

There is a very pretty back road from Veles to Prilep through the Babuna Mountains. The mountain section is not paved, and a lot of the original cobbling from over a century ago can still be seen, as well as the original mile markers. Although it is the extension of the E27 coming from Štip, the road out of Veles is not signposted, and so can be a little hard to find. Taking the second exit into Veles from Skopje (or the third if you are approaching from the south) cross the bridge into the centre of town and take the second right off the double roundabout. Follow the road around through the north of the town, and take the next left after the sign for the hospital (*bolnica*) and the railway station (*Železnička stanica*). Keep going straight until the T-junction with Blagoj Gorcev high street and then turn right. This will take you through the one-way system to pop out at the end of the high street.

The road follows the railway line to Prilep until shortly before Izvor, when the road takes a sharp turn to the left over a picturesque old bridge into Izvor itself. **Izvor**, meaning 'water spring', does indeed have a large built-up spring right next to the main road. All the locals take their drinking water from here and you might want to fill up any spare water bottles too as the water is very good. After Izvor, the road rises sharply into the Babuna Mountains and at mile marker 144, just after the water fountain and the sheep pens, is the turn-off to the monasteries of **Sv Stepanci** and **Sv Dimitri**. Watch out for turtles crossing the road here as they are not used to cars. After this, hairpin bends snake all the way around the **Pig's Head** (Svinska Glava) and just before the pass at 1,134m above sea level is the dirt track turn-off to the local mountaineering lodge. A couple of kilometres later stop at the **Monastery of Sv Gjorgi** for a good view of the descent to Prilep.

ŠTIP

Today Štip is still seen as the capital of the east of Macedonia, but it is a relatively sleepy town, worth a stop on the way to places further east, but probably not worth an overnight stay unless you are coming for the Makfest international music festival in October. The town is associated with two older names, that of Astibo from during the Kingdom of Macedonia, and Stipion from the early Byzantine era. In the 14th century, prior to the Ottoman Empire taking over the whole of Macedonia, five important churches were built in and around the town: the Church of Sv Archangel Michael, the Church of Sv Jovan, the Church of Sv Nikola, the Church of Sv Spas and the Church of Sv Basilius. In 1689 large parts of the town were burnt down during the Karpoš uprising.

Like many Macedonian towns, Štip has its claims to its own crucial role in forming a consciousness of independence in the minds of Macedonians and in so doing contributing to the struggle for that independence. Three hundred years after the town was set alight during the Karpoš uprising, the founders of the next big uprising for Macedonian independence, Goce Delčev and Dame Gruev, both taught at schools in Štip.

The stream running through the centre of Štip brings torrents in the spring when the snow melts off the Plaškovica Mountains, but by May it is practically dry and turns into a welcome bed of green river plants. The stream is built up on either side to prevent the spring torrents flooding the town, and a pleasant walkway runs alongside. On the south side of the stream is the old cobbled road that forms part of the ancient road joining the valleys of the rivers Vardar and Struma.

The centre is where Ulica Kiril i Metodi joins Ulica Vančo Prke. Legend has it that the saints Kiril (Cyril) and Metodi travelled along the River Bregalnica through Štip on their way to Moravia (now in the Czech Republic) in order to preach the Gospel to the locals in their mother tongue. For this purpose Cyril invented the Cyrillic alphabet.

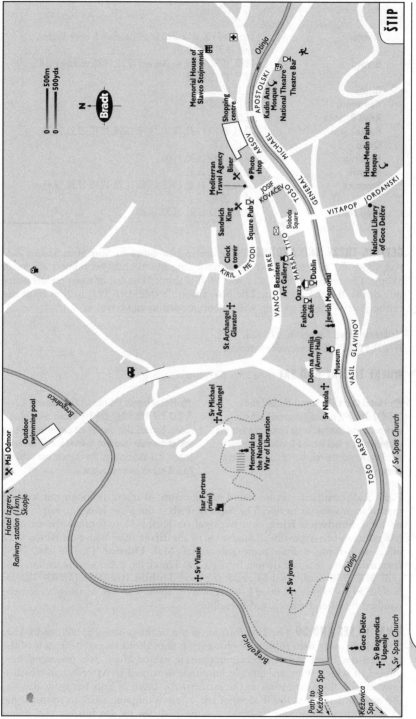

Memorial House of Slavco Stojmenski

Shopping centre

APOSTOLSKI

Kadin Ana
Mosque
National Theatre
Theatre Bar

Otinja

MICHAEL

Husa-Medin Pasha
Mosque

JORDANSKI

ARSOV

Mediterran
Travel Agency
Biser

Photo shop

JOSIF
KOVACEV

TOŠO

GENERAL

VITAPOP

Sandwich
King

Square Pub

Sloboda
Square

National Library
of Goce Delčev

Clock
tower

PRKE

VANČO Bezisten

MARŠAL TITO

KIRIL I METODI

Art Gallery

Dublin

St Archangel
Glavatov

Oaza
Fashion
Café

Jewish Memorial

Bregolnica

Dom na Armija
(Army Hall)

Museum

VASIL GLAVINOV

Sv Nikola

TOŠO ARSOV

500m
500yds

N

Bradt

0
0

Hotel Izgrev,
Railway station (1km),
Skopje

Mal Odmor

Outdoor
swimming pool

Sv Michael
Archangel

Memorial to
the National
War of Liberation

Isar Fortress
(ruins)

Sv Vlasie

Sv Jovan

Otinja

Bregalnica

Sv Spas Church

Path to
Kežovica Spa

Goce Delčev

Sv Bogorodica
Uspenje
Sv Spas Church

Kežovica Spa

Skopje	first bus 05.00 (Mon–Fri), 06.00 (Sat–Sun) & every 45mins until 19.30 (260MKD)
Berovo	09.35, 10.50, 11.20; via Delčevo 10.25, 14.35, via Vinica 15.15, 17.15, 18.15, 19.35
Bitola	13.30, 00.45
Kumanovo	15.15, 18.30
Kriva Palanka	15.00
Kočani	07.15, 09.10, 11.45, 12.00, 14.10, 15.30, 18.15, 20.55, 21.30
Ohrid	07.15, 15.15
Probistip	08.45, 11.45, 16.30, 19.00
Radoviš	14.40, 17,00, 20.30
Strumica	07.30, 08.00, 11.40, 15.05, 15.40, 16.20, 17.10, 17.30, 18.45, 19.35, 20.40
Sveti Nikole	08.00, 12.30, 13.30, 15.30, 18.30

GETTING THERE AND AROUND There are regular buses to Štip from Skopje (see box above for timetable) and the surrounding towns and two trains a day from Skopje. The train station (✆ 032 392 904) is about 1km out of town on the other side of the River Bregalnica. The bus station (✆ 032 391 391) is 2km from the centre. A travel agent to help with accommodation and travel is:

Mediteran Travel Agency Vančo Prke bb; ✆ 032 397 021; f 032 397 001; www.mediteran.com.mk

WHERE TO STAY AND EAT (See also *Kežovica Spa*, page 252.)

⌂ **Hotel Oaza** (27 rooms) Maršal Tito bb; ✆/f 032 394 899; e info@oazahotel.com.mk; www.oazahotel.com.mk. In the centre of town, this establishment is well located & modern. Formerly called the Astibo, the refurbished hotel also has a sauna. $$$

⌂ **Hotel Izgrev** (16 rooms) Vasil Vlahovikj 1; ✆ 032 394 919; f 032 394 918. Nicely refurbished rooms. Located 1km outside the centre on the east side of the main road into town near the railway station. It is also close to the Olympic-size outdoor pool & has its own restaurant. $$

Cafés and restaurants can be found in the centre of town, although much more than *skara* is difficult to find. The **Square Pub** is the main hangout, but it offers no food. **Sandwich King** over the road on Kiril i Metodi offers the standard Macedonian one-type-fits-all sandwich, or the **Biser** *skara* house on Bančo Prke offers something a little more substantial. **Mal Odmor** (✆ 032 380 187) restaurant outside town, owned by the Oaza Hotel, has patio seating, an outdoor grill and serves traditional Macedonian food. **Dublin** Irish Pub (*Maršal Tito bb;* ✆ 032 391 099; ⊕ 08.00–24.00) is new in town and has certainly raised the standard on offer. Relaxed and friendly.

WHAT TO SEE AND DO The **Isar** fortress on top of the prominent hill overlooking Štip is little more than ruins now. However, it does afford an excellent view of the modern-day town and of the inappropriately named Novo Selo (meaning 'new village' of which there are literally hundreds so named in Macedonia), which is now in fact older than most of the modern-day town of Štip, but in its day was the new settlement in the shadow of Isar. There is ongoing work to restore some of the fortress ruins and to build a stone path up to the fortress but, unless significant restoration is carried out, one can only stand on the top of the hill, imagine the grandeur of the fortress and gaze in awe at the magnificent view that the hill still commands of the surrounding countryside.

To drive there take the obvious road up the hillside as soon as you have passed over the flyover leading from the main highway into town. This road will lead you past the little **Church of Sv Michael Archangel** built in 1332. It is set in small but beautiful grounds, but is rarely open to the public. The path then leads onto the bottom of the National War of Liberation memorial site. There is limited parking here if you come by car, and only just enough space to turn and avoid the drinking fountain. Take the steps up to the war memorial and then go on to the fortress remains. You'll get a great mobile phone signal up there, but sadly the two mobile phone towers also detract from the enchantment of the site.

On each of the four sides of Isar is a church built during the Middle Ages to help protect the fortress. To the south at the bottom of the hill is the **Church of Sv Nikola**, rebuilt in 1876 on the site of an older church dating back to 1341. It is the only church that is open every day, and if you ask inside, one of the priests should be able to take you to the other churches. The upper floor of the church has an extensive gallery of icons.

Opposite the church there are several sets of steps leading up past the Church of Sv Michael Archangel on the east of the fortress, which was the first of the four churches to be built. The **Church of Sv Basilius**, on the northwest side of the fortress, was built in 1337, and little remains of it today. The last church, **Sv Jovan**, was built in 1350 on the right bank of the River Otinja. Opposite it on the left bank of the River Otinja is the **Church of Sv Spas** built in 1369.

Walking along the riverbank into town from the Church of Sv Nikola, you will come to the next main building which is the renovated **memorial house to the Arsovi brothers** (✆ 032 392 044; f 032 385 369; ⊕ Mon–Fri 07.00–15.00; entry free), two local heroes renowned as revolutionaries fighting for Macedonian independence in the pre-World War II and World War II period. It was converted into the **city museum** in 1956. Outside are numerous marble Roman artefacts on display on the lawn. If you go in and speak to the museum curator, Zoran Čitkušev, he may be able to furnish you with a bilingual Macedonian/English guidebook to the town, and if you phone in advance he can also arrange a visit to the Roman ruins at Bargala.

Between the museum and the neighbouring Dom na Armija military club is a small memorial to the 561 Jewish citizens of Štip who were deported to Treblinka gas chambers in Poland on 11 March 1943. Like many towns in Macedonia, Štip had a thriving Jewish community prior to the war and though the lives of these citizens are well documented, little remains to be seen of their influence now.

Behind the Oaza Hotel is the **Bezisten**, the old covered market built in the mid 17th century. It is now a modern art gallery (⊕ Tue, Wed, Thu & Sat 09.00–12.00 & 17.00–19.00, Fri 09.00–13.00, Sun 10.00–12.00). Štip's two mosques are south of the River Otinja. The **Kadin Ana Mosque**, built in the mid 19th century, is by the river next to the **National Theatre** (built between 1924–36). It is unclear when the older **Mosque of Pasha Husa-Meda** just off Vitapop Jordanski Hill was built. Some say as early as the 14th century, others say not until the 16th. What is clear, however, is that it was built on the foundations of the much older church of Sv Ilija. Within the grounds of the mosque is the turbeh containing the remains of the mosque's architect.

Festivals Štip hosts a number of events and festivals throughout the year. On the **first day of spring**, Štipites walk to the top of Izar fortress, where they throw a pebble off the top of the hill and make a wish for the future. In July is the Štip

International Film Festival, and in October is the **Makfest**, a music festival featuring a variety of world music. This is a popular event in Macedonia, so book a room early if you want to stay over for it. For more exact information on festival artists and films contact Mediteran Travel Agency on page 250.

OUTSIDE ŠTIP

Kežovica Spa (✆ *032 308 560*) The spa is located just off the River Bregalnica past Novo Selo. The water emerges at the L'gji spring at a temperature of 66.8°C, and is then mixed with cold water before it enters the baths. The baths themselves are separated for men and women, and are relatively pleasant and spacious. Entrance to the baths is 40MKD per person, and showers are an extra 50MKD. The baths are open 06.00–20.00 every day, except on Monday when the women's bath is closed for cleaning until 09.00, and on Friday when the men's bath opens at 09.00.

Aside from 100 beds for those booked in for physical therapy and treatment, the spa also offers 40 beds in 15 rooms to those wishing to stay overnight. Although the rooms are extremely basic and cheap at 250MKD per person per night, the spa setting alongside the River Bregalnica is very tranquil, and makes a good base for those on a shoestring budget to explore other places in the region. The spa also offers limited buffet facilities, but you are better off eating in town. It's a 3km walk from the spa along the river through Novo Selo to the centre of Štip.

Remains of the ancient city of Bargala The remains can be found in the foothills of the Plačkovica Mountains near the village of Goren Kozjak, 18km northeast of Štip. The city itself was one of the major urban centres, along with the now lost cities of Kelenidin, Armonia and Zapara, of the Roman Province of Macedonia Salutaris. Though the first written references to Bargala date from late antiquity (around the 4th century BC), archaeological finds from the site suggest that the site itself was inhabited from a much earlier date. The city thrived into the 6th century AD before being overrun by the Avars. During its heyday it was enclosed in fortified walls some 300m by 150m, whose main entrance in the northwest wall can still be partly seen. Of the many antique and Roman structures to be discovered in the city, the most impressive are those of the antique bathhouse, which had a number of baths of differing temperatures as well as a sauna, and also the early Christian Church of Sv Gjorgi. The monumental tri-nave basilica and associated complex is still visible, with its impressive entrance and its eight tiers of stairs leading to a room adorned with luxurious marble columns. Such architectural grandeur reflects the importance that the city held up until the 6th century AD. The associated complex housed the bishop's palace with its wide porch and colonnaded walkways. Bargala later became a bishopric in the Byzantine Empire.

Plačkovica mountain range This offers a whole host of hiking opportunities and beautiful scenery. Take the Kozjak road from Karabinci to access the Plačkovica summit of Lisec (1,754m), Crkvište peak (1,689m) and the mountain villages of Šipkovica and Vrteška. At the latter village you can stay at the mountain hut **Vrteška** (*64 beds;* ✆ *032 384 788, 032 384 299*). The hut warden is Marjan Ljubotenski. Beds are 250MKD per person per night.

KOČANI

From Štip, Highway 27 follows the River Bregalnica to Kočani. There is not much in the town itself as, until communist industrialisation, it had mostly been a farming settlement since the time of Aleksandar III of Macedon. Around 330BC, Aleksandar sent back rice from India, which was planted in these fertile fields. The

Hotel Gradče
4km

0 ————— 250m
0 ————— 250yds

Bradt

N

ASNOM
Park

14 BRIGADA

GOCE DELČEV

KIRIL I METODI

IVAN MILUTANOVIC

ILINDENSKA

MARŠAL TITO

9 NEN REVOLUCIJATA

BRAKJA STAVREVI

TOŠO ARSOV

LJUPČO SANTOR

STAMEN MANOV

Library

KIRIL I METODI

Sv Gjorgi †

Shopping
centre

MILAN ZEČAR VLAHOV

DIMITAR VLAHOV

Market

22 OKTOMVRI

LENINOVA ←

Beli
Murgi
Theatre

29 NOEMVRI

Park
Na
Revolu-
cijata

ASNOM

4 JULI

EDVARD KARDELJ

RAJKO ŽINZIFOV

9 MAJ

$

ROZA PETROVA

SKOPSKA

RADE KONČAR

→ IVO LOLA RIBAR

LAZAR
ANDONOV

KOTORKA
VERA

NIKOLA KARAEV

Kočanska

Courts

Police
station

Railway
station

PAVLINA VELJANOVA

Vinica,
Delčevo

Štip,
Skopje↙

KOČANI

ancient paddy fields in the region are still worked today, many by hand, and they provide most of Macedonia's rice. Surrounding Kočani are the archaeological sites of Morobyzdon and Vinica, and several hot springs.

GETTING THERE There are 13 buses a day to Kočani from Skopje running 08.15–19.30, for 280MKD. The bus station (✆ *033 272 206*) is at 29th Noemvri 26, and the train station (✆ *033 274 075*) is a little further down the street at Pavlina Veljanova 11. There are two trains a day from Skopje (see train timetable, page 74).

WHERE TO STAY The best places to stay are outside Kočani itself.

🏠 **Hotel Šagal** (16 rooms) 6km outside Kočani, before the turn-off to Vinica; ✆ 033 361 151/165. Completely refurbished in 2006, the hotel has

indoor & outdoor restaurants, a covered outdoor pool heated with water from underground hot springs, as well as a fitness centre, sauna, Turkish baths & tennis courts. This is the first modern spa-like facility in the country $$ 🏠 **Motel Sliv** (30 rooms) Less than 1km on the turn-off to Vinica from the Kočani to Delčevo road; ☎ 033 360 502, 033 362 502; e motelsliv@ mail.mt.net; www.motelsliv.com.mk. Nice restaurant, outdoor swimming pool & plenty of greenery. Each room is en suite with a TV. $$

🏠 **Hotel Gradče** (29 rooms) 4km north of Kočani; ☎ 033 274 202; e hotelgradce@ t-home.mk; www.hotelgradce.com.mk. Well worth the winding drive for its tranquil setting in the woods & its nice rooms. $$ 🏠 **Motel Dončo** (10 rooms) 2km outside Kočani in the village of Orizari; ☎ 033 294 343. The hotel has an unexciting restaurant. $

WHAT TO SEE AND DO The more important town in the region in the 5th and 6th centuries BC was the religious complex of Morobyzdon near present-day **Morodvis**, 7km almost directly south of Kočani on the south side of the River Bregalnica. The site spans the late Roman period (4th century AD) to the 10th century AD and is one of the most significant in the Kočani region. The visible architectural remains of a monumental basilica date from the 5th and 6th centuries AD; it was furnished with a luxurious marble floor, massive columns and capitals. A large tomb, lavishly decorated in a multitude of colours, is incorporated into the basilica. Kočani became a bishopric in the 10th century AD under the Byzantine emperor Basilius the Great. Later, a small church, dating to the 13th century was built over the earlier basilica. This town was probably on the ancient Diagonal Way, as was the neighbouring town of Vinica.

Vinica, named after its renown in Byzantine times for wine growing, is famous for the remarkable and unique terracotta icons found at the old fortress on the hill above the town. Archaeological finds from the fortress date to the Neolithic period. The site itself saw its heyday between the 4th and 6th centuries AD and is closely associated with the dawn of Christianity in Macedonia. The Vinica terracottas found there are ceramic tiles depicting Christian scenes in relief of traditional saints and betray an artistic style atypical of the region. The scattered pottery, stone and tile on the ground are all from the late antique settlement beneath the soil and point to the hidden city beneath your feet. The terracotta icons themselves are on display at the National Museum of Macedonia in Skopje. When the Bregalnica was dammed at **Kalimansko Ezero** in early communist times, Vinica gave up wine growing for rice and tobacco. From Vinica, the road east-southeast leads along the River Osojnica to Berovo.

To the west and east of Kočani are two dilapidated communist-style hot springs. Istibanje, 7km to the east, is generally not open. Banja, 9km to the west, is open every day 12.00–21.00. The water is allegedly good for healing stomach problems and the locals also drink the water for its general medicinal properties. The small communal baths are separated into men's and women's, costing 40MKD per visit, and a private bath cabin costs 100MKD. The spa hopes to re-open some rooms for accommodation, although this does not look as though it is going to happen any time soon.

DELČEVO

Continuing along the River Bregalnica, Highway 27 passes the manmade Kalimansko Ezero. Then, 10km before the border crossing of Arnautski Grob (meaning 'grave of the Arnauts') into Bulgaria is the small town of Delčevo, named after the Macedonian revolutionary leader Goce Delčev. As a leader of the Ilinden Uprising of 1903, Goce Delčev is resoundingly honoured every year with a festival in his name on 2 August, the day of the uprising. Prior to its renaming in 1950, the town had been known by the name of Carevo Selo, meaning 'Tsar's Village' and in Ottoman times it was called Sultania.

If you need to stop to eat in Delčevo there is a fantastic kebab house called **Buffet Cinco**, on the other side of the bridge across from the centre of town. The buffet is well located with an outside terrace from which to watch the town market on Saturday afternoon, and serves the best, most succulent *ražnič* in all of Macedonia. There are frequent **buses** (*Delčevo bus station* ↘ *033 413 684*) in and out of Delčevo on their way between Skopje and Berovo.

Three kilometres to the southeast of Delčevo are the ruins of the Byzantine village of **Vasilevo**, which was named after the Byzantine emperor Basilius II. Three kilometres to the southwest on the road to Golak is the new **Monastery of Sv Bogorodica**. The small church has bright new frescoes of all the familiar saints, but check out the new dance moves of Sts Eleuša and Ana on the right-hand side as you go in. The monastery inns have been left unfinished for years, but even if you can't overnight there, it's a great place for a picnic as the rock formations along the stream bed are a sight unto themselves and many have been converted into covered eating areas with tables and benches.

The road to Golak leads to Mount Čavka at 1,536m and the **Golak Recreation Centre** (*256 beds;* ↘ *033 411 733*), where there are some ski runs, plenty of hiking and several ball courts. The views of the Delčevo Valley on the way up are superb.

BEROVO

Turning south at Delčevo, following the River Bregalnica part way, the road comes to the quaint eastern village of Berovo. Unlike most villages and towns in Macedonia, this one does not hark back to Roman, medieval or Byzantine times, but first resembled something like a village only in the late 19th century, barely 150 years ago. It got its name from the Macedonian word *bere* meaning 'to gather', probably because outsiders were so surprised that anyone would gather in a place where there wasn't already a significant settlement.

Now people come here because of the outstanding beauty of the mountains and for the cool, refreshing mountain air. At almost 900m above sea level, Berovo lies in the Maleševo Valley of the upper reaches of the Bregalnica River. Sheltered by mountains, this valley records the coldest average temperatures in winter, and it is fairly cool here in the summer too, rarely getting into the high 20°Cs. It is an excellent getaway from the scorching heat of Skopje in June, July and August, but bring an extra sweater for the evenings.

GETTING AROUND Considering how far away it is from the capital, Berovo is reasonably well served by bus. The bus station (↘ *033 471 139*) is right in the centre of town next to 23 Avgust bridge. A journey from Berovo to Skopje is 380–420MKD one-way, and takes about 3½ hours. See timetable above.

At the taxi stand opposite the bus station, the taxi firms Central (↘ *033 9190*) and Slivka (↘ *033 9196*) run for a minimum fare of 10MKD.

Thanks to a local economy regeneration programme supported by UNDP and USAID, a **map** of the town and of hiking in the area is available commercially in Skopje and in Berovo.

BUS DEPARTURES FROM BEROVO	
Skopje via Vinica serving Kočani, Štip, Veles	04.20, 07.30, 10.15, 16.15
Skopje via Delčevo (90mins longer than via Vinica)	07.00, 08.20, 14.30

WHERE TO STAY

Loven Dom (Hunters' Lodge) (4 rooms) ✆ 033 470 454. This small state-run lodge has become somewhat rundown & charges double the price for foreigners. Nevertheless, it has a beautiful view of the mountains, its own tennis courts & a restaurant serving traditional Macedonian food. To get there turn north uphill between the church in the centre of the village on the cobbled road & the City Pub café. Keep following the road uphill for another 500m until you reach the spacious well-kept grounds of the Hunters' Lodge with its distinctive black & white, almost Tudor-style house. $$

Hotel Monastir (14 rooms) Kiril i Metodi 6, next to the Sv Michael the Archangel Monastery; ✆ 033 279 000; f 033 279 037; e info@

hotelmonastir.com.mk; www.hotelmonastir.com.mk. Brand-new comfortable hotel with apt-type rooms in a quaint setting. Popular restaurant. Excellent value. $$

Recreation Centre Maleševo (44 rooms) On the edge of Lake Berovo; ✆ 033 471 212, 033 471 555, 070 206 850. Well designed for large groups of people, & beautifully situated. It is often used for group & company retreats so ask for a discount if you are more than 10 people. $$

Motel Idila (16 rooms) 20km southeast of Pehčevo; ✆ 033 441 323, 070 233 720. A beautiful location almost on the border with Bulgaria, this trout farm has an outdoor pool (murky) & nice rooms. Good little restaurant. $

For bed and breakfast options in the area phone Atlantis Travel Agency in Strumica (✆ *034 346 212*). Prices are around 650MKD per person per night.

WHAT TO SEE AND DO Aside from hiking in the beautiful mountains, there is skiing in the winter from the Maleševo Recreation Centre, and fishing in the summer in **Lake Berovo**. The lake used to be known as Ratevo Lake, because it lies near the village of Ratevo, but now that Berovo draws more visitors it has come to be known by that village's name and the only road access to the lake is in fact from Berovo. To reach the lake take the turning downhill at the entrance to Maleševo Recreation Centre. The high road continues on to the border crossing at Klepalo. The Bulgarian side has not yet reciprocated the desire to open the border and so the road on the Macedonian side simply leads to an empty border and customs building. The lake itself is completely natural, unlike many of the reservoir lakes in Macedonia, and stays cold year round as it draws its water from the surrounding mountains.

The **Monastery of Sv Michael the Archangel** is at the eastern edge of the village, and pre-dates the village by less than half a century. The site was originally built in order to train teachers in Macedonian, away from the watchful eyes of their Ottoman rulers, who feared that the development of Macedonian language and literature would lead to revolt. A famous Macedonian literary figure, Joakim Kršovski, taught here. The monastery is surrounded by some inns where the nuns live and has a small informative museum. You will need to phone the museum keeper, Dvonko (✆ *033 472 733*), if you want to look inside, as it is usually shut.

Nine kilometres north of Berovo is the village of **Pehčevo**. The village started out as an iron-mining town in Roman times and continued to produce iron ore throughout Ottoman rule. Remains of the mine at the foot of Mount Bukovik can still be found. Hiking in the vicinity is a popular pastime and there are a number of rooms for accommodation along the River Ravna.

KUMANOVO

The third largest town in Macedonia after Skopje and Bitola is Kumanovo with almost 70,000 inhabitants. It is not an especially historically significant town, as it lies in the upper reaches of Macedonia, which did not see much development in

Roman times, and only saw a settlement of any size when the Kumani tribe settled there in the Middle Ages, hence its name Kumanovo.

One incident in history that does stand out for Kumanovo is the Karpoš Uprising of 1689, when Petre Vojnički-Karpoš, advancing from Kriva Palanka against the Turks, took Kumanovo and was then declared the King of Kumanovo by the Austrian Emperor Leopold I (see box, page 11). Unfortunately for Karpoš and his men, the tale ends in Skopje, where they were beheaded by the Turks and Karpoš's head was displayed for all to see on the Stone Bridge in Skopje as a deterrent to other upstarts.

The border to the northwest of Kumanovo neighbours Kosovo, and the town's large Albanian population have more often looked to Priština in Kosovo for leadership, trade and cultural ties than to Skopje. In the Kosovo crisis of 1998 and 1999, thousands of Kosovar Albanian refugees fled into the Kumanovo area as well as other parts of northwestern Macedonia.

During the conflict of 2001 between National Liberation Army guerillas and the local Macedonian authorities, fighting broke out in the villages surrounding Kumanovo including Tanuševci (see page 20) on the border with Kosovo, where fighting here marked the beginning of the conflict of 2001; Matejče 17km to the west of Kumanovo, where the 14th-century monastery has been ransacked and reprisals inflicted on local villagers; and Sopot, less than 3km from the border crossing into Serbia north of Kumanovo, where two Polish soldiers and one civilian were killed on 4 March 2003 by a land mine laid by former insurgents in an effort to destabilise the region.

Security in the area has improved significantly since the Ohrid Framework Agreement of August 2001, and even ethnic Macedonians have returned to hiking in the area.

GETTING THERE AND AROUND There are regular buses (see timetable below) and seven trains a day (see timetable, pages 74) to Kumanovo, including two direct trains from Skopje. The **train station** (↘ 031 423 310) is located at the end of 11th Oktomvri, a good 2km out of town. There are plenty of taxis waiting at the station, and if perchance they are all out with passengers then you can call 9182 or 9197 for a taxi. The **bus station** (↘ 031 428 570) at Industriska bb is near the train station.

⌂ WHERE TO STAY AND EAT

⌂ **Mimoza** (8 rooms) Goce Delčev district; ↘ 031 413 232; e hotel_mimoza@yahoo.com. Located on the southwest edge of town off the main road, this hotel is quiet & updated. $$$

⌂ **Hills** (4 rooms) Vasil Smilevski Bato 91; ↘ 031 452 536. In the same area of town as Mimoza but even further out. Nice location & rooms. $$$

⌂ **Rim-Pariz** (6 rooms) III MUB 56; ↘ 031 415 800. Above the pizza restaurant of the same name.

Centrally located, clean & modern but a little noisy. $$

⌂ **Lovečki Dom** (6 rooms) III MUB bb, on cnr with Vasil S Bato; ↘ 031 452 773. Basic rooms. $$

⌂ **Lav** (17 rooms) Železnički 13; ↘ 031 413 999; e hotel_lav@yahoo.com. Opposite the train station, & although a bit 1980s in style, it is at least quiet. $$

BUS DEPARTURES FROM KUMANOVO

Skopje	First bus 05.00 then every 30mins until 21.00
Kriva Palanka	07.00, 09.45, 11.30, 15.00, 16.45, 19.10
Kratovo (via Probistip)	08.30, 14.00, 16.30
Štip via Sv Nikole	05.30, 12.30, 15.30
Ohrid (seasonal)	06.00

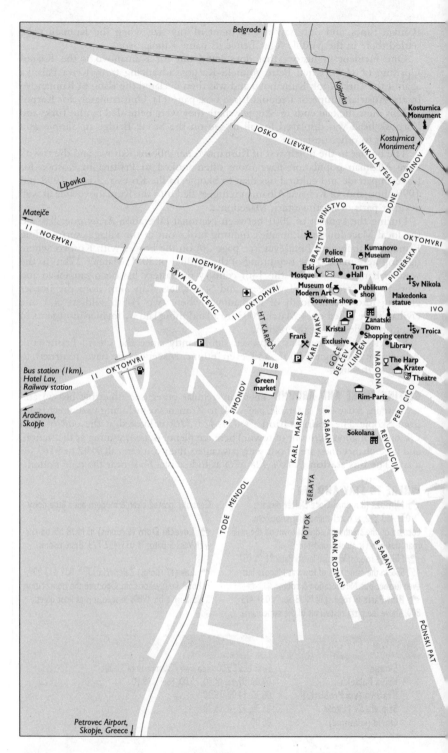

Belgrade

Kojnarka

Kosturnica
Monument

JOSKO ILIEVSKI

Kosturnica
Monument

NIKOLA TESLA

DONE BOŽINOV

Lipovka

Matejče

II NOEMVRI

OKTOMVRI

BRATSTVO EPINSTVO

PIONERSKA

II NOEMVRI

Kumanovo
Museum

Police
station

II NOEMVRI

SAVA KOVAČEVIC

II OKTOMVRI

Eski
Mosque

Town
Hall

Sv Nikola

II OKTOMVRI

HT KARPOŠ

Museum of
Modern Art

Publikum
shop

Makedonka
statue

IVO

Souvenir shop

P

Zanatski
Dom

Sv Troica

KARL MARKS

Kristal

Franš

Shopping centre

Library

Exclusive

GOCE DELCEV

ILINDEN

NARODNA

The Harp

Krater

P

Theatre

Bus station (1km),
Hotel Lav,
Railway station

II OKTOMVRI

PERO CICO

3 MUB

Green
market

Rim-Pariz

REVOLUCIJA

Aračinovo,
Skopje

S SIMONOV

KARL MARKS

B SABANI

Sokolana

TODE MENDOL

POTOK SERAYA

FRANK ROZMAN

B SABANI

Petrovec Airport,
Skopje, Greece

PČINSKI PAT

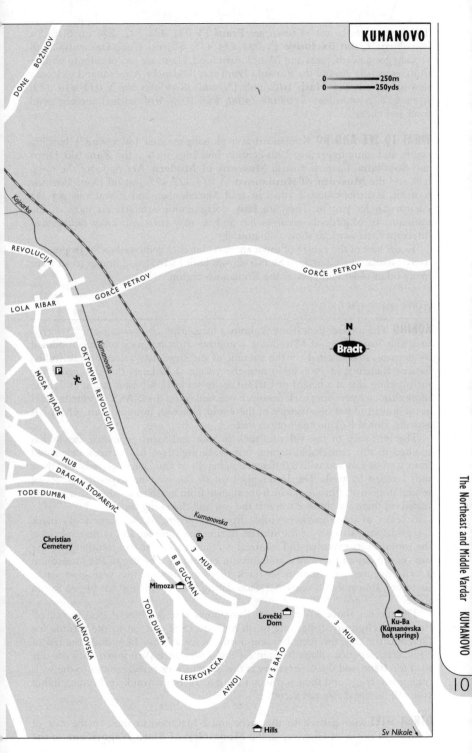

The best places to eat in town are **Franš** (✆ *031 428 842;* *$$*) on Narodna Revolucija 1, and **Exclusive** (✆ *031 454 445;* *$$*) on Goce Delčev bb, both serving good salads, pizza and Macedonian food. There are lots of cafés to choose from, especially around the Zanatski Dom and Ilindenska. A recent and welcome new edition is the **Harp** Irish pub (*Narodna Revolucija bb;* ✆ *031 418 123;* e *murfo76@ yahoo.com;* ⊕ *08.00–24.00;* *$$*), 100% Irish owned, serving good food and cheer.

WHAT TO SEE AND DO Kumanovo is a pleasant enough town with a bustling centre and some impressive 19th-century buildings, such as the **Zanatski Dom** and **Sokolana**. There is a small **Museum of Modern Art** opposite the town hall, and the **Museum of Kumanovo** (✆ *031 422 495*) just off Done Bozinov is small, but interesting if you can read Macedonian, and if you can get the curators to let you in. They are busy documenting artefacts (as most of the museums in Macedonia seem to be) and so may turn you away rather than interrupt their work to show you around.

To the east of the centre of town are two churches dedicated to Sv Trojica and to Sv Nikola. The Church of Sv Nikola was built in 1851 and houses icons from many other older churches in the Kumanovo region.

OUTSIDE KUMANOVO

KOKINO The archaeological site Kokino, a megalithic observatory often referred to as the Stonehenge of Macedonia, comprises a natural rock outcrop modified by humans. It is situated on the summit of the large neo-volcanic peak (called Taticev Kamen grid 7906 8036 near the village of Kokino) that dominates the surrounding area at a height of 1,013m above sea level. Whilst it might look little more than an interesting rock feature, it was ranked on the NASA website in 2005 as the fourth oldest observatory in the world, although nobody from NASA has actually visited Kokino to confirm that.

The tendency of the volcanic rock to split and form geometric cracks has resulted in this remarkable natural feature; though two flat surfaces, orientated from west to east and with a difference in height of 15m, have certainly had their tops levelled by tools. The lower platform to the west preserves the traces of several stone seats (thrones), which are aligned from north to south, so that anyone seated on them would face towards the east and the rising sun.

A series of stone markers visible from the centre of the observatory mark the positions variously of the sunrise during the summer and winter solstices, the moon in its maximal and minimal declines in winter and summer, and the sun on the day of the vernal and autumn equinoxes. The use of the location as a primitive research station to track the sun through the year goes back, therefore, almost 4,000 years. Artefacts dating back to 1815BC have been found there.

The site lies about 30km outside Kumanovo. Take the Prohor Pčinski exit off the E871 (Highway 2) heading north for 7km until you get to the turning for Dragomance. Take this turn, heading northeast for another 14.6km. At the rise of a hill after Slepenče village is a sign for the observatory. Turn north onto the dirt road for 100m and the observatory is the obvious rock feature 300m to the west (unless it is foggy and then you won't see it at all, but if you keep heading uphill you will unmistakably get there).

OTHER SITES Going back to the more usual Macedonian sites, to the east of Kumanovo north of Highway 2, the **Monastery of Staro Nagoričane** in the village of the same name houses the early 14th-century **Church of Sv Gjorgi**, which was built in 1313 by the Serbian king Milutin on the foundations of an 11th-century church. The church's frescoes are almost completely intact, but the narthex has been destroyed. The monastery is surrounded by a low stone wall and has no inns. The yard, containing a few old graveyards, is unkempt and the site is usually locked. To get the key ask the police officers in the small police station opposite the church. They will contact the church warden, who should be able to come over with the key in a few minutes. Note that photography inside the church requires permission.

To get to the site, take the Prohor Pčinski exit off the E871 (Highway 2) heading north. After 100m, turn left at the T-junction and then immediately right, signposted for Prohor Pčinski. Follow this road north for 2.5km, and at the top of a small hill take the new road left to the village of Staro Nagoričane. You will come across the monastery in a few hundred metres at the edge of the village.

Before you get to the turn-off from the E871 for Prohor Pčinski is an obvious rock feature to the north called **Kostoperska Karpa**, which was also an important ritual location in the past. At the same time to the south, you will make out in the middle distance a large ruined building on top of a hill. It stands out for many miles like a nipple on the landscape. This modern ruin is what is left of the once six-storey Kosturnica monument of **Zebrnjak**, commemorating soldiers who died here fighting against the Turks in the Kumanovo battle of the first Balkan War of 1912. The monument was erected on the 25th anniversary in 1937, but blown up six years later in 1943 by the Bulgarians during their occupation of Vardar Macedonia. The 360° view from the monument across the Pčinja plain is the reason why this point was such a strategic location for occupying armies. There is no signage leading you to the monument, but you can get there by turning south off the E871 at a large white house almost 4km after the start of the E871. Turn left past the house for 1km and take the first right. This road leads straight to the monument.

Forgotten in the delta of the River Kriva near the village of Konjuh (best accessed by 4x4 or a 6km hike) are an ancient cave village and a **Roman rotunda** from the 6th century. The place makes for an interesting half day out and, unlike Kokino observatory, there are lots of obvious manmade rooms, waterholes, stairs and windows. To get there continue another 15.1km on Highway 2 (E871) beyond the exit to Prohor Pčinski to grid 8024 6729 where a dirt-track road heads south. At 4.8km, just after the tunnel under the yet-to-be-constructed railway, take the turning to the south across the Pčinski River. The rock formation on the left after the river is the cave settlement (grid 8016 6211). The rotunda, barely visible, is another 100m to the southwest, and the old Church of Sv George is 200m to the southeast of the settlement.

There are probably 100 more Roman ruins in this valley, which was a route linking Skupi to Kustendil. In August 2003, a **Roman amphitheatre** was unearthed near the village of Klečevce. The **Kumanovo Hot Springs**, also popular in Roman times, are near the village of Proevce, 4km southeast of Kumanovo. There is a small outdoor pool heated by thermal waters. Entry is 50MKD.

KRIVA PALANKA

Kriva Palanka is now most famous for the 12th-century monastery dedicated to **Sv Joakim Osogovski** 3km to the east of the town. The town is named after the river it straddles, the Kriva, which is the Slavic translation of the name first given to the town when it was founded by the Ottomans in 1633. Then it was called Egri Dere, meaning 'Winding River'. The town was originally built as an important stronghold for the Ottomans on the road from Üsküb to Istanbul, but despite its supposed impregnability, it was taken by Karpoš (later given the title of King of Kumanovo, see box, page 11) during the Karpoš Uprising of 1689. When Karpoš and his men were captured and beheaded six weeks later, the town returned to Ottoman rule.

GETTING THERE AND AWAY The new bus station (✆ *031 375 033*) is north of the centre of town behind the police station. There are 11 buses a day from Skopje to Kriva Palanka for 220MKD, starting at 06.00 until the last bus at 18.30. Buses to Skopje via Kumanovo leave at 06.00, 07.00, 08.00, 09.30, 11.10, 13.00, 14.00, 15.30, 16.00 and 17.00. Buses to Strumica via Kratovo, Probištip and Štip leave on Monday, Wednesday and Friday at 05.30.

⌂ WHERE TO STAY AND EAT

⌂ **Monastir Sveti Joakim Osogovski** (100 beds) 3km northwest of Kriva Palanka; ✆ 031 375 063–5. By far & away the best place to stay in the vicinity. The monastery is well frequented & often full, so book a few days ahead during the day as monastery life closes down after evening prayers. Ask to speak to the innkeeper, Velin, as he deals with all the bookings. Sister Igoumina, who answers the phone in his frequent absence, can only defer to him on questions of bookings. You will need to register yourself at the local police station at the bottom of the hill soon after your arrival at the monastery. There is no food available so bring your own, but there are indoor kitchens, an outdoor grill & a small shop/café that sells a few soft drinks, tea & coffee. The monastery is popular with locals as a site for Sunday b/fast before church. Macedonian music from a ghetto blaster may accompany b/fast as well as the evening meal, so don't count on your stay there always being tranquil. Often, however, due reverence to the sanctity of the courtyards is observed, & you'll also see people playing a quiet board game to watch the evening sunset by. ⑀

⌂ **Hotel Turist** (30 rooms) Maršal Tito bb; ✆ 031 375 209. Classic dilapidated socialist tourism right in the centre of town. Definitely a rip-off & not even a TV in the room although it is en suite. ⑀

WHAT TO SEE AND DO

Sveti Joakim Osogovski The Monastery of Sv Joakim Osogovski probably takes number one position as the most visited monastery in Macedonia. The location was first sought out as a monastery during the middle of the 12th century, and now houses two churches, the older one dedicated to the Virgin Mary (Sv Bogorodica), and the new church of the mid 19th century is dedicated to Sv Joakim Osogovski himself (see box, page 261).

The monastery was founded in the middle of the 12th century by the priest Teodor from Ovče Polje who decided to dedicate his life to God at this spot after the death of his wife. Located on a major thoroughfare to Constantinople (*Carigrad*, Town of the Tsar, in Macedonian) the monastery was frequented and honoured by Muslims as well as Christians. In 1585 the *bey* of Kriva Palanka received permission to renovate the dilapidated buildings. The old church was first converted into a mosque and then later a church. Some of the original 12th-century walls and 14th-century frescoes still exist, although most of the church is now being completely re-frescoed.

During the Austro–Ottoman War, led in Serbia and Macedonia by General Piccolomini in 1690, the monastery buildings and original church suffered extensive damage, and the Ottomans even ordered it to be destroyed as a punishment against local Macedonians who had sided with the Austrian general. Legend claims that on arrival at the monastery, the Ottomans were so overpowered by its spiritual force that they turned back leaving the buildings

KRIVA PALANKA

Monastery
Sv Joakim
Osogovski 1 km

Border crossing
Deve Bair

Outdoor
pool

MARŠAL TITO

Kriva

KP BALTAŠA

PARTIZANSKI

Domački Dol

II OKTOMVRI

Duračka

NIKOLA TESLA

Police
station

VARDAR

MOŠA PIJADE

MARŠAL TITO

HEROJ KARPOŠ

MAKEDONSKA

Turist

B KIDRIČ

IVANOVSKI

ORCE NIKOLOV

HEROJ KARPOŠ

EDINSTVO

GOCE DELČEV

17 MAKEDONSKA BRIGADA

DR I TAMBURKOV

MARŠAL TITO

Puškarska
Maala

Kumanovo,
Skopje

N

Bradt

500m
500yds

0
0

undamaged. One of them, however, had taken a bone out of the tomb of Sv Joakim Osogovski, which proceeded to make the thief more nauseous the further he took it from the monastery. The thief soon realised that, for his own well-being, he needed to take the bone back to its rightful resting place, and so he returned it. The sultan was so overwhelmed by this account when he heard it that he ordered a protective marker of stone to be delivered to the monastery, which would signify to all Ottomans, Turks and Muslims that this monastery was not to be harmed in any way. The stone still stands on the wall near the new church, to the right as you enter the exonarthex, and is usually blessed by the residing Turkish ambassador to Macedonia at least once during his term in office.

The new church is an intricate complex with 12 cupolas in the main nave, two further naves and an exonarthex on two sides of the church. The 12 cupolas represent the 12 apostles, one for each containing a fresco of the apostle, and the remainder of the main nave is brimming with well-kept frescoes. Frescoes of the four brothers (see box, page 267) can be found, as well as of the church donors, and on the outside wall to the right of the main entrance are some interesting frescoes of hell and Satan. In the base of the belfry, on the western side of the new church, is the ossuary of the senior monks and priests.

Near the monastery is an ancient milk pipeline, which used to transport milk from the surrounding mountains to the monastery dairy. The pipe is no longer used, and Pop Dobri, the father of the monastery, requests that visitors refrain from visiting it as the pipeline requires some renovation to prevent further damage by careless visitors. Pop Dobri is happy to talk to visitors about the monastery although he can't always be found there as he lives in Kriva Palanka. The only monastic inhabitant is Sister Igoumina.

During the summer, the monastery holds a young artists' convention, usually in late July or early August. The church's saints' days are on 28 August, dedicated to Sv Bogorodica (the Virgin Mary), and 29 August dedicated to Sv Joakim, when the monastery is visited by several thousand visitors who come to pay their respects. Their generous offerings have allowed almost €5 million to be invested in the church since the revival of monastic life in Macedonia in 1995.

Osogovski mountain range Starting from the entrance to the monastery is the hiking path up to **Mount Carev** (2,084m). It is the highest point in this range completely in Macedonia, and has an excellent all-round view at the summit. An almost 20km hike from the monastery, it is not to be attempted in a single day, and even in two days only by the fit. For the less fit with a 4x4 the last turning before the Bulgarian border, towards Toranica village, turns into a fair-weather dirt track which comes to within 6km of the summit and then makes its way back down the other side of the mountain via the **Sasa Zinc Mine** and onto Highway 27 at Lake Kalimansko. The same road also comes within 4km of **Mount Ruen** (2,252m) on the border with Bulgaria. The road takes you above the treeline so the views of the surrounding mountains and into Bulgaria are extensive. It is a popular place for wild berry pickers in the summer.

If you do take this road, you may need to present identification to the mine wardens at either Toranica or Sasa where the road is gated. From Toranica gates, make sure you turn off left onto the dirt track (unsignposted) after almost 3km, just before an old building on the left and a white building on the right. For those with GPS, this is at grid 2290 7039. Do not continue on the tarmac until it becomes dirt road as this simply takes you into a logging maze. The dirt track becomes tarmac 1km before Sasa mineworks.

Midway between the start of the E871 (Highway 2) at Kumanovo and Kriva Palanka is the turn-off for Kratovo and Probištip, which joins Highway 2 to Highway 27. On this road, deep in the belly of an ancient and burnt-out volcanic crater, is the small village of Kratovo. Nearby are Stone Age observatories at Cocev Kamen and Kokino, cave dwellings at Konjuh, volcanic droplets from the volcano that once was, and the place is littered with Stone Age rock art.

In Roman times this mining town was known as Kratiskara, meaning crater, and variations of its name, Koriton and Koritos in Byzantine times, have centred around this meaning. The crater-like hollow of the village has demanded high-arched bridges to cross the river and ingenious architecture to scale the steep ravine. The difficulty of getting to Kratovo has also left the town relatively free of communist concrete. Six defensive towers hark back to the time of King Karpoš.

GETTING THERE There are four buses a day from Skopje to Kratovo at 07.30, 13.00, 15.30 and 17.30. Monday, Wednesday and Friday there is also a bus at 05.30 from Kriva Palanka on its way to Probištip, Štip and Strumica.

WHERE TO STAY AND EAT Kratovo has only one hotel, the **Kratis** (*25 rooms; Gorni Salaj bb;* \ *031 481 201*), which is another state-run rip-off at 900MKD per person including breakfast. Much nicer accommodation is available outside Kočani. Eating establishments line the village square and along Ulica Partizanska. The Kratovo version of *pastrmajlija* is *pastrmajka; mantijas* (small square meat pasties) and *mezelek* (offal casserole) are also special Kratovo dishes. You can taste these at the restaurants **Kanu** with its typical old town architecture, **Alexandria** and **Solun**. The **Café Amor** at the top end of Partizanska outside the last tower up the river has a pleasant atmosphere and good music.

WHAT TO SEE AND DO The River Tabačka runs deep at the bottom of the crater and four of the stone bridges across the river, named Radin, Johčiski, Caršiski and Krajniot, date from the early Ottoman period. Unfortunately, the first and most obscure of these bridges, the Radin, was destroyed and, although it has been repaired, it is not in its original likeness. Near the Radin bridge is the old Turkish

---

TOWERS WITHOUT STAIRS

Originally there were 12 towers in Kratovo, but now only six remain. The last to be damaged in 1929, the Hadži Kostova tower, was rebuilt in 1957. The remaining towers, Saat (meaning 'clock'), Simitčeva, Krsteva, Emin-beg and Zlatkovičeva, have stood the test of time well, and it is unfortunate that they are not kept in good repair and open regularly to the public. If you ask near one of the towers, one of the villagers might be able to get hold of the keys to the towers and let you in.

Now they are mostly abandoned although a couple are still used for storage. If you manage to get a look inside you will see that they all have wooden stairs going up to the higher floors. The towers originally had no stairs at all, following an architectural trait also seen in similar defensive towers in the Caucasus, so that access to higher levels was only by ladder. If enemy forces attacked the town, then villagers could hide in the upper levels of the tower and drag the ladder up with them. If the enemy succeeded in blowing the floor of a lower level then the villagers could again ascend to a higher level, from which they would normally defend themselves by throwing projectiles, using weapons or pouring hot oil.

amam (public baths) and the clock tower. The town museum is in the former inn Saraj, close to the old Ottoman prison.

The **bey's house**, on the lower side of town between the bottom two bridges, has been renovated in recent years but is rarely open to the public. There are six defensive **stone towers** (see box, page 265) that were used in Ottoman times by the local mine owners to store iron ore. Each of the towers is connected by underground **tunnels**, and it is possible to view these if you take a paid tour (enquire at the Rock Art Centre below). It was the miners of Kratovo who first rallied to Karpoš's call in 1689 (see box, page 11) when he went to fight on the side of the Austrians against the Ottomans.

The Kratovo **Rock Art Centre** at Planinski 1 (✆ *031 481 572;* e *lcfrockart@ yahoo.com* or *stevcedonevkratovo@yahoo.com; www.rockart.50webs.com/index-en.html;* ☉ *Mon–Sat 08.00–20.00, Sun 09.00–16.00*) explains the rock art to be found in the area (see below) and sells replicas and other associated items.

OUTSIDE KRATOVO

GORNI KRATOVO There is a lovely hike from the centre of Kratovo up the River Kratovska to the old village of Gorni Kratovo. The 4km hike takes about 90 minutes, and the babbling stream used to host a number of working water mills. The top of this route is littered with rock art, possibly dating back to the Iron Age, and large volcanic droplets wedged in the mud from when Kratovo was an active volcano. Look in at the Rock Art Centre (see above) before you go, to check what you are trying to spy among the undergrowth.

COCEV KAMEN Some 15km directly east of Kratovo (grid 8211 6044 on map 682-4-4 (Pezovo)) is Cocev Kamen, a Palaeolithic (early Stone Age, some 12,000 years ago) sacrificial megalithic observatory. Unlike Kokino (page 260) there are still megaliths scattered around the site, and there are very obvious signs of human use, including hewn steps, an amphitheatre, sacrificial chamber, constructed entry path, as well as the necessary seat or throne from which to divine star charts, sun and moon movements, and time of year. The site is possibly the oldest in the Balkans and had been used over many centuries. It too has rock art possibly from the Iron Age and currently the only find of a painting of a human figure on rock in Macedonia. Some say the site is on a par with Stonehenge in the UK.

The site is currently free to visit and has several panel boards explaining about the site in English and in Macedonian.

To get there take the road towards Kratovo from the north. At the village of Fab (grid 9368 6049), 5km before Kratovo, turn south towards Sekulica and Šopsko Rudare. Follow the main road southwest for 10km until the village of Novakovci (grid 8769 5632). At the T-junction in the village, take the road north following a northwesterly direction for another 9km (towards the villages of Donja Maala and Gornja Maala and Konjuh) until you reach a crossroads (grid 8309 6057), 5.5km before Konjuh village. At the crossroads, turn southwest for 1.8km to the hamlet of Šopsko Rudare. At the crossroads here turn north for 0.5km to the village of Cocevi, after which the road becomes a dirt track continuing north towards Cocev Kamen for 0.3km before heading off west-northwest. It's a 300m walk from the dirt track to Cocev Kamen, which is an obvious rock formation 0.6km directly north of the village of Cocevi.

MONASTERY OF SVETI GAVRIL LESNOVSKI To the south just above the village of Lesnovo is the **Monastery of Sv Gavril Lesnovski**, built in 1341 by the feudal lord Tyrant Oliver. The monastery is one of only three to contain an iconostasis by the famous woodcarvers Makarije Frčkovksi and the brothers Filipovski (the other two are in the monasteries of Sv Jovan Bigorski near Debar, and the church of Sv Spas in Skopje; a fourth in Kruševo was burnt down after the Ilinden Uprising). The church stands on the foundations of an earlier 11th-century church, whose mosaic floor is still the floor of the present church, and contains many interesting frescoes from the time it was built. The donor fresco of Tyrant Oliver holding the church is still in good condition to the left in front of the chancel, and frescoes of King Dušan, his wife and Tsar Uroš can be found on the left wall of the narthex above the baptism basin. Unfortunately, the fresco of Tsar Uroš has practically been lost. To the right on the ceiling of the narthex are frescoes of the sun and the moon and 12 animals or people seen in the night sky. Despite their amazing likeness to the zodiac signs, the friar will tell you that these are not designed to depict them.

A strict dress code is adhered to in the monastery: men must wear long trousers and women must wear ankle-length skirts. Spare clothing is provided at the door if you forget to bring such items with you.

To get there, head for Drenovo and ask there for the turning for Lesnovo. The Lesnovo road winds up the mountain and at a fork in the asphalt road follow the road to the right going up to get to the monastery rather than down to the village of Lesnovo. This road takes you past some interesting rock outcrops and the entrances to some old rock mines where millstones used to be cut. With a torch you can see where half-hewn millstones are still visible in the rock.

STONE DOLLS Halfway back to Highway 2 from Kratovo are the *kukla* or stone doll natural rock formations near the village of Kuklica. Formed from the weathering of porous volcanic rock, large stones teeter on top of tall columns and create imaginary animals and human forms in the rock. Several hundred stone figures are scattered over three sites. Legend says the figures are the result of a petrified wedding: once upon a time a young man from the village of Kuklica decided to marry both his sweetheart from Upper Kuklica as well as his sweetheart from Lower Kuklica. On the day of the wedding, when the brides saw each other, one was so jealous that she cursed the entire wedding party, turning them to stone. There is an obvious pair of stone dolls at the site, who do look indeed as if they might be going through a wedding ceremony.

At the halfway point between Kratovo and the E871 highway (about 10km either way) are two bridges that cross the River Tabačka before it empties into the River Kriva. At the southerly end of the northern bridge (grid 8984 6322) is a turn-off to the west. Turn immediately left on the dirt track and keep going past

THE BROTHERS OSOGOVSKI, PČINSKI, LESNOVSKI AND RILSKI

Sketchy details going back to the 10th and 11th centuries claim that the four brothers Joakim Osogovski, Prohor Pčinski, Gavril Lesnovksi and Jovan Rilski were amongst God's most dedicated monks. In order to serve God better, they all decided to follow a hermit's life and so they went the four directions of the compass, to found the monasteries named after each of them. Today, the beautifully painted Rilski Monastery is in Bulgaria, the Pčinski Monastery is in Serbia just over the border from Kumanovo, the Lesnovski Monastery containing the third iconostasis of Frčkovski and the Filipovski brothers is in the village of Lesnovo near Probištip (see page 266), and Osogovski Monastery is near Kriva Palanka.

Although the four are said to have been brothers, historical data show that Rilski lived at least a century earlier than the others.

a bridge on your right (do not cross the bridge) until you get to a fork in the road and turn right. Follow this road along the river valley until you get to a stone factory where a right turn will take you across a bridge. Turn left once over the bridge and in less than 1km you will see the stone formations to your right (grid 870 628).

SVETI NIKOLE

This small town lies on top of a hill in the middle of the fertile Ovče Pole plain. Known as the 'sheep fields' the plain has been inhabited since Neolithic times and remains have been found in the vicinity of the town, mostly around the villages of **Amzibegovo** to the south of Sveti Nikole, and **Gorobinci** to the northwest on the road back to Skopje. Sveti Nikole takes its name after the church built by Serbian king Milutin in 1313. The church stands prominently on top of the hill and can be seen on the approach to the town. It is enclosed within the monastery grounds, which are often closed, so ask in the town for the key if you would like to have a look in.

11

The Southern Wine Region

We wound our way up the mountains, past horses and carts, through a village and on to the top where we found the monastery of Veljuša with its jewel of a tiny thirteenth-century church whose foundations were seven centuries older. It stood, remarkable and unlikely as a Tardis, between a dark-furrowed vegetable patch and some recently refurbished but already tatty monastery buildings.

Why Angels Fall, Victoria Clark, 2000

The rich Tikveš plain running from Veles along the River Vardar to Demir Kapija is renowned for its wines. Kavadarci is the **wine capital** where Macedonia's biggest vineyard, Tikveš Wines, is based. Demir Kapija is home to the old royal Yugoslav winery Elenov, as well as the newest and most imposing winery Popova Kula. The climate is mild, the area being only 45m above sea level at the lowest point of the River Vardar at Gevgelija border town. Although Macedonian wines are little known, they easily rival better-known wines from the Balkans. Vineyard visits and wine tastings are a great way to get to know Macedonia's wines.

The south of Macedonia was well populated by the Romans so there are lots of Roman remains, including the town of **Stobi** on the crossroads of the Axios and Diagonal ways, and the best-preserved **Roman baths** at Bansko. There are also waterfalls at Smolari and Kolešino, a tectonic lake at **Dojran**, rock climbing at the **Iron Gate** and throughout the region you'll find the usual assortment of monasteries, good hiking and pleasant swimming holes. From Dojran, through Gevgelija, and along the entire southern border, lay the **Saloniki Front of World War I**. A new dedication to the fallen of 22 Division (UK) at Devil's Eye commemorates the 90th anniversary of the end of World War I. A good town to stay at to explore the region further is **Strumica**.

STRUMICA

Between the Belasica and Ogražden mountain ranges is the town of Strumica. It lies in a little-visited area that is teeming with history, sites and natural beauty. The town itself is one of the oldest in Macedonia to have remained in its original location and not be moved by earthquake or ransacked by marauding invaders. Neolithic remains have been found on the hill above the town, and a fortress has existed there since at least the 4th century AD. Archaeological excavation there continues and is well worth a visit.

Strumica is commonly thought to be the site of the ancient city of Doberos, mentioned by Thucydides in the 5th century BC in his tales of the exploits of King Sitalces, an ally of the Athenians in the Peloponnesian War against the Paeonians and Macedonians. Later in the 2nd century BC, the town came under the name Astraion, meaning 'City of Stars' and named after the Astrai tribe of the Strumica Valley. In Roman times the town was called Tiveriopolis after its first

Roman patron, Tiberius Claudius Menon. The arrival of Slavic tribes in the 7th century gave the town its current name.

In 1902, Strumica hit world headlines when America's first international hostage incident ended with the missionary Ellen Stone walking into town (see text box, below). Later, she discovered that she had been held for some of her captivity in a house in Nivičino village, just north of Strumica. The starry night sky above the valley is, of course, still visible today, although from Strumica's fashionable pedestrian area the only bright lights to be seen are those of the café bars.

AN AMERICAN HOSTAGE FREES MACEDONIA

In 1878, the Treaty of Berlin returned Macedonia to Ottoman control, thus dividing what had become Bulgaria under the Treaty of Stefano earlier that year. The people of Bulgaria tried, without success, to reunite, and many from Macedonia fled north of the border to the free municipality of Bulgaria. There they formed the Supreme Committee, with the explicit aim of reuniting the former 'Greater Bulgaria'.

Within Macedonia, a faction of the Supreme Committee was established named the Internal Macedonian Revolutionary Organisation (today's VMRO). The poorer sibling of the Supreme Committee, it settled for the more practical aim of Macedonian independence rather than re-unification with Bulgaria, as re-unification clearly did not appeal to the Great Powers at the time. Money and munitions for this 'lesser' aim was not forthcoming from the Supreme Committee, however, and so in 1901, the VMRO drew up a number of plans to 'raise' funds.

The idea to kidnap Miss Ellen Stone, an American missionary working in Bankso (in today's Bulgaria) came from Jane Sandanski (many streets in Macedonia are named after him). Although the local Bansko VMRO committee eventually bought into the idea, the top VMRO leadership, including Goce Delčev, did not. Sandanski went ahead nevertheless.

The act of the kidnap itself on 3 September 1901 went ahead relatively smoothly, with nobody hurt. Sandanski was not to know at the time though, that Mrs Katerina Tsilka, taken along with Miss Stone to act as chaperone in regard to Victorian values, was pregnant with her second child.

It took five months of negotiation for the original sum of US$110,000 to be whittled down to US$63,000, raised from the American public through a huge nationwide campaign, and for the 210lb of gold bricks to be smuggled past Turkish and Bulgarian officials into the hands of the revolutionaries. In the meantime, baby Elenchie was born on 4 January 1902 in a hut near the village of Troskovo (today in Bulgaria, some 30kms northeast of Berovo). After the money was 'deposited', it took another three weeks of traipsing through the mountains before Miss Stone, Mrs Tsilka, and baby Elenchie were finally left by the revolutionaries outside Strumica.

America's first modern hostage crisis had all the hallmarks of modern-day diplomacy, intelligence conundrums, public relations scandals, the terrorist versus the freedom fighter, personal advancement in the halls of power, escape and evasion. Reaching the desk of the US president Theodore Roosevelt, there was no question of setting a dangerous precedent by paying the kidnappers from state or federal funds, but every diplomatic means, including the implied threat of US warships to the Black Sea, was applied. Teresa Carpenter's excellent book, The Miss Stone Affair, delves into all these angles and sets the incident out in a page-turner worth reading of its own accord.

In the end, the money helped to fuel the Ilinden Uprising of 2 August 1903 (see page 14). But it was almost another 90 years before VMRO's dream of an independent Macedonia finally came to fruition.

Skopje (via Štip)	03.30, 05.00, 06.30, 08.30, 09.30, 11.30, 13.30, 15.00, 16.00, 18.00 (400MKD)
Ohrid, Resen, Bitola, Prilep	06.00, 17.00 (350–500MKD)
Gevgelija	08.00, 10.00, 15.00, 17.00 (150MKD)
Dojran (summertime only)	08.00, 10.00 (150MKD)

GETTING THERE AND AWAY Strumica is served by buses from all over the country. The new bus station (↘ *034 346 030*) is on Ulica Kliment Ohridski on the north side of town. See timetable above.

TOUR OPERATORS

Atlantis Dimitar Vlahov 18; ↘ 034 346 212; f 034 347 212; e strumica@atlantismk.com; www.come2macedonia.mk. Helpful friendly staff. Informative map of Strumica & the local region available.

Salonika Battlefield Tours ↘ 070 364 318; e director@salonikabattlefieldtour.com; www.salonikabattlefieldtour.com. Provides knowledgeable English-speaking guides who, for about €100 a day, can take you around the extensive battlefield, conduct research, provide mapping & photos, arrange cemetery visits, & book your accommodation & food. Director Romeo Drobarov is a former border policeman from the area & is well informed & very helpful.

WHERE TO STAY

🏠 **Sirius** (71 rooms) Ulica Maršal Tito, near Kukliš on the Valandovo exit out of town (or left at the 1st traffic lights if you are coming from Berovo direction); ↘ 034 345 141; f 034 335 077; e sirius@mt.net.mk; www.hotel-sirius.com.mk. The best hotel Strumica has to offer, although a short taxi ride from the centre. Wi-Fi, tennis courts & a very clean outdoor swimming pool, as well as a restaurant. Nestled right against the Belasica foothills it is in a lovely setting. 5-bed dorms available. $$$

🏠 **Hotel 404** (11 rooms) Blagaj Jankov Mučeto; ↘ 034 345 404; e hotel404@hotmail.com; www.hotel404.mk. Opened in 2009, this tiny hotel at the foot of the old town is good value & has Wi-Fi in all rooms. $$

🏠 **Ilinden** (26 rooms) Balkanska bb; ↘ 034 340 010–11. Located near the old town, this well-kept hotel offers all the mod cons & Wi-Fi in your room. $$

🏠 **Tiveriopol** (40 rooms) Bratstvo i Edinstva 20; ↘ 034 340 421–2. Centrally located but in a quiet backstreet, this Macedonian-standard hotel is showing signs of wear & tear despite recent refurbishment. Wi-Fi; friendly staff. Nearby is Beauty Spa Centre Tina (↘ 034 328 787) offering massage, beauty treatments & a spa jet pod. All treatments less than 700MKD. $$

🏠 **Tsar Samoil Hotel & Hot Springs** (165 beds) Bansko village; ↘ 034 377 210. Lodging at the hotel gives free access to the indoor pool, which is naturally heated by thermal waters, but the hot springs can be accessed only with a doctor's prescription. This is a classic former Yugoslav dilapidated facility. Entry to the pool for non-lodgers is 60MKD. 300MKD for a taxi into Strumica. $

✗ WHERE TO EAT The main area to eat or go out for a drink in Strumica is Ulica Josif Josifovski leading into the old town and in Global Gradski Pazar (shopping centre). Ulica Blagoj Jankov Mučeto leading to the park comes alive in summer evenings with stalls selling food and knick-knacks and teenagers strutting their stuff on the way to the park.

✗ **Loven Dom** Neretva bb; ↘ 034 345 206; ⊕ daily 11.00–23.00 in summer only. Unrivalled view of the town, with average food for the price. $$$$

✗ **Maredo** Mito Hadživasilev Jasmin 111; ↘ 034 326 618; ⊕ Sun–Thu 11.00–24.00, Fri & Sat 11.00–01.00. Local atmosphere, local food. Although

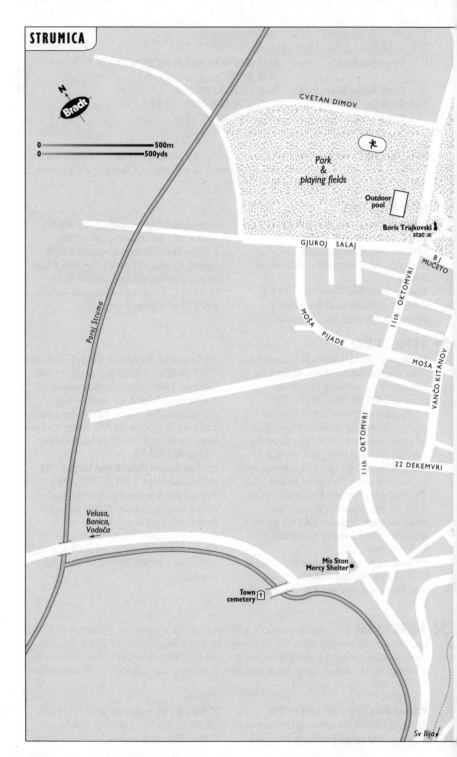

STRUMICA

N

Bradt

0 — 500m
0 — 500yds

CVETAN DIMOV

Park
&
playing fields

Outdoor
pool

Boris Trajkovski
statue

GJUROJ SALAJ

B J
MUCETO

11th OKTOMVRI

MOŠA PIJADE

MOŠA

VANČO KITANOV

11th OKTOMVRI

22 DEKEMVRI

Poroj Struma

Velusa,
Banica,
Vodoča

Mis Ston
Mercy Shelter

Town
cemetery

Sv Ilija

KLIMENT OHRIDSKI

Hotel Sirius,
Valandovo,
Dojran

Bansko,
Smolare,
Monospitovo,
Berevo

Pilikatnik
restaurant

JANKO CVETINOV

MITO HADŽIVASILEV JASMIN

LENINOVA

Gradski
Park

Srbakov

Maredo

BD GOCE DELČEV

24hr baker

Bonita

24 OKTOMVRI

Prince

BRATSTVO I EDINSTVA

Arkada

Dion

Extreme

B J MUČETO

LENINOVA

Letnica

Global
Gradski Pazar

Tiveriopol

PIJADE

BD MARŠAL TITO

BALKANSKA

Ilinden

Cultural Centre
Anton Panov

Goce Delčev
statue

Biser

Dalfufo

Centar

JOSIFOVSKI

Hotel 404

MARŠAL TITO

MARŠAL TITO

MARŠAL
TITO

Select

Park

DIMITAR

M & M

Town hall

Atlantis
Travel Agency

B J MUČETO

GJAKOVIKJ

Methodist
church

Police
station

CVETOZAR MARKOVIKJ

VLAHOV

OHRIDSKI

KOČO

RACIN

HEROI

GJURO

KARPOŠ

Orta Džamija
(ruin)

Museum of
Strumica

TOŠO ARSOV

REPUBLIKA

STIV NAUMOV

KIRIL

Sv Kiril i Metodi

KIRIL

5 NOEMVRI

5 NOEMVRI

NIKOLA

KARAEV

Maršal Tito
School

PARTIZANSKI

METODI

Loven Dom

NERETVA

KRUŠEVSKA

Hadžitosevi
House

Carevi Kuli

Sv Kozman
i Damjan

Sv Petnaeset
Tiveriopolski
Sveštenomačnici

a little out of town, it is run by the former chef of President Trajkovski, & the standard of food is high. Excellent lamb chops & their cordon bleu (*Gordomble*) are cheese wrapped in several layers of delicious ham, coated in breadcrumbs & deep fried. **$$$**

✘ **Dalfufo** Ploštad Maršal Tito 10; ☎ 034 326 112; ⊕ Sun–Thu 11.00–24.00, Fri & Sat 11.00–01.00. Behind Goce Delčev's statue: pizzas & pastas just like in Skopje. **$$$**

✘ **M & M** Josif Josifovski bb; ⊕ Sun–Thu 10.00–24.00, Fri & Sat 09.00–01.00. Only restaurant that has free internet wireless access. Dark upstairs, but a light sunny lounger downstairs. Some specialities like the chicken medallions or the *fefer* steak are great. **$$**

✘ **Pilikatnik** Boro Pockov bb; ☎ 034 331 926; ⊕ Sun–Thu 11.00–24.00, Fri & Sat 11.00–01.00. Excellent fish & fish *chorba*, but a little out of town to the southeast. **$$**

✘ **Bonita, Elizabet & Dion** pizzerias on the edge of the park are open long hours & are popular hangouts in the summer. **$$**

✘ **Letniza** Leninova bb; ☎ 034 344 072; ⊕ daily 11.00–23.00. Cheap cafeteria meals if you need a quick bite. **$**

✘ **Biser** Ploštad Maršal Tito bb. Under Goce Delčev statue, follow the marble steps to an underground found-court like place. Best *bourek* in town & also serves *boze*. Their ice cream is gelatto homemade & a great summertime treat. **$**

✘ **Srbakov** Janko Cvetinov bb; ☎ 034 327 585; ⊕ Sun–Thu 11.00–24.00, Fri & Sat 11.00–01.00. Serves the best *čorba* in town. Near the old market *Shukadum*, which sells food everyday except Sat when it sells clothes. **$**

✘ **Centar** Maršal Tito 72; ☎ 034 328 425; ⊕ daily 11.00–23.00. Good for *čevapi* as well as for enjoying the Stara Čaršija old main street. **$**

CAFÉS AND NIGHTCLUBS

⊑ **Select** Josif Josifovksi. The most popular café in the old town.

⊑ **City** Global Gradski Pazar. The most popular café on the 1st-floor entrance of Global.

⊑ **Inside** Global Gradski Pazar. Midway along the 1st floor of Global. The café spills out into the middle of the shopping centre where it is a quiet refuge for those wanting an actual conversation.

♀ **Extreme** Midway towards the park, is always lively in the summer.

The bars Pepe and Shaban in Dabile village are open from midnight to dawn for those who need to party all night to Balkan turbo-folk music.

WHAT TO SEE AND DO Strumica is a charming little town in itself and there are a whole host of things in the vicinity to keep you occupied for a good couple of weeks. The old town does not take long to get around and leads up to the restored **Loven Dom** (hunter's lodge – now a swish town-style restaurant more than a rural inn) boasting the best view over the town, for which the steep climb is also worth an expensive coffee. On the way up, Kiril i Metodi Street passes the **Church of Sv Kiril i Metodi**, completed in 1912; Maršal Tito school, built in the early 1900s; the disused court building; and the beautiful **old house of the Hadzitosevi family**, which is in dire need of preservation.

The **Museum of Strumica** (*27th Mart 2;* ☎ *034 345 925*) is a smart new building, housing a very manageable collection of prehistoric, ancient, medieval, Ottoman period and early 20th century artefacts gathered from around Strumica. Unique to Strumica is an early 20th-century printing press; and an exhibition dedicated to America's first international hostage incident, the Miss Stone case (see box, page 270). Among the photos of the incident is one of the house in the village of Nezilovo, north of Strumica, where she was held for a while. To get to the museum from Kiril i Metodi Street, take the steps leading down to 27th Mart Street. The museum ethnologist, Ilijas, is proud to use his English and will give you a quick tour around.

The heart of Strumica is dominated by a larger-than-life-size **statue of Goce Delčev** for his part played in the Ilinden Uprising in 1903 against the Ottomans.

To the north is the pedestrian street dedicated to the Strumica hero Blagoj Jankov Mučeto leading to the well-kept **Gradski Park** with its stadium and outdoor public pool, Aquarius. The park also has a bust of the late President Trajkovski, who was born in Strumica and died in a plane crash in 2004 over Bosnia.

From the southern end of Blagoj Jankov Mučeto is **Ulica Maršal Tito** (as opposed to the main boulevard further north) running east–west. This was the old high street and is picturesquely lined with buildings from the early 20th century. Like a miniature Širok Sokak in Bitola, people come to Maršal Tito Street to shop and meander. At the east end is the imposing **town hall** overlooking the **Mal**

TURKS UNRECOGNISED   *KUD Kardešlik*

In the Strumica region, an ethnic Turkish population goes about its business, working as farmers or field labourers, wood cutters, manual labourers, and whatever it takes to pay the bills. Their work is largely seasonal, with fathers and mothers working and living in shelters several hours from home in order to save enough money to send their children to school in the autumn, and to pay for firewood for the ensuing winter. Although some estimates place the Turkish population in Strumica at approximately 8,500 to 9,000, they are mostly unrecognised within Macedonia, and are mistakenly confused with the Roma population, which itself may be an additional 5,000 in Strumica. (However, statistical information is difficult to come by, hence there is room for disagreement.) The Turkish dialect here is known as Balkan Turkish, and while understood by the Turkish in Turkey, is comparable to the differences between French proper, and the French spoken in Canada, or the Spanish spoken in Spain, and that of South America.

Here in the Strumica area, inter-ethnic marriage between the Roma and Turkish does occur more frequently than in Skopje, although it is certainly not widespread. Turkish and Roma children are educated in the same classrooms in the Turkish language by Turkish teachers in the primary schools, grades levels 1–4. Many ethnic Macedonians do not know the linguistic or cultural differences between the two ethnicities, and use skin colour as a rough – though highly inaccurate – proxy to determine ethnicity. These factors make it difficult for foreigners, and Macedonians, to understand the full cultural richness, complexity and awesomeness of a sleepy agricultural city such as Strumica.

There is no doubt that these Turks love all things Turkish: Atatürk, the Children's Day (a *bayram* celebrated only amongst the Turkish both within Turkey and among the Turkish diaspora), *meze* platters of food, colourful headscarves, and, of course, Turkish folklore dances. Within the past several years, festivals have been increasingly organised around traditional folklore dancing, attracting both ethnic Turks and a broad international audience. For example, the Day of Spring Festival is celebrated annually for a few days around 6 May (the holiday of Gurgovden) in the small village of Čalikli. Here, dancers and performers from all ethnicities (Bosnian, Azerbaijan Greek, Albanian, Turkish from Turkey, Turkish from Macedonia, Kosovo, etc) dance and perform their unique dances that are peculiar to each particular city and ethnicity. Though the ethnic Turks have little, their love of music, dance, and tradition allow for a spectacular sight to behold.

To learn more about the ethnic Turks, their lives, customs and culture, or how you can help send Turkish and Roma children to school, visit KUD Kardešlik's website (*www.kudkardeslik.wordpress.com*).

KUD Kardešlik, of Strumica, is a cultural NGO that also provides educational, health, and social services to the ethnic Turks and Roma in Macedonia.

Gradski Park. Mal Park café is a relaxing place to stop in the shade and mull over the day.

On Stiv Naumov Street is the abandoned **Orta Džamija**. A national monument itself, it is plain on the inside, and is not the main point of interest here. Rather it is the **11th century church** underneath that is of current archaeological importance. Although little is known about the true significance of the church, its size indicates a certain importance for the region, especially coupled with the medieval Carevi Kuli (see below) and what is likely to have been a sizeable medieval walled town at the time. The necropolis complete with skeletons is still being excavated, and some of the findings from the church are housed in the Strumica Museum.

In the very poor Turkish part of town (sadly with little Turkish architecture) is the **Church of Sv Petnaeset Tiveriopolski Sveštenomačnici** (*Holy 15 Martyrs of Tiveriopol; Ul Slavčo Stojmenski bb*). This is where 15 Christians, who fled from Nicea (now Iznik in today's Turkey) during the persecution of Christians in the mid 4th century, are buried. Much of the lower half of the church has been uncovered, including 16 vaults, and some large mosaics, all of which can be seen. Underneath the new church, built to one side in the last century, is the icon gallery (⊕ *Tue–Sun 10.00–19.00; entry 100MKD*) housing some 50 icons ranging from the medieval period to the late 19th century.

On the top of the hill overlooking the town are the **Carevi Kuli** (Tsar's Towers) of **Strumica Fortress**. Although this site has been fortified since at least Roman times, the current structure dates from Tsar Samoil's time early in the 11th century. Expansive excavation has restarted in recent years, and there are plans to rebuild the entire structure. Noticeboards in English and Macedonian dot the site. To get there, you can take a steep 20-minute hike along very narrow paths above Loven Dom. Or, for a much more enjoyable approach, hike from Sv Ilija Monastery (see next) to join the newly tarmacked road that comes around the back of the mountain through Raborci and Popčevo villages.

A nice little walk from the centre of Strumica is the one-hour hike to the small **Monastery of Sv Ilija** (2km from Loven Dom). Once at Loven Dom the trail is a wide path leading behind Loven Dom along the valley. The path quickly joins and runs along the valley stream and is well maintained. A short cut up to Carevi Kuli starts halfway along the path behind some benches, but is steep and narrow. Sv Ilija Church is only open on Sundays, but outside seating and grill pits are used throughout the week in the summer, and outdoor pit toilets can be found at the start of the path behind the monastery inns. To continue to Carevi Kuli, take the path behind the monastery for 15 minutes (it descends slightly to the valley stream before rising again) to the saddle at the top of the stream. There the path joins the brand-new asphalt road from Popčevo village directly to the fortress. The asphalt road is an easy half-hour walk from the saddle. It is a steep and narrow 15-minute descent from the northern end of the fortress to Loven Dom.

For the first three days (*trimeri*) of Orthodox Lent (usually in March), Strumica holds a colourful and friendly **carnival** (*www.strumickikarneval.com*), which includes a special children's carnival as well as the main event and a masked ball.

OUTSIDE STRUMICA

VODOČA Out to the west of town through the Roma village of Banica is the very small settlement of Vodoča. This village is famous for the defeat of Tsar Samoil's army in 1014 by the army of Emperor Basilius II (see box, page 10). The 15,000 troops left of Samoil's army after their defeat on Belasica Mountain were brought here where they had their eyes gouged out. Only one man in every 100 was left with one eye to lead the remaining blinded troops back to Tsar Samoil in Prilep. The place is now called 'gouged eyes' after the Macedonian *vadi oči*.

There is no monument here explaining this piece of Macedonian history, but a monastery was built here a few years after the defeat of Tsar Samoil's empire. The present **Monastery of Sv Leonthius** is a newer construction, but right next to the church dedicated to Sv Leonthius are the ruins of the original church, which was of an early basilica style including marble columns. The columns were later moved to the Church of the Holy 15 Martyrs of Tiberiopolis, in Strumica.

An earthquake in 1931 destroyed the vaults of the church but these were finally restored in 1995 with the restoration of monastery life throughout Macedonia. Lead flashing, which can be seen on the outside of the church walls, marks where the old church walls lie. After the church was completed, the monks, who had originally been living in the Monastery of Veljusa (see below), moved into the inns here. The inns used to be open to travellers wishing to stay the night, but at the time of writing these were closed again.

The reconstructed church is now a wonderfully simple, high-domed affair, showing the beautiful patterns of the original brickwork, with the remnants of a few frescoes. It is very unfussy compared with a lot of Macedonian churches from later periods and it instils a sense of calm. Some of the frescoes, such as those of Sv Isavrij and Sv Pantelejmon, are now on display in the National Museum of Macedonia. Still remaining in the vaults of the church, however, are believed to be the relics of the wife and son of Sv Kiril. It is very unusual for a woman to have a burial place in a church, especially during those times. It is also just as unusual that Kiril's son should be buried with the mother rather than the father.

As for Sv Leonthius, to whom the church is dedicated, he was martyred in the year 320 for refusing to renounce Christianity. This imposition of the Roman emperors and their pagan gods earned him and 40 other martyrs the right to die by freezing in Lake Sebaste in eastern Turkey. By some unfathomable connection, the Day of the Newlyweds, 22 March, is dedicated to the martyrs and is also the festival day of the Church of Sv Leonthius.

A footpath along the River Vodočnica at the back of the monastery leads up to Lake Vodoča, sometimes called Lake Strumica. The 5km hike is shaded and cool and, once at the lake, gives a good view of the valley.

VELJUSA Continuing along the same road from Vodoča, the next village is Veljusa. This is quite a large village, which rises up into the hills and has two more churches as well as the church at the **Monastery of the Holy Mother of God – Eleusa**. The grounds of this monastery are extremely well kept and look out over the village and the plain of Strumica. The church was originally built in 1080 although the exonarthex was built in the 14th century. It is a small church that suffered two fires in the last century, one in 1913 and the other in 1968. Soot marks can still be seen over some of the frescoes, many of which have been destroyed over time, but some still remain, the most interesting of which is the one of Jesus at the age of 12 in the ceiling of the eastern cupola. The floor of the church shows the original mosaic construction although some of it has been renovated over the years. Some of the original marblework of the church was taken to Bulgaria during World War I and is now kept in the Archaeological Museum of Bulgaria in Sofia. Copies in marble have been made since and are now in place in the church above the entrance to the nave.

Since 1996, when the monks moved down to the Monastery of Sv Leonthius, this monastery has housed nuns.

11

BANSKO Bansko, 12km southeast of Strumica, is the hot springs capital of Macedonia. It may not seem much when you first arrive, but the potential is there. Aside from the rehabilitation baths for the disabled, and the medicinal baths at the Tsar Samoil Hotel, there are also the last original working Turkish baths (sadly closed in 2005) and the **ruins of a Roman bathhouse**. The Roman complex of thermo-mineral balnae dates from the 3rd and 4th centuries AD. Some ten rooms, most with vaulted ceilings, are still visible covering an area of 1,000m², and several of these rooms are almost totally preserved. As a museum of hot spring baths throughout the ages, from Roman to Turkish to communist, all that remains to be added is a swish first-class

HOME OF THE FISH-EATING SPIDER   *Kyungah Suk*

For an authentic off-the-beaten-path experience, make a stop at the Monospitovsko Blato near Monospitovo village, itself an authentic rural village where time seems to have stood still. The Blato, as it's affectionately known by its nearby residents, is a marsh, purported to be one of the last and biggest in Macedonia. It lies sprawled at the base of Mount Belasica, 17km southeast of Strumica, and has been officially designated as an environmentally protected site conferring upon it the status 'monument of nature'.

Currently, the Blato covers approximately 400ha. It encompassed a much greater area in the past but how much bigger depends on whom you talk to. (The marsh is said to have been drained and destroyed in part during Yugoslavian times due to a malaria epidemic, which did affect World War I soldiers fighting in the area, although mysteriously, there are no local hospital records which support this epidemic.) Regardless, the Blato continues to be a rich haven for biodiversity with abundant vegetation and wildlife.

In 2007, the Municipality of Bosilovo applied and received a grant from the European Union to develop the Blato as an eco-rural tourism site. The grant provided funds to develop a structure within the marsh that could be used by tourists, recreational hunters and fishermen, local village people and nature enthusiasts. The structure consists of a wooden boardwalk that extends in three directions of approximately 1km in length, in total. The boardwalk further branches out so that there are seven extensions in total. At the end of each extension stands a thatched wooden hut built for resting and observing the biodiversity in the Blato.

The Blato also boasts two wooden birdwatch towers from the top of which one has a breathtaking panoramic view of the marsh and the land that stretches beyond it with the majestic Mount Belasica mountain range as its backdrop. Academic and amateur nature enthusiasts have been known to spend the night at the birdwatch towers so that they could catalogue the cacophony of sounds made by the teeming wildlife in the marsh. Depending on the season, the marsh is filled with water or covered in rich vegetation.

An ecological study of the Blato was also conducted by experts from the Macedonian Ecological Society (MES) as part of the project. There is a published text containing a catalogue of flora and fauna, some of them extremely rare, found in the Blato. Unfortunately, as of this writing, the text is only in Macedonian. The text catalogues over 130 species of endemic and migratory birds like little bitterns, water rails, lapwings, marsh harriers, grey heron, little egrets and many others. The marsh also contains numerous species of butterflies, fishes, lizards and other amphibians, insects and vegetation. Some of the wildlife which are rare or on the endangered or protected lists include the black stork, European otter, and the fen raft spider, which is a fish-eating carnivorous spider.

modern outdoor complex complete with sauna, massage rooms and a restaurant serving the latest health salads and smoothies. While we wait for that to arrive, the Roman baths are being renovated. A water outlet in the side of the excavation emits plenty of hot water direct from the ground, and will give you an idea of how hot the Turkish baths next door are.

To get to Bansko there are several buses a day from Strumica Bus Station, or drive out towards the Bulgarian border and turn off to Murtino and Bansko. If you have a 4x4 it is possible to drive directly from the Hotel Sirius by turning right out of the hotel through the village of Kukliš.

MONOSPITOVO WETLANDS Monospitovo Blato (see text box, page 278) lies between Bansko and Kolešino in the municipality of Bosilevo. To get there take the road to Bansko and Murtino, and at Murtino turn east towards Monospitovo village. The entrance to the wetlands lies to the south of the village. In the village of Bosilevo itself, a good place to eat is at **Restoran Park**, famous for its *bosilanka* deep-pan pizza. Made with pork, or with chicken and vegetables, it is served with a delicious tomato sauce on the side.

KOLEŠINO The road from Bansko continues on through the pretty villages of Kolešino, which boasts the beautiful 36m waterfall (*vodopad*), then on to Mokrievo and Mokrino, where the asphalt road ends. Mokrino springs (*Mokrinski izvori*), a popular visit with locals, has been given a new lease of life with maintenance and signage making it a pleasant and easy spot to visit. A dirt track continues directly to Smolari or the asphalt road can be taken from between Mokrievo and Mokrino back up to the highway at Novo Selo, after which there is a turning down to Smolari. To get to the waterfall, head to the southwest of the town and, along the side of the village cemetery, follow the stream and footpath into the hills for 40 minutes.

This part of Macedonia clearly lies in an area influenced by Methodism. The main evangelical Methodist church is in Kolešino, but there are also lots of others around, some converted back to Orthodoxy, but they are given away by their church towers, which unlike Orthodox churches, are attached directly to the church or stand over the narthex.

A newly opened popular **national restaurant and inn** is Podgorski An on the western entry to Kolešino village (*10 rooms;* \ *034 351 100;* e *podgorski-an@hotmail.com; www.podgorskian.com;* $$). Taking advantage of a local watermill, the restaurant is a welcome respite and, amusingly, the restaurant chairs sport wagon wheels, making them seem a little like wheelchairs. Excellent food and setting, worth the long taxi ride from Strumica for 450MKD. Rooms are basic.

SMOLARI In a corner of Macedonia equidistant from the borders of Bulgaria and Greece is the village of Smolari, above which is the 40m drop of the Smolari Waterfall. It is a small site but set in beautiful surroundings and the half-hour hike to get there is along well-maintained grounds. There are a couple of makeshift cafés on the way serving *skara*, beer and soft drinks, and many people bring their own picnics.

To get there, there are several buses a day from Strumica bus station, or Atlantis travel agency can arrange a special bus if there is a big enough group. To drive there, head towards the Bulgarian border and after Novo Selo turn off for Smolari. Take the first right turn at the edge of the village, which is marked Vodopad (waterfall), then the next left after the village shop. This will take you to a car park. Follow the path at the side of the stream uphill for about half an hour to reach the waterfall.

VALANDOVO The road south out of Strumica goes past the town of Valandovo and on to Lake Dojran and the border town of Gevgelija. Valandovo is renowned for its pomegranates and for a number of Roman ruins in the vicinity, such as the lost town of Idomena outside the village of Marvinci where Aleksandar III of Macedon is thought to have his burial chambers, and the necropolis at Dedeli. The town also holds Macedonia's yearly competition, the Rakijada, when local people compete in mid-October to make the best *rakija*.

Just to the west outside Valandovo is the 14th-century tower of King Marko, and to the north is the Monastery of Sv George in the hills above Valandovo. Valandovo was also the site of the fighting during World War I between the Irish 10th Regiment and the central powers of Germany and Turkey. A small graveyard to the fallen of the Irish can be found on the outskirts of the town.

For a good little website on Valandovo visit the fascinating English and German pages of Mama Stina's www.valandovo.com.

WINES FROM THE TIKVEŠ PLAINS

Wines from Macedonia are little known outside of Yugoslavia even though Macedonia is the fourth largest supplier of bulk wine to Germany and supplies a fair portion of wine to the UK too. The wine, however, comes as a blend with wines from other countries and is used for house wines or a supermarket's own label. The entire course of the Vardar Valley all the way down to Thessaloniki is fertile grape-growing country, and within Macedonia the Tikveš plains between Titov Veles and Demir Kapija produce some of the best national wines. Near Demir Kapija, the ex-royal vineyard Elenov, and the new boutique vineyard Popova Kula are well worth a visit and a stay in their fine hotels. There are also vineyards further north around Skopje, and you'll find the local wines of smaller vineyards served in plastic bottles and cardboard cartons at any petrol station or local store.

Macedonian wines are unique amongst European wines for being made with very little, if any, additional sugar or sulphite preservatives. They are preserved, therefore, mostly by the grapes' own natural sugars and it is for this reason that almost all Macedonian wines are dry rather than sweet, and why you won't get such a big hangover the next day after drinking a bottle of T'ga za Jug (Longing for the South) or Alexandria.

A visit to one of the vineyards in September and October or around Sv Trifun day in February (see box, page 284) is always well worth the time if you'd like to try out the season's newest, or the best of last year's stock. Macedonia's wine tours are becoming more frequent. To get on the next tour, go to www.exploringmacedonia.com and navigate to the Wineries page under Tours on the left-hand column. A tour, including lunch, travel and drinks, costs in the region of €35–45.

KAVADARCI

Kavadarci was founded in the late Roman period, but most of the records of this period in its history are buried beneath **Tikveš Lake**, a manmade lake constructed in 1968 to provide irrigation and hydro-electricity to the surrounding area. To celebrate the start of the wine-making season, Kavadarci now holds a grape harvest **Wine Festival** on 1 September, including grape-crushing barefoot! Kavardarci is home to the largest winery in Macedonia, Tikveš, and if you get the opportunity, try to dine in their recently renovated **wine vaults**. Situated on the main road outside Kavadarci, reservations are a must for evenings and weekends, but they

Gradsko,
Rosoman,
Tikveš wine vaults

Skopje

Feni

Unipalas

EDVARD KARDELJ

Ludа Mara

Taxis

Library

7TH SEPTEMVRI

Swimming
pool

Maršal Tito
Square

Town Museum
and Gallery

Municipality
of Kavadarci

Balkan

N

Prilep,
Tikveš Lake

Bradt

0   500m
0   500yds

Ludа Mara

Kožuf,
Zelen Breg

might be able to serve you impromptu for lunch during the week (☎ *043 414 987
ext 224;* **m** *071 338 195;* **e** *aleksandar.ristovski@tikves.com.mk*).

Two interesting churches in the area are **Marko's Cave Church** in Dradnija
4km west of the Tikveš Lake dam, and the 14th-century **Monastery of Polog**
in the village of Poloski on the cliffs of Tikveš Lake. The church there, dedicated
to Sv Gjorgi, is practically windowless, despite the number of window arches built
into the walls, and the vaults of the church are claimed to hold the remains of
Dragutin, the brother of the Serbian king Dušan. The monastery is accessible only
by boat, or a 10km hike overland from the village of Pravednik.

If you need to stay overnight, **Balkan** (*24 rooms; Maršal Tito bb;* ☎ *043 410
305*) is basic and conveniently located on the town square, Maršal Tito.

NEGOTINO

Negotino is a distinctly communist-block town with little left from ancient or
Turkish times to give much character beyond the concrete and mid-rise flats.
The town of Negotino dates back to the 3rd century BC when it was called
Antigona after its founder, the Macedonia king Antigon Gonat (277–240BC).
Rivalling Kavadarci as the wine capital of the country, Negotino celebrates Sv
Trifun Day, 14 February, with a **parade and wine competition**. The town
museum also has the country's only **wine history exhibition** at the renovated
wine merchant's villa Zelkova Kuka, Aco Adzi-Ilov 2, on the outskirts of

The Southern Wine Region   NEGOTINO

11

0 ——————————— 20km
0 ——————————— 10 miles

Karbinci

Kožjak **Bargala**

Kozjak

Bregalnica

STIP
Hot springs

Kodžalija

Alikoč

Kriva Lakavica

✗ Pilav Tepe

Veles,
Skopje,
Kumanovo

Gradsko

Lake Mantovo

Stobi

K o n e č k a

Rosoman
Kral ✗
Džo

Crna

NEGOTINO

Vardar

see page 303

Volčak
1159m

Konče

M t n s

Korešnica

KAVADARCI

Demir Kapia

Marko ✝
Dradnija

Bosava

Gališka 🏛

Lake
Tikveš

Poloski ✝

Dve Uši
1766m

Kovansci

Smrdlevo
Voda

N

Bradt

Mušov Grob
1019m

Konjsko

Kožuf
Ski Area

Zelen Breg
2165m

TIKVEŠ WINE REGION

There are over 50 small private wineries in Macedonia and the number is growing, as is quality. Below is a quick overview of some of the most commonly found wines in larger shops in Macedonia, although only a few restaurants offer more than Tikveš or maybe Bovin. To find out more about other wineries in Macedonia go to www.mkwineriesguide.com.mk or www.winemk.com.

Aside from tours to the wineries themselves, **Macedonian Wine Club** (\ *02 307 4284;* ⊕ *Mon–Sat 12.00–20.00;* e *info@mwc.org.mk; www.mwc.org.mk*) regularly holds wine-tasting events on a Thursday in Skopje to provide its members with the opportunity to try wines from the more obscure as well as the better-known wineries in Macedonia.

Makedonska Vinoteka (*Ilindenska 138a, Karpoš 3, Skopje;* \ *02 307 4949;* e *info@wineshop.com.mk; www.wineshop.com.mk;* ⊕ *Mon–Sat 11.00–19.00*) in the rear courtyard of Imes Restaurant is a small shop selling every wine available in Macedonia. Sadly, only Tikveš and Bovin were on sale at Skopje Airport duty free at time of writing, so if you want to take anything else home then stock up at Makedonska Vinoteka.

Alternatively, there are two places to get Macedonian wine when back in the UK. One is **Vardar** (*69 Askew Rd, London W12;* \ *020 8746 1844;* ⊕ *Mon–Fri 11.00–19.00, Sat 11.00–1800, Sun 12.00–17.00*), a small shop near Shepherd's Bush Market in west London, selling Tikveš and Bovin wines, as well as some from Serbia and Croatia, as well as other Macedonian food products. The other is **www.winedirect.com**, who sell Popova Kula wines and deliver to your door. In Austria www.onlinewein.at sells Bovin direct to your door.

Bovin (*www.bovin.com.mk*) has for a long time been Macedonia's most prestigious label. Its award-winning Venus, Daron and Dissan red wines are distributed as far as California, while their Pinot Noir and Riesling are very recommendable, affordable wines. Bovin is open for wine tasting for groups of ten or more.

Čekorov (*www.cekorovi.com.mk*), based in Kavadarci, specialises in Macedonia's indigenous Vranec grape and in Riesling. As expected, quality comes with the specialisation.

Negotino (towards Kavadarci). Should you get stuck in Kavadarci, the state-run Hotel Park at Partizanski 1, offers 54 rooms and dilapidated charm (\ *043 370 960/961;* f *043 361 033;* e *hotelpark@mt.net.mk; www.hotelpark.com.mk*).

STOBI

To the northwest of Negotino and just south of Gradsko, nestled into the crook of the Black River and the Vardar River, lies the ancient city of Stobi. Although many Macedonians would rate the ancient city of Heraklea (see page 110), near Bitola, higher than Stobi, in my opinion Stobi is nicer to wander around. The cities were founded at the same time and both flourished under the Roman Empire, Heraklea becoming the capital of the region. With views of the surrounding mountains and riverways, it is easy to stand on the site and imagine the hustle and bustle of the ancient city, with its numerous travelling traders plying their wares and telling their tales of far-off lands. Stobi has a good little information centre and café. Entrance to the ruins costs 150MKD.

HISTORY The ancient city of Stobi was founded at the confluence of the rivers Crna (the ancient river Erigon) and Vardar (ancient Axius), at the crossing point of the Via Egnatia, the Via Axia and the Via Diagonale. The original settlement, slightly to the north of the current archaeological site, is thought to be Bronze Age in

Chateau Kamnik (*www.chateaukamnik.com*) is a bijou winery, hotel and restaurant based in the outskirts of Skopje. The hunting-themed restaurant has an extensive wine collection from around the world and of course is open for wine tasting.

Dudin (*www.dudinwinery.com.mk*), near the old Roman town of Stobi, specialises in four wines: Chardonnay, Sauvignon Blanc, Cabernet Sauvignon and Merlot; and has a pleasant wine-tasting luncheon room.

Ezimit (*www.ezimitvino.com.mk*) near Veles is one of only four producers worldwide to receive the Honorable Panel of the Vine Knights of Austria. The award was received for their Vranac Reserve and Vranac Barrique, both of which are truly deserving of the award.

Fonko (*www.fonkowines.com*) based in Negotino offers seven wines, the most prestigious of which is their 2002 special limited edition Chardonnay.

Popov (*www.popowinery.com.mk*) family wines went commercial in 2001, since when they have produced several excellent wines for public consumption. Their Temjanika (the Macedonian variety of Muscat-Frontignan), Vranec-Cabernet Sauvignon, Zilavka, and Rose (Pinot Noir and Stanushina) are particularly noteworthy.

Popova Kula (*www.popovakula.com.mk*) is a delightful new winery with an impressive hotel/restaurant overlooking the ravine of Demir Kapija. Of their seven wines, Stanushina is the most remarkable for being an indigenous grape of the Tikveš region produced only at Popova Kula. The restaurant tower holds wine tastings (700MKD) every evening at 18.00.

Skovin (*www.skovin.com.mk*) based near Skopje produces a variety of wines including a very good Muscat and a rosé.

Tikveš (*www.tikves.com.mk*) is by far the largest winery in Macedonia. Previously state-run and now producing over 55 million litres of wine a year, it produces the famous T'ga za Jug red wine (Vranec grape). Their impressive wine-cellar restaurant is also open for lunch (preferably by reservation a day in advance).

Winery Ohrid (*www.wineryohrid.com.mk*) offers four wines, including the Ohrid white made from the R'kaciteli grape.

origin, dating to around 1900BC. Bronze objects from the classical and archaic periods have been found there along with pottery from the Neolithic period and the Iron Age. The later Hellenistic city was established in the 4th century BC.

Excavation in the newer, central part of the city has revealed archaeological stratigraphy dating to the 2nd and 3rd centuries BC. Its heyday, however, came following the Roman victory in the third Macedonian war in 168BC, when Macedonia was divided into four regions, and Stobi became one of the major urban centres in one of them. The Goths destroyed the town when they invaded Macedonia in AD479, and although it was rebuilt shortly afterwards, the earthquake of AD518 damaged the town further. Rebuilt again, further earthquakes took their toll on the town, and by the end of the 13th century the town was completely abandoned in favour of towns like Veles further north along the Vardar, and Negotino further south.

GETTING THERE Stobi is just south of the town of Gradsko, and signposted. It is accessible right off the Skopje–Negotino highway on the east side. Travelling south take the first exit after Gradsko, some 3km, and go underneath the highway into the car park.

There is no public transport to the site, but you could take a bus or train to Gradsko or a bus to Rosoman and then a taxi for about 150MKD, or walk from Gradsko south alongside the railway for about 3km until you reach the ruins.

Along the walk on the southern outskirts of Gradsko is a cemetery with German graves from World War I.

WHERE TO STAY AND EAT The café has some snacks and Gradsko has a larger shop. **Rosoman**, 7km from the ruins, has a well-known restaurant, **Kralj Džo** (King Jo), offering traditional Macedonian grill, fish and salads. The restaurant is on the main street through town where all the buses stop on their way to Bitola. In the evening there is live music after 20.30 and sometimes performances of local dances. The nearest place to stay is in Veles (see page 243).

WHAT TO SEE Stobi was first discovered in 1861, but excavation did not start until 1924, and even today only a fraction of the city has been uncovered. The site is not very big and can easily be covered in a couple of hours. Aside from the ruins themselves, most of the pottery, jewellery and sculptures are in the museums of Skopje and Veles. Two of the most famous pieces, a pair of bronze satyrs, are in Belgrade's city museum.

There are numerous main buildings and town roads in Stobi. A **2nd–century amphitheatre**, which was later turned into a gladiatorial ring, has the names of family holders engraved on some of the seats. There are at least five basilicae: a northern basilica, a civilian basilica, a central basilica and synagogue, an extra mural basilica, and the **Episcopal basilica**. The Episcopal basilica was built in the 5th century AD in a Hellenistic manner with an atrium, narthex (with a mosaic floor) and an exonarthex with a double apse. This was the seat of the bishop Philip. On the south of the Basilica is the baptistery with a magnificent mosaic composition. There are a set of small baths (*thermae minores* or *balneum*) and a set of large baths (*thermae*), complete with three earthenware *pithoses* (vats). The **House of the Psalms** is a sumptuous urban villa or *domus* with a large reception room or *tablinium* with exceptional mosaics, as well as a collonaded peristyle/atrium and central trichlinium with an apse. Several other houses that have been identified include the House of Peristeria, the House of Parthenius, and the Episcopal residence. The **Palace of Theodosius** is one of the biggest buildings with a floor of marble plates, a peristilus with mosaics and marble pedestal platforms on which statues once stood. **Domus Fullonica** was a house with a fullery for treating leather or retting cloth. The roads of Stobi include the Via Axia, Via Principalis Inferior, Via Theodosia, Via Principalis Superior and Via Sacra. Finally, there is also a semicircular *plataea* (public open space), and the city well.

DEMIR KAPIJA – THE IRON GATE

From Veles via Stobi the southerly flow of the Vardar River takes it through the plains of the Tikveš region. The valley then narrows to a gap of barely 50m across where the surrounding mountains force the river through the Iron Gate mountain gorge. The Turkish word for the gorge 'Demir Kapija' means 'iron gate' and is still the name used today for the small settlement at the foot of the rocks. Beyond the Iron Gate the valley sides remain steep for another 20km. This geographical formation has forced centuries upon centuries of invaders into upper Macedonia through this narrow corridor. They are effectively funnelled into a killing zone on exiting the Iron Gate into the Tikveš plain and hence the ominous name of the rock feature.

The train ride from the north through Demir Kapija to Gevgelija is pretty, although the drive is probably more so, because of the stopping place on the road between two rock towers. This stopping place, barely big enough for half a dozen cars, gives the appearance of being in an open-topped cave. The towering rock faces are favourites among rock climbers (routes are marked), and hiking in the surrounding hills is also popular (see *Chapter 12* for a river hike from the Iron Gate itself and a map of the region, page 302).

GETTING THERE There are six buses a day to Demir Kapija from Skopje leaving Skopje at 08.30, 11.00 (not weekends), 14.00, 15.00 (not weekends), 16.00 and 17.30. The 90-minute journey costs 270MKD. Demir Kapija is also a stop on the main line between Skopje and Gevgelija (see train times on page 74) and costs only 147MKD Skopje to Demir Kapija (*train station* ☎ *034 367 230*). It is a 2km hike to Popova Kula winery and hotel-restaurant, some of which was still unpaved at time of writing. Taxis wait outside the train station or can be called on 400300, 400400, 417777, 416001, 411545.

WHERE TO STAY, EAT AND DRINK

⌂ **Popova Kula Winery** (11 rooms) Wine Boulevard 1; ☎ 043 367 400; f 043 367 404; e reservation@popovakula.com.mk; www.popovakula.com.mk. In the hills behind Demir Kapija, this boutique vineyard commands an impressive view from the rooms & restaurant tower, & is worth the visit alone. Rooms in the hotel are currently the best on offer in Macedonia, especially for the price. Vineyard tours available; wine-tasting sessions take place in the restaurant tower every evening at 18.00 for 700MKD pp, including cheese & meats. Popova Kula specialises in indigenous grape varieties such as Stanushina & Žilavka, as well as regional varieties (Vranec) & popular Merlot, Pinot Noir & Cabernet Sauvignon. $$$$

✘ **Vodenica** ☎ 043 366 111; ⊕ Tue–Sun 11.00–23.00. Serves good Macedonian food in a traditional setting. To get there turn right immediately at the end of the bridge & turn right again off the tarmacked road. The track forks immediately; keep to the right-hand fork alongside the river & the restaurant is at the end of this lane. $$
⌂ **Elenov, the Old Royal Winery** Just outside Demir Kapija; ☎ 043 367 231–2; e vinarija_elenov@mt.net.mk. Dates from the days of Royalist Yugoslavia. If you can get on a tour you will see all the old wooden wine barrels still in use as well as some of the old presses (no longer in use). The former queen's house is currently being renovated to become a restaurant in 2011, & a hotel is due to open in 2010.

GEVGELIJA

As part of the defensive line of medieval Byzantium, and the World War I Saloniki Front, Gevgelija is an archaeological treasure. Once a sleepy little border town, it now sports several casinos predominantly serving Greek visitors. It is also the main town serving Kožuf ski resort. The town has an interesting legend attached to its name, a small old town and a couple of large garish casinos near the highway. Allegedly the name comes from the Turkish, *gel geri*, meaning 'come again', which was called to a dervish monk who had been banished by the locals. The monk had only stopped to rest overnight when he expressed his desire to stay because it was such a nice place. The locals of non-dervish religion took umbrage with the statement and made it very clear that neither he nor his religion were welcome. As he left, the locals feared that the monk's god might take vengeance on them for banishing the monk and so they called after him, '*Gel geri, gel geri.*' No-one knows if he ever did return.

GETTING THERE Gevgelija is probably Macedonia's busiest border crossing. The train to Greece stops at the border train station (☎ *034 212 033*), just outside town. Four trains a day leave for Skopje at 04.59, 10.37, 15.52 and 18.05, taking almost three hours for 200MKD. For the full train timetable see page 74.

The bus station (☎ *034 212 315*) on 7th Noemvri in the centre of town serves buses to the rest of Macedonia, but none to Greece. Taxis can cross the border, however.

Negorski Banja,
Mrzenci,
Jabor restaurant

Vardar

Thessalonika

Vardarski
Rid

BLVD GEVGELIJA

GOCE DELČEV

BORIS KIDRIČ

7 NOEMVRI

INDUSTRISKA

BLVD GEVGELIJA

II OKTOMVRI

SLOBODAN MITROV DANKO

26 APRIL

Pelagonia

Railway
station

MILE PECANOV

DEKO KOVACEV

RADOVAN
KOVAČEVIĆ
MIĆO ŠARENKOV

7 NOEMVRI

SMILEVA

TALIA BIKOVA

KOCO RACIN

PITU GULI

ŽELEZNICKA

Gevgelija
Museum

PETAR MUSEV

SKOPSKA

B KARAPUZOV

GP
ODREDI

GPODREDI

Ašikot

MARŠAL TITO

MIRCE ACEV

ILINDENSKA

Apolonija

Library

IL RIBAR

PETAR MUSEV

VLAHOV

DIMITAR

KIRIL I
METODI

V KARANANOV

RAJKO ZINZIFOV

SAMOILOVA

Sv Spas

RISTO FRSININ

MARŠAL TITO

Sv Kiril i
Metodi

N

Bradt

JOSIF JOSIFOVSKI

SOLUNSKA

TANCE KAMBEROV

0   500m
0   500yds

GEVGELIJA

Ski Kožuf

WHERE TO STAY

Apolonija (44 rooms) Gevgelija Partizanski Odredi 1; 🕾 034 213 222; f 034 213 223; e info@apollonia.com.mk; www.apollonia.com.mk. Largely serving Greek clients of the hotel's casino. All mod cons, Wi-Fi, Macedonian handicrafts sold in the lobby downstairs. $$$$

Vardar (24 rooms) Around the back of Vardarski Rid archaelological site; 🕾 034 213 267; www.hotels-macedonia.com.mk/motel_vardar.html. Basic, but quiet, & friendly staff. $$

✕ WHERE TO EAT

Gevgelija's best restaurants are outside the town, and if you're driving to Thessaloniki from Skopje (or vice versa), it is worth trying the following short diversions:

✕ Jabor Village of Mrzenci; 🕾 034 212 920; ⊕ daily 11.00–23.00. Although quite expensive by Macedonian standards, the cuisine is truly outstanding for traditional Macedonian fare. The restaurant receives a lot of Greek visitors who seem to be meeting their Macedonian cousins. Mouth-watering spit-roast lamb & all the usual Macedonian fare. To get there turn off the main highway into Gevgelija & take the 2nd right heading

north towards Negorci & Mrzenci. The restaurant stands out on the right before the small bridge 3km outside Gevgelija. $$$

✕ Elita Village of Bogdanci; 🕾 070 881 146, 071 602 043; e elita_ribnik@yahoo.com; ⊕ daily 10.00–24.00. Situated on little Lake Bolovan, 2km from Nov Dojran, the setting is relaxing, the fishing is good, & the food is delicious. $$

WHAT TO SEE AND DO The **Gevgelija Museum** (*Maršal Tito 26;* 🕾 *034 213 660;* ⊕ *Tue–Sun 09.00–15.00; entry 50MKD*) mostly displays finds from Vardarski Rid (see below), as well as other local finds of pottery and money.

The small hill above the city, which displays a prominent communist monument to the National War of Liberation, ie: the partisan uprising, is also the site of **Vardarski Rid**, on which once stood a Bronze Age settlement called Gortynia of some standing during the 2nd millennium BC. It was only discovered as the foundations were being laid for the partisan monument.

Gortynia is first mentioned by the Greek historian Thucydides, writing in the 5th century BC. The oldest finds from the site date back to the Neolithic period but the earliest evidence of structural remains dates to the end of the Bronze Age. Occupation continued throughout the Iron Age and the town thrived between 800 and 500BC, characterised by rich finds of jewellery and the so-called 'Macedonian Bronzes' (bronze pendants with ritual and symbolic meaning associated with an as yet unknown cult).

The city played an important regional role between the 2nd and 3rd centuries BC, and numerous buildings have been discovered from this period, along with a rich hoard of over 500 coins, from the Antigonid dynasty (294–168BC). This dynasty, descended from one of Alexander's generals, Antigonese the One Eyed, ruled over the ancient Kingdom of Macedonia and the Greek city-states.

For more information on the site visit www.vardarskirid.org.mk. There is a nice café for coffee in the Vardar motel around the corner.

Another 1.5km along this road from Mrzenci are the hot springs of **Negorski Banja**. These baths are well kept compared with some of the other baths in the country, as they are mostly used for medicinal purposes. Male and female baths are separate, and there are additional rooms for massage and therapies as prescribed by the resident doctor. Public entry into the hot springs alone is 50MKD. Full board at one of the three accommodation houses is 1,500MKD per person per day. Recently privatised, there are plans to turn it into a Western-standard spa serving the ski resort of Kožuf.

Towards Valandovo, the site of the **Roman town Idomenae**, situated on a hill to the southwest of the village of Marvinci, offers splendid views towards the Valandovo and Vardar valleys.

The earliest incarnation of the city, spread over some 5,000m² within the circuit of a defensive wall, dates to the Hellenistic period (323–168BC). The visible architectural remains relate mainly to private buildings and dwellings, but there are also the remains of a pottery workshop to be seen. Although the site is not presented for the public and can be somewhat arduous to visit, several public buildings can be seen, among which is a temple dedicated to the Emperor Commodus (AD180–192) in the form of the Greek god Hercules. Commodus, the son of the warrior philosopher Emperor Marcus Aurelius, called himself the Roman Hercules and famously partook in the gladiatorial arena (played by Joaquin Phoenix in the film *Gladiator*).

KOŽUF SKI RESORT AND MOUNTAIN RANGE

The newest ski resort in Macedonia is at Kožuf on the mountain range bordering Greece. Going up to 2,200m, and with a chair lift rising over 500m, it boasts being the highest and best ski resort in the region, after Bankso in Bulgaria. Like Popova Šapka, its height can make it prone to wind, but the skiing opportunities are considerably greater than at Mavrovo. At the time of writing, it was still in its early days, with limited access and minimal overnight facilities. As a result a day pass is only 800MKD. To get the most up-to-date information, including all the accommodation available see www.skikozuf.com.mk

There are plans to re-mark the mountain trails in the range, including the 85km ridge trail from Kožuf to Kajmakčalan (near Bitola). Check the skikožuf website under 'Things to do' for more information as it becomes available.

To get to Kožuf, take the train or bus to Gevgelija and then a taxi to Smrdlevo Voda (25km, 400MKD) passing through the mountain village of Konsko on the way. At Smrlevo Voda (meaning 'smelly water' due to the sulphurous hot springs there) there is a *kombe* minibus which ferries people up the 18km to Kožuf at 08.30 (and back down at 16.00) for 100MKD each way. There are plans to tarmac the dirt road from Demir Kapija to Kožuf, but this may not materialise for a few years.

If you would prefer to stay in Smrdlevo Voda, Šuklev Roman has a beautiful new house located along the stream (*4 rooms with 2 shared bathrooms; ↘ 071 251 433; 900MKD pp*). There is a small restaurant next door, and other rooms available throughout the village if Šuklev's is full.

LAKE DOJRAN

Lake Dojran, once known for its beauty, its curative reed waters (for healing skin ailments) and its very good air quality, is now turning into an ecological disaster zone. The lake is the third tectonic lake of its kind in Macedonia, after Ohrid and Prespa, having been formed from tectonic shifts in the earth's land plates four million years ago. It is the shallowest of all the lakes, being a mere 10m deep when the lake is at its fullest.

Unfortunately, recent years have seen the surrounding inhabitants drain the lake of its precious water in order to irrigate outlying crops and feed the demands of growing nations. Sadly this problem is not being tackled and Lake Dojran is now counted in the Earth Policy Institute's top 15 most endangered lakes. As the EPI wrote in 2005 (*www.earth-policy.org/Updates/2005/Update47_data.htm*):

Overuse of water from the lakes and streams that feed Dojran Lake has caused the lake to shrink to a third of its former size and the water temperature to rise. More than 50 islands have appeared in the middle of the lake as the water level has dropped by up to 3.48 meters below the minimal water level established in a 1956 bilateral agreement between Greece and Macedonia. Now with an average depth of 1.5 meters, the lake is turning into a swamp to the detriment of local plants and animals, especially fish. It is unlikely that the lake will ever return to its original size, and without action it soon may disappear.

At some points the old shore road lies over 1km away from the current shoreline. This has more or less killed recreation and tourism around the lake in an already depressed economic climate for Macedonia. The Macedonians blame the Greeks, as the water runs out of the lake on the Greek side. Sadly, the continued dispute between Greece and Macedonia over the official naming of Macedonia, and Greek fears of a 'greater Macedonia' have prevented this ecological mess from being rectified, and who knows how soon is too late, if it is not already too late, to restore the biological and ecological diversity of the lake.

Some effort is being made on the Macedonian side to refill the lake, and at the Hotel Istatov turning towards the lake you can find the canal-way that funnels the water into the lake (and helps to prevent it being siphoned off). It is a small step, however, considering the number of outlets and inlets where water can be siphoned away from the lake.

The new shoreline is made up of a mixture of reeded banks and stretches of sharp splintered and bleached freshwater shells, making it difficult to simply sit around and lounge in the sun, never mind run around in bare feet. The shoreline, however, is still teeming with wildlife, and on a sunny spring day you can see more frogs than you can shake a stick at, water snakes eating tadpoles, and a host of birds, butterflies and insects. If you are lucky, you'll also see some fish.

If you would like to find out more about how to contribute or campaign to save Lake Dojran, contact one of the environmental organisations on page 38.

GETTING THERE AND AWAY Entering Macedonia from Greece via the Greek village of Doirani is a simple affair. The small border control station is usually very quick compared with the main Gevgelija crossing in and out of Greece, and although the road to Doirani is not a highway, it has relatively light traffic, making the journey fast and easy. There is still the usual police presence on the roads around the border, though.

Once through the Greek border control, there is a small Orthodox church in the border zone. Less than 50m from the Macedonian border control is the old Hotel Mlaz, which now only houses Hit Casino.

Two buses a day from Skopje (06.00 and 14.00) serve Star Dojran and a 16.00 bus from Skopje serves Nov Dojran for 350MKD. Five more buses serve nearby Bogdanci from Skopje, from where you can take a taxi the remaining 18km to Nov Dojran. Ask at your hotel for returning bus times as there is no dedicated bus station at Nov or Star Dojran. A taxi to Dojran from Strumica is 700MKD.

WHERE TO STAY

Atlantik (64 rooms, 32 bungalows) Star Dojran, on the road to the Greek border; 034 225 203. This hotel, like others in Star Dojran, caters to Greeks who want to gamble with a little more freedom than is allowed in Greece. The hotel was in its prime during the heyday of Yugoslavia, when there was water in the lake, but has since become quite dilapidated. No TV, no AC & the mosquito screens are broken. The surroundings remain tranquil. $$$

Istatov (44 rooms) Entrance to Nov Dojran; 034 227 556; f 034 227 555; m 075 421 848; e hotel.istatov@yahoo.com; www.hotelistatov.com. Also the Istatov physical training centre, this motel is owned by Blagoj

Istatov, the Belgrade Partisani football team goalkeeper in 1973, & later coach in the Netherlands & coach of the Macedonian national team. Frequented by Macedonia's football & handball teams, it is a little pricey for the quality, although it does have an outdoor pool, gym & restaurant (usual local fare). $$$

Villa Dojrana (3 rooms) Partizanska 41; 071 584 186, 075 707 770; e villadojrana@ yahoo.com. Self-catering apt including an outdoor pool. Villa Dojrana can recommend other local houses if it is full. $$

Metropol (50 rooms) Maršal Tito bb, Star Dojran; 034 225 324. Basic accommodation, conveniently located in the old village. $$

WHERE TO EAT
The old village, Star Dojran, stretches for over 1km along the lake. From here you can access the innermost bank of the new shoreline by boat to fish for carp (*krap* in Macedonian). Many restaurants, pizzerias, buffets and cafés line the road and spill onto the receding shoreline.

Fooktak Maršal Tito 15, Star Dojran; 034 255 320; daily 11.00–23.00. Although this small restaurant can't boast views overlooking the drying lake, it is the oldest & most famous in the town (& well known across all Macedonia). The restaurant is over 120 years old, going back to the days of Macedonia's struggle to overthrow Ottoman rule. On the wall just inside the main entrance hang original photos of 8 of the founders of VMRO (Revolutionary Organisation for an Independent Macedonia). Opened just after the new train line through (now Greek) Doirani,

the restaurant is named after the sound that the train engine makes: 'fook-tak, fook-tak, fook-tak'. The menu offers the usual Macedonian fare, & the freshly caught carp from the lake is exquisite, extremely tender with no trace of a muddy taste at all – undoubtedly, the best carp you'll find anywhere. After 20.30 at the w/ends there is live music. $$

Graniko At the far end of Star Dojran; 034 225 166; daily 11.00–23.00. With a lovely terrace overlooking the lake offering traditional food. $$

Abridged text from the panel boards at Kale Tepe memorial site.

The World War I Salonica Front stretched from the Gulf of Orfano in the east to Ohrid in the west, traversing variously Dojran, Strumica, Gevgelia, Prilep, Krusevo and even touching Skopje. The British offensive lay at Dojran from 1915–18, with the decisive battle of September 1918 fought by the 22 Division (UK) and the Serres Division (GR) on the Allied side. Most of 22 Div was drafted from Wales and northern England, with a few chance volunteers from elsewhere. After tragic losses, 22 Div survivors erected a memorial to their fallen comrades shortly after the war at the strong point and observation position they fought so hard to attain, which was known then as the Devil's Eye on top of Kale Tepe, or the Grand Couronne.

OPEN TO THE PUBLIC The original memorial was rediscovered among thick undergrowth and vegetation in 2007. To mark the 90th anniversary of the end of World War I, the British Embassy in Skopje, in conjunction with the Municipality of Dojran, placed a replica memorial, inspired by the original, on the site. After sweeping for unexploded ordnance by the Directorate for Protection and Rescue, the area around the memorial was cleared of undergrowth and a path and benches prepared by the Dojran Municipality. Panel boards depicting the battle at Dojran have been erected, and the original memorial can still be seen, with the new memorial above it.

The hollow in front of the 22 Div memorial represents part of a large bunker that has been demolished. Other bunkers and positions stood to the east and north, parts of which can be seen today. The bunker complex at the memorial site served a supply and command system of trenches and defences. It was known to the Bulgarians as the Ferdinand and was so named to commemorate the Bulgarian victory of 1915. Images from the time clearly show the memorial fountain, which is passed on entering the newly re-opened site. Dugouts and other strong points can also be seen from there.

WHAT HAPPENED AT DOJRAN In 1914, what was later to become the territory of the Republic of Macedonia was part of Serbia and was allied to Britain and France. Austro-Hungarian and German military divisions found Serbia more difficult to conquer than they had imagined, and by early 1915 they were encouraging Bulgaria, with the promise of territorial gains, to join them. On 21 September 1915 Bulgaria mobilised its forces on the border. On 11 October 1915 the Bulgarian army began their drive towards Skopje, splitting the Serbian army in two, part of which began to retreat towards Albania and the west and part of which began to retreat towards Greece and the south.

✕ **Kaldrma** Just inside the road sign for Nov Doijran on the Star Dojran side of town; ☏ 034 277 122; ⊕ daily 11.00–23.00. Its upstairs dining area commands great views of the lake & the mountains. Has basic local food & a variety of lake fish. If you like crunchy deep-fried fish, try the *kerpija* (redfin). $$

WHAT TO SEE AND DO Star Dojran was largely destroyed during the World War I and hence Nov Dojran sprang up. The **old clock tower** and the **Turkish baths** can still be seen in the backstreets of the Star Dojran and at the northern end of Star village are the tall ruins of the **Sv Ilija Church**. The lake **museum**, specialising in the flora, fauna and structure of Lake Dojran, is in the town hall. The lake with its **abundant wildlife** (take the *Bradt Guide to Central and Eastern European Wildlife* with you) can be enjoyed from both villages.

The World War I **Dojran battlefield** on Pip Ridge above Star Dojran is the main attraction for military buffs. Macedonia is mostly associated today with

In order to support Serbia and try and stem the retreat, the French and British landed in Salonica (Thessaloniki) and marched north. French forces marched up the Vardar Valley as far as Veles, while the British 10 (Irish) Division marched towards Strumica forming a defensive line between Kosturino and Prstan. The amassed, well-trained, Bulgarian, Austrian and German forces were unstoppable and forced the French onto the defensive to cover the retreat of the Serbs. Meanwhile, 10 Div fought fiercely in the east in a series of battles between 7 and 10 December 1915 to cover the eastern flanks of the Serbian and French withdrawal.

The Bulgarian army, in pursuit of the British and French, then occupied the southern border area and proceeded to dig in. They fortified the hills above Dojran with a well-planned system of redoubts, concrete observation positions, bunkers and machine-gun nests, the remains of which are clearly visible today.

There were two main battles in the hills above Dojran; the first in the spring of 1917 was a failure. The second battle of Dojran took place on 18 and 19 September 1918, as part of a co-ordinated assault and succeeded in tying down Bulgarian reserves so that they could not be deployed to fight the French and Serbians to the west. Following the successful breakthrough by the French and the Serbs to the west, the Bulgarian forces above Dojran retreated, leaving their positions here deserted save for British troops moving up in pursuit.

AN ICOFORT SITE There is growing international concern about the preservation and conservation of both military archaeology and what are known as 'landscapes of conflict'. In 2005 The International Council on Monuments and Sites (ICOMOS) created a subcommittee, the International Scientific Committee on Fortifications and Military Heritage (IcoFort), specifically tasked with dealing with the preservation of military archaeology and advising UNESCO. Much of what is termed military archaeology is encompassed by existing international conventions and European treaties on archaeology and heritage and in principle they are afforded the same status for preservation as would older remains, such as historic places of worship, historic buildings and other archaeological sites.

Macedonia is rich in landscapes of conflict from mid 19 century through to World War II. Dojran itself was not only a site of conflict, but also part of the physical remains of a momentous point in European and world history, one which led, ultimately, to the creation of modern Europe. It is part of a wider and very well-preserved landscape of conflict across the entire Salonica Front, with trenches and redoubts, bunkers and machine-gun nest, foxholes and shell craters all still visible in the undergrowth and largely untouched by modern-day development.

the Yugoslav conflict of the 1990s. Few now remember its part in the World War I Salonica Front, also known as the Macedonia Front, and even at the time better known as the 'forgotten front'. 'Muckydonia', as it was known in a theatre performance held by British troops in the Balkans during the war, was too small for the headline news, yet troops on the Salonika front suffered the fog of war as much as troops in Flanders, the Somme, or Verdun. Casualties were born from poor communications, malaria was endemic and life behind the lines (unlike in France and Belgium) was woefully unexciting. From 1915–18, the British were held up in trenches to the southeast of Dojran whilst the Germans and Bulgarians held the northwest (see text box above, *Winning the Devil's Eye*). In addition to almost 10,000 men dying in combat (the majority of whom were British), many men died of malaria in the much marshier conditions a century ago.

Although Dojran Municipality opened up the battlefield in 2008, it remains a difficult site to access. At the time of writing there were no signposts to the site, and even with a 1:25,000 map (sheet 784-3-2 available from *www.katastar.gov.mk*) and excellent navigations skills it is easy to get lost on Pip Ridge (as many did in World War I). In addition, walking restrictions are often imposed in the summer due to the risk of wildfires (which swept through the area in 2008), and illegal loggers and their pursuant forestry patrol can cause the unannounced hiker considerable hassle. For a hassle-free and informative day, Salonika Battlefield Tour (see page 271) can arrange a guided tour for approximately €25 per person (excluding travel and subsistence, and depending on any research requests you may have). Books and web resources on the Dojran battlefield are listed in *Appendix 3*.

A Dozen Hikes

We descended to the Dibra–Gostivar road, climbed to the Bistra Plateau, descended to the Dibra–Kicevo road and climbed again in the direction of Struga and Lake Ochrid … On the 20th we camped in some beautiful high meadows with views of spendid mountains stretching in every direction …

Albania, Macedonia and the British Military Missions, 1943 and 1944, Reginald Hibbert (from *The New Macedonia Question*, edited by James Pettifer, 1999)

Macedonia is brimming with beautiful countryside that makes splendid hiking for a range of fitness and experience levels. There are several multi-day hikes, including two 200km hikes from Ljuboten to Struga along the border with Albania (permit still required) and from the capital Skopje to the beautiful Lake Ohrid. There are also many shorter hikes of an hour or less to waterfalls, caves, glacial lakes, hidden monasteries, or other points of interest.

The **Macedonian Mountaineering and Sports Federation** (*MMSF, 11 Oktomvri 42a, 1000 Skopje;* ✆ *02 3165 540;* e *contact@fpsm.org.mk; www.fpsmf.org.mk*) are starting to put together hiking booklets and guides in English with an aim to providing western European-standard information on trails and huts. Together with brand-new 1:25,000 hiking maps being published on the whole country by the State Authority for Geodetic Works (see page 78), only a fresh coat of paint on some of the old hiking-trail markings and some much neglected trail maintenance is needed to bring hiking up to the recreational standards enjoyed in the US, and France, Germany or elsewhere in western Europe.

Other guidebooks are available in Macedonian (see box on page 311). However, even if you can read Macedonian, information on how to get to the trailhead, good route descriptions, a basic route map, water supply locations, etc are somewhat obscure, never mind grid references. Admittedly grid references are difficult to give when maps were once a state secret and only officers were taught how to read them!

This chapter offers information on 12 hikes of differing grades to whet your appetite. More routes are available at www.summitpost.org (type in the name of a mountain peak or hut) and at www.mkdmount.org, including GPS tracks, huts and further links. As with mountaineering anywhere in the world, respect the terrain and know your own limits especially if you intend to venture out without a guide. (See *Chapter 4*, page 84, for *Health and safety in the mountains*.) If you would like a guide and none of the clubs below can help, then **Dea Tours** (*www.deatours.com.mk*) based in Ohrid can arrange multi-day hikes starting from €195 depending on the number of hikers, length of tours and type of accommodation.

For more on where and how to buy maps, and the peculiarities of the new Macedonian maps, see page 78.

HIKING CLUBS

There are over 70 hiking clubs in Macedonia, some more active than others. You'll find somebody who speaks English at most of these clubs. A few are listed here, and are mentioned in relevant sections throughout this guidebook. For a complete list of all the clubs contact MMSF (see above).

Makedon Planinarski Klub ↘ 076 493 301 (075 554 595 for English-speaking club secretary Nikolov Bogoljub); e kps@makedon.mk; www.makedon.mk. This new, young club meets every Wed at 20.00, at the municipality Karpos (barrack No. 5).
Korab Planinarski Klub ↘ 071 564 086; e contact@korab.org.mk (for English-speaking club secretary Slobodan); www.korab.org.mk (including their annual programme in English). Based in Skopje, the club's weekly meet takes place at the Sports Association Hall at Jordan Hadžikonstantinov-

Džinot 12a (↘ 02 3117 687, 02 3227 672). Their national day (8 Sep) annual hike is to Mount Korab.
Ljuboten Planinarski Klub ↘ 075 649 393 for English-speaking club president Jovan Božinovski; jovan@pkljuboten.org.mk; www.sharamountainguide.com.mk. Based in Tetovo, the club's national day hike is along the River Pena to Lešnica Waterfall. Their website highlights a number of hiking options in the Šar Mountains, & their costs include a guide.

MOUNTAIN HUT SYSTEM

Serving the needs of the clubs and individuals is an extensive system of over 30 mountain huts in Macedonia. Although most of these rarely require you to book ahead, it is best to phone before arrival as some are only staffed if they know there will be overnight visitors. The huts offer clean sheets in a dormitory bed space, and cost around 300MKD for the night. This does not include food and most huts offer only small snacks and drinks, so bring your own food. Here is a list of most of the huts (called *planinarski dom* in Macedonian).

OUTSIDE SKOPJE
Dare Džambaz (50 beds) ↘ 02 3234 365, 02 3143 236; hut warden: Živko Temelkoski; location: 1,066m, peak of Mount Vodno, south of Skopje.
Karadžica (50 beds) ↘ 02 3112 199 ext 630; hut wardens: Atanas Ovnarski or Blagoja

Petrusevska; location: 1,450m on Karadžica Mountain near the village of Aldinci, south of Dračevo.
Kitka (60 beds) ↘ 070 246 419, 02 3117 100; hut warden: Sašo Popovski; location: 1,560m on Kitka Mountain near the village of Crvena Voda.

VELES AREA
Breza (44 beds) ↘ 043 228 622; hut warden: Vasko Gjorjievski; location: on Mount Golešnica.
Čeples (60 beds) ↘ Same contact details as Breza above; location: at 1,445m near the village of Nežilovo on Jakupica Mountain. Eat at the Nežilovo Trout Farm (↘ 043 811 812, 070 594 682) on the way up or down to the hut.

Maslodajna (30 beds) ↘ 043 221 110; hut warden: Mičo Kirov; location: near the village of Oreov Dol on Babuna Mountain.
Šeškovo (50 beds) ↘ 043 411 964 (for Ljubčo Binor, the president of Mountaineering Club Orle who run the hut); hut warden: Momčilo Gjorgjevik; location: near the village of Šeškovo, southwest of Lake Tikveš & Kavadarci.

STRUMICA AREA
Ezero (20 beds) ↘ 034 325 282 (for hut warden Krume), 043 343 122 (for Ilija or Lenče Končaliev of Mountaineering Club Ezero who run the hut); location: on Lake Vodoča near the village of Popčevo, southwest of Strumica.

Dedo Kožjo Murtinski (8 beds) ↘ 034 347 409; hut warden: Gjorgje Krmzov; location: 1,160m on Belasica Mountain near Strumica.
Gorna (30 beds) ↘ 034 178 150; hut warden: Slave Spasov; location: 1,420m on Pljačkovica Mountain near Radoviš.

☖ Šarena Češma (16 beds) Contact details as for Dedo Kožjo Murtinski above; location: 1,300m near Šarena springs on Belasica Mountain near Strumica.

POPOVA ŠAPKA

☖ Smreka (100 beds) ☎ 02 322 5958; hut warden: Duško Boskovski; location: ski resort of Popova Šapka.

NORTHEAST

☖ Divlje (20 beds) ☎ 02 2781 686; hut warden: Mijalčo Nikolov; location: near the village of Divlje, east of Katlanovo.

☖ Kozjak (15 beds) ☎ 031 430 990; hut warden: Momšilo Jakimovski; location: near the village of Malotino, northeast of Kumanovo, towards Prohor Pčjinski.

BABA MOUNTAIN

☖ Golemo Ezero (50 beds) Lies 600m below Pelister peak at 2,225m. To arrange an overnight stay contact Zlatko Sterjov, ☎ 047 221 605 (afternoons only). Staffed at w/ends in summer only. No food available. Water & washing facilities are outside.

☖ Kopanki (110 beds) 1,630m Mt Baba; ☎ 047 222 384. Serves food & drink (including alcohol);

GOSTIVAR-KIČEVO

☖ Sarski Vodi (8 beds) ☎ 042 214 505; hut warden: Gojko Gegovski; location: near the village of Gorno Jelovce, west of Gostivar.

☖ Tajmište (35 beds) ☎ 045 323 102; hut warden: Bosko Talevski; location: near the village of Tajmište, northwest of Zajas, Kičevo.

☖ Vrteška (64 beds) ☎ 032 393 044 or 032 384 788/299; hut warden: Marjan Ljubotenski; location: on Plačkovica Mountain.

☖ Tri Vodi (60 beds) ☎ 044 397 680; hut warden: Stojce Krstevski; location: near the village of Tearce north of Tetovo.

☖ Pojak Kalman (20 beds) ☎ 031 373 216; hut warden: Ljubisa Ivanovski; location: near the village of Dejlovce, northeast of Kumanovo, south of Mount Peren.

☖ Toranica (15 beds) ☎ as above; hut warden: Stojko Velkovski; location: near the village of Kostur, east of Kriva Palanka.

washing facilities are indoors; TV & video available. A very popular outing for Bitolites & local people.

☖ Neolica (70 beds) 1,440m on the east side of Mt Baba. Contact Slobodan Lazarevič, president of the Gjorgji Naumov Mountaineering Club to book ahead ☎ 047 242 879. Staffed during the w/ends.

☖ Treška (30 beds) ☎ 042 214 505; hut warden: Marjan Kuzmanovski; location: between the villages of Izvor & Drugovo, near Kičevo.

MOUNT GOLEM KORAB

At 2,753m, Mount Golem Korab (grid 627 275) is the highest peak touching Macedonia and shares the border with Albania. Mal Korab (2,683m), and beneath it the longest waterfall (138m) in the country, can be seen from the hike. Although permission is no longer required from the Ministry of the Interior Border Police to hike in the border area, it is a good idea to notify the border police hut at the start of the climb, in case of an accident. Once a year Korab Mountaineering Club arrange their annual climb on the weekend closest to Independence Day (8 September). It is a big event attracting over 1,000 hikers from all over the Balkans and further afield. It is usually a long and arduous walk of 25km in nine hours or more, and many enthusiasts go for the day out even if they don't make it to the top. Police escorts, guides and medical staff attend on the day. To find out more, contact Korab's English-speaking secretary, Slobodan (☎ 071 564 086; e contact@korab.org.mk).

SAGW map sheet 730-1-3 (Korab Sever, 1:25,000, January 2009) covers the hike. Type in 'Korab' at www.summitpost.org for a good route description, photos and a map.

A Dozen Hikes **MOUNTAIN HUT SYSTEM**

12

Distance	10.5km (18km from the centre of Skopje)
Altitude	Skopje 245m, Sredno Vodno 600m, Vodno Cross 1,066m, Matka 310m
Rating	Moderate: ridge walk followed by steep downhill section
Timing	4 hours (+2 hours from Sredno Vodno to Vodno Cross)
In reverse	Possible, better light for taking photos of the lake if starting from Matka, but more dramatic to end at Matka and then eat a late lunch afterwards
Start of trail	Taxi or hike to Sredno Vodno, then hike to Vodno Cross or during the week a taxi can take you to the Cross
Accommodation	Dare Džambaz mountaineering hut (see page 296) at Vodno Cross; Hotel Vodno (✆ 02 3178 866); Skopje town; Matka mountaineering hut (see page 148)
Map	1:25,000 SAGW Map Sheets Matka 731-2-1 and Skopje 731-2-2, January 2007. See pages 144–5 for route sketch

ROUTE DESCRIPTION The route is west-southwest along Vodno ridge and mostly gently downhill for about the first 7km. The last 3.5km is a steep descent, which ends with terrific views of the lake and a small boat crossing to reach Matka Hut and Sveta Andreja Monastery. The route is well marked until the last 4km when the trail veers off into the woods and is lost in overgrown fields and poor markings. For good orienteers with GPS, there is a detailed route card opposite. Grid bearings are not given here due to the lack of reliable mapping available at the time of writing. For the less orienteering-savvy, take a guide, such as one from **Korab Mountaineering Club** (✆ 071 564 086; e *contact@korab.org.mk*), where the club secretary, Slobodan, can set you up with a guide.

For a description of the route from Skopje to Sredno Vodno and to Vodno Cross see page 143.

Bring plenty of water for this hike as there is none along the way once you leave Vodno Cross until you reach the spring at Leg 10, some 7km into the hike and halfway down the other side. Hikers have been known to suffer from heat exhaustion hiking this route in the summer. If the Dare Džambaz Hut is (unusually) shut, there is signage for a tap pointing around the back of the cross. In fact it is for a spring that is very difficult to find unless somebody shows it to you.

Matka Hut serves refreshments year round, and the Restoran Peštera (see page 148) and other restaurants at Matka dam serve good traditional food. You can also ask to order a taxi at the restaurant for the return trip to Skopje (approx 400MKD), or take the number 60 bus (hourly service, 60MKD).

START POINT: DARE DŽAMBAZ HUT AT VODNO CROSS 1,066M

Leg	From Grid	Distance/ Time	To Grid	Height
1	332 468	approx 3km/40mins	3045 4658	907m

Starting at Dare Džambaz Hut at Vodno Cross – tank hideouts to left, right track goes to Krušopek. Continue straight on.

2	3045 4658	approx 2.8km/40mins	2812 4588	898m

To this point is easy, frequently marked with fresh red and white paint along an easy trail. This point is the first key turn in the entire route, and turns SSW off main track into woods between recently burnt and cut-down trees. At the turning point there is a faded red and white mark on a pine tree. From here on the path is marked but infrequently, with faded paint and the path is often not visible for several metres ahead.

3	2812 4588	250m	2780 4567	908m

Top of small wooded hill

4	2780 4567	250m	2756 4563	874m

Bottom of hill, no trees, bear left along wide track for 50m then turn right up hill along small track

5	2756 4563	800m	2710 4547	880m

Alpine field

6	2710 4547	100m	2695 4545	889m

Follow ridge line SW

7	2695 4545	150m	2678 4524	888m

Turn W down gully

8	2678 4524	400m	2653 4532	836m

Turn NW down track (to right)

9	2653 4532	900m	2618 4590	732m

Turn W off the track

10	2618 4590	500m	2605 4587	700m

Spring running into a concrete container

11	2605 4587	400m	2586 4542	488m

Fork in the track; up to Sv Nikola Church (recommended), or down to the bottom of Matka dam (bridge currently destroyed)

12	2586 4542	200m	2564 4538	598m

Sv Nikola Church. From here descend to the lake and sound the gong for a boatman to fetch you from the hut across the lake.

13	2564 4538	900m	2525 4520	310m

End Destination: Matka Hut (☏ 02 205 2655) and Sv Andrea Church

A Dozen Hikes VODNO CROSS TO MATKA DAM

12

Distance	6.5km
Altitude	Prilep town centre 640m, Markovi Kuli 945m, Treskavec Monastery 1,260m
Rating	Easy to moderate
Timing	2½ hours
Circular trail	Possible
Trailhead	Train or bus to Prilep, taxi or hike to Markovi Kuli entrance
Accommodation	Prilep town (page 206) and Treskavec Monastery (page 208)
Map	1:25,000 SAGW Map Sheet Prilep 782-1-3, January 2007

ROUTE DESCRIPTION There are three routes to the monastery.

Route 1 By foot from Markovi Kuli (for directions to Markovi Kuli see page 207). This is the easiest route and is well trodden and relatively well marked by red and white hiking marks, paintings of saints, and a spring just over halfway along the route. Part of the hike is along some steep rocks, but the way is aided by a steel rope. The rocks along all three routes are what make Prilep's scenery famous.

Route 2 By foot along the old cobbled road from Dabnica. This route is only 4.5km if you take a taxi through the disgracefully neglected Roma slums of Prilep to within 1km of Dabnica. It is steeper over the shorter distance, however. Your hike begins when the road is no longer fenced off on the left and comes to the obvious opening onto the foothills of Zlatovrv. At the end of the fence there is another dirt track to the left leading to a nearby house. The cobbled path you require, which is not obvious at first, heads straight up the ridge of the spur leading up to Zlatovrv. It lies directly between where the dirt track divides, and if you have a compass, set it to 6,000 mils or 340° and follow this bearing until you come across the obvious path uphill. After an hour, the path, with large chunks of cobbling still intact, starts to wind back and forth and comes upon a water fountain. From the fountain the path is practically straight until you get to the back gate of the monastery. Follow the path around to the left and to the front of the monastery. If you drive yourself to the start point of the hike, then head west through the Roma settlement (ask for Dabnica).

Route 3 By 4x4 or foot along a dirt track to the southwest. To reach the dirt track head out of Prilep on Marksova and Orde Čopela, past the Tobacco Institute and Museum, and turn towards the town cemetery 5km from the centre of town. Follow the road left around to the back of the cemetery. At the junction where you lose the tarmac (500m from the main road) is a small sign, marked Monastir Sveta Bogorodica, Treskavec, pointing the way straight ahead. After another 2.5km turn right when you join another track through the valley, then left after another 250m. Follow this road uphill to the monastery in about 3km.

PRILEP AREA

- 1392m
- 1303m
- Treskavec Monastery †
- Mount Zlato 1262m
- Water fountain
- Dabnica †
- Kičevo
- Prilep Lake
- Dani
- Kičevo Tobacco Museum
- 1044m
- Water fountain
- † Cemetery
- Zelenik 993m
- Sv Michael Archangel †
- Markovi Kuli
- Skopje
- N
- Bradt
- Bangkok Oriental
- Roma settlement
- University
- Kristal Palas
- Old Town
- PRILEP
- Kruševo
- Railway station
- 0 — 1,000m
- 0 — 1,000yds
- Makedonsko Sonce
- Tomb of the undefeated
- Bitola
- Bitola
- Selce

Distance	12km
Altitude	Demir Kapija 110m, Silananba Čuka 620m
Rating	Easy to moderate: short, steep wooded section at the summit
Timing	5–6 hours
In reverse	Possible, but more difficult to get a taxi back to Demir Kapija
Trailhead	Bus or train to Demir Kapija village, taxi to stopping place in the Iron Gate tunnel
Accommodation	Popova Kula Winery (see page 287)
Map	1:25,000 SAGW Map Sheets Demir Kapija West 783-1-2, Demir Kapija East 783-2-1, January 2007

ROUTE DESCRIPTION A good summer hike directly from the stopping place between the two rock towers of Demir Kapija tunnel. The path goes along the canyon stream that created the rock feature and flows between them into the River Vardar. The sides are almost vertical and offer good shade in the hot summer. The path through the canyon is easy to follow but requires fording the stream several times in the first 1km, so sandals such as Tevas which have a good grip in water are advisable. Thereafter the path and stream come into a more open area where the path is wider and used by farm vehicles from **Čelevec** village (just over 1hr from trailhead).

The path continues northeast alongside big boulders in the ever smaller stream and leads up to the mountain village of **Iberlija** (grid 0821 8997, 2hrs from trailhead). A couple of very old *babas* still tend sheep and tobacco leaves here, but most of the houses have long been abandoned. At Iberlija, go through the village and follow the track round to the west and up a steep narrow ravine. As the trickle of water and the path seem to run out (0759 9040) keep heading up the hill and in 30–40 minutes from Iberlija you will pop out of the brush at the service road (0674 9045 dirt track) for the water pipes feeding Korešnica village. A few hundred metres southeast is the trig point Silananba Čuka (620m) while the service road back to Korešnica heads off to the southwest. Some 2–3 hours gently downhill will lead you to the village shop where you can get refreshments and phone for a taxi to take you back to Demir Kapija.

The 06.17 train from Skopje stops in Demir Kapija at 08.21. There is a 16.42 train from Demir Kapija and the last train leaves at 20.42. The best (and very popular) wine hotel in Macedonia, Popova Kula, offers rooms above Demir Kapija.

There is much more hiking to be had higher up the Čevlečka River, including to the ruined fortress of Prosek. To the southeast of Demir Kapija, towards the new ski resort Kožuf on the border with Greece, are some of Macedonia's many caves including the beautiful Golem Zmejovec (large dragon) and Mal Zmejovec (small dragon). Hiking the old road and railway on the right bank of the Vardar is also pleasant. The Demir Kapija canyon is home to some rare birds of prey including the griffon vulture *(Gyps fulvus)*, Egyptian vulture *(Neophron percnopterus)*, golden eagle *(Aquila chrysaetos)*, harrier eagle *(Circaetus gallicus)*, foxy buzzard *(Buteo rufinus)* and various falcons *(Falco peregrinus, Falco naumanni)*.

Distance	7km round trip
Altitude	Oktisi 780m, Varoš 1,072m, Crni Kamen Park 1,195m, Vevčani Springs 910m
Rating	Easy to moderate
Timing	3–4 hours
In reverse	Possible
Trailhead	Bus to Oktisi and Vevčani every hour from Struga
Accommodation	Vevčani (see page 183), Struga
Map	1:25,000 SAGW Map Sheet Vevčani 780-3-1, January 2007

ROUTE DESCRIPTION A pretty and gentle hike taking in a mixed ethnic village, the alleged eighth stopping point of the Via Egnatia, and the Republic of Vevčani Springs. Starting in the centre of Oktisi, head to the top of the village and ask for Vajtos Kale. You will head up an eroding sheep herd track for about 1km towards the obvious hilltop appearing on your left to the west. At a dip in the hillside, skirt round the valley and upwards onto a wide leafy avenue that could be imagined as once part of the Via Egnatia Roman network of roads. At the top of the avenue, a turn-off leads to the site of Vajtos Kale (grid 6600 6525). Once a Paeonian fortress, perhaps, there is little left to see here now except some very large rocks and a lot of digging, probably from site robbers with a metal detector.

Back on the leafy avenue, continue for another kilometre until you come out to some meadows, pass a crossroads in the path and onto a 4x4 dirt track. This road winds its way for 1.5km NNW along the 1,220m contour offering good views of both Vevčani and Oktisi. After the road appears to head west away from the direction of Vevčani for some 350m, it turns to head northeast and downhill into the park area called Crni Kamen. Here there are a number of park benches and tables, places to hold barbecues and a couple of huts. The road continues over a small stream at the bottom of the park and slightly uphill for a 3km gentle trek back down into Vevčani. A shortcut by foot is to follow a narrow path before the stream heading down the right-hand bank of the stream following the electricity pylons into Vevčani. After almost 2km the path crosses a small bridge into the back of the village.

Head left of the bridge to get to the Vevčani Springs, eat at the quaint Domakjinska Kukja or Kutmičevica, and visit Sv Nikola Church (see page 183). Head right to get to the main road through Vevčani and follow it downhill alongside the stream for 1.4km to get back to Oktisi. A number of old watermill houses adorn the road that criss-crosses the stream.

Other hikes in the area go up to Gorna Belica village, Labuništa village and its glacial lakes and the fabled Church of Perumba on the border with Albania.

OKTISI TO VAJTOS & VEVČANI

Velešta, Debar

Matica

Vevčanska

Oktisi

Struga, Ohrid, Skopje

▲ 830m

Premier

Sv Nikola

Vevčani

Domaḱijinska Kuḱa

Springs

Kutmičevica

Vajtoš Kale 1072m

Crni Kamen Picnic Area

Pisanik ▲ 1457m

Esenca

Podolgja

N

Bradt

0   1km
0   1 mile

Distance	3km north to Galičica 1,985m; 3.5km south to Albanian border ridgeline 2,100m, a further 3km along the ridge
Altitude	Lipova Livada saddle 1,568m to highest point on Galičica range in Macedonia 2,275m
Rating	Easy to moderate: initially steep
Timing	To the viewpoint: north 1½ hours; south 2–3 hours
Alternative	2 hours to Bugarska Čuka from the plateau road
Trailhead	Bus to Trpejca, taxi to Lipova Livada
Accommodation	Bed and breakfast in Trpejca (☏ 070 261 751), Hotel Sveti Naum (page 174), camping in Ljubaništa (page 167)
Map	1:25,000 SAGW Map Sheets Ohrid 780-4-3, Gorno Dupeni 780-4-4, Ljubaništa 830-2-1, Oteševo 830-2-2, January 2007

ROUTE DESCRIPTION The route north is a steep climb to gain the Galičica peak (grid 8629 3648). It is the shortest route to gain the view of both Lake Ohrid and Lake Prespa. From Galičica peak, there is a good ridge walk all the way to Bugarska Čuka (5km, grid 8751 4018) that maintains the view of both lakes. The easier but slightly longer climb is to the south. This route is also to the highest point on the Galičica range inside Macedonia. The route is obvious at the bottom and peters out towards the top, but head towards the summit where you can see both lakes and then along the ridge.

NAISMITH'S RULE

When planning a hike, it is useful to apply Naismith's rule – rule of thumb developed by Scottish hiker, William Naismith, in 1892.

THE RULE The basic rule is as follows:

Allow 1 hour for every 5km (3 miles) forward, plus ½ hour for every 300m (1,000ft) of ascent.

Over the years the rule has been expanded and the following can generally be applied: assuming you are carrying a well packed rucksack, allow 1 hour for:

- 5km easy going (on a road, flat / paved path, bridleway etc)
- 3km easy scrambling (walking through fields etc)
- 1.5km in extreme rough country (deep sand, snow, howling blizzard, etc)
- every hour after 5 hours walking due to fatigue.

In addition, on a gentle decline (about 5–12°), subtract 10 minutes per 300m, of descent. On a steep decline (over 12°), add 10 minutes per 300m of descent.
　　Very experienced walkers can lower the total time by one third. If your party contains very inexperienced walkers or young children, the rules may be optimistic. Always calculate for the slowest walker. These rules do not include breaks, which must be added to the calculation.

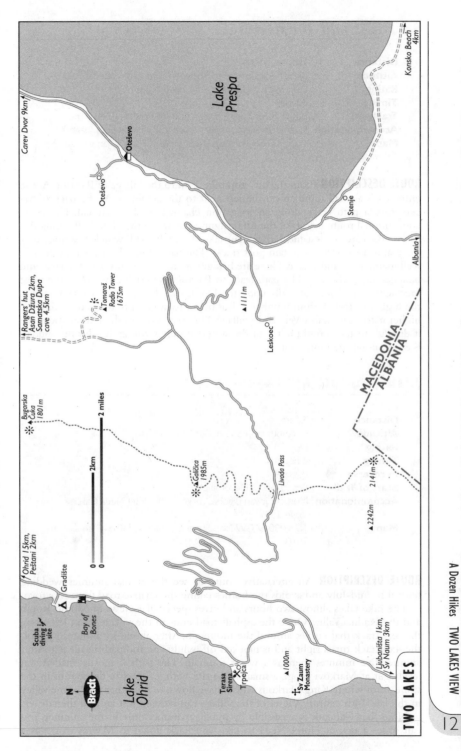

TWO LAKES

6 ROSTUŠE AND DUF WATERFALL

Distance	5km round trip
Altitude	River Radika bridge to Rostuše 700m, Duf Waterfall 840m
Rating	Easy, but narrow parts with steep drops
Timing	3 hours
Trailhead	Bus to River Radika bridge stop for Rostuše (Debar line)
Accommodation	Jovan Bigorski Monastery (page 238), Hotel Besa (page 235)
Map	1:25,000 SAGW Map Sheet Debar 730-3-3, January 2010.

ROUTE DESCRIPTION From the bus stop hike 1km to the village of Rostuše. At the entrance is a small fountain on the left next to the cemetery. At the back of the cemetery a path leads along an irrigation channel to the waterfall. The more conventional route is to take the route signposted above the church. If taking this route take care to descend rather than take the high road, which becomes very steep and turns into mountain goat tracks. The path along the irrigation ditch is well maintained and scenic. There are bridges at crossing points over the river and benches along the way. The path leads to Rostuše Waterfall 2, which is the most spectacular of all six waterfalls along the Duf ravine. It is not safe to try to access the higher waterfalls from number 2. It is better to attempt to do so by taking the higher path from before Vele Brdo village. The steep sides of the Duf ravine make it difficult to take good photos of the waterfall unless you arrive during midday. Return along the same route.

7 JANČE TO GALIČNIK (WEDDING FESTIVAL)

Distance	4.5km
Altitude	Janče bus stop 660m, Galičnik 1,415m
Rating	Easy
Timing	2 hours
In reverse	Possible
Start of Trail	Bus to Janče (Debar line)
Accommodation	Monastir Jovan Bigorski (page 238), Hotel Neda Galičnik (page 230)
Map	1:25,000 SAGW Map Sheet Lazarapole 730-3-4 January 2010

ROUTE DESCRIPTION An alternative route to see the annual summer wedding festival in mid-July and avoids the hordes taking the tarmac road from Mavrovo.

The hike takes almost two hours and gives spectacular views of Mount Korab and the Radika Valley. Once the asphalt road ends in the village, head left along the 4x4 track that curves around the mountain. After about 45 minutes by foot, the 4x4 track turns right and is blocked off, whilst the footpath heads left. After another five minutes there is a water fountain. The path is mostly shaded and levels out at Markovi Nogi, a small stone site with a foot-size depression in the stone, from where King Marko is said to have flown to the other side of the valley in the late 14th century. Views of the village can be seen just around the corner.

Note that Galičnik is accessible by public transport only in the summer. You can order a taxi at Hotel Neda to take you back down to Mavrovo or it is a

ROSTUŠE WATERFALL, JANČE TO GALIČNIK HIKE

N

Bradt

0 —————————— 2km

0 —————————————— 2 miles

▲1334m

Bistuše

Trebište

▲1548m

Duf
Waterfall
840m

Duf

Rostuše

Vele

Radika

Mavrovo,
Skopje

Debar,
Struga,
Ohrid

Adžievci

Radika

Sv Jovan Bigorski
monastery

Burkov

Janče

Bela Krasta
1911m

Galička

Galičnik

Desov Tor
2011m

Mavrovo,
Skopje

beautiful 15km hike along the Mavrovo plateau and down to the lake. Alternatively, take the ski lifts down (even in the summer) if they are working (usually at the weekends).

Distance	8km round trip
Altitude	Tresonče 1,005m, Alilica Cave 1,268m, Biljana Waterfall 2 1,296m
Rating	Easy: last 200m to the waterfall is impassable after rain
Timing	3–4 hours
Start of Trail	Bus to Tresonče /Gari/Lazaropole stop (Debar line), taxi to Tresonče (12km)
Accommodation	Hotel Kalin (page 230) or Hotel Besa (see page 235)
Map	1:25,000 SAGW Map Sheets Lazaropole 730-3-4 and Bistra 730-4-3, January 2010

ROUTE DESCRIPTION The ride to Tresonče along the pretty Mala Reka in the summer is beautiful. From the village church head along the valley and the 4x4 route through the meadows along the river. After about 1.5km the road becomes steeper, narrower and more damaged making it difficult even for a 4x4 to pass. There is a spring at this point. Another 1.5km takes you to Obesen Izvor, a small waterfall-like spring on the right-hand north bank of the Tresončka River. There is also a small hut here for wood cutters and water service tools. A single-track path continues another 500m along sometimes slippery rocks to Dolna Alilica Cave, again on the north bank. Some large branches across the now narrow river will aid you across it. Hiking poles are useful at this stage. If you don't have a torch there are usually church candles on either side of the entrance, but you will need your own lighter. While the entryway is small and requires a bit of crouching, it is possible to stand up towards the rear. Back outside, it is only 200m or so to Biljana Waterfall 2, but this is difficult to negotiate unless it is the end of the summer and the water level is low. To reach the remaining ten waterfalls a higher path needs to be taken from Tresonče village. Access to the higher waterfalls is difficult.

BILJANA SLAP WATERFALL & ALILICA CAVE

Sanne van den Heuvel

Although Macedonia's natural beauties and countryside have long attracted people's interest and desire to go out in the mountains, organised mountaineering in Macedonia did not start until the 1920s. Before that time, visits were mainly organised around religious holidays, where people gathered at the monasteries often located in remote places. Soon after the first mountaineering club was founded in Prilep in 1924, the same initiative followed in other towns. Today's clubs offer weekend trips and courses for their members in a variety of outdoor disciplines: alpinism, speleology, mountaineering, climbing and orienteering. All mountain sports organisations in Macedonia are united under the umbrella of the Macedonian Mountaineering Sports (MMSF – see contact details on page 295). Located in Skopje, they are the contact point for all information and details about visiting the Macedonian mountains. The MMSF supports the protection of nature, mountains and hiking trails in close co-operation with local communities. Besides awareness campaigns and maintenance of mountain trails, MMSF has set up a training centre for professional mountain guides. Members of mountaineering clubs can follow the training for the Mountain Guide A Certificate through which they receive qualifications to guide organised mountain trips. Because of the remoteness of the Macedonian landscape it is highly recommended to make use of experienced mountain guides. If you wish to contact a mountain guide, contact the MMSF.

Another way to get in touch with active members of mountain clubs is to enlist on the forum at www.mkd-mount.org. The forum has over 100 members from inside and outside Macedonia. Although most of the messages are in Macedonian, the webmaster speaks excellent English and one part of the forum is reserved for international guests and questions. The website itself functions as an on-line magazine for mountaineering activities in Macedonia, of which most of the pages are translated into English.

If you prefer, however, to travel without a guide, there are a couple of ways to find more information. A few descriptions of hikes, and even the GPS co-ordinates of a couple of routes can be found on the website above under 'Mountains/GPS'. MMSF also publish two booklets with a concise description of the most well-known tracks: *The Mountains and the Mountaineering Huts in the Republic of Macedonia* and *Eastern Macedonian Mountaineering Transversal*. The first one covers hikes from all over Macedonia. Unfortunately the booklet lacks good maps and, since most tracks were last marked when Macedonia was still a part of Yugoslavia, only a few of the hikes are described extensively enough to be taken without mountain guide. The maps in the second booklet are better, although the scale is still fairly large for orientation in an area visited for the first time. The booklet describes the newly marked international hiking trails, which connect with hikes in Bulgaria. In contrast to the more popular mountaineering destinations in western Macedonia, this booklet highlights less-trodden trails in the east. A long overdue promotion!

A Dozen Hikes **BILJANA WATERFALLS AND DOLNA ALILICA CAVE**

12

9 TITOV VRV

Distance	14km one-way
Altitude	Popova Šapka 1,782m, Titov Vrv 2,748m
Rating	Moderate, lengthy, steep ascent to the summit
Timing	5 hours one-way
Alternative	Return via Kriva Šija Waterfall (see below) possible
Start of Trail	Bus or train to Tetovo, taxi to Popova Šapka
Accommodation	Smreka Hut (page 297), B&B at Popova Šapka (see page 225)
Map	1:25,000 SAGW Map Sheets Bešala 680-4-3, Tetovo 680-4-4, Titov Vrv 730-2-1, January 2010; 1971 maps available now

ROUTE DESCRIPTION The fit can achieve the 37km round trip via Kriva Šija Waterfall (see below) in a long day, otherwise keep the hikes separate.

Titov Vrv is the highest mountain completely within Macedonia. Starting from Smreka mountain hut, head towards the top of the ski lifts until you cross the 4x4 track heading southeast. Follow this road just below the 2,000m contour for almost 5km until you reach a ravine. Follow the left/north bank of the ravine along a marked mountaineering path (red and white) in a northeasterly direction. The path crosses the ravine after 2km and heads southwest continuing to rise steeply for another 1.5km. The path then levels out and follows the 2,450m contour line for another 2km and rises onto the saddle southeast of Titov Vrv. From here there is a less trodden path directly to the summit or the well-trodden path heading west around the southern base of Titov Vrv to the shorter ascent to the summit. It's a 28km return hike on this route. A steep drop to the west of Titov Vrv will take you almost 4km to the beautiful Kriva Šija Waterfall (see below).

10 KRIVA ŠIJA WATERFALL

Distance	19km round trip
Altitude	Popova Šapka 1,782m, Kriva Šija waterfall 1,865m,
Rating	Moderate, lengthy, steep ascent to the summit
Timing	7+ hours
Alternative	Continuation over Titov Vrv (see above) possible
Start of Trail	Bus or train to Tetovo, taxi to Popova Šapka
Accommodation	Smreka Hut (page 297) B&B at Popova Šapka (page 225)
Map	As above for Titov Vrv

The hike from Popova Šapka can be shortened considerably if you can take a 4x4 to the end of the northern dirt track where the Lešnica River enters the Pena (the disused homes here were burned down in the 2001 conflict). From there it is a half-hour steep hike along the right/north bank of the Lešnica River to the **Lešnica Waterfall**, or a 1½–2-hour hike to Kriva Šija Waterfall. The path along the Pena requires you to jump or ford the river several times. Once across the river of the Kriva Šija ravine, the path follows the left/west bank until it plateaus out after almost 3km. The waterfall can be seen across the other side of the alp.

TITOV VRV & KRIVA ŠIJA WATERFALL

Distance	10km round trip
Altitude	Kitka trailhead 903m, Kitka mountain hut 1,320m, Kitka peak 1,675m
Rating	Easy
Timing	4–5 hours
Alternative	14km round trip from Gorno Količani
Trailhead	Bus to Dračevo, taxi to Gorno Količani or Motel Kitka crossroads
Accommodation	Kitka Hut (see page 296) or in Skopje town (page 123)
Map	1:25,000 SAGW Map Sheet Umovo 731-2-4, January 2010; 1971 map available now. See pages 144–5 for a sketch map

ROUTE DESCRIPTION Mount Kitka is the beginning of the next mountain range behind Vodno, south of Skopje. At 1,675m the peak has a mountain hut and lots of adventurous hiking trails in the beautiful forests of the Jakupica mountain range. Sadly, bus services to Količani, Crvena Voda and Motel Kitka (disused) have been discontinued for the time being.

To get to the Motel Kitka trailhead by car from Skopje, take 11th Oktomvri heading southeast out of town until it becomes Sava Kovačevič and follow the road around to the left as it becomes Ulica 1st Maj (Sava Kovačevič continues straight onto Markova Sušica). Ulica 1st Maj will take you to the village of Dračevo where you should turn right (south) opposite the village petrol station to get to Kitka Mountain. The turning is signposted in Cyrillic for Kitka and the Količani villages, and the road will take you past the Dračevo village graveyard and the red and white radio mast. Just before the village of Dolni Količani are many old marble Muslim gravestones. Keep right when you get to the village itself in order to continue on to Kitka.

The trail from Motel Kitka starts (grid 3935 3140) 200m before the prominent Motel Kitka crossroads after the village of Crvena Voda. The path winds along the northeast side of the mountain for 3km to **Kitka mountain hut**. From the hut it is another 1.5km along a winding path to the summit.

Beyond the Motel Kitka crossroads, the left-hand fork heading east follows the steep Kadina ravine to the Torbeshi (Macedonian Muslim) village of Paligrad. Here the asphalt road runs out and a 4x4 is required to continue. Back at the crossroads there is a dirt track turn-off on the right that is signposted for Karadžica mountain hut, and the road ahead, signposted for Solunska Glava, becomes a dirt track going to the village of Aldinci and beyond.

Distance	12km Brajčino to Golemo Ezero Hut. Another 3km to Malo Ezero or 6km descent to Nižepole. From Malo Ezero 3km to Pelister peak, and another 5km to Hotel Molika
Altitude	Brajčino 1,020m, Golemo Ezero 2,235m, Malo Ezero 2,250m, Nižepole 1,028m, Pelister peak 2,601m, Molika Hotel 1,400m
Rating	Moderate
Timing	5–7 hours to Golemo Ezero, plus 5–6 hours to Nižepole or Molika
In reverse	Possible
Trailhead	Bus to Brajčino (page 199), taxi to/from Molika or Nižepole
Accommodation	Brajčino (page 200), Golemo Ezero Hut (page 297), Molika Hotel (page 198)
Map	1:50,000 Geomap of Pelister (in Cyrillic); 1:25,000 SAGW Map Sheets Nakolec 831-1-1, Ljubojno 831-1-2, Kažani 781-3-4, January 2007; see sketch map on page 197

ROUTE DESCRIPTION This is a rewarding hike, which can be attempted in one day for the fit, or broken into two sections by overnighting at Golemo Ezero mountain hut. Taxis to Bitola from Molika can be ordered at the hotel.

The section from Brajčino to Golemo Ezero (Big Lake) has been well marked and several information boards about the surrounding area and wildlife are set at intervals on the way. Golemo Ezero mountain hut sits right on the edge of the waters of this glacial lake and is arguably the most picturesque of all Macdonia's mountain huts. It lies in the shelter of Veternica Peak (2,420m) and surrounding ridges. The original name of the hut is Dime Ilievski after the first and only Macedonian who died climbing Mount Everest in 1989. Pictures of his life and the Everest expedition adorn the walls of the hut. The most common route to Golemo Ezero and back is from Nižepole although this route is also the steepest.

The ridge hike from Golemo Ezero to Malo Ezero (Little Lake) and along the Pelister Peak is above the treeline and affords beautiful vistas of the mountain range and surrounding countryside. Together the two lakes are called the Eyes of Pelister. Malo Ezero sits in the shelter of Partizanski Vrv (2,349m).

For those who can no longer face the remaining 400m ascent to Mount Pelister, or want a more gentle (and longer) descent to Molika, there is a 4x4 dirt track from Malo Ezero heading west around the next peak of Široko Stapalo (2,435m) and to the west of Pelister. The track heads down through the woods and ends up at the tarmacked road just below the hotel.

Otherwise the ascent to Pelister heads north, passing Široko Stapalo and two more ridge peaks before summiting. The return route from Pelister heading northeast to Molika takes in two more panoramic viewpoints at Ilinden (2,542m) and Stiv (2,468m) and then descends into the woods. At the top of the ski lifts, 1km before Hotel Molika, is Kopanki mountain hut. Quite a wide range of food to eat and take away is for sale at Kopanki. The restaurant at Molika is also inviting after a long hike.

A Dozen Hikes **BRAJČINO TO PELISTER LAKES AND NIŽEPOLE**

Appendix 1

LANGUAGE
MACEDONIAN

Pronunciation and transliteration Like most languages (English being the prime exception) Macedonian is pronounced (almost!) exactly as it is written, so once you have mastered the sounds of each letter it is fairly straightforward to pronounce. Verbs are conjugated, but gratefully, unlike Serbian, nouns are not declined. There is no indefinite article, so the word for 'one' is used instead, and the definite article is added at the end of the noun (or adjective if one precedes the noun). There is a formal and informal conjugation of 'you' singular, as in French or Old English, and in this appendix the informal conjugation follows the formal where applicable. There are male, female and neuter genders for nouns, adjectives and verbal conjugations. For more information on the rules of the Macedonian language see Christina Kramer's excellent language book (full reference in *Appendix 3*, page 337).

Finally, a tip on sounding the correct stress on Macedonian words: with the exception of words of foreign origin, stress falls on the antepenultimate (third last) syllable. The stress in words of fewer than three syllables falls on the first or only syllable. The stress in words of foreign origin tends to fall as it would in the native language.

As it is usually too difficult for short-term visitors to learn a new alphabet like Cyrillic, it is not used in this book, but the standard transliteration is. Cyrillic, transliteration and pronunciation are given in the table below.

А	A	as in f<u>a</u>ther
Б	B	as in <u>b</u>ed
В	V	as in <u>v</u>ery
Г	G	as in <u>g</u>ood
Д	D	as in <u>d</u>oor
Ѓ	Gj	as in Ma<u>gy</u>ar
Е	E	as in b<u>e</u>t
Ж	Ž	as in plea<u>s</u>ure
З	Z	as in <u>z</u>oo
Ѕ	Dz	as in ad<u>ds</u>
И	I	as in f<u>ee</u>t
Ј	J	as in <u>y</u>oung
К	K	as in <u>k</u>it
Л	L	as in <u>l</u>og
Љ	Lj	as in Anato<u>l</u>ia, soft l pronounced at the back of the mouth
М	M	as in <u>m</u>ade
Н	N	as in <u>n</u>ot
Њ	Nj	as in ca<u>ny</u>on
О	O	as in l<u>o</u>t
П	P	as in <u>p</u>ut

П	R	as in ma**r**k
C	S	as in **s**it
Т	T	as in **t**able
Ќ	Kj	as in **c**ute
У	U	as in t**oo**k
Ф	F	as in **f**arm
X	H	as in lo**ch**
Ц	C	as in ca**ts**
Ч	Č	as in **ch**ur**ch**
Џ	Dž	as in e**dge**
Ш	Š	as in **sh**ovel

Words and phrases
Courtesies

Hello	Zdravo
Goodbye	Prijatno/čao
Please	Ve/te molam
Thank you	Blagodaram/fala
Good morning	Dobro utro
Good afternoon	Dobar den
Good evening	Dobra večer
Good night	Dobra nokj
How are you?	Kako ste/si?

I'm fine	Dobro/super
Pleased to meet you	Milo mi e što se zapoznavme
My pleasure	Milo mi e
Excuse me	Izvenete
You're welcome/ help yourself	Povelete
Welcome!	Dobredojde!

Basics

yes/no	da/ne
OK	može/važi
maybe	možebi
large/small	golemo/malo
more/less	povekje/pomalku
good/bad	dobro/lošo

excellent/terrible	odlično/lošo
hot/cold	toplo/ladno
toilet	toalet/WC (pronounced ve-tse)
men/women	maž/žena

Basic questions

How?	Kako?
How do you say in Macedonian?	Kako se vika na makedonski?
What?	Što?
What is that?	Što e toa?
When?	Koga?
When does the shop open/close?	Koga otvora/zatvora prodavnicata?
Where?	Kade?
Where is there a telephone?	Kade ima telefon?
The bill please?	Smetkata molam?

Who?	Koj?
Why?	Zošto?
Do you speak English?	Zboruvate-li angliski?
Do you understand French/German?	Razbirate-li francuski/germanski?
I do not understand Macedonian	Ne razbiram makedonski
How much does it cost?	Kolku čini?
What time is it?	Kolku e saat?
Which?	Koj/koja/koe?

Essentials

My name is...	Jas se vikam/Jas sum ...
What is your name?	Kako se vikaš?
I am from ...Britain/America/Australia	Jas sum od ...Anglija/Amerika/Avstralija
Please would you speak more slowly	Ve molam zboruvajte posporo
What is your telephone number?	Koj e vašiot telefonski broj?

What is your address?
My address in Britain/America is ...
I want to change dollars to denar
How many denar for US$1?
I need a telephone

Koja e vašata adressa?
Mojata adresa vo Velika Britanija/Amerika e ...
Sakam da smenam dolari vo denari
Kolku denari za eden dolar?
Mi treba telefon

Numbers

0	nula	21	dvaeset i eden
1	eden	30	trieset
2	dva	40	četirieset
3	tri	50	pedeset
4	četiri	60	šeeset
5	pet	70	sedumdeset
6	šest	80	osumdeset
7	sedum	90	devedeset
8	osum	100	sto
9	devet	200	dvesta
10	deset	300	trista
11	edinaeset	400	četiristo(tini)
12	dvanaest	500	petsto(tini)
13	trinaeset	one thousand	iljada
14	četirinaeset	two thousand	dve iljadi
15	petnaeset	one million	milion
16	šesnaeset	two million	dva milioni
17	sedumnaeset	quarter	četvrt
18	osumnaeset	half	pola/polovina
19	devetnaeset	three-quarters	tri četvrtini
20	dvaeset		

Time

hour	čas/saat	yesterday	včera
minute	minuta	morning	utro
week	nedela/sedmica	afternoon	popladne
day	den	evening	večer
year	godina	night	nokj
month	mesec	already	vekje
today	denes	soon	naskoro
tonight	večerva	now	sega
tomorrow	utre	this week	ovaa nedela
next week	slednata nedela	last week	minatata nedela
in the morning	sabaile	tonight	večerva
Monday	ponedelnik	Friday	petok
Tuesday	vtornik	Saturday	sabota
Wednesday	sreda	Sunday	nedela
Thursday	četvrtok		
January	Januari	July	Juli
February	Fevruari	August	Avgust
March	Mart	September	Septemvri
April	April	October	Oktomvri
May	Maj	November	Noemvri
June	Juni	December	Dekemvri

spring	*prolet*	autumn	*esen*
summer	*leto*	winter	*zima*

Getting around
Public transport

I'd like...	*Sakam ...*	to	*do*
... a one-way ticket	*... billet vo eden pravec*	airport	*aerodrom*
... a return ticket	*... povraten billet*	port	*pristanište*
I want to go to ...	*Sakam da odam ...*	bus	*avtobus*
How much is it?	*Kolku pari čini?*	train	*voz*
What time does it	*Vo kolku časot trgnuva?*	plane	*avion*
leave?		boat	*brod*
What time is it now?	*Kolku e časot?*	ferry	*feribrod*
The train has been	*...Vozot ...*	car	*avtomobil/kola*
... delayed	*... docni*	4x4	*pogon na četiri trkala/*
... cancelled	*... e otkažan*		*džip*
first class	*prva klasa*	taxi	*taksi*
second class	*vtora klasa*	minibus	*minibus*
sleeper	*vagon za spienje*	motobike/moped	*motor/moped*
platform	*peron*	bicycle	*velosiped*
ticket office	*biletara*	arrival/departure	*pristignuvanje/*
timetable	*vozen red*		*trgnuvanje*
from	*od*	bon voyage!	*srekjen pat!*

Private transport

Is this the road to ...?	*Dali e ova patot za ...?*
Where is the service station?	*Kade e benziskata stanica?*
Please fill it up	*Ve molam napolnete do gore*
I'd like ... litres	*Sakam ... litri*
diesel	*dizel*
leaded petrol	*benzin*
unleaded petrol	*bezoloven benzin*
I have broken down	*Mi se rasipa avtomobilot/kolata*

Road signs

give way	*prednost za premin*	toll	*patarina*
danger	*opasnost*	no entry	*zabranet vlez*
entry	*vlez*	exit	*izlez*
detour	*skršnuvanje*	keep clear	*zabraneto parkiranje*
one way	*ednonasočna*		

Directions

Where is it?	*Kade e?*
Which way is the ...?	*Na kade e ...?*
... mosque/church	*... džamija/crkva*
... fortress/museum	*... zamok (kale)/museum*
... archaeological site/hotel	*... arxeologska naogjalište/xotel*
... cave/bridge	*... peštera/most*
Go straight ahead	*Odi pravo*
turn left	*svrti levo*
turn right	*svrti desno*
... at the traffic lights	*... na semaforite*
... at the roundabout	*... kaj obikolnicata*

behind	*pozadi*		
in front of	*pred*		
near	*blisku*		
opposite	*sproti*		
here/there	*tuka/tamu*		
on the left/right	*na levo/na desno*		
straight on	*pravo*		
forward/behind	*napred/nazas*		
east/west	*istok/zapad*		
north/south	*sever/jug*		
Where is there a ...?	*Kade ima ...?*		
taxi rank/travel agency	*taksi stanica/putovanje agencija*		
bus station/train station	*avtobus stanica/železnička stanica*		
doctor/hospital	*doktor/bolnica*		
police station/bank	*policiska stanica/banka*		
restaurant/shop	*restoran/prodavnica*		
town/village	*grad/selo*		
house/flat	*kukja/stan*		
cinema/theatre	*kino/teatar*		
When does the train arrive/leave?	*Koga stignuva/poagja vozot?*		

Street signs

entrance	*vlez*	closed	*zatvoreno*
exit	*izlez*	toilets – men/women	*toalet – maži/ženi*
open	*otvoreno*	information	*informacija*

Accommodation

Where is a cheap/good hotel?	*Kade možam da najdam eftin/dobar hotel?*
Could you please write the address?	*Ve molam napišete ja adresata*
Do you have any rooms available?	*Dali imate slobodni sobi?*
I'd like ...	*Bi sakal ...*
... a single room	*... ednokrevetna soba*
... a double room	*... soba so francuski krevet*
... a room with two beds	*... soba so dva kreveta*
... a room with a bathroom	*... soba so kupatilo*
... to share a dorm	*... da delam soba*
How much it is per night/person?	*Kolku čini za edna nokj/eden čovek?*
Where is the toilet?	*Kade e toaletot?*
Where is the bathroom?	*Kade e kupatiloto?*
Is there hot water?	*Dali ima topla voda?*
Is there electricity?	*Dali ima struja?*
Is breakfast included?	*Dali e vklučen doručekot?*
I am leaving today	*Zaminuvam deneska*

Food

Do you have a table for ... people?	*Dali imate masa za ... lugje?*
... a children's menu?	*... detsko meni?*
I am a vegetarian	*Jas sum vegetarijanec*
Do you have any vegetarian dishes?	*Dali imate vegetarijanska hrana?*
Please bring me ...	*Ve molam donesete mi ...*
... a fork/knife/spoon	*... viljuška/nož/lažica*
Please may I have the bill?	*Ve molam donesete ja smetkata*
What do you have to drink?	*Što imate za pienje?*

I would like to drink ...		Sakam da pijam ...	
water/juice		voda/sok	
sparkling/non-sparkling		gazirane/negazirane	
tea/coffee		čaj/kafe	
turkish coffee medium sweet/bitter		tursko kafe sredno/gorko	
without sugar/milk		bez šeker/mleko	
with lemon/honey		so limun/med	
milkshake/milk		frape/mljeko	
white coffee		kafe so mleko	
red/white wine		crno/belo vino	
beer/rakija		pivo/rakija	
mulled wine		vareno vino	
What do you have to eat?		Što imate za jadenje?	
I want some bread, please		Sakam malku leb, ve molam	
I want ...		Sakam ...	
fish/meat		riba/meso	
trout/eel		pastrmka/jagula	
soup/salad		supa/salata	
yellow cheese/white cheese		kaškaval/sirenje	
tomatoes/eggs		partližani/jajca	
vegetables/fruit		zelenčuk/ovošje	
rice/potatoes		oriz/kompir	
apples/oranges		jabolko/portokal	
pears/grapes		kruška/grozje	
figs/apricots		smokva/kaijsija	
sugar/honey		šeker/med	
hazelnuts/walnuts		lešnici/orevi	
ice cream/pancakes		sladoled/palačinke	
I don't eat meat/fish		Ne jadem meso/riba	

Shopping

I'd like to buy ...	Bi sakal/a da kupam	Do you accept ...?	Dali primate ... ?
How much is it?	Kolku čini?	credit cards	kreditni kartički
I don't like it	Ne mi se dopagja	travellers' cheques	čekovi
I'm just looking	Samo razgleduvam	more	povekje
It's too expensive	Premnogu e skapo	less	pomalku
I'll take it	Kje go kupam	smaller	pomalo
Please may I have ...	Ve molam dali može ...	bigger	pogolemo

Communications

I am looking for ...	Baram ...	embassy	ambasada
bank	banka	exchange office	menuvačnica
post office	pošta	telephone centre	telefonska govornica
church	crkva	tourist office	turističko biro

Health

diarrhoea	dijarea	antibiotics	antibiotici
nausea	mi se loši	antiseptic	antiseptik
doctor	doktor	tampons	tamponi
prescription	recept	condoms	kondomi
pharmacy	apteka	contraceptive	kontracepcija
paracetamol	paracetamol	sunblock	zaštiten faktor

EMERGENCY

Help!	Pomoš!	police	policija
Call a doctor!	Povikajte doktor!	fire	požar
There's been an accident	Se slu i nesre a	ambulance	ambulantna kola
		thief	kradec
I'm lost	Se izgubiv	hospital	bolnica
Go away!	Odi si!	I am ill	Bolen sum/bolna sum

I am ...	Jas sum ...	I'm allergic to ...	aleričen sum na ...
asthmatic	astmatičar	penicillin	penicillin
epileptic	epileptičar	nuts – walnuts,	orevi,
diabetic	dijabetičar	hazelnuts, almonds	lešnici, bademi
		bees	pčeli

Travel with children

Is there a ...?	Dali ima ...?
... baby changing room	... soba za presoblekuvanje bebinja?
... a children's menu?	... detsko meni?
Do you have ...?	Dali imate ...?
... infant milk formula	... deštačko mleko za bebinja?
nappies	peleni
potty	nokšir
babysitter	bebisiter
highchair	stolče za bebinja
Are children allowed?	Dali e dozvoleno za deca?

Other

my/mine/ours/yours	moj/moe/naše/vaše	good/bad	dobro/lošo
and/some/but	i/nekoi/no, osven, tuku	early/late	rano/kasno
this/that	ova/toa	hot/cold	toplo/ladno
expensive/cheap	skapo/eftino	difficult/easy	teško/lesno
beautiful/ugly	ubavo/neubavo	boring/interesting	dosadno/interesno
old/new	staro/novo		

Basic verbs

to be	da se bide		
I am	jas sum	we are	nie sme
you are	ti si	you are	vie ste
he/she/it is	toj/taa/toa e	they are	tie se
to have	ima		
I have	imam	we have	imame
you have	imas	you have	imate
he/she/it has	ima	they have	imaat
to want/like/love	saka		
I want	sakam	we want	sakame
you want	sakaš	you want	sakate
he/she/it wants	saka	they want	sakaat

Hand gestures in Macedonia are the same as in the rest of Europe, but do not offer your left hand to Muslims, nor show them the soles of your feet or shoes.

ALBANIAN

Pronunciation Albanian nouns are declined and they are either feminine or masculine. There is no neuter, except in certain set phrases. The indefinite and definite articles are used, the latter being added to the end of the noun, as in Macedonian. Verbs are conjugated, and there is a formal and informal conjugation of 'you' singular, as in French or Old English. Here the informal conjugation follows the formal where applicable, and 'they' is translated as in standard representation with the masculine version first, followed by the feminine version. Unlike English, Albanian spelling is completely phonetic, so once you have mastered the sounds, you shouldn't have too much trouble with pronunciation. Good luck!

A	as in father
B	as in bed
C	as in cats
Ç	as in church
D	as in door
Dh	as in the
E	as in bet
Ë	as in along; it is often not pronounced at all
F	as in farm
G	as in good
Gj	as in Magyar
H	as in hit
I	as in feet
J	as in young
K	as in kit
L	as in log
Ll	as in fall, pronounced at the back of the mouth
M	as in made
N	as in not
Nj	as in canyon
O	as in lot
P	as in put
Q	as in cute
R	as in mark
Rr	as in burrito, pronounced with a resonant roll
S	as in sit
Sh	as in shovel
T	as in table
Th	as in thin
U	as in took
V	as in very
X	as in adds
Xh	as in jam
Y	as in mural
Z	as in zoo
Zh	as in pleasure

Words and phrases
Courtesies

Hello	*Tungjatjeta*	How are you?	*Si jeni/si je*
Goodbye	*Mirupafshim*	I'm fine	*Jam mirë*
Please	*Ju lutem/të lutem*	My pleasure	*Kënaqësia është e imja*
Thank you	*Faleminderit*	Excuse me	*Më fal*
Good morning	*Mirëmëngjes*	You're welcome	*S'ka përse*
Good afternoon	*Mirëdita*	Help yourself	*Shëbehuni vetë*
Good evening	*Mirëmbrëma*	Welcome!	*Mirëseardhët!*
Good night	*Natën e mirë*	Pleased to meet you	*Më vjen mirë*

Basics

yes/no	*po/jo*	good/bad	*mirë/keq*
OK	*mire/në regull*	hot/cold	*nxehtë/ftohtë*
maybe	*mundqë/mundet*	toilet	*nevojtore*
large/small	*madhe/vogël*	men/women	*mashkull/femër*
more/less	*më shumë/më pak*		

Basic questions

How?	*Si?*
How do you say ... in Albanian?	*Si thuhet ... në shqip?*
What?	*Çfarë?*
What is that?	*Çfarë është ajo?*
When?	*Kur?*
When does the shop open/close?	*Kur hapet/mbyullet shitorja?*
Where?	*Ku?*
Where is a public telephone?	*Kuka telefon publik?*
Who?	*Kush?*
Why?	*Pse?*
Which?	*Cili?*
Do you speak English?	*A flisni anglisht?*
Do you understand French/German?	*A kuptoni frëngjisht/gjermanisht?*
I do not understand Albanian	*Unë nuk kuptoj shqip*
How much does it cost?	*Sa kushton?*
What time is it?	*Sa është ora?*
The bill please?	*Llogarinë ju lutem?*

Essentials

My name is ...	*Unë quhem ...*
What is your name?	*Si quheni?*
I am from ... Britain/America/Australia	*Unë jam nga... Anglia/Amerika/Australia*
Please would you speak more slowly	*Ju lutem, mund të flisni më ngadal*
What is your telephone number?	*Cili është numri i telefonit tënd/të juaj?*
What is your address?	*Cila është adressa tënde juaje?*
My address in Britain/America is ...	*Adresa ime në Angli/Amerikë është ...*
I want to change dollars to lek (the currency in Albania)	*Dua të këmbej dollarë për lekë*
How many leks will you give me for US$1?	*Sa lekë do më japish për një dollar?*
I need to make a telephone call	*Duhet të marr në telefon*

Numbers

0	*zero*	21	*njëzet e një*
1	*një*	30	*tridhjet*
2	*dy*	40	*dyzet*
3	*tre*	50	*pesëdhjet*
4	*katër*	60	*gjashtëdhjet*
5	*pesë*	70	*shtatëdhjet*
6	*gjashtë*	80	*tetëdhjet*
7	*shtatë*	90	*nëntëdhjet*
8	*tetë*	100	*njëqind*
9	*nëntë*	200	*dyqind*
10	*dhjetë*	300	*treqind*
11	*njëmbëdhjetë*	400	*katërqind*
12	*dymbëdhjetë*	500	*pesëqind*
13	*trembëdhjetë*	one thousand	*një mijë*
14	*katërmbëdhjetë*	two thousand	*dy mijë*
15	*pesëmbëdhjetë*	one million	*një miljon*
16	*gjashtëmbëdhjetë*	two million	*dy miljonë*
17	*shtatëmbëdhjetë*	quarter	*çerek*
18	*tetëmbëdhjetë*	half	*gjysmë*
19	*nëntëmbëdhjetë*	three-quarters	*tre çerekë*
20	*njëzet*		

Time

hour	*orë*	yesterday	*dje*
minute	*minutë*	morning	*mëngjes*
week	*javë*	afternoon	*pas dite*
day	*ditë*	evening	*mbrëmje*
year	*vit*	night	*natë*
month	*muaj*	already	*veç më*
today	*sot*	soon	*së shpejti*
tonight	*sonte*	now	*tani*
tomorrow	*nesër*	this week	*këtë javë*
next week	*javën e ardhshme*	last week	*javën e kaluar*

Monday	*e hënë*	Friday	*e premte*
Tuesday	*e martë*	Saturday	*e shtunë*
Wednesday	*e mërkurë*	Sunday	*e dielë*
Thursday	*e ejte*		

January	*Janar*	July	*Korrik*
February	*Shkurt*	August	*Gusht*
March	*Mars*	September	*Shtator*
April	*Prill*	October	*Tetor*
May	*Maj*	November	*Nëntor*
June	*Qershor*	December	*Dhjetor*

spring	*pranverë*	autumn	*vjeshtë*
summer	*verë*	winter	*dimër*

Getting around
Public transport

I'd like ...	Dua ...
... a one-way ticket	... një biletë njëdrejtimshe
... a return ticket	... një biletë kthyese
I want to go to ...	Dua të shkoj në ...
How much is it?	Sa kushton?
What time does it leave?	Kur niset?
What time is it now?	Sa është ora tani?
The train has been ...	Treni do të ...
... delayed	... vonohet
... cancelled	... anulohet

first class	klasa e parë	plane	aeroplan
second class	Klasa e dytë	boat	anije
sleeper	vagon-shtrat	ferry	ferribot
platform	platformë	car	veturë
ticket office	sportel	4x4	foristadë
timetable	orar	taxi	taksi
from	prej	minibus	minibus
to	gjer	motobike/moped	motoçikletë
airport	aeroport	bicycle	biçikletë
port	liman	arrival departure	ardhje - nisje
bus	autobus	bon voyage!	rrugën e mbarë!
train	tren		

Private transport

Is this the road to ...?	A është kjo rruga për ...?
Where is the service station?	Ku është pikë furnizimi?
Please fill it up	Ju lutem, mund ta mbushni plot?
I'd like ... litres	Dua ... litra
diesel	dizel/naftë
leaded petrol	benzin me plumb
unleaded petrol	benzin pa plumb
I have broken down	mu prish makina

Road signs

give way	jep përparësi	toll	tarifë
danger	rrezik	no entry	ndalohet hyrja
entry	hyrje	exit	dalje
detour	rrugë e tërthortë	keep clear	mos ndalo
one way	njëkahshe		

Directions

Where is it?	Ku është?
Which way is the ...?	Nga është rruga për në ...?
mosque/church	xhami/kishë
castle/museum	kala/muzeum
archaeological site/hotel	vend arkeologjike/hotel
cave/bridge	shpellë/urë
Go straight ahead	Shko drejt
turn left	kthe në të majtë
turn right	kthe në të djathtë

... at the traffic lights	... te semafori
... at the roundabout	... te qarkorja
behind	prapa
in front of	përpara
near	afër
opposite	përballë
here/there	këtu/atje
on the left/right	në të majtë/djathtë
straight on	drejt
forward/behind	përpara/mbrapa
east/west	lindje/perëndim
north/south	veri/jug
Where is ...?	Ku është ...?
taxi rank/travel agency	vendqëndrim i taksive/agjensioni turistik
train station	stacioni i trenit
taxi rank	vendqëndrim i taksive
bus station	stacion i autobusave
ferry/train	target/tren
doctor/hospital	doktor/spital
police station/bank	stacioni policior/bankë
restaurant/shop	restorant/shitore
town/village	qytet/fshat
house/flat	shtëpi/apartament
cinema/theatre	kinema/teatër
When does the train arrive/leave?	Kur arin/niset treni?

Street signs

entrance	hyrje	closed	mbyllur
exit	dalje	toilets – men/women	tualet – burra/gra
open	hapur	information	informacion

Accommodation

Where is a cheap/good hotel?	Ku ka një hotel të lirë/mire?
Could you please write the address?	A mund ta shkruani adresën ju lutem?
Do you have any rooms available?	A keni dhoma të lira?
I'd like ...	Dua ...
... a single room	... një dhomë njëkrevatshe
... a double room	... një dhomë me krevat dopio
... a room with two beds	... një dhomë me dy krevatë
... a room with a bathroom	... një dhomë me banjo
... to share a dorm	... të ndaj dhomën me dikë
How much it is per night/person?	Sa kushton për një natë/person?
Where is the toilet?	Ku është tualeti?
Where is the bathroom?	Ku është banjoja?
Is there hot water?	A ka ujë të nxehtë?
Is there electricity?	A ka rymë elektrike?
Is breakfast included?	A është mëngjesi i përfshirë?
I am leaving today	Unë shkoj sot

Food

Do you have a table for ... people?	A keni një tavolinë për ... persona?
... a children's menu?	... meny për fëmijë
I am a vegetarian	Unë jam vegjetarian

328

Do you have any vegetarian dishes?	*A keni ndonjë ushqim vegjetarian?*
Please bring me ...	*Ju lutem më sillni ...*
... a fork/knife/spoon	*... një pirun/thikë/lugë*
Please may I have the bill?	*Ju lutem, mund ta sillni llogarinë?*
What do you have to drink?	*Çfarë ka për të pirë?*
I would like to drink ...	*Do të doja të pi ...*
water/juice	*ujë/lëng*
sparkling/non-sparkling	*i gazuar/i pa gazuar*
tea/coffee	*çaj/kafe*
hot chocolate/milk	*çokollatë e nxehtë/qumësht i nxehtë*
white coffee	*kafe me qumësht*
red/white wine	*verë e kuqe/bardhë*
beer/rakija	*birrë/raki*
mulled wine	*verë e nxehtë*
What do you have to eat?	*Çfarë ka për të ngrënë?*
I want some bread, please	*Dua pak bukë, ju lutem*
I want ...	*Dua ...*
fish/meat	*peshk/mish*
(Ohrid) trout/eel	*troftë/ngjalë*
soup/salad	*supë/sallatë*
cheese	*djathë*
tomatoes/eggs	*domate/vezë*
vegetables/fruit	*zarzavate/fruta*
rice/potatoes	*oriz/patate*
apples/oranges	*mollë/portokaj*
pears/grapes	*dardha/rrush*
figs/apricots	*fiq/kajsi*
sugar/honey	*sheqer/mjaltë*
hazelnuts/walnuts	*lajthi/arra*
ice cream/pancakes	*akullore/petulla*
I don't eat meat/fish	*Unë nuk ha mish/peshk*

Shopping

I'd like to buy...	*Dua të blej ...*
How much is it?	*Sa kushton?*
I don't like it	*Nuk më pëlqen*
I'm just looking	*Vetëm shoh*
It's too expensive	*Është shumë shtrenjtë*
I'll take it	*Do ta marr*
Please may I have ...	*Ju lutem, mund të ma jepni ...*
Do you accept ...?	*A pranoni ...?*
credit cards	*kartela kreditore*
travellers' cheques	*çeqe udhëtarësh*
more	*më shumë*
less	*më pak*
smaller	*më e/i vogël*
bigger	*më e/i madh*

Communications

I am looking for ...	*Kërkoj ...*
bank	*bankë*
post office	*postë*
church	*kishë*

A1

329

Help!	Ndihmë!	police	polici
Call a doctor!	Thirni mjek!	fire	zjarr
There's been an accident	Ka një aksident	ambulance	ndihmë e shpejtë
		thief	vjedhës
I'm lost	Kam humbur	hospital	spital
Go away!	Largohu!	I am ill	Jam i sëmurë

embassy	ambasadë
exchange office	këmbimore valutash
telephone centre	qendër telefonike
tourist office	zyrë turistike

Health

diarrhoea	diarre	contraceptive	kontraceptiv
nausea	të përzier	sunblock	mbrojtje nga dielli
doctor	mjek	I am ...	Unë jam ...
prescription	recetë	asthmatic	asmatik
pharmacy	barnatore	epileptic	epileptik
paracetamol	paracetamoll	diabetic	diabetik
antibiotics	antibiotik	I'm allergic to ...	Jam alergjik në ...
antiseptic	antiseptik	penicillin	penicilin
tampons	tampona	nuts	lajthi, bajame, arra
condoms	prezervativ	bees	grera

Travel with children

Is there a ...	A ka ...
... baby changing room?	... dhomë pë të ndruar beben?
... a children's menu?	... meny për fëmijë?
Do you have ...?	A keni ...
... infant milk formula	... qumësht pluhur për bebe?
nappies	pelena
potty	oturak
babysitter	dado
highchair	karrige për fëmijë
Are children allowed?	A janë fëmijët të lejuar?

Other

my/mine/ours/yours	imi/ imja/ jona/ jotja	good/bad	mirë/ keq
and/some/but	edhe/ disa/ por	early/late	shpejt/ vonë
this/that	kjo/ ajo	hot/cold	nxehtë/ ftohtë
expensive/cheap	shtrenjt/ lirë	difficult/easy	rëndë/ lehtë
beautiful/ugly	e bukur/ e keqe	boring/interesting	banal/ interesant
old/new	e vjetër/ e re		

Basic verbs

to be	të jesh		
I am	unë jam	we are	ne jemi
you are	ti je	you are	ju jeni
he/she/it is	ai/ ajo është	they are	ata/ ato janë

to have	*të kesh*		
I have	*unë kam*	we have	*ne kemi*
you have	*ti ke*	you have	*ju keni*
he/she/it has	*ai/ajo ka*	they have	*ato/ata kanë*

to want	*të duash*		
I want	*unë dua*	we want	*ne duam*
you want	*ti do*	you want	*ju doni*
he/she/it wants	*ai/ajo do*	they want	*ato/ata duan*

Appendix 2

GLOSSARY OF ARCHITECTURAL TERMS

acropolis	a fortified hill
amam	Turkish baths, usually using water from natural hot springs
amphitheatre	a Roman theatre, circular or semicircular in shape with tiered seats, used for animal or gladiatorial fights
an	an inn for travellers, usually four-sided around a well in an open courtyard, where travellers would sleep upstairs and animals and produce would be stored downstairs
apse	a semicircular recess in a wall
atrium	the inner courtyard of a Roman villa
basilica	a roofed Roman public hall which by the 5th century BC had become a place of early Christian worship or formalised church
capital	distinctively decorated upper end of a column
cardac	a large niche in the wall on the second floor of a Turkish house
chancel	the altar end of a church. In the Orthodox Church this area is usually prohibited to women
čardak	first-floor balcony
cupola	domed roof
dolap	wardrobe or drawers for clothes
exonarthex	an open hall or lean-to built onto the side of a church
forum	a Roman marketplace or public square
fresco	a wall painting
icon	portrait or likeness of a saint, often inlaid with silver and gold, and having holy and healing powers
iconostasis	the screen dividing the chancel from the nave of a church
konak	formerly describing a large Turkish house, now used for the inns of a monastery
madrese	a school teaching the Koran
methoses	land or estate owned by the Church
mihrab	the niche in the eastern wall of a mosque indicating the direction of Mecca
mimbar	the pulpit of a mosque, from where the sermon is preached
minaret	a thin circular or many-sided tower attached to an outside wall of a mosque
minder	cushion
minderlik	narrow fitted wooden benches with fitted cushions built into a room
mosaic	pictures usually depicting flora and fauna, people or buildings, made of small coloured tiles, usually laid as a flooring, but occasionally on a wall or ceiling
musandra	a built-in wardrobe for linen and bedding
narthex	the front lobby, porch or entrance hall of a church

nave	the main room of worship in a church
necropolis	a Roman graveyard
pithos	a large clay jar or jug used for storing foodstuffs
plinth	a square block of stone or marble at the bottom of a column
portico	a row of columns holding up the exonarthex roof of a church or mosque
sergen	a glass cupboard or shop window
teke	the Bektaši equivalent of a monastery
turbe	a tomb usually found outside a mosque but within its grounds
zograph	title of a skilled fresco painter

GLOSSARY OF NAMES

As one might expect in a Balkan country as diverse as Macedonia, the names of famous people differ by language, and it can be quite confusing to figure out which names apply to which people. Here are some of the more commonly confusing names:

Aleksander III of Macedon	as usually found in Macedonian literature; more commonly known as Alexander the Great, especially by the Greeks, or as Aleksandar Veliki by some Macedonians; known as Iskander in Albanian, Turkish and lands further east; abbreviated to Aco
Skenderbej	also Skenderbeg, meaning literally 'Lord' (bej/beg) Iskander/Alexander
Basilius II	the Byzantium Emperor known as Basil II in English, Vasilius II in some renditions (b and v are often interchangeable) and as Vasilie in Macedonia
Sv Kliment	St Clement in English
Jovan	John
Pavle	Paul
Gjorgi	George, also sometimes transliterated into English as Džordži
Bogorodica	the Holy Mother of God (the Virgin Mary)
Spas	the Holy Saviour

A2

Appendix 3

FURTHER INFORMATION

BOOKS If you are new to Macedonia and want to know where to start with further reading, I suggest the works of John Phillips and Robert Kaplan. There are a whole host of books written on Macedonia by Macedonians, some of which have been translated into English but are generally only available in Macedonia. These are listed separately below the more internationally available books (which can be ordered through most bookshops or amazon.co.uk (or .com), or can be borrowed from a good university library). Old, rare and out-of-print titles can often be found on abebooks.co.uk (or .com). All the Macedonian books listed are available from Ikona, Kultura, Matica or Tabernakul bookshops in Skopje. Books specifically on ethnic Macedonians outside the Republic of Macedonia are not especially covered here, but many can be found at www.pollitecon.com.

History/politics

Brown, Keith *The Past in Question: Modern Macedonia and the Uncertainties of Nation* Princeton University Press, 2003. Looks at Macedonia's work on historiography of the Kruševo Republic of 1903 and how this has been an effort to create an identity for a nation uncertain of itself. Engaging reading in parts.

Carpenter, Teresa *The Miss Stone Affair: America's First Modern Hostage Crisis!* Simon & Schuster, 2003. A page-turner of a book on the kidnap of the American missionary, Ellen Stone, and her pregnant chaperone, Mrs Tsilka, by Jane Sandanski, a member of the Internal Macedonian Revolutionary Organisation (VMRO).

Cartledge, Paul *Alexander the Great: The Hunt for a New Past* Pan Books, London, 2005. This latest book on Alexander the Great by a professor of Greek history at Oxford University gives some clarity to all those who struggle with whether Alexander/Aleksandar was Greek or Macedonian. Interesting reading.

Chiclet, Christophe and Lory, Bernard (eds) *La République de Macédoine* Editions L'Harmattan, Paris, 1998. This is a useful update (in French) on a lot of Hugh Poulton's book (see below).

Clark, Victoria *Why Angels Fall: A Journey through Orthodox Europe from Byzantium to Kosovo* Picador, 2001. The 44 pages covering Macedonia also include Aegean Macedonia. They give an insight into the relationship between these two sides of geographical Macedonia and the role that the Church still plays.

Glenny, Misha *The Fall of Yugoslavia* Penguin (3rd edition), London, 1996; and *The Balkans: Nationalism, War and the Great Powers, 1804–1999* Penguin, USA, 2001. Both books by this journalist are an excellent read, although depending on where you are in your knowledge of the Balkans, the books can either be too broad or too detailed! With the advantage of hindsight, the latter book has a weak ending.

Hammond, N G A *History of Macedonia*, Duckworth, 1979–88. The standard reference on the history of Macedonia up to the early 20th century. Three volumes.

Jezernik, Božidar *Wild Europe: The Balkans in the Gaze of Western Travellers* Saqi Books, 2004. An interesting critique of many of the books listed here. Good exposé of the Macedonian question in chapter 9, 'A True Comedy of Errors'.

Kaplan, Robert D *Balkan Ghosts: A Journey through History* Vintage, New York, 1993. The one chapter on Macedonia is a fascinating read of historical and contemporary views of the country, especially considering it was written in 1990, before the country had even become independent.

Karakasidou, Anastasia *Fields of Wheat, Hills of Blood: Passages to a Nationhood in Greek Macedonia 1870–1990* University of Chicago Press, 1997. Originally banned in Greece and the source of death threats to the author, this book is a must-read for anyone wanting to understand Macedonia.

Moody, Simon and Wakefield, Alan *Under the Devil's Eye: Britain's Forgotten Army at Salonika 1915–1918* Sutton Publishing, 2004. Detailed reading taken from soldier accounts of their time on the Salonika Front, including the Battle of Dojran

Mulley, Clare *The Woman Who Saved the Children: A Biography of Eglantyne Jebb* Oneworld Publications, 2009. Chapter 8 concentrates on Jebb's first and only trip to Macedonia and Kosovo to deliver aid to tens of thousands of refugees after the first Balkan War. The plight of children in particular spurs her to co-found Save the Children, and to author the Declaration of the Rights of the Child. A fascinating read. All book proceeds go to Save the Children.

Pekar, Harvey and Roberson, Heather *Macedonia: How Do You Stop a War?* Villard, 2007. Roberson's search to answer this question, through meetings with Macedonians as well as with foreigners working in Macedonia's many international organisations, is rendered into comic-book script and drawings by Pekar and illustrator Ed Piskor. The comic-book style leaves a lot out.

Pettifer, James (ed) *The New Macedonian Question* Palgrave, 2001. This is a collection of essays and articles covering a wide variety of topics concerning Macedonia. Extremely informative.

Phillips, John *Macedonia: Warlords and Rebels* I B Tauris, 2004. This book by a reporter for *The Times* is the first to give full coverage of the 2001 conflict in English. It is insightful and balanced until the last few pages, when his attempt to catch up on the last two years when he was not reporting on the country paints far too pessimistic a picture. Excellent review of Macedonian history.

Poulton, Hugh *Who Are the Macedonians?* Indiana University Press, Bloomington, 1995. A somewhat dry book that explores the origins of the peoples who now occupy the Republic of Macedonia and what they may mean in terms of their identity.

Silber, Laura et al *The Death of Yugoslavia* (revised edition) Penguin, 1996. An in-depth account of the ins and outs and minutiae that led up to the death of Yugoslavia. It is much easier to watch the BBC TV series.

Sokalski, Henryk J *An Ounce of Prevention: Macedonia and the UN Experience in Preventive Diplomacy,* United States Institute of Peace, Washington, 2003. Analysis by the head of UNPROFOR/UNPREDEP of the UN's first military mission in preventive diplomacy. Could the conflict of 2001 have been avoided if UNPROFOR had not been pulled out of the country?

Thucydides *History of the Peloponnesian War,* Penguin, 1972. This is *the* account of the wars over the Greek city-states and islands, a foundation work in political science, and describes the beginning of the end of the Greek Empire. Paeonia and the royal house of Macedon are referred to in Book Two.

Macedonian authors

Koneska, Elizabeta *Yoruks* Museum of Macedonia, Skopje, 2004. Beautiful colour photos by Robert Jankuloski and succinct text about the little-known Yoruk community of Macedonia.

Kumanovski, Risto *Ohrid and its Treasures* Mikena Publishing, Bitola, 2002. Gives an introduction to Ohrid's best sites, including 25 of its churches and monasteries.

Pavlovski, Jovan and Pavlovski, Mishel *Macedonia Yesterday and Today* (3rd edition) Mi-an Publishing, Skopje, 2001. A very readable, if very pro-Macedonian and anti-Bulgarian, account of Macedonia's history up until the first session of the Anti-fascist Assembly of the National Liberation of Macedonia (ASNOM) in October 1943.

Šeldarov, Nikola and Lilčikj, Viktor *Kralevite na antička Makedonija i nivnite moneti vo Republika Makedonija* (The Kings of Ancient Macedonia and their Coinage) National and University Library of Kliment Ohridski, Skopje, 1994. A good reference book on the ancient kingdom of the Macedons including maps of the kingdom, its tribes and towns, as well as drawings of many of their coins. Macedonian only.

Stojčev, Vanče *Military History of Macedonia*, Military Academy General Mihailo Apostolski, Skopje, 2004. Just what it says it is, covering the period from 7BC through World War II. A beautiful compendium of maps accompanies the main 777-page volume. Hard copy.

Natural history

Gorman, Gerrard *Central and Eastern European Wildlife* Bradt Travel Guides, 2008. Although this guide does not cover Macedonia specifically, most of the animals to be found in Macedonia are covered in this guide, and it is a lot more affordable and easier to travel with than the Mitchell-Jones atlas below.

Mitchell-Jones, A J et al al *The Atlas of European Mammals* Academic Press, Oxford, 1999. A weighty tome with lots packed in.

Polunin, Oleg *Flowers of Greece and the Balkans, a Field Guide* Oxford University Press,1987. Invaluable.

Hoffman, Helga and Hoffman, Marktanner, Thomas *Butterflies and Moths of Britain and Europe* HarperCollins, 1995. Small with a plastic cover, very handy for expeditions.

Svensson, Lars *Collins Bird Guide* (new edition) HarperCollins, 2001.

Karadelev, Mitko *Fungi Makedonci, Gabite na Makedonija* PGUP Sofija Bogdanci, Skopje, 2001. Available only in Macedonian, this is an excellent book with page-by-page descriptions and colour photos of all the mushrooms to be found in Macedonia.

Historical travel writing

Čelebi, Evlija *Book of Travels: The Seyahataname*, volumes 1–9, Brill Academic Publishers, Leiden, 1999. This is the best and often only source of what went on during the 17th century in the Ottoman Empire. Massively informative, if sometimes a bit dense.

Lear, Edward *Journals of a Landscape Painter in Greece and Albania* Century,1851, reprinted 1988. The more serious side of this most famous limerick writer offering sobering views on the region.

Maclean, Fitzroy *Eastern Approaches* Penguin, 1991. An excellent account of Maclean's missions through the Balkans during World War I.

Moore, Frederick *The Balkan Trial* Smith, Elder and Co, 1906. An American journalist writes about his travels with other European travellers, including an English journalist, through Monastir (Bitola), Prilep and Üsküb (Skopje) and about the Kruševo uprising from his time there in 1903, aged 29.

Pouqueville, F C H L (ed James Pettifer, Classic Balkan Travel Series, 1998) *Travels in Epirus, Albania, Macedonia, and Thessaly*, Loizou Publications, Paris, 1820. Early 18th-century travels through Ottoman-held territories with only a few pages on Vardar Macedonia.

West, Rebecca *Black Lamb and Grey Falcon* Canongate Books, Edinburgh, 1941, reprinted 1993. On the one hand it is one of the few accounts available of the Balkans in the early 20th century; on the other hand it is the account of a privileged upper-class lady with undisguised ethnocentric tendencies.

Willis, Martin P L *A Captive of the Bulgarian Brigand: An Englishman's Terrible Experiences in Macedonia* Ede, Allum & Townsend, 1906. A revealing thriller, highlighting only one account of a more widespread problem debated by the Great Powers at the time.

Modern travel writing

Cho, Carol *A Hitchhiker's Guide to Macedonia . . . and My Soul* Forum Publishing, 2002. Written by an Amerasian woman who spent three years living in the Macedonian community over the 2001 conflict period. Although the book mentions little of the conflict itself, it offers excellent insights into the trials and tribulations of a young woman coming to terms with her own self and with Macedonia.

Delisso, Christopher *Hidden Macedonia, The Mystic Lakes of Ohrid and Prespa* Haus Publishing, London, 2007. Delisso, a long-time Balkan-hand, brings his insights as editor of balkananalysis.com to bear on his 2006 journey through three countries around lakes Ohrid and Prespa. A short and readable introduction to the history, religions and races of the region.

Palin, Michael *New Europe* Weidenfeld & Nicholson, 2007. Palin's documentary takes him through all of New Europe and a few days in Ohrid and Prilep.

Macedonian literature

Pavlovski, Božin *The Red Hypocrite* AEA Publishers (Australia), 2001. One of the most famous modern authors to emerge from Macedonia, who now lives in Australia. Other books by Pavlovski available in English include: *Duva and the Flea; Eagle Coat of Arms; Egyptian Dreamer; Home is Where the Heart is; Journey with my Beloved; Miladin from China; Neighbours of the Owl; Return to Fairy Tales.*

Miscellaneous

Biegman, Nicolaas *God's Lovers: A Sufi Community in Macedonia* Kegan Paul, 2007. Biegman, a former Dutch diplomat in Macedonia and an expert on Islam, has produced a masterful photographic treatise of the little-understood Sufi community of Macedonia.

Biegman, Nicolaas *Living Sufism: Sufi Rituals in the Middle East and the Balkans* American University in Cairo Press, 2009. Complementing many of the gorgeous photos from *God's Lovers*, this book compares the Sufi rituals across the Middle East and the Balkans and how they have developed over time and distance.

Biegman, Nicolaas *Oil Wrestlers*, Stylus Publishing, 2009. Close up photography of pelivan wrestling in Macedonia. A male-only sport involving only a pair of sturdy breeches and total body coverage with sunflower oil. This author accompanied Biegman in 2004 when he shot these photos.

Kornakov, Dimitar *A Guide to Macedonian Monasteries* Matica, Skopje, 2005. A guide in English on 29 of Macedonia's most revered monasteries. In-depth information on the building and reconstruction of the monastery buildings, on their frescoes and some of their history.

Kramer, Christina E *Macedonian: A Course for Beginning and Intermediate Students* University of Winsconsin Press, Madison, 1999. An extremely well-presented and comprehensive language learning book with exercises. Explanations are in English and a separate CD-Rom can be purchased to accompany the book in order to listen to native spoken Macedonian.

Kusevska, Maria and Mitovska, Liljana *Do You Speak Macedonian?* MEDIS-informatics, Skopje, 1995. This course book, accompanied by a work book and cassette tape, is written entirely in Cyrillic Macedonian, so it is impossible to use as a beginner without the cassette tape. Vocabulary at the back is listed with English translations.

Murgoski, Zoze *Dictionary: English–Macedonian, Macedonian–English* National and University Library of Kliment Ohridski, Skopje, 1995. A handy little paperback dictionary for carrying in your back pocket or bag. The definitive *English–Macedonian Dictionary: The Unabridged Edition* also by Murgoski, is all you will ever need for finding those awkward words like 'sovereignty' and 'fennel'. And the equivalent Macedonian–English version is also now out.

WEB RESOURCES There are a lot of outdated sites on Macedonia so check when the site was last updated before acting upon any of the information.

General
www.macedonia-timeless.com Site hosting the current internationally aired tourist advert for Macedonia directed by Macedonia's most famous film director, Milčo Mančevski. Offers hundreds of links to help you get to know, and get about, Macedonia.
news.bbc.co.uk/2/hi/europe/country_profiles/1067125.stm For a good overview of the recent history of Macedonia.
www.macedonia.co.uk The Macedonian Cultural and Information Centre for lots of useful info to help you get to know the country before you go.
www.mymacedonia.net Macedonian history from a nation-state perspective, including articles from leading Macedonian historians Risto Stefov and Alexander Donski.
www.manaki.com.mk Official site dedicated to the Manaki brothers, pioneers of film and photography in Macedonia.
www.kniga.com.mk Where you can find most Macedonian books, maps and software. Only available in Macedonian at time of writing.
www.vardar.co.uk And after you've fallen in love with Macedonia and returned back home, this is where you can buy all your favourite Macedonian things, including Macedonian, Serbian and Croatian wine (*69 Askew Rd, London W12*).
www.cybermacedonia.com Extremely good on the history of towns and famous Macedonians and all sorts of other facts. Last updated 2003.
faq.macedonia.org Another very informative site on all aspects of Macedonian life.
www.pollitecon.com A site offering books and views supporting the argument that there are ethnic Macedonians in Greece.
www.mhrmi.org The website of the Macedonian Human Rights Movement International, based in Toronto, Canada. Interesting dialogue in 2006 between MHRMI and *The Times* regarding the use of the word 'Slav'.

Travel and accommodation
www.exploringmacedonia.com The official tourist site for Macedonia. Very useful.
www.gomacedonia.com.mk An excellent site with up-to-date, accurate information on places worth visiting in Macedonia.
www.airports.com.mk Flight information for Skopje and Ohrid.
www.mz.com.mk Train information for national and international rail travel through Macedonia.
www.jsp.com.mk The Skopje city bus website with map and timetables (sometimes only working in Macedonian).
www.sas.com.mk The national and international bus service website (English timetable not working at time of writing).
www.unet.com.mk/oldmacedonianmaps For all you map freaks.

Sports clubs and associations
www.alpinizam.org Information about rock-climbing sites around Macedonia. Latest information available in Macedonian only.
www.amfora.com.mk Diving centre in Ohrid.
www.eskimo-freeride.com For the best skiing at the cheapest rates in Europe – too awesome for words.
www.korab.org.mk Korab mountaineering club, based in Skopje.
www.makedon.mk New, young mountaineering and climbing club, based in Skopje.
www.mkdmount.org A hub of information about mountaineering in Macedonia, has links to all the clubs, how to hire a guide, and latest info on the state of mountaineering in Macedonia. English pages not as up-to-date as Macedonian pages.

www.new7wonders.com/nature/en/nominees/europe/c/VreloCave Macedonia's entry for the New Seven Wonders of Nature.

www.sharamountainguide.com.mk Homepage of Ljuboten mountaineering club, based in Tetovo, including hiring guides for Šar Planina hikes.

www.vfm.org.mk/en_clubs.html Macedonia's Aviation Association's linkpage to all the local hang-gliding and paragliding club.

www.yoga.org.mk/index_e.htm Macedonian yoga association.

Government, media, communications, etc

988.mt.com.mk Macedonia's on-line phone directory for private addresses.

www.culture.in.mk A very good site by the Ministry of Culture giving all the latest news on events and shows.

www.mia.com.mk Macedonian Information Agency, the official independent national news agency – very informative and the most up todate.

www.president.gov.mk/index_e.asp To see what the president is up to.

www.setimes.com Southeast European Times – provides a very good overview of top news coverage by country in the Balkans.

www.sobranie.mk Website of the Macedonian parliament.

www.t-home.mk Homepage of Makedonski Telekomunikacija now that it is owned by T-Mobile, with all the latest news in Macedonia and useful links to other sites.

www.vlada.mk For the latest from the government.

www.yellowpages.com.mk Macedonia's on-line business phone directory, with an optional English interface. Useful links to other Yellow Pages around the world.

www.zels.org.mk/eng_linkovi.htm A useful page from the Organisation of Local Self Government with links to all the municipalities. These sites in turn, many of which are available in English, offer the latest information on the local area including places of interest, transportation and accommodation.

World War I Salonika Front

www.1914-1918.net/salonika.htm For family historians.

www.archive.org/stream/salonikafront00mannuoft/salonikafront00mannuoft_djvu.txt On-line publication of *The Salonika Front* by Capt Arthur Mann, 1920.

www.gwpda.org/memoir/Salonica/salonTC.htm#TC On-line publication of *The Story of the Salonika Army* by G Ward Price, 1918.

memorabilia.homestead.com/files/Salonika_and_Macedonia_1916_18.htm Listing of the battalions of each division who fought on the Salonika Front.

www.salonikabattlefieldtour.com A Strumica-based company providing informative tours of the Dojran Battlefield and nearby graves.

www.srpska-mreza.com/library/facts/November-1918.html A Serbian site extolling the bravery of the Serbs in World War I using extracts from the book *November 1918* by Gordon Brook-Shepherd, 1981.

FILMS/DOCUMENTARIES

Cvetanovski, Vlado *The Secret Book*, 2005. A thriller based on a fictional search for the legendary secret Slavic book of Bogomil Gnostic religion of the 11th century. The book is supposed to have ended up in France, where a father and son duo take up the search in the 21st century. In French and Macedonian, available with English and Macedonian subtitles. À-la *Da Vinci Code*.

Horne, Robert *Edward Lear: An Exile in Paradise* Lear Productions, 2008. A fascinating reproduction of Lear's travels from Greece, through Monastir (Bitola), Prilep and Üsküb (Skopje) in 1848. Lear is better known for his nonsense poetry and sketches, but this documentary does a great job of showcasing his landscape paintings of the time and how they compare with the region today.

Leder, Mimi *The Peacemaker*, 1997. Nuclear warheads get in the wrong hands between Russia and the Balkans. A couple of the scenes are set in the church on the main square in Bitola. Starring George Clooney and Nicole Kidman. Usual Hollywood stuff.

Mančevski, Milčo *Before the Rain*, 1995. Set in London and Macedonia in the 1990s giving a chilling forecast of how inter-ethnic violence might start. English, Macedonian and Albanian with English subtitles. Gripping.

Mančevski, Milčo *Dust*, 2001. Set in New York and Macedonia at the beginning and end of the 20th century. Wild West comes to Macedonia, starring Joseph Fiennes. Action packed.

Mančevski, Milčo *Shadows*, 2008. A young doctor in Skopje has to lay to rest the wandering souls of several characters from bygone years. Not as 'insightful' of Macedonia per se, but a gripping drama all the same.

Mitrevski, Darko *Bal-kan-kan*, 2005. A fantastic parody of life in the Balkans at the turn of the 21st century. Available with English subtitles. Brilliant.

Mitrovic, Živorad *The Assasins of Salonika*, 1961. Classic feature of the fight for Macedonia at the end of the 19th century. Today's Macedonians grew up on this stuff. Macedonian and Serbo-Croat. Available with English subtitles.

Palin, Michael *New Europe* BBC documentary, 2007. Palin's documentary takes him all through New Europe stopping for a few days in Ohrid and Prilep.

Popov, Stole *Tetoviranje*, 1994. Set in Šutka detention centre and Idrižovo prison. A man is detained for having an empty suitcase and ends up being shot by a Macedonian crack sniper. English subtitles. Perks up in parts.

Stone, Oliver *Alexander*, 2004. This movie was never going to win any Oscars, not least because it is too long with too many up-close battles, but a revealing rendition of a legendary figure. Starring Colin Farrell and Angelina Jolie.

Trajkov, Ivo *The Great Water*, 2004. Based on the book of the same name by Živko Cingo, this story tells of an orphan after World War II, whose experience as a young pioneer in the orphanage allegedly creates one of the greatest democratic forces in Yugoslavia. English subtitles. Average.

Wood, Michael *In the Footsteps of Alexander* BBC documentary, 1997. An informative and interesting account of Alexander the Great's conquest of Persia.

Index